HOW TO USE THE COMPANION CD

The companion CD and the software included on it have been designed to run on Windows 95, NT 3.51, and NT 4.0. It is not compatible with 16-bit Windows. Some of the software requires that you have the latest Service Packs from Microsoft (Service Pack 5 on NT 3.51, Service Pack 2 on NT 4.0) and Visual Basic 5.0.

RECOMMENDED SYSTEM

- ▶ Pentium PC
- ▶ Windows 95, NT
- ▶ 4X CD-ROM drive
- ▶ 16MB RAM

CD START INSTRUCTIONS

1 Place the CD-ROM in your CD-ROM drive.

2 If your CD is set to Autostart (Windows 95 and NT 4.0), the file gtp.exe will run. This launches a help file from which you can install the software.

3 You can also install the software by running the program setup32.exe in the root directory of the CD-ROM. Select Open File from the File menu. Select your CD-ROM drive (usually drive D), then select the file called setup32.exe.

Dan Appleman's Developing ActiveX Components with Visual Basic 5.0

A Guide to the Perplexed

DAN APPLEMAN'S DEVELOPING ACTIVEX COMPONENTS WITH VISUAL BASIC 5.0
A GUIDE TO THE PERPLEXED

Dan Appleman

Ziff-Davis Press
An imprint of Macmillan Computer Publishing USA
Emeryville, California

Publisher	Stacy Hiquet
Associate Publisher	Steven Sayre
Acquisitions Editor	Lysa Lewallen
Development/Copy Editor	Candace Crane
Technical Reviewer	Leslie Taylor
Production Editors	Barbara Dahl and Edith Rex
Proofreader	Jeff Barash
Cover Illustration and Design	Magan Gandt
Technical Illustration	Mina Reimer
Book Design	Gary Suen
Page Layout	Bruce Lundquist
Indexer	Valerie Robbins

Ziff-Davis Press, ZD Press, and the Ziff-Davis Press logo are trademarks or registered trademarks of, and are licensed to Macmillan Computer Publishing USA by Ziff-Davis Publishing Company, New York, New York.

Ziff-Davis Press imprint books are produced on a Macintosh computer system with the following applications: FrameMaker®, Microsoft® Word, QuarkXPress®, Adobe Illustrator®, Adobe Photoshop®, Adobe Streamline™, MacLink®*Plus*, Aldus® FreeHand™, Collage Plus™.

Ziff-Davis Press, an imprint of
Macmillan Computer Publishing USA
5903 Christie Avenue
Emeryville, CA 94608

ISBN 1-56276-510-8

Manufactured in the United States of America

10 9 8 7 6 5 4 3 2 1

CONTENTS AT A GLANCE

TABLE OF CONTENTS

Part 2 Code Components

Part 3 ActiveX Controls

ACKNOWLEDGMENTS

If you had told me five years ago that I would have written not one, but four books, I would not have believed it. Even now I'm not sure I believe it, but fortunately for me, a lot of other people do.

The crew at Ziff-Davis Press has changed from when I started, but the current team is as good as ever, maybe better. Candace Crane did a phenomenal job editing and cleaning up my language without changing the tone. Barbara Dahl, Edith Rex, Bruce Lundquist, and Mina Reimer handled things on the production end. Stephen DeLacy and I struggled through yet another CD-ROM production cycle on an impossible schedule. Lysa Lewallen handled a myriad of details as usual. Les Taylor, as outside tech editor, helped keep me honest. Megan Gandt designed this cool cover. Andrea Burnett and Stephanie Rodriguez on the marketing end helped you find out about this book. And Juliet Langley—what can I say? You are always a pleasure to deal with, and this book would not be here without you.

I'd like to extend a special thanks to Dan Soha, who provided the COMics artwork in Chapter 4.

In my Win32 API book I wrote: "This book is dedicated first to the people who work at my company, Desaware. Each and every one of them was involved in one way or another, including taking over some of my responsibilities so I could work on this book."

I could think of no better way to express this—and it is just as true for this book. Franky Wong again acted as inside technical editor, catching errors and pointing out areas that needed additional explanation, not to mention handling the day-to-day operation of the company while I was off writing. My father, Gabriel Appleman, also reviewed each chapter for readability and clarity. You can find out more about the rest of the Desaware team on the help file on the CD-ROM: Stjepan Pejic, Roan Bear, Marian Kicklighter, Karyn Duncan, Josh Peck, Levy Ring, Edo Mor, Michael Dickman, and Matt Solnit—thank you all for your help.

I find words are inadequate to express how I feel. To my family, friends, those of you who have read my previous books, and those who own Desaware's products…your support made this book possible. Thank you.

Introduction:
A Different Kind of Book

I've been waiting to write a book on ActiveX technology for years.

True, it didn't used to be called ActiveX. Perhaps it was called OLE, or OLE Controls, or VBX, or Visual Basic Custom Controls. It doesn't matter. All along I've been working with the technology as it evolved and waiting for the right time to do a book on the subject. I was waiting for Visual Basic to mature to the point where it could be used to create these types of controls.

When I saw the beta for Visual Basic 5, I knew my wait was over, which left me with a problem. How do I write a book on this technology that will be both incredibly useful to Visual Basic programmers and also stand out from the myriad of ActiveX VB books that undoubtedly will appear on the bookshelves at the same time? How do I write a book detailed enough for the advanced programmer, but with enough scope to welcome even a beginning Visual Basic programmer to ActiveX development?

So I put on my programmer hat and thought about the things that I like and hate about technology books and quickly realized this: I hate manual rehashes.

Simply paraphrasing the Microsoft documentation is pointless. A certain amount of that is inevitable, I suppose, but at least an author should add a significant amount of new material—and, perhaps, a creative new way of looking at the technology that does not echo the manuals. I also hate having to read through things I know to find a few tidbits of new information. You know the kind of book I'm talking about, where a supposedly advanced book starts out by explaining how to draw controls on forms, click a mouse, and turn on the computer.

I knew I wanted to do a comprehensive book on ActiveX and object programming using Visual Basic. I knew I did not want to waste a lot of time rehashing the manual. In fact, I'll let you in on a little secret: The Visual Basic 5.0 documentation is not bad at all. I suppose that is an odd thing for an after-market book author to say. I realized as I was reading the VB5 documentation that it would be perfect…

> ▶ …if only it took the time to explain a few core concepts instead of assuming the understanding of them.

- ► …if only it had a few more examples illustrating how to go about certain tasks.

- ► …if only I could have someone watching as I read to explain some of the sections that aren't as clear as they could be and answer questions that arise as I read it.

- ► …if only it would go a little bit beyond explaining how to perform certain tasks and expand into why some tasks, which are truly important, are necessary and how to choose between different ways to perform the same task.

- ► …if only it included some information for more advanced programmers. For example, how this technology works behind the scenes or how to subclass a control off a built-in Windows control.

As I realized these things, I knew what I wanted to do. I did not want to write *The ActiveX Bible for Visual Basic 5.0*. Microsoft already wrote it; it's in the documentation. I wanted to write the commentary!

A Talmudic Sage named Maimonides wrote the original *Guide to the Perplexed* in the Middle Ages. It was a guide that did not try to replace the scripture, but rather elaborate on it, interpret it, and help ordinary people understand it. While I'm certainly not a sage of his caliber, I know he had the right idea.

What's in *A Guide to the Perplexed*?

"So what's in this book?" you may ask. Here are some of the goals I reached for and philosophies I followed while writing it.

ON CONCEPTS

There are certain core concepts a programmer must understand to write ActiveX components (not to mention to program in Visual Basic in the first place). I wanted to take a step back and cover those concepts in-depth. I wanted to cover them in such a way that even a beginning VB programmer could understand them. This was my task in Part 1.

ON MY TARGET AUDIENCE

I focused on information that is new to Visual Basic 5.0 and in some cases to Visual Basic 4.0. If you are completely new to Visual Basic, this is probably not the book to start with because I assume you already know how to use Visual Basic and are familiar with the general syntax of the language.

However, this book is definitely intended for people who have not yet made extensive use of the new object-oriented constructs introduced with Visual Basic 4.0 (such as classes). It is also for those who have not yet worked with OLE or ActiveX technology.

ON APPROACH

I assume that you have access to the Visual Basic documentation. This book is intended to supplement the Microsoft documentation, not replace it. While there is some overlap by necessity, the emphasis is always to go beyond the documentation in the following ways:

- ▶ Interpretation, clarifying those subjects that are unclear. Translating them into something that resembles English when necessary.

- ▶ Illustration, adding new examples where appropriate. Showing alternate ways to implement certain features. Showing how things crash if you do them incorrectly.

- ▶ Elaboration, demonstrating techniques that are not covered in the documentation. Explaining how some of the technology works behind the scenes.

- ▶ Commentary, discussing not just how you *can* program, but how you *should* program. Explaining why some things are done the way that they are, and otherwise adding my two cents into the fray.

ON STYLE

The entire book is written just like this introduction—in the first person. A commentary is, by definition, more than just an authoritative presentation of accurate technical information. It also includes interpretation and opinion. So, while I'll certainly make every effort to make sure that this book is technically accurate and reasonably comprehensive, there will be portions of the book that are based on personal opinion and biases. In other words, not only will I tell you about a feature, how it works and why. I might also tell you what I think of it, and whether you should use it or perhaps try a different approach.

If you find any technical inaccuracies, I will welcome e-mail on the subject (dan@desaware.com) and make corrections promptly for the next edition as well as post the correction on our Web site at www.desaware.com. If you disagree with my interpretation or commentary, I will also welcome e-mail on the subject, will read it carefully and will either post the opposing viewpoint, or delete the message—depending on the nature of your message and my personal whim.

ON SCOPE

You've probably noticed that Visual Basic 5.0 is enormous. It has evolved dramatically from version 1.0 in both size and scope. In order to make it possible to come out with a good ActiveX book in a timely manner, I had to decide how much information to cover. I have no doubt that I will receive many e-mail messages complaining that I left out the one crucial subject needed to make the book perfect. So let me start by telling you what I included and what I left out and why.

What's In and Why

Core concepts relating to ActiveX	Because I believe an expert is someone who understands the fundamentals of a subject very well. With the advent of classes and ActiveX technology in Visual Basic, a good understanding of the underlying concepts of ActiveX are essential to every Visual Basic programmer.
Classes	Working with classes is now a key part of the foundation for Visual Basic programming. Many VB programmers don't believe this yet. I intend to change their minds.
Code Components (Alias, OLE servers, EXE servers)	With the appearance of event sinking and multithreaded objects with Visual Basic 5.0, this type of component has become even more exciting than before. Plus, it is the foundation for understanding ActiveX controls and documents.
ActiveX Controls	I truly believe this is one of the two most important features in Visual Basic 5.0 (the other being native code compilation). I believe that now that it is possible for VB programmers to create ActiveX controls, they all will.
The Internet (or, ActiveX Documents)	Is the Internet the most important new technology of the decade? I don't know. I do know that it is not the most important aspect of ActiveX technology. But it is important, and it's covered here.

What's Not In and Why

The VB IDE	Using the VB environment itself is not particularly hard and is well documented in the Microsoft manuals. I'll cover this subject only enough to show you how to set attributes for ActiveX features.
Wizards	The whole idea of wizards is to simplify certain tasks, so discussing how to use a wizard seems rather pointless. But I will take a look at the code that wizards produce (a very interesting subject) and discuss when you should and should not use them.
Remote Automation	This may be a subject for a future edition, and I think you'll find the foundations covered here invaluable for using remote automation. But it's a very large subject in itself and deserving of a book of its own.
Language, controls, and almost everything else	This book is about ActiveX technology. There are dozens of other VB books on many different subjects available, For example, to study how to use the Win32 API from Visual Basic you can use my book *Visual Basic 5.0 Programmer's Guide to the Win32 API*, ZD Press, 1997.

All of the content of the book is based on the Enterprise edition of Visual Basic. However, there are very few subjects that do not apply directly to the professional edition as well. Refer to the online Visual Basic help for limitations relating to the standard edition.

FINAL COMMENTS

When I told my publisher I wanted to do a technical book that was a commentary on the actual documentation and was written entirely in first person, they said yes. Who would have figured? The result is in your hands. I hope you find it useful and, perhaps, even entertaining.

Finally, I wanted to clarify a few matters to help avoid any possible misunderstandings.

ON MICROSOFT

For the record, I like Microsoft. I believe that most of their success is not due to their lawyers (who are legendary) or marketing (which is everywhere) but ultimately because they write good software. Great software. Like Visual Basic 5.0.

I know that Microsoft bashing is a popular sport. Some people are secretly hoping they'll be taken down or split up or something. I don't feel that way at all. That said, you may notice that in any number of places in this book I take various digs at Microsoft or otherwise attempt to be humorous at their expense. So let me be perfectly clear. I have no hidden anti-Microsoft agenda. I mean them no ill-will. It's just that they are such a big juicy target, I can't resist having some fun with them now and then. And that's all there is to it.

A case in point: How many Microsoft programmers does it take to change a light bulb? Answer: None. They just redefined darkness to be the new standard.

Or take this true story. A programmer asked me what it is like to be a software vendor where Microsoft is the biggest fish in the pond. My response: Microsoft isn't the biggest fish in the pond. They *are* the pond.

ON FREE SOFTWARE

Many books you purchase claim to offer megabytes of "free software" of various types. When you look more closely, however, you find that the software is often shareware that needs to be registered, demo-ware, cripple-ware, or software that is otherwise unsupported. And I don't care what the price is. Unsupported software is always too expensive in the long run for any professional use. So this book contains no "free software."

Now don't worry. You'll find lots of software on the CD-ROM, but it's all intended for educational purposes, to help you learn about ActiveX programming. Maybe you'll look at some of it, decide that it is useful for your own applications, and adapt it to your own purposes. If so, great. Think of it as an extra bonus. But don't buy this book because of free software. If you buy it, let the reason be for the information and educational content.

ON DESAWARE

I am the president of a small software company called Desaware Inc. I founded the company in 1991 when I saw Visual Basic 1.0 and decided it represented the future of Windows programming. I think history has proven me right on that account.

You will occasionally find references to Desaware's tools and products in the text of this book. There are two reasons for this. Desaware specializes in ActiveX controls and tools that extend Visual Basic. That make it possible to take full advantage of Windows from the Visual Basic language. Since I use our tools and code in my own ActiveX development efforts, it should be no surprise that I've borrowed some of that technology to solve some of the problems described in this book. I hope that over the course of reading it, you will find it valuable to take a serious look at the Desaware products and demos on the CD-ROM that comes with this book and consider adding some into your own repertoire. If I may boast a little, I must say our products are very cool.

ON E-MAIL

I get a lot of e-mail, and many of the messages contain questions on API related questions. I suspect after this book comes out, I will begin to see questions on ActiveX-related subjects as well.

I wish I could take the time to read and respond to every question that comes my way, but I'm afraid I can't. There isn't that much time in a day. When I receive a question, I will often answer it if I know the answer off the top of my head. If I don't, I'll try to point the questioner in the right direction. But I rarely have the time to do more than that. If you send me your program and ask me to debug it (which happens more often than you might expect), I must apologize in advance. I won't be able to offer much help.

ON UPDATES AND CORRECTIONS

I wish I could promise you that this book will be perfectly correct in every way. Not only can I not do that, but I can promise you it won't be. There are bound to be errors, omissions, and typographical errors. They seem to occur no matter how many times I read the proofs and regardless of how many people review the chapters.

If you see a problem, please let me know (politely will be nice, but I'll take corrections even if they come with a flame, which also happens more often than you might expect). Also, watch for the latest corrections and updates on our Web site: www.desaware.com.

That's it for the introduction. Now, on to the good stuff.

Daniel Appleman
March 1997

Part 1

Core Technologies

I discovered something several years ago I would like to share with you now.

I discovered that an expert in a field is not someone who knows a great deal about almost every aspect of that field. Instead, an expert in a field is a person who understands the fundamentals of that field very, very well.

In this book, it is my intent to help you become an expert at ActiveX development using Visual Basic (VB). This means rather than flooding you with thousands of details and a myriad of tips and techniques, I'm going to first focus on helping you gain a rock solid understanding of the fundamentals of ActiveX. To illustrate what I'm trying to accomplish, here is a short scenario:

Let's say a chapter has just introduced a really important and elegant tip for improving your ActiveX control. Without a solid understanding of the fundamentals your reaction might be, "Wow, what a cool technique. I'll try to remember it in my own projects. Where did you come up with an idea like that? You must be some sort of genius."

But if I succeed in teaching you the fundamentals of ActiveX, your reaction is more likely to be, "Interesting, but let's face it, it's sort of obvious when you consider the way this stuff works. How could it be otherwise? Well, Dan, I guess you're not so smart after all."

The second reaction is the one I want. My goal is for you to understand the fundamentals so well that all of the tips and techniques we cover later will just flow logically—they'll make sense, and you'll never forget them because you will really understand them.

Part I of the book covers these fundamentals. My goal here is to introduce you to ActiveX technology in such a way that you will understand not only how it works, but why it works the way it does. You'll understand it so thoroughly that when we actually get to looking at Visual Basic code, the pieces will fall into place so nicely you'll wonder what all the fuss was about. Building code components, ActiveX controls, and ActiveX documents will seem easy and intuitive, because for you, it will be easy and intuitive.

"But wait!" you might say. "I really want to start coding right away." That's fine. In fact, it's not a bad idea. Here's my suggestion: Whenever you feel the urge to code, go to the Visual Basic 5.0 documentation on building ActiveX components and start walking through the examples on building the Shape control. It's a good example, and the manual is reasonably well written.

As you go through this book, if you find that something is not clear or have trouble understanding it, just skip it. You'll probably find the missing piece later in the text. You'll also find that even if I don't answer a question directly, you'll have gained enough of an understanding of the underlying technology to understand the documentation on a second reading.

ActiveX Myths

My publisher told me it's not customary or appropriate for a chapter to be only a few pages long. But length is relative. This chapter may be short in terms of length, but it is equal in terms of importance to any of the longer chapters that follow.

Any time you begin to learn a new technology, it is important to start on the right track. Erroneous assumptions or early misconceptions can get in the way of understanding a technology and make it difficult to use correctly.

There are a number of myths relating to ActiveX technology that have become quite widespread. This is due in part to the rapid changes in technology we've seen recently. It is also due to the nature of Microsoft's marketing efforts, as you will see in the next chapter.

If you are one of those individuals who is relatively new to ActiveX and have not heard any of these myths, count yourself lucky, for you'll have fewer misconceptions to overcome. Don't worry if you don't fully understand some of the terms I use in this brief chapter; they'll all be explained in the chapters that follow.

Meanwhile, let us begin by laying some of these myths to rest, so we can begin our study of ActiveX with a clean slate.

MYTH: *ActiveX is only important for Internet programming and Web sites.*

FACT: *ActiveX ≠ Internet.*

While there are certain specific aspects of ActiveX that relate to Internet programming, the vast majority of ActiveX technologies have nothing to do with the Internet.

Now, I realize that some of you reading this might be taken aback by this statement. You might point out that Microsoft created ActiveX controls to replace OLE controls. In doing so, however, you make my case—that early misconceptions can get in the way of understanding new technologies. You see, ActiveX controls did not replace OLE controls. ActiveX controls *are* OLE controls. No difference. None whatsoever. Why this is the case, and how it happened, will be covered in the next chapter.

MYTH: *ActiveX is only for advanced VB programmers.*

FACT: *ActiveX should be one of the first things any new VB programmer learns.*

There is a natural tendency to learn and teach Visual Basic in a sequence that roughly corresponds to the order in which features were added to the language. You can see this in many Visual Basic 4.0 books, where a discussion of classes appears, almost as an afterthought, at the end of the book after other language features are covered.

This is a terrible mistake.

The most important feature that appeared in Visual Basic 4.0 from a programming perspective was the class module. For the first time, Visual Basic was able to support *object-oriented programming*. True, VB was not (and is not) a true object-oriented language in the strictest definition of the term. But class modules make it possible for you to implement several key object-oriented features. The most important of these is the ability to hide information behind a clearly defined interface. In other words, the data in a class can be hidden from the rest of the program and access to that data limited to the functions you add to the class.

What does this have to do with beginning programmers?

Consider the steps many Visual Basic programmers use to create an application:

1 Draw controls on a form (create the user interface).

2 Start attaching code to various events.

3 Place additional functions in the declaration section of forms or modules, depending on whether they are shared among forms or by programmer's whim. Define variables and otherwise write the program.

This is fine for trivial programs or "throwaway" code. But if this is the approach you use in general, I would like to invite you to consider another way:

1 Think about the design of the application. Goals. Algorithms. User Interface. Data Structures. Schedules. Resources.

2 Define the classes the application will use. Classes correspond to key data structures or areas of functionality. Classes may be made up of other classes. Remember to think of forms as a type of class as well! You may wish to go through the additional step of defining user interface components (ActiveX controls) with which to implement your application.

3 Now go ahead and draw the form and implement the program.

Design always comes first. Taking the time to design your application is the single most important thing you can do to improve the quality of your code, reduce its size, increase its reliability, and accelerate its performance.

And implementing your application as a collection of classes will make your programs even better. Object-oriented programming is not a marketing buzzword that language vendors put into their ad copy to sell more software. (Well, it is, but that's beside the point.) Object-oriented programming is a design discipline and implementation methodology that will help you write better code. And it is something that should be learned by every Visual Basic programmer—even beginners.

What does this have to do with ActiveX? Simple. As you will see in Chapter 2, classes are ActiveX components. Since Visual Basic 4.0, VB was implemented internally using ActiveX technology.

MYTH: *ActiveX is only important if you are creating servers or controls.*

FACT: *ActiveX is important to every VB programmer.*

If ActiveX is the implementation technology for classes, and classes are the implementation technology for object-oriented programming, and object-oriented programming is important to all VB programmers, it follows naturally that ActiveX is important for all VB programmers. The case has already been made.

But allow me to expand slightly on this point. ActiveX is the fundamental technology for objects under Visual Basic, and this technology can be deployed in many different ways. Thus, during the design process for your application, you have two distinct issues to consider.

First, you must define the object model of your application. What are the objects and interfaces that will best implement your application? Second, you must determine how to deploy those objects. Which are public and which are private? Should an object be part of an application class, an in-process code component (DLL server), out-of-process code component (EXE server), ActiveX control (OLE control), or ActiveX document (DocObject)?

As a Visual Basic programmer, your technology options with Visual Basic 5.0 are far greater than those available under earlier versions. Learning about those options is what this book is about.

Let us begin.

ActiveX: A Historical (but Technical) Perspective

I realize that your temptation to skip a historical perspective chapter in a technical book must be nearly irresistible. But bear with me. In the case of ActiveX, understanding the history can be the most certain road to understanding the technology.

THE APPLICATION-CENTRIC ENVIRONMENT

Think back to ancient history, say the mid 1980s. DOS was king, and Windows 1.0 was a slow graphic interface that could actually run on an 8086-based machine from floppy disks. (OK, it didn't run very well, but it did run.) Every task you performed on a PC was *application-centric*. In other words, each application would work independently, and in most cases would work with its own unique data type. Figure 2.1 illustrates this situation. As long as you were working with the type of data native to the application, everything was fine.

But what if you wanted to convert the data from one program to work with another? In that case, you had to use special conversion programs or depend on the application to have an import or export routine that could handle the desired conversion. If you wanted to create a report that combined two different types of data, you had to use a special report generation program or depend on an application's ability to combine more than one type of data. Sometimes companies came out with application suites that worked together, but in most cases these were just packages of applications that had a better-than-average ability to convert each other's file formats or create reports made up of data from the various applications.

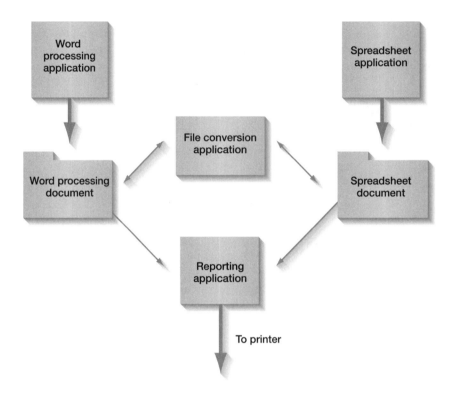

Figure 2.1: A typical application-centric environment

Let's consider a fairly common situation, in which you wished to combine financial data with text in a newsletter or report format. You had a number of possible approaches.

Most high-end word processors contain at least some support for tables. Nowadays that support can be quite extensive and can even include the ability to perform simple calculations across cells, but in the DOS time frame, this capability was still quite primitive. You could create the report using the word processor, create a simple table, and copy the financial information into the table. Of course, any time you changed your spreadsheet, you needed to correct the figures in the text document manually.

Most spreadsheet programs have some capability for adding arbitrary text. In a modern spreadsheet, such as Excel, you can perform a significant amount of text formatting—almost as much as a word processor. But back in the days of Lotus 123, you were limited to adding text to individual cells. If you created your report using a spreadsheet program, the text would look quite plain.

You could export information from the spreadsheet and place it in the word processing document. If you converted the spreadsheet to text, the word processor could probably import the data and display it in a table in the document. Of course you would need to repeat this operation any time the data changed. You could export the data as an image, but this could lead to problems if you tried to scale the image.

You could use a report generation program or desktop publishing application that understood the native data formats involved. This approach sounds perfect, except that most of those programs were limited to a relatively few data formats, were difficult to learn and use, and were limited in scope.

Let's take a closer look at one specific approach: trying to bring the spreadsheet data into the word processing document. Figure 2.2 illustrates converting the spreadsheet data into text and copying it into the document. The result does not look particularly good and does not scale well. You can, of course, proceed to reformat the data using the word processor's capabilities, but this is quite a bit of extra work.

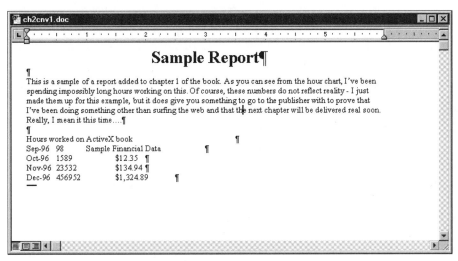

Figure 2.2: Spreadsheet data imported as unformatted text

There are a number of common data formats that can be used to transfer formatted text. In this case the word processor is smart enough to recognize this data format and place the imported data into a table format. As you can see in Figure 2.3, the results still leave something to be desired. Scaling the table once again requires manual formatting.

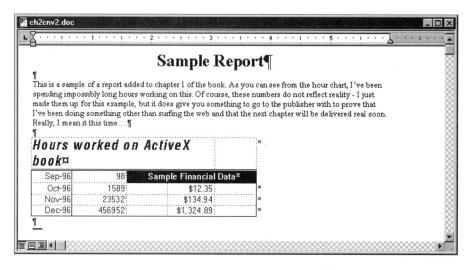

Figure 2.3: Spreadsheet data imported into a table

It is possible to obtain a perfect image of the spreadsheet by converting it into a bitmap image, as shown in Figure 2.4. Most word processors are able to handle standard bitmap formats quite well. In this case you are stuck with the image as it exists—you cannot modify the image further without either using a paint program or reconverting the information from the original spreadsheet. Furthermore, bitmap images suffer from severe scaling problems, as shown in Figure 2.5.

There is one other issue to consider when importing data in the manner shown in the previous four examples: the conversion works only in one direction. In other words, once the spreadsheet data has been converted into a format useable by the word processor, it is extremely difficult to convert the data back to a spreadsheet. In the best case, you could import it back into the spreadsheet but lose most of the formatting information. In the worst case, where the data was transferred as a bitmap, the only possible approach is to manually reenter all of the data.

THE DATA-CENTRIC ENVIRONMENT

One of the key characteristics of an application-centric environment is the conversion process required to move data from one application to another. It might be called *conversion, importing, exporting,* or *cut-and-paste,* but the principle is the same in each case. An explicit operation must take place to convert the data between the two data formats, and information is frequently lost in the process.

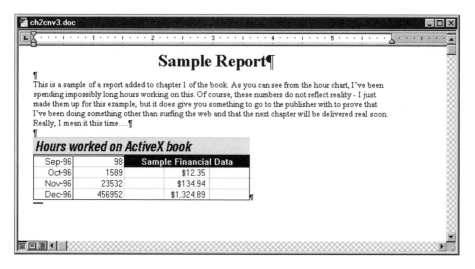

Figure 2.4: Spreadsheet data imported as a bitmap

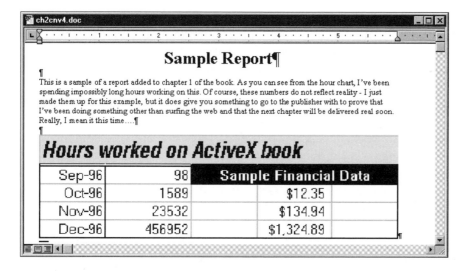

Figure 2.5: Spreadsheet data imported as a bitmap, then scaled

"Big deal" you may say. "After all, isn't that how most applications work today?"

In many cases you would be right. But we are already beginning to see the results of a fundamental shift in programming. This shift has its roots in a vision that Microsoft began promoting for PCs a decade ago. The idea was that computing should be data-centric instead of application-centric.

What does this mean? It means that instead of users concerning themselves with applications and the files associated with them, a user could be concerned only with the documents they are working with. Documents could contain any type of object, from text to images to sound to types not yet imagined. The users would never have to worry about which type of application they were using. When they opened a document, the operating system would automatically run the code necessary to view or edit the document or any object in the document. The user would never have to worry about the exact representation of the document on disk. The objects for the document might exist on one file or thousands of files and might be present on one disk or distributed throughout a network. If a file was moved, the operating system would keep track of where it was so the document could still find it when necessary.

Is this beginning to sound familiar? While most users still think in a somewhat application-centric manner, the transition to data-centric systems is well on its way. One manifestation of this is that users are becoming more and more accustomed to embedding different types of objects inside their word processing or spreadsheet documents. This can be seen in Figure 2.6; the actual Excel spreadsheet object has been embedded into the word processing document. Not only does the image look correct, but it scales very nicely. It does seem somewhat magical that a word processor can understand how to use and display a spreadsheet object in this manner, and—that's the very magic we'll be talking about for the rest of this book. The data-centric approach of embedding a spreadsheet object within a word processing document is shown in Figure 2.7.

Perhaps the greatest data-centric system in use today is the World Wide Web, where an HTML page can contain images, video, sound, applets and many other types of objects. They can be distributed throughout the world. Yet the user on the system may not even need to worry about launching a browser—they need only ask for a document. The system takes care of launching the browser, and the browser launches any applications needed to use or display the various objects on the page.

Is a data-centric environment actually better for computer users than the familiar application-centric approach? It's a good question, one for which I do

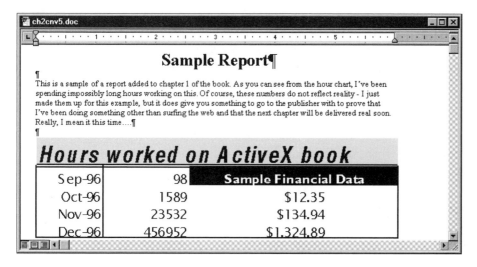

Figure 2.6: An Excel spreadsheet object embedded in a Word document

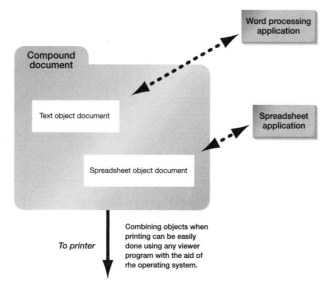

Figure 2.7: A typical data-centric environment

not know the answer. In fact, it's probably too soon to answer for sure. Today's implementations of data-centric systems are still not perfect. Lost links on documents when files are moved or servers are down and system configuration problems attest to that fact. But the truth is that as programmers we have little choice in the matter. The transition to a data-centric model of computing is continuing at a rapid pace and will increasingly affect every application you use and write.

Question: What does all this have to do with ActiveX?

Answer: Microsoft is pushing a vision of data-centric computing. ActiveX is Microsoft's implementation of that vision.

THE ROAD TO ACTIVEX

What we call ActiveX today did not appear overnight. Well, the name ActiveX did appear overnight, but the technology did not. It has evolved over the course of years, and knowing about this evolution can both help you understand today's technology and adapt to new technology as it appears.

DDE

The first step on the road to ActiveX was Dynamic Data Exchange (DDE). This capability is still supported by some applications and by Visual Basic, but only for backward compatibility with older applications. Few new applications support DDE to any substantial degree.

DDE was a first step in allowing applications to communicate with each other. This took two forms: data and commands. Applications could send or receive data to and from other applications. Data was identified by the application name and by individual topic and item names within that application. It was also possible to create hot links, so that one application could notify another when information changed.

Applications could also execute commands in another application. For example: if application MyWordProcessor had a macro command called OpenFile implemented via DDE, it would be possible to send an OpenFile execute command through DDE so that the word processor would open a specified file.

DDE was fairly limited, difficult to implement correctly, notoriously slow, and unreliable. It was also a rather application-centric approach to sharing data. It allowed applications to share data but did not allow documents to share data beyond those mechanisms built into the application.

So now that you know a little bit about DDE, feel free to forget most of what you've just read. DDE was a great step, but with one exception it ultimately turned out to be a step in the wrong direction. That exception is its ability to execute commands in other applications, a technology that was the ascendant of today's ActiveX automation.

OLE 1.0

OLE stands for Object Linking and Embedding. OLE 1 was the first step toward implementing one of the most important concepts in data-centric computing: the idea that a document can contain different types of objects. The linking and embedding term suggests the possible locations for objects that are part of a document. They can be embedded within a document, or linked, in which case the document simply contains the name of a file or other reference to the location where the object is stored.

OLE 1 also provided a way for applications to work with these compound documents. Any application could display a document consisting of many different types of objects, and you could double-click on the object in order to edit it using the application associated with the object. Consider the example in Figure 2.7. The document contains a text object and a spreadsheet object. If you opened the document using a word processor, you would see the text and the spreadsheet. The word processor would be able to handle the text directly, but if you wanted to edit the spreadsheet, you would double-click on the spreadsheet object. This would launch the spreadsheet application to edit the object. When you closed the spreadsheet, the object in the document would be updated with any changes you made.

This approach differs in two significant aspects from the application-centric techniques described earlier. First, no conversion takes place. The spreadsheet object remains a spreadsheet, even though it is in some unknown manner being displayed within a word processing application. Because no conversion takes place, no data is lost, and all of the original spreadsheet formatting is preserved. Second, because there is only one spreadsheet object, any changes made to the object from within the word processing application (if such a thing were possible) would affect the actual spreadsheet data. The problem of converting information back from the text document to the spreadsheet does not exist.

OLE 1.0 suffered from one major problem: it was a software technology that was ahead of the available hardware. This was the Windows 2.x and 3.0 era, an age where the 640K base memory limit was still quite real (even 3.0, with its virtual memory, required the lower 640K for many purposes). Attempting to run a large word processing application, such as Microsoft Word, at the same time as a large spreadsheet application, such as Excel, was a slow, frustrating, and often dangerous process. Truly, it was the age of the Unrecoverable Application

Error, as compared to the Windows 3.x era, which was the age of the General Protection Fault, as compared to the modern era which is the age of the Exception, or "Your program has performed an illegal operation," which comes in many different flavors.

Despite these limitations, OLE 1.0 was the first real step towards data-centric computing under Windows. And though it did not truly succeed, that's not surprising when you consider for a moment the challenge that implementing a data-centric environment presents.

A data-centric environment requires:

▶ A way for an application to display objects that it knows nothing about, since a true data-centric application must allow a document to contain any type of object, including those not even imagined when the application was created.

▶ A way for an application to load and save documents containing objects it knows nothing about.

▶ A way for an application to provide a visual interface that makes it possible to edit objects it knows nothing about.

And while we're at it, wouldn't it be nice to add:

▶ A way for an application to execute commands that manipulate objects it knows nothing about.

▶ A way for an application to support drag-and-drop capability on objects it knows nothing about.

Now, even a beginning programmer knows it's hard enough to work with program data when you know what it is. Manipulating data that your application doesn't even recognize is an intimidating, if not incomprehensible idea. But that's exactly what was needed, and the answer to that challenge was called OLE 2.0

OLE 2.0

In the next few pages, I'm going to attempt a task I suspect is nearly impossible: to provide a clear, understandable explanation of OLE 2.0. I've read quite a few attempts at this, and I must confess I've never been entirely satisfied. I wish I could say I am confident that I can do a better job. All I can say is that I'll do my best. You see, OLE 2.0 is possibly the most complex software technology I've ever seen. I don't think you'll find too many people who understand it completely, and I don't claim to be one of them.

But please don't let me scare you off. And please don't skip this section, going under the assumption that you can understand ActiveX without first understanding OLE 2.0 (the reasons will become obvious by the end of this chapter).

The good news is that you don't need to understand all of OLE 2.0 to use it. This is because much of the complexity is hidden by Visual Basic (and by the Microsoft Foundation Classes, for those of you using Visual C++). In fact, working with ActiveX in Visual Basic is so easy you can create ActiveX components without understanding much of anything. (OK, they may not be particularly good ActiveX components, but you wouldn't be bothering with this book if you didn't know that already.)

I have good reasons for asking you to go through the process of learning OLE 2.0 and ActiveX technology.

▶ It will help you to understand the language of ActiveX. For example: What is an interface? What is an IDispatch?

▶ It will help you to not only write good components, but to become a true expert at component development in Visual Basic (and my intent is to help you become nothing less than a guru on the subject).

▶ It's interesting stuff. After all, aside from being the easiest, most efficient and cost-effective Windows development environment around, VB is widely reputed to also be the most fun.

We'll tackle this technology in two parts. The remainder of this section will focus on the philosophy of OLE 2.0—the ideas on which it is based and the functionality it defines. Information on how it is implemented appears throughout the rest of Part I and is scattered throughout the rest of the book, as well. My hope is that a good understanding of the purpose behind the technology will help you to understand its implementation and its use.

A Technological Stew   The first thing to know about OLE 2.0 is that it is not a single technology. Rather, it is a collection of technologies that have relatively little to do with each other. The most important thing they have in common is they are all based on a standard way of working with objects.

Now, object is one of those words that essentially means whatever you want it to mean. There's object-oriented programming and objects as data structures within a program. But when we talk about objects in the context of OLE 2 or ActiveX, we are referring to a very specific type of object, sometimes called a *component object* or a *window object*. These objects follow a standard called *component object model* (COM). The COM standard defines the following:

1 A common way for applications to access and perform operations on objects. This will be the subject of Chapters 3 and 4.

2 A mechanism for keeping track of whether an object is in use and deleting it when it is no longer needed.

3 A standard error-reporting mechanism and set of error codes and values.

4 A mechanism for applications to exchange objects.

5 A way to identify objects and to associate objects with applications that understand how those objects are implemented.

Why are these factors important and how do they relate to the idea of data-centric computing? Consider our ongoing example of a document containing text and spreadsheet information in which the document is opened by a word processing application. How can the word processor display a spreadsheet object it knows nothing about?

If the spreadsheet object is a COM object, it's relatively easy. The COM object can support a standard set of functions that tell an object to display itself (COM standard #1). But what does it mean when we say that an object supports a set of functions? The word processor document contains the data for the spreadsheet. (How it keeps the spreadsheet data separate from the text data will be discussed shortly.) The document also contains an object identifier that tells the system the object is a spreadsheet. (Note that it tells the system, not the word processor!) The document does NOT contain the actual functions that draw the object. Those are kept in an application or .DLL that does understand the object, in this case, the spreadsheet application.

Where does the word processing application find the spreadsheet application that contains the drawing functions? It uses the COM mechanism for finding applications that implement objects (COM standard #5). Of course, before displaying the object it may need to launch that application and allow it to access the object's data (COM standard #4). If an error occurs while the spreadsheet object is being displayed by the other application, the word processor will understand the error (COM standard #3). And when both the spreadsheet and the word processor are done with the spreadsheet object, it will be deleted (COM standard #2).

This is a vast simplification of what goes on behind the scenes, but hopefully the point is clear. The common object model makes it possible for applications to manipulate objects they know nothing about. It is the enabling technology for data-centric computing that forms the foundation for everything from future Microsoft operating systems to ActiveX controls to Visual Basic itself.

I called OLE a technological stew. So what other tasty nuggets are contained within this sauce called COM? Here is a brief list of some of the more important features of OLE.

UUID (or GUID or CLSID)   One of the key requirements of OLE is the need to be able to identify objects. When an application works with a document that contains multiple objects, it needs to be able to identify each type of object so the system can correctly identify the application that can manage the object.

To accomplish this, COM assigns every type of object a 16-byte value. This value goes by a number of different names depending on how it is used. UUID stands for Universally Unique Identifier. GUID stands for Globally Unique Identifier. CLSID stands for Class Identifier. IID stands for Interface Identifier.

When you look at a GUID in the system registry, it typically looks something like this:

{970EDBA1-111C-11d0-92B0-00AA0036005A}

Now when Microsoft calls a GUID globally unique, they aren't kidding. Once a GUID is assigned to an object, it is effectively guaranteed to be unique throughout the entire universe, forever. Two factors go into making sure the number is unique. First, part of each GUID is generated based on the network card address in your system (assuming one exists), and every network card built has a unique address thanks to industry standards relating to these cards. Second, a GUID is a very large number, so even if you don't have a network card, a GUID generator program can create a number whose odds of duplicating another are microscopically small.

Visual Basic 5.0 will create GUID numbers for your objects automatically (in fact, you'll have a greater problem cleaning up GUID numbers you don't need than in creating new ones). The important thing to remember is that the objects you create in VB are identified by the GUID—not the object name—so even if you use the same object name as someone else (something you should avoid if possible), your program will still work; it won't confuse the objects.

GUID numbers are also used to identify sets of functions called interfaces, but you'll find out about that later.

Object Presentation   OLE defines standard mechanisms by which objects can be displayed. This means that a container application, such as Microsoft Word, can allocate a space on the screen or on a printed page and allow the object to draw itself into that space. How does this happen? Word knows the GUID of the object and the standard functions the object uses for display (and other purposes). The system can search for the GUID on the registry and find the application or .DLL that contains the actual code for these functions.

But OLE 2.0 goes even farther. It defines a mechanism by which an object's application (server) can take over portions of a document container so you can use all of the tools of that application to edit the object, even though it is still within the same container. This is called *in-place editing*, and a form of this mechanism is an essential part of what makes ActiveX controls work. Fortunately, Visual Basic automatically handles essentially all of the implementation details of this rather complex technology.

Object Marshaling   OLE defines a mechanism by which objects can be transferred between applications, a process called *marshaling*. If you are new to 32-bit programming, this may not seem to be a big issue, as it is relatively easy to transfer blocks of memory between processes in 16-bit Windows. However, you will quickly learn that transferring objects between processes is much more difficult under 32-bit Windows. Fortunately, OLE handles most of the work for you. This subject will be covered in much more depth in Chapter 6.

Windows now includes an extended form of COM called Distributed Common Object Model (DCOM). DCOM objects can be marshaled between applications running on different systems on a network.

Compound Documents (OLE Structured Storage)   If a document can contain many types of objects, how can a given container save a document? It would need to understand the file format for each of the objects, an impossible task given that the application may be totally unaware of the nature of the object or how it works. Or would it be?

OLE handles object persistence (loading and saving of objects) in the same way that it handles object display: it is the object's responsibility to know how to load and save itself from a file. Just as OLE defines a set of functions for object display, it also defines a set of functions that can be supported by an object to persist itself.

It might occur to you that this can lead to serious problems. If any one of the objects has a bug in its file I/O code, it could interfere with the portion of the file used by other objects, possibly overwriting and corrupting parts of the file. The problem of storing objects within a file is solved using an OLE technology called OLE Structured Storage. Under OLE Structured Storage, a file is divided into a hierarchy of storages and streams, where a storage corresponds roughly to a directory, and a stream corresponds roughly to a file. In effect, you have an entire file system contained within a single disk file. A container such as Word can create a storage or stream and pass it to the object, telling the object to save itself into the storage or stream. In most cases the container will also save the GUID of the object so when the document is loaded it will be able to determine the type of object that is stored in that particular storage or stream.

Figure 2.8 shows the contents of an OLE Structured Storage document created by Word for Windows (a .DOC file) containing a spreadsheet document. Storages are indicated by file folders, streams by pages. The text portion of the file is kept in a stream called WordDocument. The spreadsheet object is kept in the ObjectPool storage. The spreadsheet object in turn has as many streams of data as it wishes to use, including, in this case, streams containing summary information about the spreadsheet.

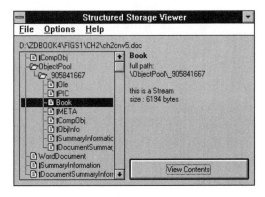

Figure 2.8: Inside a Microsoft Word .DOC file

OLE Structured Storage is not the only way for objects to save data, as you will see with regard to ActiveX controls developed in Visual Basic. However, one common theme remains: that it is the responsibility of each object to handle its own persistence.

Drag-and-Drop Few operations require more cooperation between applications than the ability to drag-and-drop objects from one application to another. Each application must decide what objects the user can select and drag and must provide a reference to that object to the system. It must also decide what types of objects it can accept from other applications and how to handle those objects. OLE 2.0 defines a mechanism for drag-drop operations not only between applications, but between applications and the operating system.

OLE Automation (ActiveX Automation)   This is definitely a case of leaving the best till last. OLE automation is the descendent of DDE's ability to allow one application to execute commands in another application, but it is far more powerful. You see, OLE allows any application to expose any number of objects to the world. OLE automation allows you to execute commands those objects make available or to transfer data to and from those objects.

OLE automation makes it possible for an application to not only call those functions, but to determine at runtime what functions an object has made available and what parameters they require (should the object wish to make that information public).

OLE automation forms the basis for much of the operation of ActiveX components, and it will, in fact, be the focus of the next few chapters. But before we delve further into this subject, there is one more step we need to go through. How do we get from OLE 2.0 to ActiveX? And where do ActiveX controls fit in?

Before we can answer that question, there is one more technology that needs to be discussed. A technology that surprised everyone by its success, and one that has absolutely nothing to do with OLE.

ENTER THE VBX

In 1991 Visual Basic was released by Microsoft. In this age of Visual Programming, it is sometimes hard to remember that Visual Basic was truly a revolutionary development in Windows programming. Until then, even the simplest Windows application consisted of hundreds of lines of C code. It was common for beginning Windows programmers to take six months of hard study to reach a level of even moderate competence. Overall, Windows programming was a complex and rather unpleasant experience.

Visual Basic changed all that. You could write a simple Windows application in minutes. For the first time it was possible to write trivial throwaway Windows applications for simple tasks. Windows programming was even fun.

Visual Basic did this by encapsulating much of the complexity of Windows into the Basic language. The forms layout package made creating a user interface easy. (Note that I did not say it made making a good user interface easy. VB makes it as easy to create a bad user interface as a good one—maybe easier.) You simply dropped controls onto forms. These controls had properties you could set from your application. The values of these properties could be set at design time and stored in the application. Most controls had their own user interface as well—they were displayed on the form and could be clicked or otherwise manipulated at runtime.

If this was all Visual Basic did, it would be a remarkable product. But Visual Basic's developers took things one critical step further. They made the language extensible. First, they made it possible for Visual Basic to directly access functions in dynamic link libraries, especially those in the Windows API. (My first book, the *Visual Basic Programmer's Guide to the Win32 API*, and its successor, *Dan Appleman's Visual Basic 5.0 Programmer's Guide to the Win32 API*, both from ZD Press, discuss this subject at length.) Next, they made it possible to add custom controls (VBX) to Visual Basic in such a way that they appear to the programmer as if they were built into the environment itself. They appear in the toolbox and behave exactly like those controls that are built into the language.

All of a sudden an entire industry sprang up to create and market a wide variety of custom controls for almost any imaginable application. (I founded a company myself, Desaware, for the sole purpose of developing Visual Basic custom controls.) An amazing synergy then took place. The availability of a wide variety of custom controls made Visual Basic more powerful and more popular. The presence of a large Visual Basic market allowed VBX developers to amortize their costs across a large customer base, allowing them to sell their controls at prices far below what it would cost a programmer to develop the same functionality on their own. This was essential because VBXs, being written in C or C++, were notoriously difficult to write—far more difficult than programming in Visual Basic. Meanwhile, Microsoft consciously supported the custom control market by encouraging and promoting these third-party vendors.

You see, Visual Basic not only realized the dream of easy Windows programming. It realized the dream of component-based programming. It made it possible to develop complex applications that are built up from low-cost reusable software components. The combination served to make Visual Basic the enormous success that it has become, selling far more copies than languages such as C or C++.

Now let's back up for a moment and reconsider the characteristics of a custom control. It is an *object* of a sort. It *contains* data. The part of the data that is set at design time can be saved in a project file, and each custom control knows how to save its own data. Visual Basic can support any type of VBX, because each VBX contains a standard set of *functions* that Visual Basic can manipulate. A custom control can have a visual appearance, and each VBX is responsible for drawing itself when instructed to do so by the Visual Basic environment. An executable contains the persisted data for a custom control, but the implementation of the control—the functions that make it work—is kept in a separate dynamic link library with the extension .VBX. Visual Basic stores with the executable, on a form, not only the data for each instance of the control (each control object), but also information identifying the control so it can load the correct VBX for each object.

Does any of this sound familiar? It should. Those are the same characteristics we described earlier for an OLE 2.0 object. Now, let me stress: A VBX is *not* a COM object. It is based on its own VB-specific technology that is implemented only in 16-bit Windows for VB3, 16-bit VB4, and environments that have tried to be more or less compatible with the VBX standard.

ENTER VISUAL BASIC 4.0

Visual Basic 1.0, as revolutionary as it was, was grafted from a number of existing technologies. It used a Basic language engine that was written in 16-bit assembly language. This language engine was grafted onto a forms package architecture called Ruby, which was originally developed by Alan Cooper, the father of Visual Basic. Clearly, Visual Basic as it was implemented in version 1.0 through 3.0 was not a sound foundation for the long term, especially with regard to the new 32-bit operating systems then under development. Microsoft therefore began work on a language engine called Object Basic, which is now known as VBA, or Visual Basic for Applications. This would become the underlying programming language not only for Visual Basic 4.0 and its successors, but for all of the Microsoft applications, or at least the programmable ones. In fact, Microsoft is now licensing VBA for use in non-Microsoft applications as well.

VBA was a complete redesign and rewrite of the language engine. Most of the details of what has changed are mysteries known only to Microsoft developers, but the most important one is clear. VBA is based on COM.

What does this mean? It means that VBA is built up of objects that are true OLE objects. Not only does VBA use OLE automation to program other objects and applications, it uses OLE internally to execute commands on its own objects. It also uses OLE when you create your own objects that can then be used either from within VBA or made public and used from other applications.

When Microsoft developers rebuilt Visual Basic 4.0 on COM technology, they knew they still needed to support custom controls. But they also knew that VBX technology was obsolete. What they needed was an OLE equivalent. Fortunately, they almost had one already. You see, OLE already provided the ability for objects to be placed in containers. Those objects could already be programmed using OLE automation. They already had the ability to save themselves into files. The only thing those objects could not do was raise events.

The answer was simple. Extend OLE. A new type of object was defined called an OLE control (OCX), which defined a way for controls to raise events in the container application. It also defined some new functions to improve performance and add some additional capabilities. Not only were OLE controls compatible with Visual Basic 4.0, but they could be used with minor modifications by virtually any OLE container.

To say that the answer was simple is perhaps misleading. The implementation of this technology is complex and took quite a while to develop. And it is still evolving. But OLE is by its very nature extendible. You'll find out how and why this is so as you read on, because you'll be using the same techniques to extend your own objects.

ActiveX: Is It Technology or Is It Marketing?

Let's review for a moment.

We started out by looking at the problems related to building complex documents in an application-centric environment.

We then took a look at what a docu-centric environment would be like, and what it would require.

We then saw how COM made it possible to implement many of the technologies that a docu-centric environment would require.

We saw that OLE was not one technology, but a whole set of technologies that are seemingly unrelated except for the fact that they are based on COM and relate to docu-centric environments.

We saw that Visual Basic combined with VBX custom control technology, became an extremely successful platform for component-based software development, but that it was not viable in the long term.

Finally, we saw how Visual Basic 4.0 was built on VBA, a COM-based language engine, and how OLE was extended to include OLE controls, a COM-based custom control technology.

As you can see, the technology has been evolving towards a more docu-centric approach for years. Yet the process is still very much in its early stages.

So far we've been talking about OLE 2.0. You may be wondering where ActiveX comes in. The answer may surprise you. But before proceeding, I want to clarify one thing. I am not an employee of Microsoft, and aside from a brief contract job several years ago, have never worked for them. Much of what I know about Microsoft and how it works is based on informal discussions with Microsoft employees, information they make public, reports in

the media, an understanding of the technology, and, sometimes, sheer specu-
lation. So, while I have little, if any, inside information that a Microsoft employee might have, I do have a correspondingly greater freedom to share my
opinions. I don't have to adhere to the "party line."

That said, here is the truth about ActiveX as I know it.

Think of the world as it existed in late 1995 and early 1996. Visual Basic 4.0
was shipping, and OLE was well on its way to establishing a dominant standard
for object embedding and programming. It was driving Microsoft's vision for
docu-centric computing.

Then, as if from nowhere, the Internet frenzy, specifically the World Wide
Web, went into a growth curve of hyperbolic proportions. Now, I truly believe
that much of what you read about the Internet is overblown media hype. Much
of the investment in Internet-related products and companies is going to prove
to be a waste of money. It is still way too early to forecast what will happen
with the Internet, what kinds of markets will develop, and what its impact on
society will be in the long run.

I do know enough about Microsoft to know that, as chaotic as it may be sometimes as an organization, it is an organization that includes a large number of extremely bright people. Yet, on the surface, it looks as if their collective reaction to
the Internet was nothing short of panic. All of a sudden, Microsoft had a strategy that seemed to be: "Whatever we do must have an Internet component."
Surely Microsoft was not actually afraid of Netscape? Could the Internet really
challenge Microsoft's vision of a computer on every desktop running Microsoft
software on Microsoft operating systems? (By the way, when I describe this as
their vision, I'm not being critical. This is, as near as I can tell, their actual corporate vision. If you don't like the idea, that's your judgment call.)

It was only when I began outlining this book that it became clear to me. I
don't think Microsoft was afraid of Netscape as a company. I think they were
suddenly tremendously afraid of the World Wide Web as a vision. You see, the
trend towards a Windows-based docu-centric programming scheme was well
under way when, all of a sudden, here came the World Wide Web, an environment clearly docu-centric by nature. Why, HTML pages routinely contain all
sorts of objects from formatted text, to picture, to sound, to video. With Java,
Web pages can include code-based objects. HTML is easily extendible to include other types of objects as well. HTML documents are easy to create, and
becoming easier as advanced tools become available.

In a way, the Web presents a conceptual leap over Microsoft's approach. Application programmers are only now getting used to the idea of embedding
different types of objects in word processing documents or spreadsheets,

where these objects are typically located on the same system or maybe a local network. Web programmers start with the fundamental understanding that documents can and should be built up of pages of different types, where each page may exist anywhere in the entire world. HTML is limited when compared to OLE technology, but it promotes a way of thinking that could jeopardize Microsoft's approach towards docu-centric computing.

I believe this is why Microsoft panicked. They weren't afraid of Netscape. They were afraid that the World Wide Web (including HTML, Java, and a non-COM-based object standard) would become the dominant implementation of a docu-centric programming environment.

So Microsoft changed its approach. They adopted the Internet. This was easier than it might seem. OLE was, by its very nature, extendible. It wouldn't take much effort to add a few Internet extensions and make OLE a strongly competitive mechanism for implementing compound documents on the Internet in a way that was fully compatible with HTML.

But technology isn't everything. Perceptions count as well. Microsoft needed an Internet message. They needed to show the world they were serious about the Internet. They didn't really have an Internet-specific technology yet, but they needed a dramatic way to show they would have one soon and a sound technological foundation that would clearly become viable on the Internet.

Here's what they did: They renamed OLE and called it ActiveX.

OLE is ActiveX. It's that simple. ActiveX automation is OLE automation. All OLE controls instantly became ActiveX controls. They were not all Internet-enabled ActiveX controls (some very useful controls have nothing to do with the Internet), but they were all, by definition, ActiveX controls. ActiveX *code components* are OLE servers. The name has changed, but the technology is the same. ActiveX documents are *Doc Objects*.

I can't stress this enough. Microsoft's marketing team has gone to great lengths to promote ActiveX as an Internet technology. This is essential from their point of view because Microsoft desperately wants it to be the dominant object technology on the Internet and on corporate intranets. But as a Visual Basic programmer, you may find that the Internet is the least important aspect of ActiveX in your own efforts. Visual Basic 5.0's ability to create ActiveX controls may prove a good way to create flashy Web pages. It *will* become the most powerful tool for component-based application development yet created. Of that I am certain.

Rest assured, this book will discuss how to deploy ActiveX controls and ActiveX documents (previously called doc objects) on the Internet. But the emphasis will be on the technology in general and on the ways you can use this technology to craft great applications that may or may not be Internet based.

This concludes our historical perspective. From now on, I'll usually refer to the technology as ActiveX, but you'll know that it and OLE are one and the same. Now it's time to take a look at how this is implemented, at least at the Visual Basic level.

Objects and Visual Basic

I remember a course from my sophomore year in college titled ICS2 (Information and Computer Science #2—go figure). It was several weeks into the course, and I was struggling to understand the concept of *class* in a language called Simula. For those of you who are curious, Simula is one of those languages college professors seem to love, but they never catch on, and nobody can quite understand why. Think of it as a "better" kind of Pascal (before Pascal fragmented into almost as many dialects as there are programmers).

Anyway, up until then I'd been programming in Basic, which also has fragmented into many dialects, but nobody seems to care. The professor must have explained the idea of class a dozen times, but I just didn't get it. How can a data structure contain a function? It just didn't make any sense.

Then one day lightning struck, figuratively speaking, and I got it. I not only understood what classes were all about, but I realized they were a phenomenal tool for building applications. I had discovered object-oriented programming and have used it ever since, at least where it was supported by the language I was using.

When people talk about the relative importance of features introduced in Visual Basic 4.0, they often talk about the 32-bit support, the support for OLE automation (excuse me, Active X) .DLLs, performance improvements, or other features. For me, the single most important feature in Visual Basic 4.0 was the introduction of the class module, not because it supported servers or OLE automation, but because I had classes back. I could finally apply object-oriented techniques in my favorite language.

Now, if you are comfortable programming with classes, if you appreciate their importance, and if your first step in designing any VB application is to consider what classes abstract the data and functionality of your project, then you can skim through and perhaps even skip this chapter. But if you routinely create applications that do not use class modules, if you think they are only important for creating programmable objects (EXE or DLL servers), or if you have no idea why I would be so excited about class modules that I would call them the single most important advance from VB3 to VB4, this chapter is for you. Even if you are an absolutely beginning Visual Basic programmer.

THE THEORY OF OBJECT-ORIENTED PROGRAMMING

An object, in the context of object-oriented programming, exhibits the following three characteristics:

- Encapsulation

- Polymorphism

- Inheritance

Whoa.... Let's back up for a moment.

Object-oriented programming is one of those terms in computer science that have a number of unfortunate side effects.

- It's intimidating—beginning programmers often look upon it as some sort of advanced technique only expert programmers can use.

- It sounds advanced—like something that a beginning or intermediate level programmer can learn later once he or she is comfortable with the language.

Wrong on both counts.

It's not surprising that the term produces this reaction when people so often use terms like *encapsulation, polymorphism,* and *inheritance* to describe it.

You know, I probably have read about the true definition of object-oriented programming, the necessity for polymorphism, and the trade-offs between inheritance and aggregation dozens of times. But I never seem to be able to remember all of the academic arguments. And since VB5 isn't a true object-oriented language anyway (by the strict academic definition), I don't think it really matters.

In fact, now that I think about it, it seems to me that studying the theory of object-oriented programming has to be about the worst possible way to learn it. Perhaps we can find a different approach and come back to the theory later if necessary.

So let's just skip the rest of this section.

OBJECTLESS PROGRAMMING

I have an ambitious goal here. I don't want to just explain object-oriented programming. I want to convert you to this way of programming. I want to convince you it is the only way to program. I believe this will not only make your ActiveX programming efforts more successful, it will also allow you to improve all of your software efforts.

Theory is very interesting, but in this case I don't trust it to prove my point. Instead, let's start by looking at the way many people program and examining how object-oriented programming techniques can improve on that approach.

In other words, let's code.

A simple application should do. Consider a simple retail sales application—the kind that you might create for a fast-food restaurant. Figure 3.1 shows the main form for the Retail1 project. There are four buttons, each for a different type of food. Clicking on a button adds the specified item to the bill. The clear button clears the current order. When you enter an amount paid, the change box will show the amount of change due. You can double-click on an item in the list box to reduce the order for the specified item.

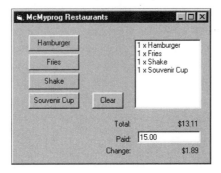

Figure 3.1: Main form for Retail1 application

It's a simple application and relatively foolproof, even though it lacks some of the data validation one would add to a commercial quality application. For example, if you add a $ sign to the Paid box, it will not parse the value correctly.

This sample was coded by drawing the user interface, adding a couple of arrays to hold the price and item count, then attaching code to events where it makes sense. Listing 3.1 shows the code for this implementation. Two zero-based arrays are used in this application. Zero-based simply means that index zero of the array contains useful information. The prices(3) menu thus contains four entries (0 to 3), each of which will be loaded with the price of a food item. The four command buttons are a zero-based control array. The captions of the buttons contain the name of the menu items. The items array contains a count representing the quantity of each menu item ordered.

Listing 3.1: Listing for Form frmRetail1.frm

```
' Retail example #1
' ActiveX: Guide to the Perplexed
' Copyright (c) 1997 by Desaware Inc.


Option Explicit


' Zero based array of items
Dim prices(3) As Currency  ' Prices of menu entries
' Zero based quantities
Dim items(3) As Integer


Private Sub Form_Load()
    prices(0) = 1.99
    prices(1) = 0.89
    prices(2) = 1.29
    prices(3) = 8.94  ' A bargain at any price
    UpdateAll
End Sub


' Add an item to the order
Private Sub cmdMenu_Click(Index As Integer)
    items(Index) = items(Index) + 1
    UpdateAll
End Sub


' Clear this order
Private Sub cmdClear_Click()
    Dim itemnum%
```

Listing 3.1: Listing for Form frmRetail1.frm (Continued)

```
   For itemnum = 0 To 3
      items(itemnum) = 0
   Next itemnum
   UpdateAll
End Sub


' Updates the contents of the list box
Public Sub UpdateListBox()
   Dim itemnum%
   lstItems.Clear
   For itemnum = 0 To 3
      If items(itemnum) > 0 Then
         lstItems.AddItem items(itemnum) & " x " & cmdMenu(itemnum).Caption
         lstItems.ItemData(lstItems.NewIndex) = itemnum
      End If
   Next itemnum
End Sub


' Delete an item on double click
Private Sub lstItems_DblClick()
   Dim thisitem%
   thisitem = lstItems.ItemData(lstItems.ListIndex)
   items(thisitem) = items(thisitem) - 1
   UpdateAll
End Sub


' Calculate the total price
Public Function CalculateTotal() As Currency
   Dim itemnum%
   Dim total As Currency

   For itemnum = 0 To 3
      total = total + items(itemnum) * prices(itemnum)
   Next itemnum
   CalculateTotal = total
End Function


' Display the total and change
Public Sub UpdateTotals()
   Dim total As Currency
   Dim paid As Currency
```

Listing 3.1: Listing for Form frmRetail1.frm (Continued)

```
   total = CalculateTotal()
   lblTotal.Caption = Format(total, "Currency")
   paid = Val(txtPaid.Text)
   If paid - total > 0 Then
      lblChange.Caption = Format(paid - total, "Currency")
   Else
      lblChange.Caption = "Please pay"
   End If
End Sub



Private Sub txtPaid_Change()
   UpdateTotals
End Sub



Public Sub UpdateAll()
   UpdateListBox
   UpdateTotals
End Sub
```

How is this code flawed? The major obvious error is that the number of items on the menu is hard coded. This means not only can the menu items not be changed dynamically, but changing them requires recoding the application. This may be fine for a quick and dirty prototype, but it's terrible design.

We won't even discuss the user interface. Its only saving grace is that it is simple. It wouldn't take you more than a few minutes to train someone to use the program.

And it could have been worse—much worse.

You can see that even in this quick throw-together code, there are some good ideas. The prices are in an array. True, its size is hard coded, but it suggests the possibility of run-time price changes in the future. The command buttons are in an array as well. Perhaps run-time menus will be possible? What about custom pricing—you might want to have a separate senior menu? Having the pricing in an array makes this possible.

The code has some modularity. The list box updating is centralized, as is the totaling. This means that anytime code changes something that might affect the current order, it need only call the UpdateAll function—it does not have to worry about dealing with the list box or total fields directly.

Let's implement some of these obvious improvements as shown in Listing 3.2.

Listing 3.2: Listing Form frmRetail2.frm

```
' Retail example #2
' ActiveX: Guide to the Perplexed
' Copyright (c) 1997 by Desaware Inc.


Option Explicit


' Zero based array of items
Dim prices() As Currency   ' Prices of menu entries
' Zero based quantities
Dim items() As Integer
' ID of the next menu item
Dim NextItem As Integer


' Clear this order
Private Sub cmdClear_Click()
    Dim itemnum%
    For itemnum = 0 To UBound(items)
        items(itemnum) = 0
    Next itemnum
    UpdateAll
End Sub


' Add an item to the order
Private Sub cmdMenu_Click(Index As Integer)
    items(Index) = items(Index) + 1
    UpdateAll
End Sub


Private Sub Form_Load()
    mnuStandard_Click
End Sub


' Updates the contents of the list box
Public Sub UpdateListBox()
    Dim itemnum%
    lstItems.Clear
    For itemnum = 0 To UBound(items)
        If items(itemnum) > 0 Then
```

Listing 3.2: Listing Form frmRetail2.frm (Continued)

```
                 lstItems.AddItem items(itemnum) & " x " & cmdMenu(itemnum).Caption
                 lstItems.ItemData(lstItems.NewIndex) = itemnum
            End If
        Next itemnum
End Sub



' Calculate the total price
Public Function CalculateTotal() As Currency
    Dim itemnum%
    Dim total As Currency


    For itemnum = 0 To UBound(items)
        total = total + items(itemnum) * prices(itemnum)
    Next itemnum
    CalculateTotal = total
End Function



' Display the total and change
Public Sub UpdateTotals()
    Dim total As Currency
    Dim paid As Currency
    total = CalculateTotal()
    lblTotal.Caption = Format(total, "Currency")
    paid = Val(txtPaid.Text)
    If paid - total > 0 Then
        lblChange.Caption = Format(paid - total, "Currency")
    Else
        lblChange.Caption = "Please pay"
    End If
End Sub



' Delete an item on double click
Private Sub lstItems_DblClick()
    Dim thisitem%
    thisitem = lstItems.ItemData(lstItems.ListIndex)
    items(thisitem) = items(thisitem) - 1
    UpdateAll
End Sub



' Set a standard menu
Private Sub mnuStandard_Click()
```

Listing 3.2: Listing Form frmRetail2.frm (Continued)

```
    ClearMenuItems
    AddMenuItem "Hamburger", 1.99
    AddMenuItem "Curly Fries", 1.32
    AddMenuItem "Side Salad", 2.39
    AddMenuItem "Chicken", 2.32
    AddMenuItem "Stuff Delux", 5.39
    UpdateAll
End Sub


' And a senior citizen's menu
Private Sub mnuSenior_Click()
    ClearMenuItems
    AddMenuItem "Hamburger", 1.79
    AddMenuItem "Fries", 1.12
    AddMenuItem "Chicken Soup", 2.39
    AddMenuItem "Salad", 2.12
    AddMenuItem "LoCal Delux", 5.19
    UpdateAll
End Sub


' and, of course, a programmer's menu
Private Sub mnuProgrammer_Click()
    ClearMenuItems
    AddMenuItem "Hamburger", 2.19
    AddMenuItem "Pizza", 2.52
    AddMenuItem "Cheetos", 0.89
    AddMenuItem "Jolt", 1.19
    AddMenuItem "More Jolt", 2.19
    UpdateAll
End Sub


Private Sub txtPaid_Change()
    UpdateTotals
End Sub


Public Sub UpdateAll()
    UpdateListBox
    UpdateTotals
End Sub
```

Listing 3.2: Listing Form frmRetail2.frm (Continued)

```
' Create a menu item
Public Sub AddMenuItem(ByVal itemname$, ByVal itemprice As Currency)
    Dim currenttop%
    If NextItem > 0 Then
        ' Don't bother creating button 0
        Load cmdMenu(NextItem)
    End If
    ReDim Preserve items(NextItem)
    ReDim Preserve prices(NextItem)
    prices(NextItem) = itemprice
    items(NextItem) = 0
    cmdMenu(NextItem).Caption = itemname
    cmdMenu(NextItem).Top = cmdMenu(0).Top + NextItem * 450
    cmdMenu(NextItem).Visible = True

    NextItem = NextItem + 1
End Sub


' Clear all of the menu items.
Public Sub ClearMenuItems()
    Dim itemnum%
    Dim currenttop%
    If NextItem = 0 Then Exit Sub ' Already clear
    currenttop = UBound(items)
    For itemnum = 1 To currenttop
        Unload cmdMenu(itemnum)
    Next itemnum
    ReDim items(0)
    ReDim prices(0)
    NextItem = 0
End Sub
```

Some of the changes here are obvious. All of the looping routines are now based on the upper bound of the arrays, so they will work correctly regardless of the number of items on the menu. The menu items themselves are created dynamically using the AddMenuItem and ClearMenuItems functions. A popup menu (Windows menu, not food menu) has been added to support multiple menus.

Take a few minutes to look over these two samples. Try running them from the CD. You'll want to be sure you understand how they work when considering the scenario in the next section.

HAS THIS EVER HAPPENED TO YOU?

So, you've just delivered your simple point-of-sale program, on time and under budget, of course. The customer (or your manager) looks it over, tests it out using real employees, and everybody is raving about it. Then you hear those words that send chills down every programmer's spine: "I'd just like a few minor changes."

They continue, "You see, we think we can really improve efficiency by having each register hold several orders at once. That way the cashier can take a second order while waiting on the first. All you need to do is add a few buttons so the cashier can switch between orders. But don't worry, we don't need to support more than three or four menus at a time, and I can see there is plenty of space on the form."

What do you need to do to change the retail2.vbp example to support this "minor" modification?

Well, you need multiple orders, and since each order is kept in an array, that means multiple array—perhaps a two-dimensional array? But then how can we get the redimensioning to work properly? Remember that each order may have a different menu associated with it. And every time you switch between orders you need to switch the menu.

You suddenly realize you are in deep trouble, because your program simply wasn't designed with this possibility in mind. Sure, you can fix the problem—but the changes will affect virtually every function in the program. It will almost be like writing the program from scratch.

ONCE AGAIN, WITH OBJECTS

Let's look at the problem again, but this time with some thought toward proper design.

This time, we'll use Visual Basic's ability to define objects when designing the application. This section does assume that you have at least a beginner's familiarity with how to add a class module to your application, and how to add methods and properties to your class module. If this is completely new to you, you may want to take a look at the Visual Basic 5.0 programmer's guide in the VB5 books online.

In this book, the chapter "Programming with Objects" in Part 2 includes a section called "Class Module Step by Step" that walks you through the process of creating a class module and adding a method. The process of adding functions and subroutines to a class module is identical to adding them to a form, so you should find the code in the following examples easy to follow even if you have never used class modules before.

The register application allows a cashier to select items from a fixed menu to build an order. Each item on the menu has a price and a name. The order may contain one or more items from the menu. An order also has a total price that can be derived from the list of items. Conceptually, we're looking at three objects: a menu, menu items, and an order.

Each menu contains one or more menu items, each of which has a price and a name. An order contains one or more menu items, with an associated quantity for each one.

Keep in mind here that I'm referring in this section to a food menu in a fast-food cash register application. This has nothing to do with Visual Basic menus and menu objects, the kind that drop down from the top of a window. (I realize that this may seem obvious to you, but I assure you that if I did not clarify this here, I would be destined to receive any number of e-mail messages from people wondering about the relationship between hamburgers and pop-up menus.)

On a more serious note, as with most of the examples in this book, there is no one right design for a given application. In most cases there will be many different solutions, even if you take an object-oriented approach.

One critical decision to make when implementing the menu object is to decide whether a menu item will be an object or an entry in an array. In the Retail1 and Retail2 samples, each menu item had its price stored in the prices array and the name stored in the button caption. This was a rather awkward solution, to put it kindly. Two obvious solutions come to mind:

1 Keep the menu items in an array of prices and names. This approach is efficient—redimensioning an array is a fast process. But it makes it difficult or impossible to work with individual menu items outside of the menu class.

2 Define a new class to hold the menu items. This approach makes it possible to expose the menu item object as a subobject for a menu or to easily pass it as parameters to other routines in the application, should it become necessary.

In this case, I decided that menu items will only be an internal construct for the clsMenu1 class. As such, it really doesn't matter to the rest of the program how they are implemented. The item list exists as an array of a user-defined type. This eliminates the need to manipulate separate arrays for each item. Using a user-defined type is also consistent with an object-oriented methodology. You can think of a user-defined type as a very simple type of object that only has properties, though it is not implemented as a COM object. Listing 3.3 shows the implementation for a menu object.

Listing 3.3: Listing for clsMenu1, the Menu Object

```
' Retail example #3
' ActiveX: Guide to the Perplexed
' Copyright (c) 1997 by Desaware Inc.


Option Explicit
' A type describing the item
Private Type MenuItem
    ItemName As String
    ItemPrice As Currency
End Type


Private MenuList() As MenuItem    ' Array of menu items
Private NextItem As Integer        ' Next item to load
' Method to add menu items to the clsMenu object
Public Sub AddMenuItem(ByVal ItemName$, ByVal ItemPrice As Currency)
    Dim currenttop%
    ReDim Preserve MenuList(NextItem)
    MenuList(NextItem).ItemPrice = ItemPrice
    MenuList(NextItem).ItemName = ItemName
    NextItem = NextItem + 1
End Sub


' Retrieve the number of items in this menu
Public Function ItemCount() As Integer
    ItemCount = NextItem
End Function


' Expose the price and name as functions
Public Function ItemPrice(ByVal itemnum As Integer)
    ' We can do error checking
    If itemnum >= NextItem Then Exit Function
    ItemPrice = MenuList(itemnum).ItemPrice
End Function


Public Function ItemName(ByVal itemnum As Integer)
    ' We can do error checking
    If itemnum >= NextItem Then Exit Function
    ItemName = MenuList(itemnum).ItemName
End Function
```

The clsMenu1 object has an AddMenuItem method for adding individual menu items. The ItemName and ItemPrice functions allow you to retrieve the name and price for any item.

An order consists of an array of quantities for each item on a menu. This means each order must have an associated menu, which in this case is whichever menu is currently in use by the application. This was implemented by the "items" array in the Retail1 and Retail2 example, but we can isolate that implementation from the rest of the program by encapsulating it into a class, as shown in Listing 3.4.

Listing 3.4: Listing for clsOrder1, the Order Object

```
' Retail example #3
' ActiveX: Guide to the Perplexed
' Copyright (c) 1997 by Desaware Inc.


Option Explicit
Dim ItemList() As Integer
' Start the array off with at least one entry
Private Sub Class_Initialize()
    ReDim ItemList(0)
End Sub


' Clear the current order
Public Sub Clear()
    Dim entry%
    For entry = 0 To UBound(ItemList)
        ItemList(entry) = 0
    Next entry
End Sub


' The quantity of a particular menu item


Public Property Get Quantity(ByVal itemnum%) As Integer
    ' Invalid value, just return zero
    If itemnum > UBound(ItemList) Then Exit Property
    Quantity = ItemList(itemnum)
End Property
```

Listing 3.4: Listing for clsOrder1, the Order Object (Continued)

```
Public Property Let Quantity(ByVal itemnum%, ByVal iNewQuantity As Integer)
    If itemnum > UBound(ItemList) Then
        ReDim Preserve ItemList(itemnum)
    End If
    ItemList(itemnum) = iNewQuantity
End Property
```

The clsOrder1 class has a number of methods and properties that expose the internal array to the rest of the program. The Quantity property allows you to set or retrieve the quantity for any given menu item. Using Get/Let functions to access the property allows error checking and array management to be handled automatically during the property access.

The Clear method clears the order. Could you create a function at the form level or module level to clear an order simply by setting all of the Quantity property values to zero? Of course you could. But the whole idea of object-oriented programming is to associate code with a set of data. If you have an operation that needs to be performed on the data within an object, you should almost always implement it as a method for the object.

From the user's perspective, the Retail3 and Retail2 projects are identical. They work exactly the same way. However, the Retail3 project is implemented using the clsMenu1 and clsOrder1 projects, as shown in Listing 3.5.

Listing 3.5: Listing for frmRetail3.frm, the Main Form for the Retail3 Project

```
' Retail example #3
' ActiveX: Guide to the Perplexed
' Copyright (c) 1997 by Desaware Inc.


Option Explicit


Dim HighestButtonIndex As Integer
' The menu to use
Dim CurrentMenu As clsMenu1


' The three standard menus
Dim StandardMenu As New clsMenu1
Dim SeniorMenu As New clsMenu1
Dim ProgrammerMenu As New clsMenu1
```

Listing 3.5: Listing for frmRetail3.frm, the Main Form for the Retail3 Project (Continued)

```
' The current order
Dim CurrentOrder As New clsOrder1


' Load the menu selection here.
' It goes without saying that in a real application
' these would probably be loaded from a database.
Private Sub Form_Load()
   With StandardMenu
      .AddMenuItem "Hamburger", 1.99
      .AddMenuItem "Curly Fries", 1.32
      .AddMenuItem "Side Salad", 2.39
      .AddMenuItem "Chicken", 2.32
      .AddMenuItem "Stuff Delux", 5.39
   End With
   With SeniorMenu
      .AddMenuItem "Hamburger", 1.79
      .AddMenuItem "Fries", 1.12
      .AddMenuItem "Chicken Soup", 2.39
      .AddMenuItem "Salad", 2.12
      .AddMenuItem "LoCal Delux", 5.19
   End With


   With ProgrammerMenu
      .AddMenuItem "Hamburger", 2.19
      .AddMenuItem "Pizza", 2.52
      .AddMenuItem "Cheetos", 0.89
      .AddMenuItem "Jolt", 1.19
      .AddMenuItem "More Jolt", 2.19
   End With


   ' Default to the standard menu
   Set CurrentMenu = StandardMenu
   ' Load the menu buttons for the current menu
   LoadCommandButtons CurrentMenu
   UpdateAll
End Sub


' Clear this order
```

Listing 3.5: Listing for frmRetail3.frm, the Main Form for the Retail3 Project (Continued)

```
Private Sub cmdClear_Click()
    CurrentOrder.Clear
    UpdateAll
End Sub


' Add an item to the order
Private Sub cmdMenu_Click(Index As Integer)
    CurrentOrder.Quantity(Index) = CurrentOrder.Quantity(Index) + 1
    UpdateAll
End Sub


' Updates the contents of the list box
Public Sub UpdateListBox()
    Dim itemnum%
    lstItems.Clear
    For itemnum = 0 To CurrentMenu.ItemCount
        If CurrentOrder.Quantity(itemnum) > 0 Then
            lstItems.AddItem CurrentOrder.Quantity(itemnum) & " x " &_
            CurrentMenu.ItemName(itemnum)
            lstItems.ItemData(lstItems.NewIndex) = itemnum
        End If
    Next itemnum
End Sub


' Calculate the total price
Public Function CalculateTotal() As Currency
    Dim itemnum%
    Dim total As Currency

    For itemnum = 0 To CurrentMenu.ItemCount
        total = total + CurrentOrder.Quantity(itemnum) *_
        CurrentMenu.ItemPrice(itemnum)
    Next itemnum
    CalculateTotal = total
End Function


' Display the total and change
Public Sub UpdateTotals()
    Dim total As Currency
    Dim paid As Currency
```

Listing 3.5: Listing for frmRetail3.frm, the Main Form for the Retail3 Project (Continued)

```
    total = CalculateTotal()
    lblTotal.Caption = Format(total, "Currency")
    paid = Val(txtPaid.Text)
    If paid - total > 0 Then
        lblChange.Caption = Format(paid - total, "Currency")
    Else
        lblChange.Caption = "Please pay"
    End If
End Sub


' Delete an item on double click
Private Sub lstItems_DblClick()
    Dim thisitem%
    thisitem = lstItems.ItemData(lstItems.ListIndex)
    With CurrentOrder
        .Quantity(thisitem) = .Quantity(thisitem) - 1
    End With
    UpdateAll
End Sub


' Select the appropriate menu
Private Sub mnuStandard_Click()
    Set CurrentMenu = StandardMenu
    MenuChanged
End Sub


Private Sub mnuSenior_Click()
    Set CurrentMenu = SeniorMenu
    MenuChanged
End Sub


Private Sub mnuProgrammer_Click()
    Set CurrentMenu = ProgrammerMenu
    MenuChanged
End Sub


Private Sub txtPaid_Change()
    UpdateTotals
End Sub
```

**Listing 3.5: Listing for frmRetail3.frm, the Main Form for the
Retail3 Project (Continued)**

```
Public Sub UpdateAll()
   UpdateListBox
   UpdateTotals
End Sub


' Loads the command buttons needed for a specified
' menu object
Public Sub LoadCommandButtons(mnu As clsMenu1)
   Dim buttonindex%
   buttonindex = 1
   ' Unload current buttons
   Do While buttonindex <= HighestButtonIndex
      Unload cmdMenu(buttonindex)
      buttonindex = buttonindex + 1
   Loop
   ' Now load new buttons
   cmdMenu(Ø).Visible = False ' In case menu is empty

   ' Load and display the menu items
   For HighestButtonIndex = Ø To mnu.ItemCount - 1
      If HighestButtonIndex > Ø Then Load cmdMenu(HighestButtonIndex)
      With cmdMenu(HighestButtonIndex)
         .Visible = True
         .Top = cmdMenu(Ø).Top + HighestButtonIndex * 450
         .Caption = mnu.ItemName(HighestButtonIndex)
      End With
   Next HighestButtonIndex



   ' Decrement HighestButtonIndex if any were added
   If HighestButtonIndex > Ø Then HighestButtonIndex = HighestButtonIndex - 1
End Sub


' Update the menu command buttons and clear the current
' order.
Public Sub MenuChanged()
   CurrentOrder.Clear
   LoadCommandButtons CurrentMenu
   UpdateAll
End Sub
```

The application defines a current clsMenu1 object and a current clsOrder1 object. In this example, only a single Order object exists, but three different menus are defined. In this example the menus are loaded during the form load event. However, it should be clear that you could just as easily load the menu object from a database or external file, eliminating the need to hard code the items. In fact, you would probably implement the code to load the object as a class method, not as part of the form.

Most of the code was intentionally kept as similar as possible to the Retail2 project. The one big difference is in the command button handling. The form needs a way to define the command buttons for a given menu. This is accomplished by the LoadCommandButtons function.

MINOR CHANGES, REVISITED

When you look at the Retail3 example, you may still wonder what all of the fuss is about with regard to object-oriented programming. Perhaps the code is slightly more organized and easier to read, but it also looks like a bit more work. Where is the benefit?

Well, let's go back to our friendly manager or client who has suddenly realized that efficiency would double if only you could store several orders in the register at once. Modifying the Retail2 application to support this change would be a major hassle. Are things different with the Retail3 sample?

Here are the changes that were made to the Retail3 application to create the Retail4 example. First, all references to clsOrder1 were changed to clsOrder2 and clsMenu1 to clsMenu2. This has nothing to do with the functionality of the application. It was done only to distinguish between the example files. Then, add the following line to the clsOrder2 module:

```
Public AssociatedMenu As clsMenu2
```

This property is needed so that the clsOrder2 object can keep track of which menu it is using.

In the form declarations section, change the CurrentOrder declaration and add an array to hold the three orders that this example will implement:

```
Dim CurrentOrder As clsOrder2
    Dim Orders(2) As New clsOrder2
```

In the form load event, add the following:

```
Set CurrentOrder = Orders(0)
    Set CurrentOrder.AssociatedMenu = CurrentMenu
```

This initializes the current order.

Now add a label control to the form called lblOrder and three command buttons in a control array called cmdOrder1, as shown in Figure 3.2.

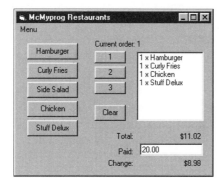

Figure 3.2: Runtime view of form frmRetail4

Add the following code to the form:

```
' Switch to a different order
Private Sub cmdOrder1_Click(Index As Integer)
    Set CurrentOrder = Orders(Index)
    If CurrentOrder.AssociatedMenu Is Nothing Then
        ' First time the order is selected, use the default menu
        Set CurrentOrder.AssociatedMenu = CurrentMenu
    End If
    Set CurrentMenu = CurrentOrder.AssociatedMenu
    LoadCommandButtons CurrentMenu
    UpdateAll
    lblOrder.Caption = "Current order: " & Index + 1
End Sub
```

When you change orders, the current menu is set based on the order, the menu command buttons are set according to the menu in use, and the list box and totals are updated to reflect the selected order. (Adding a checkbox by the appropriate pop-up menu entry is left as an exercise for the reader.)

That's it.

All of the code that works with orders deals with the clsOrder2 object. Switching between orders is thus a simple matter of switching objects.

You would probably make a number of other changes to this design to make it more robust in a real application. For example, you can change the menu to an array or dynamically allocate and load menu objects from a database. These objects could be kept in an array or a collection. The VB menu can be defined as a menu array, which could reflect the objects in the collection. This eliminates all of the hard-coded clsMenu1 objects.

Now that the clsOrder2 object contains a reference to the menu it uses, you can easily implement the CalculateTotal function as a function in the clsOrder2 class. This is left as an exercise for the reader.

The clsOrder2 object can be extended to hold the item description and price instead of just referencing an entry in the current menu. This makes it possible to change the price of an individual item instead of always using the menu price. You could thus sell one hamburger for $1.99, and another at $1.12 (though whether you want to do this or not may depend on how much you trust your cashiers).

THE THEORY OF OBJECT-ORIENTED PROGRAMMING REVISITED

Object-oriented programming is not just a buzzword. It is not a marketing term. Well, actually it is both of these, but don't let that get in the way of what's important. Object-oriented programming is a practical methodology.

This was demonstrated in the Retail2 and Retail3 examples. The two programs are virtually identical except for their use of objects. Yet they are worlds apart in design. A major enhancement that would have been extremely difficult to implement with one becomes almost trivial with the other.

What are the characteristics of object-oriented programming that make this possible? Think of it this way: Software has become increasingly complex. The process of developing software consists largely of managing complexity. Anything you can do to break a large problem into manageable tasks is good. And object-oriented programming is fundamentally a tool for breaking large problems into small objects.

When we created the clsMenu1 object, we effectively defined a type of data and a set of functions that could work with the data. The class functions AddMenuItem, ItemCount, ItemPrice, and ItemName provide everything we need to manage menu objects. You might think of these functions as the *interface* for the object (in fact, you will see later that interface is the actual technical term for a set of functions exposed by an object).

The object itself contains data structures (an array of MenuItem structures) and code to manage those data structures. An object may also contain its own internal functions to work on the object's data, though clsMenu1 does not take advantage of this capability.

Now here's the payoff. Once you implement an object, design its data structures, and write (and test) the code to work with those data structures, you are at liberty to forget all about it! You need never worry again about the code and data structures within that class. All you need to know about is the interface—the functions the class exposes.

Not only can you forget about this code in order to concentrate on other matters, you can also stop worrying that changes in one part of your program might somehow interfere with the functioning of the object, or that some other function or object might accidentally corrupt the data structures in the object. The object data is accessible only through the interface functions. This separation between objects can contribute greatly to the long-term reliability of an application, especially if it has multiple authors. It can also make it easier to add features to an application, by extending the interface of a few classes instead of rewriting global application code.

This ability to hide data and functionality behind a set of methods and properties is a characteristic of object-oriented programming called encapsulation. A second characteristic of object-oriented programming can be seen by answering this question: What does the Clear command do in Visual Basic?

Well, if you are referring to the Clear method for a list box, the command is used to clear a list box. But if you are referring to the Clear method of the clsOrder1 object, the command is used to clear the order object. In fact, you can have as many Clear methods as you wish. Each object will perform on its own internal data whatever operation is defined for the command. This ability to have a single command name shared by multiple objects is called Polymorphism.

Once again, the benefit of polymorphism is its contribution to reducing complexity. Without it VB would need separate commands for each object. For example, ClearListBox to clear a list box and ClearClsOrder1 to clear the Order1 structure. If 20 different objects had a Clear command, you would need 20 different functions. That's 20 functions to learn and remember and perhaps look up in the documentation when necessary. A single polymorphic Clear command is much easier to manage.

A third characteristic of object-oriented programming is called inheritance. Inheritance in the classic sense is not implemented in Visual Basic. Thus, Visual Basic does not meet the classic definition of a true object-oriented language. But don't worry about that now. Visual Basic allows you to accomplish many of the tasks that inheritance usually supports. You'll read more about this in Chapter 5.

The Component Object Model: Interfaces, Automation, and Binding

CHARACTERISTICS OF COM OBJECTS

THE SUNDAY COMICS

AUTOMATION (DISPATCH) INTERFACES
AND BINDING

W hen I read the VB5 documentation, I realized that VB has encapsulated ActiveX functionality so well I could probably get away with
writing the entire book without mentioning COM at all, more or less
the way Microsoft did. The problem was, every now and then they would use a
term such as *automation interface* or *QueryInterface* without really explaining
it, leaving the reader who is ignorant about COM with no clue as to whether
the term is important or not and what the manual is actually trying to say. It
seems to me that if you really want to write top-quality ActiveX components,
you need to understand about interfaces, type libraries, dispatch IDs, early versus late binding, process spaces, and all of those other concepts that are mostly
(but not entirely) handled by Visual Basic. In other words, you need to understand at least the fundamentals of the component object model. The challenge
is to introduce these concepts so clearly that even a beginning programmer
can understand them. Can I succeed where so many others have, how shall I
put it, crashed and burned? That is for you to judge.

CHARACTERISTICS OF COM OBJECTS

In Chapter 2 we introduced the idea of COM, where a COM object (sometimes called a Windows object) has the following characteristics:

▸ A COM object may contain data.

▸ It has one or more sets of functions called interfaces that can be called to operate on the data or perform other operations, such as display and data persistence.

▸ The functions for the object are contained in an application or *dynamic link library.* These are typically the only functions that can directly access the data in the object.

▸ COM objects may be identified by a GUID, which is an identifier that uniquely identifies a particular type of object across all time and space.

▸ The GUID may be used by the system to associate a particular instance of an object with the application or .DLL that contains the functions for that object (that implements the object).

So far so good.

You've also seen that classes provide the fundamental mechanism for Visual Basic programmers to create their own objects and that because VBA is based on COM, these class objects are also COM objects. The properties and methods of an object become the interface for that object—the set of functions that are exposed by the object.

At this point, those C++ programmers who truly understand COM fire up their e-mail and send me a nasty message along the lines of, "Dan, how dare you say that the properties and methods of the object become the interface for the object—you're supposed to be explaining COM and have just succeeded in misdirecting those of your readers who are learning this for the first time and confusing most of the rest. Your explanation is just plain wrong."

Mea Culpa. They are right.

You see, conceptually the properties and methods of an object can be thought of as an interface to the object. But when we talk about COM objects and ActiveX, the term *interface* has a very specific meaning. Well, actually meanings. And that's the subject of the rest of this chapter. The good news is this: once you understand what interfaces are from the COM perspective, you will be well on your way to becoming an expert on ActiveX technology, because these concepts form the basis for virtually everything you will be doing.

INSIDE COM

You already know that a COM object will be called on to expose a set of functions. In Chapter 2 we talked about a COM object being able to expose a set of functions that would allow it to draw itself into a device context. Not every COM object has a visual interface, so clearly not every COM object needs to contain the particular set of functions used for drawing. In other words, not every COM object has an interface for viewing the object.

We also talked about a COM object being able to expose a set of functions that would allow it to save itself into a file, or into a stream or storage using OLE structured storage. But again, not every object needs to persist in its state, so not every COM object will support that set of functions. Not every COM object has an interface for saving and loading itself to and from streams and storages.

Put these two paragraphs together and you can logically see one of the key features of COM: that a COM object can support more than one interface! A COM object may, if it so chooses, implement an interface named IViewObject2 that allows it to draw itself into a device context. (Allow me to duck the subject of interface names for a short while. Suffice it to say that a particular interface can always be identified by a GUID, but that we use human readable names for convenience.) An object may, if it so chooses, implement an interface named IStream that allows itself to save its data into a stream. The author of the object may choose to have his or her object implement as many interfaces as desired. If an interface is implemented, all of the functions that define that interface must be implemented.

I realize this may seem confusing, but allow me to go on just a bit further before we backtrack and tackle this subject again in a slightly different way.

Every object must implement at least one interface. This is a special interface named IUnknown. This interface consists of three functions:

- ► AddRef

- ► Release

- ► QueryInterface

Every COM object has an internal reference counter that keeps track of how many times it is being referenced. The AddRef function in the IUnknown Interface increments the reference counter. The Release function decrements it. If you release an object and the reference count becomes zero, the system knows it can delete the object.

We're going to talk more about reference counting later in this book. But for now, here is a short code fragment that illustrates what Visual Basic is doing with these functions behind the scenes.

```
Dim ob As Object        ' Defines variable ob. No object exists
Dim ob2 As Object       ' Defines variable ob2. No object exists
Set ob = new myobject   ' Creates object myobject. Calls AddRef for
                        ' the object. Reference count is now 1
```

```
Set ob2 = ob              ' Sets ob2 to reference the object. Calls
                          ' AddRef for the object. Reference count is
                          ' now 2
Set ob2 = nothing         ' Sets ob2 to nothing. Calls Release for the
                          ' object. Reference count is now 1
Set ob = nothing          ' Sets ob to nothing. Calls Release for the
                          ' object. Reference count is now 0
                          ' Object is freed and it's termination
                          ' function is called.
```

Now that you've seen reference counting, forget about it for the time being. It's a big subject that will be covered in Chapter 13, "Object Lifetime."

What we're interested in now is the third function of the IUnknown Interface, the function QueryInterface. QueryInterface has one purpose. It allows you to ask an object if it supports a particular interface and, if it does, to obtain a pointer to the code containing the functions for that interface. But what is a pointer to a function?

The code for an interface must exist somewhere in memory. This means each function has an actual memory address associated with it. A variable that holds a memory address is called a pointer. Now you may think that Visual Basic does not support pointers, but that is not quite true. You may not be able to define pointer variables, but an object variable is really nothing more than a pointer variable. It's just a specialized kind of pointer variable that can only point to OLE interfaces, the code for a group of functions that implements an interface.

So when you set an object variable to an object, what you have really done, behind the scenes, is obtain a pointer to an interface for the object and assign it to an object variable, which is really a pointer variable.

You will never explicitly call QueryInterface (or AddRef or Release) in your Visual Basic programs. But you will do so implicitly all the time.

You will never explicitly create an interface of this type in Visual Basic. But you will be creating a special kind of interface called an automation interface.

Now all of this may still be a bit confusing. I know I wrestled with it for quite awhile. I've found that sometimes the best way to learn a concept is to stop fighting it and relax. In that spirit, let's strip away the technical jargon, turn the page, and allow me to invite you to enjoy the Sunday COMics.

THE SUNDAY COMICS

WRITTEN BY DANIEL APPLEMAN
ILLUSTRATED BY DAN SOHA

Imagine a world where restaurants don't exist. Everyone eats at home. Everyone bakes from scratch. Nobody knows what other people eat, so each may be called something different by each family.

Without COM, objects only exist within the context of their own application. Even if they have similar functions, those functions have different names and parameters. One object might be displayed using a function called "Display", another might use "View" - there is no standard.

Mr. G visits a banker who is skeptical. How will people tell the waiter what they want to eat?

The restaurant object has two interfaces, Breakfast and Lunch. Breakfast has ID #1, Lunch has ID #2. The Breakfast interface has 4 functions: the first is Omelet, the second Waffles and so on. The Lunch interface has 5 functions.

The interface does not describe exactly how to cook each item— implementation is up to each chef. But if you order Waffles and on one menu, you can be sure that you'll receive pretty much the same thing when using the same menu at any other restaurant. In other words, if you call a function on an interface for one object, you will perform pretty much the same operation when using the same menu on any other object.

QueryInterface requests the Breakfast interface. They have one, so you can call function #2 on the interface and obtain a waffle. Function #2 is always a waffle, everywhere in the world, so there is no need to remember the actual name of the meal.

The restaurant idea caught on like wildfire. In no time people could order meals that they liked anywhere in the world. Mr G. became wealthy beyond his wildest dreams.

Some restaurants specialized in one menu only.

An object does not need to support every possible interface. In fact, most don't. If an interface is not supported, QueryInterface fails.

But not everyone was happy…

Mrs. C. decides to open her own restaurant chain that has a new kind of menu.

This was a shocking turn of events for people who were used to just ordering with the two numbers. Would the idea catch on?

It's a success! The special Dispatch menu allows a restaurant to use a standard menu, yet offer many different meals.

A dispatch interface has functions that allow the object to define other functions. You can obtain a list of the functions that are available and their parameters.

The dispatch interface provides a way for each object to expose as many different functions and properties as it wants. You can call a function by its dispatch ID number (food item number in this example), or ask the dispatch interface for the dispatch number associated with a function or property name.

Sometimes, however, problems would occur. People would get used to ordering from the Dispatch menu using numbers, and sometimes a restaurant would change the meals for a given number.

Curiously enough, this exact scene happened to me. There's a local sandwich chain called Togo's that has been a long time favorite of mine. My favorite was their #13, an Italian sub. One day I ordered a 13 as usual and got a different sandwich. They had changed the numbers. I was not happy.

When you define a dispatch menu, it's OK to add functions but you had better not change the functions for a given dispatch ID number or programs using that object will fail and people will get quite upset. You can avoid this problem by always ordering by name. This is a difference betweem early binding and late binding, a subject that will follow later in this chapter.

The Dispatch menu became extremely popular. In fact, some restaurants had several dispatch menus available, each with its own set of meals. But what of Mr. G?

People would still use the standard menus which were, after all, a worldwide standard. But more and more used Dispatch menus to create customized selections unique to their own restaurant. It was easy to do, and the new restaurants, with all of their variety, attracted far more attention than they did.

A Dispatch Interface is also called an Automation interface. And ActiveX automation is used to implement all of the functions and properties that your VB classes and ActiveX objects define.

INTERFACE NAMES AND THE NATURE OF THE CONTRACT

As a Visual Basic programmer, you're going to be creating automation interfaces, the *dispatch interfaces* described earlier. You will be deeply concerned with the functions and methods for the interface that are in the dispatch table. But before going into the subject of automation, let's take a more detailed look at the nature of non-dispatch interfaces (standard COM interfaces). This is important because, as you will see, many of the principles apply to automation interfaces as well.

Every COM object exposes at least one interface called *IUnknown*. But what does IUnknown mean? Interfaces, by convention, are given a name that begins with the letter I, which obviously stands for Interface. But this name is simply a human convention for naming the interface. Windows actually identifies interfaces by their GUID. The GUID for the IUnknown Interface is:

`{00000000-0000-0000-C000-000000000046}`.

GUIDs, as you recall, are globally unique. So once a GUID is assigned to an interface, you can absolutely rely on the fact that when you request an interface with a particular GUID you will receive the same one, regardless of the object you are working with. OLE (or ActiveX) defines a large number of standard interfaces. They are used to implement everything from data exchange to object embedding. In fact, any time Microsoft wants to extend the functionality of ActiveX, all they need to do is define a new interface. The list of interfaces available on a system can be found in the system registry under the HKEY_CLASSES_ROOT\Interface key as shown in Figure 4.1.

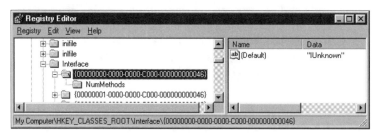

Figure 4.1: Finding standard interfaces in the registry

We've established that once you define an interface it can be uniquely identified throughout the universe through the use of its GUID. But there is one more critical requirement towards making COM work: **You see, an interface represents a contract.**

A contract is an agreement. What does it mean when we say that an object supports an interface? It means that the object implements all of the functions for that interface in a standard way. When we say that every object implements IUnknown, what we are really saying is that when you obtain the IUnknown Interface for an object, you will be able to call three functions: AddRef, Release, and QueryInterface. Those functions will always take the same parameters and return the same values regardless of whether the object is a picture, an animation, or a sound object. The functions will always appear in the same order in the declaration for the interface. The functions will always perform exactly the same operations.

However, the way those functions perform their task—the actual implementation in code—is not dictated by COM. An interface is a contract and a specification, but it does not dictate implementation.

The ramifications of this are significant. It means that objects can be implemented using different languages, even different types of processors. As long as the object exposes interfaces (which consist of pointers to functions) in a standard way and the functions for those interfaces can read the parameters and return values as specified by the COM standard, the object will work. This is why objects created with Visual Basic 5.0 can be accessed by C++ programmers or by Access programmers. The language and implementation does not matter. Only the interface and the COM standard matter.

Thus when a word processor wants to display an object, it can request the IViewObject2 Interface using the QueryInterface function. If the object supports that interface, the word processor can display the object. The word processor does not need to know what type of object it is, only that it supports the requested interface. This also implies that if an object claims to support an interface, it must support it fully and correctly. Failure to do so will lead to problems ranging from functional errors all the way up to system exceptions.

The interface contract specifies the following:

- ▸ GUID—The ID that uniquely identifies the interface
- ▸ The order of functions in the interface
- ▸ The parameters to each function
- ▸ The return values of each function
- ▸ The operation that the function performs

It does not specify:

- ▸ How to implement the function
- ▸ The language in which the function should be implemented

But what happens if you need to change an interface?

You don't.

You see, if you remove a function or change its parameters, every application that is currently using that interface will fail to work with objects defined under the newer definition. If you add a function, then applications designed for the newer definition will fail to work with objects defined under the older definition. Either way, you have major problems.

The solution is to create a new interface with a different name. That's why we have interfaces such as IViewObject2. It is similar to IViewObject, except that it contains a new function. This solves the problem in both directions. Newer applications and objects can take advantage of the newer interface if they wish, with absolute confidence that the original interface will continue to work the same way it always has.

What happens if you have an object that implements an interface and you've discovered a way to recode it to improve performance?

Go right ahead. The interface contract does not dictate implementation. As long as you don't change the function definitions, the order in the interface, or the way that they work, you can change the code as much as you wish. What's more, any performance improvements you make to the code that implements the object will be instantly propagated to every application that uses the object!

AUTOMATION (DISPATCH) INTERFACES AND BINDING

The IDispatch Interface consists of the following functions:

- ▸ GetTypeInfoCount—Used to determine if type information is available for this interface

- ▸ GetTypeInfo—Used to retrieve type information for the interface

- ▸ GetIDsOfNames—Used to find the dispatch ID for a method or property

- ▸ Invoke—Used to execute a method or set or retrieve a property value

Now, of course you'll never actually call these functions from Visual Basic. The intent here is to get a feel for what is going on behind the scenes so you'll understand better how your own components work.

Of these functions, the latter two are the most important. The GetTypeInfo-Count and GetTypeInfo functions are used to browse a list of the methods and properties for this interface. Type information includes not just the function names, but detailed information about the parameters, parameter types, and return values as well. A dispatch interface is not required to provide type information, but you need not worry about this, as your Visual Basic objects automatically implement these functions.

Each dispatch interface can provide any number of functions. There are three types of functions to consider:

1 Calling a function (often referred to as calling or invoking a method).

2 Setting a property

3 Retrieving a property

These are the only ways to operate on an object using a dispatch interface. Each method or property supported by the interface has a dispatch ID—a number that identifies that method or property. Thus, while each method has its own dispatch ID, the function to set a property and the function to retrieve that same property will share the same dispatch ID.

This has a curious impact on your Visual Basic objects you may not be aware of. I've been asked whether there is any performance difference between exposing a variable in a class as a public variable or via Property Set and Property Get statements. The answer is, it doesn't matter. Allowing you to define a variable as public is a convenience provided by the Visual Basic language. Internally, access to that variable is provided in either case by separate property set, property get functions. This is the only mechanism a dispatch table provides for accessing properties in an object.

The GetIDsOfNames function of the IDispatch Interface allows you to obtain the dispatch ID for a method or property given its name. GetIDsOfNames is also able to retrieve identifiers for the method or property arguments. So, by calling GetIDsOfNames, you can retrieve the dispatch ID and parameter types for any method or property name.

Microsoft defines a number of standard dispatch IDs, all of them with negative values. For example: The dispatch ID for the Hwnd property of an ActiveX control is -515. The use of standard dispatch IDs makes it possible for ActiveX containers to handle certain methods or properties in a consistent manner, regardless of the object in question.

The Invoke function of the IDispatch Interface is the one that does the work. It takes the dispatch ID that is specified, an array of variants and structures containing parameter information, and actually calls the function.

You may be wondering at this point if this isn't a great deal of effort to go through to call a function. Consider the simple task of invoking a method called MyMethod for an object. Using the IDispatch Interface, the program must go through the following steps:

1 Use GetIDsOfNames to find the dispatch ID for the word MyMethod

2 Prepare an array of variants containing parameters to the method

3 Call the Invoke function to execute the method.

Well, actually it is a great deal of effort. But it has one great advantage. The application using the object does not need detailed information about the interface before using the object. It can find out what it needs to know at runtime after the object already exists. This is called *late binding*.

Late binding occurs in Visual Basic when you dimension an object variable to be *As Object*. An object variable can hold any type of object. Since the variable can reference any object and must support whatever methods or properties that object may implement, it clearly can have no way of knowing until runtime what those methods and properties may be. Without late binding and the IDispatch Interface, the As Object type of variable would not be possible.

But what if you know ahead of time the type of object that a variable will reference? Isn't there a way to get around the performance hit entailed by using IDispatch?

Actually, there is. The trick is this: When an IDispatch Interface is implemented, somewhere there must exist a table of function pointers for the methods and properties supported by the interface. If a program using that object could figure out ahead of time the locations of the functions and necessary parameters, all it would need at runtime is a pointer to that table and it could call the functions directly. But how can you provide a pointer to that table at runtime? Easy—that's what a standard COM interface does! An interface that does double duty as both an IDispatch Interface and a standard interface is called a *dual interface.*

It gives applications a choice. When an application uses the direct interface for an object, it is called *early binding*. Figure 4.2 shows how this works internally.

When Visual Basic needs to access the methods or properties of an object, it starts with a reference to the object's IUnknown Interface. If the variable is dimensioned As Object, Visual Basic will use the QueryInterface function to obtain a reference to the object's IDispatch Interface (which, in this example, would actually be the same value, but it does not have to be). It can then call the Invoke function to execute the MyFunc method or access the MyProp property, which is implemented by two functions: one to set the property, the other to get it.

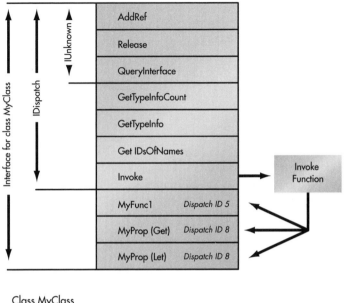

Class MyClass

```
Public Runction MyFunc1 () As Integer
Public Property Get My Prop () As Variant
Public Property Let My Prop(vNewValue As Variant)
```

Figure 4.2: Inside a Visual Basic object

If the variable is dimensioned As MyClass, early binding is used. Visual Basic can use QueryInterface to obtain a reference to the MyClass interface—an ActiveX automation dual interface. This interface contains both the IUnknown and IDispatch interfaces within it. Visual Basic can call the MyFunc method or access the MyProp property functions directly through this interface without calling the Invoke function.

In Visual Basic you can implement early binding by adding a reference to an object via the references dialog box, then declaring a variable using the specific object type instead of As Object. This can substantially reduce the time it takes to access methods and properties in the object.

Have you ever wondered why most Visual Basic variables can be assigned directly, but object variables must be assigned using the Set command? It's because a completely different operation is occurring.

If you assign one variable to another, for example:

```
Dim A As string, B As string
A = B
```

Visual Basic simply copies the value of one variable to another. VB reads the actual data of variable B and sets a copy of that data into variable A.

But if you are assigning objects:

```
Dim A As Myclass, B As New Myclass
Set A = B
```

Visual Basic actually does the following:

- ▸ B contains a pointer to the standard Myclass Interface for a newly created object.

- ▸ VB performs a QueryInterface on this interface to obtain another pointer to the standard Myclass Interface. This also increments the reference count for the object.

- ▸ The pointer is loaded into variable A.

What happens with the following code?

```
Dim A As Object, B As New Myclass
Set A = B
```

- ▸ B contains a pointer to the standard Myclass Interface of a newly created object.

- ▸ VB performs a QueryInterface on this interface to obtain another pointer to the IDispatch Interface for the object. This also increments the reference count for the object.

- ▸ The pointer is loaded into variable A.

And what if the object types don't match?

```
Dim A As OtherClass, B As New Myclass
Set A = B
```

- ▸ B contains a pointer to the standard Myclass Interface of a newly created object.

- ▸ VB performs a QueryInterface on this interface to obtain another pointer to the OtherClass Interface for the object. However, this operation fails because Myclass does not support the OtherClass Interface.

- ▸ Visual Basic reports a *type mismatch* error.

You'll read more about this in Chapter 13.

PERFORMANCE IMPACTS OF BINDING

How much of a difference does the binding type make when accessing an object's methods and properties? The Binding sample program in the Chapter 4 samples directory on your CD-ROM demonstrates this. The main form contains a list box and a button control. The listing below shows the code for the program. The project contains a single class with two functions. One of the functions simply returns an integer—a very fast operation. The other function performs a longer set of string operations, simulating a more complex function.

```
' ActiveX: A Guide to the Perplexed
' Binding example
' Copyright (c) 1997 by Desaware Inc.

Option Explicit

' A very fast operation
Public Function FastOperation() As Integer
   FastOperation = 1
End Function

' A somewhat slower operation
Public Function SlowOperation() As Integer
   Dim x&
   Dim s$
   For x = 1 To 50
      s$ = s$ & "X"
   Next x
End Function
```

The form creates a single instance of the Class1 object. Two object variables are set to reference this object during the Form_Load event. The EarlyBound variable is defined to the Class1 type. Because Visual Basic knows about the Class1 class at compile time, it is able to use the direct interface to the object and is thus early bound. The LateBound variable is defined to be As Object. Visual Basic does not know at compile time what type of object will be referenced by this variable, because you can set it at runtime to reference any type of object. This means Visual Basic must use the automation interface for all property and method access through this variable. Thus, it is late bound.

The measurement operation is very straightforward. The current time is recorded, then the FastOperation and SlowOperation functions for the object are called. This is done for both the EarlyBound and LateBound variables. The calls are performed multiple times to make it possible to measure the average duration of a call, given the rather poor granularity of the system timer. Even so, the early-bound fast operation is so fast it cannot be measured accurately with the number of repetitions defined in this example. Try varying the repeats constant to adjust the accuracy for your system.

```
' ActiveX: A Guide to the Perplexed
' Binding example
' Copyright (c) 1997 by Desaware Inc.

Option Explicit

Private Declare Function GetTickCount& Lib "kernel32" ()

' Mark the time
Dim CurrentTime As Long

Dim EarlyBound As Class1
Dim LateBound As Object

Const repeats = 50000

' An actual object to work with
Dim TheObject As New Class1

Private Sub cmdTest_Click()
    Dim ctr&
    Dim res&
    Dim EarlyFast As Long
    Dim EarlySlow As Long
    Dim LateFast As Long
    Dim LateSlow As Long

    Screen.MousePointer = vbHourglass
    CurrentTime = GetTickCount()
    For ctr = 1 To repeats
        res = EarlyBound.FastOperation
    Next ctr
    EarlyFast = (GetTickCount() - CurrentTime)
    ' Now slow operation
    CurrentTime = GetTickCount()
    For ctr = 1 To repeats
        res = EarlyBound.SlowOperation
    Next ctr
    EarlySlow = (GetTickCount() - CurrentTime)

    ' Late bound early
    CurrentTime = GetTickCount()
```

```
    For ctr = 1 To repeats
        res = LateBound.FastOperation
    Next ctr
    LateFast = (GetTickCount() - CurrentTime)
    ' Now slow operation
    CurrentTime = GetTickCount()
    For ctr = 1 To repeats
        res = LateBound.SlowOperation
    Next ctr
    LateSlow = (GetTickCount() - CurrentTime)

    Screen.MousePointer = vbNormal

    lstResults.AddItem "Early Binding"
    lstResults.AddItem "  Fast: " & GetTime(EarlyFast)
    lstResults.AddItem "  Slow: " & GetTime(EarlySlow)
    lstResults.AddItem "Late Binding"
    lstResults.AddItem "  Fast: " & GetTime(LateFast)
    lstResults.AddItem "  Slow: " & GetTime(LateSlow)
    lstResults.AddItem "Binding overhead:"
    lstResults.AddItem "  Fast: " & Format$((LateFast - EarlyFast) / LateFast,_
    "Percent")
    lstResults.AddItem "  Slow: " & Format$((LateSlow - EarlySlow) / LateSlow,_
    "Percent")

End Sub

Private Sub Form_Load()
    Set EarlyBound = TheObject
    Set LateBound = TheObject
End Sub


' Get a formatted string for the time in microseconds
Public Function GetTime(timeval As Long) As String
    ' timeval is the difference in milliseconds
    GetTime = Format$(CDbl(timeval) / repeats * 1000#, "0.###")
End Function
```

You'll probably want to run the executable version of the program; it is compiled into native code and is quite fast. You can run it in the VB environment, but be prepared to wait for a while. Figure 4.3 shows the program in action and some typical results. As you can see, for the short function, the binding overhead introduces a substantial delay—essentially 100% of the time spent for a late-bound fast operation. For slower functions, the binding overhead is correspondingly lower.

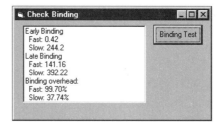

Figure 4.3: The binding program in action

Now you might think that the slower function is the more representative of the two when it comes to accessing object methods, but this is not really the case. Not only are many object methods short, but object properties tend to be very simple and short as well. Thus the advantages of using early binding are significant in many cases.

You may be wondering, why not always use early binding? Well, for one thing, there are situations where you may want a single variable to handle many types of objects. There are other situations where you may obtain an object from another server or program where the type definitions are not available ahead of time, or where an object wishes to change the properties and methods that it exposes. Some objects created using other tools have type libraries available but do not support dual interfaces. In these cases, Visual Basic can perform a limited type of early binding called *Dispid binding*. It pre-calculates the dispatch IDs for the functions and parameters at design time, and at runtime uses those values to call the functions, using the Invoke method on the IDispatch Interface.

One last comment about the IDispatch Interface. An object can have more than one. This has always been true under COM, but now it is true under Visual Basic as well, and this is a very exciting prospect indeed. You can implement multiple interfaces for an object using the Implements statement. Chapter 5 will delve further into the subjects of early versus late binding and the use of multiple interfaces with Visual Basic-created ActiveX objects.

Aggregation and Polymorphism

Did you by any chance read the Introduction? I suppose that's an odd question to ask at the start of Chapter 5, but it occurred to me that if you haven't read the Introduction, this would surely seem to be one of the oddest technical books ever written. Where are the step-by-step tutorials? Where are the introductory descriptions of how to use class modules and how to create properties?

When I made the decision early on not to just rehash the Visual Basic manuals, I didn't realize what a luxury that would be. It's not just the time and effort saved in not having to re-phrase in my own words what the manuals and other VB books say. Rather, it's the luxury of being able to focus on what I know to be truly important. It's the chance to go beyond the bare syntax of the language to really delve into how and why VB programs work the way they do and how you can take full advantage of the language features to craft software that is efficient, elegant, and cool.

Which is why I can spend a whole chapter on the subject of *aggregation* and polymorphism. These subjects may be tucked into a few relatively obscure corners in the VB manuals, but make no mistake—these features can and will change the way you program in Visual Basic. Don't blame Microsoft for not giving them more space than they did; they have a lot more material to cover and don't have other language manuals to fall back on.

BACK TO BINDING

In the last chapter you saw that Visual Basic objects are, in fact, COM objects. You learned that COM objects can have multiple interfaces. The methods and properties of a COM object are exposed by the object as a dual interface: one interface that can be called directly, the other a dispatch interface that contains in its dispatch table the list of methods and properties for the object.

The samples in Chapter 3 used early binding. All of the object references were declared as referencing the class type directly, so calls to methods and properties of the object went directly through the class interface. In Chapter 4 you saw that this type of early binding is substantially faster than late binding. I mentioned briefly three reasons why you might use late binding: cases where the interface information is not available ahead of time, cases where an object may wish to dynamically change the properties and methods it exposes, and cases where you may wish for a single variable to handle multiple data types.

The first two situations are fairly obvious. If you don't have the interface information for an object at design time, you obviously have to use the IDispatch interface, since it is able to determine the methods and properties of the object at runtime. Keep in mind that while Visual Basic objects have dual interfaces, COM objects can be created by any application, and there is no requirement that a COM object use a dual interface. Many objects that you can use from Visual Basic only support the IDispatch interface—these are always late bound. An object that only uses IDispatch does have the flexibility to change its methods and properties at runtime, though it's not common practice and you can't do it with your Visual Basic objects.

The third situation is trickier. When and why would you want a single object variable to handle multiple data types?

Let's start with a simple application that manages a portfolio of loans. The Loan1 project shown in Figure 5.1 contains two list boxes. The top list box displays information about available loans, the bottom list box displays detailed information about the loan when you click on an entry in the upper list box.

Each loan has a duration, amount available and interest rate. Listing 5.1 shows the clsBankLoan class. In addition to the AmountAvailable, Duration, and Interest properties, the class has a Payment function that returns the monthly payment on the loan, a Summary function that returns a brief description of the loan, and a SourceType function that returns a string describing the source of the loan.

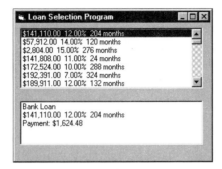

Figure 5.1: Main form for the Loan1 application

Listing 5.1: The clsBankLoan Class

```
' ActiveX: Guide to the Perplexed
' Copyright (c) 1997 by Desaware Inc.  All Rights Reserved
' Chapter 5

Option Explicit

' Amount of loan available
Public AmountAvailable As Currency


' Term of loan
Public Duration As Integer


' Interest
Public Interest As Double



' Calculate the loan payment
Public Function Payment() As Currency
   Dim factor As Double
   Dim iper As Double
   iper = Interest / 12
   factor = iper * ((1 + iper) ^ Duration)
   Payment = AmountAvailable * factor / (((1 + iper) ^ Duration) - 1)
End Function


' Obtain string description of loan
Public Function Summary() As String
   Summary = Format$(AmountAvailable, "Currency") & "  " & Format$(Interest,_
   "Percent") & "  " & Duration & " months"
End Function
```

Listing 5.1: The clsBankLoan Class (Continued)

```
Public Function SourceType() As String
    SourceType = "Bank Loan"
End Function
```

Listing 5.2 shows the main form for the sample application. The Form_Load function preloads an array of clsBankLoan objects. In a real application you might load this array from a database, or perhaps from an online service. The summary information for the objects is preloaded into the upper list box lstLoans. When you click on an entry in this list box, information about the loan is displayed in the lstInfo list box.

Listing 5.2: Listing for Form LnSel1.frm

```
' ActiveX: Guide to the Perplexed
' Copyright (c) 1997 by Desaware Inc.  All Rights Reserved
' Chapter 5

Option Explicit

' Array of available loans
Dim Loans() As clsBankLoan

' Constant for test purposes
Const LOANCOUNT = 100

Private Sub Form_Load()
    Dim loannum%

    ' Load a list of available loans
    ' In a real application, you would retrieve
    ' this information from a database, or perhaps
    ' an online service
    ' In this example, we create them randomly
    ReDim Loans(LOANCOUNT)
    For loannum = 1 To LOANCOUNT
        Set Loans(loannum) = New clsBankLoan
        With Loans(loannum)
            .AmountAvailable = CLng(Rnd() * 200000)
            .Duration = 12 * Int((Rnd * 30) + 1)
            .Interest = (7 + Int((Rnd * 80) * 0.125)) / 100
            lstLoans.AddItem .Summary
```

Listing 5.2: Listing for Form LnSel1.frm (Continued)

```
        End With
    Next loannum
End Sub

Private Sub lstLoans_Click()
    Dim loannum%
    loannum = lstLoans.ListIndex + 1
    lstInfo.Clear
    With Loans(loannum)
        lstInfo.AddItem .SourceType
        lstInfo.AddItem .Summary
        lstInfo.AddItem "Payment: " & Format$(.Payment, "Currency")
    End With
End Sub
```

So far, this is a very straightforward and simple application. And if you were a mortgage broker handling bank loans, it could serve you well. But we're in an age of rapid changes, and you never know when the government may deregulate the mortgage industry and let security brokers into the business. Your business needs to upgrade its software to handle these new loans. What happens if, for example, a brokerage loan also needs to keep track of the margin requirement for the loan?

AN OBJECT AS OBJECT

Listing 5.3 shows portions of a new class added to the loan application (see the sample program loan2.vbp on the CD that comes with this book) to handle the brokerage mortgages. Otherwise, the class is identical to the clsBankLoan class. You'll notice there is some duplication here, in that the clsSecurityLoan class has an exact copy of the Payment function that appears in the clsBankLoan class. This is somewhat wasteful, and shortly we'll take a look at a way to reduce that overhead.

The Loans() array in the frmLoan1 form was defined to reference the cls-BankLoan object. Now we need this array to also support the clsSecurityLoan object. Any attempt to assign a clsSecurityLoan object to the Loans() array as it stands now would result in a type error. One solution, shown in Listing 5.4, solves this problem by changing the Loans() array to reference the Object type.

Listing 5.3: Modifications to the clsSecurityLoan

```
' Margin requirement
Public Margin As Double

' Obtain string description of loan
Public Function Summary() As String
   Summary = Format$(AmountAvailable, "Currency") & "  " & Format$(Interest,_
   "Percent") & "  " & Duration & " months. Margin: " & Format$(Margin, "Percent")
End Function

Public Function SourceType() As String
   SourceType = "Brokerage Loan"
End Function
```

Listing 5.4: Modifications to the frmLoan Form

```
' Array of available loans
Dim Loans() As Object


Private Sub Form_Load()
   Dim loannum%

   ' Load a list of available loans
   ' In a real application, you would retrieve
   ' this information from a database, or perhaps
   ' an online service
   ' In this example, we create them randomly
   ReDim Loans(LOANCOUNT)
   For loannum = 1 To LOANCOUNT
      Select Case Int(Rnd() * 2)
         Case 0
            Set Loans(loannum) = New clsBankLoan
         Case 1
            Set Loans(loannum) = New clsSecurityLoan
            ' Margin only applies to this type
            Loans(loannum).Margin = Rnd()
      End Select
      With Loans(loannum)
         .AmountAvailable = CLng(Rnd() * 200000)
         .Duration = 12 * Int((Rnd * 30) + 1)
         .Interest = (7 + Int((Rnd * 80) * 0.125)) / 100
         lstLoans.AddItem .Summary
      End With
```

Listing 5.4: Modifications to the frmLoan Form (Continued)

```
   Next loannum
End Sub
```

Now here's an interesting observation. The *only* changes needed to implement this new type are changing the type in the Loans() array and loading the correct object type into the array. The Margin property is only set for the clsSecurityLoan type.

Consider for a moment what happens when the Summary function is called for an object in the Loans() array. Visual Basic correctly calls the correct function for the actual object being referenced. This is a demonstration of polymorphism, where the same function name can be used by two different objects. As you see here, it is more than a convenience to the programmer in terms of reducing the number of functions that need to be remembered. Polymorphism allows you to use the same code to reference different object types by the shared method or property name.

AGGREGATION

Your mortgage software business has really taken off, and along the way you've gained many new customers, some of whom have a clientele you perhaps weren't anticipating. Now you find you need to update your program to handle loans for clients who are, how can we put it, somewhat less than creditworthy? These loans require not only that you add a new type of object but that the object support a method that calculates a late penalty based on the value of the loan.

Before coding it might occur to you that this object will require yet another copy of the Payment method. Now, not only is this wasteful, but it opens the door to a maintenance nightmare. What happens if one day you find a bug in the payment code? (I realize this is unlikely in this simple example, but extrapolate this example to a real application with a dozen class methods substantially more complex, and you'll see this is a very real concern.) You could add a code module and create a global function to calculate payment values, but this is a step away from the encapsulation that object-oriented programming offers. More important, the problem will return, should you ever decide to deploy these classes as individual ActiveX code libraries (DLL servers), where each class will be implemented in its own DLL. Surely there must be a solution that follows an object-oriented methodology, right?

Right. The answer is aggregation, and it is demonstrated in Listing 5.5. The new clsLoanShark class is based on clsBankLoan, which serves as our reference loan type. But instead of simply copying the method and property code from clsBankLoan, a private instance of clsBankLoan is actually created whenever a clsLoanShark object is created. In other words, a clsLoanShark object is an aggregate of new code with an object of type clsBankLoan (hence the term aggregation). In most cases, instead of handling methods and properties directly in the clsLoanShark object, they are delegated to the internal clsBankLoan object. For example: Instead of including the code for the Payment function in the class, it simply calls the Payment method of the LoanTemplate object, which is the variable name of the private clsBankLoan object.

Note that LoanTemplate is dimensioned with the New option. This is necessary because you actually need to create an instance of the object. Without the New option, the LoanTemplate variable remains empty (set to nothing), and you obviously cannot access methods and properties for an object that does not exist.

Listing 5.5: clsLoanShark Class Object

```
' ActiveX: Guide to the Perplexed
' Copyright (c) 1997 by Desaware Inc.  All Rights Reserved
' Chapter 5

Option Explicit

' Internal class object used in aggregation
Private LoanTemplate As New clsBankLoan


Public Property Get AmountAvailable() As Currency
    AmountAvailable = LoanTemplate.AmountAvailable
End Property

Public Property Let AmountAvailable(ByVal vNewValue As Currency)
    LoanTemplate.AmountAvailable = vNewValue
End Property

Public Property Get Duration() As Integer
    Duration = LoanTemplate.Duration
End Property

Public Property Let Duration(ByVal vNewValue As Integer)
    LoanTemplate.Duration = vNewValue
End Property
```

Listing 5.5: clsLoanShark Class Object (Continued)

```
Public Property Get Interest() As Double
   Interest = LoanTemplate.Interest
End Property

Public Property Let Interest(ByVal vNewValue As Double)
   If vNewValue < 0.5 Then vNewValue = vNewValue + 0.5
   LoanTemplate.Interest = vNewValue
End Property

Public Function Payment() As Currency
   Payment = LoanTemplate.Payment
End Function

Public Function Summary() As String
   Summary = LoanTemplate.Summary
End Function

Public Function SourceType() As String
   SourceType = "Loan Shark"
End Function

Public Function LatePenalty() As String
   Select Case AmountAvailable
      Case 0 To 25000
         LatePenalty = "Broken Fingers"
      Case 25000 To 75000
         LatePenalty = "Broken arm"
      Case Else
         LatePenalty = "You don't want to know"
   End Select
End Function
```

You may be wondering why the AmountAvailable, Duration, and Interest properties are delegated to the LoanTemplate object. Wouldn't it be easier to simply declare these as public variables? Wouldn't that also improve performance by eliminating an extra function call?

It might be easier, but it wouldn't work. Remember, you are delegating the Payment function, and that function uses these three properties to calculate the monthly payments. This function operates on the values it finds within the LoanTemplate object, so you must delegate these properties to the internal object in order for the Payment function to work with the correct values.

The delegation need not be exact, however. You can add your own error checking to the property access functions as shown in the Property Let function for the Interest property. No self-respecting loan shark would accept under 50 percent interest, and this is reflected in the handling of this property.

The clsLoanShark object does not need to delegate all of its methods and properties to the LoanTemplate object. The SourceType method, for example, is handled directly within the class. This makes sense because the result from the LoanTemplate object would be Bank Loan, which is incorrect. Overriding the methods or properties of the delegated object is one of the reasons you might create a new class based on another. Another reason is the ability to add new methods or properties, as shown with the LatePenalty method, which does not exist in the clsBankLoan class.

Aggregation allows you to easily reuse code from the contained object. But does it have any disadvantages? Only one major one: each time you create a clsLoanShark object, you are in fact creating a new clsBankLoan object as well. This involves some additional overhead, and the impact on performance may be difficult to calculate.

The overhead of creating a contained object when the object is a class within your own application is negligible, but if the object is in an ActiveX server, the impact on the system may be substantial. This will be discussed further in the next chapter. A more significant issue comes into play if the contained object has code in its Initialization and Termination events. That code is executed any time an object is created and destroyed.

Now let's take a look at how the main program handles this new object. Figure 5.2 shows the program in action. Since we are following good object-oriented programming design here, it's not surprising that the changes needed to incorporate this class into the Loan3 project are fairly simple. The Form_Load event (see Listing 5.6) is modified to load the new object type. Once again, this only simulates a real application that would load the loan information from a database or online service.

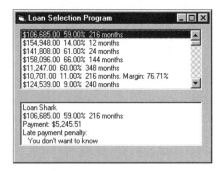

Figure 5.2: Main form for the Loan3 application

Listing 5.6: Listing for LnSel3.frm

```
' ActiveX: Guide to the Perplexed
' Copyright (c) 1997 by Desaware Inc.  All Rights Reserved
' Chapter 5

Option Explicit

' Array of available loans
Dim Loans() As Object

' Constant for test purposes
Const LOANCOUNT = 100

Private Sub Form_Load()
   Dim loannum%

   ' Load a list of available loans
   ' In a real application, you would retrieve
   ' this information from a database, or perhaps
   ' an online service
   ' In this example, we create them randomly
   ReDim Loans(LOANCOUNT)
   For loannum = 1 To LOANCOUNT
      Select Case Int(Rnd() * 3)
         Case 0
            Set Loans(loannum) = New clsBankLoan
         Case 1
            Set Loans(loannum) = New clsSecurityLoan
            ' Margin only applies to this type
            Loans(loannum).Margin = Rnd()
         Case Else
            Set Loans(loannum) = New clsLoanShark
      End Select
      With Loans(loannum)
         .AmountAvailable = CLng(Rnd() * 200000)
         .Duration = 12 * Int((Rnd * 30) + 1)
         .Interest = (7 + Int((Rnd * 80) * 0.125)) / 100
         lstLoans.AddItem .Summary
      End With
   Next loannum
End Sub

Private Sub lstLoans_Click()
   Dim loannum%
   Dim LatePenaltyValue$
```

Listing 5.6: Listing for LnSel3.frm (Continued)

```
   loannum = lstLoans.ListIndex + 1
   lstInfo.Clear
   With Loans(loannum)
      lstInfo.AddItem .SourceType
      lstInfo.AddItem .Summary
      lstInfo.AddItem "Payment: " & Format$(.Payment, "Currency")
      LatePenaltyValue = GetLatePenalty(Loans(loannum))
      If LatePenaltyValue <> "" Then
         lstInfo.AddItem "Late payment penalty:"
         lstInfo.AddItem "     " & .LatePenalty
      End If
   End With
End Sub


' Generic function to obtain LatePayment value
Public Function GetLatePenalty(obj As Object) As String
   On Error GoTo nofunction
   GetLatePenalty = obj.LatePenalty
   Exit Function
nofunction:
End Function
```

Perhaps the most interesting modification to the code is the handling of the LatePenalty method. Any attempt to call this function for the clsBankLoan or clsSecurityLoan object will result in an error, because those objects don't support that method. This means that you have two choices on how to handle this new method:

▶ Check to see if the object is of type clsLoanShark. If it is, call the LatePenalty method. You can test the type of an object by using the "If Typeof … Is" statement or by checking using the TypeName function to obtain the name of the object.

▶ Try calling the LatePenalty method for every object, simply ignoring any errors that occur.

This sample takes the latter approach. The GetLatePenalty function handles the operation, simply returning an empty string if an error occurs. The nice thing about this approach is that it is generic—it will work correctly for any future objects that incorporate the LatePenalty function without requiring further modification to the main form code.

A third approach is to test for the presence of the method name directly. The apigid32.dll utility DLL provided with this book includes the function agIsValidName(), which lets you test whether a method or property name is supported by an object. It does this internally by obtaining the IDispatch interface for the object, then using the GetIdOfNames function of the IDispatch interface to see if the requested name has a valid identifier.

AN OBJECT IMPLEMENTS

You've seen the power of the object data type in implementing both aggregation and polymorphism. Unfortunately, this data type has two major problems.

1 Since an object variable can reference any object, it opens the door to new types of bugs. What happens to your program if you accidentally assign one of these variables to a form or control object? Or to another object that is not a loan? This type of bug cannot be detected at design time, only at runtime when the program attempts to access a property or method for the object that does not actually exist. This places an additional burden on the testing process. It's always better to let the compiler find these kinds of problems if possible.

2 All access to these objects is late bound, which tends to degrade performance. This may not be noticeable in such a small sample program, but in a program handling millions of transactions the difference can be critical.

Visual Basic 5.0 adds a powerful new way of solving these problems. Think back for a moment to the interface discussion of Chapter 4. An object can expose more than one interface. For example, our clsBankLoan object exposes at least three interfaces: IUnknown (because all objects support IUnknown), IDispatch (the automation interface used for late binding), and _clsBankLoan (the early-bound dual interface containing the methods and properties of the object. By convention, it is preceded by an _ to indicate that it is hidden).

These interfaces are shown in Figure 5.3. This figure also illustrates the standard schematic used by Microsoft to describe COM objects. Each circle indicates an interface to the object.

In our earlier example we needed to use the object data type because it was the only way to have a variable reference more than one type of interface.

But a second approach is possible. Instead of having a single object variable reference multiple interfaces, why not have each object implement a common interface?

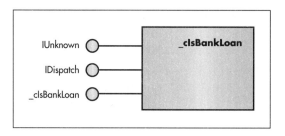

Figure 5.3: The interfaces for the clsBankLoan object

If the clsLoanShark object could expose the clsBankLoan interface as well as its own, then instead of using an object data type variable, you could continue to use a clsBankLoan data type variable. This is illustrated in Figure 5.4.

Visual Basic 5.0 makes it possible for one object to expose multiple interfaces by using the Implements statement, possibly the most important new feature in Visual Basic 5.0.

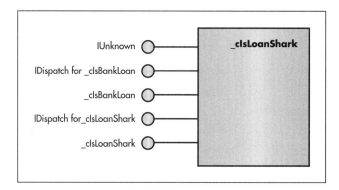

Figure 5.4: The interfaces for the clsLoanShark object

The Implements statement is used by adding the command:

```
Implements otherclassname
```

to the beginning of a class. For example: if you have class2, which implements class1, and class 1 has a method mymethod(), class2 must contain code for the implemented method. The declaration for the code takes the form:

```
class1_mymethod()
```

The class1 prefix indicates that the code implements the class1 interface instead of the class2 interface. Class2 must implement all of the methods and properties of the class1 interface—that is fundamental to the way COM interfaces work. Remember, an interface is a contract, and if class2 is going to implement the class1 interface, it must implement all of it.

Let's take a look at how this is accomplished using the various loan sample objects one step at a time in the Loan4 sample application.

First, the clsBankLoan object is shown in Listing 5.7.

Listing 5.7: The clsBankLoan Object, Version 2

```
' ActiveX: Guide to the Perplexed
' Copyright (c) 1997 by Desaware Inc.  All Rights Reserved
' Chapter 5

Option Explicit

' Amount of loan available
Public AmountAvailable As Currency

' Term of loan
Public Duration As Integer

' Interest
Public Interest As Double


' Calculate the loan payment
Public Function Payment() As Currency
    Dim factor As Double
    Dim iper As Double
    iper = Interest / 12
    factor = iper * ((1 + iper) ^ Duration)
    Payment = AmountAvailable * factor / (((1 + iper) ^ Duration) - 1)
End Function

' Obtain string description of loan
Public Function Summary() As String
    Summary = Format$(AmountAvailable, "Currency") & "  " & Format$(Interest,_
    "Percent") & "  " & Duration & " months"
End Function

Public Function SourceType() As String
    SourceType = "Bank Loan"
End Function
```

Don't spend too much time looking for differences between this and Listing 5.1. There aren't any.

Most of the documentation that refers to the Implements statement emphasizes the creation of an *abstract class*—that is, a class that contains methods and properties that don't actually have any code attached. You see, a class that implements an interface only needs the method and property definitions—it doesn't actually need any of the code to define the interface. It will add its own code for implementing the interface methods and properties.

But you don't need to use an empty abstract class as the source for your interface definition. Having code in the source class does no harm whatsoever. Now, we could have created a generic loan class that could be implemented by all of the other loan objects. But, in this case, the clsBankLoan object is treated as the standard interface. This makes it possible to use aggregation (as you saw earlier) to use the code in the source class. This provides a form of inheritance, where an object can inherit both the definition and some of the code of the source class.

And inheritance, as you may recall from Chapter 3, is the third requirement of an object-oriented language!

Now, this type of inheritance is not true language inheritance according to the theoretical definition of the term. But it lets you accomplish most of the same tasks, and arguing the theory of whether VB is or is not a true object-oriented language accomplishes little from a practical point of view.

The Microsoft documentation tends to stress the use of abstract classes as sources for interface definitions. I can't really argue with them on this count, but I suspect that many programmers will find fully implemented classes much more valuable in general use. So be sure you take the time to learn both approaches. In fact, let's do so.

Listing 5.8 shows the clsSecurityLoan object revised to implement the clsBankLoan object. There are two issues to stress in this listing.

First, because this object does not use aggregation, the methods and properties of the clsBankLoan object are never called by this class. It implements its own versions of the functions in each case (just as its predecessor did in the earlier examples). This means the object is only using the clsBankLoan class to define the methods and properties for the interface. The code in the clsBankLoan class is not used at all.

Next, note that all of the properties and methods are in fact implemented twice! This is because they appear on both of the object's interfaces. For example: The Interest property is part of both the clsBankLoan interface and the clsSecurityLoan interface. You will see shortly that this is not necessary.

Also note how the class implements all of the functions of the clsBankLoan interface.

Listing 5.8: The clsSecurityLoan Object, Version 2

```
' ActiveX: Guide to the Perplexed
' Copyright (c) 1997 by Desaware Inc.  All Rights Reserved
' Chapter 5

' Implements the clsBankLoan interface
Implements clsBankLoan

Option Explicit

' Amount of loan available
Public AmountAvailable As Currency

' Term of loan
Public Duration As Integer

' Interest
Public Interest As Double

' Margin requirement
Public Margin As Double


' Calculate the loan payment
Private Function Payment() As Currency
    Dim factor As Double
    Dim iper As Double
    iper = Interest / 12
    factor = iper * ((1 + iper) ^ Duration)
    Payment = AmountAvailable * factor / (((1 + iper) ^ Duration) - 1)
End Function

' Obtain string description of loan
Public Function Summary() As String
    Summary = Format$(AmountAvailable, "Currency") & "  " & Format$(Interest,_
    "Percent") & "  " & Duration & " months. Margin: " & Format$(Margin, "Percent")
End Function


Public Function SourceType() As String
    SourceType = "Brokerage Loan"
End Function
```

Listing 5.8: The clsSecurityLoan Object, Version 2 (Continued)

```
' The clsBankLoan Interface
Private Property Let clsBankLoan_AmountAvailable(ByVal RHS As Currency)
   AmountAvailable = RHS
End Property


Private Property Get clsBankLoan_AmountAvailable() As Currency
   clsBankLoan_AmountAvailable = AmountAvailable
End Property


Private Property Let clsBankLoan_Duration(ByVal RHS As Integer)
   Duration = RHS
End Property


Private Property Get clsBankLoan_Duration() As Integer
   clsBankLoan_Duration = Duration
End Property


Private Property Let clsBankLoan_Interest(ByVal RHS As Double)
   Interest = RHS
End Property


Private Property Get clsBankLoan_Interest() As Double
   clsBankLoan_Interest = Interest
End Property


Private Function clsBankLoan_Payment() As Currency
   clsBankLoan_Payment = Payment()
End Function


Private Function clsBankLoan_SourceType() As String
   clsBankLoan_SourceType = SourceType()
End Function


Private Function clsBankLoan_Summary() As String
   clsBankLoan_Summary = Summary()
End Function
```

The clsLoanShark object uses aggregation as shown in Listing 5.9. This object acknowledges the fact that since clsBankLoan properties and methods are in reality only accessed through the clsBankLoan interface. Including them in the clsLoanShark interface is overkill. This also reduces the amount of code in the class. In fact, the only function in the clsLoanShark interface is the Late-Penalty function, which is unique to this object!

Listing 5.9: The clsLoanShark Object, Version 2

```
' ActiveX: Guide to the Perplexed
' Copyright (c) 1997 by Desaware Inc.  All Rights Reserved
' Chapter 5

Option Explicit

' Implements the clsBankLoan interface
Implements clsBankLoan

' Internal class object used in aggregation
Private LoanTemplate As New clsBankLoan


Public Function LatePenalty() As String
    Select Case LoanTemplate.AmountAvailable
        Case 0 To 25000
            LatePenalty = "Broken Fingers"
        Case 25000 To 75000
            LatePenalty = "Broken arm"
        Case Else
            LatePenalty = "You don't want to know"
    End Select
End Function

Private Property Let clsBankLoan_AmountAvailable(ByVal RHS As Currency)
    LoanTemplate.AmountAvailable = RHS
End Property

Private Property Get clsBankLoan_AmountAvailable() As Currency
    clsBankLoan_AmountAvailable = LoanTemplate.AmountAvailable
End Property

Private Property Let clsBankLoan_Duration(ByVal RHS As Integer)
    LoanTemplate.Duration = RHS
End Property

Private Property Get clsBankLoan_Duration() As Integer
    clsBankLoan_Duration = LoanTemplate.Duration
End Property

Private Property Let clsBankLoan_Interest(ByVal RHS As Double)
    If RHS < 0.5 Then RHS = RHS + 0.5
    LoanTemplate.Interest = RHS
End Property
```

Listing 5.9: The clsLoanShark Object, Version 2 (Continued)

```
Private Property Get clsBankLoan_Interest() As Double
    clsBankLoan_Interest = LoanTemplate.Interest
End Property

Private Function clsBankLoan_Payment() As Currency
    clsBankLoan_Payment = LoanTemplate.Payment
End Function

Private Function clsBankLoan_SourceType() As String
    clsBankLoan_SourceType = "Loan Shark"
End Function

Private Function clsBankLoan_Summary() As String
    clsBankLoan_Summary = LoanTemplate.Summary
End Function
```

All that remains is to take a look at the Loan4 program itself. Listing 5.10 shows the main form modified to take advantage of the fact that all of the objects implement the clsBankLoan interface.

Listing 5.10: Listing for InSel4.frm

```
' ActiveX: Guide to the Perplexed
' Copyright (c) 1997 by Desaware Inc.  All Rights Reserved
' Chapter 5

Option Explicit

' Array of available loans
Dim Loans() As clsBankLoan

' Constant for test purposes
Const LOANCOUNT = 100

Private Sub Form_Load()
    Dim loannum%
    Dim secLoan As clsSecurityLoan

    ' Load a list of available loans
    ' In a real application, you would retrieve
    ' this information from a database, or perhaps
    ' an online service
```

Listing 5.10: Listing for InSel4.frm (Continued)

```
    ' In this example, we create them randomly
    ReDim Loans(LOANCOUNT)
    For loannum = 1 To LOANCOUNT
        Select Case Int(Rnd() * 3)
            Case 0
                Set Loans(loannum) = New clsBankLoan
            Case 1
                Set Loans(loannum) = New clsSecurityLoan
                ' Margin only applies to this type
                Set secLoan = Loans(loannum)
                secLoan.Margin = Rnd()
            Case Else
                Set Loans(loannum) = New clsLoanShark
        End Select
        With Loans(loannum)
            .AmountAvailable = CLng(Rnd() * 200000)
            .Duration = 12 * Int((Rnd * 30) + 1)
            .Interest = (7 + Int((Rnd * 80) * 0.125)) / 100
            lstLoans.AddItem .Summary
        End With
    Next loannum
End Sub

Private Sub lstLoans_Click()
    Dim loannum%
    Dim LatePenaltyValue$
    Dim LoanSharkObject As clsLoanShark

    loannum = lstLoans.ListIndex + 1
    lstInfo.Clear
    With Loans(loannum)
        lstInfo.AddItem .SourceType
        lstInfo.AddItem .Summary
        lstInfo.AddItem "Payment: " & Format$(.Payment, "Currency")
        ' LatePenaltyValue = GetLatePenalty(Loans(loannum))
        ' This won't work now!
        'If LatePenaltyValue <> "" Then
        '    lstInfo.AddItem "Late payment penalty:"
        '    lstInfo.AddItem "   " & LatePenaltyValue
        'End If
        If TypeOf Loans(loannum) Is clsLoanShark Then
            Set LoanSharkObject = Loans(loannum)
            lstInfo.AddItem "Late payment penalty:"
            lstInfo.AddItem "   " & LoanSharkObject.LatePenalty
        End If
```

Listing 5.10: Listing for InSel4.frm (Continued)

```
   End With
End Sub



' Generic function to obtain LatePayment value
'Public Function GetLatePenalty(obj As Object) As String
'    On Error GoTo nofunction
'    GetLatePenalty = obj.LatePenalty
'    Exit Function
'nofunction:
'End Function
```

The first and most important change to note is that the Loans() array is defined as clsBankLoan again. You can do this because every object has a clsBank-Loan interface, which can be assigned to this array. The Form_Load event still creates the different types of objects, but as soon as the object is assigned to the Loans() array, Visual Basic performs a QueryInterface to obtain a pointer to the clsBankLoan interface for the object. This pointer can be placed into the array.

The clsSecurityLoan object requires special treatment, since the Form_Load function must also set its Margin property. The problem is that the Margin property is not part of the clsBankLoan interface. In order to set it, the program must create a temporary variable called secLoan, which can access the full clsSecurityLoan interface. Once this variable is assigned from the object, the Margin property can be set.

There is one other major change in this code. The previous technique for checking the LatePenalty doesn't work! (Go ahead and try commenting out the code and test it out for yourself if you wish.) The LatePenalty property will never be found! Now, this may be confusing. After all, the GetLatePenalty function accepts an object reference, which uses the IDispatch interface, which is late bound, right? And the IDispatch interface can safely be used to check whether the LatePenalty property is implemented, right? (That's what we did last time.)

The catch can be seen by taking a second look at Figure 5.4. Yes, the Get-LatePenalty function does use the IDispatch interface for the clsLoanShark object, but which one? The clsLoanShark object has two IDispatch interfaces, one for the clsBankLoan interface, and one for the clsLoanShark interface (remember, in a dual interface you have both the direct interface and a corresponding IDispatch interface).

The GetLatePenalty function receives the IDispatch interface for the cls-BankLoan interface, which never has a LatePenalty function, so this approach does not work. We must go back to checking the individual object type to see if it is one that we know supports the LatePenalty function.

How does Visual Basic decide which IDispatch interface to use in cases like these? It doesn't—so it always returns a pointer to the one most recently accessed. In this application, the previous access to the object is through the Loans() array, which uses the clsBankLoan interface. You should never assume that a particular interface will be chosen when passing an object with multiple interfaces to a function that takes a generic object parameter, unless you explicitly choose that interface by first assigning the object to a variable with the desired interface type.

Is there a way to avoid testing for individual object types and generically test for the LatePenalty property?

Yes. You could redefine the clsBankLoan interface to add a function that always returns a reference to the object's other IDispatch interface. If it was called MainInterface, it might be implemented something like this in the clsLoanShark class:

```
Public Function clsBankLoan_MainInterface() As Object
        Dim myobj As clsLoanShark
        Set myobj = Me
        Set clsBankLoan_MainInterface = myobj
End Function
```

This is demonstrated in the Loan5 sample application. Here the lstLoans_Click function uses the following code to obtain the late penalty, if it exists:

```
LatePenaltyValue = GetLatePenalty(Loans(loannum).MainInterface)
If LatePenaltyValue <> "" Then
   lstInfo.AddItem "Late payment penalty:"
   lstInfo.AddItem "    " & LatePenaltyValue
End If
```

There's one catch with taking this approach: You had better decide on it ahead of time. As you will see if you look closely at the Loan5 example, adding a function to the clsBankLoan project required the addition of the MainInterface function to every class that implements this interface. This is not a big problem in this example, but what if you had created ActiveX components based on the interface? What if other projects used the same class? What if they were already in distribution? You run the risk of breaking all of those components because you have effectively violated the interface contract by changing it.

The COM object model used by Visual Basic and ActiveX provides many capabilities and advantages, but it demands something in return: that you take care in defining your objects ahead of time. There is no harm in adding and changing an interface while you are developing it, but once you release an object based on that interface to the outside world or to other developers or projects, you will have to live with that interface forever.

In taking one last look at these samples, you will see that the Loan4 project has one great advantage over the Loan3 project: all of the object method and property accesses are early bound. The Loan5 project maintains this advantage except in the LatePenalty test which is, in this case, late bound.

TRADE-OFFS

This chapter demonstrates a variety of techniques for developing objects in Visual Basic. I've tried to illustrate some of the trade-offs involved in choosing a particular approach. You should be considering:

- ▶ The performance impact of early versus late binding.

- ▶ The code reusability and long-term reliability achieved by using aggregation and delegating to contained functions.

- ▶ The performance and resource cost entailed in the creation and destruction of contained objects when using aggregation.

All of these techniques are available to you as a VB programmer. But it's up to you to choose the ones most suitable to your own tasks.

So far, all of the objects that we've looked at have been implemented as classes within an application. Now that you understand a little bit (well, actually, a great deal) about how COM objects work, it's time to take the next step and look at other places where COM objects can live: in dynamic link libraries and even in other applications.

The Life and Times of an ActiveX Component

Objects: Are They Real or Are They Memory?

Process Spaces: The Final Frontier

The Life Cycle of a DLL Object

The Life Cycle of an EXE Object

Performance Issues

Chapter

6

You can probably tell from what you've read so far that I'm one of those people who like to understand how things work. But it's not idle curiosity. The way I see it, understanding how something works can help you to understand how to use it.

The trick is to set a balance. If you go into too much depth trying to understanding how a technology works, you can find yourself with no time left to do anything with it. Not enough depth and your application of the technology will become nothing more than applying formulas based on sample programs that other people wrote. This is fine if what you are trying to accomplish matches the sample. But as soon as you try to go beyond the sample, you find it impossible to proceed because you don't really know what you're doing.

Setting that balance with regard to ActiveX is the challenge that I've faced in writing these chapters. I've tried to provide the conceptual background without bogging you down in the details of how COM objects are actually implemented. (Refer to Kraig Brockschmidt's book, *Inside OLE,* second edition, Microsoft Press, 1995, for a good text on OLE/ActiveX that covers the internal implementation details.)

One more subject remains to be covered before we can dive into the specifics of creating Visual Basic components. You need to understand a little bit about how ActiveX objects are created and how they exist in your system. Without this knowledge you will not be able to easily determine the trade-offs involved in choosing between the different types of ActiveX objects that Visual Basic 5.0 supports.

Objects: Are They Real or Are They Memory?

Let's think back for a moment about COM objects. What are the characteristics of an object?

- ▶ It has a GUID—A globally unique identifier.

- ▶ It supports one or more interfaces.

- ▶ It may have data associated with it, but the only way that you can access that data is through the interfaces. (Remember that even public variables in a Visual Basic class are actually accessed behind the scenes as separate Property Get and Property Let functions belonging to the class interface.)

Now, if you think about it, the above list is really quite intangible. A GUID is a number. Interfaces are a list of function declarations—a contract, so to speak. Data is an abstraction until you actually point to a block of memory and say, "Here it is."

This is all very nice, but you can't load a number, execute a contract, or manipulate abstractions. (Well, actually, I had a number of college professors who seemed to be able to do all of these quite readily, but I never particularly enjoyed their classes, so let's just move on.) An object must have a tangible reality in order to use it in an application. Specifically, an interface must be implemented with actual code that can be loaded into actual memory and executed. An object's data must also exist somewhere in memory, and there has to be some mechanism in the operating system to take a GUID and somehow create the object that it refers to.

Let's skip the GUID issue for later in the chapter. For now, let's concentrate on two ideas:

- ▶ A interface must be implemented in code.

- ▶ An object's data must exist in memory.

Sounds simple enough, but consider this: Nothing that I've said up until now suggests that there is a one-to-one correspondence between an object's interface and a particular implementation of that interface. This raises an interesting question: Is it possible for a dozen different programs and DLLs to each have its own code implementation for a particular interface on a particular object?

Also, nothing I've written suggests that an object's data must exist in memory belonging to any particular application or even a particular system on a network. Is it possible for code to execute functions in an interface on one system that manipulates object data that exists on another system half way around the world?

The answer to both of these question is yes. So perhaps there is more to this subject than meets the eye.

The good news is that some of the more esoteric variations can be safely ignored. With Visual Basic, the only time you will have multiple code implementations for an object is when you create new versions of your object handler. And managing objects across a network is handled nicely with remote automation, a subject this book will cover only briefly.

But there is one issue that will have a major impact on your components. It will determine not only their potential capabilities but have a dramatic impact on their performance. You see, on a 32-bit operating system, different applications are separated into their own process spaces, and though they may exist on the same machine, in many ways they might as well be on different ones.

Now, if you are a knowledgeable Win32 programmer, your reaction to the term *process space* is most likely to nod your head in understanding. And chances are that the next section in this chapter will not only be clear to you but quite superfluous, so feel free to skip it.

However if you are among the multitude who has worked extensively under 16-bit operating systems and applications, but you are still a bit uncertain with regards to the 32-bit world, read on. But first, a short interlude.

AN INTERLUDE

To be sung to the tune of *The Way We Were*.

Memory
Like the code I've left behind
Misty-banked extended memory
oh, the way things were.

Six-forty K
And the crashes that we saw.
From UAE to GP fault,
oh, the way things were.

Could it be that things were all so simple then
wasting time rebooting one more time?
If we could write each application once again,
Tell me would we?
Could we?

Memory
Wasn't bountiful and yet
What we used to squeeze in 10K
Now takes over 20 meg!
So let's remember
Whenever we assemble,
Who has time to remember?
The way things were
The way things were…

PROCESS SPACES: THE FINAL FRONTIER

Whether you're dealing with code or data, one truth remains. The information must exist in memory in order for the processor to deal with it. But how that memory is organized can have an enormous impact on the computing environment, both in terms of performance and stability.

In the days of 16-bit operating systems (Windows 3.x), system memory was a giant sea in which applications lived. Code and data could be intermixed, even among different applications. Figure 6.1 illustrates this situation, showing two applications and a dynamic link library. Purists may note that this does not illustrate either the linear way in which memory is physically organized or the internal architecture, which would distinguish between low memory and extended memory, or between physical memory and virtual memory.

But what the purists know in this case really has no impact on how, as programmers, we usually look at memory. From our perspective under the Windows operating system, memory can be thought of as a sea in which blocks are allocated. We don't really care where those blocks are, or what order they are in, or whether they are loaded into physical memory or currently swapped out onto disk.

Let's take a moment and reflect on the differences between dynamic link libraries (DLLs) and executable programs. First, it is important to realize that both DLLs and executables are fundamentally the same—they use the same file format (with slightly different options) and are loaded in much the same way. Both can contain code and data. The only real difference is the way Windows interacts with them.

When Windows loads a DLL, it runs its initialization code, then leaves it alone. Functions in the DLL will only be called if they are explicitly referenced by an application. When Windows loads an executable, the application's initialization code is responsible for creating what is called a *message pump*, essentially

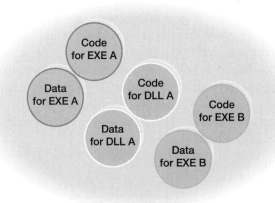

Figure 6.1: Memory organization under Windows 3.x

a program loop that runs as long as the application is running. The message pump requests messages from the operating system. Windows keeps track of the application as a separate task, sending messages as necessary and allocating a share of CPU time to it.

Dynamic link libraries are designed to be loaded by an application whenever it needs to access functions in what is, in effect, a shared library. Calling a function in a DLL once it is loaded is a very fast operation. You might think that calling a function in another application is just as fast. After all, the memory is directly accessible; but this is not the case. The reason is that programs almost never call functions in another application directly. Instead, they send messages to the other application. Sending a message involves quite a bit of overhead when compared to a simple function call.

There is one serious problem with the type of memory organization shown in Figure 6.1. Since all of the code and data for all of the executables and DLLs exist in the same sea of memory, there exists the possibility that they can interfere with each other. As long as all of the code is bug-free and only references its own data areas, everything works fine (and we all know how common bug-free code is). But if a program accidentally modifies memory belonging to another application, or to the operating system itself, not only is the program likely to crash but it can also bring down the entire system.

Microsoft's 32-bit operating systems use a radically different memory architecture that largely solves this problem. Each executable runs as its own process, and the operating system divides available CPU time among the running processes. The sea of memory that it runs in is called the process space for the application. This is shown in Figure 6.2. As you can see, the process space for each application is walled off from other applications and from the operating system. It is impossible for code in one application to access memory belonging to another process unless both processes take explicit action to define a shared memory space through specialized techniques built into the operating system. Applications can also communicate with each other by sending messages to each other and using the operating system's ability to copy data from one process space to another.

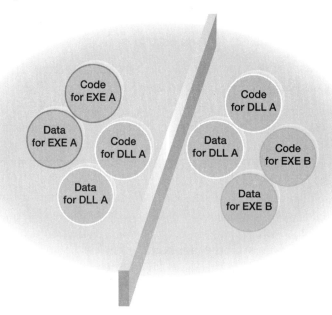

Figure 6.2: Memory organization under Win32

One subtle issue relates to the use of dynamic link libraries under Win32. Figure 6.2 suggests that a DLL is loaded into memory separately for each process that uses it. Conceptually, this is accurate. It may seem like a waste of memory; after all, one of the advantages of DLLs is that multiple applications can share the same code. Fear not. Even though the DLL appears to be loaded multiple times from the application's point of view, at a lower level the physical memory for the DLL's code is usually shared. The data segments are separate for each process, however, so you cannot share data using a DLL in the manner that you can under a 16-bit operating system. In addition, this description applies most accurately to Windows NT. Under Windows 95, DLL and operating system memory is shared globally—one of the reasons Windows 95 is not as stable and reliable as Windows NT.

For a more low-level and in-depth look at Win32 memory organization and processes, along with the API functions used to work with them, refer to Chapters 14 and 15 of my book, *Dan Appleman's Visual Basic 5.0 Programmer's Guide to the Win32 API,* ZD Press, 1997.

BACK TO COM OBJECTS

As mentioned earlier, a COM object exists in memory both as code (to implement the interfaces) and as data. The code for a COM object can be in an executable file or a dynamic link library. The data must always exist within a single process space (and for obvious efficiency reasons, this will be the same process space containing the implementing code).

Which leaves an interesting problem. If 32-bit operating systems define unbreakable walls between processes, how can one application reference an object that is created and implemented by another application?

The first thing to realize is that the data portion of the object is inconsequential. An object's data is only accessible by the code that implements it, and that code will always be in the same process as the data. So when we talk about accessing an object belonging to another application, we are really talking about the ability to obtain an interface pointer to that object and call the functions belonging to that interface. The data is never accessed directly.

But even the interface poses a problem. Because of the separation between process spaces, it is not possible to call functions belonging to another process directly. OLE solves this problem in a rather clever way. When you request an interface to an object implemented in another process, OLE creates a proxy object in your application's process space. This fake object exposes the same interface as the actual object. When you call a function on the proxy object, Windows collects all of the parameters to the function and, using the interprocess capabilities of the operating system, copies the parameter values to the process that contains the object's implementation code and data. It then calls the matching function on the real object's interface. This process, called *marshaling,* is illustrated in Figure 6.3.

How does Windows know enough about an object to be able to create this proxy object? After all, to do this, it would need a list of the functions for each interface of the object, along with the parameters to each function. There are actually a number of answers to this question, depending on the programming language in use. Suffice it to say this is exactly the kind of information that a

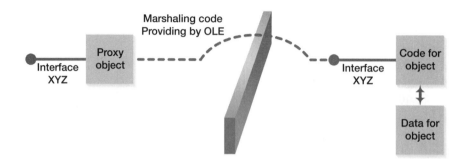

Figure 6.3: How objects cross process spaces

type library is designed to provide, and type libraries are created automatically for your Visual Basic classes when you create them. It is possible for people implementing objects in C or C++ to define their own marshaling code, but as a VB programmer you are unlikely to ever do this.

The concept of marshaling can be extended even farther. After all, once you have the ability to marshal function calls across process spaces, how much extra effort can it be to marshal them across a network to another system?

This leaves us with a number of scenarios for where a COM object can exist:

Within Your Own Application   The interfaces for the object are implemented in your executable (typically as class modules). The data is allocated and managed by the application.

Within an ActiveX DLL   The interfaces for the object are implemented in the dynamic link library. The data is allocated and managed by the DLL. Because the DLL is loaded into the process space of the application, no marshaling is required.

Within an ActiveX EXE   The interfaces for the object are implemented in the executable. The data is allocated and managed by the executable. Windows creates a proxy object any time you need to access the object. All function calls to the proxy object are marshaled to the other process. This involves a certain amount of overhead.

On a Remote System   The interfaces for the object are implemented in a DLL or executable that is present on another system. The data exists there as well. Distributed COM (DCOM) or remote automation creates the necessary proxy object on your system and takes care of marshaling the data across the network. Not only do you have the overhead of the marshaling between processes, you also have overhead due to the marshaling between systems. The main benefit of remote automation comes into play when the remote system already contains the data you need to work with (perhaps in the form of a large database). The overhead of marshaling a few function calls may be negligible compared to the alternative of transferring megabytes of data across the network.

You may be wondering why I have not yet mentioned ActiveX controls or ActiveX documents. This is because both of these types of objects are just specialized cases of the scenarios described above. Once you understand these scenarios, you'll find it easy to apply them to specialized ActiveX components. So much for theory. Let's take a look at a couple of these scenarios in practice.

THE LIFE CYCLE OF A DLL OBJECT

Throughout this book I've been stressing the idea that ActiveX technology in fact permeates every aspect of Visual Basic and that COM objects are substantially the same, regardless of whether they are implemented as classes within your own application or as DLL objects. This is important because if all of these objects are essentially the same (which they are), once you understand how to work with one, you really do know how to work with any of them. This implies that the best way to learn ActiveX technology is not to initially deal separately with each type of ActiveX component, but instead to first understand thoroughly the core COM technology. After that, it becomes relatively simple to cover those features that are unique to a particular type of component. So to begin our exploration of a DLL-based object, rather than creating one from scratch, let's turn an existing class into a DLL object so it can be easily shared by other applications.

The obvious candidate is the clsBankLoan class from Chapter 5. Not only is this class used directly by the application, but its interface forms the basis for the clsSecurityLoan and clsLoanShark classes. It serves as a contained object for clsLoanShark class as well. The steps to convert it into a stand-alone DLL object are simple.

1 Copy the Loan5 project into a new directory, possibly renaming the files for convenience (you can find the modified code with the name Loan6 in the samples\ch06 directory on your CD-ROM).

2 Create a new DLL project called gtpBankLoan (gtp stands for *Guide To the Perplexed*).

3 Add the existing clsBankLoan class to the project.

4 Remove the default class1 class created by VB.

5   Select the clsBankLoan class in the Project window, and in the Property window change its instancing property to 5-Multiuse (this tells VB to make the object public).

6   For testing purposes, add the original Loan project (now named Loan6) to the workspace.

7   Remove the clsBankLoan class from the project. (Note: the ability to support multiple projects in a workspace is new to Visual Basic 5.0. If this operation is not clear, you should review the Visual Basic documentation relating to the File menu commands or the chapter titled "Managing Projects" in the programmer's guide.)

8   Use the menu command **Project, References** to add a reference to gtpBankLoan to the Loan6 application.

9   In the Project window, click on the Loan6 project entry with the right mouse button and select **Set as Startup**.

10   Now run the Loan6 program. It works just as it did before, except that now it is using the clsBankLoan object exposed by the gtpBankLoan project. Note that not a single line of code needed to be changed.

11   Now, let's continue the process by compiling the program into a DLL. In the Project window, select the gtpBankLoan project.

12   Select the Properties tab.

13   In the General tab, add a project description.

14   In the Make tab, select the auto-increment checkbox (this should be done routinely) and add any copyright information that you need.

15   In the Compile tab, select native code compilation. (We're going to be doing some performance tests shortly, and use of native code lets us duck the native versus P-code question for now.)

16   Using the menu command **File, Make**, make the DLL.

17   Close the project workspace and open just the Loan6.vbp project. If you look at the project references, you will see that the clsBankLoan reference is implemented by the DLL instead of the project.

Once again, you will see that the Loan6 project works just as it did before. For now, don't worry about the various settings in the Project Settings dialog box—this subject will be covered in greater depth later in this book.

To run the Loan6 example, you have to make sure the objects are registered. This requires two operations:

▸ Register the gtpbkln.DLL objects using the command line: 'regsvr32 gtpbkln.dll'.

▸ Register the gtpPln.exe objects by running the program. (You'll find out more about this object later in the chapter.) You won't see anything happen, but the program will be registered.

A LOOK BEHIND THE SCENES

How does the Loan6 project know that the clsBankLoan object is implemented by the gtpbkln.dll dynamic link library? How does any application know which DLL or EXE contains the code that implements that object? The answer is in the registry.

In the Tools directory on your Visual Basic 5.0 CD-ROM you'll find a subdirectory called OLETOOLS, which in turn contains a program called OLEView (or OLEVW32.EXE). Refer to the readme file in this directory for more details on installing this application.

OLEView is a great tool for seeing what is going on behind the scenes in the system registry. It also makes it easy to launch the registry editor regedt32.exe that is in the system directory of your Windows system. Use caution when running regedt32.exe—if you change the contents of the registry you can seriously damage your system, perhaps making it impossible to reboot. The registry editor provides the ability to dump information about an entry to a text file.

Note: The directory locations, times, and actual GUID or CLSID values that you find on your system may differ from the ones shown here. The values shown here are for illustration purposes only!

If you look in the HKEY_CLASSES_ROOT key for the registry, lo and behold, you'll find an entry much like this one for the clsBankLoan class:

```
Key Name:       gtpBankLoan.clsBankLoan
Class Name:     <NO CLASS>
Last Write Time: 10/24/96—4:27 PM
Value 0
    Name:           <NO NAME>
    Type:           REG_SZ
    Data:           gtpBankLoan.clsBankLoan

Key Name:       gtpBankLoan.clsBankLoan\Clsid
Class Name:     <NO CLASS>
```

```
Last Write Time:    10/24/96-4:27 PM
Value 0
    Name:           <NO NAME>
    Type:           REG_SZ
    Data:           {CBBEF242-2DEE-11D0-92E4-00AA0036005A}
```

The system registry is made of a hierarchy. Each level of the hierarchy has an associated name called a *Key*—it's similar to a directory name on disk. Each key can have a default (unnamed) value and as many named values as desired. The gtpBankLoan.clsBankLoan key has a default value that is a string containing the name of the object. It has a subkey called Clsid. As you may recall, Clsid is short for class ID, or class identifier. In this case, the Clsid key contains the string representation of the 16-byte number that uniquely identifies the object. When an application requests an object by name, for example, when you use the CreateObject function, this is where Windows can go to find the identifier for the object.

Once you have the object's identifier, you need to find an executable file (DLL or EXE) that knows how to create the object and contains the code to implement its interfaces. This can be found in the HKEY_CLASSES_ROOT\CLSID section in the registry, where you will find the following key.

```
Key Name:           CLSID\{CBBEF242-2DEE-11D0-92E4-00AA0036005A}
Class Name:         <NO CLASS>
Last Write Time:    10/24/96-4:27 PM
Value 0
    Name:           <NO NAME>
    Type:           REG_SZ
    Data:           gtpBankLoan.clsBankLoan

Key Name:           CLSID\{CBBEF242-2DEE-11D0-92E4-00AA0036005A}\Implemented
Categories
Class Name:         <NO CLASS>
Last Write Time:    10/24/96-4:27 PM

Key Name:           CLSID\{CBBEF242-2DEE-11D0-92E4-00AA0036005A}\Implemented
Categories\{40FC6ED5-2438-11CF-A3DB-080036F12502}
Class Name:         <NO CLASS>
Last Write Time:    10/24/96-4:27 PM

Key Name:           CLSID\{CBBEF242-2DEE-11D0-92E4-00AA0036005A}\InprocServer32
Class Name:         <NO CLASS>
Last Write Time:    10/24/96-4:27 PM
Value 0
    Name:           <NO NAME>
    Type:           REG_SZ
```

```
  Data:              D:\ZDBOOK4\Samples\CH06\gtpBkLn.dll


Key Name:            CLSID\{CBBEF242-2DEE-11D0-92E4-00AA0036005A}\ProgID
Class Name:          <NO CLASS>
Last Write Time:     10/24/96-4:27 PM
Value 0
  Name:              <NO NAME>
  Type:              REG_SZ
  Data:              gtpBankLoan.clsBankLoan


Key Name:            CLSID\{CBBEF242-2DEE-11D0-92E4-00AA0036005A}\Programmable
Class Name:          <NO CLASS>
Last Write Time:     10/24/96-4:27 PM


Key Name:            CLSID\{CBBEF242-2DEE-11D0-92E4-00AA0036005A}\TypeLib
Class Name:          <NO CLASS>
Last Write Time:     10/24/96-4:27 PM
Value 0
  Name:              <NO NAME>
  Type:              REG_SZ
  Data:              {CBBEF1B4-2DEE-11D0-92E4-00AA0036005A}


Key Name:            CLSID\{CBBEF242-2DEE-11D0-92E4-00AA0036005A}\Version
Class Name:          <NO CLASS>
Last Write Time:     10/24/96-4:27 PM
Value 0
  Name:              <NO NAME>
  Type:              REG_SZ
  Data:              2.0
```

Let's tackle these one at a time. The default value for the
CLSID\{CBBEF242-2DEE-11D0-92E4-00AA0036005A} key is the name of the
object: gtpBankLoan.clsBankLoan. Under this key there are additional subkeys
as shown in Table 6.1.

The most important piece of information here is clearly the InProcServer32
field. Now you can see how an application can find the DLL or EXE that implements an object.

You can retrieve most of this information in a somewhat easier fashion by
using the OLEView application and searching for the gtpBankLoan.clsBank-
Loan object.

Table 6.1: Object Subkeys

Subkey	Description of Entry
Implemented Categories	Contains one or more subkeys that are GUID values for a key in the HKEY_CLASSES_ROOT\Component Categories entry in the registry. Each entry under this key describes something about the object. In this case, the object is marked as Programmable. As a VB programmer, you are unlikely to ever care about this entry.
InProcServer32	This entry tells the system which DLL contains the code to implement this object in process (within the same process of the application trying to use the object).
ProgID	The programmatic identifier of the object. In other words, the name you would use within a program to identify the object. In this case it is gtpBankLoan.clsBankLoan.
Programmable	Another way of indicating that this object is Programmable (via ActiveX automation)
TypeLib	This key contains the value of the GUID for the type library, which is the library that defines the interfaces supported by the object.
Version	The version of the object, in this case, 2.0. Versioning will be discussed at great length later in this book.

There's one more trail to follow: the TypeLib value. To look at a type library, you can use the OLEView application (there are entries in the HKEY_CLASSES_ROOT\Typelib key, but these once again reference the DLL containing the type library). The easiest way to load the type library is to use the menu command, File, View Type Library, and load it from the DLL directly. (Even though the file types listed show .TLB and .OLB, you can load the type library resource from a DLL as well.) OLEView can save a summary of the type library information to a text file. Here is the summary for the clsBankLoan class:

```
' ================================================================
' Type Library: gtpBankLoan, Library Version 2.000
' GUID: {CBBEF1B4-2DEE-11D0-92E4-00AA0036005A}
' LCID: 0X00000000
' Documentation: gtpBankLoan: Chapter 6 sample object for Guide To The Perplexed.
' Help:
' ================================================================


' ================================================================
```

```
' Type Info: _clsBankLoan, TypeInfo Version 1.000
' GUID: {CBBEF241-2DEE-11D0-92E4-00AA0036005A}
' LCID: 0X00000000
' TypeKind: dispinterface
'----------------------------------------------------------------

' Function: QueryInterface
'
Declare Sub QueryInterface (ByRef riid As Variant, ByRef ppvObj As Variant)

' Function: AddRef
'
Declare Function AddRef () As ULONG

' Function: Release
'
Declare Function Release () As ULONG

' Function: GetTypeInfoCount
'
Declare Sub GetTypeInfoCount (ByRef pctinfo As Variant)

' Function: GetTypeInfo
'
Declare Sub GetTypeInfo (ByVal itinfo As UINT, ByVal lcid As ULONG, ByRef pptinfo
As Variant)

' Function: GetIDsOfNames
'
Declare Sub GetIDsOfNames (ByRef riid As Variant, ByRef rgszNames As Variant,
ByVal cNames As UINT, ByVal lcid As ULONG, ByRef rgdispid As Variant)

' Function: Invoke
'
Declare Sub Invoke (ByVal dispidMember As Long, ByRef riid As Variant, ByVal lcid
As ULONG, ByVal wFlags As USHORT, ByRef pdispparams As Variant, ByRef pvarResult
As Variant, ByRef pexcepinfo As Variant, ByRef puArgErr As Variant)

' Function: AmountAvailable
'
Declare Function AmountAvailable () As Currency

' Function: AmountAvailable
'
Declare Sub AmountAvailable (ByVal  Currency)

' Function: Duration
```

```
'
Declare Function Duration () As Integer

' Function: Duration
'
Declare Sub Duration (ByVal  Integer)

' Function: Interest
'
Declare Function Interest () As Double

' Function: Interest
'
Declare Sub Interest (ByVal  Double)

' Function: Payment
'
Declare Function Payment () As Currency

' Function: Summary
'
Declare Function Summary () As String

' Function: SourceType
'
Declare Function SourceType () As String

' Function: MainInterface
'
Declare Function MainInterface () As LPDISPATCH


'=========================================================
' Type Info: clsBankLoan, TypeInfo Version 1.000
' GUID: {CBBEF242-2DEE-11D0-92E4-00AA0036005A}
' LCID: 0X00000000
' TypeKind: coclass
'---------------------------------------------------------
```

The programmed interface used for this object is called _clsBankLoan. Note how the first seven functions in the interface correspond to the functions from the IUnknown and IDispatch interfaces. This is what you would expect from a dual interface. Note also how properties that were defined as public variables in the class are actually implemented as two functions. The OLEView application provides more detailed information for each function, much of which is comprehensible only to OLE gurus, and most of which is of interest only to Visual Basic and other object containers.

The type library also contains a reference to the class GUID (the *co-class* type shown at the end of the list). This allows VB to go from the type library to the CLSID for an object.

With this background, it's now easy to follow the life cycle of an object implemented in a DLL.

At Registration Time: Before any application (including Loan6) can access the gtpBankLoan.clsBankLoan object, information about the object must be stored in the system registry. Visual Basic does this for you automatically at compile time. When distributing applications, the various components are typically registered by the installation program or by using the regsvr32.exe program.

Visual Basic DLLs contain the exported functions DllRegisterServer and DllUnregisterServer, which can be called to perform the registration (or clear the registration) for the objects supported by the DLL. These functions are called by regsvr32.exe or the installation program as needed.

During Design Time: A reference to the gtpBankLoan.clsBankLoan object was added to the Loan6 project.

- ▶ Visual Basic can use the program ID (gtpBankLoan.clsBankLoan) to search the registry for the CLSID for the object.

- ▶ Visual Basic looks in the registry to find the server for the object. It finds gtpbkln.dll.

- ▶ Visual Basic reads the type library from the DLL. It now knows all about the interface for the object.

- ▶ When you save a project, the TypeLib identifier is stored in the project file. When Visual Basic loads a project it can read the type library first and obtain from it the CLSID for the object.

During Compilation: (This stage also occurs when running in the VB environment.) Because the interface information is available at design time, all calls to object variables defined as clsBankLoan objects can be early bound. Visual Basic can compile direct calls to the functions on the interface instead of depending on the IDispatch interface for the object.

At Runtime: When Loan6 tries to create a clsBankLoan object, it uses the CLSID of the object when searching the registry for the name of the DLL that implements the object.

- ▶ Visual Basic then loads the DLL.

- ▶ Visual Basic uses functionality built into OLE to create objects as needed. When OLE creates an object, it returns a pointer to the IUnknown interface for the object. Visual Basic then uses QueryInterface to obtain the _clsBankLoan interface, which it can assign to a clsBankLoan object variable. The object is created with a reference count of 1.

▶ Properties and methods for the object interface are executed by calling functions in the interface directly (early bound).

▶ When the project is closed or the object variable is set to Nothing, the reference count for the object is set to zero. The gtpbkln.dll DLL sees that the reference is zero and frees the memory for the object. When all objects implemented by the DLL are freed, the DLL can be unloaded.

THE LIFE CYCLE OF AN EXE OBJECT

The DLL object described in the previous section has two major characteristics: it is implemented in a dynamic link library, and it runs in process.

What happens when an object is implemented in an executable file that runs in a different process? To demonstrate this, let's add another object type to the Loan6 application.

Interest rates have risen, and more and more people purchase their homes using loans from their parents. The Loan6 example has been extended to handle parent loans. Parent loans are implemented using a class in an EXE server called gtpPln.vbp. This project has a single-class module called clsParentLoan (ParLn.cls), which is shown in Listing 6.1.

Listing 6.1: Listing for Class clsParentLoan

```
' ActiveX: Guide to the Perplexed
' Copyright (c) 1997 by Desaware Inc.  All Rights Reserved
' Chapter 6

Implements clsBankLoan

Option Explicit

' Amount of loan available
Public AmountAvailable As Currency

' Term of loan
Public Duration As Integer

' Interest
Public Interest As Double
```

Listing 6.1: Listing for Class clsParentLoan (Continued)

```
' Margin requirement
Public Margin As Double


' Calculate the loan payment
Private Function Payment() As Currency
    Dim factor As Double
    Dim iper As Double
    iper = Interest / 12
    factor = iper * ((1 + iper) ^ Duration)
    Payment = AmountAvailable * factor / (((1 + iper) ^ Duration)-1)
End Function


' Obtain string description of loan
Public Function Summary() As String
    Summary = Format$(AmountAvailable, "Currency") & "  " & Format$(Interest,_
    "Percent") & "  " & Duration & " months."
End Function


Public Function SourceType() As String
    SourceType = "Loan from parents"
End Function


' The clsBankLoan Interface
Private Property Let clsBankLoan_AmountAvailable(ByVal RHS As Currency)
    AmountAvailable = RHS
End Property


Private Property Get clsBankLoan_AmountAvailable() As Currency
    clsBankLoan_AmountAvailable = AmountAvailable
End Property


Private Property Let clsBankLoan_Duration(ByVal RHS As Integer)
    Duration = RHS
End Property


Private Property Get clsBankLoan_Duration() As Integer
    clsBankLoan_Duration = Duration
End Property


Private Property Let clsBankLoan_Interest(ByVal RHS As Double)
    If RHS > 0.02 Then
        RHS = RHS / 10
    End If
```

Listing 6.1: Listing for Class clsParentLoan (Continued)

```
    Interest = RHS
End Property


Private Property Get clsBankLoan_Interest() As Double
   clsBankLoan_Interest = Interest
End Property


' Get reference to other interface
Private Function clsBankLoan_MainInterface() As Object
   Dim myobj As clsParentLoan
   Set myobj = Me     ' Get correct interface
   Set clsBankLoan_MainInterface = myobj
End Function


Private Function clsBankLoan_Payment() As Currency
   clsBankLoan_Payment = Payment()
End Function


Private Function clsBankLoan_SourceType() As String
   clsBankLoan_SourceType = SourceType()
End Function


Private Function clsBankLoan_Summary() As String
   clsBankLoan_Summary = Summary()
End Function


Public Function LatePenalty() As String
   LatePenalty = "Don't worry about us, we'll be fine"
End Function
```

This class is based on the clsSecurityLoan class from the Loan6 application. As you can see, it also implements the clsBankLoan interface. In order to make this possible, the project also has to reference the gtpBankLoan.clsBankLoan class. This is accomplished by using the Project, References command to add a reference to gtpBankLoan.

Could this class use aggregation in the same manner as the clsLoanShark class? Absolutely!

This again demonstrates an important fact. The choice of whether to implement an object in a class, DLL server, or EXE server may depend on many factors, including the logical division of functionality, performance issues, distribution issues, and special features associated with each (which will be discussed later). But once you've chosen where to implement the object, the code itself is essentially identical in each case.

An object in an EXE server can be registered in several ways. It is registered automatically when the program is compiled. It is registered when the executable is run, or when run with the command line option /regserver. You can unregister EXE objects by running the program with the /UnRegServer command line option.

The entries created for an EXE server in the registry are similar to those created for a DLL server. The biggest difference is that the server appears under the \LocalServer32 key instead of the \InProcServer32 key. This indicates that the server implementing the object runs on the local system but is not in process. The registry entries are shown below:

```
Key Name:        CLSID\{2B8BE8E9-2E0D-11D0-92E4-00AA0036005A}
Class Name:      <NO CLASS>
Last Write Time: 10/24/96-8:04 PM
Value 0
  Name:          <NO NAME>
  Type:          REG_SZ
  Data:          gtpParentLoan.clsParentLoan


Key Name:        CLSID\{2B8BE8E9-2E0D-11D0-92E4-00AA0036005A}\LocalServer32
Class Name:      <NO CLASS>
Last Write Time: 10/24/96-8:04 PM
Value 0
  Name:          <NO NAME>
  Type:          REG_SZ
  Data:          D:\ZDBOOK4\Samples\CH06\gtpPLn.exe


Key Name:        CLSID\{2B8BE8E9-2E0D-11D0-92E4-00AA0036005A}\ProgID
Class Name:      <NO CLASS>
Last Write Time: 10/24/96-8:04 PM
Value 0
  Name:          <NO NAME>
  Type:          REG_SZ
  Data:          gtpParentLoan.clsParentLoan
```

The type library for an EXE implemented object is essentially the same as that of a DLL implemented object.

Now let's take a look at the life cycle of an EXE implemented object.

At Registration: Registration performs the same task as with the DLL object, but with an EXE it is accomplished by running the application as described earlier.

During Design Time: A reference to the gtpParentLoan.clsParentLoan object was added to the Loan6 project. Then:

- ► Visual Basic uses the program ID (gtpParentLoan.clsParentLoan) to search the registry for the CLSID for the object.

- ► Visual Basic looks in the registry to find the server for the object. It finds gtpPln.exe.

- ► Visual Basic reads the type library from the EXE. It now knows all about the interface for the object.

- ► As with the DLL case, Visual Basic stores the TypeLib information in the project file so that it can load the reference information via the type library when you reload the project.

During Compilation: (This occurs also when running in the VB environment.) Because the interface information is available at design time, all calls to object variables defined as clsParentLoan objects can be early bound. Visual Basic can compile direct calls to the functions on the interface instead of depending on the IDispatch interface for the object.

At Runtime: When Loan6 tries to create a clsBankLoan object, it uses the CLSID of the object to search the registry for the name of the EXE that implements the object.

- ► Visual Basic then launches gtpPln.exe.

- ► Visual Basic uses functionality built into OLE to create objects as needed. When OLE creates an out-of-process object, it first creates the object in the process space of the gtpPln.exe application. It then creates a proxy object in the process space of the Loan6 application and returns a pointer to the IUnknown interface for the proxy object. The proxy object can reproduce the interfaces of the real object. Visual Basic can thus use Query-Interface to obtain the _clsParentLoan on the proxy object, which it can assign to a clsBankLoan object variable. The object is created with a reference count of 1.

- ► Properties and methods for the object interface are executed by calling functions in the interface of the proxy object. The proxy object marshals the function calls and parameters, and OLE sends the information to the real object in the gtpPln.exe process space. If the function returns a value or any of the parameters are passed by reference, Windows marshals those results back to the Loan6 process space so that they can be returned to the calling application.

▸ When the project is closed or the object variable is set to Nothing, the reference count for the object is set to zero. The gtpPln.exe program sees that the reference is zero and frees the memory for the object. When all objects implemented by the program are freed, the application terminates.

The life cycle of an out-of-process object is almost identical to that of a DLL object, and those differences that do exist are hidden from the programmer. Why then, is it so important that you understand the differences between objects? One reason is that your choice of implementation can have a major impact on performance.

PERFORMANCE ISSUES

The perform.vbp project in the samples\ch06 directory on your CD-ROM demonstrates the performance impact involved in implementing an object out of process. The code for the main form for the project is shown in Listing 6.2. The code is very similar to that used in the binding.vbp example in Chapter 4.

This project uses the actual objects defined for the Loan6 application. References are added to the clsBankLoan and clsParentLoan objects using the Project References command. The clsSecurityLoan class is added directly into the project.

Three objects are defined, one for each class. The number of repetitions for the out-of-process example is much smaller than the two in-process examples. This is necessary in order to avoid taking hours to perform the test. (Once again, you can choose any values for these constants that run in a reasonable time on your system.)

The first operation during the cmdTest_Click event is to access a property in each of the objects. This is necessary because Visual Basic does not actually create an object until it is referenced. The New modifier in the dimension statement does not actually create the object—it merely indicates to the application that the object should be created as soon as it is referenced. In this case, we want to create the objects before beginning to measure the access times in order to avoid distorting the results.

Since we want to measure the time to perform a function call, it makes sense to choose a function that does as little as possible. The function that retrieves the Duration property is as simple as a function gets, since all it does is return an integer.

Listing 6.2: Listing for the Perform Project

```
' ActiveX: A Guide to the Perplexed
' Performance example
' Copyright (c) 1997 by Desaware Inc.

Option Explicit

' System API call to retrieve time in milliseconds
Private Declare Function GetTickCount& Lib "kernel32" ()

' Mark the time
Dim CurrentTime As Long

Dim InApp As New clsSecurityLoan
Dim InProcDLL As New clsBankLoan
Dim OutProcEXE As New clsParentLoan

Const repeats = 1000000
Const oprepeats = 10000&


Private Sub cmdTest_Click()
    Dim ctr&
    Dim res%
    Dim InAppTime As Long
    Dim InProcTime As Long
    Dim OutProcTime As Long

    ' Access each object to make sure they are loaded
    ' We don't want load time as part of this measurement
    res = InApp.Duration
    res = InProcDLL.Duration
    res = OutProcEXE.Duration

    Screen.MousePointer = vbHourglass
    CurrentTime = GetTickCount()
    For ctr = 1 To repeats
        ' Duration is fast, so this is a good measure
        res = InApp.Duration
    Next ctr
    InAppTime = (GetTickCount()—CurrentTime)
    ' Now inproc operation
    CurrentTime = GetTickCount()
    For ctr = 1 To repeats
        res = InProcDLL.Duration
```

Listing 6.2: Listing for the Perform Project (Continued)

```
    Next ctr
    InProcTime = (GetTickCount()-CurrentTime)

    ' Now out of proc operation
    CurrentTime = GetTickCount()
    For ctr = 1 To oprepeats   ' use less time out of process
        res = OutProcEXE.Duration
    Next ctr
    OutProcTime = (GetTickCount()-CurrentTime)

    Screen.MousePointer = vbNormal

    lstResults.AddItem "Within application"
    lstResults.AddItem "  " & GetTime(InAppTime) & " microseconds"
    lstResults.AddItem "In Process DLL"
    lstResults.AddItem "  " & GetTime(InProcTime) & " microseconds"
    lstResults.AddItem "Out of Process EXE"
    lstResults.AddItem "  " & GetTime(OutProcTime) * CDbl(repeats / oprepeats) &_
    " microseconds"
End Sub


' Get a formatted string for the time in microseconds
Public Function GetTime(timeval As Long) As String
    ' timeval is the difference in milliseconds
    GetTime = Format$(CDbl(timeval) / repeats * 1000#, "0.###")
End Function
```

Figure 6.4 illustrates a typical set of results. Be sure to use the executable provided or compile the project into your own native code executable before running the test, otherwise you'll also be measuring the difference between performance with PCode compilation and that of native code compilation, which will give you incorrect results. Also remember that both gtpPln.exe and gtpBkln.dll must be registered for this program to run.

As you can see, there is no real difference in performance between implementing an object in a DLL and implementing it within a project. The minor differences that you will see are due to poor resolution in the timer, and the fact that each of the loops may take different amounts of times depending on what else is going on in the system. (Remember, Windows 32-bit operating systems are multitasking, so other operations may be taking place on your system while these measurements are taking place.)

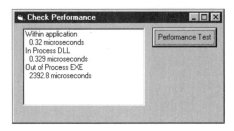

Figure 6.4: Main form of the Perform project in action

The difference between the in-process calls and out-of-process calls is, on the other hand, staggering. Minimizing cross-process operations is therefore an important goal if you want to improve an application's performance.

Here's a subtle point that you may have missed. Even though the access to the clsParentLoan object is out of process, it is nonetheless early bound! Since the Perform object added a reference to the object and uses an object variable of type clsParentLoan, it is able to bind directly to the class interface of the object. But since the object is out of process, it is actually binding to the class interface of the proxy object.

If you compare the results shown here with those of the binding application in Chapter 4, you'll see that the performance degradation of using an out-of-process object is substantially greater than that of using late binding. Using late binding in this case with the clsParentLoan object would indeed slow things down even further, but the slowdown would hardly be noticeable given the delays caused by the out-of-process marshaling.

All ActiveX components ultimately fall into the category of either in-process or out-of-process servers. But within those broad categories you'll find a number of variations—as you will see in the next chapter.

ActiveX Components: What's in a Name?

ActiveX Controls and Documents

ActiveX Trade-offs

I was considering folding the material in this chapter into Chapter 6. But once again it struck me that sometimes the size of a chapter is better measured by its importance than word count.

With the variety of ActiveX component types available, the question arises: Which type should you use? Fortunately, now that you are an expert on ActiveX and COM technology, you'll find it relatively easy to understand the trade-offs involved in choosing the right type of object for your needs.

But let me make one thing clear from the outset. Neither I nor any other author can tell you how to solve your particular programming problems. All I can hope to do is help you ask the right questions and teach you what you need to know to answer them yourself.

ActiveX Controls and Documents

So far we have focused on three types of ActiveX components: classes within an application, DLL servers, and EXE servers. Let's ignore classes within an application for the moment, since they are the fundamental building block for all of the other types of ActiveX components. The primary difference between DLL and EXE servers is whether they run in process or out of process, although there are a number of other differences that will be covered later.

In many cases these are referred to as ActiveX Code Components, because the objects that are exposed by these components are typically treated by your application as object or function libraries. In our loan application, for example, each loan type was a component that was accessed from the loan program—

from code that you write. The components did not have a visual interface and could not be manipulated directly by the user.

Now, in truth, code components can have a user interface as well. They can bring up their own forms or message boxes. In practice this is not very common except in the case of an application exposing its object model for programming by other applications. There are a number of reasons for this:

▸ One of the major reasons for creating an ActiveX code component is to allow you to reuse code. In most cases this means designing the component to be somewhat generic and avoid features that are likely to be specific to a particular application. There are many situations where the user interface would not fall into this category.

▸ ActiveX code components under Visual Basic 5.0 support multithreading in certain situations, but only if you turn off all user interface features for the component. This will be covered later in this book.

▸ Forms brought up by ActiveX code components are not contained in the forms of the calling application. In the case of an EXE server, they don't even exist in the task of the calling application. This can make the user interface rather awkward.

▸ Visual Basic 4.0 did not handle forms within DLL servers particularly well. Those problems seem to have been solved, but it's not clear that the technique will suddenly catch on now that it is properly supported.

ActiveX code components are not really intended to have an extensive user interface, but, as you might expect, there are technologies that fall under the term "ActiveX" that do support user interaction.

The first and best known of these technologies is ActiveX controls (previously known as OLE controls).

ACTIVEX CONTROLS

In Chapter 2 you read a little bit about what happens when you embed a spreadsheet or other object into a word processing document. An Excel spreadsheet is in-place editable, a concept we addressed in Chapter 2. This means that you can double-click on the object in the Word document and have Excel take over the window so that you can edit the spreadsheet directly. Excel's menus appear instead of Word's as long as you are editing the spreadsheet object. This type of in-place editing involves a great deal of overhead, in part because Excel spreadsheets are quite complex, and in part because Excel runs in another process space.

ActiveX controls are a special type of in-place editable object. They run in-process, and they are activated as soon as you select them. In addition to properties and methods, ActiveX controls can raise events. The Visual Basic environment integrates ActiveX controls seamlessly into the environment.

Like other ActiveX components, ActiveX controls are built up of COM objects. The code that implements these COM objects is contained within dynamic link libraries that typically have the extension .OCX. Let me stress this point: an OCX file is a DLL—it just has a different extension.

ActiveX controls are currently the most important form of reusable component available to Visual Basic programmers. Curiously enough, with the ability of code components to support events, it is quite likely that many applications that previously required ActiveX controls will now be implemented using code components instead.

ACTIVEX DOCUMENTS

Visual Basic 5.0 also supports creation of objects called ActiveX documents, previously known as DocObjects.

To understand ActiveX documents, let's first consider a more familiar document type—a word processing document. Microsoft Word uses documents that have the extension .DOC. You know that you can work with .DOC files by opening Word and using it to open the document. The data is contained in the .DOC file, and the code to view and edit the document is in the Word program.

You may also know that you can edit a .DOC file by opening it or double-clicking on it using the Windows Explorer. When you do this, Word is automatically launched and instructed to load the document. Explorer can do this because there is an entry in the system registry that tells the system that files with the extension .DOC should be opened using Microsoft Word—this presumes that you have Word on your system. If you do not, the .DOC extension may be associated with some other word processor that is able to read the .DOC file format.

Let's extend this idea to a new type of document. This document will be of a type called mydoc, which has a unique GUID.

A VB program called mydocserver.exe has the ability to read and edit this type of document. The mydoc document data will be stored in a file with the extension .VBD. This file will also contain within it a GUID that identifies the type of object. This way, the .VBD extension can be used for any type of object, and the GUID can be used to identify the correct object server to use.

When a container that supports ActiveX documents attempts to open the mydoc document, it reads the GUID from the .VBD file, then loads the server.

The server has the ability to display the document within the container application, in much the same way a Visual Basic form displays an ActiveX control. The server can display additional forms as needed.

ActiveX documents are currently being promoted as a way to distribute "smart" documents across the Internet. Your browser can download the server and the .VBD file, which can then be viewed within the browser window.

Perhaps the most interesting aspect of ActiveX documents is that they provide an easy way to distribute Visual Basic applications across a network. Think about it: You can take a VB form and quickly turn it into an ActiveX document, which will appear identical under an Internet browser. That could just about eliminate the need for HTML; Internet scripting languages, such as Java Script or VB Script; and Java Applets all in one bold stroke, at least for Windows platforms and those that support ActiveX documents.

But will this catch on? Will ActiveX documents become common on the Internet or on corporate intranets? Is there a practical use for ActiveX documents outside of Internet browser applications? (The MS Office binder supports them, but does anyone use it?) I don't know.

But I would like to. So if you find that you are actually making good use of ActiveX documents, please take a moment and let me know about it. (And no, you don't count if you're a Microsoft employee; your choice of technologies is too likely to be biased.)

ACTIVEX TRADE-OFFS

Let's take a quick look at the trade-offs involved in choosing different types of ActiveX components.

CLASSES

The advantages are excellent performance and no registration issues.

The disadvantages are twofold:

▶ Code is compiled into the application. If you use a class in many applications, this duplication can be wasteful.

▶ If you find a bug in a class module, you must recompile every application that uses the class in order to correct the problem. To distribute the fix, you must distribute every executable and component that uses the class.

In summary, classes are ideal for objects that are specific to an application and do not need to be reused.

ACTIVEX DLLS (CODE COMPONENTS) (IN PROCESS)

The advantages with DLLs are:

▶ Code can be easily shared among applications.

▶ They offer excellent performance due to the in-process nature of the component.

▶ Fixing a bug in a DLL Implement object only requires distributing an updated DLL. All applications using the DLL are immediately fixed.

▶ They can be used by any OLE automation client, including all VBA-based applications (such as Microsoft Office) and other Windows development languages.

The disadvantages are:

▶ If an updated DLL is incompatible with its predecessor, you can break every application that uses the DLL.

▶ It does not support multithreaded objects in VB 5.0.

▶ It increases the complexity of deploying an application.

▶ It requires registration, version checking, and component verification for safe distribution.

In summary, it is ideal for implementing standard objects that you may wish to reuse or share among applications. It is also ideal for defining interfaces to be implemented by other objects. And it is the preferred way to create high-performance objects that do not have a user interface.

ACTIVEX EXE SERVERS (OUT OF PROCESS)

The advantages here are:

▶ Objects can execute in their own thread.

▶ Objects can be created and used both by client applications and by running the server as a stand-alone application.

Disadvantages are that:

▶ Performance is considerably worse than ActiveX DLLs or classes.

▶ There is a higher system overhead due to the necessity of launching a separate task to support the object.

▶ The complexity of deploying an application is increased.

▸ Registration, version checking, and component verification are required for safe distribution.

In summary, a server is ideal for exposing an application model to other programs. It is also useful for implementing objects that can run in the background (separate threads) asynchronously to your main application.

ACTIVEX CONTROLS

There are many advantages to ActiveX controls:

▸ Good performance. ActiveX controls always run in process. However, there is additional overhead involved in using an ActiveX control that does not occur with an ActiveX DLL server. This will be discussed further in Part 3.

▸ Controls are compatible with many containers, including Microsoft Office applications and Internet browsers.

▸ Controls offer seamless integration into the VB environment.

▸ Property pages allow design time user interface, as well as runtime interface within Visual Basic.

▸ Controls have the ability to persist design time properties in most containers.

Disadvantages are:

▸ Controls are considerably faster than ActiveX EXE servers, but somewhat slower than ActiveX DLL servers due to the ActiveX overhead.

▸ There is some complexity involved in creating good quality controls.

▸ Controls increase the complexity of deploying an application.

▸ Registration, version checking, and component verification are required for safe distribution.

In summary, controls are ideal for implementing reusable objects that have a user interface. They are useful in many cases for improving the modularity of an application.

ACTIVEX DOCUMENTS (DOC OBJECTS)

Advantages here are:

▸ A doc object associates data in a document file with a user interface object. This allows distribution of arbitrarily complex data across the Internet and across intranets.

▶ Doc objects may provide an effective way to distribute software across the Internet. They offer a potential alternative to VBScript and Java for some applications.

▶ A doc object makes it easy to convert stand-alone Visual Basic applications to applications that run across a network.

There are two disadvantages:

▶ Features vary considerably from container to container.

▶ It's not clear at this time if the idea will really catch on.

In summary, this may be a good way to create applications that run across the Internet and intranets.

Part 2

Code Components

There are two reasons to learn about code components (DLL and EXE servers) before learning about ActiveX controls. First, almost everything you learn about code components applies directly to ActiveX controls. Second, thanks to their new ability to support events, many of the tasks that used to be performed using ActiveX controls can now be handled nicely with code components.

The wealth of new features offered by Visual Basic 5.0 is a double-edged sword. With its new support for ActiveX and COM features, VB5 is far more capable than version 4.0, and is suitable for many more tasks that were previously the domain of Visual C++ and other languages. On the other hand, Visual Basic 5.0 is in many ways far more complex than version 4.0. The availability of additional features also imposes the need to make additional choices. And you cannot make good design choices without understanding the technologies and trade-offs involved.

Part I of this book covered the underlying technology on which the ActiveX-related features of Visual Basic 5.0 are based. In Part 2 we'll be taking a look at each of those features specific to code components.

The Project

Chapter

8

So you're ready to create a code component. You have a task in mind—one you can envision encapsulated into an object with a clearly defined interface. Perhaps you expect this object to be used by multiple programs simultaneously, or perhaps you expect it to be reusable in some future project. Perhaps you expect that the implementation of this particular object may need to be updated frequently, and you don't want to have to redistribute the entire application with every update. Perhaps you need to take advantage of some of the unique capabilities of objects implemented within an executable.

There are many options. What counts first is that you ask the questions. You must understand what you want to accomplish before you can take that critical first step of creating your project.

PROJECT OVERVIEW

Your project, in an ActiveX code component, is made up of four elements: The project, the class modules, the standard modules, and the forms.

The project defines some key characteristics about the code component, including whether it runs in process or out of process, whether it is single or multithreaded (more on this later), and how your component is made accessible to the outside world. A project may expose multiple objects or none at all.

The class modules, if present, are used to define your component's objects. Those objects that are visible to the outside world make up the object model of your project. Objects that are private to the project may also prove valuable for implementation purposes.

Standard modules, if present, are never exposed to the outside world. They are often useful for providing global functions and variables to your project. However, the meaning of "global" can depend on the type of component you are creating.

Forms are the primary user interface objects for Visual Basic. Many code components do not have a user interface—in fact, it is possible to create code components in which all user interface elements are disabled. Other code components, such as those that belong to stand-alone applications that expose an object model, rely extensively on forms. Some code components use forms only as holders for controls. Keep in mind that forms are also objects; they can have methods, properties, and events.

Every project ultimately demands that you take the following steps (though you may not take them in the order shown):

▶ Define what you are trying to accomplish.

▶ Design an object model to suit.

▶ Configure the project settings according to the needs of the component.

▶ Define the classes and forms that you will use to implement the component. These will become the objects that the component will use, though not all of them may be exposed to the outside world.

▶ Define the global variables and functions that will be used by the component.

DESIGNING THE OBJECT MODEL

It's difficult to design a component if you do not yet fully understand the capabilities of the language you are using. It is difficult to understand and demonstrate the capabilities of a language if you do not understand how to define an application's requirements and create an object model for it. So where do you start?

Microsoft's documentation takes the approach of leading you through a step-by-step example that demonstrates many language features, while ducking (or only briefly mentioning) the trade-offs and choices implied by the sample. The documentation then goes into a more in-depth, feature-by-feature review of the language.

Theirs is really not a bad approach. And since this book is intended to supplement the Microsoft documentation rather than rehash it, it seemed appropriate that I take a different tack. Given that I've just recommended a sequence for creating a component, it seems reasonable that I follow through with a demonstration. But instead of a simple step-by-step description of building a sample component, I'll go into as much depth as possible so you can see some of the choices and trade-offs that are possible.

The first step is to define a task.

We had a recent investment craze at work. You know how fads sometimes appear in the workplace? Everyone got excited about a particular stock. You see, the company's stock had dropped suddenly due to some very public bad news, and it seems that our crew really liked their products and believed the stock would quickly recover. People were frequently interrupting their work to check the progress of the stock.

Now, I like to think I'm a very enlightened employer, and I must confess that I, too, was interrupting my work to check out the latest market figures. But things were getting out of hand. Clearly what was needed was a program that would just sit in the background and check the stock value, notifying us whenever it changed beyond a certain threshold. But it had to be a simple program—one that could be thrown together in 10 or 15 minutes—because spending any longer would defeat its purpose, which was to save time. Spending several days coding a stock monitor program in order to save a few minutes here and there would be a complete waste of time.

Logically, the program is fairly simple. You can imagine a form with a text box in which you can enter a stock symbol. It would have a variable to hold the current stock price. Every few minutes the application would retrieve the stock price and check it against the previous value. If the price changed, it would beep or otherwise notify the person to take a look. You could even set a threshold so the program would warn you only if the price changed by a substantial amount. An advanced version of the program could verify a list of stocks. Why, you could even tie it into a database and check an entire list—but I'm getting ahead of myself.

Now, to an intermediate level Visual Basic programmer, almost everything in the above project should sound absolutely trivial. You already know about forms, timers, and text boxes. The idea of a program that compares a stored value with a new value during a timer event should be clear and obvious.

But in fact, the chances are good that you'll see the catch in the project. Visual Basic does not provide a function that lets you retrieve a stock quote.

So in looking at the design of this stock monitor program, you have one critical decision to make. Do you figure out how to obtain a stock quote and add that functionality to the monitor program? Or do you create a component of some sort that has the ability to obtain stock quotes?

To answer this question, let's look at a pseudo-code description of this program. Pseudo code, for those of you who are unfamiliar with it, in this context is code for a language that doesn't exist. This is different from P-code (pseudo code), which is an intermediate compiled language used by interpreted VB programs. When you use pseudo code to document a program, you simply write a plain English-language description of what the program will do. The stock monitor program in pseudo code might look something like this:

```
Get the current price of the stock and store it.
On each timer event
        Get the current price of the stock
        If the current price does not match the stored value then
                Notify the user
        End If
End timer event
```

See what I mean? No compiler (that I know of) can run this program, but it clearly describes what the program does and could form a starting point for the actual implementation.

The only thing you cannot do using Visual Basic functions is the operation "Get the current price of the stock." Notice that this operation is performed twice in the program. Note also that while the program depends on this operation, the operation itself does not depend on any other part of the program. This means the operation can stand alone as an independent function.

Another way of looking at it is this: if you changed the "Get the current price of the stock" function, it would require that you change the rest of the program. But if you changed the rest of the program, it would have no impact on the stock pricing function. The dependency is one way only.

The question you need to ask now is this: Is the operation of getting a current price of a stock unique to this application? Or is it likely to be useful at other times by other applications?

This is a critical question. You see, if you think you will want to reuse the code that implements this functionality, you will certainly want to isolate it in some way. There are a number of ways of isolating code for reuse:

▸ Place the code in its own function and cut-and-paste the code to other applications as needed.

▸ Place the code in its own module and add the module to applications that need it.

▸ Place the code in an ActiveX component and let any applications that need the functionality access it through the component.

Let's look at the trade-offs for this particular example.

Placing the code in a function within one of the application's forms or modules has several disadvantages. Cutting-and-pasting code from one application to another is awkward; you have to remember which module contained the function each time you need it. Of course, there are some third-party tools that support code libraries that can alleviate this problem. However, if the function is one you'll use often, in no time at all your system will have multiple copies of the function scattered among many different applications. Now, if a bug turned up in the code, you would not only have to recompile each of those programs, you would have to correct the function in each and every one of the modules that contain it. Not that you would ever have a bug in one of your functions, but...

Another major disadvantage is that this approach is very poorly suited to tasks that cannot be implemented in a single function. Complex tasks may need to be implemented with multiple functions, objects, or custom controls. Using cut-and-paste techniques to share code in these cases borders on the ridiculous, if not the impractical.

Surely there must be some advantage to keeping the function within the application? Well, yes—you can be fairly certain that no changes in another application or another application's code modules will affect your program. This approach provides the best control over the code associated with your application.

Is this approach applicable to the stock quote problem?

It is not. The operation of getting a stock quote is clearly defined. If you had a bug in your implementation, you would certainly want it to be fixed on recompilation at least, without having to search through the application's modules. The chances of having changes to a common module cause problems with the monitor program are slim. Finally, what you may not know (because I have not yet even hinted at how the stock quote operation is actually implemented) is that obtaining a stock quote is a somewhat complex task that (as far as I know) cannot be implemented in a single Visual Basic language function.

So let's look at the next option.

Placing the code in a shared module solves most of the disadvantages of the previous approach. A single module can be added to many applications. Changes to the module will be incorporated into each application that uses it as soon as the application is recompiled. Because the code is kept in a single shared module, the problem of multiplying versions is eliminated. You may still run into trouble with complex tasks that require objects or custom controls. In those cases you may actually need a set of modules, forms, and classes to implement the functionality but, depending on your situation, this may not be a significant problem.

The big issue with this approach is the fact that changes to the module do not take place until the program is recompiled. You can consider this either an advantage or a disadvantage. If the functionality is in an ActiveX component and you need to fix a bug in the code, you need only redistribute the component. Your application and any other application using the component is instantly updated. However, any new bugs planted into the ActiveX component immediately appear in those applications as well! The shared module approach places the code in your executable (leading to a larger EXE size), but it eliminates the need to distribute a separate component and handle versioning of that component as well.

Is this approach applicable to the stock quote problem? It's possible, but there are numerous factors that suggest that the ActiveX component approach might be better. For example:

▶ An ActiveX component effectively adds an easy-to-use stock quote capability to your system, accessible not only from Visual Basic but from any application that supports ActiveX automation (Excel, for example).

▶ Thinking ahead, anyone who wants a stock quote would probably also want other statistics on the stock, the daily high and low, the prior closing price and other statistics as well. This sentence should raise all sorts of warning bells in your mind. Think about it: Many different data values. Functionality associated with those values (in this case, obtaining the values and perhaps performing calculations based on them). By now Data + Associated functionality should positively scream the word "object" to you. ActiveX components work by exposing objects. Bingo!!!

▶ Let's say the technique you are using to obtain stock quotes involves connecting to a quotation service via a dial-up account or the Internet. What happens when the technique suddenly fails because the quote provider has gone out of business? You need to implement a new technique—fast! The last thing you want to do is recompile and redistribute dozens of different applications that might be using the quotation component. Instead you'll want to update the quotation component to handle the new quote provider and distribute the component. All of the applications that use it will immediately work with the new provider.

So the choice is now clear. If you are not interested in reusing the stock quoting code, you can place it in the application itself. But if you are going to reuse it, the task should definitely be implemented as an ActiveX component—and as an object no less.

Now since I am basically a lazy person (in the sense that I don't like to repeat work I've already done), code reuse is a high priority. If I'm already going to go to the trouble of writing code to obtain a stock quote, once is enough. So an ActiveX component it will be.

But what type of component? Should it be a DLL or an EXE? Good question, so hold that thought. We're not quite ready to answer it.

Let's first conclude this section by following up on one key thought that came up regarding the "object" nature of the task. While the current price of a stock might be enough at first, clearly a stock quote program will want to retrieve other information associated with a stock. You can thus imagine an object related to a particular stock quotation that has the following properties:

- ▶ Symbol—The ticker symbol for the stock
- ▶ LastPrice—The current, or most recently traded, price
- ▶ High—Today's high
- ▶ Low—Today's low
- ▶ PriorClose—The closing price at the end of the previous trading day
- ▶ QuoteTime—The time of the most recent quote
- ▶ CompanyName—The full company name

You can imagine this object having a method to load the current information for the stock. It could be called GetQuote, for example. From here on we'll call this the StockQuote object.

You can imagine an ActiveX component that simply allows you to create StockQuote objects. This is a very simple object model. We'll be looking at building more complex object models later in this chapter and throughout the remainder of this book.

CHOOSING THE PROJECT TYPE: EXE OR DLL

Should the stock quote server be implemented as an in-process DLL, or out-of-process EXE? Based on the discussion in Part I of this book, the choice might seem obvious. In-process code runs substantially faster than out-of-process code, so of course it should be implemented as a DLL.

Or should it?

If the choice was this obvious, there would never be a need for EXE servers at all. Clearly out-of-process servers must have some advantages. There are a number of areas to consider:

- ▸ Performance
- ▸ Background operations
- ▸ Ability to share resources among multiple processes
- ▸ Multithreading issues

Before beginning, let's remove multithreading-threading issues from the equation. But only temporarily, because this subject will receive an entire chapter later on.

Performance We'll also give short shrift to performance, since that subject has already been covered in Part I. The important point to keep in mind here is that you cannot simply describe the relative performance of the two approaches by saying that "EXE servers are slower than DLL servers." It is more correct to say that accessing properties and methods on components implemented by EXE servers is slower than accessing properties and methods on components implemented by DLL servers. The code within the component itself runs as quickly. We've already seen that a short operation, such as a property read, can take substantially longer on an EXE server. But what if what you are doing is calling a function that takes several minutes to execute (for example, executing a large database query or generating a report)? In this case the difference between a few microseconds or milliseconds is a negligible part of the total time spent in the function.

The StockQuote object is a good example in this respect. You would expect the property accesses to the object, such as obtaining the last price or quote time, to be fast operations. Thus, the marshaling overhead would be significant. But you can expect the GetQuote operation to be relatively slow, since it will involve communication with an outside quote provider.

You should also consider how often your application will be accessing the object when estimating the performance impact. An object that your program will be accessing continuously may best be implemented in a DLL because the marshaling process does impose a load on the system. However, the impact of marshaling on your overall system performance becomes negligible with an object that your program accesses infrequently. In the case of the StockQuote object, the time to retrieve a quote will probably be measured in hundreds of milliseconds if not seconds, which is quite infrequent by the performance standards of today's machines.

Does this mean that the StockQuote object should be implemented as an ActiveX EXE component? Not necessarily. It only means that for this particular object, the performance issues are relatively unimportant. We must look at the other two issues to make the decision.

Background Operations If you've been reading closely, you may have noticed that I mentioned the term multithreading in several places, along with a caveat that it was either unimportant at the moment or would be covered later. Both of these caveats still apply. However, to understand one of the key differences between DLL and ActiveX servers, you must know something about threads and the way Windows 32-bit operating systems multitask. Those of you who have a thorough understanding of multithreading and multitasking may want to skip what follows. For everyone else, let's start with the fundamentals.

You know that Windows allows you to run multiple applications at once. You probably also realize that this involves more than just switching quickly between applications. The Counter.vbp example demonstrates this. It contains a label control and a timer. The timer has an interval of 200 ms. The code is shown below:

```
Option Explicit

Dim countval&


Private Sub Timer1_Timer()
    countval = countval + 1
    lblCounter.Caption = countval
End Sub
```

Run two instances of the counter.exe executable. Both of them will count simultaneously. How is it possible for a single processor to run two different applications at once? (We'll duck the issue of computers with more than one processor, since the principle is the same.) It is possible because the operating system can rapidly switch between the applications. In fact, at any given time your system may have many processes running, some of them that are launched and managed by the operating system itself.

Figure 8.1 illustrates multitasking between two applications. The first application runs for a while, then the operating system interrupts the flow of execution and starts running the other application. This happens very rapidly, giving the perception that both applications are running at once. This perception does not apply just at the user interface level.

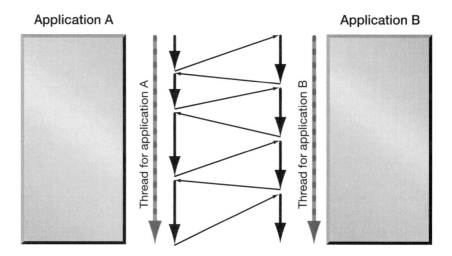

Figure 8.1: Impact of multitasking on program flow

As a programmer, you generally need not worry about the fact that your application has been interrupted. You can rely on Windows to continue running your code from the point of interruption. From your perspective as a programmer, your application runs as a continuous sequence of instructions. This sequence is called an execution *thread*. The operating system sees two different processes, each with its own thread. It can switch between the threads, but from your point of view, the thread is unbroken, as illustrated by the vertical lines.

Whereas Figure 8.1 shows multitasking from the operating system viewpoint, Figure 8.2 illustrates a system timeline from the programmer's perspective. Application A and Application B each run in their own thread, and those threads run simultaneously (as far as you can tell).

A thread can exist in three possible states. It can be running. It can be idle, meaning it is ready to run, but the CPU is currently running a different thread. Or it can be blocked, meaning that the thread is waiting for either a system resource or a system event. The operating system will not schedule the thread to run until the resource is available or the event occurs.

Each application runs as its own process. Each process has a main thread. It is possible for processes to have more than one thread, but Visual Basic 5.0 does not allow you to create multithreaded applications. (VB does allow you to create a limited type of multithreaded component server, which will be covered later.)

The nature of Windows multithreading does impact the choice between EXE and DLL servers because they work differently. Let's first look at the DLL

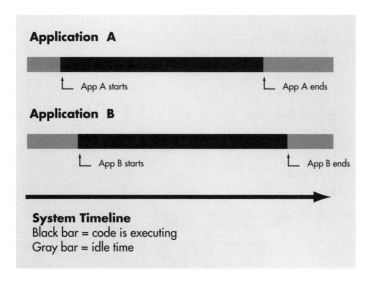

Figure 8.2: Applications run in their own thread

server case. Figure 8.3 shows the program flow for two applications and a DLL server. Application B runs in its own thread and has no impact on either Application A or the DLL server. But, as you can see, whenever Application A executes code in the DLL server, it is not executing its own code. In other words, DLL code runs in the same thread as the calling process.

An EXE server runs as a separate process. We've already discussed the impact this has on performance due to the fact that it has its own memory space. With this introduction to multitasking you can probably see what follows next: An EXE server also runs in its own thread!

This has two major ramifications. First, when one application is executing a function in an EXE server, other applications that try to access that server are blocked by default (multithreading servers will be discussed later). The server will wait until one method/property call is complete before the next is allowed to run, regardless of which application is calling the method.

Next, it is possible for an application to launch a background operation that will be run by the EXE server while the application continues to run its own code. This can be seen in Figure 8.4, where EXE server code is shown running simultaneously with the Application A code.

Let's take a look at this again from a different perspective.

An object implemented by a DLL server runs in the thread of the calling application. If 50 different applications each create an object using the same DLL

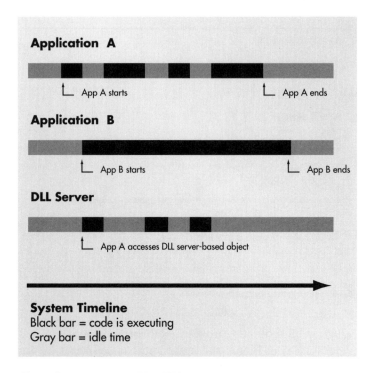

Figure 8.3: Execution sequence with a DLL server

server, each of the 50 objects will exist in the process space of the calling application and run in the thread of the calling application. Even though they are using the same server, there will be no communication between the objects, and they will not interfere with each other in any way.

An object implemented by an EXE server runs in the thread of the server application. If 50 different applications each create an object using the same instance of an EXE server, each of the 50 objects will exist in the process space of the server and will run in the server's thread. While the server is executing a method or property call from one application, it cannot execute a method or property call from another—the thread is already running code based on the first application's request. Requests will thus be queued and executed in an order determined by the operating system.

Is there any way to prevent this blocking effect? Yes. One solution is to specify that a new instance of the EXE server be run for each object created. That way each object will be run by its own process; it will have its own process space and thus its own thread. While this is appropriate for some situations,

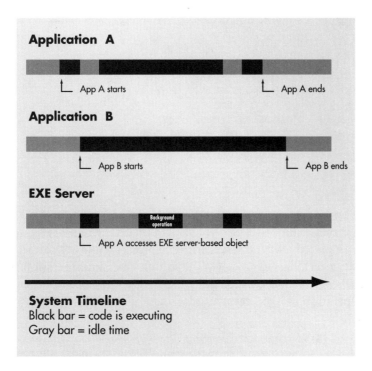

Figure 8.4: Execution sequence with an EXE server

especially when the one object acts as the top level for a complex object model that can all be run by a single instance of the server, it does involve quite a bit of overhead. Taking this approach for our 50-object example would effectively run 50 copies of the server, which is sure to impact your system's performance.

The other solution involves turning on multithreading for the server. I know I keep putting this subject off by saying that it is covered in a later chapter. The reason for this is that Visual Basic 5.0's implementation of multithreading is only appropriate for a certain class of problems and also has major impacts on global variable scoping. It's also a more advanced technique that has potential side effects. The dilemma is that I can't really talk about side effects until after the "normal" effects are discussed. If you really want to find out more now, you can skip ahead to Chapter 14.

The Chapter 8 sample directory on the CD-ROM contains several programs that demonstrate this situation. First, there are two server applications. Both servers implement a public object called TestObject1, which has the following class code:

```
Option Explicit

Public Sub SlowOperation()
    Dim counter&
    For counter = 1 To 10000000
    Next counter
End Sub

Public Sub FastOperation()
End Sub
```

The MTTstSv1.vbp project implements this object as an ActiveX EXE server with the project name MTTestServer1. The MTTstS1D.vbp project implements this object as an ActiveX DLL server with the project name MTTestServer1DLL.

The TestObject1 class exposes two functions. The SlowOperation method performs a very long loop, which demonstrates a time-consuming operation. The FastOperation method returns immediately, demonstrating a very fast operation.

A test program called MTTest1.vbp tests the behavior of these objects. The following listing shows the code for the frmMTTest1 form. This form contains a label control and four buttons. Each button calls a method in one of the TestObject1 objects and upon return increments a counter and displays the count in the label control. The project creates two objects. Both are named TestObject1, so you can distinguish between the objects by qualifying them with the project name. Figure 8.5 shows the layout of the form.

```
' Threading demonstration program #1
' Guide to the Perplexed
' Copyright (c) 1997, by Desaware Inc. All Rights Reserved

Option Explicit

Dim counter&

' We can reference two different test objects
Dim mtserve As New MTTestServer1.TestObject1
Dim mtserveDLL As New MTTestServer1DLL.TestObject1

Private Sub cmdFast_Click()
    mtserve.FastOperation
    counter = counter + 1
```

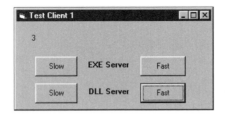

Figure 8.5: The MTTest1 project in action

```
    lblCount.Caption = counter
End Sub

Private Sub cmdFastDLL_Click()
   mtserveDLL.FastOperation
   counter = counter + 1
   lblCount.Caption = counter
End Sub

Private Sub cmdSlow_Click()
   mtserve.SlowOperation
   counter = counter + 1
   lblCount.Caption = counter
End Sub

Private Sub cmdSlowDLL_Click()
   mtserveDLL.SlowOperation
   counter = counter + 1
   lblCount.Caption = counter
End Sub
```

Now, try the following:

▸ Be sure the MTTstS1D.DLL and MTTstSv1.EXE servers are registered. (Use regsvr32.exe to register the DLL and simply run the executable.)

▸ Launch two copies of the MTTest1.exe program and set them side by side on the screen.

▸ Click on the Slow (EXE) button for one of the applications to preload the EXE server. Now click it again to get a sense for how long it takes to execute. If it is faster than a few seconds, recompile the servers using a longer loop count. It is important that you not only be able to tell the difference, but that you have time to perform other operations while one is in progress.

- ▶ Click the Slow and Fast (DLL) buttons to get a sense of their performance as well. As you can see, the performance will seem to be identical to the EXE server version. This is to be expected, since you will not be able to perceive the marshaling overhead.

- ▶ Now click on the Slow (EXE) button in one instance of the program and immediately click a few times on the Fast (EXE) button in the other instance. You will see that the other instance's counter is not updated until after the first instance's slow operation is complete. This is because its access to the server is blocked. Even though each instance has its own TestObject1 object, both objects are serviced by the same EXE server, and it can only execute code for one at a time.

Now click on the Slow (DLL) button in one instance of the program and immediately click a few times on the Fast (DLL) button in the other instance. You will see that the other instance's counter is updated right away. This is because each application's object runs in the application's thread.

I've mentioned that an EXE server's ability to run in its own thread implies that it is possible to have an object run code as background operation, but I haven't yet really demonstrated how this is done. In principle the idea is this:

- ▶ Call a method in the EXE-based object method that initializes another object that will later trigger an event (a Timer object, for example).

- ▶ The method returns. The application thread continues to run.

- ▶ At some time thereafter, the event is triggered in the Server object. This event runs in the server thread at the same time as the other application continues to run in its own thread.

We'll be going into much more detail on this subject in the next chapter. In fact, the StockQuote example uses this technique, which is a strong factor to consider towards implementing it in an EXE server instead of a DLL server.

Ability to Share Resources among Multiple Processes An EXE server that supports multiple objects can also be useful for sharing a limited system resource or one that can only be used by a single object at a time.

Consider again the problem of retrieving a stock quotation. We still haven't discussed exactly how to accomplish this, but let's assume for the moment that it will require use of an ActiveX control, a form, and a communications resource of some type.

Now, these are not exactly lightweight resources. You would not notice any significant impact on the system with a single server containing these elements.

But imagine you were running 20 different applications that could perform stock quotes simultaneously. Even if you used a DLL server, that is 20 different controls on 20 different forms, all trying to access quotes through a single communications link. Assuming that the link and the quote server has enough throughput to support a single control at a time, the other 19 controls and forms represent wasted memory and resources.

However, if you use an EXE server that can support multiple StockQuote objects, all of the objects could share a single control and form. The server could queue up requests from the various objects and report to the object once the quote has been retrieved. Since the EXE server runs in its own thread, it can retrieve quotes in the background without interfering with the performance of the applications using the objects. Because the limiting factor in performance is the relatively slow communications link and server, the overhead in marshaling caused by using an out-of-process server is insignificant.

The verdict: The StockQuote object should be implemented as an EXE server. This way, a single server implements all of the StockQuote objects.

INSTANCING

Every class module has two properties, the class name and the Instancing property. Instancing is not technically a project option (which is, after all, the subject of this chapter). But it has an enormous impact on the behavior of objects in a project. It is also one of the most confusing properties to understand, though I think you'll find it quite easy to understand with the background you have gained in this book so far.

The Instancing property can have the following values:

- ▸ Private
- ▸ PublicNotCreatable
- ▸ SingleUse
- ▸ GlobalSingleUse
- ▸ MultiUse
- ▸ GlobalMultiUse

Let's look at these one by one, though not in this order, for reasons that will soon become apparent.

PRIVATE

Private objects are accessible only within a component or application. It is theoretically possible to create a private object and pass it outside of the component, but this is generally a very bad idea, since Visual Basic will not guarantee proper referencing of private objects that are used externally. Other applications cannot create private objects of a component.

Any object that you use within an application or component should be private by default.

Private objects are supported by every type of ActiveX component and standard executables.

PUBLICNOTCREATABLE

These objects are exposed in the component's type library and are accessible by applications using the component, but only if the object is created and provided by the component itself. In other words, no outside application can create an object of this type. However, if an outside application has access to a different object in the component, that object can create a PublicNotCreatable object and pass it to the outside application through a function call or property.

This is demonstrated in the PubTest.vbg project group, which contains two projects. The first project is an ActiveX DLL server project called PubTest.vbp. It contains two classes. This demonstration can be run entirely within the Visual Basic environment.

The first class is called PublicTest and has its instancing property set to 5-Multiuse, meaning that it can be created publicly. It contains the following code:

```
Public Function GetOtherClass() As PublicNotCreatable
    Dim obj As New PublicNotCreatable
    Set GetOtherClass = obj
End Function
```

The other class is named PublicNotCreatable and has its instancing property set to 2-PublicNotCreatable. It contains the following code:

```
Public Sub Message()
    MsgBox "Public Not Creatable Object"
End Sub
```

The other project is called PubTest1.vbp and is a standard executable. The project contains a single form with a command button which triggers the following code:

```
' Obtain a public not creatable object by way of
' a public object
```

```
Private Sub cmdPublic_Click()
    Dim pubobj As PublicClass
    Dim pubNCobj As PublicNotCreatable
    ' Create an instance of the public class
    Set pubobj = New PublicClass
    ' Now use it to obtain an instance of the public not creatable class
    Set pubNCobj = pubobj.GetOtherClass()
    ' Show that it worked
    pubNCobj.Message

    ' The following line won't even compile!
    ' Set pubNCobj As New PublicNotCreatable
End Sub
```

The GetOtherClass method of the public object creates and retrieves the PublicNotCreatable object.

This type of class is extremely common. It allows you to create a hierarchy of objects in which the only way to access the object model is through a limited number of externally creatable objects that act as gatekeepers to the other objects in the hierarchy. PublicNotCreatable objects are supported by all types of ActiveX components but are not supported by standard Visual Basic 5.0 executables.

SINGLEUSE

Earlier in this chapter you saw that there are two ways for an EXE server to support objects. You can have a single server support multiple objects, in which case all of the objects run in the same execution thread. Or you can have each object launch its own instance of the server, in which case each object runs in its own process, implying that it runs in its own thread. The class instancing property determines which approach your server takes.

When SingleUse instancing is chosen, each time you create an object of this type, a new instance of the EXE server is run. This is a rather inefficient way of implementing objects and is typically used only for the top-level object in a complex object model that consists of PublicNotCreatable objects. Because of the high overhead involved, you are unlikely to want too many of these types of objects running on your system at any given time.

SingleUse objects can be created by applications using the New operator or the CreateObject function. This type of object can only be used with an ActiveX EXE server.

MULTIUSE

This instancing option allows a single server to support any number of objects of a given class. The objects can be created by applications using the New operator or the CreateObject function.

In the case of an EXE server, all instances of the object run in the process space of a single instance of the server. In the case of a DLL server, each object runs in the process space of the calling application, as described earlier.

MultiUse objects can be used with ActiveX EXE servers or ActiveX DLL servers.

GLOBALMULTIUSE

If you've been using Visual Basic for a while, you are probably familiar with something called a *global object*, though you may not know it under that name. For example, when you add a form named Form1 to your application, you can refer to it in your code by simply typing in: Form1.method. For example, the command: Form1.Show, shows the form.

In the same way, you can refer to the global Printer object. In each case you can reference the object without actually creating an instance of the object. You don't actually have to create a Printer object or Form1 object in order to use it.

Visual Basic 5.0 allows you to create your own global objects.

The GlblTest.vbg group contains two projects that demonstrate creation and use of global objects. This demonstration can be run entirely within the Visual Basic environment. The GlobalTest project (GlblTst.vbp) contains class MyGlobalClass, which is set to GlobalMultiUse instancing. It contains the following method:

```
Public Sub Message()
   MsgBox "I've been accessed"
End Sub

Private Sub Class_Initialize()
   Debug.Print "MyGlobalClassObject created"
End Sub

Private Sub Class_Terminate()
   Debug.Print "MyGlobalClassObject deleted"
End Sub
```

The object's Initialize and Terminate events are used to keep track of when instances of the object are created and deleted.

The GlobalTestClient project contains a form with two command buttons. The form code is shown below:

```
' Demonstration of global instancing
Private Sub cmdGlobal_Click()
   Message    ' This works
   GlobalTest.Message    ' Fully qualified - also works
End Sub

' The other way works as well
Private Sub cmdObject_Click()
   Dim gbtest As New MyGlobalClass
   gbtest.Message
End Sub
```

As you can see, you can access the object with either the fully qualified project.method name (GlobalTest.Message) or by simply typing in the method name. In either case Visual Basic automatically creates an instance of the object when you access the method. This instance seems to remain for the life of the application (I have yet to see one destroyed) and is used for all global access from the application.

Objects that are marked as GlobalMultiUse have the same characteristics as InSameProcess instanced objects except that they can be accessed globally. This type of object is supported by ActiveX EXE servers and ActiveX DLL servers.

GLOBALSINGLEUSE

This one is easy. It is exactly like the SingleUse option except that the object is global (See GlobalMultiUse).

This type of object is supported by ActiveX EXE servers and ActiveX DLL servers.

We can now move on to look at some interesting implications related to these Instancing options.

VARIATIONS ON INSTANCING

One important point to consider is that the Instancing properties only affect how an object is exposed and used externally. The component itself can create as many instances of objects as it wishes without restriction. This opens the door to some interesting possibilities.

The EXESingle project (EXESgle.vbp) contains a single class called EXESingleUse, which has its instancing property set to SingleUse. Be sure to register the executable EXESgle.exe before running the test program. (Don't try to demonstrate this functionality within the Visual Basic environment, because it cannot provide more than one SingleUse object.) The EXESingleUse class contains the following code:

```
' Guide to the Perplexed
' Single use executable example
' Copyright (c) 1997 by Desaware Inc. All Rights Reserved

Option Explicit

Private Declare Function GetCurrentProcessId Lib "Kernel32" () As Long

Public Sub Message()
    MsgBox "Accessed EXESingle use in process " &_
    Hex$(GetCurrentProcessId())
End Sub

' Create a new instance of the object and return it
Public Function GetNewObject() As EXESingleUse
    Dim newobj As New EXESingleUse
    Set GetNewObject = newobj
End Function
```

The Message function in this example displays the unique process identifier in which the Object method is running. This makes it easy to see if two objects are being implemented by the same server or not.

The ExeSingleTest project EXESgTst.vbp has a single form with two command buttons. These command buttons trigger the following event code:

```
' Guide to the Perplexed
' SingleUse instance test program
' Copyright (c) 1997 by Desaware Inc. All Rights Reserved

Option Explicit

Private Sub cmdTest1_Click()
    Dim newobj1 As New EXESingleUse
    Dim newobj2 As New EXESingleUse
    ' These objects are in different processes
    newobj1.Message
    newobj2.Message
End Sub

Private Sub cmdTest2_Click()
    Dim newobj1 As New EXESingleUse
    Dim newobj2 As EXESingleUse
    Set newobj2 = newobj1.GetNewObject()
    ' Both of these objects are in the same process!
```

```
        newobj1.Message
        newobj2.Message
End Sub
```

When you click on the Test1 button, two different objects are created. As you will see, each of these objects runs in its own instance of the server—they will have different process identifiers.

However, when you click on the Test2 button, you will see that the two objects that are created will run in the same process. Why is this? Because when the newobj1 object creates a second instance of the object in its GetNewObject method, it creates it in the same process space (just as if it were an ordinary class). Since this object is public, it can be returned as a result to the calling application.

This technique provides you with additional control over the Instancing of objects in your object model when using SingleUse objects in ActiveX EXE servers.

IMPACT OF INSTANCING ON SHARING CLASS MODULES BETWEEN PROJECTS

The Instancing property has an impact on your ability to share a class between projects. Earlier in this chapter we explored several possible mechanisms for sharing code, including cut-and-paste, sharing classes between projects, and creating components.

Let's say you've created an ActiveX DLL that contains a really cool Text Validation object. This object is exposed by the DLL. Thus, it has its Instancing property set to something other than Private.

Later you're working on a standard executable project. You realize you could really use that Text Validation object in your application, but it is the *only* object in the ActiveX DLL you need, and you would rather not distribute the component with the application. You might think that an easy solution is to simply add that particular class to your project.

But when you do so, Visual Basic will change the Instancing property of the class to Private (posting a highly informative warning message in the process). The class will work fine in the application, but when you save the project, its Instancing property will be Private. Next time you try to rebuild your ActiveX DLL that uses the class, the build operation will almost certainly fail (typically with a compatibility warning—more on this later).

So how can you share a class that has a particular Instancing property with a project type that does not support that Instancing property value?

You can't. You'll have to create a second copy of the class module to do this. Or implement the component in a server and have your project access the object in that manner.

What if you see this problem ahead of time (which you might, if you've turned some attention towards designing your object model). In that case, you can head the problem off at the pass. Create a private class that implements the functionality you need. Then, in your ActiveX component, use aggregation to create a new public class that acts as a wrapper for the private class.

PROJECT PROPERTIES

Once you've determined the type of project to use for your component and given some thought to the object model, you can actually go ahead and create the project. To be fair, you don't really need to go through the design process first. You can almost always change the Visual Basic project type (though doing so later in a project may cause Visual Basic to change the Instancing properties on your project's classes).

Which brings us to the properties of a project. You will want to give some attention to these properties on all but the most trivial projects.

Project settings are accessed through the VB5 Properties menu command under the Project menu, or by right-clicking on the project in the Project window and selecting the Properties option. Be sure you've selected the right project in the Project window if you are using a project group; it's frustrating to complete the property settings and find that you've just completed the work for the wrong project.

GENERAL PROPERTY SETTINGS

Figure 8.6 shows the general Project Properties page for a project. Let's consider these settings in turn.

Project Type   Choosing the project type has been one of the main focuses of this chapter. Anything here would be superfluous.

Startup Object   You have a choice of startup objects depending on the type of component you are building and the modules in your project. This option gives you some control over what will happen when your component is launched.

Standard EXE projects require a startup object. It can be any form in the project or in Sub Main. If you choose a form, the form will be loaded and its Initialization and Load events triggered when the application starts. If you

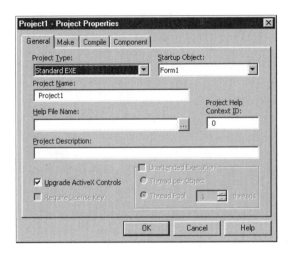

Figure 8.6: General property settings

choose Sub Main, the Main subroutine in a standard module within the project will run. This subroutine can then create additional forms as needed.

ActiveX servers do not require a startup object. You can just specify (none). In this case the first code in the component that runs will be code-executed during the initialization of one of the component's objects, or during an object method or property call if no initialization code is present.

ActiveX servers may also specify Sub Main as the startup object. The Sub Main procedure will run before any object's initialization code. Note, however, that the Sub Main procedure will not be executed until creation of the first object by the server. Once the server is loaded, Sub Main will not be run again until the server is unloaded and reloaded again. This occurrence may not be predictable, as VB5 does not necessarily unload servers immediately after their last object is destroyed.

ActiveX EXE servers under Visual Basic 5.0 may not specify a form as the startup object. If you wish to display a form on startup, you should select Sub Main as the startup object. During this subroutine you should show the form you wish to use as a startup form. You can check the StartMode property of the App object to determine if the component was started as a stand-alone object or as a server.

You can set the value of this property for test purposes for projects run within the Visual Basic environment by selecting the appropriate StartMode within the Components tab of the Project Properties dialog box. Remember that when you choose the ActiveX component server start mode, the Sub Main routine will not be executed until the first component is created by the server.

Project Name This is one of the most important properties you will choose, and you should always set it for your project. This property becomes the component name in the type library. For example: If you name your project MyProject and it contains objects MyObject1 and MyObject2, these objects will be referred to programmatically as MyProject.MyObject1 and MyProject.MyObject2, respectively. If the objects are publicly creatable, you will be able to pass this program ID to the CreateObject function to create instances of those objects, as in the example:

```
Set newobj = CreateObject("MyProject.MyObject1").
```

I don't have any great advice on choosing project names other than to try to make them somewhat descriptive and definitely unique. For example: the Stock Quote engine server that will be described in the next chapter has the project name StockMonitor.

Project Description At first glance you might think that this field exists just for documentation purposes, but it is actually quite important. This is the field used by object browsers to describe a component. Any time you use the object browser or try to add a reference or control to your project, this is the name that you see.

The Visual Basic object browser and component/reference dialog box sorts components in alphabetical order by description, using the project name only in cases where a description is not present. (It does not use strict alphabetical order; referenced components appear first.) This means that your choice of description has the side effect of determining your component's relative position in the list.

Does this mean you should produce components with descriptions like "AAAA—Alpha my cool control" in order to appear first in the list? Only if you think programmers blindly choose the first component they see in a list. (Personally, any control I see with a name like that is going to be removed from my system without a second thought.)

One useful convention that has developed is to precede the description with the company name. Thus the first word in the description for almost all of Microsoft's objects and controls is Microsoft, and these controls appear together in the browser and reference/components lists. All of the projects and controls in this book have one of two prefixes. If the description begins with gtp (for *Guide to the Perplexed*) you are dealing with a *trivial project* developed specifically for this book to illustrate some technique. It's unlikely you'll find it useful. If the description begins with Desaware, you are dealing with a component or control that was wholly or in part borrowed from Desaware's ActiveX Gallimaufry, which is a separate product.

Help File Name and Project Help Context ID   The Help File Name is the name of the help file for the project. None of the projects included with this book include help files. Any commercial-quality component should have a help file, but the whole subject of developing help files is beyond the scope of this particular book.

The Project Help Context ID represents the help context that is called when you request help on the component from the object browser.

Upgrade ActiveX Controls   Tells Visual Basic to upgrade obsolete ActiveX controls when loaded for this project.

Require License Key   Licensing applies to ActiveX Controls and is discussed in Chapter 26, "Licensing and Distribution."

Unattended Execution   Unattended execution applies to multithreading and is discussed in Chapter 14, "Multithreading."

MAKE PROPERTY SETTINGS

Figure 8.7 shows the Make property settings dialog box. The information placed here is used when Visual Basic compiles the component. Let's consider these settings in turn.

Version Number and Auto Increment   The first thing you should do when you're ready to build your control for the first time is activate the Auto Increment checkbox. This will automatically increment the revision number (or build number) each time you compile your project. The Version Number is used by installation programs to determine that a component that is about to be installed is, in fact, newer than the one already on a system. As far as I'm concerned, Microsoft should have set this checkbox on by default.

APPLICATION TITLE

The title of an application is different from the project name, which becomes the programmatic name of the component's objects. This title is the name by which the operating system knows the application. It is the name that appears in the system task list. You will typically set it to either the project name or the

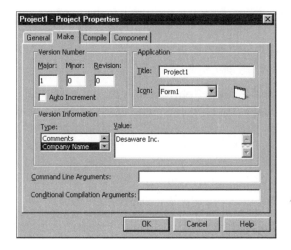

Figure 8.7: The Make property settings dialog box

component file name. Intended for use with stand-alone applications or EXE servers.

APPLICATION ICON

This is the icon representing the application in the taskbar, desktop icon, or explorer (depending on your operating system). It is intended for use with stand-alone applications or EXE servers.

Version Information   The Type list box allows you to select from among a number of strings. You can then use the Value text box to set the contents of each string. You are highly encouraged to do so, but be aware that these strings have absolutely no impact on the behavior of your component. The version information you enter here can, however, be read by the Windows Explorer or File Manager when examining the properties of the server executable file.

Command Line Arguments   This only applies when running an executable within the Visual Basic environment. It simulates running the program with the specified set of command line arguments.

Conditional Compilation   This allows you to specify constants for use during conditional compilation. This is a fantastic tool for debugging (debug code can be enabled by these constants and removed for release).

It used to be even more important with Visual Basic 4.0, since it allowed you to create both 16- and 32-bit applications from a single code base. However,

Visual Basic 5.0 does not support 16-bit compilation, so this particular usage has become obsolete.

COMPILE PROPERTY SETTINGS

Figure 8.8 illustrates the Compile property settings dialog box. This information is used by Visual Basic when it compiles the component. Let's consider these settings in order of importance.

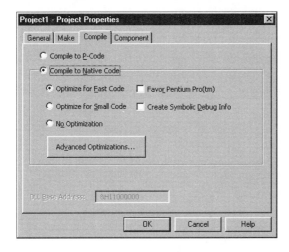

Figure 8.8: The Compile property settings dialog box

DLL Base Address   Before you release a DLL-based component (including ActiveX controls), be sure to reset this number to something over &H10000000 (and under &H80000000). Choose any 64K boundary—this means that the rightmost four digits of the address will always be 0000. Microsoft suggests you choose a random base address in that range as the base for all of your controls, then allocate addresses from that point onward. Not a bad idea.

The reason for this is as follows: When Windows loads a DLL, it tries to load it at the specified DLL base address. If the memory space is available within the process space of the application that is loading the DLL, the DLL loads extremely quickly. If, however, another DLL component is already using that space, Windows must relocate the DLL data and code to a new location. This is a time-consuming operation and one that is wasteful because it may prevent Windows from sharing the DLL code with other applications.

Since many Visual Basic programmers will never read either the part of the documentation where this is mentioned or this book, you can expect a vast number of Visual Basic-created components to appear at the default base address of &H11000000. Thus, the chance of a conflict at that address is frustratingly high.

Compile to P-Code or Compile to Native Code   Your first reaction to the appearance of native code in Visual Basic might have been a cheer (or sigh of relief, depending on your situation). Your reaction once you test it might verge on depression.

You see, if your application makes heavy use of Visual Basic native functions, API calls, other custom controls, or database access, you might be shocked to discover that the benefit gained from native code is not even noticeable. In fact, the only result you may see is a larger executable size.

Many applications spend very little time actually running P-code (the intermediate level that Visual Basic interprets), so improving the performance of that code has little effect. Microsoft claims that their people profiled many sample applications and found that typically only 5 percent of the time was spent running P-code. The rest was spent in support code. This does not surprise me.

However, if your code is computationally intensive, go right ahead and choose native code—the benefits can be enormous. This is especially the case with in-process components such as ActiveX DLL servers and ActiveX controls that are more likely to have extensive internal processing.

My suggestion is to try compiling your component both ways. If you don't notice a difference, choose the one that gives you the smaller executable size.

Some Visual Basic 5.0 programmers were disappointed to find that you still have to distribute a large run-time file with your VB 5 components and applications. Before giving up Visual Basic in frustration, allow me to point out two facts:

  ▸ If the VB5 runtime was not included, even the smallest Visual Basic executable would be hundreds of kilobytes, as with statically linked Microsoft Foundation Class (MFC)-based Visual C++ programs.

  ▸ Most Visual C++ components require both a C++ runtime and an MFC runtime. VB may not give you as many options as VC++ in this regard, but its approach is not unreasonable.

Regarding Individual Native Code Compiler Options   If you have an external debugger (such as Visual C++) and want to compile debugging information into your executable, choose the Create Symbolic Debug Info checkbox and select No Optimizations. One common reason for doing this is when you are debugging a VB-created component that is being used by a Visual C++ application. Otherwise, choose the Fast code or Small code option as you prefer.

I'm inclined to avoid the Favor Pentium Pro option for now. Maybe next year.

Regarding Advanced Native Code Compiler Options Refer to the online help for details of each of these options.

I recommend avoiding any of these optimizations until after you are confident that your component has been thoroughly tested and debugged. Be sure to do so with Break On All Errors enabled in your environment settings (you don't want an overflow error to be masked by an error handler).

After you are confident that your component has no overflow or array bounds errors, feel free to turn on the Remove Array Bounds Checks, Remove Integer Overflow Checks, and Remove Floating Point Error Checks options.

I would never recommend using any of the other options. The benefits you gain will be negligible in almost every case, and you risk adding bugs to your application that can be incredibly difficult to track down, including intermittent errors, incorrect results, and errors that are highly data dependent.

COMPONENT PROPERTY SETTINGS

This dialog box contains some of the most important project settings with regards to developing and testing ActiveX components. So it only make sense that they be covered in the chapter that discusses problems relating to creating, testing, and versioning of components, which is Chapter 9.

MOVING ON

We've looked at many different aspects of developing an ActiveX component in this chapter, ranging from the trade-offs involved in key design choices to the actual project settings. Along the way you've also learned a great deal about the different types of components and how they work.

One thing has been scarce, though. Other than a few trivial projects, there hasn't been much code. What happened to that stock quoting component that I've been promising?

Fear not, it's on its way. All of the examples in this chapter use the simplest possible code constructs: commands that any beginning Visual Basic programmer should be well acquainted with before reading this book. The stock quoting component takes advantage of more advanced language capabilities, including some that are new to Visual Basic 5.0.

But first, let's take a closer look at the process of creating and testing ActiveX components.

Creating and Testing Components

A Quick Look at the User Interface

Creating and Testing ActiveX
   Components

Referencing and Reference Order

Error Handling

Chapter
9

S ometimes I think Microsoft has a top-secret acronym lab. This is the laboratory where they come up with terms such as OLE, ActiveX, COM, and ISAPI. Given Microsoft's position in the industry, it's not surprising that these acronyms rapidly become incorporated into the vocabulary of most Windows programmers. Not that we necessarily understand exactly what they mean. . . . It's just that sometimes you have to make the right noises in order to be taken seriously (not to mention receive raises, promotions, and contracts).

The problem with these acronyms is that they can be incredibly intimidating to beginners and even to many intermediate level programmers. I remember when I first started learning about computers and was trying to understand the difference between an 8-bit bus and a 16-bit bus. I could understand that 16 bits must be twice as large as 8 bits. I just couldn't figure out the relationship between a computer and a form of mass transit!

In hindsight, I can laugh at how ignorant I was at that time. I felt so far behind I thought I would never catch up. But with the pace of change we are all facing, it is a rare programmer who does not sometimes feel overwhelmed, ignorant, and as if he or she is falling rapidly behind. The mysterious acronyms that come out of Microsoft's Acronym Labs (MAL—see, I can do it, too) don't help.

What does all this have to do with creating and testing components? Well, part of it relates to the confusion that resulted when Microsoft renamed OLE as ActiveX, but we've already defused that issue. But a large part is triggered by my reaction to my discovery that Visual Basic 5.0 had designers. This is a fact that is critical to understand when working with VB5. It's not that earlier versions of Visual Basic didn't have designers. It's just that they weren't called that. Purists will note that the term *designer* is not so much an acronym as a description or technical term. Technically they are correct—it comes from the Microsoft Institute of Terminology Extensions (MITE), which, of course, is right next door to MAL.

You've probably already noticed that a large part of what I am trying to accomplish here involves demystifying the terminology, focusing instead on what is really happening instead of what it is called. In this chapter, I'm afraid I have my work cut out for me…

A Quick Look at the User Interface

There have been any number of times when I had finally grown accustomed to a particular development environment only to install the new version and find that, not only was everything in the wrong place, but the new version was harder to use and less intuitive. True, part of this might be attributed to my conservative nature, but as I see it, if someone is going to force me to learn a new user interface, menu organization, and set of commands, the least they could do is make the new user interface so incredibly good that I cannot avoid seeing the benefits of switching over. Of course, this rarely happens, so I grudgingly force myself to learn the new interface and hope it will remain consistent for at least a short while so I can get some work done.

I suspect that somewhere in the development of Visual Basic 5.0, Microsoft let their user interface people in on the project. Make no mistake, Microsoft's user interface designers are among the best in the world. I am personally in awe of their ability to make complex applications remarkably intuitive, though I confess, there are some things about the Windows 95 interface…. But I digress.

So I faced the new Visual Basic 5.0 interface with some skepticism and trepidation. My misgivings were entirely misplaced. After just a few hours on the VB5 beta, I dreaded going back to Visual Basic 4.0. I won't list all the improvements. Microsoft documents them quite well. But here are a few of my favorites:

> ▶ I love the editor's List Members and Quick Info options. List Members displays a list of all methods and properties for an object in a pop-up list box, after you enter the name of an object variable followed by a period. QuickInfo lists the syntax for a method, including the parameters and their types. These take getting used to, but they've saved me an enormous amount of time and helped catch errors as well. (I didn't really want that parameter to be a variant, did I?)

▸ The ability to load multiple projects into a single instance of Visual Basic makes debugging DLL code components remarkably easy.

▸ I like the MDI development environment. I realize this is one of the hardest things for many VB programmers to grow accustomed to, but I do suggest that you give it a try.

▸ The instant watch capability during debugging is wonderful: just point to a variable in your code during break mode and the value of that variable instantly pops up.

IT'S NOT A FORM, IT'S A DESIGNER

Reviewing for a moment, remember that a Visual Basic 4.0 project is made up of four types of elements: forms, MDI forms, modules, and class modules. I'd like to ask you to view these elements differently.

First, let's take a look at forms and MDI forms. A form has properties that define its appearance and behavior. It also has code that defines its methods, events, and additional properties, depending on the needs of the application. In a sense, a form is defined by a set of properties plus a code module. Visual Basic allows you to set the properties of the form through a sophisticated design-time user interface. You can draw controls on the form, add menus, and so on. A separate code window is used to edit the code module for the form.

Class modules and standard modules have little in the way of predefined properties. Let me clarify this with an example: A class module can be used to define an object that has properties, but the module itself only has two properties: Name and Instancing. A class module is edited directly in a code window. Figure 9.1 illustrates the difference between the approach used to define user interface objects, such as forms, and that used to define code modules.

If a code window is used to edit code (whether it is code associated with a class module, standard module, or form), what do you call the window that is used to design a form? As of Visual Basic 5.0, you call it a designer.

A form designer allows you to edit the properties of a form using the VB properties window, to add controls by dropping them from the VB toolbox, and to edit menus using the VB menu editor. An MDI form designer is very similar to that of a standard form, but it has different properties and places restrictions on the types of components that can be placed on the form.

Visual Basic 5.0 adds two new types of built-in designers, an ActiveX control designer and a user document designer. It also makes it possible to add third-party designers called ActiveX designers. ActiveX designers cannot be created using VB5, and it is too soon to say whether they will become popular or widely available.

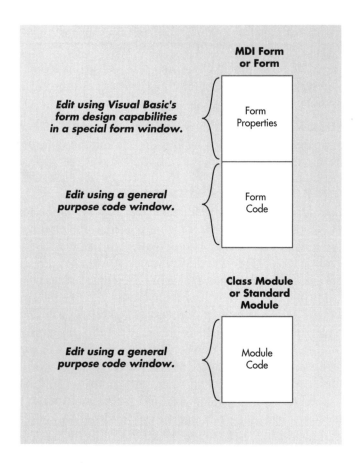

Figure 9.1: Working with forms and modules

Why is it so important to understand the difference between a designer window and a regular code window? Because, starting with Visual Basic 5.0, the behavior of a project within the Visual Basic environment can change depending on whether a designer is open (visible, maximized, or minimized) or closed.

CREATING AND TESTING ACTIVEX COMPONENTS

Sometimes people ask me how I know about the things I write about, especially in situations like this where I'm one of the first to write about a subject and thus cannot draw on information from previous authors. Do I have secret access to Visual Basic's source code? Sadly, I do not. I learn about things by reading the documentation (what there is of it) and by experimenting. I then combine the results of the experiments with my general understanding of Windows and ActiveX technology to come up with theories to explain what is going on. Usually I get it right. In this chapter, I invite you to follow along with the exact process of experimentation I went through while figuring out how Visual Basic really deals with different types of components.

The Visual Basic documentation provides step-by-step procedures for testing both in-process and out-of-process components. They are quite accurate, and if you follow them you will be able to test your ActiveX components with all of the power of Visual Basic's development environment.

Of course, you'll probably also need to keep their step-by-step procedures close at hand because there's quite a bit to do. It may be tough to remember all of the steps, most of which must be followed in the correct order. Unless, of course, you take a few minutes to understand what Visual Basic is doing and why, in which case the process of testing components becomes quite self-evident.

Shall we begin?

THE IDEAL TEST ENVIRONMENT

One of the great advantages of Visual Basic over other languages such as C++ is that it is an interpreted environment. Interpreters are great for testing and debugging. They go beyond letting you set breakpoints and view variable data in your code (which debuggers for compiled programs also support). Interpreters allow you to interactively execute commands or functions in the Immediate window, and in many cases modify your code while in Break mode. You can then continue program execution from any place you wish, using the updated code. With Visual Basic 5.0's support for native code compilation, you get the best of both worlds: an interpreted environment for testing and debugging and a native code-compiled environment for your final executable.

So when it comes to testing a component-based application, it would clearly be ideal to not only be able to run the main program within the VB environment, but to run each of the components within the VB environment as well.

But let's take this a step farther. To provide a truly excellent test environment, what you really want is to be able to run all of the in-process components with the same process as the container application. After all, you've already seen that components can behave differently when they are in process as compared to out of process.

Visual Basic 4.0 allowed you to run one project within each instance of Visual Basic, but it did let you run multiple instances of VB, which was a great improvement over version 3.0. Keep in mind though, that each instance of Visual Basic is, by definition, a separate process. So while you could run a DLL server component within the Visual Basic environment, it was always in a different process from the application using it. This means there were some features you could not test properly without first compiling them into a DLL. API-related operations that used process-specific data, whether memory or resources, were especially susceptible to these limitations.

Now I realize this might sound confusing. All along I've been saying that DLL servers always run in the same process as the application. Now I've shown that it is possible to test them out of process. How can this be? Simple: VB cheats. When you run an ActiveX DLL component within the VB design environment, it is temporarily registered in the registration database so other instances of VB, or other applications, can access that component. However, it is registered as an ActiveX EXE server, an out-of-process component.

This situation would be intolerable with Visual Basic 5.0. While you can test most DLL server features out of process, VB5 was intended to let you create ActiveX controls as well, and ActiveX controls must run in process. If Microsoft wanted to make it possible to test ActiveX controls within Visual Basic, it was absolutely essential that a single instance of Visual Basic be able to support both an ActiveX control project and a standard project (which uses the control) simultaneously.

As long as Microsoft can support one ActiveX control and standard project within a single VB instance, it couldn't be that much harder to support multiple ActiveX controls, right? And if Microsoft can support ActiveX controls, clearly they should be able to support DLL servers also, since they are based on the same underlying technology but much less complex, right?

Right. That is what they did.

Each standard executable, ActiveX control, and ActiveX server is built as a separate project. But within the Visual Basic environment you can use the File, Add Project command to load as many projects as you wish into the current environment. For your convenience, you can also define groups of projects called, remarkably enough, *project groups*. Think of a project group as nothing more than a list of projects that can be loaded as a group. You can still load or save the projects individually. The projects remain independent. But if you are testing an application with five different components and want to test all of them in the VB environment at once, it is a lot easier to define a project group than to have to add them to the environment one at a time every time you want to test your application.

Even though the projects are loaded as a group, you still work with them one at a time. For example: How do you know which project is referred to by the Option command in the Visual Basic Project menu?

All of the projects in the group are listed in the Project window. At any one time a single item in the Project window is highlighted. That determines which project you are working with. If you look at an object in the object browser what you see will depend on the project selected. For example: when a component project is selected, you will see both public and *friend functions* for objects in the component, (you'll find out about friend functions in Chapter 10). When a project that uses a component is selected, you will only see the public functions for the component. The friend functions are hidden (as they should be). Figure 9.2 illustrates the Conflict.vbg group, which contains three separate projects. The CFLTest.vbp project is the standard executable program. The group contains two additional ActiveX DLL code component projects.

Figure 9.2: Project window containing three projects

One of the projects in the Project window will have its name displayed in bold type (in this case, it's CFLTest.vbp). This determines which project will actually run when you use VB's Run command. You can choose the startup project by right-clicking on the project name and selecting the Set as startup command in the pop-up menu. Be sure that your main project (whether it is a stand-alone executable or ActiveX server) is set as the startup project. One common error that occurs when developing ActiveX components is to work on the component, then add a stand-alone test application. When you try to run the application, nothing happens. It may take several minutes to realize that the component is set as the startup project instead of the application.

Why don't you have to run the in-process component? And while we're asking questions, how does Visual Basic determine whether it should use the component within VB or within a previously compiled DLL?

To answer these questions and understand more about how to go about running applications that use both in-process and out-of-process objects, we'll need to discover a bit more about how Visual Basic loads components.

A COMPONENT IS BORN

Chapter 6 discussed in some depth how a component appears to the system. You learned that CLSIDs are kept in the registry to identify a component. That IIDs are kept in the registry to identify interfaces. That type library identifiers are kept in the registry to tell the system which file contains the type library resource. And you learned that all of these identifiers are ultimately nothing more than GUIDs that are 16 bytes long.

So let's follow the life cycle of an ActiveX component through the creation and testing cycle. We'll start with an ActiveX DLL. Feel free to follow along with this step-by-step experiment. The sample I used can be found in group Test1.vbg in the Chapter 9 directory on your CD-ROM.

First create an ActiveX DLL project within the VB environment. Give the project a name so you can identify it. Add a property to the class module for the project.

Add a standard executable to the environment that will test the DLL component by accessing the property you created. Be sure your test code accesses a property in the component to ensure that an object is actually created. You can place debug.print statements in the class Initialize and Terminate events to verify that this occurs.

Question: Does the component exist in the system registry? Answer: No. But you can nonetheless add a reference to the DLL component to your standard project! How is this possible? It is possible because Visual Basic does not need to go to the registry to obtain information about projects that are currently loaded into the environment. It checks the currently loaded projects first.

Add a reference to the component project to your test project using the project References command. Then make sure that the standard project is set to run at startup. Now run the project. Running the standard executable project also serves to run the DLL code for the first time.

Question: Does the component exist now in the system registry? Answer: Yes! Visual Basic may not need to register the component in order to use it in process, but once you run a DLL server within the VB environment, it becomes available to other applications, including other instances of Visual Basic. This makes it possible to test a DLL server in the same way it was done with Visual Basic 4.0—in two separate instances of Visual Basic. The DLL component appears in the registry as an EXE server, just as it did in VB4. Visual

Basic can provide in-process support for components only when both the component project and the client project that uses the component are loaded into the same instance of Visual Basic.

Run a separate instance of Visual Basic. Create a standard project and try adding a reference to your new component. It works! Try creating an instance of the component. This works also.

Question: When testing a DLL server as an out-of-process component, who is the server for the object? Where is the type library? Answer: The server for the object is Visual Basic itself. (Check the registry using the techniques described in Chapter 6 to see for yourself.) The type library is also provided by Visual Basic based on the project file, the name of which is recorded in the registry in the typelib section for the object. If you are testing a project that has not yet been saved, Visual Basic creates a temp file with a filename in the form VB??.TMP to hold the project information.

Now stop the project in the instance of Visual Basic that contains the component (close the standard executable project). Question: Is the information still in the registry? Answer: No. Visual Basic deletes the temporary file and removes the information from the registry. If you try creating the component using the other instance of Visual Basic, the operation will fail.

Now save the project. You'll need it later in the chapter, if you are following along with the experiment.

Our conclusions are that to debug in-process components (ActiveX DLL servers, ActiveX controls), you add the projects for the controls to an instance of Visual Basic, set the main application project to be the startup project, and run the application. You can now use all of Visual Basic's debugging features for all of the projects that are running in the environment. You can even single-step through both your main application and the components.

Again, with EXE Components   The situation for EXE components is similar in some ways, radically different in others.

The first point to consider is this: ActiveX EXE server components run in separate process spaces. This means that each server component must be tested in its own instance of Visual Basic.

So let's start with the same experiment, this time using two instances of Visual Basic. The sample I used can be found as projects EXETest2.vbp and gtpTest2.vbp in the Chapter 9 sample directory on your CD-ROM. But to reproduce the steps and errors shown here you'll have to create a project from scratch, because some of the project settings in these examples already reflect the later parts of the test sequence.

In the first instance, create an ActiveX EXE project, give it a unique name, and add a property to the class. Be sure the instancing property for the class is set to MultiUse. In the second instance, create a standard EXE project that will test the object.

Question: Can you add a reference to the ActiveX EXE server yet? Answer: No. The test application cannot add a reference to the component until it has been registered. This differs from the in-process case, where Visual Basic was already aware of all of the component projects that were loaded with the test application.

Now run the component. You can add a reference to the component to your test application. Visual Basic registers the component when it was run (just as it did with DLL components). Just as before, Visual Basic registers itself as the server for the object.

Next, run the test application. It should now be able to create objects provided by the component. Try stepping through a property call on the component. You will see that as you single-step, you will automatically switch between the two instances of Visual Basic as you move between the component code and that of your test application!

Finally, save both projects. You will need them shortly.

In conclusions, we find that to debug out-of-process components (ActiveX EXE servers, some ActiveX Documents), each component must be run in its own instance of Visual Basic. Be sure to run each component so that Visual Basic will be able to create objects as needed.

Keep in mind that you can combine these techniques! If an ActiveX EXE component uses an ActiveX DLL component, you can add the DLL component project to the same instance of Visual Basic as the EXE component and debug them both.

So far the testing process seems quite simple. Brace yourself, it's about to become a bit more complicated. But first, let's take a quick look at ActiveX controls.

About ActiveX Controls   ActiveX controls will be discussed in more depth in Part 3, but here is a quick preview. ActiveX controls are created and tested just like ActiveX DLL servers, with the following exceptions:

▶ Controls are referenced through the Components command of the Project menu instead of the References command.

▶ When an ActiveX control project is added to the VB environment, it is automatically added as a component reference for any other projects loaded into the environment that request it.

▸ ActiveX controls are disabled when their designer is open. Thus you must close the designer before you attempt to add the control to another project.

▸ Since ActiveX controls can't be run out of process, VB does not bother creating a temporary registry entry for controls each time they are run.

You'll read more about this in Part 3.

THE COMPONENT COMPILED

The first time you create and test a component, everything should work fine, just as it did in the experiments described in the previous section. But to introduce some of the complexities that are possible, try the following.

▸ Close Visual Basic so that you are starting with a clean slate.

▸ Open the DLL test project that you created earlier.

▸ Run the test program. Everything should work just as it did before.

▸ Close the DLL project.

▸ Open the ActiveX EXE component in one instance of Visual Basic. Run the program.

▸ Open the EXE component test program in a second instance of Visual Basic.

▸ Try running the test program. It will fail!

Depending on how you accessed the component, you may get a compile-time error or an error when accessing the property. You will also see the reference dialog box appear showing that the component is missing!

Uncheck the entry in the reference list where the missing component is indicated and close the dialog box. Bring up the References dialog box again, and find the reference to the component. Activate the checkbox to add the reference back in. Now run the program. It will work again. What happened?

Visual Basic and GUIDs   Using the registry editor, find the program identifier for your component in the HKEY_CLASSES_ROOT key in the registry (techniques for doing this were shown in Chapter 6). Look at the CLSID sub-key and write down the number that you find.

Now reload the component project. You can do this by either exiting Visual Basic and restarting it, then reloading the project, or by simply opening the project again using the File, Open command.

Run the component project and try running the test project. You will get the message: "Connection to Type Library or object library for remote process has been lost. Press OK for dialog to remove reference." This is effectively the same error you saw earlier.

Look at the CLSID subkey for the object again. (Be sure to use the Refresh command in the registry editor to reload the registry based on the current settings.) The CLSID is different!

Now, this is serious!

If you remember our earlier discussion of COM you'll remember that a key part of COM is that types of object and interfaces are uniquely identified, not by name, but by their class or interface identifiers. If the class identifier changes, as far as Windows is concerned you have a completely different type of object. No wonder the test program couldn't reference the component— once the class identifier had changed, the old component no longer existed.

When you delete the old "missing" reference and add a new reference, you are, in effect, telling your test program that you are using a completely different component. This new component just happens to work because the names of its classes and properties are the same as the old one, but when Visual Basic saves or compiles the test project, it will now save the identifiers to the new component instead. If you eliminate this component (by reloading the project), your test program will once again fail because the component that it expects no longer exists. You could avoid this problem by creating objects dynamically (using the CreateObject function) and using only late binding. In that case Visual Basic does not store GUID information with the project but also retrieves it each time the object is used. This solution is obviously less than ideal.

Why isn't this a problem with the ActiveX DLL server? Because Visual Basic is smart enough to update the references to components that are running in the same instance of Visual Basic. It knows that you added a reference to a component in the project group and can go ahead and update the test application to the new GUIDs as needed.

Does this mean that there is never a problem with testing DLLs?

Not at all, because the GUIDs for DLL servers are changing in the registry as well. If you were to test the DLL out of process (as described earlier), you would run into exactly the same problem you faced with the EXE server. However, there are worse problems to consider. What happens when you start compiling the DLLs and EXEs? If the GUIDs changed each time, you would never be able to recompile them, because client applications would never be able to find objects between one version and the next.

Clearly there must be some way to tell Visual Basic to keep using the same GUID values between sessions. Well, let's see....

Project Compatibility   Reload your EXE server component, and this time make the executable using the File, Make command. This accomplishes two things. First, the component is now registered in the system registry. The new executable is listed as the server for the component. Second, if you look at the Component tab of the Project-Properties dialog box, you will see that the version compatibility option has been set to project compatibility with the executable.

Run the component project. Update the References dialog box in your test program to reference this component. This is necessary in this particular case because you reloaded the EXE server project, thus creating a new type of object. You will see that there are now two different components with the same name in your References dialog box: one implemented by the executable, the other implemented by your project. (Look at the bottom of the References dialog box where it displays the server name. The executable will have an .EXE extension; the component running in the VB environment will have the .VBP extension.) Be sure you reference the one that is implemented by the component project running within Visual Basic.

Now run the test program. It will work. You will be able to step into the project just as before.

Let's take a closer look at this.

In my implementation of this experiment, the component name was gtpEXETest2.EXEClass2. If this name is registered in the registry as being implemented by the compiled executable, how is it possible for the object to also be implemented by VB so that a test application can debug it?

Once again, VB cheats. When you run a component in an instance of Visual Basic, Visual Basic changes the registry entry for the program ID to refer to a CLSID that is implemented by Visual Basic instead. This CLSID is *not* the same as the one for the compiled executable. That's why you can see two separate entries for the component in the References dialog box. One is for the compiled executable. The other is the temporary one that is created by Visual Basic when the component is running in the design environment. Your test program refers to the temporary CLSID, not the executable one.

So why bother with the executable at all? It is never actually used by the test program, right?

Right. The compiled executable is not used by the test program at all. But it *is* used by Visual Basic to determine the GUID values for the temporary component registration.

When you made the executable for the first time, the executable was assigned a complete set of GUID values for the component type, interfaces, and type libraries. Visual Basic also set the project compatibility option, which tells VB to preserve those GUID values if possible on future builds of the project.

Visual Basic is also smart enough to use those values when running the component in design mode. Of course it can't use the exact values—they would conflict with the compiled program. But VB can modify them slightly, by adding an offset to the GUID values.

The important thing is that Visual Basic can use the same values every time. Try the following: Stop the instance of VB that is running the EXE server and reload the server project. Run the server project. Now run the test program again. The missing reference problem has vanished. Visual Basic uses the information in the executable file to make sure that the server has the same GUID values, even when run within the environment. When you are finished testing the server object, you can change the reference of the test program to the executable.

Visual Basic's ability to preserve GUID information is extremely important. It makes it possible to upgrade components and still have them work with older applications that use them. However, what you have seen so far is just the tip of the iceberg with regards to compatibility issues. These issues will be discussed in much more depth in Chapter 25, "Versioning." The intent at this point is to provide you with enough information to create, test, and debug your applications.

Single Use EXE Servers   Create two projects in much the same way as you created the ActiveX EXE server example earlier. You'll find projects gtpSingle-EXE (the component server) and EXETest2.vbp (the test program) in the Chapter 9 sample directory on your CD-ROM. The test program creates an instance of the server's object every time you click on a command button.

In fact, the only difference between this example and the prior one is that the component's object class has its Instancing property set to Single Use. Now try the following:

- ▶ Run the server.
- ▶ Run the test program.
- ▶ Click the command button to create an object.
- ▶ Click the command button again to create another object.

At this point the test program will fail with the message that the Visual Basic design environment can provide only one instance of a class. The fact that your test application released the first object that it created has no bearing on this issue. Once an instance of Visual Basic creates an instance of a single use object, it cannot create another until it has been stopped and restarted.

This makes single-use EXE servers a bit more difficult to debug. Your best bet in cases like this might be to use the compiled EXE server for most of the objects, using CreateObject on the one object that you wish to test (but you'll probably have to use late binding in this case).

TIPS AND TECHNIQUES

Here are some tips that should prove helpful while creating and testing ActiveX components.

Registry Clutter Visual Basic temporarily registers components when they are run within the VB environment, then unregisters them when you stop execution. If VB terminates abnormally, those components may never be unregistered, thus leading to increasing clutter in your system registry.

Microsoft has developed a program called RegClean that is designed to remove registry entries to objects that no longer exist. You should delete the Visual Basic .TMP files before running RegClean. Now I must caution you: I've heard reports from people claiming that RegClean has messed up their registration database. I have used earlier versions of this program without problems, so I can't attest to that myself. I would strongly recommend under Windows NT that you make an emergency repair disk before running RegClean so you can restore your system registry if worse comes to worst. Look for the NT rdisk.exe program to accomplish this task.

Full Compile Visual Basic supports three compilation modes while working within the VB environment. These modes are set by selecting the Compile on Demand and Background Compile checkboxes in the General tab of the Options dialog box, which is under the Tools menu. The three modes are as follows:

- ▶ Full Compile: This mode is set by clearing the Compile on Demand checkbox. All projects in the environment are compiled each time they are run.

- ▶ Compile on Demand: This mode is set by selecting the Compile on Demand checkbox but leaving the Background Compile checkbox cleared. In this mode, code is compiled as it is needed. For example: if your program doesn't actually create an instance of a class object, the class module may never be compiled.

- ▶ Background Compile: This mode is set by selecting both the Compile on Demand and Background Compile checkboxes. This mode is similar to Compile on Demand, except that it will use any available idle time to start compiling additional modules.

You can use any of these modes when working with objects, but it is very disconcerting to be running a project and suddenly have an object that it is using fail due to a compilation error. (It's bad enough when they fail because of *real* bugs.) Personally, I do almost all of my work in Full Compile mode. That way I can deal with all syntax errors before I begin the real test and debug process.

This approach can be inefficient for very large projects that take a long time to compile. So at the very least you should use full compilation on your EXE server projects. It will save you a lot of extra effort switching between instances and dealing with timeout errors. Use Ctrl+F5 or the menu command Run, Start with full compile.

Who Implements Servers?   Let's say you have a component named MyExe-Server. The component has been compiled to MyExeServer.exe. You are also running the component in an instance of Visual Basic. When you run an application that uses the component, which one will you get?

If your application uses early binding (in other words, you added a reference to the component and defined object variables using the component type), your object will be created by whichever component you referenced. If you chose the compiled program in the References dialog box, your object will be created by that program. If you chose the VB project in the References dialog box, your object will be created by VB and you will be able to debug the component.

If your application uses late binding (in other words, you reference the component As Object and you use the CreateObject function to create the object), you will receive an object created by VB when it is running the component project. Objects created while the project is not running will be provided by the compiled executable. Be careful not to stop VB while using a component that it provides. This will cause an error in your client application.

What if you have a project that references a compiled EXE or DLL server and you want to test the component as a VB project instead?

It depends. If your program is using the component with late binding (it uses the CreateObject function to create objects from the component), you will automatically receive components from a running VB project because Visual Basic modifies the program ID to reference the VB-provided component when it starts running. However, if you have added the component as a reference to your project, you will need to bring up the References dialog box and explicitly set your project to use the components provided by the running VB instance. (Once again, look for the component that is implemented by a VB project using the VBP extension.)

StartMode   When does a Visual Basic application stop running? When its last form is closed.

When does a Visual Basic ActiveX EXE server stop running? When its last object is released and last form closed.

What happens when you try to run an ActiveX server application directly? If it has a Sub Main in a standard module, the subroutine will run. When the subroutine ends, assuming no forms have been loaded in the meanwhile, the application will close. If there are no forms loaded and no Sub Main, the application will load, then end immediately. The only thing it will accomplish is to register itself into the system registration database.

What happens when you try to run an ActiveX server application in the VB design environment? Pretty much the same thing. But you've already seen that it is necessary to place the component into run mode in order for Visual Basic to provide instances of the component to other applications. How do you prevent the server program from ending immediately?

The answer is in the Components tab of the Project dialog box under the Options menu. If you set the Start Mode option to ActiveX Component, Visual Basic keeps the project in run mode until you explicitly stop the project, even though it has no forms open or no objects outstanding. This option only affects the behavior of the component within the VB environment.

By the way, during the Sub Main routine of an ActiveX EXE server you can read the App.StartMode property to see if the program was started due to a client object request (in which case it will have the value vbSModeAutomation) or was launched by the user (in which case it will have the value vbSMode-Standalone). Remember that Sub Main in an ActiveX server launched to provide components is not called until the first object is created.

REFERENCING AND REFERENCE ORDER

What happens when methods or properties in two objects conflict with each other? This can occur when two objects define global method, properties, or enumerated constants.

In these cases, Visual Basic uses whichever one comes first in the reference order. This is demonstrated by the Conflict.vbg group of projects in the Chapter 9 directory on your CD-ROM.

The Conflict and Conflict2 projects both contain a property called My-Global, which is accessible globally (the Instancing property of the class is set to Global MultiUse).

The code in the Conflict project for this property is as follows:

```
Public Property Get MyGlobal() As Variant
    MyGlobal = "Global from Conflict"
End Property
```

And in the Conflict2 project:

```
Public Property Get MyGlobal() As Variant
    MyGlobal = "Global from Conflict2"
End Property
```

The CFLTest project contains the following code to verify which property is accessed:

```
Private Sub cmdMyGlobal_Click()
    MsgBox MyGlobal
End Sub
```

What value will be displayed? It depends on the reference order displayed in the References dialog box. If Conflict appears ahead of Conflict2, the first one will be accessed. You can use the Priority buttons to change the positions of object references in the list. However, you cannot move an added reference ahead of the Visual Basic libraries. This issue is especially important with regard to enumerated constants, which are global in all cases.

ERROR HANDLING

The Microsoft Visual Basic documentation discusses two approaches for handling errors. The API style requires that you return an error status to indicate that a function succeeded or failed. The Basic style uses Visual Basic's built-in error handling (the notorious "on error" statement).

Microsoft also suggests that you remain consistent in your choice. Functions should consistently return error values, or use a ByRef parameter to return an error value, or raise errors that can be handled by the client.

This is a rather frustrating subject to deal with, because no matter which approach I recommend, a large number of readers will declare that I'm wrong. The truth is that there is no clear right or wrong on this issue. So instead of going right into recommendations, let's take a closer look at how ActiveX errors are handled.

The ErrTest program group in the Chapter 9 directory on your CD-ROM contains two projects, ErrTest.vbp and ErrClient.vbp. The ErrTest project contains a DLL server with a single class whose Instancing property is set to Global MultiUse (to save the hassle of creating objects just to test object functions).

This class contains three functions that perform a simple division. The first of these, DivideBy1, uses API-style error checking. Because the function returns a numeric value, the error result must be returned in a separate ByRef parameter, errval. The function is shown below:

```
' This one demonstrates an API like approach
Public Function DivideBy1(numerator As Long, denominator As Long, errval As Long)
As Long
    If denominator = 0 Then
        ' Catch the error situation
        errval = -1
        Exit Function
    End If
    DivideBy1 = numerator / denominator
End Function
```

When using this function, the client must first define a long variable to pass as the errval property, then check the result after the call. You could make errval optional so clients who don't care about the resulting value can avoid passing the extra parameter.

The DivideBy2 function takes the approach of allowing the client to handle the error. It is shown below:

```
' Let the client handle the error
Public Function DivideBy2(numerator As Long, denominator As Long) As Long
    DivideBy2 = numerator / denominator
End Function
```

The DivideBy3 function uses OLE error handling. It uses its own internal error handling to detect the division error (it could also use the DivideBy1 technique of checking the denominator value first). When an error is detected using either technique, it raises the error in the client application. We'll take a closer look at the raise operation shortly.

```
' Basic (exception style) error handling
Public Function DivideBy3(numerator As Long, denominator As Long) As Long
On Error GoTo problem3:
    DivideBy3 = numerator / denominator
    Exit Function
problem3:
    Err.Raise vbObjectError + 1000, "clsErrorMaker", "Error Maker Numeric Error"
End Function
```

Figure 9.3 shows ErrClient program that is used to test this component. The array of option buttons determine which function to call. The buttons perform either a simple division (which does not cause an error), and a division by zero. This code is shown in the listing below.

```
' Guide to the Perplexed: ErrTest - Error testing program
' Copyright (c) 1996 by Desaware Inc. All Rights Reserved
Option Explicit

Dim CurrentOptionIndex As Integer

' Set the current option
Private Sub cmdOp_Click(Index As Integer)
    Dim numerator As Long
    Dim denominator As Long
    Dim errval&
    Dim result&
    Select Case Index
        Case Ø  ' Any legal values to show correct operation
            numerator = 1Ø
            denominator = 5
        Case 1  ' Divide by zero error
            numerator = 1Ø
            denominator = Ø
    End Select

    Select Case CurrentOptionIndex
        Case Ø  ' API style
            result = DivideBy1(numerator, denominator, errval)
            If errval = -1 Then
                MsgBox "Error occurred"
            End If
        Case 1  ' No handling
            result = DivideBy2(numerator, denominator)
        Case 2  ' Basic style
            result = DivideBy3(numerator, denominator)
    End Select
```

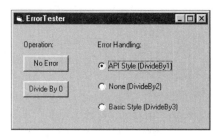

Figure 9.3: The ErrClient application in action

```
End Sub

Private Sub optFunction_Click(Index As Integer)
    CurrentOptionIndex = Index
End Sub
```

In the General tab of the Options dialog box under the Tools menu, you will find an error trapping selection. There are three options. Break on all errors causes VB to break as soon as an error occurs regardless of the setting of the error handlers. Break in class module causes unhandled errors to cause VB to break in the component module. Break on unhandled errors causes VB to break in the client at the line that caused the error.

Let's explore these permutations one at a time.

The DivideBy1 case is the simplest. No Visual Basic error is ever raised. It is up to the client to check for errors.

The DivideBy2 case is somewhat trickier. When the error trapping mode is set to break on all errors or to break in the class module, Visual Basic will break in the clsErrorMaker class where the division occurs. Otherwise it will break in the ErrClient application on the line that called the DivideBy2 method. This is because a client automatically handles errors generated by a component, so the error within the component is considered to be handled by the client.

The DivideBy3 case includes error handling, which in turn raises an error to the application. When the error trapping mode is set to break on all errors, Visual Basic will again break on the line in the clsErrorMaker class where the division occurs. When the error trapping mode is set to break in the class module, the error is triggered on the line: Err.Raise vbObjectError + 1000, "clsErrorMaker," "Error Maker Numeric Error." Why is this? The line with the division is not considered an error in the class module because it was handled by the class module. But the Err.Raise command triggers an error that is not handled in the class module and will be passed upward to the client. This is the first real error in the class module and will thus cause a break in this trapping mode. When the error trapping mode is set to break on unhandled errors, VB will break on the line in the ErrClient application that called the DivideBy3 method.

OLE ERROR HANDLING AND "BASIC" ERROR HANDLING?

Way back in Chapter 4 when we looked at some of the fundamental technologies of OLE, one of the important items on the list was

A standard error reporting mechanism and set of error codes and values.

Why is this necessary? Because COM objects can be created by many different languages. Without a standard error reporting mechanism, there would be no way for clients to handle component errors without having specialized knowledge of each component. And the whole idea of COM was to allow clients to work with generic objects without such specialized information.

The exact method OLE uses to raise errors is not important. What is important is that every OLE error value be a 32-bit value. The value is broken up as shown in Table 9.1.

Table 9.1: Breakdown of an OLE Error Value

Bit Values (31 Is High, 0 Is Low)	Meaning
31	1 = Failure, 0 = Success
27-30	Reserved or used internally by OLE
16-26	Facility: Indicates the subsystem that generated the error. For example: Windows is 8. ActiveX automation is 2.
0-15	The actual error number

Many errors are assigned standard numbers. For example: Let's say you attempted to execute a method on a dispatch interface that did not exist. You would probably get error code &H80020003. This is comprised of the following values combined:

▶ &H80000000—Bit 31 is set, indicating an error.

▶ &H00020000—Bits 16-26 are 2, indicating that an automation error occurred.

▶ &H00000003—Bits 0-15 are 3, indicating the "member not found" error.

You can define your own errors. In fact, the clsErrorMaker object does this by returning the value vbObjectError + 1000.

What is vbObjectError? It's the value &H80040000. This is comprised of the following values combined:

▶ &H80000000—Bit 31 is set indicating an error.

▶ &H00040000—Bits 16-26 are 4, indicating that the error is interface specific (each interface defines its own errors).

What error numbers can you use? You share vbObjectError with VB itself, so you should not use any values below 512. You can't use values over 65536 because they would overflow into the facility field. That's why all errors that you raise should be in the range vbObjectError+512 to vbObjectError + 65536.

Now here's a question: Instead of raising errors in this range, could you use API techniques to simply return a result in this range to indicate an error?

Of course you can. In fact, if you were to call OLE DLL functions directly (which is possible), you would find that many of them return an HRESULT value that is exactly that: an OLE error value.

Raising an event using the Err.Raise method provides an effective way to trigger errors in clients that use your component. You should provide a source name and description as well. I like to use the name of the object as the source name.

EXE SERVER COMPONENTS

EXE server components deserve extra attention because they can trigger a unique set of errors that are associated with the fact that they run in a separate process space. The EXEErr.vbp project is a simple server that demonstrates some operations that you should never intentionally place in a server. They are shown in the listing below.

```
' GTP EXEErr - EXE error server
' Copyright (c) 1997 by Desaware Inc.
' All Rights Reserved

Option Explicit

' Don't ever do this!
Public Sub KillThisComponent()
    End
End Sub

' Don't do this either
Public Sub NeverReturns()
    Do
    Loop While True
End Sub

' Loads a form that after a few seconds will
' end the program
Public Sub LoadBadForm()
    Load BadForm
End Sub

' Function to call that does nothing
Public Sub SafeFunction()
End Sub
```

The KillThisComponent method terminates the server during the method call. It should go without saying that you should never, ever do this. But it does provide an excellent simulation of what happens when a memory exception or illegal operation (previously known as General Protection Fault) occurs in a component. Not that an exception would ever occur in one of your components, but...

The NeverReturns method simulates a component that hangs, whether through an infinite loop bug or other long operation. This type of problem has been known to happen.

The LoadBadForm method loads an invisible form that contains a timer control set with a 2-second timeout. When the timeout expires, the End statement is executed, terminating the server. When running the server in the VB environment, this can be used to demonstrate what happens when you attempt to access an object that cannot be created.

The SafeFunction method provides one safe function to call for testing.

The ErrTest2.vbp project shown in the listing below shows the code for some tests that you can perform on the server to illustrate and handle some of these errors. The form for this project contains five command buttons that simply call the Click functions shown in the listing.

```
' gtp - Tests gtpEXEError
' Copyright (c) 1997 by Desaware Inc. All Rights Reserved
Option Explicit


Private Sub cmdBadError2_Click()
    Dim obj As New BadClass
On Error GoTo BadError2
    obj.KillThisComponent
    Exit Sub
BadError2:
    MsgBox "The error was caught"
End Sub


Private Sub cmdBadError_Click()
    Dim obj As New BadClass
    obj.KillThisComponent
End Sub


Private Sub cmdEnd_Click()
    Dim obj As New BadClass
    obj.LoadBadForm
End Sub
```

```
Private Sub cmdNever_Click()
    Dim obj As New BadClass
    obj.NeverReturns
End Sub


Private Sub cmdSafe_Click()
    Dim obj As New BadClass
On Error GoTo safeerror
    obj.SafeFunction
    Exit Sub
safeerror:
    MsgBox "Couldn't call the safe method"
End Sub
```

The cmdBadError_Click and cmdBadError2_Click functions demonstrate what happens when a server operation fails. Fortunately, this is not a common occurrence. Should you take care to have error handling enabled in every place where you use an EXE server? It depends on your application. In many cases you might be just fine with having your application terminate in this rather unusual case. However, you should be aware that any error handling you do have enabled will also be triggered by this type of error; take that into account in your error-handling routine.

The cmdNever_Click routine starts the server into an infinite loop. The trick for testing this situation is to run a second instance of the ErrTest2 application and click on the cmdSafe_Click button (a safe operation). Because this EXE server runs in a single thread, the infinite loop started by the first ErrTest2 program prevents the second instance from accessing the server, causing a "server busy" error.

The cmdEnd_Click method causes the server to terminate after a couple of seconds. Try selecting this command and then the cmdSafe_Click operation. This shows what happens when the server cannot provide an object of the specified type.

RECOMMENDATIONS AND TRADE-OFFS

The following are some recommendations I hope you will find helpful.

The most important form of error handling is to prevent errors through good design. Responding to errors caused by invalid client operations or parameters is one thing, but you don't really want to be raising errors due to bugs in your code.

If your component uses other components that may raise errors, you should use error handling in your component, then raise your own errors to the client. People using your component will generally want to deal with the methods and properties you define. The last thing they want to do is deal with a myriad of unhandled errors triggered by subcomponents. You should document the errors your component can raise.

Rather than raising errors in each function that can trigger an error, consider using a centralized error-handling function for the object. This eliminates the need to specify the source each time. It also allows you to centralize description strings to make localization easier. (I often put all description strings into a single standard module.)

Use error numbers that are equal to, or a fixed offset from, the context identifiers used in your help file. For example: if your errors have context identifier numbers 1000–2000, you could use error numbers 600–1600 and just add 400 to calculate one from the other. This makes it easy to include the context ID in the Err.Raise statement.

The API style error handling has the advantage of often being easier to both read and debug. Unlike the Basic style, there are no sudden jumps in the flow of the program to keep track of (one of the reasons that the Goto statement is so hated by programmers). I personally prefer it for most situations, especially within my own applications and when creating ActiveX components. I tend to use Basic style errors more often with ActiveX controls because VB programmers are accustomed to controls raising errors when they occur. Hopefully Visual Basic will one day evolve to support true structured exception handling, a more block-structured form of raising errors that does not have the radical changes in program flow that the On Error Goto statement causes.

When in doubt, you can always support both the API and Basic style error reporting. Just implement a property that lets your object's user choose between the two. Then raise errors only if they have enabled Basic style error reporting.

Now that you know how components work within your system, it's time to look inside at the Visual Basic class module, for it and its close relatives the form, ActiveX control, and ActiveX document modules, form the foundation of every Visual Basic object.

Code and Classes—Beyond the Manuals

METHODS AND PROPERTIES

PROCEDURE ATTRIBUTES

OBJECT PROCEDURES: PUBLIC, PRIVATE, AND FRIEND

SELECTED TOPICS

Chapter 10

Y ou know about functions and subs. You've seen property procedures and methods. You're familiar with the techniques of building classes. You've taken the course or read the manual. In other words, you're not a beginner anymore.

I won't trouble you with the material any novice already knows, at least not with more than a quick introduction here and there. Instead, here you'll find commentary, illustration, and even an opinion or two. Consider this chapter an exploration of selected topics related to coding and constructing classes.

METHODS AND PROPERTIES

Let's start out by exploring some topics related to class methods and properties, or is that functions and subs?

Sample code for this section can be found in the Misc1.vbp sample in the Chapter 10 sample directory on your CD-ROM.

GET, SET, LET—GO!

A class module interface is made up of functions, subs, and properties.

But wait a minute. A function and a sub are really the same thing except for the fact that one returns a value and the other doesn't—not a great difference. In fact, both are commonly referred to by the term *method*.

And you already know from earlier in the book that a property is internally implemented by two methods, one to set the property and one to retrieve the property value.

So, really, when you come right down to it, functions, subs, methods, and properties are really all the same thing. They only differ in the language syntax used to call them and to implement them.

This is perhaps why it can be so tricky to figure out whether to implement a particular operation as a method or property. They are so similar. Even the syntax to define them is similar:

```
Public Sub mysubroutine(Parameter list)
Public Function myfunction (Parameter list) As ReturnType
Public Property Get T(Parameter list) As Variant
Public Property Set T(Parameter list, ByVal vNewValue As Variant)
Public Property Let T(Parameter list, ByVal vNewValue As Variant)
```

You may be wondering: what is a parameter list doing in property procedures? Visual Basic does support parameterized properties, though you don't see them very often. We'll get to that in a moment, but first…

MORE ON PROPERTIES

A property can be implemented in two ways: by simply declaring a public variable in a form or by implementing separate property procedures. The Get property procedure returns the value of the property. The Let property procedure is used to assign a value to the property. The Set property procedure is used to set an object reference to the property.

In most cases you will want to use property procedures. This is because property procedures allow you to add data validation, error checking, and other functionality to the process of accessing a property. Even if you are sure that you will never need this additional functionality, it's a good idea to use property procedures just in case you change your mind in the future. Keep in mind that Visual Basic implements a property internally with property procedures, even if you declare it as a public variable.

You can make a property read-only by not writing a Property Set or Property Let method for the property. You can make it write-only by leaving out the Property Get method.

IS IT A PROPERTY OR IS IT A METHOD?

The Microsoft documentation presents four arguments to help you decide whether to implement an interface item as a method or a property. In brief they are the following.

The Data versus Action Argument Properties should be used to access data in an object, methods to perform an operation. For example: The Color or

Caption attributes of an object are properties—they relate directly to the object data. The Move or Show operations are methods—they do something.

The Syntax Argument   The syntax of assigning the results of a function is identical. Take these two implementations for a method/property called Error-Result.

```
Public Function ErrorResult() As Long
      ErrorResult = 5
End Function


Property Get ErrorResult() As Long
      ErrorResult = 5
End Function
```

Both can be assigned as follows:

```
Myresult = AnObject.ErrorResult
```

However, the reverse direction is not true. You can add a Property Let function for ErrorResult such as this:

```
Property Let ErrorResult(vNewValue As Long)
     ' some internal operation that is appropriate for this property
End Function
```

And now perform the assignment:

```
AnObject.ErrorResult = somenumber
```

You can't do this with a method. You would instead have to come up with a separate method, perhaps one called SetErrorResult, which accepted the "somenumber" value as a parameter.

The Property Window Argument   This one is directly applicable to ActiveX controls but can serve a useful tool for deciding between methods and properties on other components as well. Would you want this property to appear in the property sheet for the control? If so, it is definitely a property. If not—well, there are still many cases where you would want it to be a property. This argument can help resolve the issue for some properties, but is useless for others.

The Sensible Error Argument   Trying to assign a value to a read-only property produces the error: "Can't assign to read-only property."

Trying to assign a value to a function (assuming the function does not return a variant or object that can be a target for assignment) produces the error "Function call on left-hand side of assignment must return Variant or Object." Choosing between the two based on an error statement sounds almost like an act of desperation, but not as desperate as the next argument.

The Argument of Last Resort   Flip a coin.

The truth is, all of these arguments are good. There are many cases where it is extremely difficult to decide whether something should be a property or a method. Allow me, however, to add a few additional "rules" that might help.

The VBX Consistency Argument   The old VBX technology did not allow custom control designers to define their own methods. As a result, we were forced to sometimes use properties in creative ways. You can see this with the common dialog control that has an Action property. Assigning a value to this property brings up the requested common dialog box.

Based on the Data vs. Action argument, Action should clearly be a method. Better yet, there should be separate methods to bring up the different common dialog boxes.

Yet if you were rewriting this control using Visual Basic 5.0, I would recommend strongly that you keep the Action property simply because people are already familiar with it and preserving it would minimize the changes required to use this control in existing projects. Of course, you could also implement a new set of methods in addition to this property for use in new projects.

The Parameter List Argument   You saw earlier that properties do, in fact, support multiple parameters in addition to simple assignments. Except for very rare situations where an array effect is desired, if you find yourself wanting to use parameters, you should implement a method rather than a property.

Speaking of parameterized properties…

PARAMETERIZED PROPERTIES

Let's say, for example, that you want your object to expose a property as an array. You might want to declare it as follows:

```
Public T(8) As Variant
```

But if you do so, Visual Basic will report that it does not support public arrays. Fortunately, you can easily implement this functionality using a parameterized array as follows:

```
Private m_t(8) As Variant

Public Property Get T(idx As Integer) As Variant
   T = m_t(idx)
End Property

Public Property Let T(idx As Integer, ByVal vNewValue As Variant)
   m_t(idx) = vNewValue
End Property
```

The following code can be used to verify this property:

```
Dim tx As New clsMisc1
tx.T(1) = 5
tx.T(2) = 6
Debug.Print tx.T(1)
Debug.Print tx.T(2)
```

It will print 5 and 6 in the Immediate window.

You could implement a two-dimensional array by including two index parameters and so on. This will work as long as the parameter lists for the Get and Let properties are identical. By the way, in a real application you might want to add some error checking to test for a valid idx parameter.

Now that you know about parameterized properties, try to forget about them. In most cases where parameters are required you should use a function or sub. More on this later.

PROPERTIES THAT ARE OBJECTS

Earlier in this book you saw that the Set operation differs from a normal assignment because it performs an object reference rather than a simple variable assignment. This applies to properties that are objects as well.

The Misc1.vbp project includes class clsMisc2 that contains the following property:

```
Public Property Get ClassName() As String
    ClassName = "clsMisc2"
End Property
```

This is the default property for the class, so if you have object obj of type clsMisc2 and perform the operation

```
Debug.print obj
```

the word clsMisc2 will be printed to the Immediate window. An Object property in clsMisc1 that holds a clsMisc2 object can be defined as follows:

```
Private m_Object As clsMisc2

' Example of object property
Public Property Get O1() As clsMisc2
    Set O1 = m_Object
End Property

Public Property Set O1(ByVal vNewValue As clsMisc2)
    Set m_Object = vNewValue
End Property
```

The following code can be used to verify this property:

```
Dim tx As New clsMisc1
Dim tobj As New clsMisc2
Set tx.O1 = tobj
Debug.Print tx.O1
```

This will print clsMisc2 to the Immediate window. Note that the tx.O1 property must be assigned using the Set operator.

OVERLOADED PROPERTIES AND FUNCTIONS

You are probably aware of variants, that super-duper amazing magical variable type that can hold just about any type of data. I'll have more to say about variants in a moment, but I thought that before I tell you how terrible they are, I should show you something good you can do with them.

There is a concept often used in C++ and other object-oriented languages that is rarely discussed in the context of Visual Basic. It's the ability of an object to have several different functions with the same name that are distinguished by the type of data.

For example: An object might have two Print functions, one that takes a string and the other that takes a bitmap object as a parameter. If your code calls Print("mystring"), the string printing function will be called and the string will be printed. If it calls Print(BitmapObjectHandle), the other function will be called and it will print a bitmap instead.

A C++ programmer actually implements two separate functions. The compiler determines at compile time which Print function to call depending on the type of parameter passed to the function.

Visual Basic does not support this functionality at design time, but it can handle a slightly limited form of overloading at runtime through the use of variants. Since a variant can hold almost any type of data and you can tell at runtime what type of data is contained in a variant, it is relatively easy to execute code based on the type of parameter.

But what if you decide to create a variant property that may contain either an object or another data type, such as the code below. Would this code work? No.

```
Public Property Get V1() As Variant
    V1 = m_Variant
End Property

Public Property Let V1(ByVal vNewValue As Variant)
    m_Variant = vNewValue
End Property
```

Why not? Because while it will work fine for most variant types, it will fail with object types that require an assignment using the Set command. Instead, you need to base the operation on the type of variant. If the variant parameter contains an object, you need to use the Set command. The following code works:

```
' Example of variant property
Public Property Get V1() As Variant
    If VarType(m_Variant) = vbObject Then
        Set V1 = m_Variant
    Else
        V1 = m_Variant
    End If
End Property

Public Property Let V1(ByVal vNewValue As Variant)
    If VarType(vNewValue) = vbObject Then
        Set m_Variant = vNewValue
    Else
        m_Variant = vNewValue
    End If
End Property
```

You can test this property using the following code:

```
Dim tv As New clsMisc1
Dim obj As New clsMisc2
tv.V1 = 5
Debug.Print tv.V1
tv.V1 = obj
Debug.Print tv.V1
```

This will print 5 and clsMisc2 into the Immediate window.

The principle shown here for handling object and other data types differently can be extended to any variant data types. For example: the Remove method of a collection can take a string or a number as a parameter. If it's a string, the parameter is interpreted as a key. If it is an integer, the parameter is interpreted as an index in the collection. While I obviously haven't seen Microsoft's source code for the collection object, I'll lay odds they use exactly this technique.

By the way, if you did try implementing a variant property in the first way shown here (without the overloading), this particular example would still seem to work correctly (go ahead and try it). But it really isn't doing what you might expect. What happens in this function when you actually try to assign the v1 property with the obj object?

```
Public Property Let V1(ByVal vNewValue As Variant)
   m_Variant = vNewValue
End Property
```

During the m_Variant = vNewValue assignment, the object is *not* assigned to the m_Variant variable. Instead, the default property of the object is accessed (in this case, the ClassName property) and the m_Variant variable is loaded with a string containing the current value of that property. To verify this, try changing the test code to access a property on the object instead of relying on the default property. This kind of side effect is one of the reasons I tend to discourage use of default properties.

A SLIGHTLY QUIRKY WAY OF OVERLOADING PROPERTIES

The clsMisc1 contains a second property, V2, which demonstrates yet another way to overload a property. But in this case the technique only applies to distinguishing between variable assignment and object assignment. The approach begins with the question: What happens if a Class property has both a Property Let and a Property Set method?

```
Public Property Get V2() As Variant

End Property


Public Property Let V2(ByVal vNewValue As Variant)
   MsgBox "I'm in Let V2"
End Property


Public Property Set V2(ByVal vNewValue As Variant)
   MsgBox "I'm in Set V2"
End Property
```

Try the following test code:

```
Dim tv As New clsMisc1
Dim obj As New clsMisc2
tv.V2 = 5
tv.V2 = obj
Set tv.V2 = obj
```

The first two assignments are identical to the prior case. In both situations, the value (5 or obj) is converted into a variant and passed to the Property Let procedure. In the third assignment, obj is still converted into a variant, but it is passed to the Property Set procedure instead.

One can't help but wonder if there isn't a way to avoid the variant conversion. It turns out there is:

```
Public Property Set V2(vNewValue As Object)
    MsgBox "I'm in Set V2"
End Property
```

This is definitely more efficient than the variant approach. In fact, vNewValue can be defined to any object type as well (such as clsMisc2 in this case) and still work fine.

But doesn't this violate the rule that the type of data returned from a property must match the type while setting the property? It turns out that the Property Set function makes its own rules. The parameter to a Property Set function can be any object type regardless of the type of the property (the type returned by the Property Let). This makes the following property possible:

```
Public Property Get T() As Integer
End Property

Public Property Let T(ByVal vNewValue As Integer)
End Property

Public Property Set T(x As Object)
End Property
```

Yes, you are reading this correctly. T is an integer property that can also be set to an object! Given an object containing this property, named myobj, the following are both valid:

```
obj.T = 5
Set obj.T = obj   ' or any other object
```

Now that you know this is possible, don't do it. It serves no practical purpose (that I can see) and creates code guaranteed to confuse anyone else working with the code.

Another thing you might notice in these test programs is that assigning an object to a variant property does not require an explicit Set operation. This is because Visual Basic is smart enough to convert the object into a variant when passing it as a parameter. Of course, sometimes Visual Basic can be too smart for its own good.

EVIL TYPE COERCION

What do you think will print with this code?

```
Dim s$
s$ = "1"
s$ = s$ + 5
Debug.Print s$
Debug.Print s$ + 8
Debug.Print s$ + "8"
```

15, 158, 158 perhaps?

If you run this under Visual Basic 3.0 you'll get an error message indicating a type mismatch. That's right—VB3 will not let you add a string and a number. It says this operation doesn't make sense. You would first have to explicitly convert the number to a string, for example: s$ = s$ + str$(5).

In Visual Basic 4.0 and 5.0 this will print: 6, 14, 68. In other words, Visual Basic will attempt to coerce variables to different types if necessary to make an operation work.

Now there is a bit of a philosophical difference here. Personally, I was taught in school that strong type checking is a good thing. It's just barely possible that statement s$ = s$ + 5 is exactly what I want, but it is far more likely that this represents a bug in my code. True, Microsoft would suggest that I use the concatenation operator & to append strings, but that's just ducking the issue; it just makes it more likely that the above is a bug in my code. Visual Basic will happily convert other data types as well.

As a professional programmer, I want the compiler to detect as many bugs as possible. Take a look at the following code:

```
Dim I As Integer
I = 55.5
Debug.Print I
```

This will print 56. From one perspective (Microsoft's), this is a good thing. Obviously the programmer who is assigning a floating point variable to an integer knows what he or she is doing and will be glad that the language automatically performs the necessary conversion.

Personally, if I want to assign a floating point value to an integer variable, I don't mind performing an explicit conversion by calling a conversion function such as CInt. If you saw this code in one of my applications, chances are very good that it represents a programming error on my part. Perhaps I intended it to be a floating point variable? If the compiler caught this as a type mismatch, I would have the opportunity to catch the problem and either perform my own conversion or fix the problem. As things stand, I risk having the bug remain uncaught until someone notices that I've lost some precision in my calculations, possibly long after the program ships.

This is a fundamental difference in philosophy. I've often heard the current situation called Evil Type Coercion. (If you know who coined this name, I'd love to hear about it.) Quite a few programmers along with myself have been pleading with Microsoft not to eliminate the current way of doing things but to add an option to the environment that enables a stricter form of type checking (much as they added the Option Explicit functionality after Visual Basic 1.0).

If you agree with this point of view, I would like to invite you at this point to contact Microsoft directly and send them the following message (or better yet, your own message): "I support adding a strict data type checking option to future versions of Visual Basic." Feel free to refer to this book in your message. Send the message via e-mail to vbwish@microsoft.com, or via their Web site at http://www.microsoft.com/vbasic/vbinfo/vbfeed.htm.

Naturally, if you disagree with this point of view, I would encourage you to keep it to yourself.

Aside: I suppose some readers might feel this type of commentary is out of line. How dare I air a criticism about VB in such a public way in a book that, if anything, is supposed to be telling you how great Visual Basic is? How dare I proclaim what is so obviously a personal opinion in a serious technical book, which by its very nature should be objective? If you feel this way, then I am sorry, but not sympathetic. I warned you during the introduction that this book would take the form of a commentary to the documentation, not a replacement. This is a technical book, and it's a serious one (more or less), but I never promised objectivity, except, perhaps, when it comes to the facts.

OPTION EXPLICIT

On the same theme: the very first thing you should do after installing Visual Basic is bring up the Options dialog box through the Tools menu, look at the Editor tab code settings, and make sure that Require Variable Declaration is checked. This ensures that if you mistype a variable name the compiler will at least warn you about it instead of automatically creating a new variable under the incorrect name.

MORE ABOUT VARIANTS

You've just seen that variants can be useful for overloading functions and properties. They can also be useful when you need to hold a variable but are not certain at design time what the variable type will be or when a list of variables may need to contain different types of data. It's possible there are a few other situations where variants are useful.

Now here's the most important thing to know about variants. Except for those specific cases where you clearly must use a variant to accomplish a task that cannot be performed otherwise, you should *never use them*. Why?

- They are slow.

- They are slow and inefficient.

- They are slow and waste memory.

- They lead to extra data conversions, many of which are out of your control and slow down your application.

- They impose additional testing requirements when used as function parameters (the function must be able to handle any type as well as any value).

The Visual Basic documentation and environment does not really stress this enough, especially considering that:

- If you dimension a variable or parameter without specifying a type, Visual Basic defaults to using variants.

- If you forget to specify a return type for a function, Visual Basic defaults to using variants.

- When you use the Tools, Add Procedure command to add a new property procedure, VB defaults to a variant property.

So fight back for code efficiency! Remember to specify types for all of your variables and function parameters. Change properties to the actual type you need. At the very least, add a Def… command at the start of each module to change the default variable type from variant.

This is especially true now that Visual Basic supports native code compilation, since native code can handle some data types (like integers and longs) extremely efficiently.

The VarTest.vbp project in the Chapter 10 directory demonstrates a simple comparison between variant and native data type performance. It measures the time it takes to repeatedly execute the following two subroutines:

```
Public Sub LongTest()
   Dim l As Long
   Dim ctr As Long
   l = 100
   For ctr = 1 To 1000
      l = l + 1
   Next ctr
End Sub
```

```
Public Sub VariantTest()
   Dim v As Variant
   Dim ctr As Variant
   v = 100
   For ctr = 1 To 1000
      v = v + 1
   Next ctr
End Sub
```

Is this a fair test? Of course not. Who knows what data type the Variant test is using in its loop. It could well be a floating point type.

The results are telling. On my tests I found that within the Visual Basic environment, the VariantTest function was 2.2 times slower than the LongTest function. In a compile P-code executable, the factor rose to 2.7 times. And when compiled to native code, the VariantTest function took 45 times as long as the LongTest function.

This is not surprising. The variant functions are part of OLE and the Variant-Test subroutine probably uses the Visual Basic runtime as well. Even when compiled to native code, those functions must be called, so there is little difference between native code and P-code in the functions' performance. (This is additional evidence for the suggestion made in the last chapter that in many cases native code compilation will buy you little if any benefit.) On the other hand, the LongTest function is precisely the kind of computationally intensive operation that native code compilation is best at. This is not an obscure example— loops are one of the most common constructs in any programmer's toolkit.

The conclusions:

▶ If you have counter loops in your application, always use long or integer variables if possible.

▶ If you have many of these loops or they are relatively long, your application may gain more than most from native code compilation. There is certainly no harm in trying.

▶ Unless you have an overriding clear need to use variants, don't.

OPTIONAL PARAMETERS AND PARAMETER ARRAYS

It's worthwhile to take a brief look at two other features supported by Visual Basic with regard to function parameters: optional parameters and parameter arrays. These features are demonstrated in the Misc2.vbg project group that consists of two projects: Misc2.vbp and Misc2tst.vbp.

You can make function parameters optional by preceding them with the keyword "optional." One or more optional parameters may be included in a function's parameter list. However, no non-optional parameter may follow an optional parameter. In other words, all optional parameters must appear at the end of the list.

Optional parameters may be of any data type. However, there is a difference between the way Visual Basic handles Variant data types and other data types. When an optional parameter has the variant data type, the IsMissing function can be used to determine whether the parameter was passed as a parameter. This is demonstrated in the Optional1 sample, where the clsMisc2 function Optional1 appears as follows:

```
Public Function Optional1(Optional vr As Variant) As Variant
    If IsMissing(vr) Then
        Debug.Print "Variable vr is missing"
    Else
        Debug.Print "Variable vr is present"
    End If
End Function
```

It is tested using the cmdOptional1_Click command in the Misc2tst main form code:

```
Private Sub cmdOptional1_Click()
    Dim obj As New clsMisc2B
    Debug.Print "Calling with no parameter"
    obj.Optional1
    Debug.Print "Calling with parameter"
    obj.Optional1 "Hello"
End Sub
```

The situation changes when a different data type is used, as shown in the Optional2 and cmdOptional2_Click code shown here:

```
Public Function Optional2(Optional vr As String) As Variant
    If IsMissing(vr) Then
        Debug.Print "Variable vr is missing"
    Else
        Debug.Print "Variable vr is: " & vr
    End If
End Function

' IsMissing doesn't work with non-variant types
Private Sub cmdOptional2_Click()
    Dim obj As New clsMisc2B
    Debug.Print "Calling with no parameter"
```

```
    obj.Optional2
    Debug.Print "Calling with parameter"
    obj.Optional2 "Hello"
End Sub
```

In this case you will never get the "Calling with no parameter" message in the Immediate window. The optional parameter is instead initialized with the default value for the parameter type in question (for example: number 0 or an empty string).

Visual Basic 5.0 also introduced default parameter values as illustrated in the Optional3 and cmdOptional3_Click function shown here:

```
' With default values
Public Function Optional3(Optional vr As String = "A Default Value") As Variant
    If IsMissing(vr) Then
        Debug.Print "Variable vr is missing"
    Else
        Debug.Print "Variable vr is: " & vr
    End If
End Function


' Demonstration of default parameter values
Private Sub cmdOptional3_Click()
    Dim obj As New clsMisc2B
    Debug.Print "Calling with no parameter"
    obj.Optional3
    Debug.Print "Calling with parameter"
    obj.Optional3 "Hello"
End Sub
```

In this case, if you do not pass the string parameter to the function, the string will be initialized with the default value specified in the function declaration.

You may find it tempting to make extensive use of optional parameters. I discourage you from doing so. Optional parameters are most useful when you have a function that is typically called with certain parameters and only rarely with the optional parameters. Large numbers of optional parameters tend to make code harder to understand and support. You've already seen that variant parameters are best avoided if possible.

One place where you sometimes see large numbers of optional parameters is with public methods from applications such as Microsoft Word that expose the functionality of a complex dialog box. Each parameter corresponds to a field or control in the dialog box. In most cases a better approach would be to expose a new object that corresponds to the dialog box and expose properties that correspond to the dialog box fields. You can then have a few methods to actually invoke the dialog box functionality.

Visual Basic also supports parameter arrays, in which you may pass any number of parameters of any type to a function (ParamArray arguments must be variants). This is demonstrated in the ParamArrayDemo class method and cmdparamArray_Click function shown here:

```
Public Function ParamArrayDemo(ParamArray vr())
    Debug.Print "Parameters range from: " & LBound(vr) & " to " & UBound(vr)
End Function

' Demonstration of paramarray
Private Sub cmdparamArray_Click()
    Dim obj As New clsMisc2B
    obj.ParamArrayDemo "Hello", 1, 2.5
End Sub
```

If optional parameters impair the readability of a function, parameter arrays are surely worse. At the very least, you should try to make sure that parameters are related. For example: if you are going to perform a database sort operation, you might allow the programmer to specify a list of zero or more keys as a parameter list.

PARAMETERS THAT HANDLE LARGE BLOCKS OF DATA: ARRAYS AND USER-DEFINED TYPES

On occasion you may find yourself in a situation where you need fast access to large blocks of data that are encapsulated by an object. After all, the whole idea of an object is that it encapsulates data behind a clearly defined interface. The only way to access the object's internal data is through the methods and properties of the interface.

But what if the object contains a lot of data? Perhaps a large image or multimedia file? What if it has hundreds of different properties rather than a few dozen?

The simple case of an image or multimedia file that can be represented by an array of a standard data type (such as a Byte array) is relatively easy. You could expose a byte parameter that accepts an index value (parameterized array) and copy the data one byte at a time, but the overhead in calling the method for each byte is significant—disastrous if the object exists in another process space (as with an ActiveX EXE server). Fortunately, Visual Basic allows you to use arrays as function parameters and to transfer them to and from properties (the array can be held by a variant).

The Chapter 10 misc2.vbg group described earlier contains the following method in its clsMisc2 class:

```
Public Function ArrayParam(param() As Byte)
    Debug.Print "Param() range is: " & LBound(param) & " to " & UBound(param)
End Function
```

The method is called using the following test code in the frmMisc2 form in the misc2tst.vbp project:

```
' Demonstration of array parameter
Private Sub cmdArray_Click()
    Dim obj As New clsMisc2B
    Dim x(5) As Byte
    obj.ArrayParam x()
End Sub
```

As you will see, the method correctly detects the lower and upper bound of the array, proving that it is passed correctly.

But what happens when the object's data is more complex? For example, let's say the object represents a piece of test equipment that has 250 settings that are all contained internally in a single user-defined structure that can be read by the equipment's driver. Or instead of an array of bytes, the object's data is contained in an array of user-defined structures? In these cases the need to access hundreds of properties or items may severely impact performance, especially if the object is in a different process. And Visual Basic does not allow you to use user-defined types as method parameters or properties in a public object.

Before rushing to use the technique I'm about to show you (which is somewhat advanced), be sure you consider the following possibilities:

▸ Is it possible to break up the object into multiple objects? Could you replace the array of user-defined structures with an array of objects (which can be passed both in an array and as part of a collection)?

▸ Do you really need to access the data? Perhaps the object itself can perform the desired operation. One classic example of this is loading or saving the data to a disk file, which is best implemented in the object's own code.

▸ Does access to the data have to be public? If you can remain with the context of a project, you can use a Friend function, which is able to handle user-defined types as parameters to properties and methods.

▸ Do you really need block access? In-process property calls are, after all, very fast.

In other words, the need to expose large blocks of data may be an indication of poor design.

But there are cases where accessing block data is critical. It can significantly improve the speed of copying an object. It may be necessary when a high performance driver requires fast access to an object using block data in a particular format. It can be useful when working with the larger Windows API data structures.

One approach is truly a hack. It involves obtaining the address of the data within the object and returning it as a long variable. You can obtain the address of a variable using the agGetAddressForObject function included in the apigid32.dll library included with this book. There are also other third-party tools that can do this. Once you have the address, you can copy the data to or from another variable (user-defined structure, array, or any other data type that corresponds to the data format within the object itself) using a memory copy function such as agCopyData, which is also included in apigid32.dll.

The one catch with this technique is that, with one exception, it only works when the object is in process. The exception is if you use a cross-process memory copy routine that supports cross-process memory allocation. Examples of these routines include ReadProcessMemory, WriteProcessMemory, and the cross process memory functions included in Desaware's SpyWorks package.

A more reliable approach is shown in the misc2 project. This example shows the assignment of block data to and from a property that has the variant data type. This mimics the way a user-defined type property might work. Both the DLL server and the test program have the following definitions:

```
Private Declare Sub agCopyData Lib "apigid32.dll" (source As Any, dest As Any,
ByVal count As Long)

Private Type usertype
    x(20) As Byte
    y As Integer
End Type
```

The agCopyData function copies data from any source to any destination. You should call this function with great caution, because if you make any mistake (such as adding or forgetting a ByVal call as appropriate), you can cause a memory exception that will crash your program (and possibly the system if you are using Windows 95 instead of NT).

The object has a single internal variable defined to hold the data for this property:

```
Private m_UserType As usertype
```

The property Let and Set functions are shown here:

```
' This process converts a user defined type into an array
' and returns the array
Public Property Get UserTypeEquiv() As Variant
   Dim TempArray() As Byte
   ReDim TempArray(Len(m_UserType))
   m_UserType.y = 77 ' New value for demo purposes
   agCopyData m_UserType, TempArray(0), Len(m_UserType)
   UserTypeEquiv = TempArray()
End Property


' This process receives an array, and
' converts it into the user type
Public Property Let UserTypeEquiv(ByVal vNewValue As Variant)
   Dim TempArray() As Byte
   If VarType(vNewValue) <> vbArray + vbByte Then
      MsgBox "Invalid data type"
      Exit Property
   End If
   TempArray() = vNewValue 'Must do this - see text
   agCopyData TempArray(0), m_UserType, Len(m_UserType)
   Debug.Print "UserTypeEquiv set: Y = " & m_UserType.y
End Property
```

The trick on the Get side is to copy the private user-defined structure into a byte array and return that array as the property value. This is possible because variants can hold arrays. On the Let side, after you verify that the parameter is, in fact, a byte array, you must still copy the data into a temporary array. This is because a variant does not necessarily copy all of the array data into a buffer when you pass the first byte of the data as a ByRef parameter. It can make a temporary copy of the byte value, pass the temporary variable to the DLL function, then copy the data back on return. The DLL function cannot assume that the byte it receives is, in fact, the first byte of the actual array.

The following code in the Misc2tst.vbp project demonstrates how to access the UserTypeEquiv property.

```
' Faking it with user defined types
Private Sub cmdUserType_Click()
   Dim obj As New clsMisc2B
   Dim TempArray() As Byte
   Dim TempUserType As usertype
   TempUserType.y = 55  ' Test value
   ReDim TempArray(Len(TempUserType))
   agCopyData TempUserType, TempArray(0), Len(TempUserType)
   obj.UserTypeEquiv = TempArray()
```

```
    TempArray() = obj.UserTypeEquiv
    agCopyData TempArray(0), TempUserType, Len(TempUserType)
    Debug.Print "User Type Y value is " & TempUserType.y
End Sub
```

There are some limitations to watch with this approach:

▸ The structure cannot hold dynamically allocated strings or arrays.

▸ Any fixed length strings will be converted from Unicode into ANSI.

▸ You may run into problems with string conversions of string variables within structures that are themselves in arrays.

▸ The Len function may not return the correct length if the fields within the structure do not fall on their natural alignment points (integers on 16-bit boundaries, longs on 32-bit boundaries). In these cases you should calculate for yourself the array size needed or use one of the User Defined Type (UDT) packing and unpacking functions that are included in Desaware's SpyWorks package or other third-party tools.

▸ You must be absolutely certain that the layout of the data within the array is identical for every client that uses this object. Visual Basic packs structures and performs string conversions when the user-defined type is passed to the agCopyData function, as it does any time a user-defined structure is passed to a DLL function. All applications that use these properties must expect the data in that format. This is trivial with Visual Basic, since it will simply reverse the process when copying in the other direction, but it may be more complex with other applications. It is especially critical when going between operating systems, where even the byte order may be reversed.

The good news is that these limitations apply relatively infrequently. The better news is that since the data is actually being transferred as a byte array, you need not worry about whether the object is in process or out of process. OLE knows how to marshal byte arrays between processes.

There clearly is overhead in this approach. The need to copy the data into temporary byte buffers may be prohibitive in some cases. Keep in mind, however, that the copying is taking place in the process that contains the data. In many cases where objects are implemented in EXE servers, the overhead will be minimal compared to the overhead involved in multiple cross-process calls.

The subjects of data organization within arrays and user-defined types, as well as how Visual Basic manages structures during DLL calls, string conversions, and data alignment within structures are somewhat complex and beyond the scope of this book. For more detailed information refer to *Dan Appleman's Visual Basic 5.0 Programmer's Guide to the Win32 API*, ZD Press, 1997, Chapters 3 and 15.

Procedure Attributes

Visual Basic 5.0 allows you to set a variety of attributes for methods and properties in a class, form, or ActiveX control or document. Actually it allows you to set them for functions in modules as well, but since these attributes mean nothing to methods outside of modules that support COM objects, it's rather pointless to do so other than for documentation purposes. These attributes are set using the Procedure Attributes dialog box shown in Figure 10.1. It is found through the Tools, Procedure Attributes command. Figure 10.1 shows the advanced attributes.

Figure 10.1: Procedure Attributes dialog box

Many of the attributes (especially the advanced attributes) only apply to ActiveX controls. Those will be covered in Part 3 of this book.

DESCRIPTION

You should set a description for every public method and procedure. It's not a bad idea to set the descriptions for private methods and procedures as well, especially for very large classes. The description appears in the object browser and the Properties window (for ActiveX controls).

HELP CONTEXT ID

Set this to the context identifier for this method or property in the component's help file, if one exists. This help context ID will be used by the object browser and the Properties window (for ActiveX controls).

PROCEDURE ID

In Chapter 4 we discussed the way that dispatch interfaces work. You may re-call that each method or property in a dispatch interface has an identifier called a Dispatch ID, Dispatch identifier, or Procedure ID. This Dispatch ID is used by the Invoke method of the interface to determine which method or property to call. Keep in mind that while the numbers must be unique within an interface, there is no rule that says the numbers must be sequential or have any particular values.

OLE defines a number of standard dispatch interface numbers that have spe-cial meanings. Use of these numbers does not affect the way you access meth-ods and properties in an object. However, object containers do have the ability to take special action for these standard dispatch interfaces if they so choose.

One example of this is the dispatch identifier number zero. Whichever method or property has this identifier will be considered by Visual Basic (and many other containers) to be the default method or property of the object. This means that if you try to access the object without specifying a method or property name, the language will use the default.

If you have object OBJ that has property Myprop, you would normally ac-cess this by:

```
MyVariable = OBJ.Myprop.
```

If Myprop is the default property you can just use:

```
MyVariable = OBJ
```

Many developers, including the Microsoft documents, stress the importance of choosing a default property that is logical. For example: the default prop-erty for a text control is the Text property. The default property for the Label control is the Caption property.

While I cannot in good conscience tell you not to choose a default property for your objects, I generally recommend against using default properties in your applications. The reason is purely one of readability and support.

When you see a line of code that takes the form MyVariable = MyObject, it requires extra effort on your part to understand which property is being read. You need to either know it by heart or look it up. In either case, this requires extra thought.

On the other hand, for the code MyVariable = MyObject.SpecificProperty, no extra thought is required. You know exactly which property is being accessed. The slight additional time it takes to add the property name (and it is slight indeed with VB5's new Quick-Info feature in the editor) is more than justified by the improved readability of the resulting code.

Additional procedure IDs will be covered in Part 3 in the context of their use with ActiveX controls.

HIDE THIS MEMBER

This option sets a special flag in the type library for an object that causes the member or property to be hidden. This means that the method or property will not be shown in the object browser and, in the case of ActiveX controls, will not appear in the Property window. However, your code can access the method or property.

This option is generally used to provide some security for an object. Only people who have documentation for hidden properties and methods can write programs that use them. It is also sometimes used for private methods and properties that your applications use but that you do not want available to the rest of the world.

The remaining advanced options will be covered in Part 3 in the context of their use with ActiveX controls.

OBJECT PROCEDURES: PUBLIC, PRIVATE, AND FRIEND

The word *public* is almost as much fun in Visual Basic as is the word object. Its meaning depends a great deal on the context. Are you talking about a DLL declaration? A variable declaration? A class module? In this section we'll take a look at how the Visual Basic language handles issues relating to the visibility of object methods and properties, along with some of the scoping rules relating to variables within an application.

PUBLIC IS AS PUBLIC DOES

In Chapter 8, you found out about the difference between private objects and public objects. The type of object is set using the Instancing property of the class module that implements the class.

The use of the terms public and private in this context controls the visibility of the methods and properties of the class module to clients that are not part of the component project itself. In other words: If a class module has its

Instancing property set to any of the public types, the object implemented by the class may be used by other applications. One or more of the properties of that object *may* be usable by other applications as well. If a class module has its Instancing property set to private, the object implemented by the class may not be used by other applications.

The Instancing property can be thought of as an overriding setting that determines whether the object is useable outside of the project. It has *nothing* to do with using the object within a project. A project may create and use any objects implemented by classes that are part of the project, regardless of the setting of the Instancing property.

Methods and Properties   The keywords Public or Private may be used with a method or property declaration in a module. (This includes class modules, standard modules, and form modules.). These functions control the visibility of the method or property through the application.

The rule is simple: If the method/property/function is public, it can be accessed by other modules in your application. If private, it can be accessed only within the same module.

This fairly simple rule has one side effect that some Visual Basic programmers, especially those who have been using Visual Basic for a long time, are not aware of. Because this rule applies to forms as well, it is possible for a form to expose public methods and properties. This allows one form to load a second form and set custom properties for the form (or call methods on the form) before it is shown. Public methods and properties for forms were not supported on earlier versions of Visual Basic, and some programmers never noticed when they were added. An example of this feature can be seen in the Misc3.vbp project that can be found in the Chapter 10 directory on the CD-ROM.

This simple rule defines the visibility of functions within a project, but what about outside of the project? If the method or property is in a class module and the Instancing property of the class is any of the public types, the method or property is also visible to the outside world—those clients using the component.

This poses an interesting problem with regard to public classes: What if you want a class method or property to be visible within the project but hidden by clients using the object? In other words: how do you make a method or property of a class private to the component itself accessible to any module within the component but unavailable to other applications?

This is accomplished using a function type new to Visual Basic 5.0: the Friend type. Figure 10.2 illustrates the visibility of Public, Private, and Friend methods and properties in public and private classes.

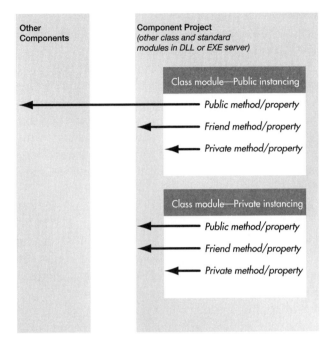

Figure 10.2: Visibility control for methods and properties

One interesting technique you can use with properties is to make the Property Let or Property Set function a Friend function while making the Property Get function public. This allows you to create properties that can be read by other applications but can be set only within your component.

There is one catch to defining methods and properties as Friends: Access to these functions must be early bound. This means, for example, that you cannot access a Friend function through a variable declared As Object. You must use a variable declared as the object type you are referencing.

Variables   The visibility rules for variables are very similar to those of methods and properties. Public variables are visible throughout the project. Private variables are visible only within the module in which they exist. Public variables within a public class are exposed to other applications (Visual Basic automatically creates hidden Property Get and Property Let/Set methods for the variable). There is no such thing as a Friend variable, however.

Privacy Is Golden A key part of the design of any object model is to determine which method and properties should be public. Generally speaking, you should maintain as much privacy as possible.

Consider a class which has function MyFunction that takes several parameters.

Let's say the function is private and is called several times within the class. In this case you can base the implementation of the function and your testing program on the way the function is used. If you only call the function with certain parameter values, you don't have to waste time and code with error handling for other parameter values. You can get away with just documenting any parameter restrictions or requirements for those who will be supporting the code in the future.

If the function is public within a project (public in a private class or a friend within a public class), the same situation applies, but on a slightly larger scale. You still maintain full code over how the function is called, so as long as you can eliminate bugs in your design and the way the function is called, you can be sure the function will always work and do not need to implement extensive error checking in the function code.

But when the function is a public method of a class, all bets are off. Any application using your component can call it with any type supported by the function and any value available to that type. This means that variant properties need to be tested both for type and value. Other properties need to be tested for any possible value. Your function must be able to correctly handle anything the calling application can throw at it.

Reduce the visibility of the variables, functions, and properties in your application as much as you can. It will make your code more modular, more reliable, and more supportable.

SCOPING RULES

Visibility is one of the attributes of a function or variable that fall under the label *scope*. Visibility defines from where the function or variable can be accessed. If it is accessible, it is visible. The scope of a variable or function refers to both its visibility and its lifetime, which is the time during which the variable exists.

You've already seen that visibility is at least in part determined by the use of the Public or Private keyword in the variable declaration. Visibility for variables is also determined by the location of the variable declaration. Variable declarations within functions or function parameters override variables of the same name declared at the module level. To see this, consider the following trivial program:

```
Option Explicit

Private x As Integer

Private Sub Command1_Click()
   Dim x As Integer
   x = 6' This has no effect on the module level variable
   Debug.Print x
End Sub

Private Sub Command2_Click()
   Debug.Print x
End Sub

Private Sub Form_Load()
   x = 5
End Sub
```

Is the value of variable x 5 or 6? In the Command1_Click function, it is 6. This is because within this function, the variable defined by the Dim statement within the function is visible. Because it has the same name as the module level x variable, it hides that variable, making it invisible within the subroutine. The variable may be set to 6, but this has no effect on the value of the module variable. The Command2_Click function does not have another x variable defined, so there is nothing to hide the module variable; it remains visible.

You've also seen that the visibility affects object methods and properties as well and is primarily determined by the Public, Private, and Friend keywords, and the Instancing property of the class module containing the method. Visibility of object methods and some application level (or Global) commands and constants can also be determined by the order of type library references in use by the application. This subject was covered in Chapter 9.

Lifetime The lifetime of a variable determines how long a variable exists. Lifetime is not the same as visibility, though they are related. For example, it is obvious that an object that no longer exists cannot be visible. Lifetime is also determined by the use of the Visual Basic *static* keyword. C and C++ programmers take note: While the Visual Basic static keyword does exhibit some of the behaviors of the C/C++ static keyword, it has major differences.

Normally, variables declared within procedures exist for the duration of a single procedure call. The variable is allocated on the stack, and when the function exits, the memory is reclaimed by the system.

When a variable is declared as static within a procedure, it is allocated in the data segment for the application instead of on the stack. The value of the variable is thus preserved from one call of the function to the next. When a procedure is declared as static, all local variables within the procedure are declared as static variables.

Table 10.1 summarizes the lifetimes of variables based on where they are declared and the use of the static keyword in either a variable or function declaration.

Table 10.1: Lifetime of Variables

Declaration	Location of the Declaration	Lifetime	Creation
Module Level— No static keyword	Standard module	Life of the application or thread*	One per application*
	Form module	Life of the form	One per form
	Class module	Life of the class object	One per class object
Module Level—Static keyword	Not allowed	N/A	
Within non-static procedure—No static keyword. Includes procedure parameters.	Any module type	Single procedure call	One per procedure call
Within non-static procedure using static keyword, or within static procedure	Standard module	Life of the application or thread*	One per application*
	Form module	Life of the form	One per form
	Class module	Life of the class object	One per class object

*Special circumstances apply when implementing a multithreading server. See Chapter 14.

The lifetime of global variables is typically the life of the application. However, special rules apply when implementing a multithreading server. (These cases are indicated in the table with an asterisk.) These are discussed in Chapter 14 during the discussion of multithreading.

When you define a procedure as static, all of the local variables within the procedure are defined as static. The problem with this is that you are no longer able to create dynamic variables in that procedure. Worse (static procedures are so uncommon that other people supporting your code later are likely to become confused), programmers are so used to procedure declared variables being dynamic.

In over five years of Visual Basic programming, I don't think I have ever created a static procedure. I have, however, often used static variables within procedures. Static variables provide a mechanism to create a variable that is effectively private to a particular procedure. It is much better than using a global variable in this case because it eliminates the possibility that some other function in the project might accidentally change the value of the variable. You see, while the static keyword does promote the lifetime of the variable to the level of a module variable, the visibility of the variable remains limited to the procedure in which it is defined.

The lifetime of an object also suggests when the specified variable is created. A variable declared in a non-multithreading standard module is created when the application loads and exists for the life of the application.

When declared in a form module, a new instance of the variable is created with each form object. Each form object has a unique instance of the variable. But both variables may be visible! Let's say a form has a public variable named ThisFormName and you have two global form objects in a standard module that reference the same type of form: MyForm1 and MyForm2. This can be accomplished using the following code from the Misc4.bas module in the Misc4.vbp application:

```
' Guide to Perplexed - Misc4 sample
' Copyright (c) 1997 by Desaware Inc. All Rights Reserved

Option Explicit

Public MyForm1 As frmMisc4
Public MyForm2 As frmMisc4

Sub Main()
    ' Set initial object variables
    Set MyForm1 = New frmMisc4
    Set MyForm2 = New frmMisc4
```

```
        MyForm1.ThisFormName = "MyForm1"
        MyForm2.ThisFormName = "MyForm2"
        ' Now show both forms
        MyForm1.Show
        MyForm2.Show
End Sub
```

The project is set to run SubMain first. ThisFormName is a public module level variable of the form. The public keyword makes the visibility of the variable application wide. Declaring the variable at the module level of the form (the declaration section) makes its lifetime the life of the form, with a new variable created for each form object (as shown in Table 10.1).

The form has a single command button and the following code:

```
' Guide to Perplexed - Misc4 sample
' Copyright (c) 1997 by Desaware Inc. All Rights Reserved

Option Explicit

Public ThisFormName As String

Private Sub Command1_Click()
    Debug.Print "Clicked" & ThisFormName
    Debug.Print MyForm1.ThisFormName
    Debug.Print MyForm2.ThisFormName
End Sub

Private Sub Form_Load()
    Caption = ThisFormName
End Sub

' Clean up the global variables when the forms
' are closed
Private Sub Form_Unload(Cancel As Integer)
    If MyForm1 Is Me Then Set MyForm1 = Nothing
    If MyForm2 Is Me Then Set MyForm2 = Nothing
End Sub
```

When you click on the command button, the ThisFormName variable by default refers to the one in the current form. Each form has a hidden object reference called Me referring to the form on which the code is acting. Specifying ThisFormName without an object reference results in an implied call to Me.ThisFormName. But because ThisFormName is public, it is possible to reference the variable for any form object as you can see in this example. The lifetime of the variable is per form, and the visibility is project wide.

You can duplicate the identical effect with class objects. Just create a public variable in a class, and create class objects instead of form objects. Next, try accessing the object variables both from within the standard module and within methods of the class module. You will achieve the same results.

What if you want a variable that is private to a class, but public to all instances of a class? In other words, one whose visibility is limited to a specific class, but which is created once and whose lifetime is the life of the application. With this type of variable, data can easily be shared among any objects belonging to a class. This can be accomplished in C or C++ by using the static keyword at the module level (class declaration level), but it is not possible directly in Visual Basic. Instead, you simply create a public global variable in a standard module and be careful not to use it anywhere except within the class module. It's not an ideal solution because it remains possible for code elsewhere in your project to modify the variable, but if you are careful to use a unique variable name, you can minimize the chances of this happening.

Keep in mind that a variable declared in a non-static procedure is created each time a procedure is called and exists until the procedure exits. This also applies to parameters to the procedure, which are treated as if they were allocated locally and initialized by the calling routine. This applies also to ByRef parameters—they may refer to a variable in the calling function but the reference variable itself is passed on the stack and is thus local to the procedure. In either case, if a function calls itself (a technique called recursion), you may find yourself creating a large number of variables.

A classic demonstration of recursion is shown in the listing that follows. The Debug.Print statement lets you track the creation and deletion of the procedure level variable (the function parameter).

```
' Guide to Perplexed - Recursion example
' Copyright (c) 1997 by Desaware Inc. All Rights Reserved


Option Explicit



Private Sub cmdCalculate_Click()
    Dim N As Integer
    Dim result As Double
    N = Val(txtValue.Text)
    result = Factorial(N)
    lblResult.Caption = "Factorial of " & N & " is " & Str$(result)
End Sub

' Factorial N is N * (N-1) * (N-2), etc.
' i.e. Factorial 5 is 5 * 4 * 3 * 2 * 1
```

```
Public Function Factorial(ByVal N As Integer) As Double
   Debug.Print "N is created with value " & N
   If N <= 1 Then
      Factorial = 1
   Else
      Factorial = CDbl(N) * Factorial(N - 1)
   End If
   Debug.Print "N with value " & N & " is about to be destroyed "
End Function
```

SELECTED TOPICS

"Selected Topics" is a nice way of describing something that I want to write about but isn't big enough to deserve its own chapter and doesn't seem to fit anywhere else.

ENUMS

This is the first place in the book where I will mention Enums, a new feature to Visual Basic 5.0. You'll see more about Enums in Part 3, where they will be discussed in relation to ActiveX control properties.

Enums are in some ways a very cool technology, and in other ways are totally useless. You see, they don't really do anything when used in code components. And while they do have a practical use with ActiveX controls, they suffer from some serious limitations, as you will see later. First some background.

You've seen that ActiveX components can publish information about objects so they can be used by other applications. This information includes the methods and properties of the object, as well as such items as the object's programmatic name and GUID. You've also learned that the way that this information is published is by writing information about the component into your system registry (which occurs when a component is registered). Part of the information in the registry is the location of the type library for the component, which is the resource that defines all of the properties and methods for the component. This resource is automatically added by Visual Basic to your component's executable file (EXE, DLL or OCX, depending on component type).

It turns out, however, that a type library is not limited to describing just methods and properties. It can expose constants as well. For example, if you create the following Enum:

```
Public Enum TestEnum
      Test1 = 1
      Test2 = 2
End Enum
```

Any application that has referenced your component can use Test1 and Test2 to represent the values 1 and 2. More important, you can create properties that have the Enum type, for example:

```
Public Property Get TestEnumProp() As TestEnum

End Property


Public Property Let TestEnumProp(ByVal vNewValue As TestEnum)

End Property
```

You might be thinking this is very cool—a property that automatically restricts itself to the values in an enumeration. But you would be wrong.

You see, enumerations allow you to define constants. That's all. Each Enum value is a 32-bit-long value, so the TestEnumProp property has effectively been defined as a long property. Visual Basic does no range checking. Given an object called myObject, where the object contains the above code, both of the following lines will work:

```
myObject.TestEnumProp = Test1
myObject.TestEnumProp = 528249
```

So why are Enums useful? They are useful because if you have the VB environment's Auto List Members feature enabled (Look for it in the Tools-Options dialog box under the Editor tab), when you type the code "myObject.TestEnumProp=", VB will automatically display all of the elements in the enumeration so that you can easily select one without looking it up.

In other words, when it comes to ActiveX components, Enums are useful to improve code readability and programming efficiency. But they don't really do anything.

So use them, but don't forget to implement range error checking on your public properties that have an enumeration type.

Here are a few other things that you should know about Enums.

▶ In ActiveX components you can precede an Enum name with an underscore to make it hidden. I see no practical use for this, however. Example: [_Test1] = 1.

▶ Use brackets to create enumerations that violate variable naming rules (have illegal characters or spaces). Example: [My Enumerated Value]= 5.

▶ Enumerations do not have to be consecutive values. This makes enumerations useful for exposing constants of all types.

▸ Different elements in an enumeration do not have to have unique values. For example: Test1=1: Test2=1 is legal.

▸ Beware of creating Enum constant names that are used by other components or by Visual Basic itself. In case of such conflict, Visual Basic will use the one that is in the type library that is first on the reference list. Microsoft recommends preceding each Enum name with a consistent prefix to help differentiate constants. Thus most constants used by VB or VBA have the prefix vb, as in vbArrow.

TO WIZ OR NOT TO WIZ

Visual Basic 5.0 comes with a number of wizards including a Class Builder Wizard. Whether you choose to use wizards or not is really a matter of personal preference. I've found that the Class Builder Wizard has some value in making in possible to get an overview of the methods, properties, and events in my object, but that it is generally more hassle than it's worth. Classes are straightforward enough so that code generated by the wizard is not substantial, and much of the time I find I end up deleting the wizard-generated code because it doesn't perform the task that I'm looking for it to perform. I'd rather build from scratch than have to go back and clean up after a wizard. But let me stress that this is a personal preference and not a recommendation. Try it both ways and see what you like.

The ActiveX Control Wizard, which is used to help create ActiveX controls, is far more useful. It is especially handy for implementing standard properties, and it's a great way to see how certain common techniques can be implemented. You'll read more about this in Part 3.

Events

A Method By Any Other Name

Back to COM

Combining OLE Callbacks and OLE
Events

How is it possible to reach Chapter 11 in a book on developing ActiveX components and not mention events even once? Well, the truth is, you have already read a great deal about events. In fact, you know almost everything that you need to know about how they work.

How is this possible? Read on…

A METHOD BY ANY OTHER NAME

Looking back: What is the difference between a method and a property?

- ▸ The syntax you use to access them is slightly different in Visual Basic.

- ▸ A property is implemented with two methods: a Get method and a Set method.

In other words, they are really nothing more than two slightly different ways to invoke functions belonging to a COM interface.

There is a strong tendency in most ActiveX documentation (including that of Visual Basic) to deal with events as a unique entity. But in truth, they are the same as methods and properties—just a slightly different way to invoke functions on a COM interface.

The only real difference is one of perspective. If your application as a client calls an object method, then it is called a method. If the object calls a method belonging to one of your application's objects, it is an event.

Let's back up for a moment and see how this works without resorting to what is commonly called *events*.

OLE CALLBACKS

Imagine you have a client application that is using an object provided by a DLL or EXE code component. This object is going to perform an operation in the background. When the background operation is complete, you want the object to somehow notify your application that it is finished. In Visual Basic 4.0 the only way to accomplish this was through a technique called *OLE callbacks*.

The scenario for this type of operation can be seen in Figure 11.1. First, choose an object in your own application that you want to have notified when the event occurs. Add a method to this object, which will be called to signal the event. In the TickTst1.vbp example, this method is called DelayedCall.

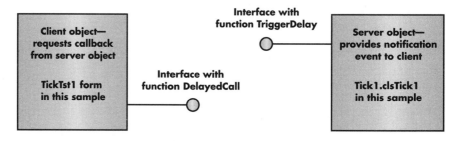

Figure 11.1: OLE callback scenario

The TickTst1 form, shown below, uses an object provided by the Tick1.vbp code component. The application creates an instance of this object when it loads (and frees it when it unloads). In this particular case late binding was chosen, but early binding could be implemented as well. You'll shortly see why, in this example, I chose to use an EXE server.

```
Dim TimerObj As Object

Private Sub Form_Load()
    ' Be sure Tick1 is running
    Set TimerObj = CreateObject("Tick1.clsTick1")
End Sub

Private Sub Form_Unload(Cancel As Integer)
    Set TimerObj = Nothing
End Sub
```

The Tick.clsTick1 object is very simple. It sets a timer to a specified delay and notifies your form when the time has expired by calling the form's DelayedCall method. How can it access the DelayedCall method in your form? Obviously, you must give it a reference to the form, which it will hold until the timer is triggered. This is done in the TimerObj.TriggerDelay method, where a reference to the form is passed by providing Me as a parameter.

The cmdTest button is disabled in order to avoid invoking the TriggerDelay method while a time operation is in progress. The Tick1 sample, being a very simple program, is not designed to handle re-entrancy. The cmdTest_Click function and its associated callback are shown here:

```
Private Sub cmdTest_Click()
    ' 2000 ms delay
    TimerObj.TriggerDelay Me, 2000
    cmdTest.Enabled = False
End Sub


Public Sub DelayedCall()
    MsgBox "DelayedCall 'Event' received"
    cmdTest.Enabled = True
End Sub
```

Referring again to Figure 11.1, you can see the two objects. The TickTst1 form includes the DelayedCall method on its default interface. The clsTick1 object includes the TriggerDelay method on its default interface. The client object (TickTst1) obtains a reference to the clsTick1 object and calls the TriggerDelay method for the object. This method includes a reference to the TickTst1 form as one of its parameters. The object holds on to that form reference in a private variable. When it is ready, it can call the DelayedCall method on the form.

Now, which one is an event? Both components are performing exactly the same operation—a method call. But the DelayedCall method is acting like an event because it is being called in response to some occurrence in the server. You see, it's mostly a matter of perspective.

Now, let's take a look inside the clsTick1 object. First, let me warn you: this object, while very short, actually takes advantage of a variety of advanced techniques. Some of these have already been discussed, but some won't be covered until later.

The Tick1 Project   This project implements a simple alarm type application. You provide it with a time delay, and after the time expires, your client object is notified. In the real world, you would probably implement this functionality with a timer in your own application. But this is actually an excellent learning example because a timer event is representative of any external event. The principles shown here can be applied directly to applications such as:

▸ Waiting for a remote query to complete

- ▸ Waiting for a child process to terminate

- ▸ Waiting for a system event

- ▸ Waiting for a download of a large file over the Internet

This project includes a single class (clsTick1.cls) and a module modTick1.bas. The class module contains two private variables. DelayToUse holds the delay value. CallbackObject is used to hold a reference to the client object. This object must contain a method named DelayedCall. If it doesn't, an error will occur.

Note that this reference must be late bound because you want this object to be useable from any client object that is willing to implement the DelayedCall method. Can you change this to early bound? Yes, by defining a custom interface that contains the DelayedCall method. You can then require any client applications who wish to use this server to implement that interface in the calling object using the Implements statement. However, this particular component is implemented in an EXE server, so the benefit to be gained by early binding is negligible compared to the overhead incurred by being out of process.

The TriggerDelay function stores a reference to the client object in the CallbackObject variable. It then calls the StartTimer function in the modTick1 module (more on this shortly). The timer portion is implemented in the module, and it needs a way to inform the clsTick1 object that the time has expired. You already know how this is done: another OLE callback! The StartTimer method takes a reference to the clsTick1 object and stores it in the module. When the time has expired, the module will call the TimerExpired method for the class object. The TimerExpired method in turn calls the DelayedCall method of the CallbackObject object.

How does the module know what time delay to use? Two possibilities come to mind. You could pass the delay value as a parameter in the StartTimer method. But this seems a good place to demonstrate the value of the Friend function. By making the Delay property a Friend property, it becomes possible for other modules in this project to retrieve the value of the private DelayToUse variable without exposing it to the outside world. Listing 11.1 shows the clsTick1 module.

So how does the timer itself work? It makes use of the timer capability that is built into Windows. This is demonstrated in Listing 11.2. Two API functions are declared: SetTimer and KillTimer. SetTimer creates a timer object with a specified delay and returns an identifier to that timer. KillTimer destroys a timer object given a timer identifier.

Listing 11.1: Class clsTick1

```
' Guide to Perplexed: Tick1
' Copyright (c) 1997 by Desaware Inc. All Rights Reserved
'
Option Explicit

Private DelayToUse As Long
Private CallbackObject As Object

' Callbackparam is an object that contains
' the method 'DelayedCall'
Public Sub TriggerDelay(Callbackparam As Object, delayval As Long)
    DelayToUse = delayval
    ' This is the object that we want to callback
    Set CallbackObject = Callbackparam
    StartTimer Me
End Sub

' Allow the module to access the delay value
' It's not public though
Friend Property Get Delay() As Long
    Delay = DelayToUse
End Property

' This is the timer expiration event from
' the module
Friend Sub TimerExpired()
    ' This is late bound
    CallbackObject.DelayedCall
    ' Don't hold a reference to the object
    Set CallbackObject = Nothing
End Sub
```

Listing 11.2: Module modTick1.bas

```
' Guide to Perplexed: Tick1
' Copyright (c) 1997 by Desaware Inc. All Rights Reserved

Option Explicit

' Timer identifier
Dim TimerID&

' Object for this timer
```

Listing 11.2: Module modTick1.bas (Continued)

```
Dim TimerObject As clsTick1

Declare Function SetTimer Lib "user32" (ByVal hwnd As Long, ByVal nIDEvent As_
Long, ByVal uElapse As Long, ByVal lpTimerFunc As Long) As Long
Declare Function KillTimer Lib "user32" (ByVal hwnd As Long, ByVal nIDEvent As_
Long) As Long


Public Sub StartTimer(callingobject As clsTick1)
   Set TimerObject = callingobject
   TimerID = SetTimer(Ø, Ø, callingobject.Delay, AddressOf TimerProc)
End Sub

' Callback function
Public Sub TimerProc(ByVal hwnd&, ByVal msg&, ByVal id&, ByVal currentime&)
   Call KillTimer(Ø, TimerID)
   TimerID = Ø
   TimerObject.TimerExpired
   ' And clear the object reference so it can delete
   Set TimerObject = Nothing
End Sub
```

The StartTimer method stores a reference to the calling object in variable TimerObject, which exposes the TimerExpired method. Note that in this case the callback object (TimerObject) is early bound. This is easily accomplished because we know that it is the only object type that will call the StartTimer method—no need to define a custom interface.

The SetTimer function also requires a pointer to a function to call when the timer has expired. A function address for a function in a standard module can be obtained using the AddressOf operator as shown. It is critical that the module function be declared with the exact parameters, parameter types, and return types or you are likely to cause a memory exception. This includes getting the ByVal and ByRef qualifiers correct for each parameter.

Windows holds on to the address function provided by the SetTimer function and calls that function (in this case TimerProc) when the timer expires. The TimerProc function kills the timer, calls the TimerExpired method on the calling object, and clears the TimerObject variable so it can be deleted properly.

If you think about it, the concept of holding on to a function address and calling it later is conceptually the same as holding on to an object reference and calling a method for the object at a later time. In fact, the type of operation where you pass a function address to Windows or a DLL for it to call later is called a *callback* and the function address that you pass to the DLL is called a *callback function*. It is important, however, to distinguish between this type of *API callback* and OLE callbacks. They may be similar in concept but they are completely different in terms of implementation.

The entire scenario shown here can be demonstrated by loading the Tick1 project and the TickTst1 project into two separate instances of Visual Basic. Run the Tick1 project to make its objects available. Make sure the TickTst1 project is referencing the Tick1 project, then run the TickTst1 application and click on the Test button. The scenario shown in Figure 11.2 will occur and you will see a message box indicating the event after about 2 seconds.

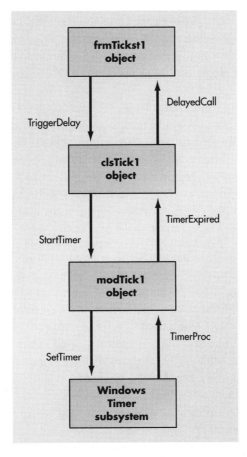

Figure 11.2: Scenario of objects and methods called during the TickTst1 and Tick1 example

Why is the Tick1 object implemented as an EXE server with the Instancing property of the clsTick1 object set to SingleUse?

A Windows timer requires use of a standard module for the callback. If the component were to support multiple clsTick1 objects, it would be necessary to keep track of those objects within the module and manage multiple timers. This is possible, and you will see later how this can be accomplished, but I decided that this sample was already sufficiently complex. By making the object single use, each instance of the object will have its own process space and thus have its own global variables. Thus, there is no need to worry about managing multiple objects—it happens automatically. The only way to make an object single use is to implement it in an EXE server.

When experimenting with the TickTst1 and Tick1 projects, you will need to stop and restart the Tick1 project each time you start the TickTst1 project if you are running Tick1 within the VB environment. This is because Visual Basic can only provide a single object from a class if the Instancing property for the class is set for single use. You can compile Tick1 into an executable to avoid this problem.

If you were actually going to implement a timer object, the approach you see here is about the last you would take. It is terribly inefficient to launch a new process just to obtain a timeout. But remember that the time delay in this example is intended to represent any long operation you wish to take place in the background. Those other scenarios that were described earlier in this chapter are often appropriate to implement in this manner. In subsequent chapters, especially Chapter 14, you'll find out a great deal more about the trade-offs involved. Meanwhile, let's take another look at events.

Events Revisited   OLE callbacks provide a way for an application to be signaled when an event occurs in another object. Event in this context is an idea—the concept that a server can notify a client when something occurs.

But when you read ActiveX documentation, including the Visual Basic documentation, the term *event* is also used to refer to a different way for a server object to notify a client. This technique is demonstrated in the Tick2.vbp and TickTst2.vbp projects. These projects were created by first copying the Tick1 and TickTst1 projects and all of their associated files. Then the suffix of the class and module names was changed from 1 to 2 (thus clsTick1 became clsTick2) and all code changed accordingly. This was done just to differentiate between the examples and prevent any confusion due to reuse of the class names.

To enable Tick2 for events, you need only add the following line to the declaration section of the clsTick2 module:

```
Event DelayedCall()
```

You'll also need to modify the TimerExpired function as follows:

```
Friend Sub TimerExpired()
    ' This is late bound
    If Not CallbackObject Is Nothing Then
        CallbackObject.DelayedCall
        ' Don't hold a reference to the object
        Set CallbackObject = Nothing
    Else
        RaiseEvent DelayedCall
    End If
End Sub
```

As you can see, the clsTick2 object still supports OLE callbacks. All you need to do is pass Nothing as a parameter to the TriggerDelay method. This tells the component to raise the DelayedCall event instead of calling a Delayed-Call method.

The changes to the client test application TickTst2 are more substantial, but only slightly so. The form code is shown in Listing 11.3.

Listing 11.3: The frmTickTst2 Module Code

```
' Guide to the Perplexed: TickTst2
' Copyright (c) 1997 by Desaware Inc. All Rights Reserved

Option Explicit

Dim WithEvents TimerObj As Tick2.clsTick2

Private Sub cmdTest_Click()
    ' 2000 ms delay
    TimerObj.TriggerDelay Nothing, 2000
    cmdTest.Enabled = False
End Sub


Private Sub Form_Load()
    Set TimerObj = New clsTick2
End Sub

Private Sub Form_Unload(Cancel As Integer)
    Set TimerObj = Nothing
End Sub

Private Sub TimerObj_DelayedCall()
```

Listing 11.3: The frmTickTst2 Module Code (Continued)

```
    MsgBox "DelayedCall 'Event' received"
    cmdTest.Enabled = True
End Sub
```

The big change is that when using events, you must use early binding. Thus before trying to run this code you must run the Tick2 application in the Visual Basic environment (not necessary if you've compiled it to an executable), then use the References dialog box to add a reference to Tick2 to the TickTst2 project. You must do this even if you are running the sample code provided. Once you have added a reference to the project, you can create an object of that class using the Dim WithEvents function.

Why did Listing 11.3 include the fully qualified class name Tick2.clsTick2 instead of just using clsTick2? Answer: No functional reason whatsoever. It just improves the readability in this example, since we just finished talking about a Tick1 project.

The form load event actually creates the object. You cannot use the New command when dimensioning an object variable using WithEvents in Visual Basic 5.0. I have no idea why; maybe they'll change it in a future version.

When the clsTick2 object uses the RaiseEvent method to raise an event, it calls the DelayedCall method on a special event interface that appears in your form with the name of the dimensioned variable, in this case, TimerObj.

So what has really changed here?

▶ We're using early instead of late binding, but that is not really a change since we could have easily used early binding on the Tick1 example as well.

▶ We're dimensioning an object variable WithEvents.

▶ We're using RaiseEvent instead of a direct method call in the Tick2 object.

▶ The event syntax is slightly different.

If the two approaches seem very similar, it's because they are. ActiveX events are really nothing more than a way to let OLE do some of the callback work for you. In a moment you'll see what's going on behind the scenes but, in short, what is happening is that the server object is calling a method on the client object. Whether it's an OLE callback or an OLE event, it's still ultimately a method call. And you already know about method calls.

So you see, I really wasn't kidding when I said that you've been learning about events all along. Whether it's a method or a property or an event, it all comes down to a method call on an IDispatch interface.

BACK TO COM

So what does OLE actually do behind the scenes to make OLE events easy to use? Let's first look at the differences between events and callbacks in terms of their use. These are shown in Table 11.1.

Table 11.1: Programming Characteristics for OLE Callbacks and OLE Events

OLE Events	OLE Callbacks
Early bound.*	Late bound or early bound.
No need to explicitly pass an object reference to the server object.	Must pass object reference to server object for it to call back.
Visual Basic automatically creates event templates in code module when the event is selected in the designer window.	Callback methods must be defined manually.
Visual Basic's Auto-List capability makes it easy to raise events in the client object.	Server does not have access to the client's type information.
Separate event routine for each object dimensioned with events.	Multiple objects of the same type will call the same callback method. You can pass parameters with the event to differentiate between objects (you can even pass a reference to the server object itself by passing 'Me' as a parameter).

* Early binding in this case means that you add a reference to the object to your project and that you can access methods and properties in the object using early binding. It does NOT imply that events are themselves early bound. Whether the RaiseEvent statement uses early or late binding to trigger the event depends on Visual Basic's implementation of the call.

Behind the Scenes   How does OLE implement events? Clearly, the following steps must occur:

▶ The client object must ask the server if it supports events.

▶ The client object must obtain a list of the events for the server object and the parameters for each event.

▶ The client object must create a new interface that contains methods that correspond to the server's events.

▶ The client object must pass to the server object a reference to this new interface. The server can then raise events by calling the methods of this interface.

Now you may begin to appreciate why it took seven chapters to reach the point of actually talking about ActiveX components. You know that an object can support more than one interface. You know that you can create multiple interfaces for an object by using the Implements statement. All that is happening here is that for each object dimensioned WithEvents, Visual Basic creates a new interface. It bases the methods of this interface on the information provided by the server (so the server determines the names and parameters of the events, which makes sense, since the server is going to invoke them). Visual Basic passes a reference to this interface to the server object, which then calls those methods.

Figure 11.3 illustrates the way OLE objects with event support are often diagrammed. An outgoing arrow called an *outgoing interface* indicates that the object is able to call methods on an interface that it defines. The server object does not actually implement this outgoing interface. It is, rather, a specification for the interface that the client object must create in order to receive events.

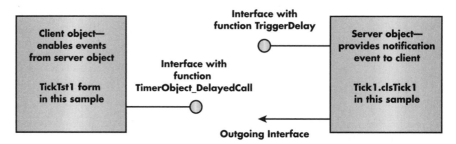

Figure 11.3: Implementation of OLE events

How does the client object obtain this interface specification? It uses Query-Interface to obtain from the server object a reference to an interface called IConnectionPointContainer. This interface provides methods that allow the object to obtain objects with an interface called IConnectionPoint.

IConnectionPoint objects have methods from which the object can obtain information on the return type and parameters of a method. The client object uses this information to create the event interface. Of course, you don't need to know anything about this process to use it from Visual Basic. It all happens behind the scenes. If you want to read more about it, you can find information about this process on the Microsoft Developer's Network Library CD-ROM available directly from Microsoft.

Isn't it amazing how many interfaces even a simple object can have? Believe it or not, only a few years ago the only way to use OLE objects was to hand-code each one of these interfaces using C or C++! No wonder OLE was so hard to code!

In the previous section you saw that the callback object was dimensioned As Object so the server could handle any type of object. But I also pointed out another approach in which you could define a custom interface that would be supported by any client object that wanted to use this server. If you are using a single object, this would produce the same effect as the OLE event mechanism, but things change if you are using multiple events of the same type.

Consider what would happen if the TickTst2 sample had a second clsTick2 object called TimerObject2. Using events, you would need to create a second event method called TimerObject2_DelayedCall. This is shown in Figure 11.4. The TickTst2 client creates a separate interface for each object dimensioned WithEvents.

With OLE callbacks, you have a choice. You can have the server dimension its callback variable As Object and call a method on the object's main interface. Or you can define a custom interface that is implemented by any client object using the server and use that interface. Either way, there is no way for the client to create a separate interface for each object. So no matter how many server objects you create, they will all call the same method. This is shown in Figure 11.5.

This raises an interesting question: Is the fact that OLE events have separate events for each object while OLE callbacks share a callback method really significant from a design perspective? This is an important question, because there may be many cases where you not only need to support multiple instances of an object that can raise events, but you need to create those objects dynamically. The answer, unsurprisingly, is yes. But the choice is not always clear-cut.

CREATING SEPARATE EVENTS WITH OLE CALLBACKS

The easiest way to differentiate between server objects is to have the server itself pass information back to the client's method as a parameter. But if you are using an object that does not do this, you can still use multiple objects and differentiate between them.

The callbk1.vbg project group demonstrates how this can be accomplished. This project group contains two projects, an ActiveX DLL server and a test project.

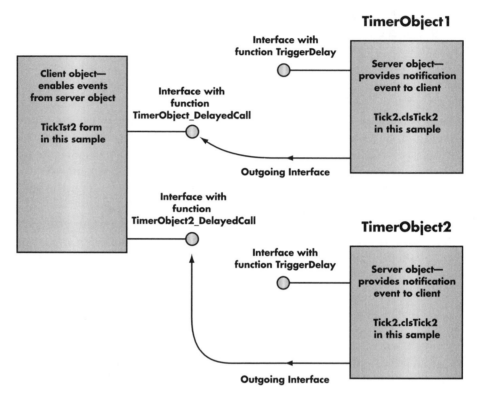

Figure 11.4: OLE events with two objects

The server project, Callback1Server (Callbk1s.vbp), contains a simple class that uses an OLE callback to signal an event. The SetCallback function takes the client object reference as a parameter and stores it in a private variable. The EventDemo function is a simple test function that triggers the event via the callback. The code for this object is shown below:

```
' Guide to the Perplexed: Callback1 Sample
' Copyright (c) 1997 by Desaware Inc.  All Rights Reserved

Option Explicit

Private CallbackObject As Object

' Sample function that sets the callback
Public Sub SetCallback(myobject As Object)
   Set CallbackObject = myobject
End Sub
```

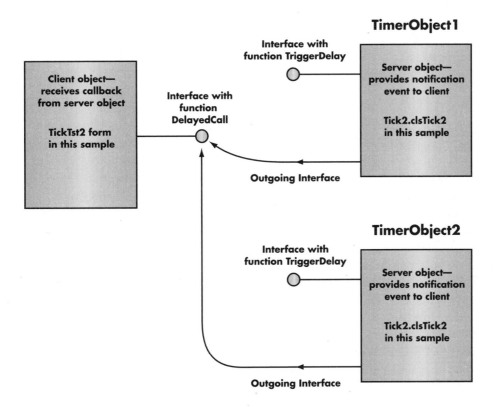

Figure 11.5: OLE callbacks with two objects

```
' Sample function that does the callback
Public Sub EventDemo()
    CallbackObject.SampleEvent "an event"
End Sub
```

This class is defined as multiple use and implemented in an ActiveX DLL. This means that the client can create as many of these objects as it wishes. However, each of these objects calls the SampleEvent method on the client object to trigger an event. Because the SampleEvent method has no parameter, there is no way for the client to determine which object made the function call.

The only answer to distinguishing between multiple CallbackObject objects is obvious: provide separate clients for each one. This is illustrated in the Callback1 project. It defines a class, clsCallbackSink, whose only purpose is to be a recipient of SampleEvent method calls from the server. The code for this class is as follows:

```
Option Explicit

' This object
Public Name As String

' Sample Event is called from the server object
Public Sub SampleEvent(ByVal msg As String)
    MsgBox Name & " received an event"
End Sub
```

Setting up the OLE callback is demonstrated in the frmCallback form, whose module code is shown in Listing 11.4. The form contains two command buttons, cmdServer1 and cmdServer2.

Two clsCallback server objects named server1 and server2 are defined. Each of these has a corresponding clsCallbackSink object that will receive the OLE callback. Instead of a reference to the form, the clsCallbackSink objects are passed to the server's SetCallback function.

The two command buttons simulate the occurrence of an event. When you click one, the EventDemo method of the server object is called, which in turn calls the SampleEvent method in the clsCallbackSink object. In this manner your project can differentiate between as many server objects as you wish.

Listing 11.4: Form frmCallback Module Code

```
' Guide to the Perplexed: Callback1 Sample
' Copyright (c) 1997 by Desaware Inc.  All Rights Reserved

Option Explicit

' Dimension two separate objects
Dim obj1 As New clsCallbackSink
Dim obj2 As New clsCallbackSink

' Here are the server objects
Dim server1 As New clsCallback
Dim server2 As New clsCallback

Private Sub cmdServer1_Click()
    server1.EventDemo
End Sub

Private Sub cmdServer2_Click()
```

Listing 11.4: Form frmCallback Module Code (Continued)

```
        server2.EventDemo
End Sub

Private Sub Form_Load()
    obj1.Name = "Object 1"
    obj2.Name = "Object 2"
    ' Each server object receives a different client
    ' object reference
    server1.SetCallback obj1
    server2.SetCallback obj2
End Sub
```

This approach closely resembles the one you saw earlier with OLE events; it's just a little bit more work.

COMBINING OLE CALLBACKS AND OLE EVENTS

To use OLE events with an object you must take the following steps:

▶ Dimension the objects with events: Dim WithEvents *myobject* as *objecttype*

▶ Create the object: Set *myobject* = New *objecttype* (or use CreateObject)

▶ Implement the event function: Sub *myobject_myevent(paramlist)*

And you must do this for each object for which you want to support events.

Clearly this approach does not lend itself to dynamic allocation of objects that use events. If you want dynamically allocated objects to signal your application, you must use OLE callbacks, but you can hide the callbacks behind another class to simplify their use. In doing so, you can also eliminate the overhead of creating a separate object and method for each server object.

The Callbk2.vbg group contains two projects that demonstrate how this can be accomplished. The server project, Callback2server (clsCbk2.cls), now contains two classes. The first class is essentially identical to the previous Callback-server class with the addition of an object name property and the fact that it is now designed to work with the clsCallback2col class, the new class in this project. Both classes are shown in Listing 11.5.

Listing 11.5: The clsCallback2 and clsCallback2 Class Modules

```
' Guide to the Perplexed: Callback2 Sample
' Copyright (c) 1997 by Desaware Inc.  All Rights Reserved

Option Explicit

Public Name$

Private callbackobject As clsCallback2Col

' Sample function that sets the callback
Public Sub SetCallback(myobject As Object)
   Set callbackobject = myobject
End Sub

' Sample function that does the callback
Public Sub EventDemo()
   callbackobject.SampleEvent Name$
End Sub

' Guide to the Perplexed: Callback2 Sample
' Copyright (c) 1997 by Desaware Inc.  All Rights Reserved
' Class clsCallback2Col

Option Explicit

' This is the OLE event definition for the
' event combining object. Note that it is in
' a different name space
Event SampleEvent(ByVal objectname$)

' This is the OLE callback method on the main interface
' for the event combining object
Sub SampleEvent(ByVal objectname$)
   RaiseEvent SampleEvent(objectname)
End Sub

' A utility function to initialize the OLE callback
' for the object
Public Sub SetCallbackServer(obj As clsCallback2)
   obj.SetCallback Me
End Sub
```

The clsCallback2col class serves as a go-between to multiple clsCallback2 objects. The SetCallbackServer method of this class sets the OLE callback for the object to reference the clsCallback2col object. The object contains a SampleEvent method, which is called by the OLE callback in the clsCallback2 object. The object then raises the SampleEvent event on the client form.

How can an object have an event and a property of the same name? It's easy—remember that the event actually becomes a method on an interface belonging to the client object. It never exists in the server object that triggers the event. Thus, there is no naming conflict.

The result of this approach can be seen in the form code. It is quite different from that of the frmCallback form in the previous example, as you can see in Listing 11.6.

Listing 11.6: Listing for Form frmCallback2

```
' Guide to the Perplexed: Callback2 Sample
' Copyright (c) 1997 by Desaware Inc.  All Rights Reserved

Option Explicit

' Dimension two separate objects
Dim WithEvents multievent As clsCallback2Col

' Here are the server objects
Dim server1 As New clsCallback2
Dim server2 As New clsCallback2
Dim server3 As New clsCallback2

Private Sub cmdServer1_Click()
    server1.EventDemo
End Sub

Private Sub cmdServer2_Click()
    server2.EventDemo
End Sub

Private Sub cmdServer3_Click()
    server3.EventDemo
End Sub

Private Sub Form_Load()
    Set multievent = New clsCallback2Col
    server1.Name = "Object 1"
    server2.Name = "Object 2"
```

Listing 11.6: Listing for Form frmCallback2 (Continued)

```
    server3.Name = "Object 3"

    multievent.SetCallbackServer server1
    multievent.SetCallbackServer server2
    multievent.SetCallbackServer server3

End Sub


' All of the server objects ultimately trigger this
' event
Private Sub multievent_SampleEvent(ByVal objectname As String)
    MsgBox "Event received from " & objectname
End Sub
```

Take a close look at the procedures that create the server objects. The objects are dimensioned, but without the WithEvents keyword. The Name property is then set and the object is passed as a parameter to the Multievent object's Set-CallbackServer method. This sets up the server objects to use OLE callbacks to call the SampleEvent method in the Multievent object. Can you see any reason why you could not use this technique on an array of clsCallback2 server objects? Or use it with objects that are allocated and freed as needed? I hope not, because there isn't any.

Meanwhile, all of the server events (triggered via OLE callbacks) are mapped into a single OLE event on the client form. You no longer have the overhead of separate event functions for each object, or of secondary objects that serve as intermediaries for the server.

As you may gather, there are many possible ways of handling events, whether they are OLE callbacks, OLE events, or some combination of the two. We'll be going into more possibilities later. The important thing to keep in mind is that no matter how you handle it, ultimately you are just calling a method on an interface, which is really what COM is all about in the first place.

Collecting
Objects

The Characteristics of Collections

The ~~Three~~ Four Approaches to Exposing Collections in Components

Chapter 12

This is a chapter about collections.

Well, actually it isn't. It is really a chapter that deals with managing groups of objects. I suspect that you can divide Visual Basic programmers into three groups on this subject:

- There are those who "know" that the best way to manage groups of objects is to use a collection.

- Then there are those who aren't really familiar with collections and thus manage groups of objects using arrays.

- And finally, there are those who understand the advantages and disadvantages of both collections and arrays and thus wrestle with the decision on which one to use each time they have to deal with more than one object in a project.

By the end of this chapter, I hope you will find yourself firmly in the third group—though you may not always enjoy it.

The Characteristics of Collections

You may be wondering why I don't start with an introduction to arrays before diving into the somewhat more complex subject of collections. It's quite simple really: arrays are a fundamental language construct that should be very familiar to any Visual Basic programmer past the level of absolute beginner. In other words, by the time you tackle this book, you should already know what an array is and how to use it. If you don't, I would encourage you to take a break and visit the Programming Fundamentals section in Part 1 of the VB programmer's guide.

So what exactly is a collection? You already know that a variant is a special kind of variable that can hold any type of data. A collection is an object that holds a bunch of variants—as many as you care to place in it. For our purposes we will focus exclusively on collections as a tool to hold objects. Just keep in mind throughout this chapter that almost everything discussed here can apply to other types of variables as well. It's just that in component development, the most common use of collections is to hold object references.

Each item in a collection has two values associated with it. First is the position within the collection (starting from one up to the number of items in the collection). Second is an optional *key value*, which is a string that uniquely identifies the object.

A collection has the following properties and methods:

- ▶ Count property: This read-only property allows you to obtain the number of items in the collection.

- ▶ Item method: Returns a variant containing the value of the item specified in a variant parameter. You can specify the item by passing either a number containing the position (index) of the item or a string containing the key of the item you want to retrieve. Refer to the section on "Overloaded Properties and Functions" in Chapter 10 for more information on how the operation of a method can change based on the type of data passed in a variant parameter.

- ▶ Add method: This method takes four parameters: *item, key, before, after*. All but the first are optional. The item is a variant containing the item to add. The key is a unique key identifying the object or an empty string if you don't wish to use a key. The before and after parameters are variants that contain either a number or a string that refer to the position or key of an existing item in the collection. The Add method then adds the current item before or after the specified item (depending on whether you are using the before or after parameter; you can't use both).

- ▶ Remove method: This removes an item specified in a variant parameter that contains a numeric position or a string key value.

The Collection object is discussed extensively in the Microsoft documentation, and I'm devoting quite a bit of space to it here. How can such a simple object be deserving of such a fuss? To answer this question, let's take a look at some of the advantages that this component offers Visual Basic programmers. These include:

- ▶ It's easy to use.
- ▶ It automatically handles all necessary memory allocation and deallocation.
- ▶ It can handle any data type.
- ▶ Its support for keys makes it easy to retrieve items based on the identifier of your choice.
- ▶ Like any other variable that supports objects, it handles object reference counting for you (so you don't have to worry that objects in a collection will vanish or be freed accidentally).
- ▶ Collections make it easy to transfer large amounts of data between objects—simply pass a reference to the collection.

Of course, the Collection object does have a number of disadvantages:

- ▶ It's so easy to use that sometimes it is used inappropriately.
- ▶ It imposes memory allocation and deallocation overhead that may not be necessary.
- ▶ Like any use of variants, it is less efficient and suffers performance limitations when compared to use of a specific data type.
- ▶ Objects are identified by variants containing either key strings or numeric indexes. When using an index you have the internal overhead involved in testing a variant. When using keys you have the overhead of allocating and deallocating strings.
- ▶ By holding references to objects, it may prevent an object from ever being freed if you do not handle cleanup properly.
- ▶ Collections make it easy to expose large amounts of data from your component, which can potentially be modified in dangerous ways by the component's client.

Call it the law of conservation of collections: for every advantage there is an equal and opposite disadvantage. If ever an object can be considered to be a double-edged sword, the Collection object is the one. So let's tackle some of these features and consider how and when they should really be used by component builders.

EVALUATION CRITERIA

You will face many situations in your components where you need to manage groups of objects (or other types of data). Visual Basic provides two mechanisms for doing this: collections and arrays.

When should you use arrays and when should you use collections? I can't tell you. You see, before you can decide which one is better for your application, you need to evaluate the task at hand by a number of criteria:

▸ How critical is performance? Are you willing to spend extra time coding to obtain better performance?

▸ How critical is development time? Will you take a performance penalty to finish your program more quickly?

▸ Are you exposing the objects to other applications or using the group only within your component. If the group is within your component, you have less need to implement a robust external interface with extensive type and error checking.

These criteria will be addressed in each of the sections that follow.

THE ~~THREE~~ FOUR APPROACHES TO EXPOSING COLLECTIONS IN COMPONENTS

The Microsoft documentation on collections discusses three approaches to working with collections of objects. The example used deals with managing a group of employees using a form. The three approaches are as follows.

In the House of Straw approach, the form uses a public Collection object to manage employee objects. This example shows how another part of the program can access this object and possibly add an invalid object to the collection.

In the House of Sticks approach, the form uses a private Collection object to manage employee objects and exposes a limited number of public methods and properties to allow other parts of the program to manipulate the collection. This makes the collection more robust as far as the rest of the program is concerned but does not protect the collection from bugs within the form code. It also makes it impossible to use the For…Each statement to iterate the collection.

In the House of Bricks approach, a separate collection class is created to manage employees.

Now, this is a fine example for what it is intended to show, which is different ways of grouping objects within an application. But this book focuses on developing components, and while these examples do apply within components, they miss a more critical issue. How can, and should, components expose groups of objects to client applications?

To demonstrate this, let's look at three examples that demonstrate the same principles on a component level.

THE HOUSE OF STRAW

As a breeder of prize rabbits, you've created an application to manage your breeding program. The Rabbit1.vbp component forms the basis of this application. It exposes a public object called PetStore1 that creates Rabbit1 objects. The PetStore1 module contains the following code:

```
' Guide to the Perplexed:
' Rabbit1 example
' Copyright (c) 1997 by Desaware Inc. All Rights Reserved

Option Explicit


' The petstore lets you buy a collection of rabbits
Public Function BuyRabbits(ByVal RabbitCount As Integer) As Collection
    Dim counter%
    Dim col As New Collection
    Dim obj As clsRabbit1
    ' Create the requested number of rabbits
    For counter = 1 To RabbitCount
        Set obj = New clsRabbit1
        col.Add obj
    Next counter
    ' Return a collection containing the rabbits
    Set BuyRabbits = col
End Function
```

This is a common technique for creating and retrieving a collection of objects.

The clsRabbit1 object describes a single rabbit and is quite simple. Each rabbit has a color and a number. Numbers are created sequentially as rabbits are born. The clsRabbit1 class module code is shown in the listing below.

```
' Guide to the Perplexed:
' Rabbit1 example
' Copyright (c) 1997 by Desaware Inc. All Rights Reserved

Option Explicit


' The color of the rabbit
Public Color As String
```

```
Private m_RabbitNumber As Long

Public Property Get Number() As Long
    Number = m_RabbitNumber
End Property

' We use a counter in a standard module to
' obtain a count of rabbit objects that have been
' created
Private Sub Class_Initialize()
    RabbitCounter = RabbitCounter + 1
    m_RabbitNumber = RabbitCounter
    ' Assign a random color
    Select Case Int(Rnd * 6)
        Case 0
            Color = "White"
        Case 1
            Color = "Pink"
        Case 2
            Color = "Grey"
        Case 3
            Color = "Blue"
        Case 4
            Color = "Brown"
        Case Else
            Color = "Black"
    End Select
    Debug.Print "Rabbit " & m_RabbitNumber & " born."
End Sub

Private Sub Class_Terminate()
    Debug.Print "Rabbit " & m_RabbitNumber & " died."
End Sub

' Inoculates this rabbit
Public Sub Inoculate()
    ' Doesn't actually do anything in this example
End Sub
```

The Color property is a string that contains the color of the rabbit. It is initialized randomly during the class initialization event. In a robust component you would probably implement this with a read-only property and a private variable, as is done here with the Number property and the m_RabbitNumber variable.

How can a class assign a sequential number to each object created? To do this you need a counter that is global to the project. The RabbitCounter variable is defined in module modRbt1.bas. The counter variable must be kept in a standard module because all global and static variables within a class module are associated with a single object of the class. The counter is incremented when an object is created during the class initialization function, and the current value assigned to a class member. Note that even this technique will not work with multithreaded servers—but that is a subject for Chapter 14.

The Class_Initialize and Class_Terminate events also use a debug.print statement to help you keep track of object creation and destruction. This combination of using a global variable to assign a unique object identifier and debug.print statements to track object creation and deletion is a common and useful technique which you will see more of in the next chapter.

Meanwhile, let's take a look at the test program, RbtTest1.vbp. This project contains a form and a single class module of its own that describes a Fox object. The frmRabbitTest form is shown in action in Figure 12.1.

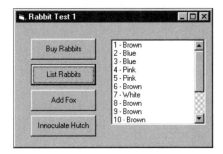

Figure 12.1: The RabbitTest form in action

This form contains four buttons and a list box. The Buy Rabbits command button, which triggers the cmdBuy_Click event is used to invoke the BuyRabbits method of the PetStore1 class. This loads the Hutch collection, which is a form module level variable. The following listing shows this and the rest of the form code.

```
' Guide to the Perplexed - Rabbit Test
' Copyright (c) 1997 by Desaware Inc. all Rights Reserved

Option Explicit

' We need a petstore to buy from
Dim PetStore As New PetStore1

' A hutch to hold rabbits we buy
Dim Hutch As Collection
```

```
' Buy some rabbits
Private Sub cmdBuy_Click()
    Set Hutch = PetStore.BuyRabbits(15)
End Sub

Public Sub ListRabbits()
    Dim obj As clsRabbit1

    lstRabbits.Clear    ' Clear the list
    For Each obj In Hutch
        lstRabbits.AddItem obj.Number & " - " & obj.color
    Next
End Sub

' List all rabbits in the hutch
Private Sub cmdList_Click()
    ListRabbits
End Sub

' This subroutine fakes a bug
Private Sub cmdAddFox_Click()
    Dim obj As New clsFox1
    Hutch.Add obj
End Sub

' Inoculate all rabbits
Private Sub cmdInoculate_Click()
    Dim obj As Object
    For Each obj In Hutch
        obj.Inoculate
    Next
End Sub
```

The ListRabbits button triggers the cmdList_Click event when clicked. This function displays the list of rabbits in the Hutch variable in a list box.

There are disadvantages to having the BuyRabbits method of the PetStore1 object return a collection. Because a collection can hold any type of object, it is possible for your code to accidentally add the wrong kind of object to the collection. This is demonstrated by clicking the Add Fox button to trigger the cmdAddFox_Click event. This function adds a clsFox1 object (one that belongs to the application) into the hutch.

After clicking on this button, try clicking on the ListRabbits and Inoculate hutch buttons. The ListRabbits function will fail during the enumeration of the hutch (the For…Each operation). Visual Basic will try to obtain a clsRabbit1 interface for the clsFox1 object during the enumeration because the obj enumeration variable is defined as type clsRabbit1. This will fail because the clsFox1 object does not have a clsRabbit1 interface. (You could make this work using the Implements statement, but what point is there in having a fox implement a rabbit?)

The cmdInoculate event will fail differently. With this function the obj enumeration object is defined *as object*, so it can refer to a clsFox1 object. This function does not fail until Visual Basic attempts a late-bound call to the Inoculate method. This method does not exist in the clsFox1 object, so an error will occur when VB attempts to invoke it.

These error scenarios are bad enough, but what would happen if, instead of returning a collection containing a hutch, the Hutch collection was instead exposed as a public property of the PetStore class? (In other words, your component manages the collection instead of having the form manage it.) Then you open the door to client applications placing illegal data into your component's variables—a very big problem.

What can we conclude from this? Objects in a component should never contain collection object variables that are public. Allowing client applications to arbitrarily access your component's collections is asking for trouble.

Returning Collection objects that are created by a component is not nearly as bad. At least your client application knows that the collection is valid when it receives it. Invalid data placed in the collection is likely to only impact the client application unless you provide a mechanism to pass the collection back to your component. If your component returns collections that are intended for temporary use, say, as a technique to provide a large amount of data to a client application quickly for it to examine, and it is unlikely that the client will hold the collection or add items to it, then returning collections is quite safe. It may not be worth your trouble to find an alternate approach.

THE HOUSE OF STICKS

A somewhat more robust example of this application can be created by placing the Hutch collection in the PetStore class. However, it is not exposed as a public variable (which would be equivalent to the preceding House of Straw example). Instead it is implemented as a private collection, and functions are added to the PetStore class as shown in the listing below. PetStore2 is part of projects Rabbit2.vbp and RbtTest2.vbp, which are part of the Rabbit2.vbg group. All of the file suffixes (except for the clsFox1 class, which remains unchanged) have been incremented from 1 to 2 for this example.

```
' Guide to the Perplexed:
' Rabbit1 example
' Copyright (c) 1997 by Desaware Inc. All Rights Reserved

Option Explicit

Private m_Hutch As Collection

' The petstore lets you buy a collection of rabbits
Public Sub BuyRabbits(ByVal RabbitCount As Integer)
    Dim counter%
    Dim col As New Collection
    Dim obj As clsRabbit2
    ' Create the requested number of rabbits
    For counter = 1 To RabbitCount
        Set obj = New clsRabbit2
        col.Add obj
    Next counter
    ' Return a collection containing the rabbits
    Set m_Hutch = col
End Sub


' Access items in the rabbit hutch
Public Function Hutch(ByVal idx%) As clsRabbit2
    Set Hutch = m_Hutch(idx)
End Function

' Retrieve the number of rabbits
Public Function RabbitCount()
    RabbitCount = m_Hutch.Count
End Function
```

Since you can no longer access the Hutch collection directly, it is necessary to implement a separate RabbitCount function to retrieve the number of items in the collection.

The clsRabbit2 object is essentially unchanged from the clsRabbit1 class (only the name has been changed). However, this approach does require changes in the RabbitTest form, as shown in the following listing.

```
' Guide to the Perplexed - Rabbit Test
' Copyright (c) 1997 by Desaware Inc. all Rights Reserved

Option Explicit
```

```
' We need a petstore to buy from
Dim PetStore As New PetStore2

' Buy some rabbits
Private Sub cmdBuy_Click()
    PetStore.BuyRabbits 15
End Sub

Public Sub ListRabbits()
    Dim obj As clsRabbit2
    Dim counter%

    lstRabbits.Clear      ' Clear the list
    For counter = 1 To PetStore.RabbitCount
        lstRabbits.AddItem PetStore.Hutch(counter).Number & " - " & _
        PetStore.Hutch(counter).color
    Next
End Sub

' This subroutine fakes a bug
Private Sub cmdAddFox_Click()
    MsgBox "Can't add a fox to a hutch"
End Sub

' Inoculate all rabbits
Private Sub CmdInoculate_Click()
    Dim obj As Object
    Dim counter%

    For counter = 1 To PetStore.RabbitCount
        PetStore.Hutch(counter).Inoculate
    Next
End Sub

' List all rabbits in the hutch
Private Sub cmdList_Click()
    ListRabbits
End Sub
```

The biggest advantage of this approach is that you can no longer add illegal objects to the Hutch collection because you no longer have access to that collection.

What is so wrong with this approach that Microsoft would slap the label House of Straw on it? Well, you can no longer use the For...Each operator to enumerate it. Second, while you no longer have to worry about insertion of invalid data by external clients you still need to worry about it within the PetStore2 class.

My gut reaction to both of these points is: big deal. Unless the PetStore2 class is extremely complex, chances are that you will not have problems with insertion of invalid objects into the collection, or that you will catch those problems early in the testing process.

And frankly, I have a hard time seeing what the fuss about the For...Each operator is in cases such as this one. It simply isn't that hard to implement the same functionality using a counter. Take a look at the code to inoculate all rabbits as implemented in the PetStore2 module:

```
' Enumerate Rabbits using For..Each
Public Sub InnoculateAll1()
    Dim obj As clsRabbit2
    For Each obj In m_Hutch
        obj.Inoculate
    Next
End Sub

' Enumerate Rabbits using counter
Public Sub InnoculateAll2()
    Dim obj As clsRabbit2
    Dim counter As Integer
    For counter = 1 To m_Hutch.Count
        Set obj = m_Hutch.Item(counter)
        obj.Inoculate
    Next
End Sub
```

The only other time where there is a significant difference between the approaches is when it is possible for an object to be deleted during the enumeration. In this case, the For...Each method is somewhat easier to implement because it automatically keeps track of the next object to be enumerated. With the counter approach you need to decrement the counter in order to avoid skipping objects.

So if you don't expect to need to reuse the code that manages groups of objects (in this case, rabbits), go ahead and implement them using this approach if you find it easier. Especially use it if you don't need to implement all of the functionality of a collection.

THE HOUSE OF BRICKS

The most robust solution to managing a group of objects may be to create your own collection that is designed specifically to handle those objects. Projects

Rabbit3.vbp and RbtTest3.vbp, which are part of the Rabbit3.vbg group, illustrate this technique. All files in this project have a numeric suffix of 3. This project goes back to the approach taken in the Rabbit1 groups, where the Hutch collection is a collection that is stored in a form variable and created and returned by the BuyRabbits method of the PetStore project. The difference is that instead of returning a generic collection, it returns a new collection called RabbitCollection3, shown in the following listing. The RabbitCollection3 object only holds clsRabbit3 objects. It uses an internal m_Hutch collection to hold the collection's data.

```
' Guide to the Perplexed - Rabbit Test
' Copyright (c) 1997 by Desaware Inc. all Rights Reserved

Option Explicit

'local variable to hold collection
Private m_Hutch As Collection

' Delegate to the collection
Public Sub Add()
    'create a new object
    Dim obj As New clsRabbit3
    m_Hutch.Add obj
End Sub

Public Property Get Count() As Long
    Count = m_Hutch.Count
End Property

Public Property Get Item(IndexKey As Long) As clsRabbit3
    Set Item = m_Hutch(IndexKey)
End Property

Public Sub Remove(IndexKey As Long)
    m_Hutch.Remove IndexKey
End Sub

' Enable For...Each support
Public Property Get NewEnum() As IUnknown
    Set NewEnum = m_Hutch.[_NewEnum]
End Property

' Initialize and destruct the internal collection

Private Sub Class_Initialize()
```

```
      Set m_Hutch = New Collection
End Sub

Private Sub Class_Terminate()
      Set m_Hutch = Nothing
End Sub
```

There are a number of advantages to this approach. First the NewEnum function allows you to use the For...Each operation to enumerate items in the collection. To use this you must have a public NewEnum property that returns an IUnknown object type (the generic interface for any object). This property obtains the _NewEnum property from the internal collection (you must surround it with brackets to handle the illegal underscore character, which indicates a hidden property). You must use the Procedure Attributes dialog box (under the Tools menu) to set the procedure ID (dispatch ID) for this property to -4. When Visual Basic sees this dispatch ID, it knows that it represents an enumerator. You should also set this property to be hidden.

The second advantage is that even though the internal m_Hutch collection within the RabbitCollection3 object can hold any type of object, the RabbitCollection3 object's Add method only allows you to add clsRabbit3 objects to the collection. This makes it impossible for the client application to add an invalid object to the collection.

Third, because all access to the internal m_Hutch collection is by way of methods and properties that you implement, you have complete control over the types of objects supported. You can do additional data validation and error checking as needed to maintain the robustness of the collection.

In addition, a private collection of this type is easily reusable. And the Visual Basic Class Builder Wizard can speed the process of building a custom collection class. Unlike the regular Class Builder Wizard, I've found that this one does save some time.

Finally, you need not limit yourself to the standard Collection object methods and properties when implementing your own collections. Any general purpose method that you might want to apply to all objects in the collection can and should be added to the collection class.

Let's look at this last feature more closely. For example: you might want to create a method that returns a new RabbitCollection3 object that only includes the White rabbits. To do this, add the following functions to the RabbitCollection3 class:

```
' The AddExisting function should not be exposed externally
Friend Sub AddExisting(ExistingRabbit As clsRabbit3)
   m_Hutch.Add ExistingRabbit
```

```
End Sub

' Function to obtain a new collection containing
' only white rabbits
Public Function GetWhiteRabbits() As RabbitCollection3
    Dim col As New RabbitCollection3
    Dim obj As clsRabbit3
    For Each obj In m_Hutch
        If obj.Color = "White" Then
            col.AddExisting obj
        End If
    Next
    Set GetWhiteRabbits = col
End Function
```

AddExisting is a project-only function that allows you to add an existing rabbit reference to the class (since the Add method creates a new rabbit from scratch). You can test this by adding the following code to the form:

```
' Obtain a list of white rabbits
Private Sub cmdWhite_Click()
    Set Hutch = Hutch.GetWhiteRabbits()
    ListRabbits
End Sub
```

There are some disadvantages to this approach as well. The major disadvantage is that there is more coding involved in this approach—slightly more than the House of Sticks approach and substantially more than just returning a collection. A minor disadvantage is the extra overhead in requiring two objects—the high level object and the contained collection object—for each collection.

Conclusion: If you are exposing a collection as a property from your component, always use a custom collection (though, as you will soon see, there may be better ways to implement it). If you are returning a collection that the client will be holding and working with, as is the case in this example, you should seriously consider this approach.

THE CUSTOM HOME

If you'll pardon my extending the analogy, all of the houses you've seen up to now are ultimately tract homes. They are based on the generic Collection object, which, like any tract house, is designed to satisfy most of the people most of the time. It usually works pretty well. It isn't necessarily the most efficient approach, and it may not have all of the features you want, but you can make do with it. It's good enough.

But if you have time to spare, or if you really want a home that fits you to a tee, nothing matches finding an architect and designing and building your dream house from scratch.

So much for analogies.

The Rabbit4.vbg program group contains two applications, Rabbit4.vbp and RbtTest4.vbp. Once again, all of the project files have had their suffix character incremented, in this case from 3 to 4. The DLL server in Rabbit4.vbp is similar to the one shown in the Rabbit3 project, except that it contains two different solutions to grouping clsRabbit4 objects. The RabbitCollection4 object is collection-based just like RabbitCollection3. Only three functions are changed. The GetWhiteRabbits( ) function shown here now returns a collection instead of another RabbitCollection4 object. This change was made to provide a fair comparison with the new array-based approach.

```
' Function to obtain a new collection containing
' only white rabbits
' We'll use a generic collection in this case
' to provide a fair comparison
Public Function GetWhiteRabbits() As Collection
    Dim col As New Collection
    Dim obj As clsRabbit4
    For Each obj In m_Hutch
        If obj.Color = "White" Then
            col.Add obj
        End If
    Next
    Set GetWhiteRabbits = col
End Function
```

A new SellRabbit function is used to remove a rabbit from the collection. It takes a clsRabbit4 object reference as a parameter and scans the collection to find the matching object. It then removes the matching object.

```
' Sell a specified rabbit
Public Function SellRabbit(rabbit As clsRabbit4) As Long
    Dim counter&
    Dim RabbitCount As Long
    ' Note simple optimization of taking m_Hutch.Count out of the loop
    RabbitCount = m_Hutch.Count
    For counter = 1 To RabbitCount
        If m_Hutch(counter) Is rabbit Then
            m_Hutch.Remove counter
            Exit Function
        End If
    Next counter
```

```
    SellRabbit = -1 ' API style error reporting
End Function
```

A completely different approach to collecting clsRabbit4 objects is in the RabbitArray4 class (RbtArry4.cls) shown in the next listing. In this class, the clsRabbit4 objects are kept in an array rather than in a collection. Because it uses an array, it cannot take advantage of all of the features of an embedded collection such as keys, support for the For…Each syntax, and support for any data type. However, this particular example does not require features such as keys, support for For…Each syntax and support for data types other than clsRabbit4 objects. Thus it avoids the overhead that collection objects must have to support these features. Could you add those features if you wish? Yes! You could use an array of variants to support any type of object. You could have a separate array of strings, longs, or variants to support keys. And you could use a third-party product, such as Desaware's SpyWorks, to add For…Each support to array-based collections.

```
' Guide to the Perplexed - Rabbit Test
' Copyright (c) 1997 by Desaware Inc. all Rights Reserved

Option Explicit

'local variable to hold array of rabbit objects
Private m_Hutch() As clsRabbit4
Private m_LastValidEntry As Long
Private m_HutchSize As Long

' Delegate to the collection
Public Sub Add()
    'create a new object
    Dim obj As New clsRabbit4
    ' Make sure array is large enough
    On Error GoTo AddResizeError
    If m_HutchSize = m_LastValidEntry Then
        ' Granularity on additions is arbitrary
        m_HutchSize = m_HutchSize + 4
        ReDim Preserve m_Hutch(m_HutchSize)
    End If
    m_LastValidEntry = m_LastValidEntry + 1
    Set m_Hutch(m_LastValidEntry) = obj
    Exit Sub
AddResizeError:
    ' Raise a memory allocation error here
End Sub
```

```
Public Property Get Count() As Long
    Count = m_LastValidEntry
End Property

Public Property Get Item(IndexKey As Long) As clsRabbit4
    Set Item = m_Hutch(IndexKey)
End Property

' Removes a rabbit at the specified position
Public Sub Remove(IndexKey As Long)
    Dim counter&
    If IndexKey < 0 Or IndexKey > m_LastValidEntry Then
        ' You would probably want to raise an error here
        Exit Sub
    End If
    For counter = IndexKey To m_LastValidEntry - 1
        Set m_Hutch(counter) = m_Hutch(counter + 1)
    Next counter
    Set m_Hutch(m_LastValidEntry) = Nothing
    m_LastValidEntry = m_LastValidEntry - 1
    ' Shrink the array to avoid accumulating too much space
    If m_LastValidEntry + 4 < m_HutchSize Then
        ReDim Preserve m_Hutch(m_LastValidEntry + 4)
        m_HutchSize = m_LastValidEntry + 4
    End If
End Sub

' Initialize and destruct the internal collection



' Clears all the objects in the array
Private Sub Class_Terminate()
    ReDim m_Hutch(0)
End Sub

' Function to obtain a new collection containing
' only white rabbits
' We'll use a generic collection in this case
' to provide a fair comparison
Public Function GetWhiteRabbits() As Collection
    Dim col As New Collection
    Dim counter&
    For counter = 1 To m_LastValidEntry
        ' Array itself is early bound by definition
        If m_Hutch(counter).Color = "White" Then
            col.Add m_Hutch(counter)
        End If
```

```
    Next counter

    Set GetWhiteRabbits = col
End Function

' Sell a specified rabbit
Public Function SellRabbit(rabbit As clsRabbit4) As Long
    Dim counter&
    Dim RabbitCount As Long
    For counter = 1 To m_LastValidEntry
        If m_Hutch(counter) Is rabbit Then
            ' The class method does the removal
            Remove counter
            Exit Function
        End If
    Next counter
End Function
```

The Add function first increases the size of the m_Hutch array. It keeps track of the number of objects in the array separately from the size of the array. When you add an object into the collection, the Add routine first checks to see if space is available by comparing the m_HutchSize variable to the m_LastValidEntry variable. If new space needs to be allocated, the function uses the ReDim statement with the Preserve option to preserve the current values in the array. It redimensions the array size to a larger size than is actually needed to hold the new item. This is because the object assumes that if you add one object, you are likely to add more. By allocating four spaces in the array each time, you potentially reduce the number of redimension operations by a factor of four.

This is a typical memory vs. performance trade-off, risking a potential waste of memory space to improve performance. Most array-based collections use this technique. The number of extra spaces to allocate is up to you to determine. Larger values waste additional memory but can lead to even further improvements in performance.

The Count and Item properties are identical to the collection-based approach.

The Remove property is somewhat more complex. Since there is no embedded collection to delegate the operation to, you must remove the object from the array yourself. This particular implementation does not allow for empty spaces in the array, so once the location to delete has been found, all subsequent objects in the array are moved forward.

The GetWhiteRabbits function is virtually identical to that of the Rabbit-Collection4 object. One difference has to do with the internal access to the collection or array. With an internal collection, you must assign the object you are working with to an object variable with the clsRabbit4 type. This is demonstrated in the RabbitCollection4 objects using the For…Each construct as follows:

```
Dim obj As clsRabbit4
For Each obj In m_Hutch
```

If you do not do this, access to the object will be late bound, which will have a significant impact on performance. With the array approach shown in the RabbitArray4 object, this is not necessary. All access to items in the array can be early bound because they are already defined as clsRabbit4 objects. Thus the line

```
If m_Hutch(counter).Color = "White" Then
```

is early bound. The SellRabbit function takes an object reference as a parameter, searches for it in the array, and removes it once found.

Both the RabbitCollection4 and RabbitArray4 objects provide exactly the same functionality. Which one works better?

Performance Testing Benchmarking is always tricky. The RbtTest4 project attempts to provide a fair comparison between the collection and array-based approaches. The code listing can be found in the following listing.

```
' Guide to the Perplexed - Rabbit Test
' Copyright (c) 1997 by Desaware Inc. all Rights Reserved

Option Explicit

' We need a petstore to buy from
Dim PetStore As New PetStore4

' Once again we hold the collection
Dim Hutch1 As RabbitCollection4
' But this time we have an array as well
Dim Hutch2 As RabbitArray4

' Buy some rabbits
Private Sub cmdBuy_Click()
    Dim tempdouble As Double
    Dim repetitions As Long
    repetitions = 1
    Dim counter As Long

    ' We use a clsElapsedTime object to measure the time
    Dim time1 As New clsElapsedTime
    Dim time2 As New clsElapsedTime
```

```
    tempdouble = Rnd(-1)     ' Reset random number sequence
    time1.StartTheClock
    For counter = 1 To repetitions
        Set Hutch1 = PetStore.BuyRabbits(10000)
    Next counter
    time1.StopTheClock
    tempdouble = Rnd(-1)     ' Reset random number sequence
    time2.StartTheClock
    For counter = 1 To repetitions
        Set Hutch2 = PetStore.BuyRabbitArray(10000)
    Next counter
    time2.StopTheClock
    lstRabbits.AddItem "Collection Adds: " & time1.Elapsed(repetitions) _
    & " ms/10000"
    lstRabbits.AddItem "Array Adds: " & time2.Elapsed(repetitions) & " ms/10000"
End Sub

' Sell starting at the beginning of the collection
Private Sub cmdSell_Click()
    Dim time1 As New clsElapsedTime
    Dim time2 As New clsElapsedTime
    Dim col1 As Collection
    Dim col2 As Collection
    Dim obj As clsRabbit4
    Set col1 = Hutch1.GetWhiteRabbits
    Set col2 = Hutch2.GetWhiteRabbits
    If col1.Count = 0 Then Exit Sub
    time1.StartTheClock
    Call Hutch1.SellRabbit(col1(1))
    time1.StopTheClock
    time2.StartTheClock
    Call Hutch2.SellRabbit(col2(1))
    time2.StopTheClock
    lstRabbits.AddItem "Sell White Col: " & time1.Elapsed() & " ms"
    lstRabbits.AddItem "Sell White Array: " & time2.Elapsed() & " ms"

End Sub

' Sell starting at the end of the collection
Private Sub cmdSell2_Click()
    Dim time1 As New clsElapsedTime
    Dim time2 As New clsElapsedTime
    Dim col1 As Collection
    Dim col2 As Collection
    Dim obj As clsRabbit4
    Set col1 = Hutch1.GetWhiteRabbits
    Set col2 = Hutch2.GetWhiteRabbits
```

```
        time1.StartTheClock
        Call Hutch1.SellRabbit(col1(col1.Count))
        time1.StopTheClock
        time2.StartTheClock
        Call Hutch2.SellRabbit(col2(col2.Count))
        time2.StopTheClock
        lstRabbits.AddItem "Sell White Col: " & time1.Elapsed() & " ms"
        lstRabbits.AddItem "Sell White Array: " & time2.Elapsed() & " ms"
End Sub

' Time to extract the white rabbits
Private Sub cmdWhite_Click()
        Dim time1 As New clsElapsedTime
        Dim time2 As New clsElapsedTime
        Dim col1 As Collection
        Dim col2 As Collection
        Dim repetitions As Long
        Dim counter As Long
        repetitions = 5
        time1.StartTheClock
        For counter = 1 To repetitions
            Set col1 = Hutch1.GetWhiteRabbits
        Next counter
        time1.StopTheClock
        time2.StartTheClock
        For counter = 1 To repetitions
            Set col2 = Hutch2.GetWhiteRabbits
        Next counter
        time2.StopTheClock
        lstRabbits.AddItem "Find White Col: " & time1.Elapsed(repetitions) & _
        " ms/" & col1.Count
        lstRabbits.AddItem "Find White Array: " & time2.Elapsed(repetitions) & _
        " ms/" & col2.Count
End Sub


Private Sub Form_Unload(Cancel As Integer)
        Set Hutch1 = Nothing
        Set Hutch2 = Nothing
End Sub
```

This test program contains two module level variables, Hutch1, which uses the RabbitCollection4 object, and Hutch2, which uses the RabbitArray4 object. These objects are loaded with 10000 clsRabbit4 objects by the cmdBuy_Click command. There is a call to the function Rnd(-1) in the PetStore BuyRabbits and BuyRabbitArray routines that create the rabbit lists. This is because each list uses random numbers to assign colors, and the positions and numbers of rabbit colors will have an impact on later tests. The Rnd(-1) call resets the random number list so that both Hutch1 and Hutch2 will contain the exact same rabbit types.

The times to load the collections are measured using two clsElapsedTime objects. These objects are based on the elapsed time code that was used in early examples in the book. I finally decided I was using it often enough to turn it into a reusable class. The listing for this object can be seen in the following listing. The initial time is set using the StartTheClock method and the ending time using the StopTheClock method. The Elapsed method returns a string containing the elapsed time in milliseconds.

```
' Elapsed time class
' Copyright (c) 1997 by Desaware Inc. All Rights Reserved

Option Explicit

Private Declare Function GetTickCount& Lib "kernel32" ()

Private m_CreationTime As Long
Private m_StopTime As Long


' Update the creation time. This should always
' be called because class initialization is not
' as controllable.
Public Sub StartTheClock()
    m_CreationTime = GetTickCount()
End Sub

' Mark the stop time. This is called automatically
' the first time you request the elapsed time for an
' object.
Public Sub StopTheClock()
    m_StopTime = GetTickCount()
End Sub

' Get a formatted string for the time in microseconds
Public Function Elapsed(Optional ByVal repetitions As Long = 1) As String
    Dim timeval As Long
    If m_StopTime = 0 Then StopTheClock
    timeval = m_StopTime - m_CreationTime
    ' timeval <0 indicates StartTheClock was never called
    ' You could raise an error here instead
```

```
    If timeval < Ø Then timeval = Ø
    ' timeval is the difference in milliseconds
    Elapsed = Format$(CDbl(timeval) / repetitions, "Ø.###")
End Function
```

There are four buttons on the form, as shown in Figure 12.2. Each one corresponds to a benchmark test. You should click the Buy Many Rabbits button before any of the others to load the Hutch1 and Hutch2 objects. The Find White button measures the time it takes to scan through the list and build a collection of clsRabbit4 objects whose color property is White. This allows you to compare the time to both scan a list and perform a property comparison.

There are two buttons that remove clsRabbit4 objects from the collections. The Sell First White Rabbit command removes the first white rabbit found. The Sell Last White Rabbit button removes the last rabbit. As you will soon see, there is a significant difference between the two.

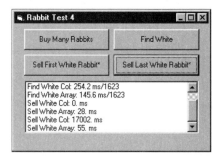

Figure 12.2: The RabbitTest4 program in action

Results   Before performing the test you should compile both the DLL and the test executable using the native code compilation option. This provides the fairest test between the two approaches. In fact, it is this kind of low-level operation that can often benefit most from native code.

Table 12.1 shows results of these tests on my test system. (Your results probably will differ.) Like all benchmarks, you need to use care interpreting these results.

The Buy Many Rabbits operation is about 10 percent faster with the array-based approach. Does this mean that the array approach is only marginally faster than the embedded collection approach in general? No. Keep in mind that this delay includes the overhead of the BuyRabbit and BuyRabbitArray functions in the PetStore object. It also contains the overhead involved in the creation of clsRabbit4 objects, which includes a string assignment during color assignment. This overhead takes up a substantial percentage of the total time,

Table 12.1: Result Times for the RabbitTest4 Project

Command	Collection-Based	Array-Based
Buy Many Rabbits	3816	2774
Find White Rabbits	248	126
Sell First White Rabbit	0	30
Sell Last White Rabbit	16554	30

which suggests that if you were to only measure the performance of a simple Add operation using both techniques, the array approach would be substantially faster than the collection approach.

The array approach is about 50 percent faster than the collection approach when it comes to scanning the array and extracting a specific type of object. The cmdWhite_Click function actually performs the operation five times and divides the result by five in order to obtain more accurate values.

The rabbit removal results differ radically depending on whether you are removing an object at the beginning of the list or at the end of the list. The results suggest that collections are extremely efficient at removing objects that are towards the start of a collection. The array approach is least efficient when it comes to objects at the start of the array because while they are found quickly, all of the rest of the objects in the array need to be moved to fill in the space that is freed in the array by the missing object.

It is truly shocking how the performance of the collection approach degrades when it comes to removing objects at the end of the collection. Because the internal implementation of collection objects is hidden, there is no way to tell exactly why this problem occurs, but the results here show that the collection approach is 250 times slower than the array approach in this example.

Conclusions   Do these results suggest that you should avoid collection objects and implement your own collections using arrays instead? Not necessarily. It does look as if collections containing thousands of objects may be too slow to be practical, but this does not mean that they are not useful for smaller numbers of objects. The array-based approach did require additional coding and testing. And the amount of code increases dramatically as you implement more of the features of a collection.

In fact, with the exception of the For...Each support, you could implement an exact clone of the collection object using Visual Basic. With a third-party product such as Desaware's SpyWorks, you could implement For..Each support as well. In fact, you can do so with more flexibility than is possible with a standard collection because it gives you full control over the enumeration order and insertion/deletion handling.

If you did decide to implement an exact clone of the Visual Basic collection object using VB, I suspect you would find that the performance is no better than the one provided with VB. The benefits of the array approach come from the fact that in most cases you do not need to implement all of the features of a collection.

Clearly there is a development time vs. performance trade-off to consider here. You will have to make your own call based on the needs of your own applications.

The true power of the array-based approach is that it is infinitely customizable. You can apply traditional computer science techniques, such as linked lists, binary searches, and hash tables to optimize searching, insertion, or deletion instead of depending on the trade-offs Microsoft chose for the Collection object.

You have the flexibility to define your own keying scheme or use multiple keys. For example: the Collection object key is always string-based, meaning that every key-based operation requires string comparisons or string allocation and deallocation. If your application can use a numeric key, you can achieve significant improvements in performance by using an array-based collection with your own keying scheme.

Keep in mind that a well-designed private collection class should be reusable, so the extra investment it demands for the initial implementation may pay off in the long run.

Finally, you can see in this example one of the overwhelming advantages of object-oriented programming. Did you notice that the RabbitTest form code that handles the Hutch1 and Hutch2 variables is identical (except for the place where they are created)? This means when you are creating a private collection it is quite practical to first implement a collection-based solution, then change it later to an array-based solution to improve performance!

Remember that with COM objects all you need to do is preserve the interface—the implementation can be changed at will.

If you are not sure whether you are writing performance-critical code, go ahead and take the easier collection-based approach and avoid using the For…Each operator. You can then change your mind later without changing any code outside of the object's class module. If the object is in a DLL, you won't even need to recompile the client applications.

You may also notice that this sample program seems to take forever to close. This is because when you close the test form, all of the objects (all 20000 of them in both Hutch1 and Hutch2) need to be deleted.

Speaking of deletion, in the current RabbitTest example, the only way to sell a rabbit is to call a Sell operation on one of the Hutch variables. Logically, you would think it would be possible to add a Sell function to the clsRabbit4 object itself. Of course to do this, the clsRabbit4 object would have to keep track of which collection it is in. (A rabbit shouldn't really be in two hutches at once.) The idea may seem simple, but as you will see in the next chapter, this idea opens the door to one of the most important, potentially confusing, and often frustrating subjects relating to ActiveX component development: object referencing.

Object Lifetime

REFERENCING

CIRCULAR REFERENCES

SELECTED TOPICS

13

When you've worked with objects for a while, they almost seem to take on lives of their own. Objects are born, they spin around your system for a while, then they die. Sometimes, however, they can get a little bit out of control. You have to be careful to kill them off when you're done with them or they can clutter up your system, taking up resources that other objects need. (Don't worry though, I know of no major religion that has an ethical problem with killing off COM objects whenever you feel like it.)

Killing off objects can be tricky. Keeping track of where they are referenced and remembering to clear those references when necessary is hard enough. The real challenge, however, is designing an object model that makes it possible to do so. It is all too easy to define an object model that will give your objects near immortality.

REFERENCING

Chapter 4 introduced the idea of object variables and how they work. Let's take a moment to quickly review this subject.

Object variables are different from other types of variables. The major difference is that unlike regular variables, object variables do not actually hold any data. Instead they contain a pointer to one of the interfaces for an object.

Consider the process of declaring two data variables and assigning one to another. Figure 13.1 shows two string variables, variable A and variable B. Variable A is initially loaded with the string "Data in A", and B with the string "Data in B". Both variables actually contain the string data. When you assign B to A using the term A = B, the data from variable B is copied into A.

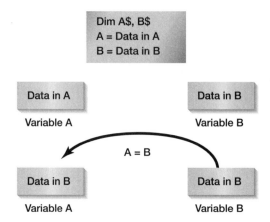

Figure 13.1: Data variable assignment

Figure 13.2 illustrates the same operation with object variables. The two variables contain pointers to the interfaces of the object variables. Each object variable keeps track of how many different variables point to the object. Initially, each object is referenced by one object, and thus has a reference count of 1.

When you perform the assignment operation: Set A=B, the operation that is performed goes beyond a simple assignment. First, Visual Basic must perform a release operation on the ObjectA interface. This decrements the reference count for the object to 0 and causes the object to be destroyed. When variable A is loaded with a pointer to ObjectB, an AddRef operation is performed on the ObjectB interface. This increases its reference count to 2.

WHAT HAPPENS WHEN...?

Let's take a look at what actually happens when some common Visual Basic object operations take place. The code for this section can be found in sample application Test1.vbp in the Chapter 13 sample directory on your CD-ROM. First, consider the process of declaring an object variable:

```
Private Sub cmdStart1_Click()
    Dim A As myobject

    Debug.Print "A is declared"
    If A Is Nothing Then
        Debug.Print "A is nothing"
    End If
End Sub
```

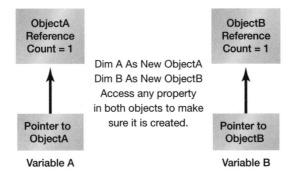

Dim A As New ObjectA
Dim B As New ObjectB
Access any property
in both objects to make
sure it is created.

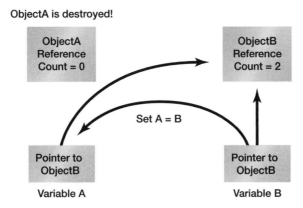

Figure 13.2: Object variable assignment

The object myobject is a simple object that contains Debug.Print statements in its Class_Initialize and Class_Terminate event to let you see when the object is created or destroyed. It contains a Name property to help identify individual objects.

In this case variable A is declared. But it does not point to an object. Internally, its pointer value is zero, which is an invalid pointer address. But this invalid address is not considered an error; it is a way of telling Visual Basic and your program that the variable has not been assigned to an object. This zero pointer is given a special name in Visual Basic called Nothing. So at this point in time, variable A is said to be equal to Nothing. You can test this using the operation: "If A Is Nothing Then…". In this case you will get the message "A is nothing" because A has never been assigned to an object. If you tried to access a property of variable A (such as A.Name) you would get an error because you cannot access a property of an object that does not exist.

Let's look at the cmdStart2_Click example:

```
Private Sub cmdStart2_Click()
    Dim A As New myobject

    Debug.Print "A is declared"
    MsgBox "Look at the immediate window"
    Debug.Print "Message box returns"
    If A Is Nothing Then
        Debug.Print "A is nothing"
    Else
        Debug.Print "A is valid"
    End If

End Sub
```

The big difference between this sample and the previous one is that A is declared with the New operator. When you run the program, you will see the following display in the Immediate window:

```
A is declared
Message box returns
Object is created
A is valid
Object is destroyed
```

One thing that might seem odd about this sequence is that the New operator does not actually create the object. It does, however, tell Visual Basic that any time you access the variable it should create a new object if one does not exist. When is the variable accessed in this example? When you perform the comparison to Nothing. In fact, a variable declared with the New operator will never be equal to Nothing—Visual Basic will create new objects any time you try to reference it. This can be seen in the following code:

```
Private Sub cmdStart3_Click()
    Dim A As New myobject

    Debug.Print "A is declared"
    If A Is Nothing Then
        Debug.Print "A is nothing"
    Else
        Debug.Print "A is valid"
    End If

    Set A = Nothing
```

```
If A Is Nothing Then
    Debug.Print "A is nothing"
Else
    Debug.Print "A is valid"
End If

End Sub
```

The result in the Immediate window is as follows:

```
A is declared
Object is created
A is valid
Object is destroyed
Object is created
A is valid
Object is destroyed
```

The first object is destroyed when you perform the operation: Set A = Nothing, but as soon as you try to test the object variable again, VB creates a new one.

Remember I mentioned earlier that killing objects in Visual Basic can be challenging. As you can see, keeping them dead can be tricky as well. This may not seem like a big deal, but what if your object performs extensive initialization and termination operations when it is created and destroyed? If you aren't careful, you might find that your application is wasting quite a bit of processing time creating and destroying objects that you never actually use. The cmdStart4_Click example demonstrates a way to avoid this problem:

```
Private Sub cmdStart4_Click()
    Dim A As myobject

    Debug.Print "A is declared"

    If A Is Nothing Then
        Debug.Print "A is nothing"
    Else
        Debug.Print "A is valid"
    End If

    Debug.Print "About to call Set A = New myobject"
    Set A = New myobject
    Debug.Print "Set A = New myobject called"

    If A Is Nothing Then
        Debug.Print "A is nothing"
    Else
```

```
        Debug.Print "A is valid"
    End If

    Set A = Nothing

    If A Is Nothing Then
        Debug.Print "A is nothing"
    Else
        Debug.Print "A is valid"
    End If

End Sub
```

This function produces the following results:

```
A is declared
A is nothing
About to call Set A = New myobject
Object is created
Set A = New myobject called
A is valid
Object is destroyed
A is nothing
```

The declaration does not create the object, and the object is not automatically created when it is accessed. It is created by the call to Set A = New myobject. Because the object is not set to be automatically created on access, it remains dead after you have set the variable to Nothing.

Generally speaking it is better to take this approach instead of dimensioning variables with the New operator. It provides you with better control over the lifetimes of objects.

Along the way you may have noticed that the object is always destroyed when the function exists. This happens because variable A is local to the function and its lifetime is limited to the duration of the function call. When the function exists, the variable is destroyed, and with it the object that it points to.

Now let's take a moment and verify the operation shown in Figure 13.2 with the code shown in the cmdStart5_Click routine:

```
Private Sub cmdStart5_Click()
    Dim A As myobject
    Dim B As myobject
    Set A = New myobject
    Set B = New myobject
    Debug.Print "A and B are set"
    A.Name = "Object A"
    B.Name = "Object B"
    Debug.Print "Name properties are set"
```

```
    Debug.Print "About to Set A=B"
    Set A = B
    Debug.Print "Set A=B done"
End Sub
```

This function produces the following results:

```
Object is created
Object is created
A and B are set
Name properties are set
About to Set A=B
Object ObjectA is destroyed
Set A=B done
Object ObjectB is destroyed
```

As you can see, the Set A = B operation does, in fact, cause object A to be destroyed.

The secret to making sure your objects are destroyed is to know where they are being referenced. But, as you are about to see, this is sometimes easier said than done.

CIRCULAR REFERENCES

It's remarkably easy to demonstrate a circular reference. Just add the line:

```
Public CircularReference as myobject
```

to the myobject class (this is already done in the test1.vbp project). Use of this property is shown in the cmdStart6_Click function:

```
Private Sub cmdStart6_Click()
    Dim A As myobject
    Set A = New myobject
    Debug.Print "About to set circular reference"
    Set A.CircularReference = A
    Debug.Print "About to set A to Nothing"
    Set A = Nothing
    Debug.Print "A is Nothing"
End Sub
```

The resulting display in the Immediate window when you run this function is as follows:

```
Object is created
About to set circular reference
About to set A to Nothing
A is Nothing
```

The object is not destroyed. Why? Because when you execute the line Set A.CircularReference = A, you set a second variable to point to the object. The fact that the variable is part of the object itself is irrelevant. The reference count for the object is still set to two.

When you set variable A to Nothing, the reference count is decremented to 1, but this is not enough to destroy the object. The object continues to live on, even though it can no longer be accessed anywhere in your program. (All of the variables referencing the object that are not part of the object itself have been cleared.) This object will continue to exist until you terminate the application. You can see this if you close the frmTest1 form (do not use the VB Stop command). The object will finally be destroyed as the application closes.

Of course, you are unlikely to have objects referencing themselves, other than by accident. So why are circular references a concern? To see this, let us take another look at our rabbit breeding program from Chapter 12.

OBJECT MODEL DILEMMAS

The rabbit breeding examples were intended to demonstrate issues relating to grouping of objects. No real effort was made to design a useful object model for the example. Circular references do not happen by accident—they result from design choices. So let's take another look at the rabbit tests, but this time turn our attention to the object model. To keep things simple, we'll start with the Rabbit3.vbp project (which was collection-based) because the method of grouping rabbit objects is irrelevant to this example. All files have been re-named with the suffix 5 instead of 3.

The rabbit class, now renamed clsRabbit5.cls, can remain unchanged for now. Each rabbit has a unique number and a color. The number of possible colors has been reduced to make the sample programs easier to follow. The Debug.Print statements are enabled so that we can track rabbit creation and sales.

By the way, for the purposes of this example, "selling" a rabbit is a nice way of saying that a rabbit object has been destroyed. Killing rabbits seemed a bit harsh for a family-oriented programming book.

The RabbitCollection5 class contains a hutch of rabbits—a group of clsRabbit5 objects. Now, we're going to invent a rule for this object model: that each clsRabbit5 object can only be in one RabbitCollection5 object at a time. This makes sense, because it would be a very talented rabbit indeed who could be in two rabbit hutches at once. There is no code yet to enforce this rule; it's just a design requirement. When we implement the code, any combination of operations that would let a clsRabbit5 object exist in two RabbitCollect5 collections at once will be considered illegal, and possibly a bug.

We're going to want to come up with a way to transfer rabbits from one RabbitCollection5 hutch to another. We're going to need a way to remove a rabbit from a RabbitCollection5 hutch (through sale or transfer to another collection).We're still going to need a way to obtain a list of rabbits of a given type. However, the resulting list will be returned as a regular collection, not a RabbitCollection5 collection. Why? Because if we returned it in a RabbitCollection5 collection, we would be violating the earlier rule that no rabbit be in two RabbitCollection5 collections at once.

Listing 13.1 shows the initial implementation for the RabbitCollection5 class.

Listing 13.1: The RabbitCollection5 Class Module

```
' Guide to the Perplexed - Rabbit Test
' Copyright (c) 1997 by Desaware Inc. all Rights Reserved

Option Explicit

'local variable to hold collection
Private m_Hutch As Collection

' Add an existing rabbit or create a new one
Public Sub Add(Optional obj As clsRabbit5)
    ' If no object was passed, create a new one
    If obj Is Nothing Then Set obj = New clsRabbit5
    m_Hutch.Add obj
End Sub


Public Property Get Count() As Long
    Count = m_Hutch.Count
End Property


Public Property Get Item(IndexKey As Long) As clsRabbit3
    Set Item = m_Hutch(IndexKey)
End Property


Public Sub Remove(IndexKey As Long)
    m_Hutch.Remove IndexKey
End Sub

' Find the index for an object in the collection
Public Function Find(findobj As clsRabbit5)
    Dim obj As clsRabbit5
```

Listing 13.1: The RabbitCollection5 Class Module (Continued)

```
    Dim counter&
    For counter = 1 To m_Hutch.Count
        If m_Hutch(counter) Is findobj Then
            Find = counter
            Exit Function
        End If
    Next counter
End Function


' Enable For...Each support
Public Property Get NewEnum() As IUnknown
    Set NewEnum = m_Hutch.[_NewEnum]
End Property


' Initialize and destruct the internal collection

Private Sub Class_Initialize()
    Set m_Hutch = New Collection
End Sub


Private Sub Class_Terminate()
    Set m_Hutch = Nothing
End Sub


' Function to obtain a new collection containing
' only white rabbits
Public Function GetWhiteRabbits() As Collection
    Dim col As New Collection
    Dim obj As clsRabbit3
    For Each obj In m_Hutch
        If obj.Color = "White" Then
            col.Add obj
        End If
    Next
    Set GetWhiteRabbits = col
End Function
```

There are a few changes from the original RabbitCollection3 implementation from Chapter 12. The Add method now allows you to add an existing clsRabbit5 object to the hutch. This capability will be necessary to transfer rabbits from one collection to another. Why not use the separate AddExisting method from the Chapter 12 example? No reason—it's another way of accomplishing the same thing.

A new Find method can be used to obtain the index of a clsRabbit5 object in the collection. The GetWhiteRabbits method returns a collection containing references to all of the white rabbits in the RabbitCollection5 collection.

The RabbitTest5 application (project RbtTest5.vbp) demonstrates the use of the modified classes. The main form for the application is shown in Figure 13.3. The listing for the form module is shown in Listing 13.2.

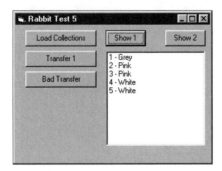

Figure 13.3: RabbitTest5 main form in action

Listing 13.2: Code for Form frmRabbitTest5

```
' Guide to the Perplexed - Rabbit5 example
' Copyright (c) 1997 by Desaware Inc. All Rights Reserved

Option Explicit

' Define two hutches
Dim Hutch1 As RabbitCollection5
Dim Hutch2 As RabbitCollection5
Dim PetStore As New PetStore5

' Load the two Hutch variables
Private Sub cmdLoad_Click()
    Set Hutch1 = PetStore.BuyRabbits(5)
    Set Hutch2 = PetStore.BuyRabbits(5)
End Sub

' Display contents of a Hutch variable
Private Sub cmdShow_Click(Index As Integer)
    Dim obj As clsRabbit5
    Dim UseHutch As RabbitCollection5
    ' Get the right hutch to display
```

Listing 13.2: Code for Form frmRabbitTest5 (Continued)

```
    If Index = 1 Then
        Set UseHutch = Hutch1
    Else
        Set UseHutch = Hutch2
    End If
    lstRabbits.Clear
    For Each obj In UseHutch
        lstRabbits.AddItem obj.Number & " - " & obj.Color
    Next
End Sub


' Transfer first rabbit from hutch1 to hutch2
Private Sub cmdTransfer1_Click()
    Dim obj As clsRabbit5
    Set obj = Hutch1(1)
    Hutch1.Remove 1
    Hutch2.Add obj
End Sub
```

The LoadCollections button loads the two Hutch variables with five rabbits each. The Show 1 and Show 2 buttons list the contents of the corresponding Hutch variable into the list box. The Transfer1 button moves the first rabbit from Hutch1 into the Hutch2 collection. You can experiment with the Show buttons to verify the operation of this code.

While this code does work correctly, it is clear that it suffers from a major design flaw within the object model.

We defined a rule that no rabbit can be in two RabbitCollection5 objects at once. But there is nothing in the object model to enforce the rule. If you forgot to remove the clsRabbit object from the first hutch, it would appear in both at once. Worse, you could add the same clsRabbit object multiple times to the same hutch if you wanted to. You can see this in the cmdBadTransfer_Click() routine in the RabbitTest5 sample program. This type of cloning may be fun in software, but it is not yet a biological possibility. So while this approach may be fine for your own use (assuming you or the programmers working with you are very careful), the lack of enforcement to the design rules makes it a poor design.

ENFORCING OBJECT MODEL RULES

The demonstration will now continue with the Rabbit6 project group, which contains the Rabbit6 server project and RabbitTest6 test program (project RbtTest6.vbp).

Adding enforcement to the rule that a clsRabbit6 object exist in only one RabbitCollection6 collection at once requires that the server be aware of all Rabbit6Collections that exist. Otherwise there is no possible way to determine which collection contains which clsRabbit6 objects. How can this be accomplished? There are two fundamental approaches you can use.

▸ Keep a list of all of the RabbitCollection6 objects at a global or higher level.

▸ Have each clsRabbit6 object keep track of which RabbitCollection6 object is holding it.

We're going to avoid discussing the global approach for now. A sample of this approach is included in the StockMonitor application in Chapter 15 (see, I haven't forgotten it).

Besides, there is a certain logical elegance to having each clsRabbit6 object know where it is. From a conceptual point of view, it makes sense that an object should know where it is, just as it makes sense that a location should know which objects it is holding. As a VB programmer you are well acquainted with this idea, though you may not recognize it. Visual Basic controls have *Parent* properties that allow them to access the methods and properties of the form or control that contains them. This is exactly the same situation (and you can be sure that Visual Basic does some work behind the scenes to avoid some of the side effects you are about to see).

Keep Track of the Container   This approach has each clsRabbit6 keep track of the RabbitCollection6 object that is holding it. This is done by adding a private object variable to the clsRabbit6 object and exposing it through two property procedures as follows:

```
Private m_Hutch As RabbitCollection6
' Anyone can find out which hutch contains the rabbit
Public Property Get Hutch() As RabbitCollection6
    Set Hutch = m_Hutch
End Property

' Only code within the project can set the Hutch for a rabbit
Friend Property Let Hutch(vNewValue As RabbitCollection6)
    Set m_Hutch = vNewValue
End Property
```

The Let property procedure is a Friend function. There is no problem with letting clients that are using your object model determine which hutch a rabbit is in, but you don't want clients to be able to set the rabbit's hutch without calling the appropriate method in the RabbitCollection6 object. This allows the RabbitCollection6 object to enforce the object model rules. The Rabbit-Collection6 object is modified to enforce the rules as shown in Listing 13.3.

Listing 13.3: The RabbitCollection6 Class Module

```
' Guide to the Perplexed - Rabbit Test
' Copyright (c) 1997 by Desaware Inc. all Rights Reserved

Option Explicit

'local variable to hold collection
Private m_Hutch As Collection

' Add an existing rabbit or create a new one
Public Sub Add(Optional obj As clsRabbit6)
    Dim IndexToRemove As Long

    ' If no object was passed, create a new one
    If obj Is Nothing Then
        Set obj = New clsRabbit6
    Else
        If Find(obj) > 0 Then
            RaiseError 0    ' Object exists error
        End If
    End If

    m_Hutch.Add obj

    ' Set the hutch for the rabbit
    If Not obj.Hutch Is Nothing Then
        ' When object belonging to a hutch is added
        ' to a new hutch, remove it from the other one
        IndexToRemove = obj.Hutch.Find(obj)
        obj.Hutch.Remove IndexToRemove
    End If
    ' And always have the object refer to this hutch
    obj.Hutch = Me
End Sub


Public Property Get Count() As Long
    Count = m_Hutch.Count
End Property
```

Listing 13.3: The RabbitCollection6 Class Module (Continued)

```
Public Property Get Item(IndexKey As Long) As clsRabbit6
    If IndexKey < 1 Or IndexKey > m_Hutch.Count Then
        RaiseError 1
    End If
    Set Item = m_Hutch(IndexKey)
End Property


' Remove an object from the hutch
Public Sub Remove(IndexKey As Long)
    Dim obj As clsRabbit6
    If IndexKey < 1 Or IndexKey > m_Hutch.Count Then
        RaiseError 1
    End If
    Set obj = m_Hutch(IndexKey)
    ' Remove object from this hutch
    obj.Hutch = Nothing
    m_Hutch.Remove IndexKey
End Sub


' Find the index for an object in the collection
Public Function Find(findobj As clsRabbit6)
    Dim obj As clsRabbit6
    Dim counter&
    For counter = 1 To m_Hutch.Count
        If m_Hutch(counter) Is findobj Then
            Find = counter
            Exit Function
        End If
    Next counter
End Function



' Enable For...Each support
Public Property Get NewEnum() As IUnknown
    Set NewEnum = m_Hutch.[_NewEnum]
End Property

' Initialize and destruct the internal collection

Private Sub Class_Initialize()
    Set m_Hutch = New Collection
End Sub


Private Sub Class_Terminate()
```

Listing 13.3: The RabbitCollection6 Class Module (Continued)

```
    Set m_Hutch = Nothing
End Sub


' Function to obtain a new collection containing
' only white rabbits
Public Function GetWhiteRabbits() As Collection
    Dim col As New Collection
    Dim obj As clsRabbit6
    For Each obj In m_Hutch
        If obj.Color = "White" Then
            col.Add obj
        End If
    Next
    Set GetWhiteRabbits = col
End Function


' Centralized error handling
' 0 = Attempt to add existing object

Public Sub RaiseError(erroffset As Integer)
    Dim e$
    Select Case erroffset
        Case 0
            e$ = "Object already exists in collection"
        Case 1
            e$ = "Invalid collection index"
    End Select
    Err.Raise vbObjectError + 1000 + erroffset, "RabbitCollection6", e$
End Sub
```

The major changes affect the Add and Remove functions, though as you see, additional error checking has been added to the Item method as well.

The Add method now has a test to make sure you are not trying to add to the collection an object that is already present. Using the Find method, it tests the object you are trying to add against the current list. If it finds it, an error is raised. The Add method tests the Hutch property of the object you are trying to add to see if it is referencing a ClassRabbit6 collection object. If it is, the object is removed from the other collection. Finally, the object's Hutch property is set to the current collection. The Remove method has to set the Hutch property for the object being removed to Nothing before it actually removes it from the collection.

The RabbitTest6 test project is similar to the RabbitTest5 program except for the two transfer tests:

```
' Transfer first rabbit from hutch1 to hutch2
Private Sub cmdTransfer1_Click()
    Dim obj As clsRabbit6
    Set obj = Hutch1(1)
    Hutch2.Add obj
End Sub

' The rules are enforced this time
Private Sub cmdBadTransfer_Click()
    Dim obj As clsRabbit6
    Set obj = Hutch1(1)
    Hutch1.Add obj
End Sub
```

The cmdTransfer1_Click() function works fine even though you do not explicitly remove the object from Hutch1. The Hutch2.Add method automatically removes the rabbit from the Hutch1 collection. In the cmdBadTransfer_Click method, an error is raised when you try to add an object a second time to the collection. Seems perfect, doesn't it? There's just one problem.

It's a Circular Reference After All   Go back to the Rabbit5 program group. Click on the Load Collections button and watch the Immediate window to see the ten rabbits get created. Click on Load Collections again. You'll see the next ten rabbits get created as the new collections are created to replace the prior ones. You'll see the previous ten clsRabbit6 objects destroyed as the original collections are destroyed.

Now try the same operation with the Rabbit6 program group. When you load the new collections, neither the rabbit objects nor the collections are destroyed! Let's take a closer look at what is going on here.

Figure 13.4 illustrates the referencing for one of the RabbitCollection5 collections. The reference count for an object can be determined from the number of incoming arrows to the object. What happens when you set the Hutch1 variable to Nothing or to another collection? The reference count on the RabbitCollection5 object is set to zero. This will cause it to terminate. This termination will cause the variables for this collection to be destroyed, including the internal m_Hutch collection. As this collection is destroyed, it will stop referencing the objects that are part of the collections. One by one the references of the clsRabbit5 objects will be decremented to 0. As this occurs they will be destroyed as well.

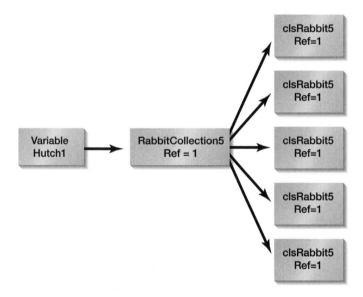

Figure 13.4: Referencing in the Rabbit5 example

Figure 13.5 illustrates the referencing for one of the RabbitCollection6 collections. As you can see, each of the clsRabbit6 objects that are part of the collection contains a reference back to the Collection object. As a result, the Collection object has a reference count of six. When the Hutch1 variable is set to Nothing or to another collection, this decrements the RabbitCollection6 object's reference count from 6 to 5. This does not cause the object to be destroyed or trigger its termination event. As a result the collection and all of the objects it references will not be destroyed until the application terminates, unless your program explicitly removes each of the clsRabbit6 objects from the collection first!

DEALING WITH CIRCULAR REFERENCES

When you come right down to it, there are only three ways to deal with the problem of circular references.

1 You can require clients to explicitly clear object references.

2 You can design them out of your object model.

3 You can break the circle.

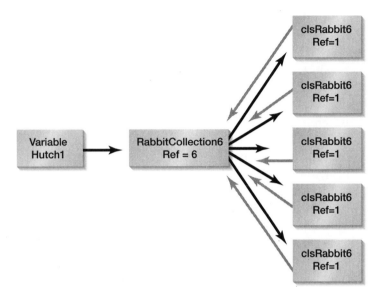

Figure 13.5: Referencing in the Rabbit6 example

Explicitly Clearing Object References   The first option is obvious. The following code is triggered by clicking the Safe Load Collections button:

```
' A way to load Hutch variables that kills
' off the prior ones first
Private Sub cmdSafe_Click()
    If Not Hutch1 Is Nothing Then
        Do While Hutch1.Count > 0
            Hutch1.Remove 1
        Loop
    End If
    Set Hutch1 = PetStore.BuyRabbits(5)
    If Not Hutch2 Is Nothing Then
        Do While Hutch2.Count > 0
            Hutch2.Remove 1
        Loop
    End If
    Set Hutch2 = PetStore.BuyRabbits(5)
End Sub
```

By removing all of the clsRabbit6 objects from the collection before the assignment, the reference count for the collection is reduced to one, then to zero when the Hutch1 variable is set to another collection.

By the way, you should keep in mind that while removing a clsRabbit6 object from the collection does destroy the object in this example, it is only because the object in this example is only referenced from the collection. If you held a reference to a clsRabbit object elsewhere (perhaps by obtaining a collection using the GetWhiteRabbits function) the object would still be removed from the collection, but it would not be destroyed until the other reference is eliminated as well.

This is one of the easiest approaches to take. It's not particularly elegant because it does require extra effort on the part of the client. In fact, your first reaction may be that it is the worst possible choice.

In general, this reaction would be a healthy one. It is certainly very poor design to expose objects that require special operations to terminate. So for a public object (such as RabbitCollection6) this is the worst possible choice. However, this approach is sound within a project. If you have a class that you are using in a well-defined manner within the project, there is no reason why you should not take this approach if it is the easiest one to implement.

In fact, this approach suggests the next one, in which we combine it with a redesign of the object model to eliminate the problem from the client's perspective.

Redesign the Object Model   The Rabbit7 program group demonstrates how you can make minor changes to the object model that resolve the circular reference problem, at least from the perspective of client applications. As before, the suffix of each of the group files has been incremented, this time from 6 to 7. The trick in this case is to redefine the current RabbitCollection7 so that it is only used internally and to create a new RabbitCollection7B, which is the public object that implements collections of clsRabbit7 objects.

The RabbitCollection7B module, shown in Listing 13.4, contains a single RabbitCollection7 object and exposes all of the RabbitCollection7 methods and properties through delegation to this internal object. Remember to set the default property in the Procedure Attributes dialog box to the Item property. Also set the Procedure ID (Dispatch ID) for the NewEnum property to -4 and its attribute to Hidden.

Listing 13.4: The RabbitCollection7B Class Module

```
' Guide to the Perplexed:
' Rabbit7 example
' Copyright (c) 1997 by Desaware Inc. All Rights Reserved

Option Explicit
```

Listing 13.4: The RabbitCollection7B Class Module (Continued)

```
Private m_Internal As RabbitCollection7

' All methods delegate to internal collection
Public Sub Add(Optional obj As clsRabbit7)
    m_Internal.Add obj
End Sub

Public Property Get Count() As Long
    Count = m_Internal.Count
End Property

Public Property Get Item(IndexKey As Long) As clsRabbit7
    Set Item = m_Internal.Item(IndexKey)
End Property

Public Sub Remove(IndexKey As Long)
    m_Internal.Remove IndexKey
End Sub

Public Function Find(findobj As clsRabbit7)
    Find = m_Internal.Find(findobj)
End Function

Public Property Get NewEnum() As IUnknown
    Set NewEnum = m_Internal.NewEnum
End Property

Public Function GetWhiteRabbits() As Collection
    Set GetWhiteRabbits = m_Internal.GetWhiteRabbits
End Function

Private Sub Class_Initialize()
    Set m_Internal = New RabbitCollection7
End Sub

' On termination of this object, the contained
' object will be deleted properly
Private Sub Class_Terminate()
    Do While m_Internal.Count > 0
        m_Internal.Remove 1
    Loop
End Sub
```

All references to the rabbit collection objects in the PetStore module and RabbitTest7 project are changed to refer to RabbitCollection7B instead. However, the references in the clsRabbit7 class module remain set to the RabbitCollection7 object. One result of this is that the Hutch property can no longer be public. Making it public would expose the RabbitCollection7 object, and we are now using it only internally. It has been changed to also be a Friend function for this example.

The real work is done in the class initialization and termination events for the RabbitCollection7B object. The initialization event creates the internal object. The termination event deletes all of the clsRabbit7 objects contained within the embedded collection, allowing it to terminate properly.

How do we know that the termination event will trigger properly for the RabbitCollection7B object? Figure 13.6 shows the referencing for this object. As you can see, while the RabbitCollection7 object still carries multiple references, the RabbitCollection7B object does not. When the Hutch1 variable is reassigned, the RabbitCollection7B object will terminate. In the process of terminating, it will explicitly clean up its embedded RabbitCollection7 object.

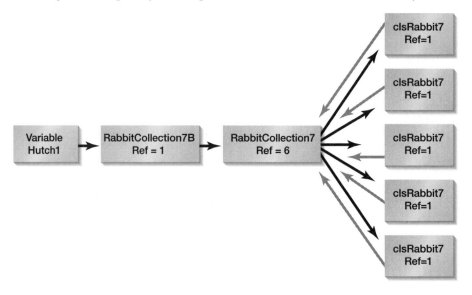

Figure 13.6: Referencing in the Rabbit7 example

This approach also requires one minor change to the RabbitCollection7 object. The Count property has been changed as follows:

```
Public Property Get Count() As Long
    If Not m_Hutch Is Nothing Then
        Count = m_Hutch.Count
    End If
End Property
```

Why is this necessary? Because when an application terminates, you do not know the order in which objects are destroyed. What happens if the embedded RabbitCollection7 object is terminated before the RabbitCollection7B object that is holding it? The termination function sets the m_Hutch variable to Nothing. When the termination event for the RabbitCollection7B object executes, it calls the Count method for the object, which in turn tries to access the m_Hutch variable that no longer exists. This raises the question: How can an object call methods in an object that has already had its termination event called?

The automatic termination of objects when an application ends is a special case where the termination order is undefined. Visual Basic is trying to clean up any objects that are left. This problem would not occur if the container application was kind enough to clear its Hutch1 and Hutch2 variables when the form was terminated as follows:

```
Private Sub Form_Terminate()
    Set Hutch1 = Nothing
    Set Hutch2 = Nothing
End Sub
```

You cannot assume that your component's clients will clean up after themselves properly. Your components should be tested by terminating an application while objects are still held by the client.

Break the Circle   With Visual Basic 5.0, you have an interesting new technique for breaking circular references. You can take advantage of VB's ability to raise events to break the circular reference. This is done in the Rabbit8.vbg group, in which all files have had their suffix incremented to 8.

A new object called clsGetContainer8 is defined to act as a sink object that the clsRabbit8 objects will be able to point to instead of the RabbitCollection8 object. Having the clsRabbit8 objects connect to a different object is an obvious solution and easy to implement. The question is: How can that object obtain references to the container? The answer is to use an event. The clsGetContainer8 object contains the following code:

```
' Guide to the Perplexed - Rabbit Test
' Copyright (c) 1997 by Desaware Inc. all Rights Reserved


Option Explicit


Public Event ContainerRequest(ContainerObject As Object)


' This method raises an event in the container which
' retrieves an object reference to its container
Public Function GetContainer() As Object
    Dim obj As Object
    RaiseEvent ContainerRequest(obj)
    Set GetContainer = obj
End Function
```

Each RabbitCollection8 collection object will contain a single clsGet-Container8 object. It will also support the ContainerRequest event. When the clsGetContainer8 object needs an object reference to its container, it raises an event in the container. The event code then sets the Container-Object parameter to refer to the container itself.

The clsGetContainer8 subobject for the collection is defined as follows:

```
Private WithEvents ContainerSubObject As clsGetContainer8
```

The object is created during the RabbitCollection8_Initialize event as follows:

```
Set ContainerSubObject = New clsGetContainer8
```

The event code is as follows:

```
Private Sub ContainerSubObject_ContainerRequest(ContainerObject As Object)
    Set ContainerObject = Me
End Sub
```

The clsRabbit8 object needs to connect to the subobject instead of the container itself. It will need the following function to obtain that reference:

```
Friend Function GetContainerSubObject() As clsGetContainer8
    Set GetContainerSubObject = ContainerSubObject
End Function
```

In the clsRabbit8 object, the Hutch property is declared as follows:

```
' Which hutch is holding this rabbit?
Private m_Hutch As clsGetContainer8


' Anyone can find out which hutch contains the rabbit
```

```
Public Property Get Hutch() As RabbitCollection8
    If m_Hutch Is Nothing Then Exit Property
    Set Hutch = m_Hutch.GetContainer()
End Property

' Only code within the project can set the Hutch for a rabbit
Friend Property Let Hutch(vNewValue As RabbitCollection8)
    If vNewValue Is Nothing Then
        Set m_Hutch = Nothing
        Exit Property
    End If
    Set m_Hutch = vNewValue.GetContainerSubObject()
End Property
```

Let's walk through the sequence in more detail.

When a clsRabbit8 object is created, it is added to a RabbitCollection8 collection object.

The clsRabbit8 object needs to hold a reference to the collection, but if it holds a reference to the collection itself, a circular reference problem will occur. Instead, the Hutch property setting uses the GetContainerSubObject function to retrieve a reference to a clsGetContainer8 object that is held by the RabbitCollection8 object.

Any time a clsRabbit8 object needs a reference to its container, it calls the GetContainer method of the clsGetContainer8 object it is referencing. This method raises an event in the RabbitCollection8 object. The collection uses this event to return a reference to itself to the clsGetContainer8 object, which returns the reference back to the clsRabbit8 object.

When the Hutch1 variable is set to Nothing or assigned to a different variable, the RabbitCollection8 object is destroyed. This works because an event sink does not add a reference count to the client object. During the collection's terminate event, the internal collection is deleted, which in turn deletes all of the clsRabbit8 objects. Once these objects and the Collection object are deleted, the clsGetContainer8 object will have no more references and will be deleted as well.

Why does this work? Because an event server holds a reference to an internal event sink subobject instead of the client object that is receiving the events. Events work this way in order to prevent exactly the kind of circular reference problems that we are dealing with here. In effect, this approach takes advantage of the event mechanism's method for eliminating circular references and applies it to a more general case. The architecture is illustrated in Figure 13.7.

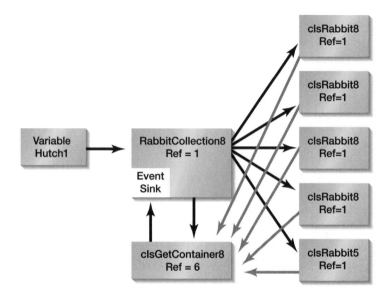

Figure 13.7: Referencing in the Rabbit 8 example

SELECTED TOPICS

There are a few more topics to cover before we conclude our discussion of object lifetime.

INITIALIZATION EVENTS

Visual Basic class, form, MDI Form, and control and document modules all support initialization and termination events.

Use the initialization event to initialize object data. One common use that was demonstrated in the various Rabbit examples is the actual creation of sub-objects that are referenced by the object. Remember that the initialization event is triggered for each object that is created.

What if you have class-specific initialization that must take place the first time an object of a certain class type is created? An example of this would be if you wanted the rabbit number in the Rabbit examples to start with some number other than 1. To do this you would have to initialize the global Rabbit-Counter variable in the modRabbit8 module the first time any object in the RabbitCollection8 class is created. You do this by setting up a Boolean variable in the global module that indicates whether the initialization has taken place. Test the value of this variable during each object's initialization event. If the variable is False, perform initialization and set the variable to True to indicate to other objects that the first-time initialization is complete.

Try to limit the amount of code in initialization events. This is especially important for EXE servers where a long initialization event could cause an OLE time-out in the client application.

TERMINATION EVENTS

Use termination events to set object references in your object to Nothing.

Be sure to test your application shutdown by closing the client application and verifying that the objects in your application are, in fact, destroyed and that the client application really terminates.

Remember that during application shutdown the order of object destruction is not guaranteed.

Be sure to test termination in the compiled version of the component as well. The behavior is slightly different from the behavior in the design environment. (For example: in the design environment, a DLL server is never actually unloaded from VB's process space.)

UNKILLABLE APPLICATIONS

The Rabbit examples we've used in this chapter have one advantage over EXE servers. All of the objects are in process. When you finally close the main application, Windows is smart enough to destroy all of the objects—even those you've lost track of due to circular references.

This does not work with EXE servers. If you have an EXE server named ServerA that holds an object reference to another executable named ServerB, and ServerB also holds a reference to an object in ServerA, neither application will ever terminate. This is because an EXE server can only close once all of its objects have been destroyed. So be extra careful to clean up your objects when working with EXE server components.

PRIVATE OBJECTS

Never pass a reference to a private object to a client that is not part of the component itself. Yes, it will work most of the time, but private objects will not prevent a server from being unloaded. This means that you may leave your client with an object reference to an object that does not exist, which will likely lead to either a memory exception or other corruption of your application's memory.

Private objects are not the same as objects whose Instancing property is set to Public Not Creatable. Public-Not Creatable objects are public and are designed to be passed to clients and other components as needed. It's just that a client cannot create one of these objects on its own—it must obtain a reference to one that was created by another object in your component.

TRACK YOUR OBJECTS

The Rabbit sample program demonstrates how you can use a module counter and debug.print statements to keep track of object creation and deletion. Visual Basic 5.0 preserves and allows you to display the contents of the Immediate window after the application stops running, so it is easy to verify that your objects are being destroyed properly.

DON'T STOP YOUR APPLICATION

There are two ways to stop a program in the VB environment. One is to close the application by using the System menu on the main form (the same way you would close a compiled application), the other is to use the Run, End command or its toolbar equivalent.

In a related way, there are two ways to terminate a running application. One is to unload its main form. The other is to use the End statement.

As a general rule, within the Visual Basic environment, always close the application using the System menu or other exit mechanism that you've programmed into the application. Do not use the Run, End command or its toolbar equivalent.

As a nearly absolute rule for compiled applications, never use the End statement to terminate a program or component. The only exception I can think of is when you've detected an internal application error so terrible that you don't dare run another line of code. I don't think I've ever used the End statement in a VB program other than to demonstrate how bad it is.

Why is this? Because when you use the Run, End command, its toolbar equivalent, or the End statement, you are telling Visual Basic to immediately stop all code execution. Visual Basic will proceed to clean up memory wherever it can. However, it will not execute any of your termination code.

Not only does this prevent you from testing your termination code, you may find that some objects were not cleaned up properly. For example: if you have used API functions to create system objects, Visual Basic and Windows may not be able to clean up those objects when your application ends. Visual Basic definitely will not close or free those objects before you try to run the application again. Thus, you may find that a file you opened the first time fails on the next attempt due to a permission error or lock condition.

So get in the habit of closing your applications using the System menu. With VB5's toolbar customization, you can even remove the Run, End button from the debug and top-level toolbars, which will help force you into better VB programming habits. And speaking of avoiding bad programming habits: it's just possible that you've heard about Visual Basic's new support for multi-threading and are dying to try it out. As you will see in the next chapter, multi-threading can be fun to play with, and it can be extremely useful, but only when used judiciously.

Multithreading

On Threads and Processes

Multithreaded Components

Testing and Debugging
   Multithreaded Components

Multithreading Examples

Background Operations Revisited

Chapter 14

M ultithreading. It's a subject that can send chills up the spines of even veteran programmers. The good news is that Visual Basic's support for multithreading is about as safe and easy as it gets. So take a deep breath and let us proceed.

ON THREADS AND PROCESSES

Until now we've taken a rather simplistic approach towards the idea of threads and processes. Chapter 8 introduced the idea of *threads of execution,* where a thread is the sequence of operations that will take place within a given application.

Each application runs as its own process, and has its own thread of execution. The operating system may be switching rapidly between the threads, but this is transparent to you as a programmer.

Each process runs in its own memory space, and its ability to interact with other applications is tightly controlled. From our perspective this interaction takes the form of method and property calls on COM objects. We trust OLE to marshal our commands and data from one process to the next.

COM objects can be implemented by in-process servers, in which case the object runs in the execution thread of the calling application. They can be implemented by EXE servers, in which case the object runs in the execution thread of the server. If you want each object in an EXE server to run in its own execution thread, you set the object to single-use, in which case a separate server instance (with its own process and execution thread) is created for each object.

The scenario described so far represents the way things work under Visual Basic 4.0, which first introduced COM object support under Visual Basic. However, this scenario suffers from two major weaknesses.

▸ Using a separate process to implement each EXE server object when you need each object in a separate thread can have a severe impact on system performance, especially when more than a few objects are involved.

▸ DLL-based objects perform poorly with multithreaded clients.

The first of these is easy to understand. Launching a new application in order to implement a single object has to be just about the most inefficient approach you can imagine. Yet you've already seen that there are situations where you want each object to run in its own execution thread, primarily in order to prevent one application from blocking the execution of others, but also to allow asynchronous background operations.

The second case is likely to be obscure to many Visual Basic programmers. This is in part because Visual Basic does not allow you to create multithreaded clients, but also because until recently there have not been too many multithreaded clients for which you might want to write in-process objects. But now with the increased use of both client server databases and Internet/intranet servers and browsers (all of which are frequently multithreaded), the need to write components for multithreading applications has become critical.

Visual Basic 5.0 addresses both of these issues by allowing you to create multithreaded components. But before we talk about developing components for multithreaded environments, perhaps we should take a look at the nature of multithreading and why it can be such a challenge.

MULTITHREADING

You saw in Chapter 8 how the Windows operating system is able to multitask between different execution threads. In the simplistic approach we took earlier, each thread was in its own process. The operating system switches rapidly between the threads, so they seem to run simultaneously.

If every process was restricted to having a single thread, we wouldn't need to distinguish between threads and processes. But it is possible for a single process to have multiple threads. The operating system divides available processor time among threads, not among processes. This is illustrated in Figure 14.1, which extends on Figure 8.1 in Chapter 8, which showed two single-threaded processes.

In this example, application A actually has two separate threads of execution. If you follow the arrows that indicate how the processor is spending its

Application A   Application B

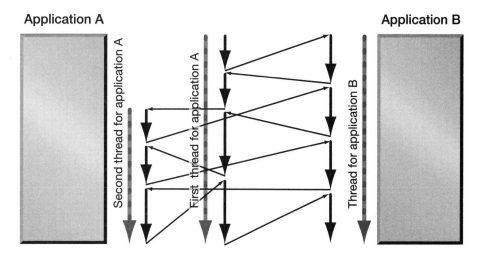

Second thread for application A

First thread for application A

Thread for application B

Figure 14.1: Multithreading

time, you'll see that the system is effectively running two different parts of application A at the same time in two separate execution threads.

Why would you want to multithread an application or component? There are a number of common situations that would cause you to want multithreading. We will discuss these next.

Data or Information Servers Say you are developing an information server that receives requests from many different clients. Examples of this include database servers or Internet/intranet servers. Some of the requests can be very slow. Rather than locking out all of the other clients while the slow request is taking place, you can launch each request in its own thread so they will be perceived to be executing at the same time. You only have a finite amount of CPU time, so the slow operation will take longer with this approach (since it has to share time with the other client requests), but, with luck, the shorter client requests will not have to wait as long as they might have to otherwise.

For example: If you have one 30-minute request ahead of four 1-minute requests, in a non-multithreaded server the long request will take 30 minutes and the others 31, 32, 33, and 34 minutes, respectively. In a multithreaded server, processor time would be divided among all five requests. The long request will take about 35 minutes, but the other four will take about 5 minutes each.

This illustrates an important point. Multithreading can be very useful, but it does not have the miraculous ability to speed up your system. On the contrary, because of the overhead involved in switching between threads, the total time spent in a multithreaded server is likely to be longer than a non-multithreaded server. The four 1-minute client requests in the above example will actually take more than 5 minutes each due to system overhead.

In fact, multithreading can make your system seem slower. Let's say you had five client requests of 1 minute each. In a non-multithreaded server the client requests will be completed at 1, 2, 3, 4, and 5 minutes (average of 3 minutes per request). On a multithreading server, the client requests will all be completed after 5 minutes, increasing the average request time to 5 minutes.

So, if you are implementing a server component and are looking for multithreading to provide an improvement in performance, think again. It can only help when you have a mix of large and short operations.

Background Operations   You already read, in Chapter 11, how to implement background operations using OLE callbacks. Background operations tend to fall into two categories. The first is calculations or operations you want your application to perform in the background while the user does something else. The second is cases where you want your application to wait for an outside event and notify the main portion of your program when it occurs.

Chapter 8 also discussed how a single-use EXE server can be used to implement background operations with the help of callbacks (both API callbacks and OLE callbacks).

Advanced User Interfaces and Other Multithreaded Clients   An Internet browser is a good example of a multithreaded client. It is not uncommon for this type of application to be able to retrieve Web documents in multiple windows, perform e-mail transfers, and still be able to respond immediately to user input. These applications can be implemented by having each document retrieval operation take place in its own thread, while having a separate thread managing the e-mail window.

You might not be able to create this type of multithreaded application in Visual Basic 5.0, but multithreaded applications often support ActiveX components. That means it is important to create components that work well with them.

MULTITHREADING PITFALLS

The first thing you need to know about this section is that most of the pitfalls I'm about to discuss do not apply to Visual Basic. Why discuss them? Because they will help you understand exactly what Microsoft did to make Visual Basic thread-safe (relatively speaking), as well as both the advantages and limitations that follow from their approach.

The next thing you need to know about multithreading is that all of the threads in an application share the same process space. In Chapter 8 you learned that one of the great advantages of 32-bit Windows over 16-bit Windows is that each application runs in its own process space. As such, each application has its own independent pool of memory and one process cannot easily interfere with the operation of another. One process cannot modify the memory of another, and in the case of an application fault, it is unlikely for one application to crash another or interfere with the operating system.

This protection applies to processes, not to threads. Every thread has complete access to all of the memory in its process space. This means that one thread can (and often does) interact with others. If one thread crashes, the application—not just the offending thread—may terminate.

Let's say you have a routine in your application that opens a file, writes some data, and closes the file. In pseudo code, it might look like this:

```
Global FileHandle As Long

Procedure SaveFile(filename)
    FileHandle = OpenFile (filename)
    WriteToFile(FileHandle, "This is line 1")
    WriteToFile(FileHandle, "This is line 2")
    CloseFile(FileHandle)
End Procedure
```

As long as your program runs in a single thread, you have nothing to worry about. Once you make a call to the SaveFile procedure, the thread will continue to execute the function until it ends. The system may allow other threads in other processes to run, but they will not interfere with your program (unless you have file sharing enabled and they access the same file).

But let's say that you have a second thread enabled in your application and both threads are called upon to save a file at the same time. You have no way of knowing exactly which instructions will be called by the processor as it switches between threads. In fact, the results could look something like those shown in Table 14.1.

As you can see, the possible results are quite serious. In this particular example you have two potentially corrupt files; one invalid operation that might be caught or might simply be ignored depending on whether you implemented error checking; and one file that remains open, meaning that it may be locked until the application terminates.

Worse, this is only one possible error. What are the chances that two threads will call the SaveFile procedure at the same time? One in five? One in a million? If it is infrequent, this might easily turn into one of those intermittent problems

Table 14.1: Multithreading Operations and Their Results

Thread 1 Operation	Thread 2 Operation	Result
FileHandle = OpenFile("File1")		FileHandle is now handle to File1
WriteToFile(FileHandle, "This is Line 1")		File1 contains "This is Line 1"
	FileHandle = OpenFile("File 2")	FileHandle is now handle to File2
	WriteToFile(FileHandle, "This is Line 1")	File2 contains "This is Line 1"
WriteToFile(FileHandle, "This is Line 2")		File2 contains: "This is Line 1""This is Line 2"
	WriteToFile(FileHandle, "This is Line 2")	File2 contains: "This is Line 1" "This is Line 2" "This is Line 2"
CloseFile(FileHandle)		File2 is now closed. File1 remains open.
	CloseFile(FileHandle)	Possible error on attempt to close a file handle that is no longer valid

that don't show up until you have already widely distributed your application. And, these problems are hard to test for, hard to detect, and hard to debug.

This type of problem is not completely new to Visual Basic programmers. If you threw a DoEvents statement into the SaveFile function and did not add code to prevent it from being reentered, the same problem could occur. But most Visual Basic programmers know to avoid the DoEvents statement if at all possible and to disable controls or functions as necessary when the statement is used.

By the way, while the DoEvents statement does open the door to this type of reentrancy problem, DoEvents is not multithreading. With a DoEvents statement you are effectively giving Windows permission to have your thread start executing event code elsewhere in your application. When the events are finished, your thread continues to execute where it left off, much like a subroutine or function call. You still only have the one thread.

It is also true that this particular example is very simple and could easily be solved by avoiding the use of a global variable for the file handle. But the intent here is to demonstrate the dangers of using multiple threads within an application. Multithreading is dangerous precisely because applications and components have global variables and global functions and because they are able to access application-wide resources, be they forms, controls, or files.

And unlike the DoEvents case, where you decide exactly where in your code you are going to allow Windows to move your execution thread, Windows switches at will between threads in a multithreaded application.

Programmers who write traditional multithreaded applications must be very careful in the way they access global variables and resources. Windows provides a number of synchronization commands and objects to help programmers control when parts of their application can run.

In this example, a programmer could create an object called a *mutex*, which places a lock on the SaveFile function. When a thread tries to run the function, it checks the mutex to see if it is available. If it is, the thread begins to run the function but first locks the mutex. If another thread tries to run the function, it would see that the mutex is locked and would perform a wait operation on the mutex. This puts the thread to sleep, which means that Windows will not execute the thread until the mutex is released by the first thread.

The fact that most of the problems with multithreading derive from the use of global variables and common resources raises an interesting question. What if you could eliminate all global variables from an application or component and eliminate all forms and controls? Wouldn't this eliminate most of the danger involved in multithreading while still providing many of the benefits? The answer is: yes.

Eliminating forms and controls, the common resources in an application, is the first step. Eliminating all global variables is a bit more difficult. That would require a fundamental change to the language. On the other hand, what if you could simply allocate a separate set of global variables for each thread? In our example above, there would actually be two FileHandle variables: one for the first thread, one for the second. The code would remain the same. The variable would still be referred to as FileHandle, but Visual Basic would automatically keep track of the data for each thread so that each one would see its own copy of the variable. Table 14.2 illustrates this approach using the SaveFile example shown earlier. The (T1) and (T2) symbols indicate whether the Thread 1 or Thread 2 copy of the FileHandle variable is active.

This approach to handling multithreading is called the *apartment model* approach to multithreading, and it is supported by ActiveX EXE and DLL server components under Visual Basic 5.0.

Table 14.2: Multithreading with Apartment Model Threading

Thread 1 Operation	Thread 2 Operation	Result
FileHandle = OpenFile("File1")		FileHandle(T1) is now handle to File1
WriteToFile(FileHandle, "This is Line 1")		File1 contains "This is Line 1"
	FileHandle = Open-File("File 2")	FileHandle(T2) is now handle to File2
	WriteToFile(FileHandle, "This is Line 1")	Uses FileHandle(T2) File2 contains "This is Line 1"
WriteToFile(FileHandle, "This is Line 2")		Uses FileHandle(T1) File1 contains: "This is Line 1" "This is Line 2"
	WriteToFile(FileHandle, "This is Line 2")	uses FileHandle(T2) File2 contains: "This is Line 1" "This is Line 2"
CloseFile(FileHandle)		Uses FileHandle(T1) File1 is now closed.
	CloseFile(FileHandle)	Uses FileHandle(T2) File2 is now closed.

MULTITHREADED COMPONENTS

In order to implement apartment model multithreading, Visual Basic first requires that no user interface elements be included in the project. This includes forms, controls, and message boxes. User interface elements are, by definition, available to any object in a project, so allowing them to exist would raise the problems discussed earlier with regard to shared resources in an application. More importantly, you can easily imagine how it would be possible for Visual Basic to keep a separate copy of global data for each thread in an application. But how could you do the same for a form or control? It would be exceedingly difficult, if not impossible.

So, before allowing you to make a project multithreading, Visual Basic requires that you turn off all user interaction by the project. This effectively eliminates standard projects, ActiveX controls, and ActiveX documents from consideration, so the only components Visual Basic can multithread are ActiveX EXE servers and DLL servers. You can turn on multithreading for a component if it has no forms or other designers with user interface elements by going to the General tab of the Project-Properties dialog box and selecting the Unattended Execution checkbox. The other two options, Thread per Object and Thread Pool, apply to EXE servers only and will be discussed shortly.

You will soon see there are other critical differences between EXE and DLL based servers.

ON THREADS AND OBJECTS

What does it mean when we say that a Visual Basic component is multi-threaded? It means that Visual Basic is able to run objects in different threads. Let's take a look first at what this means for an EXE server and how it compares with non-multithreaded servers.

EXE Servers   Figure 14.2 shows a non-multithreaded EXE server that is implementing an object set to multiuse instancing. The server is providing three objects to three different applications. To be precise, it is providing three objects to three different threads. In this case those threads are in different processes, but this example applies also to objects requested by different threads in a multithreaded client.

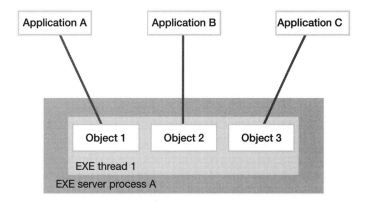

Figure 14.2: Objects implemented by a non-multithreaded EXE server using multiuse instancing

The server is represented by the lower block. There are two shaded rectangles; the outer one indicates the process space for the server, the inner one the thread. The white rectangles inside represent the objects. In this case all of the objects are contained in a single process and run in the same thread. If one of the client applications was to tie up one of the objects in a long operation, it would block the server's thread, preventing the other client applications from accessing methods or properties in the objects they are accessing until the long operation is completed.

Global variables are shared among all of the objects because they share the same thread.

Figure 14.3 shows a non-multithreaded EXE server that is implementing an object set to single-use instancing. Three separate instances of the EXE server are running as separate processes, each one implementing a single object. As such, each object naturally runs in its own thread. Because each object is in its own process space, it is evident that none of the global variables for the component can be shared among the objects.

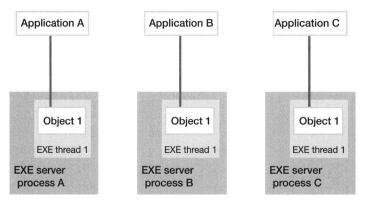

Figure 14.3: Objects implemented by a non-multithreaded EXE server set to single-use instancing

What happens when an EXE server has more than one class set to single-use instancing? Each server is allowed to implement one single-use object of each type. So if you have two objects set for single-use instancing, such as MyObjectA and MyObjectB, a single EXE server can provide one of each. In that case those two objects will both share the same global variables because they will be running in the same execution thread! This can lead to some peculiar situations.

Figure 14.4 illustrates a single-use EXE server where the following sequence of operations occurs. First, application A requests an object of type MyObjectA. The server creates an instance of this object for use by the application. Next, application B requests an object of type MyObjectB. The first server instance still has not created an object of this type, so it implements it. Note that these two objects share the same global variables within the component because they are running in the same thread. Also, a long operation by application A on its MyObjectA object will block access by application B on its MyObjectB object. If application A then requests an object of type MyObjectB, a new instance of the server will have to be launched, because the first server has already provided an object of this type.

In other words, when an EXE server component is implemented to provide multiple single-use instanced objects, you will never know which server process will actually be providing a particular object. So be careful, especially with regard to use of global variables in such situations.

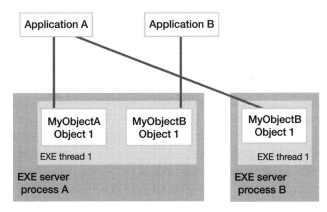

Figure 14.4: Multiple single-use instanced objects

Remember also that an EXE server that exposes a single-use object can provide additional objects of that type in the same thread by creating the objects itself and returning a reference to that object to the client.

Figure 14.5 illustrates a multithreaded EXE server implementing a multiuse instanced object. In this case the server is configured to provide one thread per object. All of the objects run in the same process space. However, due to the apartment model threading, each object has its own set of global variables within its own thread.

This approach is much more efficient than the non-multithreaded approach because it does not suffer from the system overhead of a separate process for each object. The system overhead for separate threads is not nearly as great.

Keep in mind that the server objects are running in their own threads, not in the thread of the calling process. Also that they are running in the server process, not the calling process. The efficiency that comes from running in process (which is the ability to avoid marshaling overhead) is the sole domain of DLL servers.

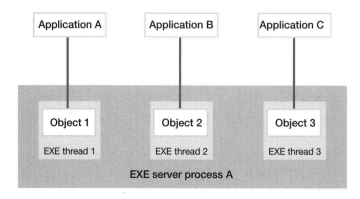

Figure 14.5: Objects implemented by a multithreaded EXE server component

Figure 14.6 takes this a step further to illustrate some of the options that are available when implementing multithreaded EXE server objects. As with single-use objects, it is possible for an object in a multithreaded server to create additional objects within its own thread and pass those objects back to the client. Application C uses this approach to obtain object 4 (which presumably was created by a method in object 3). To create an object within the same thread, an object need only dimension an object variable of the desired type and create it using the New operator. Note that if it creates the object using the CreateObject function, the object will be created in a new thread.

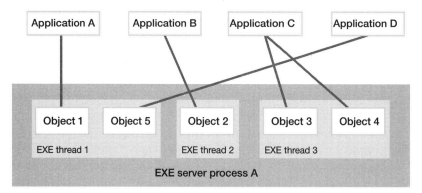

Figure 14.6: More objects implemented by a multithreaded EXE server component

But how did application D obtain object 5 in the first thread? In this example, instead of setting the project options to one thread per object, the unattended execution option in the General tab of the Project-Properties dialog box is set to thread pooling, and the thread count is set to three. This option tells the server to limit the number of threads available for implementing threads to the specified number. Once those threads are used, additional objects will be allocated in turn from the other threads.

Visual Basic does not perform any balancing; it allocates objects on threads in turn. This means that if you have four threads, each of which implements ten objects, and by coincidence all of the objects in one thread are destroyed, logic would suggest that additional objects should be allocated on the available thread to balance the load. Unfortunately, Visual Basic does not take this approach.

In this case, when application D requested an object, the object was allocated off of the next thread in the sequence (objects created by internal objects don't count here). Thus the object is allocated on EXE thread 1.

One of the side effects of this approach is that now application A and application D both have objects in the same thread. Those objects share global variables, and operations on one of them can block operations on the other.

This demonstrates one of the major disadvantages of thread pooling. You can't know which thread will implement a particular object or which other objects might be sharing that thread (with all of the blocking and shared global variable implications that apply). Why, then, would you ever want to use thread pooling? Because each thread you launch does incur additional system overhead. You can quickly reach the point where the cost of this overhead exceeds any possible benefit due to multithreading. Thread pooling allows you to limit the number of threads, essentially putting a cap on the system resources that your server will use. Just be extra careful how you use global variables when you enable thread pooling (better yet, avoid them entirely).

DLL Servers   DLL servers are somewhat different from EXE servers in that, unlike an EXE server, an object in a DLL server never runs in its own thread. The question with DLL servers is this: are objects run by the thread that launched the DLL or by the thread that creates the object? If the DLL is not multithreaded, all of the objects created by the DLL are implemented by the thread that created the object. This scenario is shown in Figure 14.7. All of the objects run in the same thread, thus they all share the same global variables.

What is wrong with this scenario? You should be well acquainted by now with the material in Chapter 6, where you learned about the performance impact of marshaling across process spaces. Well, I didn't mention it until now, but it turns out that the impact of marshaling data across threads is nearly as great. You see, OLE itself uses apartment model threading. Other models exist now under NT

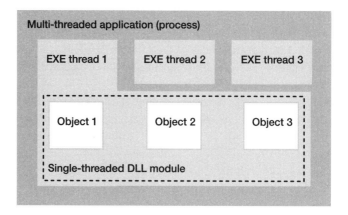

Figure 14.7: Objects implemented by a non-multithreaded DLL server

4.0 but are not supported by Visual Basic. This is necessary because if different threads were allowed unrestricted access to objects in other threads, the kinds of problems you saw earlier with multithreading could occur with every method and property call to an object. Because the objects run in the same process, marshaling of data is not as slow as it is with out-of-process objects. However, an internal proxy object is still necessary to insure that access to objects is properly synchronized—that only one thread can access an object at a time.

In this case, cross-process marshaling is necessary every time EXE thread 2 and thread 3 access object 2 or object 3. Let's say that EXE thread 2 performs a long operation on object 2 and thread 3 tries to access object 3. Thread 3 will be blocked by OLE because thread 1 is busy running the operation started by thread 2.

This problem is avoided by making the DLL multithreading (setting unattended execution), as shown in Figure 14.8. Note that the DLL does not create any new threads. When a DLL is multithreading it simply means that each object runs in the thread that creates the object. Assuming that object 1 is created by EXE thread 1, object 2 by EXE thread 2, and so forth, no cross-thread marshaling will be necessary as long as each thread accesses only those objects that it creates. Threads can still access objects created by other threads, but doing so requires cross-task marshaling again.

In this example, each object exists in the thread that creates it, and global variables are only shared by those objects that are in the same thread.

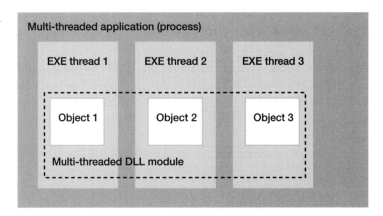

Figure 14.8: Objects implemented by a multithreaded DLL server

SCOPING REVISITED

Chapter 10 discussed scoping rules, the rules by which the lifetime and visibility of variables is determined based on where they are declared. You may wish to review that section before you continue.

In the previous section you saw many references to the sharing of global variables. The fact that global variables are not shared between threads in the apartment model of multithreading clearly suggests that some major changes to the scoping rules are necessary.

Some things haven't changed. Variables that are declared at the module level of a class are still created for each class object and exist for the lifetime of an object. Variables declared in non-static procedures or in a procedure without the static keyword are still created for each procedure call and exist until the procedure exits. Variables declared at the module level of form modules… you guessed it: there are no forms in a multithreading component, so this situation won't arise.

So the only variables we are concerned with are global variables defined in a standard module or static variables defined within procedures. These variables used to be created once per application and exist for the life of the application.

For multithreaded components, these variables are created once per thread and exist for the life of the thread. The visibility of the variable is local to an individual thread. In other words, all of the objects in a given thread share the same global variable data. Objects in other threads see their own copy of the data.

TESTING AND DEBUGGING MULTITHREADED COMPONENTS

Each instance of Visual Basic can work with a single thread. Thus, you cannot test the multithreading characteristics of your components using the Visual Basic environment. This means that your testing will have to use the compiled components. You can still run the component in the VB environment, but it will not use multiple threads.

Of course, since components have no user interface, you can't exactly bring up a message box to let you know what is going on in the component. And since they aren't running in the VB environment, you can't use debug.print statements.

One option is to compile the component to native code, including debugging information, and to use a stand-alone debugger such as the one that comes with Visual C++. But there are alternatives.

LOGGING

While multithreading does require that you disable all user interface output, it does not completely eliminate your component's ability to notify the system when problems or other events occur. The LogMode property of the App object allows you direct information to either a log file or the system event log. This includes text that would have shown up in message boxes, system errors, and text strings that are written using the App object's LogEvent method. This information will appear in the Immediate window when debugging within the VB environment.

Still, reading a log file or the system event log during debugging is awkward. Fortunately, ActiveX technology itself provides an excellent alternative.

DEBUG MONITOR

Your multithreading component may not be able to generate messages, but there is nothing to prevent it from accessing an object that can.

The DebugMonitor project (DmDebMon.vbp) in the Chapter 14 directory consists of one class module and two forms. This component is configured as an ActiveX EXE server because it will be receiving messages from many different applications and threads. Objects that it creates will be used by many threads. Yet they will all need to share the same centralized data in order to allow the server to display messages from all of the objects in the order they are received. The Trace class module is set to multiuse so all of its objects will come from the same server.

The Trace class is shown in Listing 14.1. The class exposes a single public method called Add, which takes a string parameter. Applications call this method to send a message that will be displayed on the monitor's main form. The method simply calls the Add method on the frmDebug form, the main form for the component.

Listing 14.1: The Trace Class (File DMTrace.cls)

```
' DebugMonitor trace program
' Copyright (c) 1997 by Desaware Inc. All Rights Reserved

Option Explicit

' Add the message to the form
Public Sub Add(msg As String)
    frmDebug.Add msg
End Sub
```

Listing 14.2 shows the code for the main form module. The form contains a View menu with three commands: Update, Clear, and Options. It also contains a list box called lstDebug, which displays the incoming messages in the order in which they are received. This form is shown during the Sub Main routine in the DmDebug.bas module, which is set as the Startup object for the project. That way it will automatically be loaded and displayed as soon as the component is loaded for the first time. The form also contains a single timer named Timer1.

Listing 14.2: The frmDebug Form Listing (File DmDeb.frm)

```
' DebugMonitor trace program
' Copyright (c) 1997 by Desaware Inc. All Rights Reserved
Option Explicit
Dim StartPos&
Dim EndPos&
Dim MaxStrings&

Dim StringArray() As String

Private Sub Form_Load()
    SetArraySize 200
End Sub
```

Listing 14.2: The frmDebug Form Listing (File DmDeb.frm) (Continued)

```
' Set the number of strings
' Clears the current contents
Public Sub SetArraySize(ByVal maxsize%)
    If maxsize < 10 Then maxsize = 10
    If maxsize > 1000 Then maxsize = 1000
    MaxStrings = maxsize
    ' Update the array size
    ReDim StringArray(MaxStrings)
    StartPos = 1
    EndPos = 1
    UpdateList
End Sub


' Update the listbox
Public Sub UpdateList()
    Dim counter&
    Dim currenttop&
    currenttop = lstDebug.TopIndex
    lstDebug.Clear
    counter = StartPos
    Do While counter <> EndPos
        lstDebug.AddItem StringArray(counter)
        counter = counter + 1
        If counter > MaxStrings Then
            counter = 1
        End If
    Loop
    If currenttop < lstDebug.ListCount Then
        lstDebug.TopIndex = currenttop
    End If
End Sub


' Add a string to the list
Public Sub Add(newstring$)
    StringArray(EndPos) = newstring
    EndPos = EndPos + 1
    If EndPos > MaxStrings Then EndPos = 1
    If EndPos = StartPos Then
        StartPos = StartPos + 1
        If StartPos > MaxStrings Then StartPos = 1
    End If
End Sub


Private Sub mnuClear_Click()
    StartPos = 1
    EndPos = 1
```

Listing 14.2: The frmDebug Form Listing (File DmDeb.frm) (Continued)

```
    UpdateList
End Sub

' Bring up options page
Private Sub mnuOptions_Click()
    Hide
    frmOptions.Show 1
    Show
End Sub

Private Sub mnuUpdate_Click()
    UpdateList
End Sub

Private Sub Timer1_Timer()
    UpdateList
End Sub

' Copy the contents to the clipboard
Private Sub mnuCopy_Click()
    Dim counter&
    Dim s$
    counter = StartPos
    Do While counter <> EndPos
        s$ = s$ & StringArray(counter) & vbCrLf
        counter = counter + 1
        If counter > MaxStrings Then
            counter = 1
        End If
    Loop
    Clipboard.SetText s$
End Sub
```

A simple implementation of this type of program could add information directly to the list box. This approach suffers from two major disadvantages:

- ▶ You run the risk of poor performance as the list box fills with messages. Or you must incur the overhead needed to check the list count and make sure that the list box contents do not get out of hand.

- ▶ There is substantial overhead involved in adding data to a list box. This is overhead you may not want to incur every time a message is sent to the component. This is especially true if you wish to use this component as part of the benchmarking process.

To avoid these problems, the component maintains a separate array named StringArray. The SetArraySize method sets the maximum array size and initializes the StartPos and EndPos variables. These variables implement a rotating first-in-first-out buffer. The StartPos variable indicates the first item in the buffer. The EndPos variable represents the next entry in the array to be loaded. When the two variables are equal, the buffer is considered empty.

The UpdateList method clears the list box, then reloads it from the current buffer by looping from the StartPos to the EndPos positions in the array. The function keeps track of the current display location so that excessive scrolling does not occur. This method is called by expiration of the timer or by selection of the cmdUpdate menu command.

The mnuClear menu command clears the current buffer. The mnuCopy menu command copies the buffer to the clipboard. The frmOptions form, shown in Listing 14.3, controls the timer control, allowing you to disable the timer and set the interval from 1 to 60 seconds.

Listing 14.3: The frmOptions Form Listing (File DmOpt.frm)

```
' DebugMonitor trace program
' Copyright (c) 1997 by Desaware Inc. All Rights Reserved
Option Explicit

Private Sub cmdOK_Click()
    Dim delayval&
    delayval = Val(txtInterval)
    If chkAutoUpdate.Value Then
        frmDebug.Timer1.Enabled = True
        If delayval < 1 Or delayval > 60 Then
            MsgBox "Select a delay between 1 and 60", vbOKOnly, "Invalid value"
            Exit Sub
        End If
        frmDebug.Timer1.Interval = Val(txtInterval.Text) * 1000
    Else
        frmDebug.Timer1.Enabled = False
    End If
    Unload Me
End Sub


Private Sub Form_Load()
    If frmDebug.Timer1.Enabled Then
        chkAutoUpdate.Value = 1
```

Listing 14.3: The frmOptions Form Listing (File DmOpt.frm) (Continued)

```
    End If
    txtInterval.Text = frmDebug.Timer1.Interval / 1000
End Sub
```

The chkAutoUpdate checkbox controls the timer's enabled property. The txtInterval text control is used to set and display the timer interval. The cmdOK button accepts the changes and sets them into the form.

In the next section, you will see how this component is used.

MULTITHREADING EXAMPLES

Multithreading does take getting used to. You've seen graphical descriptions, but there is no substitute for code. We'll briefly review the code, then analyze the results closely in order to understand what is actually happening.

THE PROOF IS IN THE TIMING

It's easy to see how you would test a multithreading EXE server from Visual Basic. Just create objects from several different applications and show that they don't block each other. But how can you test a multithreading DLL server from Visual Basic? The only way to see the benefits of multithreading in a DLL is through a multithreading client application, right?

Right. And Visual Basic can't create a multithreading client application. But it can create a multithreading EXE server. That server can take advantage of a multithreading client! So we test the DLL server through the EXE server.

We'll use four different projects (in addition to the DebugMonitor project described earlier) to perform these multithreading tests.

MT3.VBP and MT4.VBP Let's start on the DLL side with the MT3.VBP and MT4.VBP projects. These are both ActiveX DLL servers.

All of the projects use the clsElapsedTime class from Chapter 12 to measure elapsed time. It will not be described further here.

Listing 14.4 shows the listing for the ClassMT4 class module. The code is identical to that of the ClassMT3 class module. In fact, the only differences between the MT3 and MT4 projects are the class names, project description, and the fact that the MT4 project has the option for unattended execution set. In other words, it has multithreading enabled.

Listing 14.4: Class ClassMT4 (mt4cls4.cls) and ClassMT3 (mt3cls3.cls)

```
Option Explicit


Private CurrentMessage$
Private InProgress As Boolean
Private DebugMon As DebugMonitor.Trace

Private Declare Function GetCurrentThreadId Lib "kernel32" () As Long

' Performs a long operation
' Measures the time to do it and
' reports it
Public Sub LongOp(msg$)
    Dim ctr&
    Dim x&
    Dim s$
    Dim Elapsed As New clsElapsedTime
    CurrentMessage = msg
    ' A nice long operation that can't
    ' be optimized away
    Elapsed.StartTheClock

    For ctr = 1 To 5000
        For x = 1 To 255
            s$ = Chr$(x)
        Next x
    Next ctr
    Elapsed.StopTheClock
    Report Elapsed
End Sub

' We don't actually do anything, just marshal the string
Public Sub ShortOp(ByVal msg$)


End Sub


Public Sub ShowTID(ByVal msg$)
    DebugMon.Add msg & " TID: " & GetCurrentThreadId()
End Sub

Private Sub Class_Initialize()
    Set DebugMon = New DebugMonitor.Trace
End Sub

Private Sub Class_Terminate()
```

Listing 14.4: Class ClassMT4 (mt4cls4.cls) and ClassMT3 (mt3cls3.cls) (Continued)

```
    Set DebugMon = Nothing
End Sub


' Report the current message and elapsed time
Friend Sub Report(elp As clsElapsedTime)
    Dim msg$
    msg$ = CurrentMessage$ & " Time: " & elp.Elapsed & " TID: " &
GetCurrentThreadId()
    DebugMon.Add msg
End Sub
```

The LongOp method performs a time consuming operation that takes about 5 seconds on a medium speed Pentium machine. You'll probably want to tune this value to set the same approximate delay. The string operations within this function have no real purpose. Without them the native code optimization would optimize away most of the contents of the loop.

The ShortOp method does nothing. It demonstrates a method that can be called quickly, but since it takes a string parameter, it does perform marshaling of the string data. This will be used to demonstrate the performance impact of cross-thread marshaling.

The DebugMon object is available by adding a reference to the DebugMonitor component to this project. Its Trace object is used to send a message to the DebugMonitor component. The ShowTID option routine is used to have the component send a message to the DebugMonitor tool indicating which thread it is.

What does "which thread" mean? Every thread in the system has a unique thread identifier. You can obtain this value by using the GetCurrentThreadId() API function as shown here, or the ThreadId property of the App object you will see later.

MT2.VBP The two DLL servers will be tested by the EXE server (under instruction from a test program). The MT2.VBP project is an ActiveX EXE server that is set for unattended execution (multithreading) and is configured to create a new thread for each object. The code for the ClassMT2 module is shown in Listing 14.5. The Instancing property for this class is set to multiuse. The project has references to the DebugMonitor object and the MT3 and MT4 projects.

Listing 14.5: Class ClassMT2 (mt2cls2.cls)

```
' Guide to the Perplexed - Multithreading EXE example
' Copyright (c) 1997 by Desaware Inc. All Rights Reserved
'
Option Explicit

Private CurrentMessage$
Private InProgress As Boolean
Private DebugMon As DebugMonitor.Trace


' Performs a long operation
' Measures the time to do it and
' reports it
Public Sub LongOp(msg$)
    Dim ctr&
    Dim x&
    Dim s$
    Dim Elapsed As New clsElapsedTime
    CurrentMessage = msg
    ' A nice long operation that can't
    ' be optimized away
    Elapsed.StartTheClock

    For ctr = 1 To 1000
        For x = 1 To 255
            s$ = Chr$(x)
        Next x
    Next ctr
    Elapsed.StopTheClock
    Report Elapsed
End Sub


Private Sub Class_Initialize()
    ' Preload objects so they aren't included in elapsed time
    Set DebugMon = New DebugMonitor.Trace
End Sub

Private Sub Class_Terminate()
    Set DebugMon = Nothing
End Sub

' Report the current message and elapsed time
Friend Sub Report(elp As clsElapsedTime)
    Dim msg$
    msg$ = CurrentMessage$ & " Time: " & elp.Elapsed & " TID: " & App.ThreadID
```

Listing 14.5: Class ClassMT2 (mt2cls2.cls) (Continued)

```
    DebugMon.Add msg
End Sub

' Call a long op in a non multithreaded DLL
Public Sub CallDllNoMTLong(ByVal msg$)
    Dim dllNonMT As New gtpMT3.ClassMT3
    dllNonMT.LongOp msg
End Sub

' Call a long op in a multithreaded DLL
Public Sub CallDllMTLong(ByVal msg$)
    Dim dllMT As New gtpMT4.ClassMT4
    dllMT.LongOp msg
End Sub


' Call a non multithreading DLL
Public Sub CallDllNoMT(ByVal msg$)
    Dim Elapsed As New clsElapsedTime
    Dim dllNonMT As New gtpMT3.ClassMT3
    Dim x&
    CurrentMessage = msg
    dllNonMT.ShowTID "CallDllNoMT in TID: " & App.ThreadID & " on DLL object"
    Elapsed.StartTheClock
    For x = 1 To 4000
        dllNonMT.ShortOp "This string must be marshaled"
    Next x
    Elapsed.StopTheClock
    Report Elapsed
End Sub

' Call a multithreading DLL
Public Sub CallDllMT(ByVal msg$)
    Dim Elapsed As New clsElapsedTime
    Dim x&
    Dim dllMT As New gtpMT4.ClassMT4
    CurrentMessage = msg
    dllMT.ShowTID "CallDllMT in TID: " & App.ThreadID & " on DLL object"
    Elapsed.StartTheClock
    For x = 1 To 400000  ' Note: factor of 10 slower
        dllMT.ShortOp "This string must be marshaled"
    Next x
    Elapsed.StopTheClock
    Report Elapsed
End Sub
```

The LongOp method of the class is essentially identical to that of the MT3 and MT4 projects. It is used to demonstrate the fact that each object is in its own thread. The DebugMon object is again used to access the DebugMonitor component and provide a mechanism for tracing output.

The CallDllMTLong and CallDllNoMTLong methods create MT4 and MT3 objects, respectively, and call the LongOp methods on the objects. This allows us to see the different characteristics of objects under multithreading and non-multithreading DLL servers.

The CallDllMT and CallDllNoMT methods perform repetitive calls on the ShortOp method on the multithreading and non-multithreading DLL server objects. These are used to demonstrate the impact of cross-thread marshaling on object performance. The only difference between these two functions is that the method is called 100 times more often on the multithreading server, which should give a preview of how great an impact this marshaling can have.

MTTest1.VBP   This project includes references to the DebugMonitor and MT2 components. It also includes the clsElapsedTime class in order to measure the total elapsed time for each test. The main form for the project is shown in Figure 14.9. Listing 14.6 shows the listing for the test form.

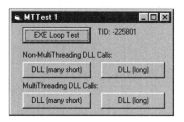

Figure 14.9: The MTTest1 project main form in action

The five tests are as follows:

▸ EXE Loop Test measures the time to perform a LongOp call on the MT2 server.

▸ DLL (many short) measures the time to perform CallDllNoMT and CallDllMT calls on the MT2 server.

▸ DLL (long) measures the time to perform a CallDllNoMTLong and CallDllMTLong calls on the MT2 server.

Listing 14.6: Listing for Form frmMTTest1 (MTTest1.frm)

```
' Guide to the Perplexed - Multithreading test program
' Copyright (c) 1997 by Desaware Inc. All Rights Reserved

Option Explicit
Dim MT2obj As ClassMT2
Dim elapse As New clsElapsedTime
Dim debugmon As DebugMonitor.Trace

Private Sub cmdDLLMT_Click()
    elapse.StartTheClock
    MT2obj.CallDllMT "Called from TID: " & App.ThreadID
    elapse.StopTheClock
    debugmon.Add "Elapsed on TID: " & App.ThreadID & " was " & elapse.Elapsed
End Sub

Private Sub cmdDllMTLong_Click()
    elapse.StartTheClock
    MT2obj.CallDllMTLong "Long - Called from TID: " & App.ThreadID
    elapse.StopTheClock
    debugmon.Add "Elapsed on TID: " & App.ThreadID & " was " & elapse.Elapsed
End Sub

Private Sub cmdDLLNoMT_Click()
    elapse.StartTheClock
    MT2obj.CallDllNoMT "Called from TID: " & App.ThreadID
    elapse.StopTheClock
    debugmon.Add "Elapsed on TID: " & App.ThreadID & " was " & elapse.Elapsed
End Sub

Private Sub cmdDllNonMTL_Click()
    elapse.StartTheClock
    MT2obj.CallDllNoMTLong "Long - Called from TID: " & App.ThreadID
    elapse.StopTheClock
    debugmon.Add "Elapsed on TID: " & App.ThreadID & " was " & elapse.Elapsed
End Sub

Private Sub cmdTest1_Click()
    elapse.StartTheClock
    MT2obj.LongOp "Called from TID: " & App.ThreadID
    elapse.StopTheClock
    debugmon.Add "Elapsed on TID: " & App.ThreadID & " was " & elapse.Elapsed
End Sub

Private Sub Form_Load()
```

Listing 14.6: Listing for Form frmMTTest1 (MTTest1.frm) (Continued) (Continued)

```
    ' We don't want the load time to be included
    ' in the elapsed time
    Set debugmon = New DebugMonitor.Trace
    Set MT2obj = New ClassMT2
    lblTID = "TID: " & App.ThreadID
End Sub

Private Sub Form_Unload(Cancel As Integer)
    Set MT2obj = Nothing
    Set debugmon = Nothing
End Sub
```

LET THE TESTING BEGIN

To exercise the mttest1 project and the various servers, be sure to first register the servers. You can do this by running the MT2.EXE and DmDebMon.exe programs and by using regsrv32.exe to register files MT3.DLL and MT4.DLL.

Testing the Multithreading EXE Server   Run three instances of the MTTest1.exe program. They will also bring up the DebugMonitor screen. (The caption for the project is Trace Display.) Arrange the three MTTest1 projects so they are easily accessible.

Each MTTest1 program displays its thread identifier. Since this is a standard VB executable, it uses a single thread, so this thread ID uniquely identifies the project.

Now click on the EXE Loop Test button of all three instances as quickly as you can. Keep in mind that the times shown here are measured on one system. Your times are sure to differ. The results are as follows:

```
Called from TID: 243 Time: 1733. TID: 241
Elapsed on TID: 243 was 1933.
Called from TID: 108 Time: 2304. TID: 242
Elapsed on TID: 108 was 2474.
Called from TID: 236 Time: 2003. TID: 213
Elapsed on TID: 236 was 2063.
```

The first message was generated as follows: The message "Called from TID: 243" was generated in the cmdTest1_Click routine. This identifies the originating thread. The elapsed time of the LongOp call on the MT2 server was 1733 ms. This is the time the server spent in the loop. The LongOp routine ran on thread 241. When the operation concluded, the total elapsed time of 1933 ms was reported.

To get an idea of how long a single LongOp operation takes, try clicking on the EXE Loop Test button for a single MTTest1 instance. Here are the results:

```
Called from TID: 243 Time: 1052. TID: 241
Elapsed on TID: 243 was 1062.
```

About 1052 ms. Now, if the three LongOp operations were taking place sequentially, you would expect each one to measure a time of about 1 second. You would expect the total elapsed time to be about 1 second for the first, 2 seconds for the second, and 3 for the third. The actual results showed all of the operations taking about the same time (2 seconds) and the total elapsed time for all of them is about the same as well. These are exactly the results you would expect when each object runs in its own thread, which is clearly the case based on the thread identifiers that are reported here.

Perhaps the most important result of this test is that we have verified that we have, in fact, created a single process (the EXE server) that can run three separate threads simultaneously. We'll be using those threads to test the DLL servers.

Testing the Impact of Cross-Thread Marshaling   Still using the three MTTest1 instances, try clicking on the DLL (many short) command button for the non-multithreading DLL. The results are as follows. (Once again, your results will differ.)

```
CallDllNoMT in TID: 241 on DLL object TID: 247
CallDllNoMT in TID: 242 on DLL object TID: 247
CallDllNoMT in TID: 213 on DLL object TID: 247
Called from TID: 243 Time: 8603. TID: 241
Elapsed on TID: 243 was 9173.
Called from TID: 108 Time: 8922. TID: 242
Elapsed on TID: 108 was 9063.
Called from TID: 236 Time: 6329. TID: 213
Elapsed on TID: 236 was 11106.
```

Each instance generates three messages. Let's follow the sequence for thread 108.

The mdDLLNoMT_Click() first passes the message "Called from TID: 108" to the server. The server saves this message. It first lets you know who it is by using the DLL object's ShowTID method to display:

```
CallDllNoMT in TID: 242 on DLL object TID: 247
```

It then calls the DLL object's ShortOp method 4000 times. After that it reports on the elapsed time by displaying:

```
Called from TID: 108 Time: 8922. TID: 242
```

It uses the stored message from earlier. We now know that MTTest1 thread 108 used server object in thread 242 to call the ShortOp method on a DLL server object in thread 247. The ShortOp loop took about 8.7 seconds. Finally, the call returns to the MTTest1 program which displays the message:

```
Elapsed on TID: 108 was 9063.
```

The total elapsed time from click to return was about 9 seconds.

It's interesting to note that all of the tests ran in about the same time and the total elapsed time was the same. How can this be when we are not using a multithreading DLL server? Simple: we're not performing a long operation. Objects on a thread only block the thread while in the middle of a method call. The method calls to the DLL are extremely short, so there is no reason why all three of the EXE server threads can't take turns, each calling its DLL object in turn!

Then what is the point of this test? Note how all of the DLL objects run in thread 247, the EXE server thread that actually loaded the component. (Yes, this is another thread in the EXE server, one that handles server overhead rather than an individual object.)

Try the same operation using the DLL (many short) command buttons under the multithreading group. Here are the results:

```
CallDllMT in TID: 241 on DLL object TID: 241
CallDllMT in TID: 242 on DLL object TID: 242
CallDllMT in TID: 213 on DLL object TID: 213
Called from TID: 243 Time: 3044. TID: 241
Elapsed on TID: 243 was 3435.
Called from TID: 108 Time: 3786. TID: 242
Elapsed on TID: 108 was 4376.
Called from TID: 236 Time: 2914. TID: 213
Elapsed on TID: 236 was 3895.
```

The big difference here is the DLL object thread ID. Note how each object runs in the same thread as the EXE server object that calls it! This is seen in the first three lines of the listing.

At first glance it may seem that the operation is only slightly faster—3 seconds instead of 9 seconds. But look back at the listing. We aren't performing 4000 calls to the ShortOp function in this case, we're performing 400,000! In other words, the performance improvement is a factor of about 200.

The conclusion is inescapable. If you are writing a DLL server object intended to be used by a multithreaded client such as a Web server or browser, turning on multithreading can improve the performance dramatically. Of course, this is a best-case scenario, where the function we call is not doing anything. Real-world improvement will be substantially less, depending on how big a factor the cross-thread marshaling is in the total time spent on each method or property call.

Testing Long Operations on DLL Servers   Now click on the button marked DLL Long for non-multithreading DLL calls. Here are the results:

```
Long - Called from TID: 243 Time: 5698. TID: 247
Long - Called from TID: 236 Time: 5508. TID: 247
Elapsed on TID: 236 was 8803.
Elapsed on TID: 243 was 11427.
Long - Called from TID: 108 Time: 5508. TID: 247
Elapsed on TID: 108 was 15793.
```

Here you can see clear evidence of blocking. The time to perform a LongOp call on the DLL object is about 5.5 seconds in each case. The total elapsed time increased for each operation because each one is blocked by the prior long operation. Once the first long operation ends, there is an additional delay before the total elapsed time is measured because the other thread is tying up CPU time. You can see that the total elapsed time to finish all three is about 15.7 seconds, very close to the sum of the three individual operations.

Now try the DLL Long button for multithreaded DLL calls.

```
Long - Called from TID: 243 Time: 14621. TID: 241
Elapsed on TID: 243 was 15162.
Long - Called from TID: 108 Time: 15302. TID: 242
Elapsed on TID: 108 was 15963.
Long - Called from TID: 236 Time: 15072. TID: 213
Elapsed on TID: 236 was 15813.
```

The total time for each call and the total elapsed time is almost the same in each case. This is exactly the situation that was described earlier in the chapter. The proof is indeed in the timing.

BACKGROUND OPERATIONS REVISITED

You've seen that Visual Basic 5.0 allows you to create multithreading components. You've seen that it does not allow you to create multithreaded applications. Or does it?

What if you could create an object in a multithreaded EXE server, call a method on the object and return immediately, then have the object begin a background operation and notify you when it is complete. Well, for all practical purposes you've just created a new thread for your application.

You saw this work with single-user EXE servers in the Tick1 project in Chapter 11. Could it work with multiple-use classes in a multithreaded EXE server? Yes, but with some caveats.

Listing 14.7 shows an implementation that is very similar to that of the Tick1 project from Chapter 11. The standard module used to implement the timer is shown in Listing 14.8.

Listing 14.7: The ClassMT5 Class Module (File cls5mt5.cls) in the MT5 Project

```
' Guide to the Perplexed: Background Thread Launcher
' Copyright (c) 1997 by Desaware Inc.
Option Explicit

Private CurrentMessage$
Private InProgress As Boolean
Private debugmon As DebugMonitor.Trace
Private CallerToNotify As Object


' Performs a long operation
' Measures the time to do it and
' reports it
Public Sub LongOp(msg$)
    Dim ctr&
    Dim x&
    Dim s$
    Dim Elapsed As New clsElapsedTime
    CurrentMessage = msg
    ' A nice long operation that can't
    ' be optimized away
    Elapsed.StartTheClock

    For ctr = 1 To 5000
        For x = 1 To 255
            s$ = Chr$(x)
        Next x
    Next ctr
    Elapsed.StopTheClock
    Report Elapsed
End Sub



Private Sub Class_Initialize()
    ' Preload objects so they aren't included in elapsed time
    Set debugmon = New DebugMonitor.Trace
```

Listing 14.7: The ClassMT5 Class Module (File cls5mt5.cls) in the MT5 Project (Continued)

```
End Sub

Private Sub Class_Terminate()
    Set debugmon = Nothing
End Sub

' Report the current message and elapsed time
Friend Sub Report(elp As clsElapsedTime)
    Dim msg$
    msg$ = CurrentMessage$ & " Time: " & elp.Elapsed & " TID: " & App.ThreadID
    debugmon.Add msg
End Sub

' Get the thread ID of an object
Public Function ObjectThreadId() As Long
    ObjectThreadId = App.ThreadID
End Function

' Tries to start a background operation using a timer
Public Sub StartBackground1(ToNotify As Object)
    Set CallerToNotify = ToNotify
    debugmon.Add "Starting timer from TID: " & App.ThreadID
    StartTimer Me
End Sub

' Background operation is starting
Friend Sub TimerExpired()
    debugmon.Add "Starting Background Op in TID: " & App.ThreadID
    LongOp "Background Op Done "
    ' OLE callback to calling object
    If CallerToNotify Is Nothing Then Exit Sub
    CallerToNotify.BackgroundNotify
    Set CallerToNotify = Nothing
End Sub
```

Listing 14.8: Module modMT5.bas

```
' Guide to the Perplexed: MT5
' Copyright (c) 1997 by Desaware Inc. All Rights Reserved

Option Explicit


' Timer identifier
```

Listing 14.8: Module modMT5.bas (Continued)

```
Dim TimerID&

' Object for this timer
Dim TimerObject As ClassMT5
Declare Function SetTimer Lib "user32" (ByVal hwnd As Long, ByVal nIDEvent As
Long, ByVal uElapse As Long, ByVal lpTimerFunc As Long) As Long
Declare Function KillTimer Lib "user32" (ByVal hwnd As Long, ByVal nIDEvent As
Long) As Long

Public Sub StartTimer(callingobject As ClassMT5)
   Set TimerObject = callingobject
   TimerID = SetTimer(0, 0, 100, AddressOf TimerProc)
End Sub

' Callback function
Public Sub TimerProc(ByVal hwnd&, ByVal msg&, ByVal id&, ByVal currentime&)
   Call KillTimer(0, TimerID)
   TimerID = 0
   TimerObject.TimerExpired
   ' And clear the object reference so it can delete
   Set TimerObject = Nothing
End Sub
```

The client application creates a ClassMT5 object and calls the StartBackground1 method to start the background thread. This method receives a reference to the form object to use as an OLE callback. The StartBackground1 method sends a debug method to the DebugMonitor component and calls the StartTimer function in the modMT5 module. This starts a short duration timer. The StartBackground1 method then returns.

When the timer event occurs, the TimerProc function is called. It kills the timer and calls the TimerExpired method in the ClassMT5 object. This method displays another debug method, then begins a long operation. This operation is running in a separate thread from the original client, the thread of the EXE server object.

When the long operation is complete, another debugging message is displayed and the OLE callback's BackgroundNotify method is called.

The MTTest2 project is shown in Listing 14.9. It creates an object in the MT5 component, then starts the background operation when you click the test button. When the operation is complete, as indicated by a call to the BackgroundNotify method, it displays the total elapsed time in the DebugMonitor application.

Listing 14.9: The MTTest2 Project

```
' Guide to the Perplexed: Background thread demonstration
' Copyright (c) 1997 by Desaware Inc. All Rights Reserved
Option Explicit

Dim MTTestObj As gtpMT5.ClassMT5
Dim Debugmon As DebugMonitor.Trace
Dim Elapsed As New clsElapsedTime

Private Sub cmdTest_Click()
    Elapsed.StartTheClock
    MTTestObj.StartBackground1 Me
End Sub


Private Sub Form_Load()
    Set MTTestObj = New gtpMT5.ClassMT5
    Set Debugmon = New DebugMonitor.Trace
    lblTID.Caption = "TID: " & App.ThreadID
End Sub

Private Sub Form_Unload(Cancel As Integer)
    Set MTTestObj = Nothing
    Set Debugmon = Nothing
End Sub

Public Sub BackgroundNotify()
    Elapsed.StopTheClock
    Debugmon.Add "Total elapsed in TID: " & App.ThreadID & " was: " &
Elapsed.Elapsed
End Sub
```

After registering the MT5.EXE component, try running two instances of the MTTest2.exe program. Then click on the Background Using Timer button on both. Here are some typical results:

```
Starting timer from TID: 59
Starting Background Op in TID: 59
Starting timer from TID: 213
Starting Background Op in TID: 213
Background Op Done  Time: 9794. TID: 59
Total elapsed in TID: 223 was: 10024.
Background Op Done  Time: 9824. TID: 213
Total elapsed in TID: 77 was: 10184.
```

As you can see, both of the long background operations took about 10 seconds, and the total elapsed time was 10 seconds. Clearly the operations were taking place in different threads.

MULTITHREADING IS NOT MAGIC

In this chapter you've seen that you have even more options for implementing components. I'd like to leave you with two final thoughts.

Before Visual Basic 5.0, many VB programmers prayed for native code compilation as the solution to all of their performance problems. Only a small fraction of them, those who created code intensive applications, actually saw the benefit they had hoped for. The rest found that native code is not a magical solution and certainly not a substitute for good design practices. Neither is multithreading.

Multithreading can serve you well in certain cases. It is very useful for in-process components intended for use with multithreaded clients. It is very useful as a replacement for single-use EXE server components that do not need to share data among objects. In other cases it can actually slow your application down. So consider your choice carefully.

YOU HAVE MORE CONTROL THAN YOU THINK

Don't forget that while the choice of multithreading and class instancing does dictate how Visual Basic will implement created objects, you always have the ability to have your server create objects for you. This means that you have a great deal of flexibility in terms of how you allocate objects to threads. If you don't like VB's allocation, create your own.

You can even get sophisticated and implement your server simultaneously as both an EXE server and a DLL server (with different server and program names, of course). Your server can look at incoming requests and estimate their complexity. Long, complex operations can be serviced by objects created on a multithreading EXE server. Shorter operations can be serviced by objects created on a non-multithreading DLL server.

This concludes our discussion of multithreading. In Chapter 15 we'll tie many of the subjects covered in the preceding 7 chapters by taking an in-depth look at the long-promised stock quoting component.

Bringing It All Together: The StockQuote Server

Top-Down Design

Implementation

Back in Chapter 8, I used the example of a stock quoting server to demonstrate the advantages of component design and the issues involved in choosing between ActiveX EXE servers, DLL servers, and other approaches. I then promised to show you how to create one.

The last six chapters have been spent discussing many of the issues relating to implementing ActiveX components—the issues we will now demonstrate in this chapter.

TOP-DOWN DESIGN

There are a number of design methodologies programmers use, and I wouldn't even begin to suggest which is the best. But my personal favorite is to design from the top down and code from the bottom up. This means that you start by figuring out at the highest level what your program will do, then determining what kind of modules, components, and functions are needed to implement that level. Then you step down again and figure out what kind of code is needed to implement those modules and so on. When it's time to actually write code, you work in the reverse direction, coding the lowest level modules and components first, then working your way back up.

HIGH-LEVEL DESIGN REVIEW

Our goal is to come up with an ActiveX EXE server that can retrieve stock quotations. The reasons behind choosing an EXE server were discussed in depth in Chapter 8. The key reasons were:

▸ An EXE server allows us to retrieve the quote in a separate thread so the requesting application is not blocked during the retrieval process.

▸ An EXE server that exposes multiple objects allows multiple clients to share the same communications link.

In principle, we want any client application to be able to request a stock quotation and receive a notification when the response is received. It should be possible for an application to request multiple quotations at once. The server must support multiple clients.

These requirements influence additional design choices. For example, there are two notification mechanisms available: OLE events and OLE callbacks. Which one should we support? To answer this you must first decide whether a single StockQuote object can handle multiple requests or only one at a time. If it can handle multiple requests, the OLE event mechanism may be reasonable. However, in this case it seemed preferable to have the client use multiple Stock-Quote objects to handle multiple requests. This suggests that the OLE callback mechanism is a better choice.

Should the server be multithreading? In this case multithreading is clearly not appropriate. We want the server to be able to queue requests from the different clients and handle them in turn. This means that the objects must be able to communicate with each other, most likely through shared data structures in the global module. The apartment model of multithreading used by Visual Basic 5.0 prevents this type of sharing. Not only that, but since we are bound by a single communications link, multithreading would have no benefit; we only need a single thread. In fact, it would probably reduce performance due to the threading overhead.

So the higher-level design is beginning to take shape. You have a Stock-Quote object that is creatable by any application. It will have a method that is called to start a quote retrieval operation. This method will take a reference to a Callback object to use for the notification. It might also take the ticker symbol of the stock to retrieve. The server will have a module in which it will keep track of queued requests. As data arrives it will use the Callback object to notify the client application that the information has been retrieved.

We can envision the following design for the StockQuote object:

- ▶ GetQuote (symbol, callback): A method to start the retrieval process.
- ▶ State: A read-only property that lets you check the retrieval status.
- ▶ Symbol: A read-only property that contains the stock symbol. It is set by the GetQuote method.
- ▶ LastPrice: A read-only property containing the last price or net asset value of the security.
- ▶ PriorClose: A read-only property containing the prior close price of the security.
- ▶ Change: A read-only property containing today's change in price.
- ▶ QuoteTime: A read-only property containing the time of the quote.
- ▶ High: A read-only property containing today's high price.
- ▶ Low: A read-only property containing today's low price.

We also need to define a Callback method, the method the Callback object must have to receive the notification:

- ▶ QuoteUpdate(Stockquote): A Callback method that passes a reference to the Stockquote object itself as a parameter
- ▶ CancelNotification: A method that allows a client to cancel a notification—say, if it wants to close

Should the price properties shown above be in the form of strings (as they are when retrieved) or should they be converted to currency values? In this object they are left as strings, because stocks are traditionally displayed as an integer followed by the fractional price in eighths, such as 1/2 or 5/8, so this makes display easier. However, it would be helpful to have some utility functions to convert to the currency type to make it easier to do numeric comparisons. The StockQuote object seems a good place to place these functions:

- ▶ QuoteToCurrency(quote as string): A function that takes a stock price in fractional string format and returns the numeric value as a currency data type
- ▶ CurrencyToQuote(quote as currency): A function that takes a stock price as currency and in fractional string format and returns the numeric value as a currency data type

LOW LEVEL DESIGN REVIEW

You may have noticed that one small detail has been left out of the discussion so far. You may have been wondering exactly where do we obtain the stock quotes? For information of this type we naturally turn to the source of all known wisdom, the Internet. OK, maybe the Internet is not the source of all wisdom, but there are places where you can easily obtain delayed quotes, if you know how to submit a request and read an HTML page.

There are many ways to access the Internet from Visual Basic. For this application I chose one that I could be confident every reader would have access to, the Internet Transfer Control included with Visual Basic 5.0 Professional and Enterprise. This control allows your VB program to access the Internet if you have an Internet connection and Winsock set up for TCP/IP. Now if you don't have these, I'm afraid you'll have to obtain them in order to use this component. (Discussing how to obtain Internet access and configure your system properly is way beyond the scope of this book. However, during my last to a local bookstore, there seemed to be several thousand other books available to help you through the process.)

We'll talk about the implementation shortly. Knowing that we'll be using an Internet control is the final piece of the puzzle for defining the architecture of the server.

Figure 15.1 illustrates the overall architecture of the StockQuote server. When the client requests a quote, the StockQuote object calls functions in the common QuoteEngine module. The module adds a reference to the object into a collection that represents a queue of objects that have requested quotations. When the first request arrives, the quote engine invokes a method on a utility form, which in turn sends an HTML request through the Internet control. When the transfer is complete (or an error occurs), an event is triggered in the control. The control then lets the QuoteEngine know that a quote has arrived and passes the HTML information to the StockQuote object. The object parses the HTML code to extract the quote information, notifies the client, and presto! Success!

Sounds simple enough. And if you are an experienced Internet programmer who has done this sort of thing before, it is simple. So you might just want to skip the rest of this chapter. However, I know that for many of you this may seem almost like black magic. So let's back up and take this step by step so you can see exactly how it all works.

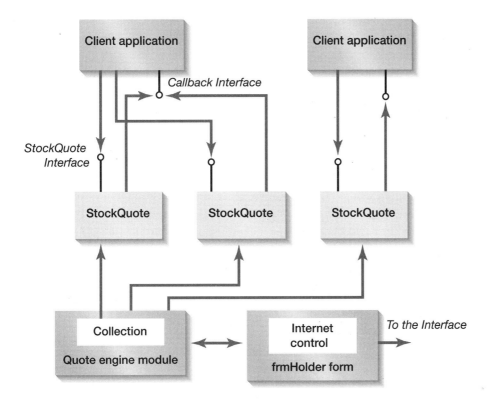

Figure 15.1: Architecture of the StockQuote server

IMPLEMENTATION

We've done the top-down design. Now it's time to do the coding, from the bottom up.

EVERYTHING YOU NEED TO KNOW ABOUT HTML

Well, perhaps not everything you need to know, but certainly all you need to know for this particular application.

The StockQuote object is currently configured to access quotes off of either Charles Schwab (www.schwab.com) or Yahoo (www.yahoo.com). There are a myriad of other quote services available through the Internet that you can add to the server if you wish. While my choice of these two services is not intended to recommend them over any others. I do tend to use Yahoo first when searching the Internet, and I have a personal account with Schwab, so I am glad to be able to mention them in this context. From my perspective, the fact that it took me less than a day to obtain their permissions to base this demonstration on their sites says something about their organizations.

I want to give you a strong caveat here. Nothing prevents Schwab or Yahoo from changing the format of their Web pages at any time. Doing so will probably cause this component to fail and cause some of the description in this section to be incorrect. If this happens, you will be able to find updated information on our Web site at www.desaware.com.

To understand how this Internet retrieval is accomplished, you'll need to know a little bit about HTML and how the World Wide Web works.

When you tell a browser (or Internet custom control) that you want a specific Web page, several things happen. First, the control uses a Domain Name Service (DNS) to find the unique 64-bit address of the computer that contains the page. This is the Internet Protocol (IP) address. Domains are set in a hierarchy. Thus www.desaware.com is, first, part of the *com* domain, the domain that contains all commercial sites. Next, it is part of a domain named desaware.

Once the control has this IP address, it opens a communications link called a *socket* to the site. The site must be running a server program that "listens" for incoming requests. This program is called a Web server.

The control sends a string containing a request to the site. The site then responds by returning the requested data. In the http protocol used for the World Wide Web, the returned data can be text or binary. For our purposes we will only be concerned with text.

When you request a page from a Web site, you receive back a text string in a format called HyperText Markup Language (HTML). This string is broken up into two types of elements:

▸ Tags—Surrounded by angle brackets < >, a tag contains formatting information that provides some sort of instruction to the browser.

▸ Data—Text to display on the page.

Any time your browser retrieves a very complex page that contains images and links and animations, your browser actually makes multiple requests. The initial page contains tags that instruct the browser where to find the other objects that belong on the page. If a tag specifies that an image must be loaded, the browser must perform a second request to retrieve the image based on the location specified in the tag. Listing 15.1 shows what a portion of a typical Schwab stock quote page looks like in HTML.

Listing 15.1: Sample Quotation HTML Page

```
<HTML>
<BODY BGCOLOR="#FFFFFF">
<CENTER>
<FORM METHOD="POST" ACTION="/fq/schwab/quote">
<TABLE BORDER=2 CELLPADDING=2 WIDTH="100%"><TR><TD VALIGN=top>Select
quote or chart:<BR>
<INPUT TYPE="radio" NAME="request" VALUE="Delayed quote"
CHECKED>Delayed quote<BR>
<INPUT TYPE="radio" NAME="request" VALUE="Intraday chart" >Intraday
chart<BR>
<INPUT TYPE="radio" NAME="request" VALUE="Daily chart" >Daily chart<BR>
<INPUT TYPE="radio" NAME="request" VALUE="Weekly chart" >Weekly
chart</TD>
<TD VALIGN=top>Enter the security symbol*, or <A
HREF="/fq/schwab/ticker">search for symbol</A>:<BR>
<INPUT NAME="symbols" SIZE=25 VALUE="MSFT"><BR>
<FONT SIZE=-1>*<B>Multiple symbols</B> may be entered for <B>quotes
only</B>.
Separate symbols with spaces.</FONT><BR><BR>
<INPUT TYPE="image" VALUE="Submit" BORDER=0
SRC="/graphics/schwab/submit.gif">
</TD></TR></TABLE>
</FORM>
<A NAME="QuoteSummaryTableAnchor"><B>Quote Summary</B></A><BR>
For more quote details, click on symbol.<BR>
Quote times are Eastern Standard Time.<BR>
<TABLE BORDER=2 CELLPADDING=2 WIDTH="100%">
<TR><TH ALIGN=left>Symbol</TH><TH>Security<BR>Type</TH>
<TH>Last<BR>Trade</TH><TH>Net<BR>Change</TH><TH>High</TH>
<TH>Low</TH><TH>Trade<BR>Time</TH>
<TH>Intraday<BR>Chart</TH></TR>
<TR ALIGN=center><TH ALIGN=left><A HREF="#MSFT">MSFT</A></TH>
<TD>Stock</TD>
<TD>97 <SUP>3</SUP>/<SUB>8</SUB></TD><TD><FONT COLOR="#008800">+2
<SUP>3</SUP>/<SUB>8</SUB></FONT></TD><TD>98
<SUP>1</SUP>/<SUB>2</SUB></TD><TD>94
<SUP>5</SUP>/<SUB>8</SUB></TD><TD>16:17</TD>
<TD VALIGN=center><FORM METHOD="POST" ACTION="/fq/schwab/quote">
<INPUT TYPE="hidden" NAME="request" VALUE="Intraday chart">
<INPUT TYPE="hidden" NAME="symbols" VALUE="NASDAQ:MSFT">
<INPUT TYPE="image" VALUE="Submit" BORDER=0
src="/graphics/schwab/submit.gif"></TD></TR></FORM>
</TABLE><P>
<A NAME="MSFT"></A><TABLE BORDER=2 CELLPADDING=2>
```

Listing 15.1: Sample Quotation HTML Page (Continued)

```
<TR><TH>MICROSOFT CORP</TH>
<TH><TABLE BORDER=0 CELLPADDING=2><TR><TH
ALIGN=right>Symbol:</TH><TD>MSFT</TD></TR>
<TR><TH ALIGN=right>Security Type:</TH><TD>Stock</TD>
</TR></TABLE></TH></TR>
<TD><TABLE BORDER=0 CELLPADDING=2>
<TR><TH ALIGN=right>Last<BR>Trade:</TH><TD>97
<SUP>3</SUP>/<SUB>8</SUB></TD>
<TH ALIGN=right>Net<BR>Change:</TH><TD><!-- Not Yet+2
<SUP>3</SUP>/<SUB>8</SUB>--></TD></TR>
<TR><TH ALIGN=right>Bid:</TH><TD>97 <SUP>3</SUP>/<SUB>8</SUB></TD>
<TH ALIGN=right>Ask:</TH><TD>97 <SUP>1</SUP>/<SUB>2</SUB></TD></TR>
<TR><TH ALIGN=right>Day High:</TH><TD>98 <SUP>1</SUP>/<SUB>2</SUB></TD>
<TH ALIGN=right>Day Low:</TH><TD>94 <SUP>5</SUP>/<SUB>8</SUB></TD></TR>
<TR><TH ALIGN=right>Volume:</TH><TD>16,157,600</TD>
<TH ALIGN=right>Last Trade<BR>Tick:</TH><TD></TD></TR>
<TR><TH ALIGN=right>Last Trade<BR>Date:</TH><TD>01/22/97</TD>
<TH ALIGN=right>Last Trade<BR>Time:</TH><TD>16:17</TD></TR>
<TR><TH ALIGN=right>52 Week<BR>High:</TH><TD>95.06</TD>
<TH ALIGN=right>52 Week<BR>Low:</TH><TD>44.50</TD></TR>
<TR><TH ALIGN=right>EPS:</TH><TD>1.71</TD>
<TH ALIGN=right>EPS Date:</TH><TD><FONT SIZE=-1>Coming
Soon</FONT></TD></TR>
<TR><TH ALIGN=right>P/E Ratio:</TH><TD>45.0</TD>
<TH ALIGN=right>Current<BR>Yield:</TH><TD><FONT SIZE=-1>Coming
Soon</FONT></TD></TR>
</TABLE></TD><TD VALIGN=top><TABLE BORDER=0 CELLPADDING=2>
<TR VALIGN=top>
<TH COLSPAN=2>Additional<BR>Information<BR><BR><BR></TH></TR>
<TR><TH ALIGN=right>Dividend:</TH><TD>0</TD></TR>
<TR><TH ALIGN=right>Option Open<BR>Interest:</TH><BR><TD>N/A</TD></TR>
<TR><TH ALIGN=right>Dividend<BR>Pay Date:</TH><TD><FONT SIZE=-1>Coming
Soon</FONT></TD></TR>
</TABLE></TD></TR></TABLE>
<CENTER><A HREF="#QuoteSummaryTableAnchor">
<IMG SRC="/graphics/schwab/schwab.return.gif" ALT="[Quote Summary]"
BORDER=0></A>
</CENTER><P>
<CENTER><FONT SIZE=-1>Security quotes are at least 15 minutes
delayed</FONT></CENTER><BR><UL><LI>Customer support, quote definitions,
 and a price
chart legend are available in <NOBR><A HREF="schwab.help.html">Quotes
and Charts Help</A>.</NOBR></LI></UL>
<P>
<TABLE BORDER=0><TR><TD>
```

Listing 15.1: Sample Quotation HTML Page (Continued)

```
<A HREF="http://www.quote.com/" TARGET=_top><IMG
SRC="/graphics/spryquotecom.gif"
        BORDER=0 ALT="Provided by Quote.com" WIDTH=165 HEIGHT=70></A>
</TD><TD>
        Market data is provided by Quote.com, Inc. By using this
service, you
        agree to the terms of the

<A _
HREF="http://www.schwab.com/SchwabNOW/SNLibrary/SNLib041/
SN041Agreement.html">User Agreement</A>.
</TD></TR></TABLE>


</center>
</BODY>
```

</HTML>If you look closely, you will see that most of the information we need for the StockQuote object can be found in this listing. You can also see examples of some of the tags. For example, here is a tag that retrieves an image.

```
<A HREF="http://www.quote.com/" TARGET=_top><IMG SRC="/graphics/spryquotecom.gif"
```

The image is not part of the page itself; a browser has to make a separate request to the specified location on the site in order to retrieve it. We'll look at this listing again later when it comes time to extract the information from the page.

The question to ask now is this: how do you request a quote for a particular stock? To do this, we have to take a look at part of a different page where you place the request:

```
<FORM METHOD="POST" ACTION="/fq/schwab/quote">
<TABLE BORDER=2 CELLPADDING=2 WIDTH="100%"><TR><TD VALIGN=top>Select
quote or chart:<BR>
<INPUT TYPE="radio" NAME="request" VALUE="Delayed quote"
CHECKED>Delayed quote<BR>
<INPUT TYPE="radio" NAME="request" VALUE="Intraday chart" >Intraday
chart<BR>
<INPUT TYPE="radio" NAME="request" VALUE="Daily chart" >Daily chart<BR>
<INPUT TYPE="radio" NAME="request" VALUE="Weekly chart" >Weekly
chart</TD>
<TD VALIGN=top>Enter the security symbol*, or <A
HREF="/fq/schwab/ticker">search for symbol</A>:<BR>
```

```
<INPUT NAME="symbols" SIZE=25 VALUE="MSFT"><BR>
<FONT SIZE=-1>*<B>Multiple symbols</B> may be entered for <B>quotes
only</B>.
Separate symbols with spaces.</FONT><BR><BR>
<INPUT TYPE="image" VALUE="Submit" BORDER=0
SRC="/graphics/schwab/submit.gif">
</TD></TR></TABLE>
</FORM>
```

The three tags that do the work are the *form method* tag and two *input type* tags. The line

```
<INPUT NAME="symbols" SIZE=25 VALUE="MSFT"><BR>
```

places a text box named "symbols" on the Web page. The current value (from a previous search) is MSFT in this particular case. The tag

```
<INPUT TYPE="image" VALUE="Submit" BORDER=0 SRC="/graphics/schwab/submit.gif">
```

places a button named "submit" on the page. The button appearance is defined by a separate graphic /graphics/schwab/submit.gif. The tag

```
<FORM METHOD="POST" ACTION="/fq/schwab/quote">
```

tells the browser how to submit the information when the submit button is clicked. The page address you will be requesting is http://schwab.quote.com/fq/schwab/quote, where schwab.quote.com is the site where this page can be found.

The server receives the rest of the information in a command line it processes to generate the response page that contains the stock quote. The command line created by a Web form consists of a question mark followed by all of the various form fields (such as the text box) with their values separated by ampersands. The commands take the generic format:

```
http://webaddress.domain/Action?firstfield=firstvalue&secondfield=secondvalue&
```

In this case, the request to retrieve Microsoft's stock price was

```
http://schwab.quote.com/fq/schwab/quote?symbols=MSFT
```

The radio button field can be ignored in this case because the default value (Delayed quote) is acceptable.

You see, you don't need to know what all of the different HTML tags mean to retrieve information from the Internet. I don't know what all of these tags mean. We will be looking at HTML in Part 3 as well, where we look at how Web pages host ActiveX controls and documents. But for now, we're ready to look at some code.

TALKING TO THE NET

The Internet control is actually quite easy to use. You start by setting the protocol property to 4 - icHTTP. This control is placed on a form named frm-Holder, which will be an invisible form belonging to the EXE server.

The form has a public property called StartQuote, which is used to start the quote retrieval process. This simple routine follows:

```
Public Sub StartQuote(symbol As String)
    Dim q$
    Select Case QuoteSource
        Case sqschwab
            q$ = "http://schwab.quote.com/fq/schwab/quote" & "?symbols=" & _
            Trim$(symbol)
            Inet1.Execute q$, "GET"
        Case sqyahoo
            q$ = "http://quote.yahoo.com/quotes?SYMBOLS=" & Trim$(symbol)_
            & "&detailed=t"
            Inet1.Execute q$, "GET"
    End Select
End Sub
```

As you can see, all we do is build the request string that the server expects to see to request a stock quote. We then use the Execute method of the control to send the request to the server.

The control does all of the work of resolving the domain and retrieving the page. You can monitor its progress by looking at the control's StateChanged event, as shown in Listing 15.2.

Listing 15.2: The Inet1_StateChanged and Form Terminate Events

```
Private Sub Inet1_StateChanged(ByVal State As Integer)
    Dim res$
    Dim ChunkVar As Variant
    Dim bDone As Boolean
    Dim st$
    Select Case State
        Case icNone
        Case icResolvingHost     'The control is looking up the IP address _
        of the specified host computer.
            st$ = "Resolving host"
        Case icHostResolved          'The control successfully found the _
        IP address of the specified host computer.
            st$ = "Host resolved"
        Case icConnecting            'The control is connecting to the host _
        computer.
            st$ = "Connecting"
```

Listing 15.2: The Inet1_StateChanged and Form Terminate Events (Continued)

```
        Case icConnected          'The control successfully connected to _
    the host computer.
        st$ = "Connected"
        Case icRequesting         'The control is sending a request to _
    the host computer.
        st$ = "Requesting"
        Case icRequestSent        'The control successfully sent the _
    request.
        st$ = "Request sent"
        Case icReceivingResponse  'The control is receiving a response _
    from the host computer.
        st$ = "Receiving"
        Case icResponseReceived   'The control successfully received a _
    response from the host computer.
        st$ = "Response received"
        DoEvents
        Case icDisconnecting      'The control is disconnecting from the _
    host computer.
        st$ = "Disconnecting"
        Case icDisconnected       'The control successfully disconnected _
    from the host computer.
        st$ = "Disconnected"
        Case icError              'An error occurred in communicating _
    with the host computer.
        st$ = "Error"
        EndQuote ""
        Case icResponseCompleted  'The request has completed and all _
    data has been retrieved
        st$ = "Response complete"
        Do
            ChunkVar = Inet1.GetChunk(1024, icString)
            If Len(ChunkVar) > 0 Then
                DoEvents
                res = res & ChunkVar
            Else
                bDone = True
            End If
        Loop While Not bDone
        EndQuote res
    End Select
    Debug.Print st$
End Sub

Private Sub Form_Terminate()
    DoEvents ' Required due to MSInet bug
End Sub
```

As you can see, the control provides detailed information on what it is doing at any given time. The sample uses the debug.print statement to let you monitor and see what is happening.

For the purposes of this component, only two states are of interest. The icError state indicates that an error occurred. The most common error you will run into will be a timeout, due to connection or server problems (on the network). The icResponseCompleted state informs the program that the data has been retrieved. The control's GetChunk method returns a string of a specified length. We loop through until the entire page has been placed into a string.

The final operation in either state is to call the EndQuote function, which is part of the QuoteEngine module. This tells the engine that a response has been received.

You may be wondering why a DoEvents statement must be placed after each GetChunk call, after the ResponseReceived state, and in the Termination event for the form, especially since, as those of you who have followed my work over the years know, I despise the DoEvents statement. In most cases it is a indication of a flawed design.

In this case, the DoEvents statements are an indication of a bug in the Microsoft Internet control. They solve a known synchronization problem with the control. This bug is documented in the Visual Basic 5.0 Readme file.

I confess that I sympathize with Microsoft's plight. As a software developer who knows full well that any non-trivial program contains bugs (and any program with more than ten lines is, by definition, not trivial), I realize that if they tried to fix every known bug in VB5, it would never ship. But as a developer, I don't have to like it.

THE QUOTE ENGINE

The code that manages the various StockQuote objects and communicates with the network by way of the frmHolder form is kept in a standard module called the Quote Engine. With all of the focus on object-oriented programming, you would think that a standard module is the last thing you would want to use in a component. Usually this would be correct. But you see, from the perspective of this component the QuoteEngine module itself represents an object, even though it is obviously not a COM object. Because the variables in a standard module are potentially global to the entire application, it presents the ideal way to share information or arbitrate between the objects in the application. The quote engine is an excellent demonstration of where you would want to use a standard module.

Listing 15.3 shows the QuoteEngine module. It uses several techniques you have seen earlier. For example: The Sub Main routine determines whether the component was started as a stand-alone program. If it was, a second form, frmQuote.frm, is shown. This form contains a text box that lets you request individual quotes and provides an easy way to test the component without using a second application. It is not unreasonable to use this technique to test ActiveX EXE servers in general; you can always remove the form before shipping the component or just disable it so it will never be shown. If the server was started as a component, we set the App.TaskVisible property to False so that it won't show up in the task list.

Listing 15.3: The QuoteEngine Module (modQuote.bas)

```
' dwQuote QuoteEngine
' Desaware ActiveX Gallimaufry
' Copyright (c) 1997 by Desaware Inc.  All Rights Reserved

Option Explicit

' Enum that indicates which service to use
Public Enum QuoteSourceType
    sqschwab = 0    ' Charles Schwab & Co.
    sqyahoo = 1     ' Yahoo
End Enum

Public QuoteSource As QuoteSourceType   ' Service in use

' This is a collection of quotes that need to be filled
' Each one is filled in turn
' All objects work with this list
Private QuotesPending As New Collection

' Set to True when a quote is in progress
Private QuotationInProgress As Boolean

' Initialization routine
Sub Main()

    ' For now, hardcode the quote source
    QuoteSource = sqyahoo

    ' On standalone operation, bring up quotation form
    If App.StartMode = vbSModeStandalone Then
        frmQuote.Show
```

Listing 15.3: The QuoteEngine Module (modQuote.bas) (Continued)

```
    Else
        ' Don't show the task in the task bar
        App.TaskVisible = False
    End If
End Sub



' Called by StockQuote object to start a quotation
' if one is not yet in progress
Public Sub StartQuote(Optional obj As StockQuote)
    Dim sq As StockQuote
    ' Add it to the list
    If Not obj Is Nothing Then
        QuotesPending.Add obj
    End If
    If (Not QuotationInProgress) And QuotesPending.Count > 0 Then
        QuotationInProgress = True
        Set sq = QuotesPending.item(1)
        frmHolder.StartQuote sq.symbol ' Start a quotation now
    End If
End Sub


' Called when quotation is done
' htmlstring is String containing the downloaded html
' html is "" if EndQuote is due to an error
Public Sub EndQuote(htmlstring As String)
    Dim htmlcol As New dwHTMLcollection
    Dim sq As StockQuote

    ' Quotation is done
    QuotationInProgress = False

    ' Remove the first item in the collection
    ' (it's the one that's been in progress
    Set sq = QuotesPending(1)
    QuotesPending.Remove 1

    ' Don't keep objects hanging around unneeded
    If QuotesPending.Count = 0 Then
        Set QuotesPending = Nothing
        Unload frmHolder
    End If

    If Len(htmlstring) = 0 Then
        sq.ReportQuote Nothing, sqError
```

Listing 15.3: The QuoteEngine Module (modQuote.bas) (Continued)

```
    Else
        htmlcol.LoadFromString htmlstring
        sq.ReportQuote htmlcol, sqIdle
    End If
    ' Start the next quotation
    StartQuote
End Sub
```

The module has two private variables. Private in this case means they can only be accessed by function in this module. Even though the standard module is shared by all of the other modules in the application, there is no reason why we shouldn't use object-oriented techniques to hide any variables and functions that are only used within the module. (And there is every reason why we should.) The QuotesPending collection contains references to all StockQuote objects that have requests pending. The QuotationInProgress Boolean keeps track of whether a request is currently in progress.

Why use a standard collection to hold the pending StockQuote objects? Why not create a custom collection or an array? Because doing so would be a waste of time, effort, and code. The primary reason for creating a custom collection is to create more robust code and to minimize the chances of clients of the collection adding an invalid object or performing an illegal manipulation on the collection. But in this case the only client for the collection is the module itself. In this case it is far easier to make sure that the module code is correct than it would be to create and test a custom collection.

The extra object involved in a custom collection is a waste of code and resources as well. As for using an array, the slight performance improvement in using an array is negligible compared to the relatively long time each quote request takes.

The module has a public variable called QuoteSource to allow you to choose the quotation service to use. This was actually a preliminary implementation of this functionality added for testing purposes. It will probably be moved to the StockQuote object for the final shipping version of this component.

The QuoteEngine module has only two public functions. The StartQuote function is called by the StockQuote objects to tell the module that it wants to make a request. The StockQuote object passes a reference to itself (Me) as a parameter. The object reference is then added to the QuotesPending collection. If a request is currently in progress, the function returns. Otherwise it checks to see if any requests are pending. If it finds one, it starts a request.

The function actually serves a dual purpose, because if you pass Nothing to it as a parameter, the function starts any pending requests if possible. This allows it to be used by the EndQuote function to start the next request. The EndQuote function is called only by the frmHolder form when a request is complete.

The first thing it does is remove from the QuotesPending collection the StockQuote object that placed the request, holding a reference to it so it won't be deleted. If no more quotes are pending, it unloads the form. This is necessary to make sure that the server terminates correctly. (Remember, an EXE server cannot be terminated unless all of its forms are unloaded.)

The EndQuote function then calls the ReportQuote method of the Stock-Quote object that placed the request. This method takes two parameters, a dwHTMLcollection object, which will be described in the next section, and a flag indicating whether the request ended in success or in error. The dwHTML-collection object is initialized using the retrieved Web page via the LoadFrom-String method.

Finally, the EndQuote function starts the next request. You can see this is really quite an elegant solution to obtaining stock quotes. The EXE server runs in its own thread; thus, it is in the background for clients using the server. The actual data retrieval across the Internet runs in the background as far as the server is concerned, leaving the server open at all times to provide additional StockQuote objects and fill requests!

PARSING HTML

You've seen that HTML pages consist of a string of tag data and content data. How do we extract the information we need from the page? The process of extracting tokens of information from a string is called *parsing*, and that is what we need to do in this case.

If this was likely to be the only time you ever wanted to parse an HTML page, then you would probably just use the Instr$ function to search for strings and extract the data. But in my case, I knew I would probably want to do this again, so I wanted to come up with a more generic solution. Besides, I wanted some nice HTML parsing components to include in Desaware's new ActiveX Gallimaufry product. They turned out to be very useful for the Stock-Quoting component and are thus included here.

The first issue that needed to be resolved was how to store the page. One possibility would be to keep it as a string, perhaps as an HTML Page object, and have methods that let you extract information from the page. The other approach would be to parse the page into multiple objects, with each object representing a single tag or content string. This latter approach is more flexible because once you break a page into its individual elements it becomes easy to add or rearrange those elements. This is ideal when it comes to creating server scripts. It also makes the searching process relatively fast. The disadvantage is that allocating a new object for each element on the page is relatively inefficient.

The implementation shown here uses the latter approach. The page is parsed into its individual elements, each of which is stored in an object called a dwHTMLelement. This object is shown in Listing 15.4.

Listing 15.4: The dwHTMLelement Class

```
' HTML element
' Desaware ActiveX Gallimaufry
' Copyright (c) 1997 by Desaware Inc.  All Rights Reserved

Option Explicit

Private intTag As String
Private intContents As String
Private separator As String

' Tag. Empty string for text
Public Function Tag() As String
    Tag = intTag
End Function

' Contents of tag element or text (if no tag)
Public Function Contents() As String
    Contents = intContents
End Function

' Loads the next tag or string element.
' Returns the balance of the string
Public Function LoadFromString(inputstring As String) As String
    Dim Bracket1Pos As Long
    Dim Bracket2pos As Long
    Dim holdstring As String
    Dim spacepos As Long
    Dim returnstring As String
    Bracket1Pos = InStr(inputstring, "<")
    Bracket2pos = InStr(inputstring, ">")
    If Bracket1Pos > 1 Then
        ' Everything up to the first bracket is content for
        ' this object
        holdstring = Left$(inputstring, Bracket1Pos - 1)
        returnstring = Mid$(inputstring, Bracket1Pos)
```

Listing 15.4: The dwHTMLelement Class (Continued)

```
    Else
        If Bracket1Pos = 0 Then
            ' No tag present. The entire input string is content
            ' for this object.
            holdstring = inputstring
        Else
            ' It's the start of a tag
            If Bracket2pos = 0 Then   ' No right bracket!
                ' This should never happen on a valid page
                ' Just treat it as a string
                returnstring = inputstring
            Else
                ' Retrieve the entire tag for this object
                holdstring = LTrim$(Mid$(inputstring, 2, Bracket2pos - 2))
                If Bracket2pos < Len(inputstring) Then
                    returnstring = Mid$(inputstring, Bracket2pos + 1)
                End If
            End If
        End If
    End If
    If holdstring <> "" Then ' Separate out the tag
        If Bracket1Pos <> 1 Then ' No tag - store the contents only
            intContents = holdstring
        Else
            ' It's a tag. Find the first delimiter character
            spacepos = StringSpan(holdstring, separator$)
            If spacepos <= 1 Then
                ' No delimiters indicates a tag with no parameters
                intTag = holdstring
            Else
                ' Place the tag in the intTag member,
                ' and the parameters in the intContents member
                intTag = Left$(holdstring, spacepos - 1)
                If spacepos < Len(holdstring) Then
                    intContents = Mid$(holdstring, spacepos + 1)
                End If
            End If
        End If
    End If
    ' Trim on left
    spacepos = StringSpan2(returnstring, separator)
    If spacepos = 1 Then
        LoadFromString = returnstring
    Else
        If spacepos > 0 Then
```

Listing 15.4: The dwHTMLelement Class (Continued)

```
        LoadFromString = Mid$(returnstring, spacepos)
      End If
    End If
End Function

Private Sub Class_Initialize()
    ' Initialize the separator string
    separator = " " & vbCrLf & vbTab
End Sub
```

Each object has two important items of data. The tag data contains the type of the tag if the object represents a tag. The contents data contains the text data either from non-tag elements or from any parameters to the tag for tag elements. Both of these items are exposed through functions.

The object is loaded via the LoadFromString function, which takes HTML code as a parameter. This method loads the object from the first element in the string. It then returns the input string with the first element stripped off. You will soon see how this can be used to quickly parse an entire page. The object uses two string utilities that are defined in a separate utility module shown in Listing 15.5.

Listing 15.5: String Functions in Module strFuncs.bas

```
' String functions
' Desaware ActiveX Gallimaufry
' Copyright (c) 1997 by Desaware Inc.  All Rights Reserved


Option Explicit

' Search string sourcestring for first occurrence of any character in _
searchchars
Public Function StringSpan(sourcestring As String, searchchars As _
String) As Long
    Dim x&
    Dim strlen&
    Dim foundpos&
    For x = 1 To Len(sourcestring)
        If InStr(searchchars, Mid$(sourcestring, x, 1)) > Ø Then
            StringSpan = x
            Exit Function
        End If
```

Listing 15.5: String Functions in Module strFuncs.bas (Continued)

```
    Next

End Function


' Search sourcestring for first character not found in searchchars
' Return 0 if entire string is in searchchars
Public Function StringSpan2(sourcestring As String, searchchars As _
String) As Long
    Dim x&
    Dim strlen&
    Dim foundpos&
    For x = 1 To Len(sourcestring)
        If InStr(searchchars, Mid$(sourcestring, x, 1)) = 0 Then
            StringSpan2 = x
            Exit Function
        End If
    Next
End Function


' Converts occurrences of HTML literal characters to real characters
Public Function ConvertHtmlLiterals(strInput As String) As String
    Dim amppos&
    Dim semipos&
    Dim lit$
    Dim res$
    Dim charval As Integer
    amppos = InStr(strInput, "&")
    If amppos = 0 Then
        ' No literals, just copy
        ConvertHtmlLiterals = strInput
        Exit Function
    End If
    semipos = InStr(strInput, ";")
    If semipos = 0 Or semipos <= amppos + 1 Then
        ' No HTML literal string, just copy
        ConvertHtmlLiterals = strInput
        Exit Function
    End If
    ' Get the string
    lit$ = Mid$(strInput, amppos + 1, semipos - amppos - 1)
    If Left$(lit$, 1) = "#" Then
        ' It's a numeric literal
        charval = Val(Mid$(lit$, 2))
    Else
```

Listing 15.5: String Functions in Module strFuncs.bas (Continued)

```
        Select Case LCase$(lit$)
          Case "lt"
              charval = 60
          Case "gt"
              charval = 62
          Case "amp"
              charval = 38
          Case "quot"
              charval = 34
          Case "emdash"
              charval = 151
          Case "copy"
              charval = 169
          Case "reg"
              charval = 174
          Case Else
              charval = 0
        End Select
    End If
    ' Yank out the unknown symbol
    If amppos > 1 Then
        res = Left$(strInput, amppos - 1)
    End If
    If charval <> 0 Then
        res = res & Chr$(charval)
    End If
    If semipos < Len(strInput) Then
        res = res & Mid$(strInput, semipos + 1)
    End If


    ' Why recursion? There may be more than one literal.
    ConvertHtmlLiterals = ConvertHtmlLiterals(res)
End Function


' Strip from the first line feed
Public Function StripLinefeeds(line$) As String
    Dim x%
    x% = InStr(line$, Chr$(10))
    If x = 0 Then StripLinefeeds = line Else StripLinefeeds = _
                  Left$(line$, x - 1)
```

End FunctionThe StringSpan function searches for the first occurrence of any character in a string that matches a character in a search string. The StringSpan2 function performs the opposite task, finding the first character in a string that does not exist in a search string. These are used to find separators between elements.

The strFuncs module also contains a function ConvertHtmlLiterals. You see, if HTML uses certain symbols to control the linking and formatting of a page, it obviously has to have a way to differentiate between those symbols as control characters and where they occur in text. For example: What if you wanted to include the line <center> in the text of a page? The browser would interpret this as a center tag. HTML thus defines a way to represent special characters. It uses an ampersand followed by an ASCII code or text code, followed by a semicolon. Thus, to include <center> in the text itself you would use:

```
&lt;center&gt;
```

The ConvertHtmlLiterals function scans a string and converts any HTML special codes into the actual characters so it can be easily used in your program. The StripLinefeeds function returns the first part of a string up to the first linefeed character that it finds. This is used later when extracting information from the page.

COLLECTING HTML ELEMENTS

Once you retrieve a stock quote HTML page, two tasks need to be performed. First, you need to parse it into a collection of dwHTMLelement objects. Next, you need to scan through that page to retrieve the quote information.

Because this collection of elements is likely to be used not only by the Stock-Quote object, but by other components as well, it seemed a good candidate for a custom collection. Using a custom collection provides two additional advantages beyond the obvious safety issues. It allows us to use a more efficient array-based approach to store the object references, and it provides an ideal location for some search utilities that are specific to dwHTMLelement objects.

Listing 15.6 shows the collection-oriented methods and properties for this class. The array-based technique shown here is virtually identical to that shown in Chapter 12. The most interesting function here is the LoadFromString function, which parses an entire HTML page and loads the collection with newly created dwHTMLelement objects from the results.

Listing 15.7 shows the searching extensions added to the collection to help find specific content on the page.

Listing 15.6: Collection Methods and Properties for the dwHTMLcollection Class

```
' HTML element collection
' Desaware ActiveX Gallimaufry
' Copyright (c) 1997 by Desaware Inc.  All Rights Reserved

Option Explicit

'local variable to hold collection
Private mCol() As dwHTMLelement
Private mColUsed As Long    ' Number of elements used
Private mColSize As Long    ' Number of elements total
Private Const GRANULARITY = 5

Public Function Append(objNewMember As dwHTMLelement)
    If mColSize = mColUsed Then
       ' Need to increase the array size
       mColSize = mColSize + GRANULARITY
       ReDim Preserve mCol(mColSize)
    End If
    mColUsed = mColUsed + 1
    Set mCol(mColUsed) = objNewMember
End Function


' Retrieve the number of objects in the collection
Public Property Get Count() As Long
    Count = mColUsed
End Property


Public Property Get item(vntIndex As Long) As dwHTMLelement
    If vntIndex < 1 Or vntIndex > mColUsed Then
      RaiseError 9    ' Subscript error
    End If
    Set item = mCol(vntIndex)
End Property

' Remove the specified item
Public Sub Remove(vntIndex As Variant)
    Dim ctr&
    If vntIndex < 1 Or vntIndex > mColUsed Then
      RaiseError 9    ' Subscript error
    End If
    ' Shift contents of array
```

Listing 15.6: Collection Methods and Properties for the dwHTMLcollection Class (Continued)

```
    For ctr = vntIndex To mColUsed - 1
        Set mCol(ctr) = mCol(ctr + 1)
    Next ctr
    Set mCol(mColUsed) = Nothing
    mColUsed = mColUsed - 1

    If mColSize - mColUsed > GRANULARITY * 2 Then
        mColSize = mColSize - GRANULARITY
        ReDim Preserve mCol(mColSize)
    End If
End Sub



Private Sub Class_Initialize()
    ' Dimension space for first element
    ReDim mCol(GRANULARITY)
    mColSize = GRANULARITY
End Sub



Private Sub Class_Terminate()
    ' mCol array objects will terminate when it goes out of scope here.
End Sub

' Parse an entire page into a collection of dwHTMLelements
Public Function LoadFromString(ByVal inputstring As String)
    Dim CurrentElement As dwHTMLelement
    Do
        Set CurrentElement = New dwHTMLelement
        inputstring = CurrentElement.LoadFromString(inputstring)
        Append CurrentElement
    Loop While Len(inputstring) > 0
End Function
```

Listing 15.7: Search Functions for the dwHTMLcollection Object

```
' Find an element that has the specified tag, content pair
' Empty content string matches all
' Case sensitive defaults to True
' Returns 0 if nothing found
Public Function Find(FirstElement As Long, ByVal Tag As String, Optional ByVal_
Contents As String, Optional CaseSensitive = True) As Long
    Dim LastElement&
```

Listing 15.7: Search Functions for the dwHTMLcollection Object (Continued)

```
Dim CurElement&
Dim thtml As dwHTMLelement
Dim bFoundTag As Boolean
Dim bFoundContents As Boolean
LastElement = Count()
' Don't bother if already past the limit
If FirstElement > Count Then Exit Function
' Compare upper case if case insensitive
If Not CaseSensitive Then
    Tag = UCase$(Tag)
    Contents = UCase$(Contents)
End If
For CurElement = FirstElement To LastElement
    Set thtml = mCol(CurElement)
    ' First check tag
    If Tag <> "" Then
        If Not CaseSensitive Then
            If Tag = UCase$(thtml.Tag) Then
                bFoundTag = True
            End If
        Else
            If Tag = thtml.Tag Then
                bFoundTag = True
            End If
        End If
    Else
        bFoundTag = True
    End If
    ' Now check contents
    If Contents <> "" Then
        If Not CaseSensitive Then
            If Contents = StripLinefeeds(UCase$(thtml.Contents)) Then
                bFoundContents = True
            End If
        Else
            If Contents = StripLinefeeds(thtml.Contents) Then
                bFoundContents = True
            End If
        End If
    Else
        bFoundContents = True
    End If
    ' Match both is a hit
    If bFoundTag And bFoundContents Then
        Find = CurElement
```

Listing 15.7: Search Functions for the dwHTMLcollection Object (Continued)

```
        Exit Function
      End If
   Next

End Function

' Searches for a sequence of tags starting with element FirstElement.
' CaseSensitive determines if the search is case sensitive
' Then follows a list of tags to find. Tags must appear in the _
specified order
Public Function FindTagSequence(FirstElement As Long, CaseSensitive As _
Boolean, ParamArray TagSequence() As Variant) As Long
   Dim CurrentBase As Long
   Dim LastElement As Long
   Dim CurrentParam As Long
   Dim FirstParam As Long
   Dim LastParam As Long
   Dim bCompareFailed As Boolean
   ' Expected and current position of tag
   Dim ExpectedPosition As Long
   Dim CurrentPosition As Long

   LastElement = Count()
   CurrentBase = FirstElement
   LastParam = UBound(TagSequence)
   FirstParam = LBound(TagSequence)
   Do
      bCompareFailed = False
      ' Try first match
      CurrentBase = Find(CurrentBase, TagSequence(FirstParam), , _
      CaseSensitive)
      ' If no match, exit now
      If CurrentBase = Ø Then Exit Function
      ' Now try the other parameters
      ExpectedPosition = CurrentBase + 1
      For CurrentParam = FirstParam + 1 To LastParam
         CurrentPosition = Find(ExpectedPosition, _
         TagSequence(CurrentParam), , CaseSensitive)
         ' If it's not the correct position, exit right away
         If ExpectedPosition <> CurrentPosition Then
            bCompareFailed = True
            Exit For
         End If
         ' Increment the expected value
         ExpectedPosition = ExpectedPosition + 1
```

Listing 15.7: Search Functions for the dwHTMLcollection Object (Continued)

```
        Next CurrentParam
        If Not bCompareFailed Then
           ' Compare succeeded on all tags!
           FindTagSequence = CurrentBase
           Exit Function
        End If
        CurrentBase = CurrentBase + 1
   Loop While CurrentBase <= LastElement

End Function


' Find next element that has no tag
' Stops search at closetag if present
Public Function FindNextNonTag(Optional FirstLoc As Long = 1, Optional _
CloseTag As String) As Long
    Dim LastElement&
    Dim CurElement&
    Dim thtml As dwHTMLelement
    LastElement = Count()
    For CurElement = FirstLoc To LastElement
        Set thtml = mCol(CurElement)
        If thtml.Tag = "" Then
            FindNextNonTag = CurElement
            Exit Function
        Else
            If thtml.Tag = CloseTag Then Exit For
        End If
    Next
End Function


' FindNextContent starts at FirstLoc,
' Looks for string "FirstContent" in a content field using _
CaseSensitive
' Then looks for the next non-tag field and returns it
' Updates the FirstLoc parameter to the location of the content tag _
returned
' Returns empty string on failure
' This function is useful for finding content pairs
Public Function FindNextContent(FirstLoc As Long, FirstContent As _
String, Optional CaseSensitive As Boolean = True) As String
    Dim HtmlFoundIdx&
    HtmlFoundIdx = FirstLoc
    HtmlFoundIdx = Find(HtmlFoundIdx, "", FirstContent, CaseSensitive)
    If HtmlFoundIdx > 0 Then HtmlFoundIdx = FindNextNonTag(HtmlFoundIdx _
    + 1)
```

Listing 15.7: Search Functions for the dwHTMLcollection Object (Continued)

```
    If HtmlFoundIdx > Ø Then
        FindNextContent = mCol(HtmlFoundIdx).Contents
        FirstLoc = HtmlFoundIdx
    End If

End Function

' AppendThroughTag  starts at FirstLoc,
' Looks for string "FirstContent" in a content field
' Then appends all non-tag fields through the specified closing tag
' Updates the FirstLoc parameter to the location of the content tag _
returned
' Returns empty string on failure
' This function is useful for combining content fields that are _
separated by formatting tags.
Public Function AppendThroughTag(FirstLoc As Long, FirstContent As _
String, ByVal CloseTag As String) As String
    Dim HtmlFoundIdx&
    Dim BuildString$
    HtmlFoundIdx = FirstLoc
    CloseTag = UCase$(CloseTag)
    If FirstContent <> "" Then HtmlFoundIdx = Find(HtmlFoundIdx, "", _
    FirstContent)
    If HtmlFoundIdx > Ø Then HtmlFoundIdx = FindNextNonTag(HtmlFoundIdx _
    + 1, CloseTag)
    If HtmlFoundIdx > Ø Then
        Do While HtmlFoundIdx <= Me.Count
            If UCase$(mCol(HtmlFoundIdx).Tag) = CloseTag Then Exit Do
            If mCol(HtmlFoundIdx).Tag = "" Then
                BuildString = BuildString & _
                StripLinefeeds(mCol(HtmlFoundIdx).Contents)
            End If
            HtmlFoundIdx = HtmlFoundIdx + 1
        Loop
        FirstLoc = HtmlFoundIdx
    End If
    AppendThroughTag = BuildString
End Function


' Raises an internal error
Private Sub RaiseError(ByVal errnum&)
    Dim ErrNumToUse&
    If errnum >= 1ØØØ Then
        ' Custom error
```

Listing 15.7: Search Functions for the dwHTMLcollection Object (Continued)

```
        Err.Raise vbObjectError + errnum, "dwHTMLcollection", _
        GetErrorString(errnum), App.HelpFile, errnum + HelpBaseOffset
    Else
        ' Raise VB error
        Err.Raise errnum, "dwHTMLcollection", GetErrorString(errnum)
    End If
End Sub
```

In this listing, the following functions are implemented.

The Find function searches for a specific element by both tag and content. It allows you to specify whether the search should be case-sensitive or not. If the tag is the empty string, the function only searches for the requested contents. If the contents is empty or missing, the function only searches for the specified tag. If both are specified, both must match. The function starts searching from a location that you specify and returns the location of the first match, or zero if no match is found.

The FindTagSequence function searches for a specified sequence of tag elements. We're going to need to find a way to uniquely identify the parts of the HTML page we are interested in. Since page formats are fairly consistent, a series of tags can be an excellent way to narrow down the search area. This function demonstrates a good use for parameter arrays, since they allow a single function to work with as many or as few tags as you wish.

The FindNextNonTag function is useful once you have found the series of tags that mark your desired location on the page. This function skips past any remaining tags in the sequence to return the location of the next non-tag element on the page. It also lets you specify a closing tag that will stop the search. This is useful for cases where the item you are searching for is blank.

The FindNextContent function is very useful for handling HTML text that looks like this:

```
<td width=130>Today's open</td><td>155 1/8</td>
```

The description for the field is a content element that is separated by one or more tags from the content element that you really want. The FindNextContent function can take the string "Today's open" as a parameter, find the element in the HTML string, skip past any tag elements to the next content element, and return the contents of that element, all in one operation. This is the function we will use most often to extract quote information from the page.

The AppendThroughTag function is useful for handling HTML code that looks like this:

```
<TH ALIGN=right>Day Low:</TH><TD>94 <SUP>5</SUP>/<SUB>8</SUB></TD></TR>
```

It searches for a specified content tag, then appends all of the content tags that follow up until a closing tag. In this case you could specify the first tag as Day Low: and the closing tag as /TD and retrieve the string "94 5/8".

The class also includes a centralized error handling function as shown. The INetErrors module (not shown here) contains the error constants for the component and the GetErrorString function.

THE STOCKQUOTE OBJECT, AT LAST

Listing 15.8 shows the actual StockQuote object. Most of the listing will be fairly clear, given your level of knowledge at this time. There are a number of private variables containing the quote information. There is the m_Notify variable, which holds the Callback object. The component uses a public enumeration to make it easy for users to interpret the value of the State function. Read-only properties are used to retrieve the quote values.

Listing 15.8: Listing of the StockQuote Object (dwQuote.cls)

```
' HTML tag
' Desaware ActiveX Library
' Copyright (c) 1997 by Desaware Inc.  All Rights Reserved

Option Explicit

' The symbol is set by the GetQuote function
Private m_Symbol As String

' These will be loaded from the web page
Private m_CompanyName As String
Private m_LastPrice As String
Private m_PriorClose As String
Private m_Change As String
Private m_High As String
Private m_Low As String
' Time of last quote
Private m_QuoteTime As String

' Object to notify when quote arrives
' Object must have function:
' Sub QuoteUpdate (QuoteInfo As StockQuote)
```

Listing 15.8: Listing of the StockQuote Object (dwQuote.cls) (Continued)

```
' We use notification instead of events because
' an app will typically use many of these objects.
Private m_Notify As Object

' 0 for idle
' 1 for busy
' 2 for error on latest quote
Private m_State As Integer

Public Enum QuoteState
    sqIdle = 0
    sqBusy = 1
    sqError = 2
End Enum



' Retrieve the state of this object
' 0 - idle
' 1 - Busy
' 2 - Error on last operation
Public Property Get State() As QuoteState
    State = m_State
End Property

' Symbol
Public Property Get symbol() As String
    symbol = m_Symbol
End Property

' Properties to retrieve stock info
Public Property Get CompanyName() As String
    CompanyName = m_CompanyName
End Property

Public Property Get LastPrice() As String
    LastPrice = m_LastPrice
End Property

Public Property Get PriorClose() As String
    PriorClose = m_PriorClose
End Property

Public Property Get Change() As String
    Change = m_Change
```

Listing 15.8: Listing of the StockQuote Object (dwQuote.cls) (Continued)

```vb
End Property

Public Property Get QuoteTime() As String
    QuoteTime = m_QuoteTime
End Property

Public Property Get High() As String
    High = m_High
End Property

Public Property Get Low() As String
    Low = m_Low
End Property

' Prevents notification. Used when you
' want to close your application - it
' forces the Quote object to release the callback
' object that it is holding
Public Sub CancelNotification()
    Set m_Notify = Nothing
End Sub

' Start the process of retrieving a quote
Public Sub GetQuote(symbol As String, Optional callback As Object)
    If m_State = 1 Then
        ' Don't try to get a quote when one is in progress
        TriggerError 4000
        Exit Sub
    End If
    If Not IsMissing(callback) Then
        Set m_Notify = callback
    End If
    ' Set the symbol
    m_Symbol = symbol
    ' Mark it as busy
    m_State = 1
    ' Start the quotation
    StartQuote Me
End Sub


' Raise an error
Private Sub TriggerError(errnum As Long)
    Err.Raise vbObjectError + errnum, "StockQuote", _
GetErrorString(errnum), App.HelpFile, errnum + HelpBaseOffset
```

Listing 15.8: Listing of the StockQuote Object (dwQuote.cls) (Continued)

```
End Sub


' Report the quote back to the notification object
' if one exists
' Remember, this is called on error - callee should
' always check state for an error code
' html is collection of dwHTMLelements
Friend Sub ReportQuote(html As dwHTMLcollection, endState As _
QuoteState)
    Dim CallbackObject As Object

    ' Parse the html page
    If Not html Is Nothing Then
        ParseHtml html
    End If

    ' Set the current state
    m_State = endState

    Set CallbackObject = m_Notify
    ' Always clear the notification - we don't want to
    ' hold the object
    Set m_Notify = Nothing
    If Not CallbackObject Is Nothing Then
        On Error GoTo NoCallbackName
        CallbackObject.QuoteUpdate Me
    End If
NoCallbackName:
    ' If a callback text error occurs, just exit
End Sub


Friend Sub ParseHtml(html As dwHTMLcollection)
    Select Case QuoteSource
        Case sqschwab
            ParseSchwabQuote html
        Case sqyahoo
            ParseYahooQuote html
    End Select
End Sub


Private Sub ParseYahooQuote(html As dwHTMLcollection)
    Dim HtmlFoundIdx As Long
    Dim IsFund As Boolean
```

Listing 15.8: Listing of the StockQuote Object (dwQuote.cls) (Continued)

```
    Dim QuoteType$
    HtmlFoundIdx = html.FindTagSequence(1, False, "Table")
    If HtmlFoundIdx = 0 Then Exit Sub
    HtmlFoundIdx = html.FindTagSequence(HtmlFoundIdx, False, "td", _
    "strong")
    If HtmlFoundIdx = 0 Then Exit Sub
    m_CompanyName = ConvertHtmlLiterals(html.item(HtmlFoundIdx + _
    2).Contents)
    m_QuoteTime = ConvertHtmlLiterals(html.AppendThroughTag(HtmlFoundIdx, _
    "Last Trade", "strong"))
    If m_QuoteTime = "" Then
        m_QuoteTime = _
        ConvertHtmlLiterals(html.AppendThroughTag(HtmlFoundIdx, "Net Asset _
        Value", "strong"))
        If m_QuoteTime <> "" Then IsFund = True
    End If

    m_LastPrice = html.AppendThroughTag(HtmlFoundIdx, "", "/STRONG")
    m_Change = html.AppendThroughTag(HtmlFoundIdx, "Change", "/TD")
    m_PriorClose = html.AppendThroughTag(HtmlFoundIdx, "Prev Close", _
    "/TD")
    ' If QuoteType <> "Stock" Then IsFund = True
End Sub


Private Sub ParseSchwabQuote(html As dwHTMLcollection)
    Dim HtmlFoundIdx As Long
    Dim IsFund As Boolean
    Dim QuoteType$
    HtmlFoundIdx = html.FindTagSequence(1, False, "/Table", "P")
    If HtmlFoundIdx = 0 Then Exit Sub
    HtmlFoundIdx = html.FindTagSequence(HtmlFoundIdx, False, "TR", "TH")
    m_CompanyName = ConvertHtmlLiterals(html.item(HtmlFoundIdx + _
    2).Contents)
    QuoteType = html.FindNextContent(HtmlFoundIdx, "Security Type:")
    If QuoteType <> "Stock" Then IsFund = True
    m_LastPrice = html.AppendThroughTag(HtmlFoundIdx, "Trade:", "/TD")
    m_Change = html.AppendThroughTag(HtmlFoundIdx, "Change:", "/TD")
    If Not IsFund Then
        m_High = html.AppendThroughTag(HtmlFoundIdx, "Day High:", "/TD")
        m_Low = html.AppendThroughTag(HtmlFoundIdx, "Day Low:", "/TD")
        m_PriorClose = ""
    Else
        m_High = ""
        m_PriorClose = ""
```

Listing 15.8: Listing of the StockQuote Object (dwQuote.cls) (Continued)

```
        m_Low = ""
    End If
    '' Retrieve the date
    m_QuoteTime = html.FindNextContent(HtmlFoundIdx, "Date:")
    m_QuoteTime = m_QuoteTime & " " & html.FindNextContent(HtmlFoundIdx, _
    "Time:")
End Sub


Public Function QuoteToCurrency(ByVal quote As String) As Currency
    Dim spacepos%    ' Location of space
    Dim fractionpos% ' Location of fraction
    Dim TempResult As Currency
    If quote = "" Then Exit Function
    quote = Trim$(quote)     ' Dump leading & trailing spaces
    spacepos = InStr(quote, " ")
    If spacepos = 0 Then
        QuoteToCurrency = CCur(quote)
        Exit Function
    End If
    ' Get the integer value first
    TempResult = CCur(Left$(quote, spacepos - 1))

    ' We know it's not a trailing space because of
    ' the initial trim operation.
    quote = Mid$(quote, spacepos + 1)

    ' Is there a fractional?
    fractionpos = InStr(quote, "/")
    If fractionpos <= 1 Or fractionpos = Len(quote) Then
        ' We don't know how to parse this
        QuoteToCurrency = TempResult
        Exit Function
    End If
    On Error GoTo MathError:
    TempResult = TempResult + CCur(Left$(quote, fractionpos - 1)) / _
    CCur(Mid$(quote, fractionpos + 1))
    QuoteToCurrency = TempResult
    Exit Function

MathError:
    ' For now, just return the current result.
    QuoteToCurrency = TempResult
End Function
```

Listing 15.8: Listing of the StockQuote Object (dwQuote.cls) (Continued)

```
Public Function CurrencyToQuote(ByVal quote As Currency) As String
    Dim IntVal As Integer
    Dim FracVal As Integer
    Dim Denominator As Integer
    IntVal = Fix(quote) ' Get integer part

    ' Get the fractional part
    ' How many 64's (lowest fraction we're likely to see)
    FracVal = CInt(Abs(quote - IntVal) * 64)

    ' Now we keep dividing while even
    Denominator = 64
    Do
        If (FracVal And 1) Then
            ' It's odd
            Exit Do
        End If
        FracVal = FracVal \ 2
        Denominator = Denominator \ 2
    Loop While Denominator > 0

    CurrencyToQuote = IntVal & " " & FracVal & "/" & Denominator

End Function
```

Perhaps the most interesting functions here are the ParseHtml and the functions it calls. These functions first look for the tags that appear before the company name. The company name has to be processed by the ConvertHtmlLiterals function because some companies have special characters in their names (AT&T, for example). The function then calls FindNextContent to extract the various quote information.

As you can see in this implementation, not every service provides all of the information the StockQuote object can use. You can search for other services or call multiple services to obtain as much information as you need.

What would happen if Schwab or Yahoo changed the format of their pages? Unless the format change is major, chances are these are the only functions that would need to be changed. What would happen if Schwab or Yahoo stopped providing stock quote information, and we had to change the server to another site? We would have to add a new parsing function and change the request line in the frmHolder form. That's all.

Clearly the server could easily be modified to handle multiple stock quoting services and even to support alternate services if one is down. Part of the work has already been started; the rest is left as an exercise for the reader.

ON REFERENCING

One subtle aspect of the operation of this server relates to the object referencing. For example: What happens if a client closes down during a request?

Surprisingly enough, this is not a problem. First of all, when a request is in progress, the object holds on to a reference to the Callback object, which prevents the client from closing down in the first place. However, the client can (and should) use the CancelNotification method to cancel a request and shut down. Also, the client does not have to use a callback. It can pass Nothing to the GetQuote function and poll the State property to determine when the request is complete.

So what happens if the client does close down? This eliminates a reference to the StockQuote object. However, if the object has a quote pending, it will not be deleted because it is still referenced by the QuoteEngine's collection. Only after the quote is complete will the object be terminated.

The same care is used to unload the frmHolder form open when no more quotes are pending. If the form was always loaded, the server would never terminate.

THE STOCKMON.VBP PROJECT

The StockMon.vbp project is a very simple project that demonstrates the original task I had in mind: a program that would monitor a selection of stock and periodically notify me if any changes occur. The project is extremely straightforward and can be found in the Chapter 15 samples directory on your CD-ROM.

This concludes the long-promised and often-delayed StockQuote component. As you have seen, it takes advantage of many of the features of ActiveX that were described throughout this part of the book.

But like any ActiveX code component, the StockQuote server operates primarily behind the scenes. It's time to look at a component type that is possibly even more exciting, and certainly more challenging: ActiveX controls.

Part 3

ActiveX Controls

When Visual Basic 1.0 first came out, there were two things I saw in it that I found really exciting.

First, Visual Basic encapsulated Windows to such a degree that anyone could quickly learn to create a Windows program. Today we sometimes forget how difficult it was to write Windows programs back in 1991. The really nice thing about VB was that even as it hid the complexity of Windows, Microsoft made it possible to make direct API calls so programmers could still take advantage of the full power of Windows. In fact, I liked the idea so much that I wrote two books about it (the original *Visual Basic Programmer's Guide to the Windows API*, ZD Press, 1993 and then its successor, the *Visual Basic Programmer's Guide to the Win32 API*, ZD Press, 1996).

I was also thrilled with the idea of custom controls. I had spent some time working as a hardware engineer and was well accustomed to the idea of building complex hardware out of components—integrated circuits that had a clearly defined electrical and functional interface. The idea of building applications out of software components was quite appealing. The idea of creating them even more so. In fact it was so appealing that I founded a company with the express purpose of creating components—specifically, the kind of components that other Visual Basic programmers could use to take full advantage of Windows. (See the common theme?)

It should be no surprise that I find Visual Basic 5.0's ability to create custom controls (now called ActiveX controls) to be possibly the most important feature in the language. The minute I heard that this feature would be included, I decided I wanted to channel my efforts toward helping Visual Basic programmers learn this technology and create the coolest and most advanced controls possible.

Part of this goal is fulfilled in the new tools from my company that extend the reach of ActiveX controls as implemented in VB. The other part is this book. In fact, I was originally thinking about writing a book that focused only on creating ActiveX controls, but I quickly realized that you can't really write great controls without a good understanding of code components and ActiveX technology in general. Besides, now that code components support events, there are many tasks that were traditionally implemented by controls that are now better suited for code components. You have to understand how to create both in order to evaluate the trade-offs involved when you make your own design choices.

It is with those trade-offs that any discussion about ActiveX controls must begin.

ActiveX Control Fundamentals

THINGS EVERY PROGRAMMER SHOULD
KNOW ABOUT ACTIVEX CONTROLS
BEFORE HE OR SHE WRITES A SINGLE
LINE OF CODE

DESIGN TIME VERSUS RUNTIME VERSUS
DESIGN TIME VERSUS RUNTIME

THE ~~THREE~~ FOUR MODELS FOR CONTROL
CREATION

A s is true with any technology, it is important to keep ActiveX controls in perspective. If you listen to Microsoft for any length of time you will quickly become convinced that ActiveX controls are not just the most important technology to hit Windows, the Internet, intranets, client-server development and so on, but that they will also bring on world peace, end hunger, eliminate political corruption, and lead to the rapid development of faster-than-light travel. If you listen to some other companies and pundits, you may come to discover that ActiveX controls are severely limited, inherently insecure, overly complex, poorly standardized and that they will lead to brain damage, World War III, and the ultimate hegemony of Microsoft as Bill Gates proceeds to buy up every software company in the world.

Ahem...

There are days when I feel that the media organizations covering our industry are taking their cue from colleagues who cover political campaigns. The problem is that this type of coverage is not necessarily helpful to programmers who are trying to decide what technologies to deploy. I feel it is important that we start our discussion of ActiveX controls by trying to place some of the conflicting claims into perspective. One of the worst things that can happen to any programmer is to invest lots of time and effort on a technology only to hit a brick wall halfway through a project, discovering that it is not suitable for the task and never was.

Hopefully this chapter will help minimize the chances of hitting brick walls, or, at the very least, help you to see them approaching in the distance.

Things Every Programmer Should Know about ActiveX Controls before He or She Writes a Single Line of Code

What is an ActiveX control? Obviously that is the subject of forthcoming chapters, but the forthcoming chapters focus on the technical answer to this question. If you look at it from the highest level, an ActiveX control potentially supports the following characteristics:

1 Everything that an in-process DLL server can do except:

▸ Expose public objects (other than the control itself)

▸ Support multithreading

2 Be sited on a container. This means the control has its own independent user interface that is contained on the window of another application, be it a form in Visual Basic or a Web page on an Internet browser. The control is able to interact with the container application in a variety of different ways.

3 Support design-time programming characteristics, including:

▸ Support for property pages

▸ The ability to store property values set at design time in a location specified by the container

▸ The ability to interact with the container's property browser if one exists

In other words: ActiveX controls = Code Components + User Interface + Container Features. We'll go into much more detail on these subjects later. The reason for mentioning them here is this: If your component does not need any of these three characteristics, there is a very good chance you should not implement an ActiveX control but should, instead, create a code component. ActiveX controls are more complex than code components. Why put in the extra work if you don't need to?

ACTIVEX CONTROLS ARE PLATFORM-LIMITED

At the time of publication of this book, ActiveX controls created with Visual Basic 5.0 were able to run on the following platforms:

▸ Windows 95 and later versions of Microsoft's "lighter" 32-bit operating system

▸ Windows NT 3.51 with service pack #5 or later

▸ Windows NT 4.0 and later

That's it. What does this mean with regard to your choice of whether to adopt this technology? Here are some situations where ActiveX controls may prove ideal:

▸ You are creating applications that are targeted for these platforms. These applications may be in Visual Basic, Office 97, other containers that support ActiveX controls, or any other VBA-based application that supports ActiveX controls. Keep in mind that Microsoft is now licensing VBA to other companies and that ActiveX controls are being adopted by many software development tools.

▸ You are creating a Web site that is targeted towards those who are using these Microsoft platforms, or you are willing to accept lesser functionality for those who are not. Microsoft takes this approach on their own Web site.

▸ You are creating a Web site for a corporate intranet and your corporation has standardized on these platforms, or you are willing to accept lesser functionality for those who are on other platforms.

These situations also suggest other times where ActiveX controls may not be appropriate:

▸ Your application needs to support 16-bit platforms. In this case you have two choices. You can use Visual Basic 4.0 and use Visual C++ to create both 16- and 32-bit ActiveX controls. Or you can use Visual Basic 3.0 or 4.0, use 16-bit technology and just run your 16-bit applications on 32-bit Windows.

▸ You need to create a general purpose Web site that supports multiple platforms, including perhaps Apple, UNIX, Windows for Workgroups, and Windows NT users who have not upgraded to 3.51 with service pack 5. For cases such as these, a generic version of Java (assuming such a thing exists) may be a better choice.

Occasionally one hears rumors coming out of Microsoft regarding support for ActiveX control technology on non-Windows platforms. With all due respect to Microsoft, I would suggest that you do not believe it until they ship it. For technical reasons, if they do end up supporting Visual Basic ActiveX controls on non-Microsoft platforms, I would expect that there may be some limitations including:

▸ They may require compilation in P-Code. Otherwise they would have to implement a full Intel native code emulation.

▸ They may not support use of API functions in a control, which as you will see is a very powerful technique for creating sophisticated controls.

It is possible that other vendors will support ActiveX controls on non-Windows platforms. Here, too, I would suggest that you do not believe it until they ship it.

I must stress, however, that when I question the support of ActiveX controls on non-Windows platforms, that is *not* the same thing as questioning the support of ActiveX controls on non-Microsoft containers. I fully expect many Windows versions of non-Microsoft products (including Web browsers) to support ActiveX controls very nicely. Unlike the case with different operating systems, there are no technical reasons why a Windows-based application or browser should not support ActiveX controls. Of course, there may be political and strategic issues—but I won't go any closer to that subject.

ACTIVEX CONTROL CONTAINERS ARE NOT ALL THE SAME

In the ideal world, every application that claimed to be a container for ActiveX controls would be able to handle every ActiveX control. In the ideal world, every ActiveX control would work perfectly in every application that is a container for ActiveX controls.

I suppose it will be no surprise to you if I inform you at this point that we don't live in an ideal world.

A Brief History of ActiveX Controls   What I'm about to tell you now has little or nothing to do with today's ActiveX control technology, or developing controls in Visual Basic. Consider, if you will, a brief historical aside, the kind that comes from the deep-seated need of those who have gone through a traumatic experience to tell their tale. Traumatic experience? Yes, for you see, I am a survivor of the ordeal that component vendors went through in the switch from VBX to OCX technology during the transition from Visual Basic 3.0 to 4.0.

And an ordeal it was. Like the other software vendors who had contributed controls to be included with Visual Basic, we were given early notice of the new technology. We were given impossible schedules. And then things began to slip. I think when all was said and done, the transition took almost a year longer than was originally forecast.

The frustrating thing from our point of view was that we were trying to create controls based on a specification that was changing, using tools that were changing, to run on a container that was changing, for an operating system that was still unreleased. There was not a stable piece of code anywhere in sight.

It was not unusual for us to get multiple drops of software every week and very common for new drops to require some major recoding.

By ship date, I think it is safe to say that we were all frustrated and exhausted. Our controls worked fairly well on Visual Basic 4.0, but those who tried to support other containers often had to add code specific to that particular platform. For example: Access 95 was released before Visual Basic 4.0 and did not support all of the ActiveX control features that were supported by VB.

Fortunately, Visual Basic 4.0 finally did ship, and so did vendors' controls. I can't speak for others, but I was quite pleased with the stability and reliability of ours. And the ActiveX control standard finally stabilized…a little bit.

The Different Flavors of ActiveX Containers You see, the ActiveX control standard is not quite as standard as one might expect. And you now know enough about ActiveX technology to understand why.

Remember that ActiveX technology is based on COM objects. ActiveX controls are COM objects that support specific interfaces. In fact, the ActiveX control specification consists mostly of definitions of those interfaces.

The problem is this: the standards focused mostly on the interfaces themselves—the methods and properties for each one. But the standards were not clear about which interfaces a container had to support to really be considered an ActiveX container. It was possible, and common, for a container to only support a minimal set of interfaces. For example: There is an interface called ISimpleFrame that a control can implement if it wants to be a container for other controls. An example of this is a picture control, which can hold other controls. An ActiveX container was not required to support this interface, and some did not.

This meant a control that wanted to be a container for other controls could not assume it would actually be allowed to do so by its own host container.

Microsoft did make an effort to specify which interfaces are required and which are optional for both containers and controls. But it remains a moving target.

You already know that the way ActiveX technology is extended is by defining new interfaces. A recent example of this involved making ActiveX controls Internet-compatible—it was simply a matter of adding new Internet-related interfaces to controls.

But when new interfaces are added to controls, they obviously cannot assume that existing containers will support those new features. On the contrary, as a control developer you must assume there will be containers that cannot support certain features of your control. This leaves you two options: You can choose not to support those containers, or you can be sure that your control degrades gracefully, using careful coding and error detection to make sure that if your control does not work, at least it does not crash the application.

There are also some areas where container behavior is not clearly defined. To see an example of this, look at the ch16ctl1.ocx control in the Chapter 16 directory on your CD ROM and register it. Try adding it to a VB5 project—take note of how it looks at design time. Note that properties TestBool1 and TestBool2 both appear in the property page.

Now try adding it to a VB4 project. Looks different, does it? And what happened to the TestBool1property? You'll find out why later.

This book will attempt to point out situations that are likely to be container-specific. However, keep in mind that I myself have only worked with a fraction of the containers that exist today, much less those that will be available by the time you read this.

VB-CREATED CONTROLS DO HAVE LIMITATIONS

I mentioned earlier that Visual Basic made Windows programming accessible by encapsulating the features of Windows into the Basic syntax. Visual Basic programming is not as easy as it once was, but that is mostly because Windows has grown considerably. Visual Basic is still one of the easiest ways to create Windows applications.

Visual Basic is also one of the safest ways to create Windows programs. Programmers who use Visual C++ and similar languages grow accustomed to dealing with frequent memory exceptions during the course of application development. Visual Basic does an excellent job of preventing these kinds of exceptions. In fact, the only ways to trigger a memory exception during VB development are:

- ▶ Invalid use of API calls or low-level API extensions
- ▶ Use of the AddressOf operator
- ▶ Bugs in Visual Basic

Perhaps the nicest thing about Visual Basic is that it gives you control over the trade-offs between power and safety. You can stay within the safe and "easy" confines of Visual Basic and perform a large percentage of the tasks that Windows makes possible. You can selectively extend the power of Visual Basic using API calls and third-party controls and DLLs to perform almost any task, but at a price. These extensions either reduce the safety level, making memory exceptions possible, or increase the overhead, as you distribute additional controls and DLLs that perform the desired tasks in a safe manner.

This situation is repeated with Visual Basic 5.0's implementation of ActiveX control creation.

Visual Basic allows you to create ActiveX controls more easily and quickly than has ever been possible. It does this by encapsulating many of the ActiveX control-related interfaces and objects into the Visual Basic language and environment. Control development under VB is remarkably safe as well.

But in doing so, Visual Basic had to sacrifice some of the features that are available to ActiveX controls written under Visual C++. These limitations fall into several major areas:

▶ Inability to create 16-bit controls.

▶ Not all events and methods of the OLE control interfaces are exposed to VB programmers.

▶ Inability to support non-dispatch interfaces.

▶ Inability to modify design-time-only properties of contained controls at control runtime.

We'll go into more details on these limitations in upcoming chapters.

The good news is that just as it was possible to use direct API calls and third-party products to extend the power of Visual Basic, it is also possible to use API calls and third-party products to extend the reach of VB-created controls to the point where they are able to handle almost any task you can perform with other control development tools.

Also, keep in mind that Visual Basic controls also have advantages over those created in Visual C++. For example: It is notoriously difficult to build a control from constituent controls using VC++.

The intent of this section, which focuses on limitations, is not to discourage you from using Visual Basic to create your ActiveX controls. On the contrary, I think you'll find that Visual Basic is the best tool around for creating controls. The intent is to get some of the "nasty surprises" out of the way, so you can approach the technology with a clearer understanding of its strengths and its limitations.

Design Time versus Runtime versus Design Time versus Runtime

When working with ActiveX controls you have to be aware at all times of whether the control that you created is in design time, meaning that its designer is open, or the designer is closed and you are in Break mode, which is also considered design time, and to differentiate between design time from your perspective as a control developer and design time meaning the mode of the container that is hosting your control—for your control will usually be at runtime while it appears to be exhibiting design-time behavior (which you programmed) from the perspective of the end user of your controls, keeping in mind, of course, that any constituent controls of your control are in runtime mode except for when your control designer is actually open.

And we haven't yet discussed what happens when the user of your control enters runtime mode as well.

And if you understood that sentence, I am very impressed. It will take me the rest of this chapter to explain it. Let us begin.

A MATTER OF PERSPECTIVE

Perhaps the single most important thing you need to do before undertaking development of ActiveX controls in Visual Basic is to gain a thorough understanding of the different objects you use to create controls, how they relate to each other, and the different operating modes they support.

Without this understanding, you might get hopelessly lost, as you try to figure out which property belongs to which object. For example: does the property "Name" refer to the name of a constituent control (and if so, which one?), the name of your control, or the name that some developer using your control assigned to your control? All of these Name properties can exist in your control simultaneously and will almost certainly have different values.

In fact, some of you reading this probably got lost as soon as I mentioned constituent controls!

So let's begin with a somewhat philosophical look at ActiveX controls. Then we'll build on your existing knowledge of COM objects and ActiveX technology to see how the pieces fit together.

First, consider a standard control type, such as a list box. As far as you're concerned at this point, the built-in controls such as a list box are identical to any ActiveX control you create yourself. The only difference is that a built-in control (also called an intrinsic control) is implemented within Visual Basic instead of a separate .OCX file.

When you draw a list box onto a blank form, you have placed a COM object on a form. Like any object, it has properties, methods, and the ability to raise events. For example, you can add an item to the list box using the line:

```
List1.AddItem
```

The events of the list box appear with the syntax List1_*eventname.* For example:

```
Private Sub List1_Click()
End Sub
```

You may have noticed that the syntax of a control event is identical to that of events raised with an ActiveX code component and of interface functions added to an object using the Implements statement. That is because this syntax defines both the event name and the name of an interface. List1_Click means the Click event on the List1 event interface.

Now, here is a question for you. When your form is in design time, do the list box properties and events exist? The answer is: yes, absolutely. But you can't do much with them. There are two reasons for this: First, Visual Basic does not run any of your application's code at design time. So if the list control raises an event, nothing happens in your code. And your code can't set list box properties if it is not running.

But you can set list box properties using the Visual Basic property window. As far as the list control itself is concerned, all it sees is a property being set. It does not care and cannot tell whether the property has been set by a property window or by your code.

However, the list control does know whether its container is in design time or runtime. It knows this because the ActiveX specification provides a way for a control to ask the container what mode it is in. The list control can decide how to handle property access based on the container's run mode. If you use the VB property window to set the background color for a list box, the change takes place immediately. However, if you drop a new list control on a form, it displays the name of the control at design time and nothing at runtime (unless you use the List property to add items at design time). There are other properties, such as the MultiSelect property, that can only be set at design time.

The key point that you must keep in mind is that these different control behaviors are not determined by Visual Basic. They are determined by the control itself. Visual Basic knows which properties can be set only at design time because the control informs Visual Basic of the fact. And the control can do this because the code that implements the control is running.

Figure 16.1 illustrates this scenario from the point of view of a developer using a control. The control itself is always running but may change its behavior based on the mode of the container. In VB design mode, most of the communication with the control is from Visual Basic's property window. In VB run mode, and in compiled executables, most of the communication is from your own application's code.

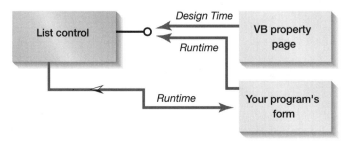

Figure 16.1: A control from the developer's perspective

The Author's Point of View   As the author of a control, you will have a different perspective.

Your job is to create a control which, when it is running, exposes properties, methods, and events. It will be up to you to ask the container whether it is in design mode or run mode, and to vary the operation of your control accordingly if you wish. The developer who uses your control will only be able to access those properties, methods, and events that you choose to make public.

This terminology follows the lead of Microsoft's documentation. You are the author of the control. The developer is the person who creates instances of your control and places them on the forms of his or her application.

Controls do not magically develop themselves. From your point of view as an author, your control will be in design mode as well as run mode. But controls are a little bit more complex than applications in this respect.

You may recall in Chapter 9 that I made quite a fuss about designers and about distinguishing between the designers that allow you to edit user interface characteristics of an object, such as a form, and code windows, which allow you to edit the code for an object. The reason for this is that the behavior of ActiveX controls you create depends on whether the control's designer is open or closed.

When the ActiveX control designer is open, your control is unavailable to clients. When the designer is closed, you can add the control to forms in the current instance of Visual Basic. You can set breakpoints in your control's code and thus trace through both your control's code and the developer code that is using the control.

So the first step you need to perform in order to test your control is to close its designer. This starts the control running. This means it is possible to close a designer, set a breakpoint in your control's code, place the control on a form, and step through your control code that is running even though the container is in design mode!

How do you create methods, properties, and events in your control? And how do you differentiate between the methods and properties you expose to the outside world and those you must use to create your control?

A CACOPHONY OF OBJECTS

A number of different objects are involved in the process of authoring ActiveX controls. The most important of these are:

- ▶ Your Control object
- ▶ The UserControl object
- ▶ The Ambient object
- ▶ The Extender object
- ▶ Constituent control objects

Let's look at these one by one as you follow the process of creating a very simple control. This control will be a private control that is built into the executable itself. You will not be able to create a public OCX for it, but this is the only difference between private and public ActiveX controls.

Create a new stand-alone EXE project. Add a UserControl object to the project. The ActiveX designer for the control will be visible. Change the name of the control from UserControl1 to MyControl. Change the project name from Project1 to Ch16CtlA.

Click on the control in the designer window. Look at the property window. The properties that you see listed are those of the UserControl object for your control. The MyControl class that you have created to implement your control contains a UserControl object you will use to implement the control.

Double-click on the designer to bring up the code window for the control. Add a property to the control by adding the following code:

```
Dim m_MyProp As String

Public Property Get MyProp() As String
    MyProp = m_MyProp
End Property

Public Property Let MyProp(vNewValue As String)
```

```
    m_MyProp = MyProp
End Property
```

Bring up the form for the project. Change the form's name to MyForm. This is the form you will use to test the control. If you look in the toolbox, you will see a grayed-out bitmap that is associated with your control.

Now close the designer for the control. The control's bitmap will become clear. Bring up the form and create an instance of the control that you authored on the form. The default name for the control instance was defined by the Name property of the control's UserControl object, in this case MyControl1. This is also the name for the object's type.

Look at the property page for the control. You'll see the MyProp string that you created earlier. You'll also see many other properties. These properties are called *Extender* properties because they are implemented by a separate object called an Extender object provided by the container (in this case, Visual Basic).

Without closing the form designer, open the control designer again by clicking on the MyControl icon in the project window. Look at the form. The image of the control has been marked with diagonal lines to indicate that the control is not available. Bring up the code window for the control again and add the following event code:

```
Event Click()    ' Add this at the top of the module

Private Sub UserControl_Click()
    RaiseEvent Click
End Sub
```

Close the designer again. In the MyForm code module, add the following code:

```
Private Sub MyControl1_Click()
    MsgBox "MyControl was clicked"
End Sub
```

Now run the project (be sure MyForm is set as the startup form). Click on the control. The message box will appear when the control's Click event is triggered.

Stop the project and bring up the ActiveX designer again. Add a command button to the control. Add the following code to the module

```
Event ButtonClick()    ' Add this at the top of the module

Private Sub Command1_Click()
    RaiseEvent ButtonClick
End Sub
```

Go back to form Myform and add the following code:

```
Private Sub MyControl1_ButtonClick()
   MsgBox "MyControl's button was clicked"
End Sub
```

Run the project. Now try clicking on both the control and the command button that is on the control. From your perspective as an author, you are handling two incoming Click events on two different COM event interfaces, one from the UserControl object, the other from the command button, which is a constituent control. You are then raising two different events on your control's event interface. The developer sees both controls as events of MyControl1.

Bring up the ActiveX designer. Add a label control to your control. Add the following code to the UserControl_Paint() event:

```
Private Sub UserControl_Paint()
   If Ambient.UserMode Then
      Label1.Caption = "Container is in Run mode"
   Else
      Label1.Caption = "Container is in Design mode"
   End If
End Sub
```

Now close the designer and look at the form in design mode. Now run the project. This demonstrates how a control can change its behavior based on whether it is in run mode or design mode. To do this, a control uses the Ambient object, which contains information about the container's environment.

Let's take a closer look at the five types of objects you have seen here.

Your Control Object   The only part of the ActiveX control you implement as an author is the control object itself, in this case, the MyControl object. This object serves two purposes: It defines the public methods, properties, and events that are available to those using your control. It defines the behavior of the control.

In addition to methods and properties you implement, you have access to properties in the UserControl, Extender, and Ambient objects and any constituent controls you add to your control. You receive events from the UserControl object and any constituent controls you add to your control.

The UserControl Object   From your perspective as a programmer, the UserControl object is a subobject of your control. You access methods in the UserControl object using the syntax: UserControl.*method*. The UserControl object can raise events in your control object you can respond to in your code. Note that this does *not* raise events in the control instances that developers create when using your control. If you want a UserControl event such as the UserControl_Click event to be exposed to developers using your control, you must define a new event in your control's object and raise an event yourself.

From the perspective of a Visual Basic application, your control object may seem like a subobject of the UserControl object. This is because it is the User-Control object that Visual Basic knows how to site and place on a container. Visual Basic and Windows direct mouse and keyboard input to the UserControl object, which processes them and raises events your code can handle as needed. The UserControl object is responsible for creating the control's window and for handling activation, input focus, and all other user interface issues. All of these activities are then exposed to your control object through events and properties.

The UserControl object is the default object for your control. To see what this means, consider what happens when you work with a form and access the property known as "Caption." In this case you will by default access the caption of the form. But if you create a new property called Caption in the form, the new Caption property will hide the default one provided by the form. This is exactly like the variable scoping rules that you read about in Chapter 10. Locally defined variables hide global variables of the same name. Locally defined properties and methods hide global properties and methods or properties and methods of the default object. You can, however, still access the Caption property of the form by explicitly specifying the form; for example: Form1.Caption.

The Ambient Object The Ambient object is used to obtain information from the container. The properties in this object allow you to determine some of the capabilities of the container and adapt your control to handle them if you so wish. One example you saw earlier is the UserMode property, which allows you to determine if the container is in run mode or design mode. Another example is the BackColor property, which allows you to obtain the background color for the container. This can be useful if you want your control to track the background color of its container. The UserControl object includes the AmbientChanged event, which allows you to detect when an Ambient property is changed.

Containers may define their own ambient properties and are not required to implement even the ones that you see in the Visual Basic object browser and VB documentation. To make life easier, the Ambient object detects properties that are missing from the container and simply returns the default value for the property.

Does this mean, for example, that a container is not required to implement a property such as UserMode? Yes. If it isn't implemented, how does your control know whether it is in design time or not? It doesn't. Some containers do not distinguish between design time and runtime. Those containers don't need to expose the UserMode property. In this case the Ambient object will always return True.

The Extender Object   There are some properties associated with controls that really have nothing to do with the functioning of the control itself. For example: Every control in Visual Basic has a Name property, and that property is really managed by the container. Other properties that fall into this category are the Visible property and the position properties, such as Left and Right.

When a developer uses your control, the container automatically adds these properties to your control's interface so the developer can access them. They are called Extender properties. The developer cannot tell the difference between properties provided by the container and those provided by the control itself. But you, the control author, can. For one thing, you don't need to implement Extender properties—in fact, you can't. But you are able to access these container-provided Extender properties using the Extender object.

There is just one catch to this object. There is no way of knowing what properties a container provides. While there are some standard properties that most containers support, you must always use error-checking when accessing these properties if you want to be sure that you can support any container.

Because Extender objects cannot be determined ahead of time, access to them is always late bound.

Constituent Objects   In a way, these are the easiest objects to deal with. They work almost exactly the same way as controls work in a form. You draw them on your control just as if you were placing controls on a form. You access them in the same way, and they raise events in the same way. Just keep in mind that developers using your control will have no access to the properties, methods, or events of constituent controls unless you explicitly expose them.

There are some interesting side effects of using constituent controls in an ActiveX control. These side effects relate to focus, accelerator keys, and tabbing between controls, but this is a subject for the next chapter.

Constituent objects in ActiveX controls suffer from one major limitation. It derives from the following question: When is a constituent control in run mode and when is it in design mode?

Table 16.1 illustrates the possible operating modes for ActiveX controls, client applications, and constituent controls. As you can see, when the designer is open, your control code cannot run (you are in control design mode). At this time you can set the design-time properties of your constituent controls using the VB property window or their property pages. As soon as you close the designer, your control begins to run and the constituent controls enter run mode, regardless of the container operating mode.

This means it is not possible with Visual Basic 5.0 to set the design time-only properties of a constituent control at runtime. For example: you cannot change a constituent list control from single selection to multiselection mode, even at the container's design time (when you might want to support this capability). There are a number of ways to work around this problem, as you will see later.

Table 16.1: Operating Modes of ActiveX Controls and Constituent Controls

ActiveX Designer	Client Application Using Your Control	Constituent Control Mode
Open—control is not running	Control is inactive	Design
Closed—control is running or in break mode	Design mode	Run mode
Closed—control is running or in break mode	Run mode or break mode	Run mode—control is running or in break mode

Figure 16.2 summarizes the object model for ActiveX controls. The gray rectangle at the upper length represents your control. Your control includes the UserControl object and any constituent controls. The other gray block indicates objects relating to the container. The Ambient object and Extender object are provided by Visual Basic to provide access to container information.

The ~~Three~~ Four Models for Control Creation

Visual Basic supports four models for creating ActiveX controls. Yes, I know that Microsoft only mentions three of them, but the fourth is really quite important. It's also quite complex and requires a somewhat advanced level of knowledge, so I can't really fault them for not discussing it.

Choosing a model is one of the most important decisions you will make when designing your control. In this section we'll review these approaches and the advantages and disadvantages of each one. At the same time, we will review some fundamental concepts that were introduced earlier in this chapter.

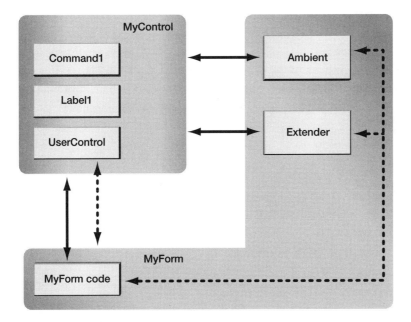

Figure 16.2: Object relationships in an ActiveX control

ENHANCE AN EXISTING CONTROL

Let's say you have been using Command buttons in your applications for years, but one day you realize something has been missing. There is one feature you really wish command buttons had, and that if it was only there, you would be perfectly satisfied with everything else relating to Visual Basic. That the one thing you wished is that the Click event included parameters telling you where in the button the mouse had been clicked.

Now, as a veteran VB programmer, you know that you can accomplish this using the MouseUp event, but you also know that anyone for whom a modified Click event is the ultimate wish is probably not thinking too clearly anyway. But that is irrelevant. The point is that almost every VB programmer has probably looked at a control and thought, "If only it had this one more feature…"

The ActiveX control designer allows you to drop other controls—called Constituent controls—onto your ActiveX control. It also allows you to create Public properties and events that can access the properties and events of the Constituent control.

The BtnTest group in the Chapter 16 sample directory on your CD-ROM demonstrates this using a simple example. It contains a BtnTest standard EXE project, which is used to test the control, and the ch16Button ActiveX control project. This control was created by dropping a command button on the User-Control designer and using the ActiveX Control Wizard to map properties and events from your class to the Command button.

You've already seen the type of code that maps properties and events. Here, for example, is the code to map the Font property:

```
Public Property Get Font() As Font
    Set Font = Command1.Font
End Property

Public Property Set Font(ByVal New_Font As Font)
    Set Command1.Font = New_Font
    PropertyChanged "Font"
End Property
```

Here is an example of an event mapping:

```
Private Sub Command1_KeyPress(KeyAscii As Integer)
    RaiseEvent KeyPress(KeyAscii)
End Sub
```

Here is how the Click event for your object is modified:

```
Event Click(ByVal X As Single, ByVal Y As Single)
Private mousex As Single, mousey As Single

Private Sub Command1_MouseDown(Button As Integer, Shift As Integer, X As Single,
Y As Single)
    mousex = X: mousey = Y
    RaiseEvent MouseDown(Button, Shift, X, Y)
End Sub

Private Sub Command1_MouseMove(Button As Integer, Shift As Integer, X As Single,
Y As Single)
    mousex = X: mousey = Y
    RaiseEvent MouseMove(Button, Shift, X, Y)
End Sub

Private Sub Command1_Click()
    RaiseEvent Click(mousex, mousey)
End Sub
```

During the Command1_MouseMove and Command1_MouseDown events, the mouse location is stored in two private variables. They are used to provide the parameters for the Click event.

It is also important to make sure that the command button fills the area of the control. This is accomplished by detecting the UserControl's Resize event and resizing the command button to fill the control area.

```
Private Sub UserControl_Resize()
   ' Let control fill the window
   Command1.Move 0, 0, Width, Height
End Sub
```

There are a number of important facts to keep in mind in this example. You should not redefine standard events, such as the Click event. Doing so is likely to confuse those using your controls. Create a new event name instead. The same thing applies to standard properties.

This control sample is not a complete implementation of a command button. It covers many of the properties and events just to illustrate how to approach the task.

This control maps most of its public properties and events directly to the command button. It does not use the properties and events of the UserControl object. Why is this?

When you click on a constituent button control, the Click event of the button is triggered, not that of the UserControl. The UserControl Click event is triggered only when you click on the control area itself. You can see this in the Ch16CtlA control described earlier, which distinguishes between events from the two sources. In this example, we don't need to use the UserControl's Click event, because we expand the button to fill the entire control. The UserControl's Click event is never triggered.

The same applies to UserControl properties, such as the Font property. There are three Font properties to consider in this control. The command button has one. The UserControl object has one. And your class object has one!

▶ The command button's Font property controls the appearance of the caption on the button.

▶ The UserControl's Font property controls text drawing operations on the UserControl object itself. But since you don't draw text directly onto the UserControl in this example, this property serves no purpose.

▶ The class Font property is the public property that can be accessed by developers who use your control. They have no access to the other two unless you expose them explicitly.

It's easy to see which Font property the developer using your control sees. But which one do you see within your application?

Try modifying the Command1_KeyPress code as follows:

```
Private Sub Command1_KeyPress(KeyAscii As Integer)
    RaiseEvent KeyPress(KeyAscii)
    If KeyAscii = Asc("A") Then
        Debug.Print Font.Name
    End If
    If KeyAscii = Asc("B") Then
        Debug.Print UserControl.Font.Name
    End If
End Sub
```

In the test program, change the font name for the design time instance of your control using the VB property window. (Click on the Font property to bring up the font selection dialog box.) When you run the program and type in the A and B keys, you will see that the Font property you access within your program is the one that you yourself defined for the object, which in turn delegates to the command button's Font property.

If you did not expose a public Font property, you would instead access the UserControl's Font property because the UserControl object is the default object for a control.

As you can see, scoping rules for properties are extremely important with ActiveX controls because you are very likely to have the same property name in use simultaneously by many different objects.

Existing Control Trade-Offs   The biggest advantage of enhancing an existing control is that it is extremely easy to do. The ActiveX Control Wizard can do much of the work of mapping public properties, methods, and events to those of constituent controls or the UserControl object.

There are, however, a number of disadvantages to this approach:

- Because each constituent control defines its own behavior and drawing characteristics, there are limits to what you can do to modify the control. There are occasions where you can use advanced subclassing techniques to perform some modifications to the behavior of the constituent controls. But this is a rather advanced technique that requires a good understanding of the Win32 API and, depending on the control, some trial and error as you attempt to figure out how the control responds to different Windows messages.

- As you read earlier, constituent controls are always in run mode when your control is active, making it impossible to set the control's design-time properties even though the control's container is in design mode.

▶ As soon as you go beyond the built-in controls or redistributable controls provided by Microsoft, you run into licensing and copyright issues. In order for your control to work in Visual Basic's design environment, each of the constituent controls must be properly licensed. This will be discussed further in Chapter 26.

BUILD A CONTROL FROM CONSTITUENT CONTROLS

This model is described by Microsoft as one of the three possible control models. In fact, it is just a superset of the Enhanced control model. The major differences are as follows:

▶ Instead of mapping your public properties and events to a single control, you map them to any or all of the constituent controls. It is also possible to map the same property to more than one control.

▶ You are also much more likely to access properties of the UserControl object.

This is demonstrated in the BtnTest project with the Ch16DualButton control. This control contains two button controls and demonstrates a number of different techniques for mapping properties.

You can map multiple events to one. The Click event from both constituent controls is mapped to a single parameterized Click event as follows:

```
Event Click(ByVal ButtonNum%)
Private Sub Command1_Click()
   RaiseEvent Click(1)
End Sub

Private Sub Command2_Click()
   RaiseEvent Click(2)
End Sub

Private Sub UserControl_Click()
   RaiseEvent Click(0)
End Sub
```

Try running the project and clicking on both command buttons and the space between them. A message describing which object has been clicked is displayed in the Immediate window.

You can map a single class property to multiple controls as shown here with the Font property:

```
Public Property Get Font() As Font
   Set Font = UserControl.Font
```

```
End Property

Public Property Set Font(ByVal New_Font As Font)
    Set Command1.Font = New_Font
    Set UserControl.Font = New_Font
    Set Command2.Font = New_Font
    PropertyChanged "Font"
End Property
```

In this particular case, mapping the Font property to the UserControl's Font property is overkill, because this example does not currently draw text directly onto the UserControl. Why do we return the Font property from the UserControl object in the Property Get statement? In truth, it doesn't matter. All of the objects reference the same Font object, so you can retrieve a reference from any of them and it will work.

This model of control creation suffers from exactly the same advantages and disadvantages as the Enhanced control approach. It also has the characteristic that the UserControl itself cannot receive the focus—only the constituent controls receive focus.

USER-DRAWN CONTROLS

User-drawn controls represent one of the most exciting approaches for control creation, though they also represent a jump in complexity. With this type of control you work primarily with properties and events of the UserControl object. You can include invisible constituent controls if you wish, but as soon as you add a visible constituent control, the behavior of the control changes in that the UserControl object can no longer receive the focus.

The ClkTest sample application contains a private control called ClkTest.ctl, which is a trivial demonstration of a user-drawn control whose code is shown in Listing 16.1. The control appears as a green rectangle when created, then switches to blue and red as it receives and loses the input focus. When you run the project, you will see the control on the clkForm test form. Try tabbing to and from the control, and try clicking on the control to see that the Click event works.

You will usually use the UserControl_Paint event to draw to the control. You'll find out more about user-drawn controls in Chapter 17 as the various methods and properties of the UserControl object are discussed.

User-Drawn Control Trade-Offs   The biggest advantage of user-drawn controls is their flexibility. Because you determine the behavior and appearance of the control at all points in its life, there are few limits on what your control can do.

Listing 16.1: Trivial User-Drawn Control

```
Option Explicit

Event Click()


Private Sub UserControl_Click()
   RaiseEvent Click
End Sub

Private Sub UserControl_GotFocus()
   UserControl.BackColor = vbBlue
End Sub

Private Sub UserControl_Initialize()
   UserControl.BackColor = vbGreen
End Sub

Private Sub UserControl_LostFocus()
   UserControl.BackColor = vbRed
End Sub
```

The biggest disadvantage of user-drawn controls derives from this fact. Not only can you determine the behavior and appearance of the control—you must do so. This can rapidly get very complex. Some of the techniques you can use for user-drawn controls will be covered in the chapters that follow, but there are so many possibilities it would be presumptuous to suggest that what you read here is more than a solid introduction.

Keep in mind that when you are implementing a user-drawn control, you are not limited to the functionality inherent in Windows. You have access to all of the Win32 API functions as well, and the Win32 API includes some extremely powerful graphic and text output functions that go far beyond what is implemented by Visual Basic (and are faster besides). Refer to the Visual Basic Programmer's Guide to the Win32 API for an in-depth description of these functions.

Also watch for third-party products that include commercial quality controls with source code. They not only offer controls that you can use in your application, but are a great way to learn advanced control creation techniques.

CREATE YOUR OWN WINDOW

The Windows operating system defines standard classes of windows such as list boxes, text boxes, outline windows, and common dialog boxes.

Many ActiveX controls and Visual Basic intrinsic controls are actually super-classes of these standard windows. For example: The Visual Basic list box control actually creates a Windows list box window. It intercepts the underlying messages for the window and maps them into control properties and events. This allows a relatively simple control to take full advantage of controls that are built into the operating system.

When you use constituent controls, you are, in effect, building another level onto this structure, as shown in Figure 16.3.

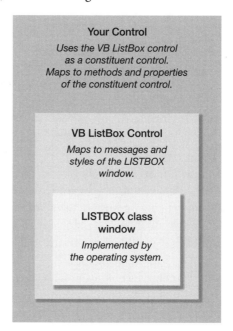

Figure 16.3: A hierarchy of controls

The problem with this approach is that your control can suffer from limitations that are introduced at either level of the hierarchy. Not every ActiveX control implements all of the functionality of the underlying Windows class. For example, even the VB ListBox control does not allow you to set tab locations in a list box, a feature that is built into the operating system's implementation. With Visual Basic 5.0-authored ActiveX controls, you are also limited in that any design time-only properties cannot be changed at runtime.

Why is this? Because with a LISTBOX class window, certain characteristics, such as whether the control can handle multiple selections, must be determined as the window is created. In order to change this characteristic, it is necessary to destroy and recreate the window. Visual Basic 5.0-created controls cannot arbitrarily destroy and recreate a constituent control, something that is necessary to change characteristics, such as support for multiple selections.

But there is a solution. Instead of using the VB list box, you can go directly to the windows class itself and create your own LISTBOX class window on top of the UserControl. Because you created the window yourself, you can destroy it and re-create it at will. This allows you to change these design-time characteristics any time you wish, even at the container's runtime if you so choose.

The advantage of this approach is that it allows you to take full advantage of window classes that are defined by the operating system. But there are a number of disadvantages:

▶ This approach requires a good understanding of Windows API techniques and the operation of the windows class.

▶ This approach can involve quite a bit of work, especially for complex controls.

But there is one factor to keep in mind. If you are creating a control for your own use, you may not need to expose all of the functionality offered by the operating system for a particular window class. A commercial developer will usually expose as many of the features of the underlying control as possible to make the control useful to as many programmers as possible. But when you take this approach for your own applications, you can concentrate on those features you need and not waste time implementing and testing others. So this model may be more practical than it seems at first glance. This approach will be discussed further in Chapter 22.

Now that you are acquainted with the fundementals of ActiveX control creation with Visual Basic, it's time to dive in and look at its heart and soul: the UserControl object.

The UserControl Object

LIFETIME-RELATED EVENTS

INTRODUCTION TO PROPERTY
   PERSISTENCE

SITING AND DISPLAY EVENTS AND
   PROPERTIES

FOCUS EVENTS AND PROPERTIES

TRANSPARENT CONTROLS

OTHER PROPERTIES AND METHODS

T he UserControl object is the heart and soul behind every ActiveX control authored in Visual Basic. It's roughly the equivalent of the form for ActiveX controls. It contains the interfaces that make an ActiveX control work and allow the container to communicate with it. But, above all, the UserControl object is a COM object. And to know a COM object, you have to know its interfaces.

Not every UserControl property and event is covered here. Many of them should be quite familiar to you from general Visual Basic programming. Instead, I've focused on those events and methods that are unique to ActiveX controls, or that behave differently in ActiveX controls than they do in forms or controls. I've tried to group properties and events that are related to each other and provide samples that illustrate specific behaviors.

LIFETIME-RELATED EVENTS

In Chapter 16 you learned about the different states a control can be in. The typical life of a control during authoring (when you are creating and testing the control) is:

- ▶ Designer open—Control is in design mode.

- ▶ Designer closed—No instance of the control exists yet.

- ▶ Control is drawn on a container—An instance of the control is created and is in run mode on a container that is in design mode.

▸ The container runs—Any existing design-time instance of the control is first destroyed, then a new instance is created and run on a container that is in run mode.

When you run an executable that uses a control, only Step 4 takes place: an instance of the control is created and run on a container that is in run mode.

While it is true that ultimately your control will spend most of its time in containers that are running, you must, as a control author, consider the container's design time. This is because, from your perspective, the control will be running in that environment as well.

The UserControl has a lot of events. It's important to understand how they work in each container mode, when they occur, and what kinds of things you can, cannot, should, and should not do during those events. The same applies to properties.

Let's start with the events that relate directly to the initialization and termination of a control. The ch17tst1.vbg group contains two projects, ch17ctl1 and ch17tst1.vbp. The ch17ctl1.vbp project contains a number of controls that will illustrate many of the issues described in this chapter.

The first control in the project is ch17ctlA. This control has a single public property called myprop, which is a variant property that can be set at design time. It includes debug.print statements for a number of UserControl events.

Open the project group and make sure the control designers are closed. You may need to first register the ch17ctl1.ocx control for the project group to open without error. When a new ch17ctlA control is drawn on the ch17tst1 form, the following events are triggered:

▸ UserControl_Initialize

▸ UserControl_InitProperties

When you run the ch17tst1 project, the following events occur:

▸ UserControl_Terminate

▸ UserControl_Initialize

▸ UserControl_ReadProperties

This proves that a control is destroyed when the container switches from design mode to run mode.

The Initialize and Terminate events are familiar to you from class modules. Initialize is always the first event that takes place when an object is created. Terminate is the last event to occur before it is destroyed.

When you switch back to design mode, the following events are triggered:

▸ UserControl_Terminate

▸ UserControl_Initialize

▸ UserControl_ReadProperties

We'll take a look at the property-related events in just a moment.

THE INITIALIZE EVENT
The Initialize event is the first event received by your control.

The Initialize Event

During this event you should:	Initialize any module level variables for your control.
	Initialize properties of constituent controls to their default values.
During this event you may:	Access or initialize the properties of any constituent controls. All constituent controls exist at this time.
	Initialize variables that are used to hold the control's property values to their default value (this will be discussed further in the next section).
During this event you may not:	Access the Extender or Ambient properties of the UserControl object or any of their properties. This is because while your control object does exist at this time, it has not yet been placed on the container (or, as they usually phrase it, the control has not yet been sited at this time).
	Access property values that were saved previously for the control. Properties have not yet been read at this time.
During this event you should not:	Rearrange constituent control or perform any operations that are based on the expected size of the control. Not only has the control not yet been sited, it has not been resized to its final dimensions.
	Perform any operations that are dependent on features, attributes, or properties of the container.
	Display anything.

THE TERMINATE EVENT

The Terminate event is triggered before the object closes. It is the last event to be triggered for a control and (with rare exceptions) the last code to run in the control module.

The Terminate Event

During this event you should:	Make sure that any objects your control is using are properly released.
During this event you may:	Perform any other "cleanup" operations that are necessary for your control.
	Access the properties of any constituent controls. All constituent controls still exist at this time.
During this event you may not:	Access the Extender or Ambient properties of the UserControl object or any of their properties. This is because your control has already been removed from the container when this event is called. In fact, when Visual Basic is the container, the form has already been unloaded by the time this event is called.
During this event you should not:	Perform any operations that are dependent on features, attributes, or properties of the container.

Termination Issues   There are a few other important things to consider with regard to the Terminate event. You cannot know the order in which controls will be terminated. This is unlikely to be a problem in most cases, but it can become an issue when an application is closing.

Consider what happens if your control contains variables or accesses global variables that reference other objects or ActiveX code components. Normally, the very act of referencing the object prevents it from terminating, but when a Visual Basic application closes, all of the objects and controls are terminated despite any references that may still be held to them. You cannot determine the order in which these objects will be terminated.

What happens if you try to access another control or object during your control's Termination event? If the Termination event for the other control has not yet been called, you are unlikely to have any problem. But what if the other object or control has terminated? Surprisingly, the operation may work. For example: you can access properties in the other control. This means that code for that control may be running after its Terminate event has been called! The real problem occurs if the other control performed some cleanup operations during its Termination event that could cause a property access to fail (for example, setting a required object reference to Nothing). In this case an error will be raised when your control attempts to access the property.

This is not a terribly common scenario, but it is one that you should test for if you access object properties or methods during a Terminate event. One way to handle the problem is to use error trapping during the event.

Another thing to remember is that you should avoid using the Visual Basic Stop or End command in your application or invoking the Run, End menu command when running a component project. These commands stop your application or component immediately and prevent the object's Terminate event from triggering.

This problem does not apply to compiled controls. When you load a compiled control into a project and stop the project using the Run, End command, the Terminate event for the project's form will not fire. However, the Terminate event for the compiled control will fire. This is because the compiled control is not considered to be Visual Basic code from the perspective of your project, and the Stop or End command only stops further execution of VB code.

INTRODUCTION TO PROPERTY PERSISTENCE

One of the features that differentiates between ActiveX code components and ActiveX controls is that controls you author can run at design time in the environment of a developer using your control. This means that ActiveX controls have the ability to allow developers to set properties at design time. These property values can be saved by the development environment in whatever format it uses to save applications that are being developed. The properties can be loaded again when the control is recreated. This process of saving and loading properties is called *property persistence*.

Consider the simple Text control. Table 17.1 shows the typical property persistence for a text control. The operations should be quite familiar to you already.

As you can see, three different operations need to be supported for properties. They need to be initialized, they need to be saved, and they need to be loaded. A control knows when to perform these operations via three events from the User-Control object: InitProperties, ReadProperties, and WriteProperties.

ON DEFAULT VALUES

One of the most confusing things about properties with regard to ActiveX controls is that there are two types of property initializations to consider. This situation arises because ActiveX control properties can have default values. Let me explain…

Table 17.1: Property Persistence with a Text Control. The Text Property.

Event in the Life of a Control	Property Operations
Control is drawn on a form for the first time.	Control properties are initialized. The Text property is initialized to the name of the control.
Project or file containing the control is saved.	Control properties are saved into the .FRM file (in the case of VB).
Project is run.	Control properties are saved into memory when the control is destroyed. The properties are read back into the control when it is created in the run-time environment.
Project is stopped.	Control properties are *not* written when the control is stopped because run-time values are not persisted. Control properties are read from memory (where they were last saved) when the control is created in the design-time environment.
Project is compiled.	Control properties are written into the executable file.
Executable is run.	Control properties are read from the executable file when the control is created.

Obviously not every property in your control needs to be persisted. The hWnd property, for example, returns the current window handle of the control. Because this is determined at runtime and changes each time the control is created, it would be silly to save this property in a project or executable file.

For those properties that you do wish to persist, you must keep one fact in mind: saving and loading property values takes time. A lot of time. The exact mechanism of persisting properties will be discussed in Chapter 19, but for now just look at a .FRM file (open one using a text editor such as Notepad). The properties of controls are all listed with the property name and a text representation of the value. Binary values (such as pictures) are stored in the .FRX file. Converting to and from a text representation of a value is obviously a fairly slow process, as is opening files and finding where in a file a particular property value can be found.

The designers of the ActiveX specification realized that in many cases control authors would initialize properties to values they expected would be the most common ones used. This implies that in many cases property values will be unchanged by developers. If a control is going to initialize a property to the correct value anyway, why bother with the overhead of saving and reloading it?

Thus each property in your control may be assigned a default value. When it comes time to write the property, Visual Basic will check to see if the property is set to the default value. If it is, there is no need to write the property. When the control is reloaded, Visual Basic will not try to read the property (it can't, since it was not written in the first place). Instead, VB will assign it the specified default value.

Now look again at Table 17.1. When the control is first drawn on a form, the Text property is the name of the control (for example: Text1). But what is the default property? You wouldn't want to use the control name because that is going to be different for each control. The empty string is a much more reasonable choice, if only because it is very common for Text controls to be empty when a form is first brought up. But how then does it get set to Text1 when a control is first added to a form? Clearly there must be a separate event to indicate when a control is first being created. This is the InitProperties event.

THE INITPROPERTIES EVENT

The InitProperties event is received by a control instance only when it is created for the very first time (for example: when drawn on a form).

The InitProperties Event

During this event you should:	Set persisted properties to their initial values. Not to their default values. Default values are set during the ReadProperties event. In the case of a standard text box, the default value for the Text property is the empty string, the initial value is the name of the control.
	Call any control initialization routines that need to be performed after a control is created. You may wish to place this type of initialization in a separate function, because you may need to perform the same operations after the ReadProperties event.
	Set non-persisted properties to their initial values. The idea of "default" values does not really exist for non-persisted properties. You may wish to place this code in a separate routine, because it will typically be called during the ReadProperties event as well.

During this event you may:	Perform most of the initializations that depend on the container. The control is already sited when this event occurs, thus the Extender and Ambient properties are valid.
During this event you should not:	Display anything. The control will not yet be visible at this time.
	Perform operations that depend on the size of the control. The control and container may not yet be at their final size.
	Perform operations that assume that the control window is actually present on the container. Examples of these include API functions that manipulate windows. The control window is not actually on the container during this event (though from the point of view of the object relationships, it has already been sited).

THE READPROPERTIES EVENT

The ReadProperties event occurs any time a control is created except for the very first time it is placed on a form.

The ReadProperties Event

During this event you should:	Use the PropBag object to read the values of persisted properties. The actual mechanism for reading and writing properties will be covered in Chapter 19.
	Call any control initialization routines that need to be performed after a control is created. You may wish to place this type of initialization in a separate function, because you may need to perform the same operations after the InitProperties event.
	Set non-persisted properties to their initial values. The idea of default values does not really exist for non-persisted properties. You may wish to place this code in a separate routine, because it will typically be called during the InitProperties event as well.

During this event you may:	Perform most of the initializations that depend on the container. The control is already sited when this event occurs, thus the Extender and Ambient properties are valid.
During this event you should not:	Display anything. The control will not yet be visible at this time.
	Perform operations that depend on the size of the control. The control and container may not yet be at their final size.
	Perform operations that assume that the control window is actually present on the container. Examples of these include API functions that manipulate windows. The control window is not actually on the container during this event (though from the point of view of the object relationships, it has already been sited).

THE WRITEPROPERTIES EVENT

This function is called any time a control is saved to a project or executable or saved to memory in preparation for entering run mode. You cannot tell which of these operations is being performed, nor do you need to. Visual Basic's property persistence functions automatically channel the data to the correct place.

The WriteProperties Event

During this event you should:	Use the PropBag object to save the values of persisted properties. The actual mechanism for reading and writing properties will be covered in Chapter 19.
During this event you should not:	Perform any required termination operations. There are situations when this event will not be triggered.
There are two situations you should be aware of in which this event is not triggered:	When switching from run mode to design mode in the VB environment.
	When Visual Basic Believes no property values have changed.

Keep in mind that the decision of when to invoke the WriteProperties event belongs to the container. Containers that don't support a design mode may never call this function.

THE PROPERTYCHANGED METHOD

Consider a control with a single text property. Every time you switch from design mode to run mode, Visual Basic must save the persisted property values in memory so they can be reloaded when the control is recreated in run mode. But why save all of the properties each time if they haven't all changed? Couldn't Visual Basic cache the property values and only update those that have changed in order to improve performance?

Absolutely. Visual Basic only writes properties it knows have changed. This means that must notify Visual Basic any time you change a property value. This is accomplished using the PropertyChanged method of the UserControl object. This method takes as a parameter the name of the property that has been changed.

Containers use this method in several different ways:

▶ To keep track of which properties need to be written when the project is saved or switches from design time to runtime.

▶ To update the value of the property in the development environment's property page. Note that it is possible (though rare) for non-persisted properties to appear in a property page. In this case you should call PropertyChanged for the property even though it is not persisted.

▶ If the control supports databinding, this method is used to inform the system that the bound property has been changed and may need to be updated in the database. This particular situation often applies when the container is in run mode as well.

There is no harm in calling the PropertyChanged method for properties that don't need it (other than perhaps a slight performance impact). Failing to call the PropertyChanged method when necessary can cause design-time settings to not be written, the VB property page to not update itself when values are changed by the control, or bound properties to fail to update their underlying databases. So be sure to ask yourself whether the method needs to be called each time a property is changed.

Here's another tip. Let's say you have a typical property defined in a control as follows:

```
'Property Variables:
Dim m_myprop As Variant

Public Property Get myprop() As Variant
    myprop = m_myprop
    myprop = UserControl.Name
End Property
```

```
Public Property Let myprop(ByVal New_myprop As Variant)
    m_myprop = New_myprop
    PropertyChanged "myprop"
End Property
```

Let's say you need to change the myprop property somewhere else in your control. Your control can access the m_myprop variable directly, but it may be preferable to use the control's myprop property instead. If you get in the habit of using existing properties within your control, you reduce the chances of forgetting to call PropertyChanged. You also gain the benefits of any error checking you've added to the property procedures.

Siting and Display Events and Properties

Siting is the process of placing a control on a container. Siting and display is one area where the behavior of a UserControl object may depend on the state and type of container.

After properties have been initialized, either through InitProperties or Read-Properties, the following three events will occur:

- ▶ Resize—Indicates that the control has been resized
- ▶ Show—Indicates that the control is sited and/or visible
- ▶ Paint—Indicates it is time for you to draw the contents of the control

Let's tackle them one at a time.

THE RESIZE EVENT

The Resize event indicates that the control's size has changed. This event occurs after a control has been sited on the container and all properties have been read. This event also occurs when the control is created.

The Resize Event

During this event you may:	Rearrange constituent controls based on the final size of the control (final, at least until the control is resized again).
	Perform other operations that relate to the size of the control or container.
During this operation you should not:	Redraw your control. Wait for the Paint event.

The ch17ctlc control in the ch17ctls1 project demonstrates some of the features control and constituent resizing. By experimenting with this control, you will discover the following.

First, you may not receive a Resize event for Constituent controls during control creation. This is because by the time you receive an Initialize event in your control, Constituent controls have already been placed and sited on your control. To see this, look for the debug message from the picture1 Constituent control. You will not see one when the control is created, but if you double-click on the control while it is running in a container (not in design mode), you will see the event when the control is resized by the following code:

```
Private Sub Picture1_DblClick()
    ' Generate picture1 resize event
    Picture1.Width = Picture1.Width + 1
End Sub
```

Second, the Resize event may not be reliable on all containers at design time. This is because containers are not required to site a control during design time. This will be discussed further in the next section that discusses the Paint event.

Setting a Fixed Size for Controls Let me start by saying that generally speaking you should allow your control to be resized by the developer. You should never move your control on the container, but there are some cases where you may want your control to have a fixed size. For example: a control that is invisible at runtime may have a simple icon display at design time. Or you may wish to force the size of a control to that of a contained bitmap.

To resize a control, you can use the Size method as shown in the following example from the ch17ctlc control:

```
Private m_AutoResize As Boolean

Public Property Let AutoResize(ByVal bResize As Boolean)
    m_AutoResize = bResize
    PropertyChanged "AutoResize"
    SetDefaultSize
End Property

Public Property Get AutoResize() As Boolean
    AutoResize = m_AutoResize
End Property

Private Sub UserControl_ReadProperties(PropBag As PropertyBag)
    m_AutoResize = PropBag.ReadProperty("AutoResize", False)
End Sub
```

```
Private Sub UserControl_WriteProperties(PropBag As PropertyBag)
   PropBag.WriteProperty "AutoResize", m_AutoResize, False
End Sub


Private Sub UserControl_Resize()
   Debug.Print "C: resize"
   SetDefaultSize
End Sub

Private Sub SetDefaultSize()
   if m_AutoResize then
       Size 200 * Screen.TwipsPerPixelX, 100 * Screen.TwipsPerPixelY
   EndIf
End Sub
```

Try resizing the control at design time with the AutoResize property set to False and the True to see how this works. The Size method does not generate additional Resize events if the control is already at the specified size.

THE SHOW AND HIDE EVENTS

The Show event occurs when your control's window is sited or is made visible on a container. Now this may be an odd way of phrasing the description, but there is a reason for describing it this way. First, it implies that the control must have a window and that the window must have the container as its parent. It also demands that we carefully define what it means for a control to be visible.

Every Visual Basic-created control has a window (it is possible to create windowless controls using other development tools). However, the window does not always have the container as its parent. For example: when a control has not yet been sited on the container, the window may exist, but it has a different parent (one that Visual Basic creates to hold control windows until they are needed). So the first condition for the Show event is that the control be sited.

Next, you need to know a little bit about visibility as it relates to Windows. Say you have a parent window and a child window and both of them are visible. When you hide the child window, its state changes to invisible. (For those of you knowledgable about the Win32 API: A window's visibility state is dictated by the WS_VISIBLE style.) When you hide the parent window, both are hidden but the state of the child window remains visible. That way it will automatically be shown when the parent is made visible again. In other words, a child window is truly visible only if it is visible and the parent window is visible as well. A visible window may still be obscured because it is behind another window, but that does not affect the internal state of the window itself. Table 17.2 illustrates the possible visibility states of a window and whether or not you can actually see it.

Table 17.2: Visibility States of a Child Window Contained in a Parent Window

Parent Window State	Child Window State	Is Another Window on Top?	Can You See the Window?
Visible	Visible	No	Both
Visible	Hidden	No	Parent
Hidden	Visible	No	Neither
Hidden	Hidden	No	Neither
Any	Any	Yes	Neither

The Show event occurs when the child window state becomes visible or when it is first sited on a container. The Visual Basic documentation suggests that this event occurs immediately after the control is sited. However, experimentation shows that the control is already sited during the Resize event, which comes before the Show event.

It occurs even if you load a form that contains a control but does not actually show the form. It occurs any time you change the Visible property of the control to True (changing its state to visible). It occurs any time an Internet browser returns to a page containing the control.

It does not occur when you change the visibility state of the container. Thus if you hide the container or minimize it, then show it again, the Show event will not be generated. It does not occur at design time on containers that do not site control windows, for example, in Visual Basic 4.0. This scenario is discussed further in the description for the Paint event.

The Show Event

During this event you may:

Perform any operations that you would like a Web-based control to do when the user returns to the page containing the control.

Set a flag variable to indicate that your control has, in fact, been sited on a container. Some development environments do not site controls at design time. This will be discussed further in the section describing the Paint event.

When this event occurs (at least on VB5), all of the other controls on a form are sited and the form's Load event has executed. This differs from the Read-Properties event, which guarantees only that your control is sited. If your control must interact with other controls on a form (which is not recommended), this is probably a safe time to do so, though this behavior is not guaranteed for every container.

The Hide event is the inverse of the Show event. It occurs when the control window is removed from the container and any time the visible property of the control is set to False.

THE PAINT EVENT

The Paint event occurs when all or part of your control needs to be drawn. The UserControl Paint event occurs before Paint events in Constituent controls. This is one of the most important events for user-drawn controls but is relatively unimportant for controls that are simply aggregates of other controls.

Visual Basic-created controls support many of the standard properties that affect drawing, including AutoRedraw and ClipControls. There is a sample project called clipctls.vbp in the Chapter 17 directory on your CD-ROM that allows you to experiment with the ClipControls property. These properties should be familiar to you from general VB programming.

Keep in mind that the Paint event will not occur for controls whose AutoRedraw property is True. I encourage you to avoid setting AutoRedraw to True in your controls. It adds substantially to the overhead of your control and has little benefit. If you do need a persistent image, it can be much more efficient to create one yourself using Win32 API techniques.

You can use subclassing to detect the update area for a control in situations where the drawing is complex and you wish to only draw those portions of the control that were changed. This involves intercepting the WM_PAINT message for the control and saving the update area. This technique is demonstrated in Chapter 22.

The Paint Event

During the Paint event you may: Perform any drawing operations (subject to siting issues that follow).

During the Paint event you should not:	Change the size of your control or call the Refresh method. These operations can trigger another Paint event and ultimately a chain of Paint events, which can cause a stack overflow.
	Modify properties that can trigger another Paint event (for example: the BackColor property).

Siting and Drawing Issues   There are two fundamental techniques for drawing onto a control: Visual Basic commands and Win32 API commands. API functions require that you draw into an object called a *device context*. An extensive discussion of how to do this is beyond the scope of this book but is covered in almost mind-numbing detail in the *Visual Basic 5.0 Programmer's Guide to the Win32 API*. I realize that readers who are not familiar with the Win32 API may be overwhelmed by what follows, and I apologize for that, but the information, though somewhat advanced, is important for those who wish to support multiple containers.

The UserControl Paint event is shown below:

```
Private Sub UserControl_Paint()
    Dim usedc&
    Dim pt As POINTAPI

    Debug.Print "C: control paint"

    usedc = GetDC(UserControl.hwnd)  ' Use DC obtained from window
    Call MoveToEx(usedc, 0, 5, pt)
    Call LineTo(usedc, 100, 5)
    Call ReleaseDC(UserControl.hwnd, usedc)
    UserControl.Line (5, 15)-(100, 15), &HFF
    Call MoveToEx(UserControl.hdc, 10, 25, pt)
    Call LineTo(UserControl.hdc, 100, 25)
End Sub
```

The question that arises when using API functions is how to obtain the device context. This code demonstrates two methods: you can obtain one from the window handle or from the hDC property of the UserControl object. Similar code is included for the Paint event of the constituent Picture control as follows:

```
Private Sub Picture1_Paint()
    Dim usedc&
    Dim pt As POINTAPI
```

```
    Debug.Print "C: picture paint"
    ' Now do the picture control
    usedc = GetDC(Picture1.hwnd)   ' Use DC obtained from window
    Call MoveToEx(usedc, 0, 5, pt)
    Call LineTo(usedc, 100, 5)
    Call ReleaseDC(Picture1.hwnd, usedc)
    Picture1.Line (5, 15)-(100, 15), &HFF
    Call MoveToEx(Picture1.hdc, 10, 25, pt)
    Call LineTo(Picture1.hdc, 100, 25)
End Sub
```

These events each draw three horizontal lines: two black lines with a red line in the middle. If you place this control on a VB 5 form, everything looks fine, both in design time and at runtime. But try placing the control on a VB4 form. (Register the OCX file provided using Regsvr32 or recompile the project.) You'll see that at design time the upper line in the user control and all three of the lines in the Picture control are missing.

Why is this? Because a container is not required to site and activate a control at design time, and Visual Basic 4.0 does not do so. The contained Picture control is not handled at all. Its window exists somewhere else in the system, and VB4 is not smart enough to realize that it needs to draw onto a different location.

But the UserControl drawing works part of the way. The Line command works, and drawing using the hDC property of the UserControl object works. Why is this? Because the ActiveX specification does handle this type of situation and provides a mechanism for the container to provide a device context to use for drawing when a control is not sited. Visual Basic is smart enough to provide this device context as the hDC property and use it for Visual Basic drawing commands. Which window does this device context belong to? The container form itself! Your control may think it is drawing into the UserControl window, but in fact it is drawing directly onto the container.

As long as you stick with the VB drawing commands, you are unlikely to have any problems. But with API functions you must be careful. In this particular example, drawing into the device context provided by the hDC property works. The coordinate system for this device context is the same as it would be for a sited control, but there is no reason this should always be the case. This code really should obtain the viewport, extents, and origins of the device context using the GetViewportOrgEx and GetViewPortExtEx functions, and draw into the area provided.

Under no circumstances should you use API functions that work with window handles to do such things as draw or perform sizing calculations. Remember that the control's window is not sited on the control, so the results you obtain are likely to be incorrect or inapplicable. Keep in mind that these problems only occur on containers that do not site controls at design time.

How can you tell if your control is sited? You have two obvious choices:

▸ You can set a flag during the Show event. This event only occurs when the control is sited.

▸ You can use the following code:

```
' If Parent.hwnd <> GetParent(hwnd) Then MsgBox "I am not sited!"
```

You can try this latter approach during the Paint event and during the ReadProperties event under both VB4 and VB5 to see the difference between the two.

THE INVISIBLEATRUNTIME PROPERTY

You can set this UserControl property to True to prevent your control from being sited on a container at runtime.

This property sets a flag for the control indicating to the container that it should not place the control on the container or activate it. It prevents user interface events such as Show, Paint, and Resize from occurring, as well as the input events (focus is obviously not applicable to invisible controls). VB Extender properties other than Name, Index, Left, Top, and Tag are unavailable.

ActiveX controls created under Visual Basic 5.0 always have a control window, even if this property is true. Constituent controls are created as well.

There is just one catch. Containers are not required to support this option. If you use your control on such a container, it will be visible. You can detect this condition by seeing if the Resize or Paint event arrives. You then have a number of options. You could use the Extender property to set the control's Visible property to False or you can move the control outside of the container's visible area. You will need to keep monitoring the Resize or Paint event to make sure the developer does not try to show your control. Also be sure to differentiate between the container design time and runtime—you do want your control to be visible at design time.

For many cases in which you would create an InvisibleAtRuntime property, an ActiveX code component might be a better choice. The advantages of InvisibleAtRuntime controls is that they allow you to have a design time user interface (including property pages) and to persist data.

FOCUS EVENTS AND PROPERTIES

There is a huge difference between user-drawn controls and constituent-based controls when it comes to focus management. When a control contains constituent controls, the UserControl object itself never receives the focus. Otherwise, it is possible for it to receive the focus. This is illustrated in Figures 17.1 and 17.2.

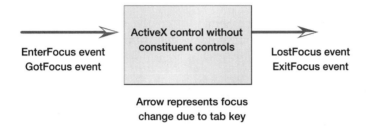

Figure 17.1: Focus sequence for a control without constituent controls

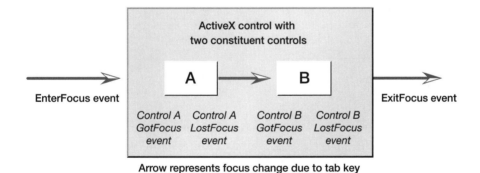

Figure 17.2: Focus sequence for a control with constituent controls

The EnterFocus and ExitFocus events are used to indicate when any constituent control in an ActiveX control has the focus.

The subject of how to use focus events in general is vast. Many Visual Basic programmers use them for data validation—a subject beyond the scope of this book. You can use the GotFocus and LostFocus events in controls in the same way as you would in ordinary Visual Basic programs.

THE GOTFOCUS EVENT

When a control receives the GotFocus event, it already has the input focus. This event occurs after the EnterFocus event for a control.

The control container may trigger its GotFocus event for a control before you receive the UserControl object's GotFocus event within your control. This is what happens in Visual Basic, but there is no guarantee that every container will behave the same way.

This means that a developer using your control might execute code during the container's GotFocus event, thinking that your control has the focus. Your control does, in fact, have the focus, but it has not yet received its GotFocus event.

The HasTheFocus method in the ch17ctlD control demonstrates a reliable way to determine if your control actually has the focus. Place the following API declaration in the module.

```
Private Declare Function GetFocus Lib "user32" () As Long
```

The HasTheFocus method tests the window handle returned from the function with the window handle of the UserControl object. You could easily modify this example to test for focus on any constituent controls as well.

```
Public Function HasTheFocus() As Boolean
   If GetFocus() = hwnd Then
      HasTheFocus = True
   End If
End Function
```

An important use of this event is to provide some indication that the control has received the focus (for a user-drawn control). It is very important that developers using your control (and their end users) be able to differentiate between the focus and non-focus states of your control.

The GotFocus Event

During the event you should:	Indicate focus state with user-drawn controls.
During this event you may not:	Try raising the Extender object's GotFocus event. That is the responsibility of the container.
During this event you should not:	Use this event to set a flag that indicates reliably whether the control has the focus.

THE LOSTFOCUS EVENT

When a control receives the LostFocus event, it has already lost the input focus. This event occurs before the ExitFocus event for a control.

The control container should trigger its LostFocus event for a control after you receive the LostFocus and ExitFocus events within your control. This is what happens in Visual Basic, but there is no guarantee that every container will behave the same way.

During this event you can set the focus back to the control that just lost the focus, but not before the next control receives the focus (and a GotFocus and LostFocus event). This is because this event does not actually trigger when the control loses the focus. It triggers later during the course of normal Windows event processing. This limits the use of this event for data validation purposes, but this problem is fundamental to Visual Basic in general and not unique to ActiveX controls.

The LostFocus Event

During the event you should:	Indicate non-focus state with user-drawn controls.

THE ENTERFOCUS AND EXITFOCUS EVENTS

The EnterFocus event occurs when an ActiveX control or any constituent control first receives the focus. The control has already received the focus when this event occurs. The ExitFocus event occurs when a control, or all of its constituent controls, loses the focus. The control has already lost the focus when this event occurs.

These are perhaps the most important events for focus management when creating controls that use constituent controls. It can be thought of as a global GotFocus and LostFocus for the entire control.

Now that you know about all four of the main focus events, let's take a closer look at the order in which they occur.

The ch17ctlD and ch17ctlE controls in the ch17tst1 project group use debug.print statements to trace the sequence of events. The ch17ctlD control has no constituent controls. The ch17ctlE control contains two constituent text box controls. Form frmTest3 contains both of these controls. When you run the project and display this form, then tab between the controls, the results are quite interesting. The most interesting result shown here relates to the EnterFocus event.

```
D:EnterFocus        ' Form is first loaded here.
Form: D: GotFocus        ' Focus is initially at ch17ctlD control.
```

```
D:GotFocus
E:EnterFocus          ' Tab to the ch17ct1E control.
D:LostFocus
D:ExitFocus
Form: D: LostFocus
Form: E: GotFocus
E:Text1:GotFocus
E:Text1:LostFocus          ' Tab to 2nd text box on ch17ct1E control
E:Text2:GotFocus
D:EnterFocus     ' Tab to the ch17ct1D control
E:Text2:LostFocus
E:ExitFocus
Form: E: LostFocus
Form: D: GotFocus
D:GotFocus
D:LostFocus            ' Close the form
D:ExitFocus
```

As you can see, the EnterFocus event occurs as soon as you tab to a control. It not only occurs before the GotFocus event for the control or its constituents, it occurs before the LostFocus or ExitFocus events of the controls losing the focus!

THE CANGETFOCUS PROPERTY

This property indicates whether an ActiveX control can receive the focus. If you set it to False, everything you have read here on focus events immediately becomes irrelevant, since they will never occur.

You can only set this property to False on user-drawn controls or controls that only contain constituent controls that cannot receive the focus (the Timer control, for example).

THE ACCESSKEYS PROPERTY

Access keys (which are also sometimes called accelerator keys) allow you to jump directly to a control by pressing an alt-key combination. From the developer's perspective, an access key can be specified in two ways. For some controls the control caption is underscored by preceding it with an ampersand character. For controls that do not have captions, it is common to set the caption for a Label control that precedes the target control in the tab order.

Thus to set Alt-A as the accelerator for a command button, you might set the caption to &A Button, which will result in the button displaying: A Button.

For a Text control, you would set a Label control ahead of it in the tab order and set its caption in the same way. For example, it would set it to &A Textbox, which will result in A Textbox. As a control author, it makes sense to ask what a control must to do internally in order to support this capability.

A first step is obviously to specify which keys should be the access keys for a control. There are two ways to specify an access key for a Visual Basic-authored control:

- ▸ You can set the caption of a constituent control as an accelerator (for example, setting an accelerator key for a constituent command button or Label control).

- ▸ You can add the character to the AccessKeys property. This property contains a string of characters that will all act as AccessKeys for your control.

The characters in this process can be upper or lower case. Either way both the shifted and unshifted character will be considered an access key. How the control reacts to the accelerator depends on the ForwardFocus property.

THE FORWARDFOCUS PROPERTY

When a Label control has an accelerator key specified, the focus is set to the next control in the tab order when the key is pressed. You can make your ActiveX control exhibit this same behavior (forwarding the focus to the next control) by setting the ForwardFocus property for the control to True.

When this property is False, the behavior of accelerator keys depends on whether the control is user-drawn or contains constituent controls. If it is user-drawn, the focus goes to the control itself. Otherwise it goes to either the first constituent control (for access keys specified by the AccessKeys property) or the constituent control associated with the accelerator.

When this property is True, the focus always goes to the next control on the container. This happens whether the access key is specified in the AccessKeys property or by a constituent control. The interaction between the AccessKey and ForwardFocus properties can be seen in Table 17.3.

THE ACCESSKEYPRESSED EVENT

This event is triggered to indicate that an access key has been pressed. It only occurs when the ForwardFocus is False.

It is triggered when the user chooses an access key that is in the list specified by the AccessKeys property (it does not trigger for access keys specified by constituent controls).

It is also triggered when the DefaultCancel property is True (more on this later) and the control is set by the developer to be the default or cancel button for the form. Refer to the DefaultCancel property description for more details.

Table 17.3: Summary of AccessKey and ForwardFocus Characteristics

In Access-Keys?	Access Key for Constituent Control?	ForwardFocus?	Result
No	Yes	No	Focus goes to next Constituent control or the control itself (if user-drawn). AccessKeyPress event is not triggered.
No	Yes	Yes	Focus goes to the next control on the container (not the next constituent control).
Yes	No	No	No effect if focus is already a constituent control. Otherwise focus goes to the first constituent control or the control itself (if user-drawn). AccessKeyPress event is triggered.
Yes	No	Yes	Focus goes to the next control on the container (not the next constituent control).

WORKING WITH ACCESS KEYS

As you have seen, there are many permutations possible between use of Access-Keys, constituent controls, ForwardFocus, and CanGetFocus. Let's look at the most useful and realistic scenarios:

Label style controls: Set the access keys using the AccessKeys property based on developer property settings. Set CanGetFocus to False and ForwardFocus to True.

User-drawn controls that receive the focus: Set the access keys using the AccessKeys property based on developer property settings. Set CanGetFocus to True and ForwardFocus to False. Indicate the focus state based on the Got-Focus event. Perform actions based on the AccessKeyPressed event.

Controls made up of constituent controls: Access keys can be set in either the AccessKeys property or using the constituent controls. Keys should be chosen by the developer using your control. CanGetFocus is, of course, True (required for this type of control). Set ForwardFocus to False to allow tabbing within the control itself.

You should never hard code the access key values into the control itself. Always provide a way for the developer using your control to select their own access keys. You wouldn't want someone dictating that part of the user interface for you, right?

Also, be sure to provide some visual indication of which access keys are set for your control.

THE DEFAULTCANCEL PROPERTY

The DefaultCancel property is used to indicate to the container that your control can act as a default or cancel button. If the container supports this capability, it will add the Default and Cancel properties to the extender to allow the developer to set your control to be the Default or Cancel control for the container. If the control is the Default or Cancel button for a container, the Access-KeyPress event will trigger when the user presses the Enter key (with keycode 13) or the Escape key (with keycode 27) depending on the setting chosen.

Curiously enough, once the DefaultCancel property is set, the Enter key will always be detected if Enter is pressed while the control has the focus. This mimics the behavior of the standard command button, which is clicked by the Enter key even if its Default property is False.

TRANSPARENT CONTROLS

Visual Basic 5.0 almost provides excellent support for transparency in all or part of your control. Transparency is turned on by setting the control's Back-Style property to 0. Why do I say almost? Because, as you will soon see, there are some minor problems with the way transparency is implemented under Windows 95.

When the BackStyle property is set to 1 (opaque), the control appears as a rectangular area and no part of the container shows through. If the BackStyle property is set to 0 (transparent), portions of the control become transparent. Those areas of the control that are transparent have the following characteristics:

▶ The container that holds the control determines the appearance of the transparent areas. In other words: the container shows through the control.

▶ Mouse events on the transparent area go to the container, not the control. This includes MouseUp, MouseDown, and MouseMove events, as well as generated Click and DblClick events.

Transparent areas in a control are specified according to the following rules:

▶ All non-transparent constituent controls are opaque.

▶ If you assign a bitmap into the MaskPicture property of a control, all areas in that bitmap that are not the color specified in the MaskColor property are opaque. The MaskColor property should always be set to white or black if you want your control to work correctly under Windows 95. Windows 95 handles transparency internally using monochrome masking. This means that during the masking process the MaskColor value is converted to either black or white, and the MaskPicture image is converted to monochrome. The only way to reliably set both properties is thus to use black or white as the MaskColor property and a monochrome bitmap as the MaskPicture property.

▶ Transparent areas in a transparent control (such as a Label or Shape control with the BackStyle property set to 0) are transparent. Opaque areas of these controls are opaque except for Label controls that are using a non-TrueType font.

These rules suggest a number of useful scenarios for control transparency.

TRANSPARENT CONSTITUENT-BASED CONTROLS

This type of control is made of up constituent controls where you want the container background to appear between the controls. To accomplish this, simply set the UserControl's BackStyle property to 0-Transparent.

This type of control is useful when you wish to use a control to effectively group a limited number of controls along with a defined functionality, and you expect these controls to appear on top of a container that has a complex pattern or image (a map, for example).

You should not take this approach as an easy way to always use the container's background color. This is because transparency increases the overhead of your control both in terms of increased resources and decreased performance. If you simply want to follow the container's background color, you should detect changes to the BackColor property of the Ambient object and adjust your control's background color accordingly. You'll see how this is done in Chapter 19.

ODDLY SHAPED CONTROLS

If you wish your control to have a non-rectangular shape, you have three choices.

1 You can place an opaque Shape control on your control to define the shape of the control. You can then draw on the area covered by the Shape control using standard drawing techniques. Constituent controls will continue to appear as you would expect. The catch to this approach is that the Shape control is drawn after the UserControl's Paint event, making it much more difficult to implement user-drawn controls. You can subclass the control and perform your drawing after default processing of the Paint event (post-default subclassing). This approach is shown in the OvalTest.vbp sample project on the CD-ROM that comes with the book. This particular example uses the dwsbc32d.ocx demo subclassing control from Desaware's Spy-Works. I would probably use Desaware's in-process dwSpyvb.dll code component subclasser for a more efficient solution in a real application. You'll read more about this component in Chapter 22.

2 You can define a bitmap to set into the MaskPicture property for the control. Only bitmaps (.BMP, .DIB, .GIF, and .JPG) are supported for this purpose. You cannot use metafiles or icons. The MaskColor property determines which color is transparent. This approach is fairly efficient but suffers from the inability to maintain a quality mask as the control is resized. Keep in mind that the MaskColor setting must be white if you wish for the transparency features of your control to work correctly on Windows 95. The Microsoft documentation recommends that you only use monochrome bitmaps for the MaskPicture property under Windows 95. This is because light colors will also be mapped to white and considered transparent, making it difficult to determine ahead of time which areas will be transparent when you use a color bitmap.

3 You can use the SetWindowRgn function to create an arbitrarily shaped region for the control's window. This is demonstrated by the OvalTst2.vbp project, which contains the following code in the control module:

```
Private Declare Function CreateEllipticRgn Lib "gdi32" (ByVal X1 As Long, ByVal _
Y1 As Long, ByVal X2 As Long, ByVal Y2 As Long) As Long
Private Declare Function SetWindowRgn Lib "user32" (ByVal hWnd As Long, ByVal _
hRgn As Long, ByVal bRedraw As Long) As Long

Private Sub UserControl_Resize()
    Dim hr&, dl&
    Dim usew&, useh&
    usew& = ScaleWidth / Screen.TwipsPerPixelX
    useh& = ScaleHeight / Screen.TwipsPerPixelY
    hr& = CreateEllipticRgn(0, 0, usew, useh)
    dl& = SetWindowRgn(hWnd, hr, True)
End Sub
```

This approach is perhaps the most efficient of the three, but it does require a good understanding of creation of Region objects using the Win32 API. This subject is covered in depth in Chapter 7 of the *Visual Basic 5.0 Programmer's Guide to the Win32 API*.

LABEL STYLE-BASED CONTROLS

By far the easiest way to implement a Label style transparent control is to use one or more constituent transparent Label controls. There are two main disadvantages with this approach:

- ▸ It only works with TrueType fonts. Transparent Label controls do not mask properly with bitmap fonts.

- ▸ You are limited to the capabilities of Label controls. Thus you cannot mix such things as fonts, styles, and colors in a single control.

The way to deal with this situation adds a bit of complexity but is infinitely flexible. It is based on the idea that the opaque areas of the control can be defined by the MaskPicture property, and that this property can be defined at runtime.

The lblTest.vbp project demonstrates a simple approach to this problem. The control contains an invisible picture control that has its AutoRedraw property set to True and its Visible property set to 0. This keeps the Picture control invisible but at the same time forces it to allocate a bitmap that saves the contents of the control at all times. Text is drawn into this Picture control using API functions. In this example the text output is placed in a Timer event as follows:

```
Private Declare Function TextOut Lib "gdi32" Alias "TextOutA" (ByVal hdc As Long, _
ByVal x As Long, ByVal y As Long, ByVal lpString As String, ByVal nCount As Long) _
As Long


Private Sub Timer1_Timer()
    Static counter&
    Dim t$
    counter = counter + 1
    t$ = "Elapsed " & counter & " seconds"
    Picture1.Cls
    Call TextOut(Picture1.hdc, 0, 0, t$, Len(t$))
    MaskPicture = Picture1.Image
End Sub
```

The default background color for the Picture control and the MaskColor property for the UserControl are both set to white in this example, so the example will work correctly on Windows 95. The Picture1.Cls command sets the entire Picture control to the current background color.

The TextOut command draws text onto the Picture1 control using the default text color—black in this case. The Win32 API includes a number of extremely flexible text output functions that can perform various types of text alignment and even word-wrap. These are also covered in the *Visual Basic Programmer's Guide to the Win32 API*.

Once the text is drawn, the MaskPicture property is set to the current image of the Picture1 control. In this example control, the text will show up as blue because that is the background color of the control itself. What in effect has happened is that only those pixels in the control that contain text are opaque and thus show the background color of the control instead of that of the container. Blue is a dark color and is unlikely to be mapped into white with regard to transparency under Windows 95.

The control also has the following code in the Click event:

```
Private Sub UserControl_Click()
    Line (0, 0)-(ScaleWidth, ScaleHeight), 0, BF
End Sub
```

When you click on the text itself (it may take a few tries, because the text is quite small), the entire control will be filled with black. But because the mask defines only the text areas as opaque, only those areas will be colored black. This will appear as if the text has simply changed color.

This approach can be extended to the creation of arbitrary masks and drawing at runtime. If you choose to take this approach, there are a number of techniques you can use to reduce the overhead involved in using a separate Picture control with a persistent bitmap. You can set the AutoRedraw property to False when it is not in use to eliminate the extra bitmap. You can also use more advanced API techniques to create a bitmap dynamically as needed and load it into the MaskPicture property directly (the OleCreatePictureIndirect OLE API function is used to do this).

BITMAP-BASED CONTROLS

You may have wondered why you would ever want to use a color bitmap in the MaskPicture property of a control to specify the mask. After all, a monochrome bitmap would do as well; you only need two pixels to specify the mask and opaque areas.

The elegance of this approach is that you can use the same bitmap in the MaskPicture and Picture properties of a control. The MaskColor property then allows you to specify a single color in the image as transparent. Of course, you can only use this approach reliably if you know that your control will only run under Windows NT, since only NT is able to handle arbitrary MaskColor property values and color bitmaps.

The ch17ctlG.ctl control in the ch17test1 project demonstrates how you can combine the techniques described here to achieve a variety of transparency effects. Keep in mind that transparent controls should not be configured as control containers.

The TranTest.vbp sample project can be found in the ch17 directory on the CD-ROM that comes with this book. This program allows you to experiment with transparency using different types of bitmaps and different MaskColor property values. I encourage you to experiment with it under both Windows 95 and Windows NT.

OTHER PROPERTIES AND METHODS

The remaining UserControl properties and events are either identical in their behavior to what you are accustomed to on forms or are so clearly described in the Microsoft documentation that I'm hard pressed to find anything else to say. In this section, I'll review those properties, methods, and events that deserve a few additional comments and are not covered more thoroughly in the chapters that follow.

The following properties are covered elsewhere in this book:

Property	Chapter
Ambient	18
AsyncRead	19
CancelAsyncRead	19
CanPropertyChange	19
Extender	18
HyperLink	21
PropertyPages	20

THE ALIGNABLE PROPERTY

When this property is set to True, a container may add an Align property to the Extender object for the control. The container will then relocate the control in the container based on the alignment selected by the developer without any further action on your part. You may, if you wish, check the Align property in the Extender object to add your own alignment characteristics.

THE CONTROLCONTAINER AND CONTAINEDCONTROLS PROPERTIES

When you set this property to True, a developer using your control can place additional controls on yours at design time. Visual Basic does most of the work to support this capability.

You can access controls the developer has placed on your control using the ContainedControls collection. This collection can be accessed once the control is sited. You cannot add or remove controls from this collection.

Some containers do not support the interfaces needed to support container controls. These containers will raise an error when you try to access the ContainedControls property.

Avoid making control containers out of controls that contain visible constituent controls. It works, but the results can be quite strange depending on where the developer places additional controls.

Container controls involve quite a bit of overhead. It may be tempting to come up with container controls that perform organizational tasks such as rearranging or resizing controls that are placed on them. It is much more efficient to perform these tasks using code on a form than to use specialized container controls.

THE EDITATDESIGNTIME PROPERTY

Setting this property to True makes it possible for a developer to actually activate and use your control within the container's design time. It enables the Edit command on the control's context menu (the menu that appears when you right-click on the control).

Normally, when a developer places your control on a form or container at design time, the entire control is treated as one unit. Clicking on the control selects the entire control and brings up sizing boxes so the control can be sized and positioned. This is all managed by the container. No user interface events are triggered in your control's code. The container intercepts all mouse and keystroke events before they get to your control.

When the EditAtDesignTime property is True and the developer selects the Edit context menu command, your control becomes active even though the container is at design time. User interface events are received by your control and need to be handled appropriately. Note that the UserMode property of the Ambient object will correctly show that the container is in design mode. The ch17ctlf sample control in the ch17tst1 program group demonstrates this.

Any events your control raises in the container in this mode will be ignored.

THE ENABLED PROPERTY

When you disable a UserControl object, the constituent controls are disabled as well, but they won't take on the appearance of a disabled control unless you explicitly disable them as well. This is identical to what happens when you disable a form. Chapter 18 includes further discussion on this property.

THE EVENTSFROZEN PROPERTY

There are certain times in the life of a container when it is not able to receive events from controls. A classic example of this is that Visual Basic forms cannot receive events while a Visual Basic MsgBox command is displaying a message box.

There are some controls that can generate events while events in the container are frozen. A Timer control is a good example of this.

When this property is True, any events raised by your control will be ignored by the container.

What do you do if the event you want to raise is important and cannot simply be discarded?

You can queue the event and raise it later when events are reenabled.

You can define some standard ways for the control to respond to the event and allow the developer to select one to use during those times when events are frozen. How can you detect when events are unfrozen? Visual Basic does not provide an easy way to do this, though you could poll the EventsFrozen property using a timer. Desaware's SpyWorks also provides an easy way for your control to be notified when the container's EventsFrozen property changes. Events are always frozen when a container is in design mode.

THE PALETTEMODE PROPERTY

In addition to the options available to forms and controls in general, ActiveX controls can be set to use the palette of the container or set to use no palette at all.

THE PARENT PROPERTY

This property allows you to access the control's container. It is similar to the Container and Parent properties on the UserControl's Extender object, except that it is always available. You can use this property to determine the container your control is running in (see the description of this property in the Visual Basic 5.0 readme file for a summary of containers). Refer to the section in Chapter 18 titled "Terrible Evil Things You Should Never Do" for a summary of things that you should not do with this property.

THE PARENTCONTROLS PROPERTY

This property is a collection of the other controls that are in the container that contains your control. You cannot add or remove controls from this collection. This property is useful for those controls intended to help manage other controls on a form. For example: you could use it to create a tool that would align controls or assign them all the same color.

Not every container supports this property.

THE PUBLIC PROPERTY

When the Public property is True, the control is exposed for use by other applications. It is possible to create private ActiveX controls to use within executables or within other ActiveX controls.

The issues to consider when deciding whether to make an ActiveX control public or private are the same as those you consider when deciding to make a class private or expose it through an ActiveX DLL code component.

THE RIGHTTOLEFT PROPERTY

When your control is running on a version of Windows that supports right-to-left formatting (such as Hebrew or Arabic Windows), this property will change the direction of text output on the control. If you wish to support this capability, you should set this property based on the AmbientProperties RightToLeft property.

THE TOOLBOXBITMAP PROPERTY

Select a 16 x 15 pixel bitmap that will appear in the container's toolbox to represent the control.

The upper left pixel defines the transparent color for the control (the background of the toolbox will show through any parts of the bitmap set to this color). I usually use a distinct color such as green to represent the background so I don't make a color transparent by accident.

Now that we've reviewed the UserControl object, we'll move on to the remaining ones: the Ambient and Extender objects.

The Extender and Ambient Objects

THE EXTENDER OBJECT

AMBIENT PROPERTIES

Chapter
18

If I'm doing my job right, by now you should be beginning to feel comfortable with the way ActiveX controls fit together. You should understand the different states in which a control exists. You should be familiar with the main events in the life of a control and a few of the most important methods and properties.

Chapter 19, which deals with the way you define properties and events in your control, is going to be extremely important when it comes to implementing your controls. You can think of this chapter, perhaps, as a long introduction to the next one. It's a chapter in which we'll introduce the rest of the fundamental building blocks on which a control is based. For if the UserControl object forms the core of your ActiveX control, then surely the Extender and Ambient objects define the environment in which it lives.

The Extender Object

Most of the properties of the Extender object are already familiar to you—they are found in almost every Visual Basic form or control. The purpose of this section is not to tell you about those properties or how they are used from the developer's perspective. Instead, the purpose is to show you how to deal with them from a control author's perspective.

To begin, try creating a new control, closing its designer, and adding it to a form. Do not add any properties—this is a completely empty control.

When you look at the properties of the control in the container's design time, depending on the property settings of the UserControl object, you will see the properties shown in the following table.

Extender Properties for an Empty ActiveX Control	Comments
Name	Standard
Align	Only appears if the control's Alignable property is True
Cancel	Standard—only appears if the control's DefaultCancel property is True
DataBinding DataChanged DataField DataSource	Only appears if the control has a property that is bound to a database. See Chapter 19.
Default	Standard—only appears if the control's DefaultCancel property is True
DragIcon	
DragMode	
Enabled	Only appears if the control has an Enabled property—more on this later
Height	
HelpContextId	Only appears if the control's CanGetFocus property is True
Index	
Left	Standard
Negotiate	Only appears if the control's Alignable property is True
TabIndex	Only appears if the control's CanGetFocus property is True
Tabstop	Only appears if the control's CanGetFocus property is True

Extender Properties for an Empty ActiveX Control	Comments
Tag	
ToolTipText	
Top	
Visible	Standard
WhatsThisHelpID	
Width	Standard

The following items about this table should be noted.

▶ Those properties labeled "standard" represent properties that most containers will support.

▶ If the control's InvisibleAtRuntime property is True, only the Name, Index, Left, Top, and Tag Extender properties are available.

▶ As design-time properties, Visual Basic automatically handles persistence of these properties (saving them with your project).

In addition to these properties, Visual Basic provides the following Extender properties that can be accessed by a developer at runtime.

Runtime-Only Extender Properties, Methods, and Events	Comments
Container property	The container (typically a form) that contains the control
Object property	References the underlying object, not the extender
Parent property	Standard—the container of the control. The UserControl object also provides a Parent property, which is always available regardless of the container.
Drag method	
Move method	
SetFocus method	

Runtime-Only Extender Properties, Methods, and Events	Comments
ShowWhatsThis method	
ZOrder method	
DragDrop event	
GotFocus event	Only appears if control's CanGetFocus property is True
LostFocus event	Only appears if control's CanGetFocus property is True
DragOver event	

From the point of view of the developer (the person using your control), there is no difference between Control properties and Extender properties. They appear as a single interface. How is this possible? When you, as a developer, reference a control, you are in fact referencing the control's extender. The Extender object reflects the properties and methods of the object itself. This is shown in Figure 18.1.

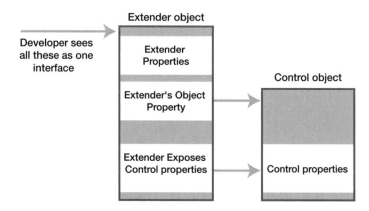

Figure 18.1: The relationship between the control and the extender

There are some things you must keep in mind with respect to the Extender object:

▸ Properties, methods, and events on the Extender object are provided by the container. You cannot assume that any given property, method, or event will be present on the Extender object, since they may vary from one container to the next.

▸ Because the Extender object can change depending on the container, all access to Extender properties and methods from your control is late bound.

▸ When a developer references your control, he or she will actually be referencing the Extender object for your control. They can access the control object directly by using the extender's Object property (if one exists).

The ch18tst1.vbg program group contains two projects: ch18ctls.vbp project contains a number of controls that demonstrate the techniques described in this chapter. The ch18tst1.vbp project is a test program that exercises those controls.

The ch18ctla control is completely empty except for two functions that allow you to access the control's internal Extender and Me objects using the following code:

```
Public Function InternalExtender() As Object
    Set InternalExtender = UserControl.Extender
End Function

Public Function InternalMe() As Object
    Set InternalMe = Me
End Function
```

You should not generally expose these objects in this manner, but it is useful for test purposes. Place the control on a form, add a command button, and add the following code to its Click event:

```
Private Sub Command1_Click()
    If ch18Ctl A1.Container Is ch18Ctl A1.Parent Then
        Debug.Print "Parent and container are the same"
    Else
        Debug.Print "Parent and container are not the same"
    End If
    If ch18Ctl A1 Is ch18Ctl A1.Object Then
        Debug.Print "Control and control's Object are the same"
    Else
        Debug.Print "Control and control's Object are different"
    End If
```

```
    If ch18CtlA1.Object Is ch18CtlA1.InternalMe Then
        Debug.Print "Extender's object property is the control's Me"
    Else
        Debug.Print "Extender's object property is not the control's Me"
    End If

    If ch18CtlA1 Is ch18CtlA1.InternalExtender Then
        Debug.Print "Control is the control's extender"
    Else
        Debug.Print "Control is not the control's extender"
    End If
End Sub
```

The results are as follows:

▸ Parent and container are the same.

▸ Control and control's object are different.

▸ Extender's Object property is the control's Me.

▸ Control is the control's extender.

From this, we can generate Table 18.1, which shows how to access the various properties as both a control author and a developer using the control.

Table 18.1: Navigating between Control, Container, and Extender

Object	Access as a Developer	Access as a Control Author
Control myctl Extender	myctl	Usercontrol.Extender
Control myctl object itself (not the extender)	myctl.Object	Me
Container of control "myctl"	myctl.Parent myctl.Container	UserControl.Extender.Container UserControl.Extender.Parent UserControl.Parent

IMPACT OF SCOPING RULES

You are already quite familiar with the general rules for scoping of variables, properties, and methods. When you define an item with the same name as an item that exists at a higher level, the other item is hidden. Thus if you have a global variable named x and define x in a procedure, the global one is hidden until the procedure exits.

The same principle applies with Control properties as they relate to Extender properties. For example: say you add a Tag property to your control. The VB extender already has a Tag property that it manages. Since the developer accesses the extender, that property takes priority. This is demonstrated in the ch18tst1.vbp project with the ch18ctlb.ctl control. This control implements its own Tag property and member variable using the following code:

```
Public Property Get Tag() As String
    Tag = m_Tag
End Property

Public Property Let Tag(ByVal vNewValue As String)
    m_Tag = vNewValue
    Debug.Print "Setting internal tag"
    Report
End Property

Public Sub Report()
    Debug.Print "Internal Tag variable is " & m_Tag
    Debug.Print "Internal Tag property is " & Tag
    Debug.Print "Extender Tag is " & Extender.Tag
End Sub
```

The test code in form frmch18test1 is attached to a second command button as follows:

```
Private Sub Command2_Click()
    ch18CtlB1.Tag = "Setting tag Property"
    ch18CtlB1.Object.Tag = "Setting object tag property"
End Sub
```

The results are as follows:

```
Setting internal tag
Internal Tag variable is Setting object tag property
Internal Tag property is Setting object tag property
Extender Tag is Setting tag Property
```

From this we can conclude that there are two separate Tag variables—one implemented and belonging to the control, the other by the container. You can access these variables as shown in Table 18.2.

Table 18.2: Scoping Example with Tag Property for ch18CtlB1

Tag Being Accessed	Access As Developer	Access As Author
Extender Tag property managed by Visual Basic	ch18CtlB1.Tag	UserControl.Extender.Tag
Internal Tag property managed by your control	ch18CtlB1.Object.Tag	Tag Me.Tag

Why would you ever want to define a property, such as Tag, which is already implemented by the container? Because you may want to guarantee that people using your control have access to a Tag property for the control, and you cannot be sure that your control's container will always support a Tag property on its extender.

ACCESSING EXTENDER PROPERTIES

The biggest catch to using Extender properties is that you can never be certain whether or not they are actually present. This means that unless you want your control to be limited to Visual Basic or a subset of containers, you must take precautions when accessing Extender properties so your control degrades gracefully. There are two approaches for doing this.

▶ You can use error trapping any time you access an Extender property or method.

▶ You can explicitly check to see if an Extender property exists before calling it.

The error trapping approach is obvious. The second approach can be handled in two ways. You can create a routine that attempts to access a property and records the results. The following code from the ch18ctlb.ctl control shows how this can be accomplished:

```
Private TagIsPresent As Boolean
Private xyzIsPresent As Boolean
Private zzzispresent As Boolean
Private Sub CheckExtender()
    Dim testnumber As Integer
    Dim v As Variant
    TagIsPresent = True
    xyzIsPresent = True
    zzzispresent = True
    On Error GoTo itp1
    testnumber = 0
    v = Extender.Tag
    testnumber = 1
    v = Extender.xyz
    testnumber = 2
    v = Extender.zzz
    Exit Sub
itp1:
    Select Case testnumber
        Case 0
            TagIsPresent = False
```

```
      Case 1
          xyzIsPresent = False
      Case 2
          zzzispresent = False
    End Select
    Resume Next
End Sub
```

The routine simply checks the desired properties one by one, setting a module level flag to indicate which ones fail. A simpler version of this routine could use a Boolean array, where each entry corresponds to a particular Extender property.

An even easier approach uses the apigid32.dll dynamic link library included with this book. This DLL was written originally for the *Visual Basic Programmer's Guide to the Win32 API* and contains a variety of useful low-level functions, one of them being the function called agIsValidName. The function is declared as follows:

```
Declare Function agIsValidName& Lib "apigid32.dll" (ByVal o As Object, ByVal_
lpname$)
```

Its use is demonstrated in the following code from the ch18ctlb.ctl control:

```
Debug.Print "Tag property present: " & agIsValidName(Extender, "Tag")
Debug.Print "xyz property present: " & agIsValidName(Extender, "xyz")
```

This function is actually quite simple internally. It simply calls the GetIDsOfNames method on the object's dispatch interface to see if it gets a valid return value. As you may recall from Part 1 of this book, Visual Basic 5.0 requires that all interfaces it uses be either dispatch interfaces or dual interfaces that contain the dispatch interface functions along with those you define.

Which approach should you take? It's really up to you. I tend to use the latter because most of the controls I create take advantage of Desaware's tools (which is not surprising, since those tools were created primarily for me and my staff to be able to create more powerful controls in the first place). Since we're distributing apigid32.dll anyway (or one of its big brothers, which also contain the IsValidName function), there is no additional cost in terms of resources or performance in using the DLL function.

CONTROL DEPENDENCIES

The Extender properties that are made available for a particular control may depend on settings in the control itself. These dependencies are entirely up to the container. The following are the most important of these dependencies that you should be aware of as a Visual Basic programmer.

Enabled The Enabled property is strange. To see why, load the EnTest1.vbp project in the Chapter 18 samples directory on your CD-ROM. This project contains a single control called EnCtl1.ctl, which contains a command button and a public Enabled property. The code for this control is as follows:

```
Option Explicit

Public Property Get Enabled() As Boolean
    Enabled = UserControl.Enabled
End Property

Public Property Let Enabled(ByVal New_Enabled As Boolean)
    UserControl.Enabled() = New_Enabled
    PropertyChanged "Enabled"
End Property

'Load property values from storage
Private Sub UserControl_ReadProperties(PropBag, As PropertyBag)
    UserControl.Enabled = PropBag.ReadProperty("Enabled", True)
End Sub

'Write property values to storage
Private Sub UserControl_WriteProperties(PropBag As PropertyBag)
    Call PropBag.WriteProperty("Enabled", UserControl.Enabled, True)
End Sub
```

This code should be quite familiar to you by now—it is the standard way in which a public property is implemented and persisted. The UserControl object's internal Enabled property is set according to the public variable. A Report function has been added to the control. It prints the state of the Enabled property, the UserControl enabled property, and the Command1 enabled property to the Immediate window as follows:

```
Public Sub Report()
    Debug.Print "Within control code - "
    Debug.Print "Enabled property is: " & Enabled
    Debug.Print "UserControl.Enabled property is: " & _
    UserControl.Enabled
    Debug.Print "Command1.Enabled is: " & Command1.Enabled
    Debug.Print "Extended Enabled is: " & Extender.Enabled
    Debug.Print "End within control code."
End Sub
```

The project contains a single form, enForm1, which contains a timer and the EnCtl1 control. During the Timer control's Timer event, the following trace routine is called:

```
Private Sub Timer1_Timer()
    Debug.Print "Enabled property is: " & Enabled
    Debug.Print "Control's Enabled property is: " & _
    EnableTestControl.Enabled
    Debug.Print "Report: ";
    EnableTestControl.Report
End Sub
```

The EnCtl1 control has two properties set in the VB property window for the form: The Enabled property is set to True, and the Name property is set to EnableTestControl. The Enabled property of the form is set to False.

Now, before you run this sample, let's take a moment and review all of the different Enabled properties we are actually dealing with. In the control (control author's point of view) the properties are these:

Syntax	What You Are Accessing
Enabled	The public Enabled property for the control.
UserControl.Enabled	The UserControl object Enabled property.
Command1.Enabled	The Enabled property of the constituent command button on the control.
Extender.Enabled	The Enabled property provided by the container as part of the Extender object. Due to the scoping rules described earlier, this is the property seen by developers using the control unless they explicitly access the control's Enabled property using the Object property and the syntax EnableTestControl.Object.Enabled.

From the container (application developer's point of view):

Syntax	What You Are Accessing
Enabled	The Enabled property for the form (actually, the Enabled property for the form's Extender object).
EnableTestControl. Enabled	The Enabled property provided by the container as part of the Extender object for the control.
EnableTestControl. Object.Enabled	The public Enabled property for the control. (Developers should never access this property.)

When you run the application, you will see the following displayed in the Debug window.

```
Enabled property is: False
Control's Enabled property is: False
Report: Within control code -
Enabled property is: True
UserControl.Enabled property is: True
Command1.Enabled is: True
Extended Enabled is: False
End within control code.
```

The Enabled property for the form is disabled. This makes sense because that is what was set for the form in the VB Property window.

The control's Enabled property, which is on the Extender object, is False. Keep in mind that it was set to True at design time. But the public Enabled property for the control, along with that of the UserControl object and the command button within the control, are all True! What's going on? Why is the control's Extender Enabled property False while the Control properties are actually enabled?

This occurs because of a convention specific to Visual Basic. First, consider how Windows works. When you disable a window, all of its child windows continue to appear as enabled. They will not receive keystrokes or mouse input because their parent form is disabled. If you want them to appear as disabled, you must disable them individually. This is similar to the situation we saw in Chapter 17 with regards to visibility, where controls on a form can have their Visible properties set to True, yet they are obviously hidden when their container is hidden.

In this example we disabled the form but did not disable the control. The developers of Visual Basic, for reasons that are probably lost in history and certainly undocumented, decided that when a container is disabled, the controls it contains should read as disabled as well (even though they have not been set explicitly to disabled). They could not, however, just disable the controls. Doing so would change their appearance, violating the standard behavior of Windows applications. So they let the controls remain enabled (as far as they were concerned), but rigged it so the Enabled property on the Extender object for controls on a disabled container would return False.

Now, in order for this trick to work, there is one important requirement. There has to be a way to let Visual Basic know which property is the Enabled property. It's not enough to assume that the property will actually be named Enabled—the control author may choose to localize the property name for different languages or use a different term entirely. How can you, as a control author, let Visual Basic know which of your properties is the Enabled property for the control?

The solution lies in one of the characteristics of the IDispatch interface discussed back in Part 1 of this book. Remember how each property in the interface has a unique dispatch identifier number (Dispatch ID or DispID)? You may also recall that negative Dispatch ID numbers are defined by COM to indicate certain standard properties. These values do not affect the behavior of the interface or property itself but may be used by a container to provide special handling for properties if it chooses to do so. Dispatch ID number -514 is the identifier number for the Enabled property.

You can use the VB Tools, Procedure Attributes menu command to bring up the Procedure Attributes dialog box. Select the Enabled property and click the Advanced button. In the Procedure ID combo box you will see that Enabled is selected. When the Enabled procedure ID is selected, Visual Basic automatically sets the Dispatch ID for the property to -514.

When you create a blank control with no properties, Visual Basic does not create an Enabled property on the Extender object by default. However, if you assign any of the control's properties to the Enabled procedure ID, Visual Basic will add an Enabled property to the extender for the control. When you set the Enabled property using code or the VB property window, Visual Basic will also set the property that you specified with this ID, regardless of the actual name of the property.

What happens if you add an Enabled property to the control but do not set the Procedure ID for the property to Enabled? Visual Basic does not create an Enabled property on the Extender! The Enabled property you see in the VB Property window for the control is the control's Enabled property.

If you set the Procedure ID for the EnCtl1.ctl control to (None) and run the program again, you will see the following debug messages in the Debug window (you may need to save and reload your project for the system to reset itself properly after this change):

```
Enabled property is: False
Control's Enabled property is: True
Report: Within control code -
Enabled property is: True
UserControl.Enabled property is: True
Command1.Enabled is: True
Extended Enabled is: True
End within control code.
```

As you can see, there is no difference between the Enabled property as seen by the developer using the control and that seen by the control's author.

To conclude: If you want your control to exhibit the standard Visual Basic behavior for the Enabled property, you must do the following:

▸ Add an Enabled property to your control (it may be any name you choose, but you should use Enabled unless you have some overwhelming reason not to do so).

▸ Set the Procedure ID for that property to Enabled.

▸ Within the property procedures for the Enabled property, set the internal Enabled property for the control and possibly any constituent controls as well (if you wish for them to look disabled when the control is disabled). For user-drawn controls, you will probably also want to change the appearance of the control to indicate its state.

▸ Persist the value of the property during the ReadProperties and WriteProperties events as shown earlier.

Align and Negotiate   If you set the Alignable property in your control to True, the extender will display an Align property and possibly a Negotiate property as well (depending on the container).

Your control can read the extender's Align property to determine whether your control has been aligned. You need not take any action in this case; the container is responsible for repositioning your control.

If your control uses a Toolbar control to implement a toolbar, the Negotiate property is provided to allow the developer to determine how the toolbar is displayed on an MDI form. Refer to your Visual Basic documentation for information on using the Toolbar control provided with Visual Basic.

Cancel and Default   If you set the DefaultCancel property of your control to True, Visual Basic will add a Default and Cancel property to your control's extender. You can then read these Extender properties to determine whether your control has been set to be the Default or Cancel control for the container.

It is customary for a Default control to show a different appearance from a standard control of the same type. You could look at the default Extender property, but Visual Basic provides an easier way to determine when this is necessary. The Ambient object has a DisplayAsDefault property that is set to True when your control should appear in its default state. Why use the Ambient property instead of the extender?

▸ Because the Ambient property can be early bound

▸ Because you can use the UserControl_AmbientChanged event to determine when the DisplayAsDefault property has changed

The ch18CtlB.ctl control demonstrates this using the following code:

```
Private Sub UserControl_AmbientChanged(PropertyName As String)
    If PropertyName = "DisplayAsDefault" Then
        UserControl.Refresh
    End If
End Sub

Private Sub UserControl_GotFocus()
    Label2.Caption = "Has Focus"
End Sub

Private Sub UserControl_LostFocus()
    Label2.Caption = "Lost Focus"
End Sub

Private Sub UserControl_Paint()
    Dim s$
    If Extender.Default Then
        s$ = "Default"
    End If
    If Extender.Cancel Then
        s$ = s$ & " Cancel"
    End If
    If s$ = "" Then s$ = "Normal"
    Label1.Caption = s$
End Sub
```

The control contains two constituent Label controls that are used to display the current state of the control. Open the frmCh18Test2 form in design mode and try changing the control's Default and Cancel property in the VB Property page (keep in mind that by doing so you are directly changing the Extender properties). When you change the Default property, the control will update immediately. When you change the Cancel property you will not see the change until the control is redrawn (try changing the size of the control after changing the Cancel property to see this).

Is there a way to determine when an Extender property has changed? I don't know of any, other than polling. If you find one, please let me know.

CONTAINER DEPENDENCIES

Allow me to close this section with two warnings. Visual Basic's Extender control and design environment is exceptionally robust. Other containers are likely to have fewer Extender properties and less sophisticated support for features you may have incorporated into your control. You should review all use of Extender properties to make sure that your control will still work if they are missing. There are a number of options for how to handle different containers with regard to Extender properties:

- Disable the feature supported by the Extender property in a way that is transparent to the developer.

- Disable the feature supported by the Extender property and notify the developer (by raising an error during the property access or by way of a message box or other notification scheme).

- Disable the control completely if the Extender property is required for your control to work. Your control will not run at all in the container if this is the case.

- Allow a run-time error to occur when the Extender property is accessed. This is the "ignore the problem and it will go away" scenario I encourage you to avoid.

Terrible Evil Things You Should Never Do   The container and parent properties give you access to the Container object and all of its properties and methods. This means your control can do the following:

- Move itself on the container.

- Change the color of the container.

- Rearrange, resize, or change the visibility of other controls on the container.

- Set its own Extender.Container property to a different container in the application.

- Unload the container!

I could probably go on for pages with variations on the possibilities. It is possible for controls to be terribly nasty to an application.

It is fundamental to the philosophy of components that the developer using your control be responsible for the container. The developer is also responsible for setting and using Extender properties and events (since those are provided by the container). As a control author, keep your hands off the container and other controls!

AMBIENT PROPERTIES

It is sometimes easy to get confused between Extender and Ambient properties. Like so many aspects of ActiveX control development, the difference between them is a matter of perspective. Extender properties are those that are added to your control by the container and are intended to be used primarily by developers who are using your control to create applications. Ambient properties are those that are provided by the container and are intended to be used by control authors.

Ambient properties are accessed through the AmbientProperties object, which is accessed via the Ambient property of the UserControl object for your control. The AmbientProperties object always includes a core set of standard properties, unlike the Extender object, whose properties vary based on the container and control configuration. However, this does not mean that all of the standard Ambient properties are, in fact, supported by each container. If an Ambient property is not supported by the container, the AmbientProperties object simply returns a default value for the property.

Consider, for example, the UserMode property. If a container does not support a design-time mode, it need not provide a UserMode ambient property. The AmbientProperties object sees that the property is missing in the container and always returns a default value of True for its own UserMode property.

A container can provide additional container-specific Ambient properties. These properties are always late bound, and you should use error trapping when accessing them. Table 18.3 shows the standard properties for the Ambient object. The default value shown indicates the value returned for the property when it is not supported by the container. The UserControl object's AmbientChanged event is triggered any time an Ambient property is changed.

Table 18.3: The Standard Ambient Properties

Property	Comments	Default Value
BackColor	Background color of the container.	&H80000005
DisplayAsDefault	If the control's DefaultCancel property is True, and the developer specifies that this is the default control, this property returns True. Refer to the description of the DefaultCancel property in Chapter 17.	False

Table 18.3: The Standard Ambient Properties (Continued)

Property	Comments	Default Value
DisplayName	The name of the control assigned by the developer.	" "
Font	The font of the container, or the default font recommended by the container for use by the control. Note that the container's FontTransparent property does not trigger an AmbientChanged event.	MS Sans Serif 8
ForeColor	Foreground color of the container.	&H80000008
LocaleID	See chapter text.	Current system default
MessageReflect	See chapter text.	False
Palette	A Picture property specifying the container-recommended palette (usually the palette in use by the container).	
RightToLeft	Indicates that the control should draw text from right to left on Hebrew or Arabic versions of Windows.	False
ScaleUnits	The name of the units in use by the container. See chapter text.	
ShowGrabHandles	See chapter text.	True
ShowHatching	See chapter text.	True
SupportsMnemonics	See chapter text.	False
TextAlign	Indicates the container's text alignment or the default text alignment for the control.	Zero
UserMode	True indicates that the control is in end-user mode, which means run-time for Visual Basic.	True
UIDead	See chapter text.	False

SPECIFIC PROPERTIES

The following Ambient properties are worthy of further comment.

Encapsulated Properties   The MessageReflect, ShowGrabHandles, ShowHatching, SupportsMnemonics, and UIDead ambient properties are important to controls but are handled entirely by Visual Basic's implementation of ActiveX controls. You can safely ignore them. Here is a short description of these properties in case you are interested:

- ▶ MessageReflect—Indicates that the container should reflect certain windows messages back to the control.

- ▶ ShowGrabHandles—Indicates that the container can display grab handles for re-sizing the control.

- ▶ ShowHatching—Indicates that the container can display a hatching pattern over an inactive control when necessary.

- ▶ SupportsMnemonics—Indicates that the container can support access keys for a control.

- ▶ UIDead—Indicates that a control should ignore all user input.

ScaleUnits   This property can be used to determine the scale units of the container. When Visual Basic is the container, ScaleUnits can take the values User, Twip, Point, Pixel, Character, Inch, Millimeter, Centimeter; these are the constant names of the ScaleMode property.

The possible values of this property are not defined by the ActiveX specification. Thus, containers can use any strings they wish. This means that this property may not be reliable under all containers for determining the actual scale mode of the container. It is intended primarily for controls to be able to display the container coordinate system when necessary.

When Visual Basic is the container, you can also access the container's Scale-Mode property directly through the Extender object's Container property.

LocaleID   A *Locale* is a 32-bit value that identifies the language and platform for the thread or system. Bits 0 through 15 (the low-order word) identify the language. Bits 16 through 19 specify how sorting works under this language. It is typically 0 but may be set to 1 for Far East Unicode environments. Figure 18.2 shows the structure of a Locale identifier.

The low-order word is divided into two parts. The low 10 bits (bits 0 through 9) indicate the language. The high 6 bits (bits 10 through 15) indicate a subset of the language—to differentiate, for example, between U.S. English and U.K. English. The values for the supported languages can be found in any good

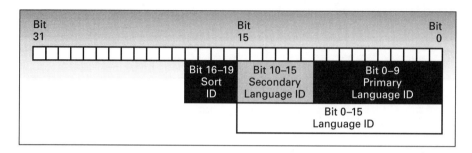

Figure 18.2: The Locale identifier

Win32 API declaration file: Look for the constants with the prefix LANG_. The subsets, or sublanguage constants, are identified with the prefix SUBLANG_. Many functions take the default system or user locales, which are given the special constant values

```
Public Const LOCALE_SYSTEM_DEFAULT = &H800
Public Const LOCALE_USER_DEFAULT = &H400
```

A great deal of information is associated with locales. For example, the country name, names of days and months (and their abbreviations), the symbol used for local currency, the format used for dates and times, and other information that tends to vary from country to country. This information can go a long way in helping you create truly international applications using Visual Basic. The subject of locales and the Win32 API functions that are available to work with them are discussed further in the *Visual Basic 5.0 Programmer's Guide to the Win32 API*.

UserMode   The UserMode ambient property is probably the most important one. It is almost certainly the one that you will use most often. A setting of True for this property indicates that the control's container is in run mode or *End-User* mode. False indicates that the container is in a design-time or developer mode. Keep in mind that not every container supports a design-time environment.

The most common uses for this property are:

▶ Making properties setable only at design time (this will be demonstrated in Chapter 19).

▶ Defining different appearances for design time and runtime.

▶ Defining different behaviors for design time and runtime (including handling activation at design time if you choose to support it).

STRATEGIES FOR USING AMBIENT PROPERTIES

There are a number of approaches you can use when working with Ambient properties. In order to illustrate this, let's take a close look at the BackColor property.

This is another one of those properties that require you to keep close track of which object you are considering. The ch18Test1 project group includes the ch18ctlD control, which contains three constituent Text Box controls. This means that you, as the control author, have to deal with six different Back-Color properties on six different objects, as shown in Table 18.4.

Table 18.4: A Plethora of BackColor Properties

Property	Description
Text1.BackColor	Author only—sets the background color of the Text1 control
Text2.BackColor	Author only—sets the background color of the Text2 control
Text3.BackColor	Author only—sets the background color of the Text3 control
UserControl.BackColor	Author only—sets the background color of the ActiveX control
BackColor	Public—Does whatever you the control author wishes
Ambient.BackColor	Public—The current background color of the control's container

This raises some interesting questions. Exactly what should this control look like? What determines the background colors of the various text boxes and the control itself? You have a number of options:

▶ You can have the control or its constituent controls share a single public BackColor property.

▶ You can have each constituent control set independently.

▶ You can have the control or its constituent controls track the container's BackColor property.

▶ You can combine these approaches in any way you wish.

I would not dare to suggest which approach you should take. But I would strongly recommend that you ask yourself these questions when you are designing your control.

The ch18CtlD control demonstrates all of these approaches in a manner that is hopefully educational and definitely unattractive. The public BackColor property defines the background color for the control and the Text1 constituent control. The property functions are as follows:

```
Public Property Get BackColor() As OLE_COLOR
    BackColor = UserControl.BackColor
End Property

Public Property Let BackColor(ByVal New_BackColor As OLE_COLOR)
    UserControl.BackColor() = New_BackColor
    Text1.BackColor = UserControl.BackColor
    PropertyChanged "BackColor"
End Property
```

There are two things to note in this code. First, the property type is OLE_COLOR. This property type is defined by referencing the standard OLE (stdole) library, which is referenced by default by Visual Basic 5.0. The OLE_COLOR variable is a 32-bit long, and variables of this type can be assigned directly to and from Visual Basic numeric variables. Why then should you use the OLE_COLOR type? Because Visual Basic is a very smart container, and when it sees a property with the OLE_COLOR type, it adds the color selection popup to the VB property window for that control.

The other point of interest is that two objects are "connected" to the BackColor property. When the property is set, both the UserControl and the Text1 control's BackColor property are set. The intent in this example is for these two objects to always have the same background color. The property is saved in the UserControl_WriteProperties function with the following code:

```
Call PropBag.WriteProperty("BackColor", UserControl.BackColor, &H8000000F)
```

It is read as follows:

```
UserControl.BackColor = PropBag.ReadProperty("BackColor", &H8000000F)
Text1.BackColor = UserControl.BackColor
```

When writing the property, we can use the value from either the UserControl or the Text1 object, since they are the same. When reading the property we must be sure to set both to the new value. It is also necessary to initialize the property in the UserControl_InitProperties event. There are two approaches for doing so. One is

```
UserControl.BackColor = PropBag.ReadProperty("BackColor", &H8000000F)
Text1.BackColor = UserControl.BackColor
PropertyChanged "BackColor"
```

The other is to simply use

```
BackColor = &H8000000F
```

In this case the public BackColor setting serves exactly the same purpose. The advantage to using the public property in this manner is obvious—it allows you to reuse the same code and helps you avoid forgetting some crucial operation (such as calling PropertyChanged or setting all of the values that are necessary). There will be cases, however, where you cannot do this; for example, when you have code or error trapping in the public property setting routine that you do not want called when reading the property settings from a file.

The Text2 constituent control takes a different approach. It is set using an independent property called BackColor2. As such it is completely independent of the other background colors, and its property procedures are quite straightforward:

```
' Background color for text2
Public Property Get BackColor2() As OLE_COLOR
    BackColor2 = Text2.BackColor
End Property


Public Property Let BackColor2(ByVal vNewValue As OLE_COLOR)
    Text2.BackColor = vNewValue
    PropertyChanged "BackColor2"
End Property
```

The Text3 constituent control is somewhat more complex. Its background color can be set to follow the container color or set independently using the BackColor3 property. This imposes some additional requirements on the control code:

▶ You need to provide a way for the developer to choose between having the Text3 control follow the ambient background color or the BackColor3 property value.

▶ Since the Text3 control's BackColor property value may reflect the container's background color, it is necessary to store the BackColor3 property value independently.

▶ You need to detect when the container's BackColor property changes so that the Text3 control can be updated if appropriate.

Listing 18.1 shows the remainder of the control module. This example takes a simple approach to letting the developer choose between the different modes for the Text3 control. It uses a separate property called Text3Ambient, which is True when the Text3 control should follow the Ambient BackColor property value. The value for this property is stored in private variable m_Text3Ambient. A second private variable, m_Text3Backcolor, is used to hold the value of the BackColor3 property.

Another possible approach would be to define an "impossible" color value, meaning the control should return to the ambient background color mode. In this case, you would examine the BackColor3 property Let function parameter. If it was some invalid value, such as &HFFFFFFFF, you would set the m_Text3Ambient property to True instead of setting the m_Text3Backcolor variable. This approach is somewhat awkward, because it requires the developer to remember that the way to reset the control to its ambient background mode is to type -1 or &HFFFFFFFF into the BackColor3 property edit box in the VB Property window. Since colors are usually set using the pop-up palette values, this is not an intuitive approach. A separate variable to control the Text3 control mode is much easier for developers to remember.

Listing 18.1: Partial Listing for ch18ctlD.ctl

```
' Should we use the ambient or back3color value
Private m_Text3Ambient As Boolean
Private m_Text3Backcolor As OLE_COLOR

Private Sub UserControl_AmbientChanged(PropertyName As String)
    If PropertyName = "BackColor" Then
        SetText3Color
    End If
End Sub

'Load property values from storage
Private Sub UserControl_ReadProperties(PropBag As PropertyBag)
    UserControl.BackColor = PropBag.ReadProperty("BackColor", &H8000000F)
    Text1.BackColor = UserControl.BackColor
    Text2.BackColor = PropBag.ReadProperty("BackColor2", &H80000005)
    m_Text3Backcolor = PropBag.ReadProperty("BackColor3", &H80000005)
    m_Text3Ambient = PropBag.ReadProperty("Text3Ambient", True)
    SetText3Color  ' Update after read
End Sub

'Write property values to storage
Private Sub UserControl_WriteProperties(PropBag As PropertyBag)
    Call PropBag.WriteProperty("BackColor", UserControl.BackColor, &H8000000F)
    Call PropBag.WriteProperty("BackColor2", Text2.BackColor, &H80000005)
    Call PropBag.WriteProperty("BackColor3", m_Text3Backcolor, &H80000005)
    Call PropBag.WriteProperty("Text3Ambient", m_Text3Ambient, True)
End Sub

Public Property Get BackColor3() As OLE_COLOR
    If Ambient.UserMode Then
        ' At runtime, return the actual color in use
```

Listing 18.1: Partial Listing for ch18ctlD.ctl (Continued)

```
      BackColor3 = Text3.BackColor
   Else
      BackColor3 = m_Text3Backcolor
   End If
End Property

Public Property Let BackColor3(ByVal vNewValue As OLE_COLOR)
   m_Text3Backcolor = vNewValue
   PropertyChanged "BackColor3"
   SetText3Color
End Property

Public Property Get Text3Ambient() As Boolean
   Text3Ambient = m_Text3Ambient
End Property

Public Property Let Text3Ambient(ByVal vNewValue As Boolean)
   m_Text3Ambient = vNewValue
   PropertyChanged "Text3Ambient"
   SetText3Color
End Property

Private Sub SetText3Color()
   If m_Text3Ambient Then
      Text3.BackColor = Ambient.BackColor
   Else
      Text3.BackColor = m_Text3Backcolor
   End If
End Sub
```

The actual setting of the Text3 background color is accomplished using the SetText3Color function. This function needs to be called any time the Text3 background color may change. This includes after the properties are read during the UserControl_ReadProperties event and any time the Text3Ambient or BackColor3 properties are set.

To see the effects of this code, bring up the frmCh18Test3 form in design mode and experiment with the various property values using the VB property window.

As you have seen, the Ambient and Extender objects interact closely with properties that you define for your ActiveX control. But as you will see in the next chapter, you have only begun to delve into issues relating to ActiveX control properties.

The Wonderful World of Properties

PROPERTY DATA TYPES

PROPERTY PROCEDURES

CONTROL PROCEDURE ATTRIBUTES

CUSTOM OBJECTS

PERSISTENCE

DATABINDING

A ll ActiveX components can have properties. But what makes properties special with regard to ActiveX controls?
    The big difference is persistence—that control properties can be
set at a container's design time and the values stored with an application. This
implies that you'll have to pay special attention to the differences between the
design-time and run-time behavior of properties.

PROPERTY DATA TYPES

You are probably quite familiar with the usual property types, such as longs,
strings, variants, and objects. With ActiveX controls, the type of property can
have a significant impact on the way the container interacts with the control at
design time. The ch19ctla control in the ch19ctls.vbp project demonstrates
some of the issues relating to property data types. There are several property
types that are deserving of special attention.

VARIANTS

When you add a new property procedure to a control using the Tools, Add
Procedure command, it defaults to the variant property type. This is a shame,
because a variant is probably the worst type for an ActiveX control property.

In order to build a robust ActiveX control it is important that the control be
able to successfully handle any values set by the container in both design and
run mode. Since a variant can contain any type of data, use of variants as a
control property clearly imposes a significant amount of extra work on a control author, both in terms of coding and testing.

Using variants as properties can potentially confuse the design-time property window as well. If the variant contains a value that it can convert into a string, the property will appear in the Property window (assuming other requirements, which will be described later, are also satisfied). But if the variant contains an object reference when the control loads, the property will not appear. If the property is initially a string, but later is set to contain an object reference, a blank line may appear on the property window (depending on when the container chooses to update its property window), leaving no indication that the property is set to a legal value.

The Visual Basic property window will always set a variant to the string data type when the developer edits the property.

When you add these facts to the long list of disadvantages associated with variants that were described in Chapter 10, the bottom line is clear: Unless you have some overriding reason, don't use variants as properties. At the very least, don't use them for properties that are visible at design time.

Now that you know the bottom line, stay tuned, because you'll shortly become intimately acquainted with one of those overriding reasons to use variants after all.

A typical set of property procedures for a variant property is shown below:

```
Private m_Variant1 As Variant

Public Property Get Variant1() As Variant
    Variant1 = m_Variant1
End Property

Public Property Let Variant1(ByVal vNewValue As Variant)
    m_Variant1 = vNewValue
    PropertyChanged "Variant1"
    Debug.Print "Variant type: " & VarType(m_Variant1)
End Property
```

OLE_COLOR

The OLE_COLOR type can be a bit misleading. You might think it is a special object type like a font or picture (which we'll discuss in a moment), but in fact, an OLE_COLOR variable is simply a 32-bit-long integer. It is not an object and thus has no properties or methods. It's just another name for a long variable and can be directly assigned to and from Visual Basic long variables.

Why, then, should you ever use this variable type? Because Visual Basic is smart enough to know that this variable type should receive special treatment in the VB property window and with regard to property pages. When a property is defined as the OLE_COLOR type, Visual Basic adds a pop-up color selection menu to the VB property window entry for the property. It also enables linking the property to the standard color selection property page.

A typical set of property procedures for an OLE_COLOR property is shown below:

```
Private m_Color1 As OLE_COLOR

Public Property Get Color1() As OLE_COLOR
    Color1 = m_Color1
End Property

Public Property Let Color1(ByVal vNewValue As OLE_COLOR)
    m_Color1 = vNewValue
    PropertyChanged "Color1"
End Property
```

OLE_TRISTATE

The OLE_TRISTATE date type is an enumerated value and, like any enumerated value in Visual Basic, is also represented by a 32-bit-long value. When Visual Basic sees this data type, it provides a dropdown list box in the Visual Basic property window that contains the three possible values for this data type: 0—Unchecked, 1—Checked, and 2—Gray.

Keep in mind that, as with any enumerated type, Visual Basic does not, itself, limit the possible values for this property. This means you must add your own code to verify that the property is not set to an invalid value.

A typical set of property procedures for an OLE_TRISTATE property is shown below. Note the use of error checking on the Property Let statement.

```
Private m_TriState1 As OLE_TRISTATE

Public Property Get MyTriState() As OLE_TRISTATE
    MyTriState = m_TriState1
End Property

Public Property Let MyTriState(ByVal vNewValue As OLE_TRISTATE)
    If vNewValue > 2 or vNewValue <0 Then
        Err.Raise 380
    End If
    m_TriState1 = vNewValue
    PropertyChanged "MyTriState"
End Property
```

OLE_OPTEXCLUSIVE

This data type is equivalent to the Visual Basic Boolean data type, meaning that it can only take on the values True and False. You can assign any value to a variable of this type, but it will automatically be set to -1 if the value is not 0.

If the default property for a control has this data type, Visual Basic assumes that this control is expected to behave like an option button. Only one control that uses OLE_OPTEXCLUSIVE will have its default property set to True at any given time. When you set one to True, other controls that have a default property of this type will be set to False.

There are a few points regarding this data type that are not completely clear in the documentation:

▶ Contrary to what the documentation says, use of the OLE_OPTEXCLUSIVE data type in this manner has nothing to do with the Value property, even though it is typically used with that property. What counts is that the property be set to be the default property using the Tools, Procedure Attributes dialog box. This is done by setting the Procedure ID (DispID) to (Default) in the dialog box. This is demonstrated in the ch19ctla control, where the default property is actually named xValue instead of Value.

▶ All controls with a default property of type OLE_OPTEXCLUSIVE that share a given container are considered a single group by the container regardless of the type of control. You can see this in the ch19tst1 form. When you click on the option button, the xValue property for both ch19ctla controls is set to False.

▶ This behavior is entirely dependent on the container. You cannot assume that this type of option exclusion will be implemented on a given container. However, most containers seem to support it correctly.

A typical set of property procedures for an OLE_OPTEXCLUSIVE property is shown below. The Debug.Print statement monitors the current state of the variable so you can see when the property is set to False after another control's OLE_OPTEXCLUSIVE default property is set to True.

```
Private m_Value As OLE_OPTEXCLUSIVE

Public Property Get xValue() As OLE_OPTEXCLUSIVE
    xValue = m_Value
End Property

Public Property Let xValue(ByVal vNewValue As OLE_OPTEXCLUSIVE)
```

```
    m_Value = vNewValue
    Debug.Print Ambient.DisplayName & vNewValue
    PropertyChanged "xValue"
End Property
```

ENUMERATED TYPES

When you assign an enumerated type to a control property, Visual Basic will use the enumeration list to build a dropdown list of possible property values in the Visual Basic property window. This can be seen in the ch19ctlA control with the EnumProp property, which is implemented as follows:

```
Enum TestEnum
    dwFirstVal = 0
    dwSecondVal = 1
    dwThirdVal = 2
End Enum
Private m_Enum As TestEnum

' Enumerated property
Public Property Get EnumProp() As TestEnum
    EnumProp = m_Enum
End Property

Public Property Let EnumProp(ByVal vNewValue As TestEnum)
    m_Enum = vNewValue
    PropertyChanged "EnumProp"
End Property
```

This actually presents a curious limitation for control authors using Visual Basic. It is desirable to use enumeration names that have a prefix such as "dw" to avoid conflicts with other enumerations that might be using a similar name. But it is also desirable to have a more easily understood name in the dropdown list provided by the Visual Basic property window. Visual Basic does not provide a solution to this problem, but Desaware's SpyWorks does provide a mechanism to customize the dropdown list in the Visual Basic property window instead of using the default enumeration list. It also allows you to override the value display in the property window.

Enumeration conflicts can cause subtle bugs if you have two different components that have the same enumeration name with two different values. As long as you are within the same project, Visual Basic will warn you about ambiguous names when attempting to run or compile the application. Otherwise, Visual Basic will choose the first name in the reference order. Reference order was discussed in Chapter 9. It is important that you resist the temptation to choose enumeration names such as "First," color names, and dates, which are all unlikely to be unique.

Keep in mind that Visual Basic does not perform range checking on the value passed to an enumerated property procedure. You should verify the values passed to the Property Let procedure and raise an error if the value is invalid.

PICTURES AND FONTS

Pictures and Fonts are encapsulated in standard OLE objects, which support the interfaces IPictureDisp and IFontDisp. Visual Basic recognizes objects with these types and provides them with special handling. The Visual Basic property window displays a summary display describing the object and a button that can be clicked to display a common dialog box or property page, which can be used to edit the object.

You should be sure that the Property Get statement for a font always returns a valid Font object. If it returns Nothing, the container may not be able to correctly set the font. One way to do this is to set the private font variable to the ambient font during the UserControl's InitProperties event. The Property Get statement for a picture may return Nothing to indicate that no picture has been specified.

A typical set of property procedures for a Font property is shown below:

```
Private m_Font1 As Font

Private Sub UserControl_InitProperties()
   Set m_Font1 = Ambient.Font
End Sub

Public Property Get Font1() As Font
   Set Font1 = m_Font1
End Property

Public Property Set Font1(ByVal vNewValue As Font)
   Set m_Font1 = vNewValue
   PropertyChanged "Font1"
End Property
```

You can create your own objects, which will be handled similarly to Picture and Font objects, but there are some subtleties involved. This subject will be covered later in the chapter.

The Font property presents an interesting choice. You can implement a single Font object or implement separate properties for the FontName, FontSize, FontBold, FontItalic, and FontStrikethru characteristics. You can even implement both, as you will see in the Banner project in Chapter 21. Regardless of which properties you expose, you also have the option of persisting the Font object with a single PropBag.WriteProperties call or separate calls for each font characteristic.

At first glance it may seem that using a single Font object both as a property and for persistence is the obvious choice, but this is not always the case. If you intend your control to be used in Web pages, you may choose to expose the individual Font properties instead of a single Font object. This is because individual Font properties will appear on the Web page in human readable form. If you persist the Font object, you will typically get a subobject on the Web page, assuming that your Web development tool knows how to handle the object at all.

There is another side effect involved in exposing the Font object at runtime. You have no way of detecting when a developer changes a property of the Font object unless you are using the ambient font, in which case you can use the PropertyChanged event to detect any change to the ambient font. When you assign a Font object from the Ambient Font property, you are not actually obtaining a reference to the Ambient font. Visual Basic makes a clone of the Font object. This prevents you from accidentally changing the Ambient font while setting the font characteristics of your control.

PROPERTY PROCEDURES

When defining properties for ActiveX controls you will always use property procedures. How you define them and what you do in them is a major part of every control.

USING BYVAL WITH PROPERTY LET FUNCTIONS

Property Let procedures can be defined with or without a ByVal in most cases. You can gain some performance benefit with string variables by passing the parameter by reference. However, to ensure the maximum compatibility with different containers, parameters should always be passed by value. This is because some containers do not handle all of the variable types correctly when passed by reference. For example: Visual Basic 4.0 does not correctly handle Boolean variables passed by reference.

RAISING ERRORS

Chapter 9 introduced the underlying concepts for OLE error handling, in which each 32-bit error code is divided into three parts: the result code, the facility code, and the error number. You might want to quickly review the section on OLE error handling before continuing.

As you have seen, the vbObjectError constant uses a facility value of 4, indicating an interface error, in which the first 512 error numbers are predefined by Visual Basic. When working with ActiveX controls, you may, on occasion, raise vbObjectError values when you have custom errors. But OLE defines facility code &H0A, which is intended specifically for use with ActiveX controls. Curiously enough, this is the same facility code Visual Basic seems to use internally for trappable errors in general. For example: the Invalid Property Value error is trappable error #380. If you execute the line

```
Err.Raise 380
```

you'll see an Invalid Property Value error message. If, however, you explicitly set the facility code as

```
Err.Raise &H800A0000 Or 380
```

you'll see the same error, and the Err object will report error number 380.

If you look at the list of trappable errors in the Visual Basic online help, you will see many that are obviously useful with ActiveX controls. Should you use them in your control? Absolutely!

You see, the error values defined for the ActiveX control facility codes are not just standard to Visual Basic; they are standard to all ActiveX controls. Error code 380 will be raised by any control when you try to set an invalid property value. This means that your Visual Basic program can handle any ActiveX control errors regardless of who developed the control and the language in which it was written. It also means that you can (and should) use these error codes in your controls so they can be supported properly by all ActiveX containers.

The ch19Tst2 project is designed to help you experiment with the behavior of errors raised by ActiveX controls in both the container's design time and runtime. Figure 19.1 shows the ch19ctl2A control included in this project.

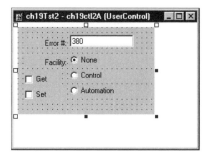

Figure 19.1: The ch19ctl2A control

The control contains a constituent text box in which you can enter an error number to raise. The three option buttons allow you to choose the facility code (null, control, or automation). The settings in the Get and Set check-boxes determine if the error should be raised when the property is read or set. The control's code is quite simple, as you can see here:

```
' Guide to the Perplexed
' Chapter 19 - ch19ctl2a
' Copyright (c) 1997 by Desaware Inc. All Rights Reserved
Option Explicit

Private m_Facility As Long

Private Const vbCtlError = &HA0000 Or &H80000000

Private Sub optFacility_Click(Index As Integer)
    Select Case Index
        Case 0
            m_Facility = 0
        Case 1
            m_Facility = vbCtlError
        Case 2
            m_Facility = vbObjectError
    End Select
End Sub

' The Get and Let check boxes determine when the error is triggered
Public Property Get TriggerError() As String
    Dim errcode&
    errcode = Val(txtErrNum.Text) Or m_Facility
    Debug.Print Hex$(errcode)
    If chkGet.Value Then Err.Raise errcode
End Property

Public Property Let TriggerError(ByVal vNewValue As String)
    Dim errcode&
    errcode = Val(txtErrNum.Text) Or m_Facility
    Debug.Print Hex$(errcode)
    If chkLet.Value Then Err.Raise errcode
End Property
```

The test form, ch19frm2.frm, contains a single instance of the control and two command buttons. The Get command button reads the control's Trigger-Error property. The Set command button sets it to an arbitrary value.

Here's a question you should be able to figure out quickly. It should be fairly clear how to test the control at runtime—all of the constituent controls on the ch19ctl2a control are active, so you can just edit the error number in the text box, select the desired options, and click the Get or Set command buttons. But how can you perform the same test during the container's design time?

If you look at the property settings for the control itself (the properties of the UserControl object for the control), you'll see that the EditAtDesignTime property is set to True. After closing the designer and drawing the control on the form, invoke the Edit command on the context menu (the pop-up menu that appears when you right-click on the control). This will make the control active, allowing you to edit the text box and set the other control options. Now click on the form. This brings the control out of edit mode. When you click on the control again, Visual Basic will attempt to read the TriggerError property in order to load the property window, allowing you to test the property read side. You can test the property setting side by editing the TriggerError string in the property window.

Why does this sample program limit itself to testing errors raised during property access? Because, generally speaking, the only time your control should raise errors is during property access or method calls. You should avoid raising errors while processing internal events. This is because the container may not be designed to handle errors that are raised at arbitrary times. If an error occurs at other times, you should keep track of it and raise the error next time the control is accessed in a method or property.

Frequently Used Error Codes   A complete list of trappable errors can be found in your Visual Basic online help (search the index for trappable errors). Most of the errors are self explanatory. Table 19.1 lists the error codes most frequently used by control authors.

The principles of error handling described for ActiveX components in Chapter 9 apply to ActiveX controls as well. If an error is raised by a component that your control is using (either a constituent control, or an object such as the UserControl object for the control), you should handle it within your control, then raise it to your control's container if it is appropriate to do so.

To make life easier on developers using your control, you should also document those errors that your control can raise. This is especially important for customer errors.

RUNTIME AND DESIGN-TIME CHARACTERISTICS

As the control author, you determine when it is legal to read or write properties. There are 16 possible permutations of read/write permissions, as shown in Table 19.2. Read indicates whether the property can be read, Write indicates that it can be set. VB property window characteristics apply to numeric or string property types. The most common configurations are shown in bold type.

Table 19.1: Errors Used Frequently by Control Authors

Error Code	Description
7	Out of Memory—Typically raised if a memory allocation fails within your control.
380	Invalid Property Value—Raise this error when the user tries to set the property to an illegal value.
381	Invalid Property Array Index—Raise this error when an invalid index value is specified for a parameterized property (property array).
382	Set not supported at runtime—Raise this error when an attempt is made to set a property you wish to be settable only at design time. Raise this error only when the Ambient UserMode property is True.
383	Set not supported—Raise this error when an attempt is made to set a property you wish to be read-only.
387	Set not permitted—Raise this error when an attempt is made to set a property that is temporarily configured as read-only.
393	Get not supported at runtime—Raise this error when an attempt is made to read a property you wish to be write-only at runtime. This type of property is typically used to trigger an action in the control and may be better implemented as a method. Raise this error only when the Ambient UserMode property is True.
394	Get not supported—Raise this error when an attempt is made to set a property you wish to be write-only. This type of property may be better implemented as a method.

Table 19.2: Property Permissions. Runtime UserMode = True, Design Time UserMode = False

Read Runtime	Read Design Time	Write Runtime	Write Design Time	Description
Yes	**Yes**	**Yes**	**Yes**	**Full access at all times—one of the most common configurations.**
Yes	Yes	Yes	No	See Note #1.

Table 19.2: Property Permissions. Runtime UserMode = True, Design Time UserMode = False (Continued)

Read Runtime	Read Design Time	Write Runtime	Write Design Time	Description
Yes	**Yes**	**No**	**Yes**	**Write-only at design time. This configuration is used frequently for properties that can be set only at design time.**
Yes	Yes	No	No	What use is a property that cannot be set? It can be used to retrieve information from the control. See Note #1.
Yes	No	Yes	Yes	See Note #2.
Yes	**No**	**Yes**	**No**	**Accessible only at runtime. Frequently used for runtime-only properties.**
Yes	No	No	Yes	See Note #2.
Yes	**No**	**No**	**No**	**Read-only at runtime. Frequently used to retrieve information from a control. Cannot be persisted.**
No	Yes	Yes	Yes	Fully settable at design time, but write-only at runtime. A very uncommon configuration but safe to use.
No	Yes	Yes	No	See Note #1.
No	Yes	No	Yes	Design-time only property. Used by a control to allow configuration by the user without any runtime access. An unusual choice—authors typically allow run-time read access instead.
No	Yes	No	No	See Note #1.

Table 19.2: Property Permissions. Runtime UserMode = True, Design Time UserMode = False (Continued)

Read Runtime	Read Design Time	Write Runtime	Write Design Time	Description
No	No	Yes	Yes	Could be used to trigger an operation in a control. See Note #2.
No	No	Yes	No	Sometimes used to trigger an operation in a control. This approach was common with VBX technology, which did not allow custom methods. Consider using a method instead to accomplish this task.
No	No	No	Yes	See Note #2.
No	No	No	No	If you can find a good use for this one, please let me know!

Note #1   The property will be displayed in the VB property window but cannot be set. While this configuration may conceivably be useful for displaying a property in the VB property window, it is non-intuitive and will probably lead to complaints from users of your control who will wonder why any attempt to edit the property leads to an error (or fails to work). If you wish to display a property in the VB property window that cannot be set, you should at least avoid raising an error.

Note #2   A property that cannot be read at design time will not appear in the VB property window. Still, such a scenario is conceivable if you have a way to set the property value internally or by way of a property page.

It is your responsibility to restrict property access if you wish to do so. This can be accomplished in two ways. You can raise an error or simply ignore the operation.

Errors 382, 383, 393, and 394 shown earlier in Table 19.1 can be raised on an attempt to access the property. For example: to make a property read-only at runtime, you can use the following code:

```
Public Property Let MyProp(ByVal vNewValue As Variant)
    If Ambient.UserMode Then
        Err.Raise 382
    End If
End Property
```

Any attempt to set the property at runtime raises the "Set not supported at runtime" error.

With ActiveX code components it is customary to create read-only properties by simply leaving out the Property Let procedure (and vice-versa for write-only properties). You may want to avoid taking this approach with ActiveX controls. It will work, but the error messages that result when you attempt the illegal operation (messages such as "Object required") will not be particularly useful to the end user. It is better to implement the procedure and raise the appropriate error.

If you want a property to appear in the Visual Basic property window but to be read-only at design time, you should not raise an error when the user attempts to set the property. Simply ignore the attempt to set the property as shown in the following code:

```
Public Property Let MyProp(ByVal vNewValue As Variant)
    If Not Ambient.UserMode Then    ' Design time
        Exit Property
    End If
    ' Perform the runtime property setting operation here
End Property
```

Control Procedure Attributes

The Tools, Procedure Attributes dialog box has a number of settings that are extremely important to ActiveX controls. Chapter 10 introduced those attributes that are applicable to any ActiveX component. Several additional attributes apply specifically to ActiveX controls. The Databinding options will be discussed later in this chapter.

PROCEDURE ID

You have already seen that the procedure ID corresponds to the dispatch ID (DispID) on an ActiveX automation interface. You know that OLE defines many standard procedure IDs, many of which you can select from the drop-down combo box in the Procedure Attributes dialog box.

Keep in mind that the procedure ID has no impact on the property itself, only on how the container deals with the property. The property or method does not have to have the same name as that of the procedure ID. The container does not look at the property name, only the procedure ID.

Table 19.3 lists those procedure IDs that have an impact on the behavior of Visual Basic. You should always assign the standard procedure ID to standard properties that you implement in your control. This will insure that your control works correctly on other containers that may provide special handling for standard properties.

Table 19.3: Standard Procedure IDs Used by Visual Basic

(None)	Non-Standard Dispatch ID Assigned to the Property
(Default)	The property that is accessed when you reference the object without specifying a property name. Choose the default property carefully (or avoid it entirely) to avoid confusing developers who use your control.
AboutBox	When this procedure ID is assigned to a method, the container will invoke this method to display an about box. Visual Basic will add an About Box entry to the VB property window.
Caption or Text	When a property is given either of these procedure IDs, Visual Basic will update the property immediately as keystrokes are entered in the VB property window. This is the standard behavior of Text and Caption properties for many controls. Note that you can use these procedure IDs for any property, even if they have no relation to a typical Text or Caption property.
Enabled	Setting this procedure ID to a property allows Visual Basic to implement standard Enabled behavior for your control as described in Chapter 18.

USE THIS PAGE IN PROPERTY BROWSER

ActiveX controls can implement property pages to allow editing design-time characteristics and properties of your control. This combo box contains a list of all of the currently defined property pages. When you assign a property to a property page, on the VB property window next to the property, Visual Basic will display a button that can be clicked to bring up the specified property page.

Assigning a property to a property page in this manner overrides the existing behavior of the entry for that property in the property window. For example, an enumerated property will typically have a dropdown combo box in the property window that lists the possible values for the property. If you assign the property to a property page, the property page dialog button will appear instead. Property pages will be discussed further later in this chapter and in Chapter 20.

PROPERTY CATEGORY

The category combo box allows you to assign a property to a category. This helps organize properties that relate to each other and specifies which properties will appear together when you select the categorized tab in the VB property window. The combo box contains a list of standard categories, but you can add your own by typing them into the edit portion of the combo box.

This setting is purely for the convenience of developers using your control and has no impact on the functionality of the control.

DON'T SHOW IN PROPERTY BROWSER

This option prevents a property from appearing in the Visual Basic property window. Other containers should follow this behavior as well. The property can still be viewed by the Visual Basic object browser and is not marked as hidden in the type library for the control. Use this option for all properties that are intended to be accessed only at runtime.

The related HideThisMember setting was covered in Chapter 10.

USER INTERFACE DEFAULT

You can specify one property and one event as the user interface default. The user interface default property is the one that will be initially selected in the VB property window when the developer brings it up. The user interface default event is the one that is initially selected when the developer double-clicks on the code window or selects your component in order to attach code to your control's events. This setting is purely for the convenience of developers using your control and has no impact on the functionality of the control.

CUSTOM OBJECTS

You can create your own objects, which will be handled similarly to Picture and Font objects, but there are some subtleties involved. Consider for a moment what you already know about working with properties and how they work with the VB property window:

- ▶ A Property Get function must return a value that can be represented as a string in order for the property to appear in the VB property window.

- ▶ A Property Get function must return an object reference if you wish it to be a true Object property.

- ▶ An Object property is always edited using a separate dialog or property page. Thus you want a dialog button to appear in the VB property window for the Object property.

- ▶ A Property Set procedure must allow you to set an object reference if you wish it to be a true Object property.

Clearly, both the Picture and Font objects meet all of these requirements. Yet, at first glance, they seem somewhat contradictory. How can the Property Get function return both a string and an object? Drat! I guess we have to use variants after all...

THE CLSMYOBJECT FRACTION OBJECT

The clsMyObject object in the ch19ctls project is an extremely simple object that stores two numbers: a numerator and a denominator for a fraction. This is not quite as ridiculous an object as you might think, because there are many fractions that cannot be represented accurately by a floating point number.

The ch19ctlA control will have a property called MyObject1, which allows you to set and retrieve an object of this type. The properties value can be set at design time using a property page and then persisted (saved with the project). I realize that property pages have not been discussed yet. You'll see a brief introduction to them in this section, followed by a much more in-depth discussion in the next chapter.

We'll look at the persistence issues later. For now, let's review the object itself.

Listing 19.1 shows the code for the clsMyObject object. The Numerator and Denominator properties are quite straightforward. You'll note that the Denominator is initialized to 1, and it cannot be set to 0. The Result property (which is read-only) could raise an overflow error, but no error checking is implemented because all it would probably do is raise the same overflow error anyway.

Listing 19.1: Object clsMyObject

```
' Guide to the Perplexed
' Chapter 19 examples
' Copyright (c) 1997 by Desaware Inc. All Rights Reserved

Option Explicit

Private m_Numerator As Double
Private m_Denominator As Double

Public Property Get Numerator() As Double
    Numerator = m_Numerator
End Property

Public Property Let Numerator(ByVal vNewValue As Double)
    m_Numerator = vNewValue
End Property
```

Listing 19.1: Object clsMyObject (Continued)

```
Public Property Get Denominator() As Double
    Denominator = m_Denominator
End Property

Public Property Let Denominator(ByVal vNewValue As Double)
    If vNewValue = 0 Then Exit Property
    m_Denominator = vNewValue
End Property

Private Sub Class_Initialize()
    m_Denominator = 1
End Sub

Public Property Get Result() As Double
    Result = m_Numerator / m_Denominator
End Property

Public Property Get DisplayName() As String
    DisplayName = Str$(m_Numerator) & "/" & LTrim$(Str$(m_Denominator))
End Property
```

THE PROPERTY PROCEDURES

In this particular example, the m_MyObject1 variable, which contains the current setting of the MyObject1 property, is always set to a valid value. Thus, it is defined and initialized as shown below:

```
Private m_MyObject1 As clsMyObject

Private Sub UserControl_Initialize()
    Set m_MyObject1 = New clsMyObject
End Sub
```

Before looking at the rest of the implementation code, let's consider what it must do in order to meet the requirements set earlier. At design time:

▶ The Property Get statement must return a descriptive string that can be displayed in the VB property window.

▶ It must ignore any changes made by the user editing the VB property window.

▶ It must have a button to bring up a property page that allows editing of the object.

▶ It must provide a way for the property page to read and write the property's object.

At runtime the property must only accept references to clsMyObject type objects on both reading and assignment.

Let's look first at the Get side of the equation. The Property Get procedure is defined as follows:

```
Public Property Get MyObject1() As Variant
    If Ambient.UserMode Then
        Set MyObject1 = m_MyObject1
    Else
        MyObject1 = m_MyObject1.DisplayName
    End If
End Property
```

At runtime, the Property Get statement always returns a reference to the object. At design time, it always returns a descriptive string for the object. This string will appear in the VB property window for the property.

But how can a property page access the property's object itself at design time if the Property Get statement returns a string? It does so through a separate procedure such as this one:

```
Friend Property Get InternalMyObject1() As clsMyObject
    Set InternalMyObject1 = m_MyObject1
End Property
```

Note that this procedure is a Friend function and is only accessible by other components in the same project. The property page will be able to use it, but it will be hidden to developers using your control.

On the assignment side, you need to deal with both the Let and Set procedures. On the Let side, you can simply detect if the variant contains an object of the correct type. If so, the internal variable is assigned the new value. Otherwise, an Invalid Property Type error is raised at runtime. At design time, errors are simply ignored; the display in the VB property window will be unchanged. You don't need to worry about incorrect values being set from the property page because you are the author of the property page and can make sure that it always uses valid values when setting the property.

A separate Property Set procedure is used to handle direct setting of the object using the Set statement instead of the variant assignment.

```
Public Property Let MyObject1(ByVal vNewValue As Variant)
    If TypeOf vNewValue Is clsMyObject Then
        Set m_MyObject1 = vNewValue
    Else
```

```
        If Ambient.UserMode Then
            Err.Raise 380
        End If
        ' Don't raise error at design time
    End If
    PropertyChanged "MyObject1"
End Property


Public Property Set MyObject1(ByVal vNewValue As clsMyObject)
    Set m_MyObject1 = vNewValue
    PropertyChanged "MyObject1"
End Property
```

With this code, you can assign the property two ways as shown in the following code from the ch19tst1 project:

```
Private Sub Command1_Click()
    Dim myobj As clsMyObject
    Set myobj = ch19ctlA1.MyObject1
    myobj.Numerator = 2
    myobj.Denominator = 3
    ch19ctlA1.MyObject1 = myobj
    Debug.Print ch19ctlA1.MyObject1.DisplayName
    myobj.Numerator = 1
    myobj.Denominator = 3
    Set ch19ctlA1.MyObject1 = myobj
    Debug.Print ch19ctlA1.MyObject1.DisplayName
End Sub
```

In the first case you are using a direct assignment without a Set statement. This works because the object is automatically converted into a temporary variant, which is then passed to the Property Let procedure. The procedure detects that the object is of the correct type and performs the assignment. In the second case, the object is passed directly to the Property Set procedure. This approach is much more efficient.

You could remove the ability of the Property Let statement to assign clsMy-Object objects (variable assignment without the Set keyword) by always raising an error if it is called at runtime. This would require developers to always use the Set command syntax. Be sure to raise an error if you take this approach. Otherwise, developers will not be able to figure out what is wrong when they accidentally leave off the Set keyword (a very common oversight).

One final comment about the above code: How many objects are you actually dealing with? If you walk through it carefully, you'll see there is only one object involved! Assigning the myobj variable to the control's MyObject1 property assigns the property to the same object that it is already referencing. You'll see the same trace results if you took out the assignments. This doesn't matter for this example, because the intent is only to prove that the assignment actually works.

INTRODUCTION TO PROPERTY PAGES

We'll look at property pages in depth in the next chapter. For now, we'll just cover enough to show how one might implement a custom object. The property page for the clsMyObject object is shown in Figure 19.2.

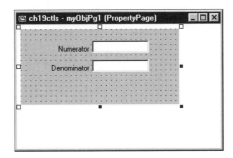

Figure 19.2: Design view of the clsMyObject property page, myObjPg1

There is one text box for the numerator and one for the denominator. Visual Basic automatically adds the OK, Cancel, and Apply buttons to the page when it is displayed.

Once you have created the property page, you can assign it to the property using the Tools, Procedure Attributes dialog box. All defined property pages appear in the "Use this Page in Property Browser" combo box.

Every property page has a PropertyPage object, much in the same way as every VB control has a UserControl object. The PropertyPage object has a property called Changed, which indicates if any of the properties for the page have been changed. It is set any time you edit either of the text boxes representing Object properties, as shown in the following code:

```
Private Sub txtDenominator_Change()
    Changed = True
End Sub

Private Sub txtNumerator_Change()
    Changed = True
End Sub
```

The PropertyPage SelectionChanged event occurs when the page is first assigned to an object. At this time, the program uses the InternalMyObject1 property of the control to retrieve the actual object to edit. It then initializes the text boxes based on the object. Finally, it sets the Changed property back to False (since it was set to True when the text boxes were initialized and we haven't actually made any changes yet). Don't worry about the SelectedControls() array yet. Just assume it provides a way to access the control that is being edited.

```
Private Sub PropertyPage_SelectionChanged()
    Dim myobject As ch19ctlA
    Dim refobject As clsMyObject
    ' We have to go early bound to get at the friend procedure
    Set myobject = SelectedControls(0)
    Set refobject = myobject.InternalMyObject1
    txtNumerator.Text = refobject.Numerator
    txtDenominator.Text = refobject.Denominator
    ' Initialization complete - override the
    ' changes that supposedly were made
    Changed = False
End Sub
```

When you apply the changes to the property or click the OK button for the page, the PropertyPage's ApplyChanges event is triggered. The program creates a new object at this time, loads the object's properties based on the text boxes, and assigns it to the control via the control's Property Set statement, as shown below:

```
Private Sub PropertyPage_ApplyChanges()
    Dim refobject As clsMyObject
    Set refobject = New clsMyObject
    refobject.Numerator = txtNumerator.Text
    refobject.Denominator = txtDenominator.Text
    Set SelectedControls(0).MyObject1 = refobject
End Sub
```

There are other approaches you could take when implementing the ApplyChanges statement, as you will see in the next chapter.

Persistence

One of the key differences between ActiveX code components and ActiveX controls is the ability of controls to save information about the state of the control that is set by a developer at design time. Chapter 17 discussed the events during which you should save property information. Now let's take a look at how it is actually accomplished.

The major portion of the work is done by the PropBag object that is provided by the UserControl object during the ReadProperties and WriteProperties event. The PropBag object has two methods. The Read method takes a property name and default value as parameters, and returns the stored property value. The function returns a variant and can thus handle any property type. The Write method takes a property name, value, and default value as parameters. The importance of Default values is also discussed in Chapter 17.

Visual Basic strives to be efficient and only saves properties when changes have been made. Thus, it is critical that you call the PropertyChanged method of the UserControl object any time a persisted property is changed. If you fail to do so, any changes you make to the properties at design time will not be saved and the VB property window will not be updated to display the current value of the property. There is no harm in calling this method at runtime, so you do not need to add a runtime/design time test to your property setting code.

You've already seen some simple persistence examples in previous code samples—it's hard to do anything in an ActiveX control without it. Unfortunately, the simple examples you see most often can lead to a somewhat limited view of property persistence. So allow me to make a somewhat radical statement: *The PropBag object and its methods and the ReadProperties and WriteProperties events have nothing to do with your control's properties.*

OK, perhaps that is a bit strong. After all, you often will use these elements of Visual Basic to persist the values of your control's properties. But my point is this: The ReadProperties and WriteProperties events are intended to signal the correct time to save or load your control's persistent data. The PropBag object is used to perform the save and load operations.

But whether your control's persistent data has any relationship with your control's properties is entirely up to you. In other words:

▶ The property name under which you save data using the PropBag object need not match the name of a property in your control.

▶ Using the PropBag object, you can save data that does not correspond to a control property.

▶ You can use more than one PropBag property to save information relating to a control property.

The property name under which you save data is just a label—it bears absolutely no relationship to the properties in your control. That said, it is obvious that when you are using the PropBag object to store control properties, you should store the data under the property name in order to minimize possible confusion when people read form files or HTML pages that use your control. But you don't have to.

The ch19ctlB control in the ch19ctls project demonstrates the difference between persisted data and control properties. The control implements a read-only property called CreationTime, which will always contain the date and time that the control instance was added to a container.

The time is stored in a date variable called m_CreationTime. This variable is initialized during the UserControl's InitProperties event. This event is only called when a control instance is created, as shown in the following code:

```
Private m_CreationTime As Date

Private Sub UserControl_InitProperties()
    m_CreationTime = Now()
    Label3.Caption = m_CreationTime
    PropertyChanged "CreationTime"
End Sub
```

The label3 constituent control is used to display the creation time. The PropertyChanged method is called to ensure that the change is stored.

The creation time is stored during the WriteProperties event as follows:

```
Call PropBag.WriteProperty("ControlCreationTime", m_CreationTime)
```

And loaded during the ReadProperties event as follows:

```
m_CreationTime = PropBag.ReadProperty("ControlCreationTime", m_CreationTime)
Label3.Caption = m_CreationTime
```

The property can be read using the Property Get procedure:

```
Public Property Get CreationTime() As Date
    CreationTime = m_CreationTime
End Property

Public Property Let CreationTime(ByVal vNewValue As Date)
    Err.Raise 383
End Property
```

The name under which the data is stored (ControlCreationTime) was intentionally chosen to be different from the property name to emphasize the point that they bear no direct relation to each other. The Property Let procedure always raises the "Set not supported" error. The property is marked with the "Don't show in property browser" option using the Tools, Procedure Attributes statement so it will not appear in the property browser (VB property window). This is the correct way to implement a read-only property in an ActiveX control.

Because there is no way to set the CreationTime property at design time or at runtime, the value will always remain as it was when the control was first placed on the container.

MAPPING PROPERTIES

The fact that persisted data has no direct relationship to a particular property or variable within a control offers enormous flexibility in how you can use this data. You have already seen several cases where a single data item can be mapped to more than one property or variable. This is demonstrated in the ch19ctlB control with both the BackColor and the Font properties.

The BackColor property is used to set the background property for the control and the two picture boxes. The Font property is used to set the fonts for the three Label controls. The property procedures for these properties is shown below.

```
Public Property Get BackColor() As OLE_COLOR
    BackColor = UserControl.BackColor
End Property

Public Property Let BackColor(ByVal New_BackColor As OLE_COLOR)
    UserControl.BackColor() = New_BackColor
    Picture1.BackColor = New_BackColor
    Picture2.BackColor = New_BackColor
    PropertyChanged "BackColor"
End Property

Public Property Get Font() As Font
    Set Font = Label3.Font
End Property

Public Property Set Font(ByVal New_Font As Font)
    Dim lbl As Object
    For Each lbl In UserControl.Controls
        If TypeOf lbl Is Label Then Set lbl.Font = New_Font
    Next
    PropertyChanged "Font"
End Property
```

The BackColor property demonstrates one way to map a single property to multiple objects. The Font property demonstrates how you can use the controls collection to do the same. The ReadProperties and WriteProperties events are implemented as follows:

```
'Load property values from storage
Private Sub UserControl_ReadProperties(PropBag As PropertyBag)
```

```
    ' By using the public property, we set all 3, but
    ' also call PropertyChanged unnecessarily
    BackColor = PropBag.ReadProperty("BackColor", &H8000000F)
    Set Font = PropBag.ReadProperty("Font", Ambient.Font)
End Sub


'Write property values to storage
Private Sub UserControl_WriteProperties(PropBag As PropertyBag)
    Call PropBag.WriteProperty("BackColor", UserControl.BackColor, &H8000000F)
    Call PropBag.WriteProperty("Font", Font, Ambient.Font)
End Sub
```

During the ReadProperties event, you can load the Object properties directly or use the control's Property Get procedure as shown here.

SELF-PERSISTING OBJECTS

Earlier in this chapter you saw how it was possible to create a custom Object property, which can be edited at design time using a property page. The ch19ctlA control demonstrates how you can persist such an object.

It is always best to have the object save its own internal properties. The clsMyObject class contains the following two functions, which are called from the control:

```
' One method to save properties
Friend Sub ReadProperties(PropBag As PropertyBag, propname$)
    m_Numerator = PropBag.ReadProperty(propname$ & "Numerator", 0)
    m_Denominator = PropBag.ReadProperty(propname$ & "Denominator", 1)
End Sub


Friend Sub WriteProperties(PropBag As PropertyBag, propname$)
    PropBag.WriteProperty propname$ & "Numerator", m_Numerator, 0
    PropBag.WriteProperty propname$ & "Denominator", m_Denominator, 1
End Sub
```

The functions are defined as Friend functions because there is no particular reason for them to be exposed to end users. You would have to make them public if the class was defined in its own ActiveX DLL. The functions are called in the ch19ctlA ReadProperties and WriteProperties events as follows. In the ReadProperties event:

```
    Call m_MyObject1.ReadProperties(PropBag, "MyObject1")
```

In the WriteProperties event:

```
    m_MyObject1.WriteProperties PropBag, "MyObject1"
```

In this particular example, the object stores its internal data in multiple properties. The name of the object must be passed to the component so it can create a unique property name (in case there is more than one property using this object).

Keep in mind that the PropBag object can also handle binary data (byte arrays), so if you have a complex object with many internal variables, you can always load them into a single array and store them in one block of data.

You'll notice that the Font and Picture properties are entirely self-persisting through the PropBag object. There does not seem to be any support in Visual Basic at this time for creating an object that is completely self-persisting in this manner, but rest assured, I'll continue to look for a way to accomplish this.

WE'RE OFF TO SEE THE WIZARD

Visual Basic includes an ActiveX Control Interface Wizard that can help you build and maintain your ActiveX controls.

As you've probably noticed by now, I tend to be somewhat skeptical of wizards. They can become a crutch that allows you to replace your own understanding and design effort with that of another programmer who may not be as smart as you and had no knowledge of the needs of your particular application. Because you did not create the underlying code, you may remain unaware of possibilities that were not implemented by the wizard but that could be useful in solving your particular problem.

That said, there are two places where wizards can be extremely useful. First, to do the grunt work of creating routines you already know how to do yourself. Second, to help learn the proper way to solve certain software problems.

This book has taken the approach of teaching you how to create ActiveX components without using a wizard. Now that you have a good understanding of the techniques involved, I encourage you to look at the wizards provided by Microsoft. The ActiveX Control Interface Wizard is especially useful. Listing 19.2 shows the code produced by this wizard with a set of default properties and events that are mapped to the UserControl object. The sample code is contained in the AsyncCtl.ctl project.

Listing 19.2: Code Created by the ActiveX Control Interface Wizard

```
Option Explicit
'Event Declarations:
Event Click() 'MappingInfo=UserControl,UserControl,-1,Click
Event DblClick() 'MappingInfo=UserControl,UserControl,-1,DblClick
Event KeyDown(KeyCode As Integer, Shift As Integer)
'MappingInfo=UserControl,UserControl,-1,KeyDown
Event KeyPress(KeyAscii As Integer) 'MappingInfo=UserControl,UserControl, _
                        -1,KeyPress
```

Listing 19.2: Code Created by the ActiveX Control Interface Wizard (Continued)

```
Event KeyUp(KeyCode As Integer, Shift As Integer)
'MappingInfo=UserControl,UserControl,-1,KeyUp
Event MouseDown(Button As Integer, Shift As Integer, X As Single, Y As Single)
'MappingInfo=UserControl,UserControl,-1,MouseDown
Event MouseMove(Button As Integer, Shift As Integer, X As Single, Y As Single)
'MappingInfo=UserControl,UserControl,-1,MouseMove
Event MouseUp(Button As Integer, Shift As Integer, X As Single, Y As Single)
'MappingInfo=UserControl,UserControl,-1,MouseUp



'WARNING! DO NOT REMOVE OR MODIFY THE FOLLOWING COMMENTED LINES!
'MappingInfo=UserControl,UserControl,-1,BackColor
Public Property Get BackColor() As OLE_COLOR
    BackColor = UserControl.BackColor
End Property

Public Property Let BackColor(ByVal New_BackColor As OLE_COLOR)
    UserControl.BackColor() = New_BackColor
    PropertyChanged "BackColor"
End Property

'WARNING! DO NOT REMOVE OR MODIFY THE FOLLOWING COMMENTED LINES!
'MappingInfo=UserControl,UserControl,-1,ForeColor
Public Property Get ForeColor() As OLE_COLOR
    ForeColor = UserControl.ForeColor
End Property

Public Property Let ForeColor(ByVal New_ForeColor As OLE_COLOR)
    UserControl.ForeColor() = New_ForeColor
    PropertyChanged "ForeColor"
End Property

'WARNING! DO NOT REMOVE OR MODIFY THE FOLLOWING COMMENTED LINES!
'MappingInfo=UserControl,UserControl,-1,Enabled
Public Property Get Enabled() As Boolean
    Enabled = UserControl.Enabled
End Property

Public Property Let Enabled(ByVal New_Enabled As Boolean)
    UserControl.Enabled() = New_Enabled
    PropertyChanged "Enabled"
End Property

'WARNING! DO NOT REMOVE OR MODIFY THE FOLLOWING COMMENTED LINES!
```

Listing 19.2: Code Created by the ActiveX Control Interface Wizard (Continued)

```
'MappingInfo=UserControl,UserControl,-1,Font
Public Property Get Font() As Font
    Set Font = UserControl.Font
End Property

Public Property Set Font(ByVal New_Font As Font)
    Set UserControl.Font = New_Font
    PropertyChanged "Font"
End Property

'WARNING! DO NOT REMOVE OR MODIFY THE FOLLOWING COMMENTED LINES!
'MappingInfo=UserControl,UserControl,-1,BackStyle
Public Property Get BackStyle() As Integer
    BackStyle = UserControl.BackStyle
End Property

Public Property Let BackStyle(ByVal New_BackStyle As Integer)
    UserControl.BackStyle() = New_BackStyle
    PropertyChanged "BackStyle"
End Property

'WARNING! DO NOT REMOVE OR MODIFY THE FOLLOWING COMMENTED LINES!
'MappingInfo=UserControl,UserControl,-1,BorderStyle
Public Property Get BorderStyle() As Integer
    BorderStyle = UserControl.BorderStyle
End Property

Public Property Let BorderStyle(ByVal New_BorderStyle As Integer)
    UserControl.BorderStyle() = New_BorderStyle
    PropertyChanged "BorderStyle"
End Property

'WARNING! DO NOT REMOVE OR MODIFY THE FOLLOWING COMMENTED LINES!
'MappingInfo=UserControl,UserControl,-1,Refresh
Public Sub Refresh()
    UserControl.Refresh
End Sub

Private Sub UserControl_Click()
    RaiseEvent Click
End Sub

Private Sub UserControl_DblClick()
    RaiseEvent DblClick
End Sub
```

Listing 19.2: Code Created by the ActiveX Control Interface Wizard (Continued)

```
Private Sub UserControl_KeyDown(KeyCode As Integer, Shift As Integer)
   RaiseEvent KeyDown(KeyCode, Shift)
End Sub

Private Sub UserControl_KeyPress(KeyAscii As Integer)
   RaiseEvent KeyPress(KeyAscii)
End Sub

Private Sub UserControl_KeyUp(KeyCode As Integer, Shift As Integer)
   RaiseEvent KeyUp(KeyCode, Shift)
End Sub

Private Sub UserControl_MouseDown(Button As Integer, Shift As Integer, _
                              X As Single, Y As Single)
   RaiseEvent MouseDown(Button, Shift, X, Y)
End Sub

Private Sub UserControl_MouseMove(Button As Integer, Shift As Integer, _
                              X As Single, Y As Single)
   RaiseEvent MouseMove(Button, Shift, X, Y)
End Sub

Private Sub UserControl_MouseUp(Button As Integer, Shift As Integer, _
                              X As Single, Y As Single)
   RaiseEvent MouseUp(Button, Shift, X, Y)
End Sub

'Initialize Properties for User Control
Private Sub UserControl_InitProperties()
   Set Font = Ambient.Font
   m_PictureName = m_def_PictureName
End Sub

'Load property values from storage
Private Sub UserControl_ReadProperties(PropBag As PropertyBag)
   UserControl.BackColor = PropBag.ReadProperty("BackColor", &H8000000F)
   UserControl.ForeColor = PropBag.ReadProperty("ForeColor", &H80000012)
   UserControl.Enabled = PropBag.ReadProperty("Enabled", True)
   Set Font = PropBag.ReadProperty("Font", Ambient.Font)
   UserControl.BackStyle = PropBag.ReadProperty("BackStyle", 1)
   UserControl.BorderStyle = PropBag.ReadProperty("BorderStyle", 1)
   m_PictureName = PropBag.ReadProperty("PictureName", m_def_PictureName)
End Sub
```

Listing 19.2: Code Created by the ActiveX Control Interface Wizard (Continued)

```
'Write property values to storage
Private Sub UserControl_WriteProperties(PropBag As PropertyBag)
    Call PropBag.WriteProperty("BackColor", UserControl.BackColor, &H8000000F)
    Call PropBag.WriteProperty("ForeColor", UserControl.ForeColor, &H80000012)
    Call PropBag.WriteProperty("Enabled", UserControl.Enabled, True)
    Call PropBag.WriteProperty("Font", Font, Ambient.Font)
    Call PropBag.WriteProperty("BackStyle", UserControl.BackStyle, 1)
    Call PropBag.WriteProperty("BorderStyle", UserControl.BorderStyle, 1)
    Call PropBag.WriteProperty("PictureName", m_PictureName, m_def_PictureName)
End Sub
```

There are a couple of things to remember when using the wizard.

▶ Be sure to check the procedure IDs of the standard properties and events and make sure they are set to the standard procedure IDs that are appropriate. This is especially necessary for the Enabled property if you wish it to work correctly.

▶ The wizard does not set properties to enumerated types. You should change the property type if you wish the Visual Basic property window to display an enumerated list of values for the property.

▶ If you change the default property of the UserControl object using the VB property window when authoring the control, be sure to change the default values in the PropBag.ReadProperty and PropBag.WriteProperty call for the property. This is illustrated in the example with the BackStyle property.

ASYNCHRONOUS PERSISTENCE

You've seen how a container can use a property bag to persist properties. When data is written to a property bag, the container can do a number of things with it, depending on the data type. If the data type is a string, number, or other type that can be represented as text, the container may save the information in text form. If you look into a form file with a text editor, you will see properties as strings. The properties for a typical command button may appear as follows:

```
Begin VB.CommandButton cmdSet
    Caption         =   "Set"
    Height          =   465
    Left            =   3420
    TabIndex        =   2
    Top             =   810
    Width           =   1005
End
```

But what about data that cannot be represented as text? Pictures and other binary data types must be stored in a separate file. A picture property might be stored thus:

```
Picture        =   "Form1.frx":0000
```

The form file contains a reference to a data file (with the .frx extension) that contains the actual data.

Now, let us take a moment and consider the implications of placing an ActiveX control on a Web page. Properties that can be represented as text are easy enough to handle—they can be included directly on the Web page. HTML also provides a way to include the binary data on the page, but who wants to force someone to download hundreds of kilobytes, if not megabytes, of encoded binary data in order to see a Web page?

Clearly there needs to be a way to direct a control to retrieve data from a different location. Plus, to provide reasonable performance, there needs to be a way to download data asynchronously in the background in cases where the control needs to be displayed or provide some initial functionality as quickly as possible. For example: you might want the Picture property of a control to be retrieved in the background so the control displays and starts running immediately, just without the correct image.

Visual Basic 5.0 ActiveX controls support this type of asynchronous downloading. The AsyncCtl.ctl control demonstrates one approach for loading a picture asynchronously. The program will work with any container, but the download will be asynchronous only on containers such as Microsoft Explorer, which support this feature. The relevant listings are shown in Listing 19.3.

Listing 19.3: The AsyncCtl.ctl Code Relating to Asynchronous Persistence

```
Const m_def_PictureName = ""
'Property Variables:
Dim m_PictureName As String

Public Property Get Picture() As Picture
   Set Picture = UserControl.Picture
End Property

Public Property Set Picture(ByVal vNewValue As Picture)
   Set UserControl.Picture = vNewValue
End Property

Public Property Get PictureName() As String
   PictureName = m_PictureName
```

Listing 19.3: The AsyncCtl.ctl Code Relating to Asynchronous Persistence (Continued)

```
End Property

Public Property Let PictureName(ByVal New_PictureName As String)
    m_PictureName = New_PictureName
    UserControl.AsyncRead m_PictureName, vbAsyncTypePicture, "Picture"
    PropertyChanged "PictureName"
End Property

Private Sub UserControl_ReadProperties(PropBag As PropertyBag)
    PictureName = PropBag.ReadProperty("PictureName", m_def_PictureName)
End Sub

Private Sub UserControl_WriteProperties(PropBag As PropertyBag)
    Call PropBag.WriteProperty("PictureName", m_PictureName, m_def_PictureName)
End Sub

Private Sub UserControl_AsyncReadComplete(AsyncProp As AsyncProperty)
    On Error GoTo AsyncErr
    Select Case AsyncProp.PropertyName
        Case "Picture"
            Debug.Print "Picture arrived"
            Set Picture = AsyncProp.Value
    End Select
    Exit Sub
AsyncErr:
    ' Errors on async operations will be reported when you try
    ' to access the value
End Sub
```

In this case, the Picture property is marked as not viewable in the property browser, using the Tools, Procedure Attributes dialog box. This is because we are not actually persisting the Picture property. Instead, we persist a property called PictureName, which does appear in the Visual Basic property window and is persisted using the ReadProperties and WriteProperties events as shown. This property will contain the location from which the control should load the picture. This location can be specified as a network URL or a local file path. When this property is set, via either the ReadProperties event or the Property Let procedure, it calls the AsyncRead method of the UserControl object.

The AsyncRead method takes three parameters. The first is the path or URL (Web address) specifying the file to retrieve. The second is the type of data, picture, file, or binary. The final parameter is a label identifying the data being retrieved. You set as many properties as you wish to load in the background, so the label is used to identify each one. This label will typically be the name of the property, but the choice is entirely up to you.

Once the data is retrieved, the AsyncReadComplete event will be triggered. This event has a reference to an AsyncProperty object as its sole parameter. This object allows you to retrieve the data type and label that was specified during the AsyncRead call. It also contains a Value property, which is a variant containing the returned data. The Value will contain a picture if you specified a picture type, the name of a temporary file if you specified a file type, or a byte array if you specified the binary type.

If an error occurred during the read operation, an error will be raised as soon as you access the Value property. Thus, it is critical to always use error handling during the AsyncReadComplete event. By the same token, you should never raise an error during this event. This event can happen at any time and containers will not be ready to handle errors you raise while it is being processed.

You can safely use asynchronous reads for local files on any container. Only browser-enabled containers will support URL paths. Whether the operation will actually take place asynchronously or not also depends on the container and whether the access is a URL or path. You can see the behavior of an asynchronous load by registering the AsyncCtl.ocx control and loading the following Web page using MS Internet Explorer 3.0 or other ActiveX-enabled browser. Note that the CLSID of the control and the URL shown here are subject to change between the time this book goes to press and when the accompanying CD is created. A later version of the page can be found on your CD ROM in file AsyncCtl.htm.

```
<HTML>
<HEAD>
<TITLE>New Page</TITLE>
</HEAD>
<BODY>
This is a test of an asynchronous control.
<OBJECT ID="AsyncControl1" WIDTH=320 HEIGHT=240
 CLASSID="CLSID:C49A2B57-6E63-11D0-91BB-00AA0036005A">
    <PARAM NAME="_ExtentX" VALUE="8467">
    <PARAM NAME="_ExtentY" VALUE="6350">
    <PARAM NAME="PictureName" VALUE="http://www.desaware.com/desaware/images/
bookcvr4.gif">
</OBJECT>

</BODY>
</HTML>
```

UPDATING CONTROLS

What happens when you add or remove persisted data when your control is updated? If you add a persisted property to a control, be sure you specify a default value. Otherwise an error may occur when the control tries to read a project saved with an older control. When a default value is specified, it will be loaded into the variable when the property is not found in the file. You can add persisted data without any problems.

A more complete discussion of the issues surrounding control upgrades can be found in Chapter 25.

DATABINDING

Databinding refers to the process of binding one or more properties of an ActiveX control to fields in a database. The problem with trying to discuss this subject is that it can rapidly grow to fill not just the rest of this book but dozens of additional volumes as well.

This section assumes that you have at least a passing acquaintance with databinding as it is implemented with standard controls, such as a Text Box or Label control. That should be enough for you to understand the "easy" way to bind controls, which will be covered very briefly because it is explained quite nicely in the Visual Basic 5.0 documentation.

After that, we'll take a look at the "hard way" of doing databinding, in which you take over from Visual Basic and do it yourself. This subject will also be covered very briefly because it is simply too large a subject to cover here. My intent is to point you in the right direction. If you are a Data Access Objects (DAO) expert, you should have no trouble extending the simple example presented here into as sophisticated a data management system as you wish. If you are not a DAO expert, that section will lose you anyway because I will make no effort to explain the intricacies of data access under Visual Basic. That is truly a subject for another time and place.

THE EASY WAY

The easy way to databind a property in a control is to let Visual Basic do it for you. This is accomplished by defining a property and setting its attributes using the Tools, Procedure Attributes dialog box. There are four available selections for databinding:

- ▶ Property is data bound. Select this checkbox to bind the property.
- ▶ This property binds to the DataField. This property becomes the default bound property if the control has more than one bound property.

 ▸ Show in DataBindings collection at design time. Allows the developer using your control to edit the databinding at design time.

 ▸ Property will call CanPropertyChange before changing. This options informs the container that your control will call CanPropertyChange before changing bound property values.

To understand these better, you need to have an idea of what happens when you set a property to be bound. Visual Basic adds four properties to the control's Extender object:

1 The DataSource property is used by the developer to select a data control to which your control will be bound.

2 The DataField property is used by the developer to select a field in the database to which one of your control's properties will be bound (the one that has its "This property binds to Datafield" checkbox selected. You should always select this checkbox for at least one property).

3 The DataBindings property appears in the VB window to allow the developer to bind other bound properties in your control to various fields in the database. All bound controls whose procedure attribute specifies "Show in DataBindings collection at design time" will appear in the DataBindings dialog box. The control's Extender object also exposes a DataBindings collection that contains a DataBinding object for each bound property. This object contains the binding information for the property.

4 The DataChanged property indicates if any of the bound properties have been changed.

One important thing to keep in mind is that databinding is supported by the container. Containers are not required to support databinding and not all that do will support binding of more than one property in a control.

Figure 19.3 illustrates the architecture of simple databinding. The DataSource property of the control selects a data control that specifies the database, the source table or dynaset, and determines at runtime which row in the recordset is being accessed. The DataBindings object binds individual properties within the control to the various fields in the RecordSet. You specify one of the properties as the default bound property by selecting the "This property binds to the DataField" attribute; the field that it is bound to is specified by the control's DataField property.

The ch19bind.ctl control in the Chapter 19 Binding.vbp project demonstrates simple binding of two control properties to a database. A simple database, dbdemo.mdb, has been provided for this example. The database contains

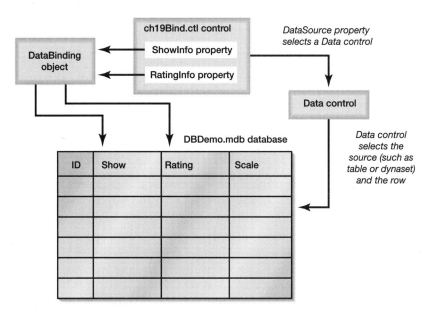

Figure 19.3: Architecture of simple databinding

a single table with several fields. Two of them are of interest here: "show," which contains the name of a TV show, and "rating," which contains a brief evaluation of the show.

The control implements a number of standard properties, which will not be shown in the listings that follow. The control contains two properties, each of which will be bound, one to the "show" field and one to the "rating" field in the table. Note that the binding is done at design time by the developer, not by you as the control author. In fact, each of these properties could be bound to any field in the database. The properties are mapped to two text boxes, txtShow and txtRating. The code for their property procedures is as follows:

```
Public Property Get ShowInfo() As String
    ShowInfo = txtShow.Text
End Property

Public Property Let ShowInfo(ByVal New_ShowInfo As String)
    If UserControl.CanPropertyChange("ShowInfo") Then
        txtShow.Text() = New_ShowInfo
        PropertyChanged "ShowInfo"
    End If
End Property
```

```
Public Property Get RatingInfo() As String
   RatingInfo = txtRating.Text
End Property

Public Property Let RatingInfo(ByVal New_RatingInfo As String)
   If UserControl.CanPropertyChange("RatingInfo") Then
      txtRating.Text() = New_RatingInfo
      PropertyChanged "RatingInfo"
   End If
End Property
```

Note that the value of the property can only be set if the CanPropertyChange function returns True. This is necessary because the procedure attributes for both properties have the "Property will call CanPropertyChange" checkbox selected. This option is not used by VB at this time—CanPropertyChange will always return True. However, by always calling CanPropertyChange, you will help ensure the correct behavior of your control on future containers (both VB and others).

The call to the PropertyChanged function is especially critical when using databinding. You may recall that PropertyChanged informs Visual Basic that a property has been changed, so it knows whether the property needs to be saved. It is also used to inform Visual Basic that the value of a bound property has changed, so it will know to write it out to the database.

If you wish the database fields to be editable, you must inform Visual Basic that they have been changed. This is done as follows:

```
Private Sub txtRating_Change()
   PropertyChanged "RatingInfo"
End Sub

Private Sub txtShow_Change()
   PropertyChanged "ShowInfo"
End Sub
```

When the Data control switches to another property, VB will access the DataChanged property of the control (or the DataChanged property for each DataBinding object). If this property is True, VB will attempt to write out the updated information to the database.

If you have used the ActiveX Interface Wizard to create the bound properties, remember to add the CanPropertyChange test on the property Let procedure and to remove the property persistence from the UserControl's ReadProperties and WriteProperties event. It's rather pointless to persist a property that is bound to a database.

Keep in mind that when a control contains multiple bound properties, it can define ways for them to interact within the control. For example, you can initialize one property to a default value that is based on another property.

THE HARD WAY

What if you want your control to contain a bound list? Or a set of lists from different tables? The rather simple binding provided by Visual Basic does not extend easily to that level of functionality.

But keep in mind that your ActiveX control has complete access to all of the database capabilities of Visual Basic. In other words, it is possible to implement binding on your own. It may not be as clean as that provided by Visual Basic, but it can be extremely powerful.

The Binding.vbp project contains a second control, ch19bnd2.ctl, which implements its own databinding. The sample shown here is just a sketchy implementation, intended only to give you an idea of how the standard database operations can be executed. The control contains a combo box and a text box. The combo box will be used to select the "show" information, and the text box will display and permit editing of the "rating" information.

The first issue the control must deal with is obtaining a reference to a Database object. You have a number of ways to accomplish this. You can actually add a property that will contain the database name and the record source name, in effect copying the properties used by the data control to choose a database and record source.

Or you can keep things simple and cheat. This example implements a DataSource property, which is a string specifying the name of a Data control on the same container as the control. The property is implemented as follows:

```
Dim m_DataSource As String

Public Property Get DataSource() As String
   DataSource = m_DataSource
End Property

Public Property Let DataSource(ByVal vNewValue As String)
   m_DataSource = vNewValue
   PropertyChanged "DataSource"
End Property

Private Sub UserControl_ReadProperties(PropBag As PropertyBag)
   m_DataSource = PropBag.ReadProperty("DataSource", "")
End Sub
```

```
Private Sub UserControl_WriteProperties(PropBag As PropertyBag)
   PropBag.WriteProperty "DataSource", m_DataSource, ""
End Sub
```

The property is also persisted in the UserControl object's ReadProperties
and WriteProperties event in the usual way. The disadvantage of this approach
is that you cannot display a dropdown list box showing the names of the data
controls already present on the container (the normal behavior of the Data-
Source property). This leaves you with a number of choices:

- ▸ You can settle for having the developer enter the name directly (perhaps
  performing validation to make sure it does match a value for a control,
  an operation not shown here).

- ▸ You can prevent direct input and perhaps use a property page to allow
  the user to select from controls on the container.

- ▸ You can use Desaware's SpyWorks to create a custom dropdown list box
  containing the names of available data controls, thus mimicking the standard behavior of the DataSource property.

- ▸ You can implement a separate bound property (which will cause the
  DataSource property to be defined for the control). You can then read
  that DataSource property at the container's design time and persist it in
  your own internal variable. This step is necessary because you cannot
  read the Extender DataSource property at runtime.

I must stress that the DataSource property implemented in the first three options above may seem to the developer to be similar and able to function the
same way as the standard DataSource property. But it is implemented differently. In the ch19Bind.ctl example shown earlier, the DataSource property is
part of the control's Extender object and is implemented by the container (as is
any Extender property). In this example the DataSource property is part of
your control's public interface and is implemented by you, the control author.

The DataSource property gives you the name of the data control. But how do
you obtain a reference to the control? One way is shown in the following code:

```
Dim m_MyRecordSet As RecordSet
Dim m_MyData As Data

Private Sub UserControl_Show()
   Dim obj As Object
   If Ambient.UserMode Then
      For Each obj In Extender.Parent.Controls
         If TypeOf obj Is Data Then
```

```
        If obj.Name = m_DataSource Then
            Set m_MyData = obj
            Set m_MyRecordSet = m_MyData.RecordSet
            LoadCombo
        End If
      End If
    Next
  End If
End Sub
```

This code shows how you can search for a specific control using the controls collection of the container, which can be accessed via the Extender property. This function is called during the Show event, during which it is safe to assume (at least with Visual Basic) that all of the other controls belonging to the container have already been sited.

Two things need to be done to this function to make it robust for use in a real control:

▶ Add error checking. Remember that you cannot assume that every extender has a Parent property or that the container has a controls collection.

▶ Add additional logic to determine whether you really want to reload the combo box each time the control is shown.

The combo box can be loaded using standard database techniques as follows:

```
Public Sub LoadCombo()
  m_MyRecordSet.MoveFirst
  Do While Not m_MyRecordSet.EOF
     Combo1.AddItem m_MyRecordSet.Fields("Show")
     m_MyRecordSet.MoveNext
  Loop
  Combo1.ListIndex = 0
End Sub
```

Once again, you should add any necessary error checking.

In this example, the DataField information is hard coded into the sample. Clearly you could specify one or more DataField properties of your own or implement your own DataBindings type collection and object with its own property page to implement more sophisticated binding. This could allow the developer to specify different fields for the different bound objects in the control.

The Text box containing the rating is loaded any time a selection is made in the combo box. This is accomplished using the following code:

```
Dim m_RatingChanged As Boolean

Private Sub Combo1_Click()
    If m_RatingChanged Then
        m_MyRecordSet.Edit
        m_MyRecordSet.Fields("rating") = Text1.Text
        m_MyRecordSet.Update
    End If
    m_MyRecordSet.FindFirst "[Show] = '" & Combo1.Text & "'"
    Text1.Text = m_MyRecordSet.Fields("rating")
    m_RatingChanged = False
End Sub
```

Once again, the field information is hard coded in this particular instance. The m_RatingChanged variable is a private Boolean variable that indicates that the Text1 text box has been changed. This variable could easily be exposed as a public property to provide identical functionality to the standard DataChanged property. When the combo box selection changes, as indicated by the Click event, the control checks to see if the text box has been changed. If so, it updates the field in the database. It then finds the record that you selected and sets the RecordSet cursor to that position using the FindFirst method. It then loads the Text1 control with the rating field for that record and marks the Text1 control as "clean." All that's left is the code that marks the Text1 box as changed:

```
Private Sub Text1_Change()
    m_RatingChanged = True
End Sub
```

One interesting thing to note about this example is that while the control does effectively bind database fields to the control (in this case, to constituent controls, but it could be to variables as well), it does not bind them to public properties of the control! Could you define public properties that would act as bound? Absolutely—just have them set the appropriate constituent control properties, just as you saw in the prior example.

Because we are not using Visual Basic's binding, we don't need to worry about calling PropertyChanged or CanPropertyChange for changes in the database. It would not be critical if you did decide to create bound public properties in this manner, but it would do no harm either.

This concludes our brief introduction to the possibilities of do-it-yourself databinding using Visual Basic ActiveX controls. It does represent more work for the author, but it can provide substantially more functionality and reduce the dependence on the container. If container-supported databinding is adequate for your needs, by all means use it.

We are almost finished with our coverage of ActiveX control fundamentals. Just one important issue remains. You've seen a quick introduction to property pages, now it's time to really put them to work.

Property Pages and Others

PROPERTY PAGE FUNDAMENTALS

PROPERTY PAGE TECHNIQUES

ABOUT BOXES AND OTHERS

I have a confession to make. I really like property pages.

Yes, I do most of my property editing using the VB property window. And yes, Microsoft recommends against doing much in property pages other than setting a control's properties. But I can't help but be intrigued by the idea of property pages.

By now you should be well acquainted with the fact that, as a control author, you are writing for both the container's runtime and its design-time environment. The control behavior that you define for runtime is ultimately intended for the end user, who is the person that the developer using your control is also coding for. But the control behavior you define at design time is intended exclusively for the developer. There isn't much room for creativity and flexibility in the control itself, mostly because Visual Basic makes it awkward to interact with the control at design time. You can allow such interaction by setting your control's EditAtDesignTime property to True, but even so, it's awkward for developers to switch to and from edit mode on controls. I rarely do so myself.

The property page, on the other hand, is designed specifically to let the developer interact with the control using whatever user interface you care to define. It's almost as if you can create your own program to allow developers to configure your control. Well, actually, that is exactly what property pages offer: the ability to create your own unique development environment for your control.

Think about it. What does a "unique development environment for your control" really mean? It is a far cry from the VB documentation, which calls property pages "...an alternative to the Properties window for viewing ActiveX control properties." I think my meaning will become clear as you read the rest of this chapter, but I offer you this one thought before beginning: There is no technical reason whatsoever that requires that a property page have anything at all to do with your control's properties. Intriguing, isn't it?

Property Page Fundamentals

The first thing you should know about property pages is that you should always implement them for your controls. The reason for this is simple: there is no guarantee that a container using your control will have its own property window like the one provided by Visual Basic. With this kind of container, property pages provide the only way to edit the properties of your control.

The next thing you should know is that property page windows exist within a property page container window. This window contains OK, Cancel, and Apply buttons, which are used by all of the property pages. The container window provides tabs to select from among the property pages. The property page container window is modeless with respect to the control under Visual Basic, but this may not be the case for every container.

Let us take a moment and review the mechanics and key properties and events of property pages.

Every UserControl object has a PropertyPages collection. When you click on the dialog button in the PropertyPages entry in the VB property window, you'll see a dialog much like the one shown in Figure 20.1.

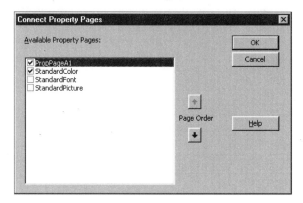

Figure 20.1: The Connect Property Pages dialog box

This dialog box lists all of the property pages that are available to your control. Three standard property pages are always available: the standard color, font, and picture property pages.

Your control's container will always provide a way to bring up the property pages for your control. With Visual Basic you can use the Properties command on the context menu or the dialog button on the Custom property in the property window.

Visual Basic automatically maps properties to standard property pages where possible. Font properties are mapped to the standard Font property pages, Picture properties to the standard picture property page, and properties with type OLE_COLOR to the standard color property page. But this default mapping does not mean that VB automatically assigns the property page to the dialog button in the VB property window.

If you want a property page to be assigned to the dialog button for the property in the VB property window, you must use the Tools, Procedure Attributes dialog box to assign the property page to the property. Select from among the available pages using the "Use this page in property browser" combo box.

The implications of this can be rather confusing. Take the BackColor property in the Trivial.vbp example for this chapter. If the BackColor property is not assigned to the standard color property page, when you click on the button in the VB property window, you will see a small palette drop down. If it is assigned to the standard property page, you will see the property page instead. Which one should you use? It's entirely up to you, but in most cases controls do not assign standard properties to the standard property pages when the container is likely to provide an alternate in its property window.

The property page mapping does become important when it comes to your own properties. You should map properties to pages wherever you wish to provide direct access to its associated property page.

The Trivial.vbp example shown in Listing 20.1 demonstrates a simple property page that handles a single String property for a control. The page contains a single text box that is used to edit a Text property named Test.

This listing demonstrates the most important events and properties for a property page. The SelectedControls collection contains references to the controls that are associated with the property page. The SelectionChanged event occurs any time one or more controls are associated with the page. At this time the Text control is loaded with the value of the Test property of the control.

If the value of the text box is changed by the developer, the txtTest_Change event fires and the property page's Changed property is set to True. This property does two things. When it is set to True, the Apply button for the property page is enabled. Also, the property page automatically triggers the ApplyChanges event when the OK button is clicked or another property page is selected.

Listing 20.1: The TrivialPg Property Page

```
Option Explicit
Private Sub txtTest_Change()
    Changed = True
End Sub

Private Sub PropertyPage_ApplyChanges()
    SelectedControls(0).Test = txtTest.Text
End Sub

Private Sub PropertyPage_SelectionChanged()
    txtTest.Text = SelectedControls(0).Test
End Sub
```

When the developer clicks the Apply button or clicks the OK button while the Changed property is True, the ApplyChanges event is triggered. This event indicates the need to write the property values to the control. Let's take a closer look at the events and properties of the PropertyPage object.

PROPERTY PAGE PROPERTIES

If you take a quick look at the VB property window for a Property Page object you will see that it supports virtually all of the properties, methods, and events of a standard form. It can contain both standard controls and ActiveX controls. This means you have effectively as much programming flexibility within a property page as Visual Basic can provide. The only limit is that you are strongly encouraged to keep your user interface within the property page. You can bring up other forms from the property page, but doing so strays considerably from what developers are accustomed to. So you should do so only when absolutely necessary.

There are a number of properties and events that are unique to property pages. These are described in the remainder of this section.

The Changed Property   When this property is True, the Apply button in the property page container window is enabled. In addition, clicking on the OK button or switching to a different property page will automatically trigger the Property page's ApplyChanges event.

If you set this property to True during the ApplyChanges event and the event has been triggered by clicking on OK or attempting to switch to another page, the page will not close.

The SelectedControls Property   The SelectedControls collection has two
properties. The Count property indicates the number of controls that are currently selected. The Item property, which is the default property for the object,
contains references to the selected controls.

How do you select more than one control for a property page? With Visual
Basic, you can do this by first bringing up the property pages for one control,
then clicking on additional controls while holding the control or shift key
down. Other containers may provide other techniques for selecting multiple
controls.

You should consider how you would like to handle multiple control selections when designing your property page. You may be tempted to just access
the first control in the list, but this could lead to confusion among developers,
not to mention taking from them the option of applying property changes to
more than one control at a time. An example of how to handle this situation
follows later in this chapter.

The StandardSize Property   When you create a blank property page, it is created with the size 395 x 233 pixels. This is a custom size that works fine with
Visual Basic containers. There are two standard sizes that can be set using this
property, 375 x 179 and 375 x 101 pixels. A well-behaved container will expand the size of its property page window to handle whatever size you choose.
That said, if you don't need the full amount of space provided by the default
size, feel free to choose one of the smaller sizes. Developers generally appreciate it when control vendors don't waste screen space unnecessarily. The Microsoft documentation recommends that you avoid using these standard settings,
as they may not adapt correctly to different display resolutions on the developer's system.

PROPERTY PAGE EVENTS

Property pages support most of the standard form events. They do not support a Load or Unload event because, frankly, these would serve little purpose.
The Initialize and Terminate events for property pages work exactly like those
of a form. You can access controls contained on the property pages during
both of these events. A property page is not destroyed when you switch between property pages by tabbing between pages for a particular control. But it
usually is destroyed when the property page container is closed or you switch
to property pages for a different control.

The SelectionChanged Event   This is one of the two truly important events
for any property page. This event is triggered any time a control is selected for

editing via the property page. It should be treated somewhat like the Load event for a form. During this event you can access the associated control using the SelectedControls collection and load the current values of properties for the control. It is during this event that you should handle the case of multiple selected controls.

If the PropertyChanged method is called for any property on the control, this event will be triggered. This can lead to interesting side effects, as you will see later.

An important part of understanding this event is to take into consideration when it does not occur. This event is not triggered when you switch between property pages, except as a result of a property being changed. Nor can you use the GotFocus or LostFocus event to detect the switch between pages. These events are not triggered if your page contains any controls (which is usually the case). Fortunately, this is rarely a problem. From your point of view, tabbing to another page is roughly equivalent to your page being temporarily covered by another window.

The ApplyChanges Event   This event is triggered any time the settings in the property page need to be written to the control. It occurs when the developer clicks on the Apply button or when the Changed property is True and the developer either clicks on the OK button, closes the page using the system menu, or selects a different page. It is not called when the page is closed via the Cancel button.

The EditProperties Event   With some containers, when you click on an individual property in the property window, instead of displaying all available property pages, the container will display the one property page associated with the property whose dialog button you clicked. In this case, the EditProperties event will be triggered to indicate which property caused the property page to appear. A typical use for this event is to set the focus to the control on the property page responsible for editing the property in question.

You should not count on this event occurring. A container has the option of bringing up all of the property pages associated with the control, in which case this event typically will not be triggered.

PROPERTY PAGE TECHNIQUES

So far you have seen two approaches for using property pages. You've seen that properties on a control can be edited on property pages. In Chapter 19 you saw that a property page can be used to edit a complex property or object. In both cases the property pages followed a standard approach:

- ▸ The property page loads property values from the control.
- ▸ The developer has the option of editing the property values in the page.
- ▸ The developer may apply or cancel the assignment of changed property values to the control.

The PrpPage1.vbg program group contains two projects: The PropPgs1.vbp project contains a control, PropPageCtlA, and a property page, PropPageA1. The PropPageTest1 project contains a form that holds two instances of the PropPageCtlA control.

The PropPageCtlA control contains four properties of interest. The Label1Caption and Label2Caption properties are reflected in the Label1 and Label2 constituent controls for the control. The Label3 constituent control demonstrates control configuration without use of properties. The BackColor property controls the background color of the control. The ButtonVisible property determines whether the Command1 constituent control is visible. The listing for the control module is shown in Listing 20.2.

Listing 20.2: The PropPageCtlA Control

```
' Guide to the Perplexed
' PropPgs1 example from chapter 20
' Copyright (c) 1997 by Desaware Inc. All Rights Reserved

Option Explicit

'WARNING! DO NOT REMOVE OR MODIFY THE FOLLOWING COMMENTED LINES!
'MappingInfo=Label1,Label1,-1,Caption
Public Property Get Label1Caption() As String
    Label1Caption = Label1.Caption
End Property

Public Property Let Label1Caption(ByVal New_Label1Caption As String)
    Label1.Caption() = New_Label1Caption
    PropertyChanged "Label1Caption"
End Property

'WARNING! DO NOT REMOVE OR MODIFY THE FOLLOWING COMMENTED LINES!
'MappingInfo=Label2,Label2,-1,Caption
Public Property Get Label2Caption() As String
    Label2Caption = Label2.Caption
End Property
```

Listing 20.2: The PropPageCtlA Control (Continued)

```vb
Public Property Let Label2Caption(ByVal New_Label2Caption As String)
    Label2.Caption() = New_Label2Caption
    PropertyChanged "Label2Caption"
End Property

'Load property values from storage
Private Sub UserControl_ReadProperties(PropBag As PropertyBag)
    UserControl.BackColor = PropBag.ReadProperty("Backcolor", &H8000000F)
    Label1.Caption = PropBag.ReadProperty("Label1Caption", "Label1")
    Label2.Caption = PropBag.ReadProperty("Label2Caption", "Label2")
    Command1.Visible = PropBag.ReadProperty("ButtonVisible", True)
End Sub

'Write property values to storage
Private Sub UserControl_WriteProperties(PropBag As PropertyBag)
    Call PropBag.WriteProperty("Backcolor", UserControl.BackColor, &H8000000F)
    Call PropBag.WriteProperty("Label1Caption", Label1.Caption, "Label1")
    Call PropBag.WriteProperty("Label2Caption", Label2.Caption, "Label2")
    Call PropBag.WriteProperty("ButtonVisible", Command1.Visible, True)
End Sub

Public Property Get BackColor() As OLE_COLOR
    BackColor = UserControl.BackColor
End Property

Public Property Let BackColor(ByVal vNewValue As OLE_COLOR)
    UserControl.BackColor = vNewValue
    PropertyChanged "BackColor"
End Property

Friend Property Get InternalLabel3() As Label
    Set InternalLabel3 = Label3
End Property

Public Property Get ButtonVisible() As Boolean
    ButtonVisible = Command1.Visible
End Property

Public Property Let ButtonVisible(ByVal vNewValue As Boolean)
    Command1.Visible = vNewValue
End Property

Public Sub About()
    frmAbout.Show vbModal
End Sub
```

There are a couple of interesting features to note about this control. The control has a third label control, Label3, that is not exposed through a public property. However, the control does include a Friend function, which exposes a reference to the Label3 control. This can allow a property page to gain direct access to the label, since it is part of the same project. It would be a major error to expose a constituent object publicly in this manner, since that would give access to the object to everyone using your control. However, it is safe to do so within your own project, since you have full control over what is done with the object.

THE PROPPAGEA1 PROPERTY PAGE

The PropPageA1 page demonstrates a number of property page techniques:

- ▶ The standard way of editing a property, used with the Label1Caption property
- ▶ The immediate update method of editing a property, used with the Label2Caption property
- ▶ Configuring a control without using a property, used to configure the Label3 constituent control
- ▶ Editing properties on multiple pages, used with the ButtonVisible property
- ▶ How to handle invalid property settings

Listing 20.3 shows the listing for the PropPageA1 property page. An in-depth explanation of how it works follows.

Listing 20.3: The PropPageA1 Property Page

```
' Guide to perplexed:
' Property page example chapter 20
' Copyright (c) 1997, by Desaware Inc.  All Rights Reserved
Option Explicit

Private Declare Function GetParent Lib "user32" (ByVal hwnd As Long) As Long
Private Declare Function EnableWindow Lib "user32" (ByVal hwnd As Long, _
ByVal fEnable As Long) As Long

Private m_ReadInProgress As Boolean
Private m_IgnoreSelectionChanged As Boolean
Private m_SavedChangedState As Boolean

Private Sub PropertyPage_Initialize()
   Debug.Print "Property page initialized"
```

Listing 20.3: The PropPageA1 Property Page (Continued)

```
End Sub

Private Sub PropertyPage_Terminate()
    Debug.Print "Property page terminated"
End Sub

Private Sub PropertyPage_EditProperty(PropertyName As String)
    lblProp.Caption = "Editing property: " & PropertyName
    Select Case PropertyName
        Case "Label1Caption"
            txtLabel1Caption.SetFocus
        Case "Label2Caption"
            txtLabel2Caption.SetFocus
        Case "ButtonVisible"
            chkButtonVisible.SetFocus
    End Select
End Sub

' Label2 is immediate update
Private Sub txtLabel2Caption_Change()
    If Not m_ReadInProgress Then
        m_IgnoreSelectionChanged = True
        m_SavedChangedState = Changed
        SelectedControls(0).Label2Caption = txtLabel2Caption.Text
    End If
End Sub

Private Sub chkButtonVisible_Click()
    If Not m_ReadInProgress Then
        Changed = True
    End If
End Sub

Private Sub txtLabel1Caption_Change()
    If Not m_ReadInProgress Then
        Changed = True
    End If
End Sub

Private Sub txtLabel3Caption_Change()
    If Not m_ReadInProgress Then
        Changed = True
    End If
End Sub
```

Listing 20.3: The PropPageA1 Property Page (Continued)

```
Private Sub PropertyPage_ApplyChanges()
    Dim ctl As PropPageCtlA
    If SelectedControls.Count = 1 Then
        If LCase$(txtLabel1Caption.Text) = "bad" Then
            MsgBox "Bad property value on Label1"
            txtLabel1Caption.SetFocus
            ' Restore the original value
            txtLabel1Caption.Text = SelectedControls(0).Label1Caption
            Changed = True
            Exit Sub
        End If
        SelectedControls(0).Label1Caption = txtLabel1Caption.Text
        SelectedControls(0).Label2Caption = txtLabel2Caption.Text
        Set ctl = SelectedControls(0)
        ' Go early bound to access friend
        ctl.InternalLabel3.Caption = txtLabel3Caption.Text
    End If
    For Each ctl In SelectedControls
        ctl.ButtonVisible = chkButtonVisible
    Next
End Sub




Private Sub PropertyPage_SelectionChanged()
    Dim ctl As PropPageCtlA

    If m_IgnoreSelectionChanged Then
        ' Triggered by immediate update to property that
        ' calls PropertyChanged
        m_IgnoreSelectionChanged = True
        Changed = m_SavedChangedState
        Exit Sub
    End If

    m_ReadInProgress = True

    SetControlsVisibility    ' handles multiple selection
    If SelectedControls.Count = 1 Then
        txtLabel1Caption.Text = SelectedControls(0).Label1Caption
        ' Initialize the value
        txtLabel2Caption.Text = SelectedControls(0).Label2Caption
        Set ctl = SelectedControls(0)
        ' Go early bound to access friend
        txtLabel3Caption.Text = ctl.InternalLabel3.Caption
```

Listing 20.3: The PropPageA1 Property Page (Continued)

```
    End If
    ' We're late bound here
    If SelectedControls(0).ButtonVisible Then
        chkButtonVisible.Value = 1
    Else
        chkButtonVisible.Value = 0
    End If

    m_ReadInProgress = False
End Sub


Private Sub SetControlsVisibility()
    Dim ctl As Object
    Dim EnableCtl As Boolean
    If SelectedControls.Count = 1 Then EnableCtl = True
    For Each ctl In PropertyPage.Controls
        If TypeOf ctl Is Label Or TypeOf ctl Is TextBox Then
            ' We could change visibility if you prefer
            ctl.Enabled = EnableCtl
        End If
    Next
End Sub

Private Sub cmdAbout_Click()
    Dim containerwnd&
    containerwnd = GetParent(PropertyPage.hwnd)
    containerwnd = GetParent(containerwnd)
    if containerwnd Then Call EnableWindow(containerwnd, False)
    frmAbout.Show vbModal
    if containerwnd Then Call EnableWindow(containerwnd, True)
End Sub
```

The Initialize and Terminate events have debug.print statements to allow you to track the creation and destruction of the property page.

The first event of real interest is the SelectionChanged event. Let's ignore the m_IgnoreSelectionChanged flag for a moment. The first thing it does is set the m_ReadInProgress module variable to True to indicate that properties are being loaded. The function loads the values of properties and displays them in the property page's text boxes, which will trigger their Change events (or Clicked events, in the case of the checkbox). The default behavior for a control's Change event in a property page is to set the Changed property to

True, which serves to enable the page's Apply button. But it is poor practice to enable the Apply button when no changes have occurred. At the very least it can be confusing to the developer. So the m_ReadInProgress variable is used in the text Change event and checkbox Click event to prevent the changed property from being set to True when the corresponding controls are being loaded with the initial property values.

Handling Multiple Selections   The next thing the SelectionChanged event code does is handle the case of multiple selections. For this example, the property page is designed to handle multiple selection only for the ButtonVisible property. A private function named SetControlVisibility checks to see if multiple controls are selected. If so, it hides the Label and Text controls that are not used with multiple selections.

Keep in mind that this example demonstrates a very simple approach to handling multiple selections. Other approaches include:

▸ Repositioning the ButtonVisible checkbox to make the box look more balanced

▸ Adding a warning display, status display, or list box showing which controls are selected

▸ Providing a completely different property page appearance for multiple selection

In other words, you have enormous flexibility in how you wish to handle this situation. An interesting application of this will follow in the PropPgT2.vbp example project later in this chapter.

The SelectionChanged event code does not access properties that are not used when multiple selections are present. There is no harm in doing so in this case, but there is overhead in accessing a control's properties, especially from property pages where the access is typically late bound. Thus, avoiding unnecessary property access improves performance at the cost of a single If...Then statement.

The ButtonVisible property is the only one on this page that is designed to work with multiple selections. How should you handle the situation where different controls may have different values for this property? The chkButtonVisible property is loaded based on the status of the first control in the SelectedControls collection. This is an arbitrary choice. It means that this example will coerce all of the controls to use the value of the first control. A more sophisticated approach would be to scan all the ButtonVisible property values for all of the controls. If they are all the same, you would set the checkbox to the appropriate value. However, if any of them differ, you could set the checkbox to the grayed state, indicating that they differ from each other. You could then modify the checkbox control logic to cycle from checked to unchecked to grayed. When the ApplyChanges event is triggered, you can set the control properties to checked or unchecked, or leave them unchanged if the checkbox is grayed. This approach is common in many dialog boxes and is left here as an exercise for the reader.

The actual mechanics of setting the property into the controls is shown in the ApplyChanges event. Simply loop through all of the controls in the SelectedControls collection and set the property to the desired value.

Immediate Update Properties   The Label1Caption property works in the manner that you are accustomed to. You edit the property in the page and, when you are finished, you have the opportunity to apply the changes to the control. The Label2Caption property, on the other hand, is updated in the control immediately as you enter text into the property page (try it!). How is this accomplished? It's actually quite simple. The Control property is set during the txtLabel2Caption_Change event.

Note that the Changed property is not set to True in this case. Nor is there any need to write the property during the ApplyChanges event, since the updates happen immediately. The update only applies to the first control in the Selected Controls list. What if more than one control is selected? That's a trick question, and there is no need to worry about it because in this example the Text control is hidden if more than one ActiveX control was selected!

The one catch to this approach is that when the Label2Caption property is changed, the control's Property Let procedure calls the PropertyChanged function. This function causes the property page's SelectionChanged event to be triggered, which reloads all of the properties and clears the Changed flag. Any pending changes to the other properties would be lost. To avoid this, two flags are set during the txtLabel2Caption_Change event. One signals that the next SelectionChanged event should be ignored. The other holds the current value of the Changed property. If the m_IgnoreSelectionChanges flag is set during the SelectionChanged event, the property page ignores the event and restores the Changed property value.

How can you avoid these immediate update problems? One solution is to avoid calling the PropertyChanged function in the control when the property is set from the property page (you can use a flag in the control to indicate whether the property is being set from the page). Another approach is to not mix immediate and deferred update properties on the same page. This is probably the cleanest solution, and it minimizes the chance that developers will confuse one type of property with the other.

This is actually a simple illustration of a whole class of property page solutions where the property page can interact instantly with the control. There may be cases where you want the control to perform an operation or be updated as the developer makes changes, instead of waiting for the Apply-Changes event to be triggered. Another example of this will follow in the PropPgT2.vbp project that follows later in the chapter.

Configuration Without Properties   The Label3Caption property demonstrates yet another technique in which a property page can perform a configuration operation on a control without going through public properties.

As you may recall, the PropPageCtlA control exposes a Friend read-only property called InternalLabel3, which returns a reference to the constituent Label3 control. Accessing this Friend function is a little bit tricky. You cannot do so directly through the SelectedControls collection, because items in the collection are referenced As Object, and Friend functions can only be accessed on an early bound interface. Fortunately, obtaining this interface is simple, as shown in the following code:

```
Dim ctl As PropPageCtlA
Set ctl = SelectedControls(0)
txtLabel3Caption.Text = ctl.InternalLabel3.Caption
```

Once you have the early bound ctl interface, you can access the internal Label3 object and its properties as well. The process is reversed for writing the property during the ApplyChanges event.

Why would anyone want to use this somewhat awkward approach to control configuration? After all, it is easy enough to configure a property for access at design time only and to prevent it from being shown in the VB property window (using the Tools, Procedure Attributes dialog box).

The truth is, in this particular case, this approach is stupid. The extra effort has no real benefit. The advantages come into play in the following situations:

- ▶ Your control contains additional complex objects that need sophisticated editing beyond what is possible using the VB property window

- ▶ Your control needs to expose a large number of properties that are not used at design time and that would unreasonably clutter the VB property window

- ▶ Your property page needs to perform complex operations directly on constituent controls or the User Control object

In the present example, exposing a constituent control just to configure the control's caption property is silly. But if I wanted to create a property page that needed to adjust a number of the Label control's properties, it might make sense to take this approach.

Handling Invalid Property Values   The Label1Caption property may seem, at first glance, to demonstrate a completely typical method for handling properties in a property page. At second glance, you will see that it is, in fact, completely typical. So, in order to prevent it from being just a waste of space in this example, I took the liberty of using it to demonstrate how you can handle invalid entries.

The error logic takes effect when you enter the word "bad" into the text box for the Label1Caption property. This logic can be found in the ApplyChanges event, which demonstrates the typical actions that your code should take in this situation:

- ▶ Bring up a message box explaining the error.

- ▶ Set the focus back to the control that has the error. This provides a clear indication to the developer as to which value needs to be fixed.

- ▶ Restore the original property value. This is useful in case the developer has forgotten what the original value was. Without some sort of feedback as to what might be a correct value, you may trap your developer in the property page forever (or at least until he or she remembers the Cancel button).

- ▶ Set the Changed property to True. This tells Visual Basic that it should not close the property page.

There is another technique you can use for validation. Instead of testing the property value and validating it within the property page, you can enable an error handler and attempt to set the property value, relying on the control to raise an error if the property value is invalid. On detecting this error, you can set the Changed property to True and abort the update operation. The only disadvantage to this approach is that if only one property is invalid, some or all of the properties that are valid will be set in the control, depending on the order in which you attempt to set the properties and the logic of your code. (For example, do you stop on first error or do you continue and attempt to set all properties?)

Bringing Up Additional Dialog Boxes   The About button on the property page shows that you can, in fact, bring up a modal form from within the property page. If you just use the Show command with the vbModal option, the form will be modal with respect to your property page. However, it is typically not modal with respect to the property page container window, leading to the rather odd effect of being able to reposition the property window under the modal dialog box.

Microsoft's documentation discourages you from showing modal forms during property pages. While I am inclined to agree with them from the standpoint of usability, it turns out that there is an easy way to improve the behavior of the property page container, at least when Visual Basic is the container. This is shown in the CmdAbout_Click event in the PropPageA1 listing. The routine uses API functions to obtain the handle of the window two levels up from your property pages (the first level up is the tabbing window, the next one is the actual container window). It then disables the window, reenabling it only after you close the modal form.

You should be aware, however, that this technique is not documented or approved by Microsoft, so there is no assurance that it will work with every container or that it will even continue to work with future versions of Visual Basic. However, if it doesn't work, the effects are likely to be harmless.

Whatever you do, do *not* show modeless forms from a property page (or an ActiveX control, or any other ActiveX DLL component for that matter). Aside from being poor programming style, the real problem is that many containers do not support modeless forms that are created by ActiveX DLLs of any kind.

Random Thoughts   The Property Page Wizard is another case of a wizard being rather useful, especially once you understand exactly what it is doing. The wizard is easy to use, allowing you to create new pages, to map properties to pages, and to select and order pages.

But the wizard focuses on the plainest of the standard techniques for handling properties. You should be sure to review carefully the code that it produces to be sure it serves your purposes, especially if you wish to handle multiple control selection correctly.

THE PROPPGT2.VBP PROJECT

The PropPgT2 project demonstrates a completely different use for property pages, demonstrating how they can be used to create design tools and utilities. The project contains a form, a private control, and a property page that is used by the control. The only reason a private control was used in this example is for convenience—it would work just as well with a stand-alone control. Listing 20.4 shows the code for the PropCtlB control module.

Listing 20.4: The PropCtlB Control

```
' Guide to the Perplexed
' Chapter 20 - Property page example
' Copyright (c) 1997 by Desaware Inc. All Rights Reserved
Option Explicit

Public Property Get Font() As Font
    Set Font = UserControl.Font
End Property

Public Property Let Font(ByVal vNewValue As Font)
    Set UserControl.Font = vNewValue
    PropertyChanged "Font"
End Property

Private Sub UserControl_InitProperties()
    Set UserControl.Font = Ambient.Font
End Sub

Private Sub UserControl_ReadProperties(PropBag As PropertyBag)
    Set UserControl.Font = PropBag.ReadProperty("Font", Ambient.Font)
End Sub

Private Sub UserControl_WriteProperties(PropBag As PropertyBag)
    Call PropBag.WriteProperty("Font", UserControl.Font, Ambient.Font)
End Sub

Private Sub UserControl_Resize()
    UserControl.Size Label1.Width, Label1.Height
End Sub

Friend Function Container() As Object
    Set Container = UserControl.Extender.Parent
End Function
```

As you can see, the control contains a single public Font property. The control contains a single constituent Label control that displays the message: "Aligner—Use Property Page to Align." The Label control has a fixed size, and the control is automatically sized to match it. This means that the developer does not have the ability to resize the control.

The only really odd function in this control is the Container function, which returns a reference to the control's container. The container, form frmtest2.frm, has no code. It does hold an instance of the PropCtlB control and five randomly positioned Label controls.

The PropPg2A Property Page   This property page contains a list box and a command button. Listing 20.5 shows the code for this property page. As you can see, it bears relatively little resemblance to a typical property page. For one thing: there are no properties!

Listing 20.5: Property Page PropPg2A

```
' Guide to the Perplexed
' Chapter 20 - Alignment property page
' Copyright (c) 1997, by Desaware Inc. All Rights Reserved
Option Explicit

Private m_LeftPosition As Long

Private Sub cmdExecute_Click()
   AdjustLabels
End Sub

Private Sub PropertyPage_SelectionChanged()
   ' Prior values may be held!
   lstLabels.Clear
   If SelectedControls.Count > 1 Then
      lstLabels.Visible = False
      ' Display warning instead
      lstWarning.Visible = True
   Else
      ' This may be overkill (is for VB)
      lstLabels.Visible = True
      ' Display warning instead
      lstWarning.Visible = False
   End If

   Set lstLabels.Font = SelectedControls(0).Font

   LoadListBox

End Sub


Private Sub LoadListBox()
   Dim MyControl As PropCtlB
   Dim ContainerObj As Object
```

Listing 20.5: Property Page PropPg2A (Continued)

```
    Dim InternalControl As Object
    Set MyControl = SelectedControls(0)
    Set ContainerObj = MyControl.Container
    For Each InternalControl In ContainerObj.Controls
        If TypeOf InternalControl Is Label Then
            lstLabels.AddItem InternalControl.Name
        End If
    Next
End Sub

Private Sub AdjustLabels()
    Dim MyControl As PropCtlB
    Dim ContainerObj As Object
    Dim InternalControl As Object
    Dim lstidx As Long
    Set MyControl = SelectedControls(0)
    Set ContainerObj = MyControl.Container
    m_LeftPosition = 0
    For Each InternalControl In ContainerObj.Controls
        If TypeOf InternalControl Is Label Then
            For lstidx = 0 To lstLabels.ListCount - 1
                ' We found a selected label with the correct name
                If InternalControl.Name = lstLabels.List(lstidx) _
                And lstLabels.Selected(lstidx) Then
                    AdjustThisLabel InternalControl
                End If
            Next
        End If
    Next
End Sub

' Note we QI for the Label IDispatch interface during the call
Private Sub AdjustThisLabel(lbl As Label)
    If m_LeftPosition = 0 Then
        m_LeftPosition = lbl.Left
    Else
        lbl.Left = m_LeftPosition
    End If
End Sub
```

The SelectionChanged event does not load any properties, since there aren't any to load. The first thing it does is clear the list box, then checks to see if more than one page is selected. This page is designed to work only with a single control, so if more than one control is selected, it hides the list box and command button and shows a label box that contains a descriptive warning message. (This Label control is behind the list box at design time. If you want to see it, load the project and temporarily move the list box aside.)

The list box is then set to use the font from the control. Note the subtle point here: the property page does not edit the font, it simply uses it. You can switch to the Font property page to edit the font, then switch back to this page and see that the list box font has been updated by way of the control's Font property. This demonstrates a mechanism for property pages to communicate with each other.

Finally, the private LoadListBox function is called to load the names of all of the Label controls from the control's container into the list box. This is illustrated in Figure 20.2.

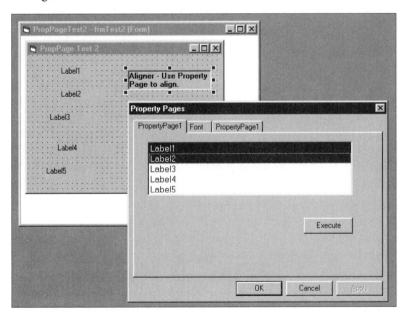

Figure 20.2: The PropPg2A property page at runtime

Hopefully you can spot the one thing that is wrong with the LoadListBox function in this code example. That's right—there is no error checking. I've taken advantage of the fact that this particular control is being tested under Visual Basic to perform operations that are sure to succeed. If you want to have any hope of this routine working under other containers (or at least failing gracefully), you should add error trapping to this example.

The Changed property is never set to True for this property page. In fact, the ApplyChanges event is not used at all. This page is designed to align the Label controls on the control's container to the left margin of the first control on the list.

To do this, the developer first selects the controls to be aligned in the list box. When the Execute button is clicked, the AdjustLabels function is called. This routine scans through all of the controls present on your control's container. If the control is a Label control, and its name is selected in the list box, it is aligned to the left position of the first Label control found.

Before concluding, take a look at the PropPg2B property page. As you can see, it contains no code. Yet it still appears because it was assigned to the control using the UserControl's PropertyPages property dialog box.

My point? That you can truly do almost anything in property pages, including giving developers powerful tools for configuring both your control and, potentially, the environment in which they exist.

ABOUT BOXES AND OTHERS

The PropPgs1.vbp project also demonstrates how to add an About Box to your control. This is easily accomplished by adding a method that will show a modal form. The method must be assigned the AboutBox procedure ID using the Tools, Procedure Attributes dialog box. This causes the VB property window to display an About property for the control at design time. The procedure will be called any time the dialog button for the About property is clicked. The procedure may have any name. All that counts is that it have the correct procedure ID.

Microsoft provides an AboutBox template that includes a system information option. It's a reasonably nice-looking About Box, and the system information option is nice, so I see no reason not to use it.

As mentioned earlier, with regard to property pages, your control should avoid bringing up any other kind of dialog boxes (modal forms). You should definitely avoid modeless forms because not every container is able to support modeless forms that are shown by ActiveX DLLs.

This concludes our coverage of property pages and dialog boxes with regard to ActiveX controls. Next, despite my best efforts to delay the inevitable, it is finally time to talk about (drum-roll please): the Internet.

ActiveX Controls and the Internet

THE HYPERLINK OBJECT

ACTIVEX CONTROLS ON WEB PAGES

DOWNLOADING, SECURITY, AND SIGNING

THE dwBANNER CONTROL

Chapter 21

I n Chapter 1, I began by trying to disassociate ActiveX controls from the Internet. And for the past 20 chapters, almost the only mention of the Internet with regard to ActiveX controls has been the discussion of control limitations in Chapter 16 and the discussion of asynchronous property downloads in Chapter 19. I think that, more than anything, should prove my original point. The value of ActiveX components and controls has little to do with the Internet.

But we can't hide from the Internet features of ActiveX controls forever. Microsoft is heavily promoting Visual Basic for creating controls for use on the Internet and on intranets. And the truth is, if you are willing to accept the fact that not everyone will be able to use your controls, Visual Basic is an outstanding tool for creating these controls. You get excellent performance, short development times, small executables and, with the occasional aid of third-party tools, as much capability as with controls that are developed using other languages such as Visual C++. In fact, in some areas, VB controls are far superior to those created in Visual C++. For example, it is significantly easier to build a control using constituent controls with VB.

This chapter will focus on those aspects of ActiveX controls that relate specifically to the Internet:

▸ Their navigation ability when placed on browsers

▸ The mechanics of actually placing a control on a Web page

▸ Issues relating to downloading controls from Web sites

And perhaps along the way, I can dispel a few myths relating to the security of ActiveX controls.

THE HYPERLINK OBJECT

The HyperLink object is accessible via the HyperLink property of the UserControl object. It has three methods: GoBack, GoForward, and NavigateTo. These methods only have an effect if the control is sited on a container that acts as a Web browser. They are ignored on all other containers.

The GoBack and GoForward methods are the equivalent of clicking on the Back and Forward buttons on the browser. The NavigateTo method is much more powerful. It takes three parameters: a target, a location, and a frame.

The target is the URL to jump to. This can be any location supported by the container, either local or on the network. The location parameter is optional and specifies the name of the file to load. If it is not specified, the default file for the site will be loaded. The frame parameter is also optional and specifies a frame to load at the specified target location.

This is demonstrated in the dwBanner control, which detects the Click event to jump to Desaware's Web site using the following code:

```
Private Sub UserControl_Click()
   On Error GoTo NoHyper
   UserControl.Hyperlink.NavigateTo "http://www.desaware.com"
NoHyper:
   RaiseEvent Click
End Sub
```

You should always have error trapping enabled when using the Hyperlink object, since an error may be raised if the container does not support Internet navigation.

Considering the emphasis Microsoft has placed on using ActiveX controls for the Internet, it is perhaps astonishing that between this short section and asynchronous properties, you now know everything you need to know about implementing Internet features in your control. Now let's look at what you need to do to actually place a control on a Web page.

ACTIVEX CONTROLS ON WEB PAGES

Chapter 15 included a quick introduction to HTML. You saw that HTML consists of tags and text. The tags, which are contained within triangular brackets, represent commands to the browser that affect its operation or text display. ActiveX controls are placed on a Web page using the OBJECT tag as shown below:

```
<HTML>
<HEAD>
<TITLE>New Page</TITLE>
</HEAD>
<BODY>

<OBJECT ID="dwBanner1" WIDTH=347 HEIGHT=39
 CLASSID="CLSID: 63B8AFC0-8E9A-11D0-91BB-00AA0036005A">
    <PARAM NAME="_ExtentX" VALUE="9181">
    <PARAM NAME="_ExtentY" VALUE="1005">
    <PARAM NAME="BackColor" VALUE="16777088">
    <PARAM NAME="FontSize" VALUE="8.25">
    <PARAM NAME="FontBold" VALUE="-1">
    <PARAM NAME="FontItalic" VALUE="-1">
    <PARAM NAME="BorderStyle" VALUE="1">
    <PARAM NAME="ScrollText" VALUE="Visit Desaware's Web site at www.desaware.com
for the coolest tools for VB developers. ">
    <PARAM NAME="XMargin" VALUE="20">
    <PARAM NAME="YMargin" VALUE="6">
</OBJECT>

</BODY>
</HTML>
```

The CLASSID field represents the unique control identifier (CLSID) that is created when your control is compiled. ActiveX controls, like all ActiveX objects, have this unique identifier (also referred to as GUID). Note that the identifier shown in the above listing will not match the one for the actual dwBanner.ocx control, as the control was recompiled into its final version after this book went to press.

The browser expects all of the information from the OBJECT tag to the /OBJECT tag to be information defining the object. The PARAM NAME tags define the initial settings for the control's properties. These are the values that will be retrieved by the control during its ReadProperties event.

If this looks somewhat cryptic, I have good news for you. You will probably never actually write this kind of HTML code. Microsoft already provides several tools that automatically create this HTML text. Perhaps the easiest one to use is the ActiveX control pad, which can be downloaded from the Microsoft Web site (currently for free). This tool allows you to insert a control into an HTML file and edit the design-time properties interactively. FrontPage 97™

and Microsoft Internet Studio™ both allow you to easily add ActiveX controls into Web pages and never worry about the HTML code that results.

If you do want your control to run on a Web page you must test it using a browser that supports it. I know this may seem like an odd statement, but I can't stress it enough. It is very easy to create controls that will run perfectly well in Visual Basic and other application containers, yet fail miserably on a Web browser. This is especially true if you use the Extender object.

DOWNLOADING, SECURITY, AND SIGNING

The most important issue with regard to using ActiveX controls on the Internet and on corporate intranets relates to the process of downloading controls from a Web site to your system. It is the subject that has perhaps raised the most controversy. To understand the nature of the controversy and Microsoft's approach to resolving it for ActiveX controls, let us begin with the issue of security.

ACTIVEX CONTROLS AND SECURITY

As long as Web pages consisted of simple text and graphics, security was not really a concern. Displaying a text file or image is unlikely to cause harm to anyone's system. That's one of the reasons that e-mail is so safe and popular. When you receive an e-mail message from someone, you don't think of it as something that can corrupt your hard drive or erase your valuable data. But Web pages that contain nothing but simple text and graphics are boring.

Or at least that is what some people say. Personally, when I use the Web to retrieve information, I would much rather have Web pages that contain plain text and some graphics. While I do have a T1 line at work, I still access the Web using a 28.8k modem at home. The large bitmaps, cluttered backgrounds, and animations some developers place on their sites is a complete waste of time. But I digress…

The point is that people did want more sophisticated content on Web pages. They wanted pages that can interact with the user, be programmed to display scrolling text or flashy animation, have complex display capabilities, or perform other operations on the user's system. Many of these capabilities require that the page be able to actually execute code on the system being used to view the page. The term *active content* is used to describe these types of elements.

The key phrase here is "execute code on the system that is being used to view the page." What does it mean? It means that the system accessing the page downloads software and runs it.

Now, chances are that if you are a serious software developer or power user, you know that downloading software is potentially the most dangerous thing that you can do. It's not the downloading that is dangerous, but the fact that you may not know who wrote the software and what's in it. It could contain viruses or harmful side effects. That's one reason why most developers tend to stick with software from reputable companies (including shareware and freeware companies) and avoid the thousands of "free" programs that tend to be worth exactly what you pay for them. The other reason that serious developers avoid free programs, for those who are wondering, is that they tend to be unsupported. And unsupported software has a nasty tendency to end up costing far more in the long run than even the most expensive commercial software.

If you want Web pages to support active content, you are effectively talking about placing code on the page itself that can be run on the end-user's system. But unless your end user is a blithering idiot, he or she would never even consider allowing a Web browser to automatically download software from a page and run it on his or her system. How can you give users a guarantee that the software on a Web page is safe to run on a system? There are two philosophical approaches to solving this problem.

THE SANDBOX APPROACH

One answer is to look at the software itself. What if you created a language that was fundamentally safe to run? Such a language might have the following characteristics:

▶ It must not be able to make direct calls to operating system functions, since operating system functions have the potential to cause harm to a system.

▶ It must not be able to write to disk, or be allowed to do so only under tightly controlled circumstances.

▶ It may not access memory arbitrarily. This means it should not directly manipulate memory pointers, because doing so could allow it to interfere with other applications or with the operating system.

The language would probably not compile directly to the native code of the target machine. Instead, it would be interpreted (perhaps in much the same way as Visual Basic compiled to pseudocode, or P-Code, is interpreted by the VB runtime). This also means that software written in the language could run on any system that supported the P-Code interpreter. It would not be restricted to any one operating system or CPU type.

A program written in this language would obviously be seriously limited as compared to a typical application that has full access to the capabilities of its target system. But it would also be safe to run, since any ability to interfere with the system on which it is running has been eliminated. You can think of the program as running in a sandbox on the system—a safe area in which it can do anything it wants to without interfering with the rest of the system.

The Java scripting language is one such language. When a Java applet appears on a Web page, it is detected by the Web browser and sent to a Java *virtual machine*, which interprets and executes the Java code. The code is platform independent in that Java virtual machines exist for almost every operating system and platform. The Java language does not support pointers, so it is fundamentally unable to corrupt your system's memory. The virtual machine does not permit any unsafe operations or direct access to the operating system.

So, when you see a Java applet in a Web page, you basically don't have to worry about downloading it.

Now, keep in mind that I am not an Internet security expert. I'm sure someone out there will be glad to point out security holes in this approach. But, in a way, that is exactly the point. Any security breaches in this approach are holes that probably can and should be fixed. The fundamental approach is sound and works quite well. Most people don't think twice about allowing their browser to run Java applets on their Web browser.

THE "TRUST ME" APPROACH

Microsoft took a completely different approach with ActiveX controls. They decided that active content should have full access to all of the capabilities of the underlying system.

If the interpretation of Microsoft's actions that I proposed in Chapter 2 is correct, they really didn't have any choice. They made the decision to extend OLE controls for the Internet and rename the technology ActiveX. But COM and ActiveX technology was never designed to be sandboxed, and existing OLE controls were written in Visual C++, which is anything but a safe language. OLE control implementation relied on extensive access to underlying system calls. In fact, OLE itself had become part of the operating system.

You must always keep in mind that every ActiveX control is a true executable. It has full access to all of the resources and functionality of a system, limited only by the security settings on the system itself.

This gives an ActiveX control enormous flexibility and power. You can do virtually anything in a control that an application can do. But it also poses extreme danger. You could write an ActiveX control that, when downloaded, erased the user's disk or registry settings, making the system unusable and un-bootable. I half expect any day now to hear about the first ActiveX control-based computer viruses, which use downloaded controls as a means for the virus to spread. Microsoft knew this, so they took another approach.

It is true that smart computer users would never allow arbitrary software to be downloaded and executed on their systems. But computer users obtain software all the time. They buy it in stores and they download it from reputable firms or other sources that are known to produce safe and reliable code. Since ActiveX controls are not designed to be safe, two things become essential:

▶ There must be a way for control authors to tell users if their control is safe to download.

▶ There must be a way for users to verify that a control is authored by a reputable, known, and otherwise trustworthy company or individual.

SAFETY ≠ SIGNING

There is a great deal of information available about distributing ActiveX controls on the Internet. There is the information included with Visual Basic that discusses how to use the setup wizard. There is the ActiveX Software Development Kit (SDK), which is available from Microsoft's Web site. There are numerous articles in magazines and other books. The subject can get very complex very quickly, especially when you start dealing with all of the variations available for installing and downloading controls.

I spent days wading through the information trying to understand it. I understood most of the ideas being presented (or at least, I thought I did), but somehow I couldn't quite figure out how to actually do the things that they were talking about. In other words, an article would describe at length how important it was to mark a control as "safe for scripting" or "safe for initialization," but it wouldn't actually explain how to do it. Authors would talk about the advantages of code signing without explaining how to actually sign a control.

After extensive experimentation, I finally figured out what they were talking about. My intent here is not to cover every aspect of control downloading and security but to offer, in as clear a manner as possible, a concise and accurate explanation of the things you actually need to know as a VB programmer to create safe downloadable controls for Web pages.

To start out, you must understand there are three completely separate issues that need to be discussed:

▶ Making your control safe

▶ Marking your control as safe

▸ Identifying (signing) your control

Make Your Control Safe Making your control safe is the process you go through as a control author to make sure your control cannot harm an end user's system. There are two types of safety to consider:

▸ Is it safe to load your control onto a container no matter what initial property settings are specified?

▸ Is it safe to use your control in an application regardless of the control methods that are called and property settings that are assigned?

The first of these is called "Safe for initialization." Your control is safe for initialization if it can accept any property settings during the ReadProperties event and not harm the system. For example, if your control has a property value that can change registry settings or manipulate the file system based on a property set during initialization, that control is not safe. Remember that a Web author can write anything they want as a PARAM field in HTML, so you can't assume that the property settings being read were written by your own control. Your control must be able to handle anything that comes its way.

The second type of control safety is called "Safe for scripting." In addition to ActiveX control objects, Web pages can contain other content in the form of Java applets or VBScript applets (two different Web scripting languages). These applets are able to call control methods and set control properties. If your control can handle any possible method call and property setting safely, then it is safe for scripting. Be sure to test your control carefully. Let's say you have a method that can save information from the control in a specified path. This is not necessarily unsafe, but what will your control do if the path name is that of a system device? The wrong method parameter could interfere with the operation of that device. Or what if you had a property that let you set a registry key. If the registry key is hard coded into the control, this might be safe. But if it is a parameter to a control property, a mischievous Web script author could wreak havoc using your control.

Keep in mind that safety, in the context of an Internet control, is different from making a control safe for application developers. There are many situations where you will want your ActiveX controls to offer functionality that would not be safe on a Web page.

For example, Desaware's StorageTools product includes a registry manipulation ActiveX control that makes it as easy for VB developers to manipulate the registry as it is to manipulate their disk file system. The control is safe in the sense that it works properly, but since it gives developers full access to the system registry, it goes without saying that the developers could use the control to write illegal information to the registry if they so chose. But when they ship their application that uses the registry control, they will be assuring their customers that their program is safe to run, so there is no problem. The registry control is unsafe in that it is possible to use it in ways that can harm a system. Thus the control, while useful to application developers, is not marked as safe for scripting.

You will see later in this chapter that it is possible for a control to support two modes: A safe mode for use on Web pages and an unsafe mode for use by application developers.

Marking Your Control   Once you have made your control safe for initialization and/or safe for scripting, the next step is to tell the end user which level of safety is supported by your control. This will be covered in depth later in this chapter. For now you need to be aware that there are two ways to mark a control as safe. One is to add information into the system registry that indicates the control is safe. The other is to add functionality to the control itself that lets the browser software request safe operation and determine if the control is safe.

When the browser downloads the control, it will try both of these methods to see if the control is safe. What it does with this information depends on the browser configuration. More on this later.

Signing Your Control   Virtually every article that discusses ActiveX control safety also talks about code signing. It is easy to come away with the impression that code signing has something to do with code safety. In fact, they are completely different things.

Earlier in this chapter I made the point that there are two requirements for ActiveX controls to become a viable component for Internet download.

▶ There must be a way for control authors to tell users if their control is safe to download.

▶ There must be a way for users to verify that a control is authored by a reputable, known, and otherwise trustworthy company or individual.

You've already read that there is a way for authors to mark a control as safe, though I have not yet shown you how to do so. But the truth is that this is not a solution. You see, anybody can mark a control as safe. There is nothing in the process of marking a control as safe that actually verifies that the control is, in fact, safe. This raises an interesting question: How do you know that a control marked safe is actually safe to install and run? The answer is, you don't. You have to trust that the control's author is telling you the truth and is competent to create a safe control.

Your first reaction to this might be to say, "Oh boy, are we in trouble now!" But when you think about it, isn't this the situation you face any time you install software on your system? How do you know the application you purchased from Lotus or Borland or IBM won't harm your system? (I don't mention Microsoft here because, after all, they *are* your system.) You know it because by and large you trust them and their programmers. You know if you do have a problem you'll be able to contact someone there to help you resolve it.

The software industry is founded on trust and accountability. Let me stress that this trust can also be extended correctly to many shareware and freeware software vendors. There are many small companies, individual software authors, and consultants who write software that is just as good or better than the large commercial applications. But the key fact remains: before you use their software you should know who they are, either individually or by reputation. It's still a matter of trust.

As long as you only load controls from sites you trust, you have no problem. You can choose to trust the Web authors of that site that they will not use a downloaded control in a way that can harm your system. It doesn't even matter if the control is marked as safe, because for a control to cause harm it must not only permit harmful operations, but the Web author must also program a harmful operation for the control using property settings or scripts.

However, the very nature of the Web makes it easy to almost unintentionally end up in places you do not know and thus should not trust. As a site author you should always assume your site will fall into that category for at least some of your visitors. As a user, you can still safely see the pages and download controls from untrusted sites if you know the control is marked as safe and comes from a source that you can trust.

Whom you choose to trust is up to you. What code signing does is provide a mechanism that ensures you that the source of the control is exactly who it says. For example, if you obtain a control that says in its version information that it was developed by Desaware, it probably is. It could be a counterfeit— someone may have modified the control's resource information. But if the control uses code signing to specify that it is from Desaware, an encrypted digital certificate embedded in the control proves to you without any doubt that it was, in fact, developed and distributed by Desaware. This certificate is issued by one of a number of companies that specialize in providing software developers with encrypted certificates (discussed more later in this chapter). Whether you choose to trust Desaware's controls or not is, of course, your decision.

DISTRIBUTING AND DOWNLOADING ACTIVEX CONTROLS

So far you have found out about the existence of two separate technologies: one for marking controls as safe for initialization or scripting, the other for identifying that controls were authored by the person or company who claims to be the author. Later, we'll get to the subject of exactly how to mark controls as safe and sign them. For now, let's look at how these two technologies fit in to the downloading process from the perspectives of the end user, the site developer, and the control author.

End User Security   Any browser that can act as a container for ActiveX controls has a number of security settings available. Microsoft Internet Explorer, which at this time provides the most thorough support for ActiveX controls, has three security settings that can be configured by the user:

- ▶ High—At this setting, the only controls that can be run are those marked as safe, signed with a certificate from a certificate-issuing authority that is acceptable by the user, and developed by a company acceptable by the user. There is a separate dialog box in Microsoft Explorer that lets you specify which certificate-issuing companies are acceptable. When the control is downloaded, the certificate is displayed. You can choose whether to accept the control and whether you would like to add the company that developed the control to your list of trusted control authors.

- ▶ Medium—At this setting, unsafe and unsigned controls can be downloaded. Explorer will display a certificate showing the author of the control and whether the control is safe for initialization and scripting. You then have the option of running the control or not.

- ▶ None—At this setting controls are downloaded and run automatically. One could conceivably use this setting in a corporate intranet situation that provided no access to outside sites. Otherwise, don't use this setting.

The digital certificate includes a hypertext link to the company that issued the certificate. It allows you to verify if the certificate is still valid. Explorer also allows you to disable future warnings for components from specific vendors or those who have digital certificates from specific authorizing companies.

The Site Developer and/or Control Author   Adding automatic downloading to a Web page is trivial. All you need to do is add the CODEBASE option to the OBJECT tag.

```
<OBJECT ID="dwBanner1" WIDTH=324 HEIGHT=49
    CLASSID="CLSID: 63B8AFC0-8E9A-11D0-91BB-00AA0036005A"
    CODEBASE="dwBanner.CAB#version=1,0,0,13">
```

```
<PARAM NAME="_ExtentX" VALUE="8573">
<PARAM NAME="_ExtentY" VALUE="1296">
<PARAM NAME="BackColor" VALUE="16777088">
<PARAM NAME="BorderStyle" VALUE="1">
<PARAM NAME="ScrollIncrement" VALUE="3">
<PARAM NAME="ScrollText" VALUE="Visit Desaware's Web site at http://
www.desaware.com - The coolest tools for VB/VBA developers. ">
<PARAM NAME="XMargin" VALUE="20">
<PARAM NAME="YMargin" VALUE="6">
</OBJECT>
```

The CODEBASE option tells the browser the name of the file to retrieve that contains the object and the version of the object it contains. The nice thing about this is, if the system already has an object with the specified CLSID with the current version or later, the browser will automatically use the existing object instead of downloading a new copy.

The .CAB file is a compressed *cabinet file* in a format specified by Microsoft. It is important that you realize you can download other types of files as well. You could, for example, place the .OCX file name directly on the line. The problem is that this does not take into account the possibility of dependencies. Most controls (and all VB-authored controls) depend on additional .DLLs in order to run correctly. The .CAB file contains an install information file with the extension .INF, which describes the list of dependencies and where the additional files can be located. You could have the CODEBASE line reference in the .INF file directly, but you cannot sign an .INF file, so the user would not be able to verify the source of the file.

The .CAB file can be created by a site developer but will typically be created by the control author. A .CAB file can (and should) have its own digital signature indicating whether it is safe to download. You should sign your controls as well. What counts is that the file specified in the CODEBASE line is signed.

Most VB programmers will use the Visual Basic setup wizard or third-party installation tool to create the .CAB files for their controls. They will also create a template for the OBJECT tag for the control, which can be added to HTML pages.

I won't go into any detail here on using the Visual Basic setup wizard. The Visual Basic documentation is adequate and the wizard is easy to use. But there are a number of issues you should consider when using the wizard. They relate to both control safety and control signing and will be covered as we continue.

The .CAB Choice The .INF file within a .CAB file can list additional files your control requires to run. If you are creating a control for Internet download, you will usually specify that the control be downloaded from Microsoft's

Web site or your own. I would tend to recommend that you use Microsoft's. Why tie up your server's bandwidth downloading the large VB run-time support files?

You can include additional files in the .CAB file if you wish, but this increases the download time for the file. This approach is more common in intranets, where download times are less important.

The ActiveX SDK, available directly from Microsoft (check their Web site for current availability), includes tools to customize sites and a more detailed explanation of the .INF file format. It is possible to create .CAB files that support multiple operating systems. The initial .INF file contains a list of .CAB and operating system dependencies. The browser then loads the .CAB file needed for the target system. This does, however, result in two digital certificates being displayed (one for each .CAB file).

MARKING CONTROLS AS SAFE

There are two approaches to marking a control as safe.

The Registry Approach   This consists of adding entries in the registry that indicate that a particular control is safe. Back in Chapter 6 (an eternity ago), you saw how an ActiveX DLL is registered. Since an ActiveX control is just a specialized type of an ActiveX DLL, it should be no surprise that it is registered exactly the same way. Under your control's class ID, there is a key called Implemented Categories, which contains additional information about the control. Two new subkeys have been defined for this key to indicate the safety state of a control. If the control can be safely initialized, the subkey is

```
HKEY_LOCAL_MACHINE\SOFTWARE\Classes\CLSID\your control's CLSID\
Implemented Categories\{7DD95802-9882-11CF-9FA9-00AA006C42C4}"
```

If the control can be safely scripted (programmed), the subkey is

```
HKEY_LOCAL_MACHINE\SOFTWARE\Classes\CLSID\your control's CLSID\
Implemented Categories\{7DD95801-9882-11CF-9FA9-00AA006C42C4}"
```

The Visual Basic setup wizard allows you to specify that your control is safe. It includes entries in the .INF file for the control that add the specified safety settings into the registry. It goes without saying that you should never add these registry entries to any control you do not know is safe.

The IObjectSafety Approach   The registry approach has two disadvantages.

▶ It requires an extra registry lookup any time the control is loaded to verify its safety.

▸ Controls using this approach must always be safe. You do not have the option of supporting unsafe operations without violating the trust expected of any control author who marks his or her code as safe.

IObjectSafety is a standard interface that allows any control to tell the system that it is safe. It also allows a control to support both safe and unsafe modes of operation, depending on the preference of the container.

Now, before going on, I must take a moment and stray from the subject. Because, you see, you cannot use the IObjectSafety technique using Visual Basic alone.

You've probably noticed that every now and then I discuss some aspect of creating controls or components that demonstrates a limitation in Visual Basic. This is not surprising. This book is intended, in part, to push the limits of what is possible using ActiveX technology, and every development environment has limits. In several places where this has occurred, I've also mentioned that you can overcome the limit using Desaware's SpyWorks package. In fact, it might seem an almost amazing coincidence that there just happens to be a SpyWorks solution for limitations that are described in this book.

It is obviously not a coincidence, but it is not a cheap advertising gimmick either. The way I see it, my responsibility in all of my Visual Basic-related books has always been to show you what can be done using Visual Basic. SpyWorks and Desaware's other tools have always been my way of extending Visual Basic so that VB programmers can go a step beyond to accomplish almost anything they could do using VC++ and other development tools.

The fact that limitations mentioned in the text often have an answer in SpyWorks is mostly due to the way they were both created. SpyWorks 5 is being written simultaneously with this book (and yes, for those who are wondering, for the five months of this project I have done virtually nothing but write, code, eat, and sleep—and precious little of the latter). Here's how it works.

Each chapter begins with research. I review the documentation and then start experimenting. Some of the experiments turn into code samples, others into text. I try to push the limits, to do things that differ from the samples provided with Visual Basic. And when I run into a fundamental limitation, I look to see whether I can solve the problem by adding a new feature to SpyWorks. In fact, the majority of the new features for SpyWorks 5 are direct results of issues or limitations I discovered while working on this book.

Once I understood the issues relating to control marking, I decided that IObjectSafety is too important to just ignore. And despite the fact that it requires SpyWorks, I decided to document it briefly here.

The work is done by a SpyWorks component called dwAXExt.dll, the Desaware ActiveX extension component. This component defines an object called DWCONTROLHOOK, which is used to add new interfaces to controls. You may ask, why not use the Implements statement to do so? Because the Implements statement works with IDispatch-compatible interfaces, and IObjectSafety is not compatible with ActiveX automation. The SpyWorks component also defines a new IDispatch interface called IdwObjectSafety, which is used to communicate with your control.

The following listing shows the steps needed to implement the interface:

```
Implements IdwObjectSafety
Dim dwActiveX As DwAXExt.DWCONTROLHOOK

Private Sub UserControl_Initialize()
    Set dwActiveX = New DWCONTROLHOOK
    Call dwActiveX.Initialize(Me)
End Sub

Private Sub IdwObjectSafety_GetInterfaceSafetyOptions(pIID As Long, _
    SupportedOptions As Long, EnabledOptions As Long)
    EnabledOptions = dwSafeToInitialize Or dwSafeToProgram
End Sub

Private Function IdwObjectSafety_SetInterfaceSafetyOptions(pIID As _
    Long, ByVal OptionMask As Long, ByVal EnabledOptions As Long) _
    As Long
    IdwObjectSafety_SetInterfaceSafetyOptions = True
End Function
```

The dwActiveX.Initialize method tells the SpyWorks component to hook into the control. If it sees that the control implements the IdwObjectSafety interface, it exposes the standard IObjectSafety interface to the outside world.

A container that requires safe operation, such as an Internet browser, will call the SetInterfaceSafetyOptions function to request that the control enter safe mode. This occurs right after the control is initialized and well before the ReadProperties event. The OptionMask parameter contains bits that define what type of safety is being requested (safe for initialization or safe for scripting). The EnabledOption parameter indicates the desired safety value for each type. For example: a container might request that your control only be safe for initialization, in which case it will not request safe for scripting.

The GetInterfaceSafetyOptions function allows the container to determine the current setting of the control. The pIID parameter will not typically be used by VB programmers but is supported for future situations where you may wish to control safety for individual interfaces. A more detailed explanation of these functions and possible parameter values is included in the Spy-Works documentation.

The important thing from a control author's view point is that you can detect the safety state requested by the container and store the current safety state in a module-level variable. You can then disable dangerous operations if the control has been requested to be safe. This is ideal for adapting existing controls for the Internet and saves you from having one Internet-safe version, and another for use in applications.

As a side effect, this approach eliminates an extra registry access. The container loads the control. If it sees that the control is safe, it proceeds to initialize it and site it on the Web page. Otherwise, it terminates the control.

SIGNING CONTROLS

The intent of a code signature is to prove that a control comes from a particular source. To understand how this works, you need to know just a little bit about a technology called *public key encryption.*

Encryption works by scrambling text using an encoding algorithm and a key. With regular encryption, both the sender and the receiver need the same key. The sender encodes the message using his or her copy of the key. The message can then be read only by someone who has the same key.

Public key encryption uses two different keys, a private key and a public key. When a person encodes a message with his private key, anyone who has the public key can then read the message. But messages encoded with the public key can only be read by someone who has the private key. How does this work? I haven't the faintest idea. With the overwhelming rate of technology change all software developers face, it is necessary now and then to do some filtering. It is enough for me to know at this time that public key encryption works as advertised. Verisign's Web site (www.verisign.com) has additional information on the subject.

How does public key encryption work in this case? Well, if you create a document using a private key that can only be decoded using a public key, a successful decoding with the public key proves that the document was created by a specific private key. If you use Desaware's public key to decode a document that claims to be from Desaware, and it decodes successfully, you know that it was, in fact, created by Desaware. This assumes, of course, that Desaware has kept its private key secret.

Let's follow the complete sequence you and your end users go through to implement ActiveX control signing.

Obtain the Certificate First go to a company that issues digital certificates. As a VB control author you will probably go to Verisign Inc. (www.verisign.com) because they issue certificates designed specifically to work with ActiveX controls. By the time you read this Microsoft may have arrangements with other companies as well, so you should check Microsoft's Web site first and read the latest about ActiveX control signing.

Whichever issuing authority you deal with will provide a way to apply for your digital certificate online. You'll be asked for basic identification information. Verisign provides two types of certificates, one for individual software developers and one for companies. The individual one cost $20 per year at the time this book went to press. The business certificate cost $400. Verisign's Web site defines the steps they go through to verify who you are. For example, they check the Dunn & Bradstreet number for businesses. The intent is that when an end user sees a business certificate he has a level of confidence that the issuing company has, in fact, verified it was issued to a real business.

You will also provide the issuing authority with a private password to be used, along with the information you provided to create a private and public key. The private key will be saved in a file with the extension .PVK. You must keep the private key secret. The public key will be sent to the issuing authority.

The issuing authority then checks your application and performs certain steps to make sure you are who you say you are. They then create a digital certificate and send it to you via e-mail. This certificate contains your public key and is, in turn, encrypted using their private key. This means anyone can use the issuing authority's public key to obtain your company's public key.

Consider the example of the dwBanner control, which you will see shortly. Let's say Verisign is the issuing authority and you have their public key. (Microsoft Explorer does have this key to use in verifying ActiveX controls.) When you successfully decode a certificate they have created, you know that it is, in fact, from them. When you pull Desaware's public key from the certificate, you have their assurance the key is from Desaware, because they obtained it from Desaware and went to the trouble of verifying that the company is who they say they are. Not only do you know you have a valid key from Desaware, but you have certain assurances from Verisign about the legitimacy of the corporation. If you believe that any company who passes their screening is trustworthy for software downloads, you could tell Explorer that you will automatically accept any control signed with one of their certificates.

Sign a Control As an author, you receive from Verisign a digital certificate, which has the extension .SPC. To sign a control you use a program called Sign-Code.exe, which is available from Microsoft and is part of the ActiveX SDK.

This program takes both your private key and the certificate. The SignCode program first runs a cryptographic algorithm to come up with a *digest* of the file you are signing. This is a large number similar to a checksum, except that the odds of two files producing the same value are extremely small. This value is encrypted with your private key. This value and the certificate information is then added to the file. You can sign .OCX files and .CAB files.

Let's continue with the dwBanner example to see what happens with a signed control once the browser has downloaded it. The browser extracts the certificate and sees that it is issued by Verisign. It uses Verisign's public key to decode the certificate and extract Desaware's public key. It then runs the same cryptographic algorithm on the file that was used during the signing process. This produces a new digest value that must agree with the one stored in the certificate. But to see the one stored in the certificate, the browser must use Desaware's public key. If the value it decodes matches the one just generated by the browser, you know several things:

- ▸ That the control was, in fact, developed by Desaware

- ▸ That Desaware does exist, based on the confirmation done by Verisign

- ▸ That the control has not been modified since Desaware signed it

That last part is very important. If anyone tries to tamper with a file, the digest value produced when the browser scans the file will differ from the one stored in the certificate. In fact, this use of code signing has nothing to do with the Internet. You can sign any control and use the ChkTrust.exe program (also part of the Microsoft ActiveX SDK) to verify that a control has not been tampered with.

Conclusion   Here is a summary of the steps you need to go through to sign your controls.

- ▸ Check www.microsoft.com to obtain a list of issuing authorities that handle ActiveX control certification. Be sure you obtain a certificate for ActiveX controls—there are many other types of certificates and digital signatures available!

- ▸ Apply for a certificate using the issuing authority's Web site. You will receive an .SPC file from them with the certificate to go along with the private key .PVK file created during the application process.

- ▸ Obtain the SignCode.exe program from Microsoft (check the ActiveX SDK).

▶ Use the SignCode program to digitally sign your .OCX file and the .CAB file that is created, using the Visual Basic setup wizard or another installation tool.

THE DWBANNER CONTROL

The dwBanner control is an example of a control designed specifically for the Internet. It is a simple scrolling banner or marquee control that is an early edition of the dwBanner control included (with full source code) in Desaware's ActiveX Gallimaufry. This is a new collection of VB-authored controls with source code that are both useful and educational. The control is, as far as I know, safe to initialize and safe for scripting. The compiled version included on your CD-ROM is signed. Remember that any version you compile will not be signed with Desaware's certificate.

There are two HTML pages in the sample directories you can use to load the control. The dwBanner.htm file in the ch21 sample directory will display the control on a Web page if you have a version of the control already registered. You can register the control using the regsvr32 program, but if you take this approach the control will not be marked as safe. The dwBanner.htm file in the ch21\swsetup directory will install and register the control using the .CAB file in that directory. This file is signed and will mark the control as safe in the registry.

The dwBanner control demonstrates many of the techniques you've seen in earlier chapters and demonstrates the steps you should take when creating a commercial quality control.

In this section we will walk through the code step-by-step. The characteristics of the control will become apparent as you read the code descriptions. You should be warned that this control does make use of some intermediate level Windows API techniques. All of the API functions used are described in my book, the *Visual Basic 5.0 Programmer's Guide to the Win32 API*, so I won't be going into an in-depth explanation of how they work.

The API declarations are found in standard module dwBanner.bas shown in Listing 21.1.

The functions will be described briefly as they appear. Listing 21.2 lists the variable declarations for the control.

Listing 21.1: File dwBanner.bas

```
' Desaware's ActiveX Gallimaufry
' Simple scrolling banner control
' Copyright (c) 1997 by Desaware Inc. All Rights Reserved

Option Explicit

Type RECT
        Left As Long
        Top As Long
        Right As Long
        Bottom As Long
End Type

' DrawText() Format Flags
Public Const DT_TOP = &H0
Public Const DT_LEFT = &H0
Public Const DT_CENTER = &H1
Public Const DT_RIGHT = &H2
Public Const DT_VCENTER = &H4
Public Const DT_BOTTOM = &H8
Public Const DT_WORDBREAK = &H10
Public Const DT_SINGLELINE = &H20
Public Const DT_EXPANDTABS = &H40
Public Const DT_TABSTOP = &H80
Public Const DT_NOCLIP = &H100
Public Const DT_EXTERNALLEADING = &H200
Public Const DT_CALCRECT = &H400
Public Const DT_NOPREFIX = &H800
Public Const DT_INTERNAL = &H1000




' API functions
Declare Function GetClientRect Lib "user32" (ByVal hWnd As Long, lpRect _
As RECT) As Long
Declare Function CreateRectRgnIndirect Lib "gdi32" (lpRect As RECT) As Long
Declare Function DeleteObject Lib "gdi32" (ByVal hObject As Long) As Long
Declare Function DrawText Lib "user32" Alias "DrawTextA" (ByVal hdc As _
Long, ByVal lpStr As String, ByVal nCount As Long, lpRect As RECT, ByVal _
wFormat As Long) As Long
Declare Function SelectClipRgn Lib "gdi32" (ByVal hdc As Long, ByVal hRgn _
As Long) As Long
```

Listing 21.2: Variable, Property, and Event Declarations from File dwBanner.ctl

```
' Desaware's ActiveX Gallimaufry
' Simple scrolling banner control
' Copyright (c) 1997 by Desaware Inc. All Rights Reserved


' dwBanner.ocx
' Desaware's ActiveX Gallimaufry
' Copyright Ö 1997 by Desaware Inc. All Rights Reserved


Option Explicit
'Default Property Values:
Const m_def_ScrollEnabled = True
Const m_def_ScrollIncrement = 2
Const m_def_AutoSizeFont = True


'Property Variables:
Dim m_ScrollEnabled As Boolean
Dim m_ScrollText As String
Dim m_ScrollIncrement As Integer
Dim m_XMargin As Integer    ' Minimum horizontal margin
Dim m_YMargin As Integer    ' Minimum vertical margin
Dim m_ReplaceText As String   ' Replacement string at runtime
Dim m_AutoSizeFont As Boolean ' Font should always be autosized


' Internal variables
Dim m_TextClippingRegion As Long    ' Clipping region for text
Dim m_TextUpper As Integer          ' Upper location for text drawing
Dim m_TextTotalWidth As Long        ' Length of total text
Dim m_CurrentXOffset As Long        ' Current offset to left for display
Dim Cliprc As RECT
Dim m_Initializing As Boolean       ' Properties are being read


Public Enum dwBorderStyle
    dwNone = 0
    dwSingle = 1
End Enum


'Event Declarations:
Event Click() 'MappingInfo=UserControl,UserControl,-1,Click
Event DblClick() 'MappingInfo=UserControl,UserControl,-1,DblClick
Event MouseDown(Button As Integer, Shift As Integer, X As Single, Y As Single)
'MappingInfo=UserControl,UserControl,-1,MouseDown
Event MouseMove(Button As Integer, Shift As Integer, X As Single, Y As Single)
'MappingInfo=UserControl,UserControl,-1,MouseMove
```

Listing 21.2: Variable, Property, and Event Declarations from File dwBanner.ctl (Continued)

```
Event MouseUp(Button As Integer, Shift As Integer, X As Single, Y As Single)
'MappingInfo=UserControl,UserControl,-1,MouseUp
Event CycleComplete()    ' Indicates that a cycle has completed


'WARNING! DO NOT REMOVE OR MODIFY THE FOLLOWING COMMENTED LINES!
'MappingInfo=UserControl,UserControl,-1,BackColor
Public Property Get BackColor() As OLE_COLOR
    BackColor = UserControl.BackColor
End Property

Public Property Let BackColor(ByVal New_BackColor As OLE_COLOR)
    UserControl.BackColor() = New_BackColor
    PropertyChanged "BackColor"
    UserControl.Refresh
End Property

'WARNING! DO NOT REMOVE OR MODIFY THE FOLLOWING COMMENTED LINES!
'MappingInfo=UserControl,UserControl,-1,ForeColor
Public Property Get ForeColor() As OLE_COLOR
    ForeColor = UserControl.ForeColor
End Property

Public Property Let ForeColor(ByVal New_ForeColor As OLE_COLOR)
    UserControl.ForeColor() = New_ForeColor
    PropertyChanged "ForeColor"
    UserControl.Refresh
End Property

'WARNING! DO NOT REMOVE OR MODIFY THE FOLLOWING COMMENTED LINES!
'MappingInfo=UserControl,UserControl,-1,Enabled
Public Property Get Enabled() As Boolean
    Enabled = UserControl.Enabled
End Property

Public Property Let Enabled(ByVal New_Enabled As Boolean)
    UserControl.Enabled() = New_Enabled
    PropertyChanged "Enabled"
End Property

'WARNING! DO NOT REMOVE OR MODIFY THE FOLLOWING COMMENTED LINES!
'MappingInfo=UserControl,UserControl,-1,Font
Public Property Get Font() As Font
    If Ambient.UserMode Then
```

**Listing 21.2: Variable, Property, and Event Declarations from File
dwBanner.ctl (Continued)**

```
          Err.Raise 393
      End If
      Set Font = UserControl.Font
End Property

Public Property Set Font(ByVal New_Font As Font)
    If (Not m_Initializing) And Ambient.UserMode Then
        Err.Raise 382
    End If
    Set UserControl.Font = New_Font
    PropertyChanged "Font"
    If Not m_Initializing Then CalculateTextMetrics
End Property


' This version does not support Transparency
'WARNING! DO NOT REMOVE OR MODIFY THE FOLLOWING COMMENTED LINES!
'MappingInfo=UserControl,UserControl,-1,BackStyle
'Public Property Get BackStyle() As Integer
'    BackStyle = UserControl.BackStyle
'End Property

'Public Property Let BackStyle(ByVal New_BackStyle As Integer)
'    UserControl.BackStyle() = New_BackStyle
'    PropertyChanged "BackStyle"
'End Property

'WARNING! DO NOT REMOVE OR MODIFY THE FOLLOWING COMMENTED LINES!
'MappingInfo=UserControl,UserControl,-1,BorderStyle

Public Property Get BorderStyle() As dwBorderStyle
    BorderStyle = UserControl.BorderStyle
End Property

Public Property Let BorderStyle(ByVal New_BorderStyle As dwBorderStyle)
    If New_BorderStyle > 1 Or New_BorderStyle < Ø Then
        Err.Raise 38Ø
    End If
    UserControl.BorderStyle() = New_BorderStyle
    PropertyChanged "BorderStyle"
    If Not m_Initializing Then CalculateTextMetrics
End Property

Public Property Get FontUnderline() As Boolean
    FontUnderline = UserControl.FontUnderline
```

Listing 21.2: Variable, Property, and Event Declarations from File dwBanner.ctl (Continued)

```
End Property

Public Property Let FontUnderline(ByVal New_FontUnderline As Boolean)
    UserControl.FontUnderline() = New_FontUnderline
    PropertyChanged "FontUnderline"
    If Not m_Initializing Then CalculateTextMetrics
End Property

'WARNING! DO NOT REMOVE OR MODIFY THE FOLLOWING COMMENTED LINES!
'MappingInfo=UserControl,UserControl,-1,FontSize
Public Property Get FontSize() As Single
    FontSize = UserControl.FontSize
End Property

Public Property Let FontSize(ByVal New_FontSize As Single)
    UserControl.FontSize() = New_FontSize
    PropertyChanged "FontSize"
    If Not m_Initializing Then CalculateTextMetrics
End Property

'WARNING! DO NOT REMOVE OR MODIFY THE FOLLOWING COMMENTED LINES!
'MappingInfo=UserControl,UserControl,-1,FontName
Public Property Get FontName() As String
    FontName = UserControl.FontName
End Property

Public Property Let FontName(ByVal New_FontName As String)
    UserControl.FontName() = New_FontName
    PropertyChanged "FontName"
    If Not m_Initializing Then CalculateTextMetrics
End Property

'WARNING! DO NOT REMOVE OR MODIFY THE FOLLOWING COMMENTED LINES!
'MappingInfo=UserControl,UserControl,-1,FontItalic
Public Property Get FontItalic() As Boolean
    FontItalic = UserControl.FontItalic
End Property

Public Property Let FontItalic(ByVal New_FontItalic As Boolean)
    UserControl.FontItalic() = New_FontItalic
    PropertyChanged "FontItalic"
    If Not m_Initializing Then CalculateTextMetrics
End Property
```

Listing 21.2: Variable, Property, and Event Declarations from File dwBanner.ctl (Continued)

```
'WARNING! DO NOT REMOVE OR MODIFY THE FOLLOWING COMMENTED LINES!
'MappingInfo=UserControl,UserControl,-1,FontBold
Public Property Get FontBold() As Boolean
    FontBold = UserControl.FontBold
End Property

Public Property Let FontBold(ByVal New_FontBold As Boolean)
    UserControl.FontBold() = New_FontBold
    PropertyChanged "FontBold"
    If Not m_Initializing Then CalculateTextMetrics
End Property



Public Property Get XMargin() As Integer
    XMargin = m_XMargin
End Property

Public Property Let XMargin(ByVal vNewValue As Integer)
    If vNewValue >= UserControl.ScaleWidth Then
        ' Invalid property value
        Err.Raise 380
    End If
    m_XMargin = vNewValue
    PropertyChanged "XMargin"
    If Not m_Initializing Then CalculateTextMetrics
End Property

Public Property Get YMargin() As Integer
    YMargin = m_YMargin
End Property

Public Property Let YMargin(ByVal vNewValue As Integer)
    If vNewValue >= UserControl.ScaleHeight Then
        ' Invalid property value
        Err.Raise 380
    End If
    m_YMargin = vNewValue
    PropertyChanged "YMargin"
    If Not m_Initializing Then CalculateTextMetrics
End Property

'WARNING! DO NOT REMOVE OR MODIFY THE FOLLOWING COMMENTED LINES!
'MappingInfo=Timer1,Timer1,-1,Interval
Public Property Get Interval() As Long
```

Listing 21.2: Variable, Property, and Event Declarations from File dwBanner.ctl (Continued)

```
    Interval = Timer1.Interval
End Property


Public Property Let Interval(ByVal New_Interval As Long)
    Timer1.Interval() = New_Interval
    PropertyChanged "Interval"
End Property


Public Property Get ScrollEnabled() As Boolean
    ScrollEnabled = m_ScrollEnabled
End Property


Public Property Let ScrollEnabled(ByVal New_ScrollEnabled As Boolean)
    m_ScrollEnabled = New_ScrollEnabled
    PropertyChanged "ScrollEnabled"
    If Ambient.UserMode Then Timer1.Enabled = ScrollEnabled
End Property


Public Property Get ScrollIncrement() As Integer
    ScrollIncrement = m_ScrollIncrement
End Property


Public Property Let ScrollIncrement(ByVal vNewValue As Integer)
    If vNewValue > 20 Then
        Err.Raise 380
    End If
    m_ScrollIncrement = vNewValue
    PropertyChanged "ScrollIncrement"
End Property



Public Property Get ScrollText() As String
    ScrollText = m_ScrollText
End Property


Public Property Let ScrollText(ByVal New_Text As String)
    m_ScrollText = New_Text & " "
    PropertyChanged "Text"
    If Not m_Initializing Then CalculateTextMetrics
    UserControl.Refresh
End Property


Public Property Get ReplaceText() As String
    If Not Ambient.UserMode Then
```

**Listing 21.2: Variable, Property, and Event Declarations from File
dwBanner.ctl (Continued)**

```
      Err.Raise 393
   End If
   ReplaceText = m_ReplaceText
End Property

Public Property Let ReplaceText(ByVal New_Text As String)
   If Not Ambient.UserMode Then
      Err.Raise 382
   End If
   m_ReplaceText = New_Text
   PropertyChanged "ReplaceText"
End Property

Public Property Get AutoSizeFont() As Boolean
   AutoSizeFont = m_AutoSizeFont
End Property

Public Property Let AutoSizeFont(ByVal vNewValue As Boolean)
   m_AutoSizeFont = vNewValue
   PropertyChanged "AutoSizeFont"
   If Not m_Initializing Then CalculateTextMetrics
End Property

'Initialize Properties for User Control
Private Sub UserControl_InitProperties()
   m_ScrollEnabled = m_def_ScrollEnabled
   m_ScrollIncrement = m_def_ScrollIncrement
   m_AutoSizeFont = m_def_AutoSizeFont
   On Error GoTo InitNoExtender
   ' Default text to developer assigned name
   m_ScrollText = Ambient.DisplayName & " "
   'Set Font = Ambient.Font
   PropertyChanged "ScrollText"
InitNoExtender:
End Sub

'Load property values from storage
Private Sub UserControl_ReadProperties(PropBag As PropertyBag)
   m_Initializing = True
   UserControl.BackColor = PropBag.ReadProperty("BackColor", &H8000000F)
   UserControl.ForeColor = PropBag.ReadProperty("ForeColor", &H80000012)
   UserControl.Enabled = PropBag.ReadProperty("Enabled", True)
   'Set Font = PropBag.ReadProperty("Font")
   FontName = PropBag.ReadProperty("FontName", "Arial")
```

Listing 21.2: Variable, Property, and Event Declarations from File dwBanner.ctl (Continued)

```
   FontSize = PropBag.ReadProperty("FontSize", 8)
   FontBold = PropBag.ReadProperty("FontBold", False)
   FontItalic = PropBag.ReadProperty("FontItalic", False)
   ' UserControl.BackStyle = PropBag.ReadProperty("BackStyle", 1)
   UserControl.BorderStyle = PropBag.ReadProperty("BorderStyle", 0)
   Timer1.Interval = PropBag.ReadProperty("Interval", 100)
   m_ScrollEnabled = PropBag.ReadProperty("ScrollEnabled", m_def_ScrollEnabled)
   m_ScrollIncrement = PropBag.ReadProperty("ScrollIncrement", _
   m_def_ScrollIncrement)
   m_ScrollText = PropBag.ReadProperty("ScrollText", "")
   m_XMargin = PropBag.ReadProperty("XMargin", 0)
   m_YMargin = PropBag.ReadProperty("YMargin", 0)
   m_AutoSizeFont = PropBag.ReadProperty("AutoSizeFont", True)
   m_Initializing = False
End Sub

'Write property values to storage
Private Sub UserControl_WriteProperties(PropBag As PropertyBag)

   Call PropBag.WriteProperty("BackColor", UserControl.BackColor, &H8000000F)
   Call PropBag.WriteProperty("ForeColor", UserControl.ForeColor, &H80000012)
   Call PropBag.WriteProperty("Enabled", UserControl.Enabled, True)
   'Call PropBag.WriteProperty("Font", Font)
   Call PropBag.WriteProperty("FontName", FontName, "Arial")
   Call PropBag.WriteProperty("FontSize", FontSize, 8)
   Call PropBag.WriteProperty("FontBold", FontBold, False)
   Call PropBag.WriteProperty("FontItalic", FontItalic, False)
   ' Call PropBag.WriteProperty("BackStyle", UserControl.BackStyle, 1)
   Call PropBag.WriteProperty("BorderStyle", UserControl.BorderStyle, 0)
   Call PropBag.WriteProperty("Interval", Timer1.Interval, 100)
   Call PropBag.WriteProperty("ScrollEnabled", m_ScrollEnabled, _
   m_def_ScrollEnabled)
   Call PropBag.WriteProperty("ScrollIncrement", m_ScrollIncrement, _
   m_def_ScrollIncrement)
   Call PropBag.WriteProperty("ScrollText", m_ScrollText, "")
   Call PropBag.WriteProperty("XMargin", m_XMargin, 0)
   Call PropBag.WriteProperty("YMargin", m_YMargin, 0)
   Call PropBag.WriteProperty("AutoSizeFont", m_AutoSizeFont, True)
End Sub
```

Let's take a closer look at the control's properties. The following properties represent straightforward mappings of standard properties to the UserControl object:

- ▶ BackColor
- ▶ ForeColor
- ▶ Enabled
- ▶ BorderStyle

Their implementation should be quite familiar to you by now.

The Font property is handled in a slightly different way from what you've seen before. The default font is the font set for the UserControl object by the control author at design time. The ambient font is not used at all in this case. Individual settings for font characteristics are exposed as the FontName, Font-Bold, FontItalic, and FontSize properties. They are persisted as separate properties in order to make control scripting easier—they appear as properties of the control itself instead of properties of an internal object. This also avoids a bug with earlier versions of the ActiveX control pad, which is not able to save Font objects into an HTML page.

The Font object is accessible at design time so the developer using the control can change the settings using the single Font dialog box. However, at runtime the Font object is not accessible. This is because this control needs to know immediately if any font value has changed. You can't detect changes to properties of the Font object unless you are using the Ambient Font object, which triggers the PropertyChanged event when any of its properties are changed. You can detect changes to the individual font properties if they are exposed as they are here. Changes to the font invoke the following line:

```
If Not m_Initializing Then CalculateTextMetrics
```

The CalculateTextMetrics function calculates the size of the font and the margins in order to be sure the text appears correctly. It also restarts the scrolling operation. Attempting to set a font size too large to display causes the font size to automatically be reduced. No error is raised in this situation.

The following properties relate to the operation of the banner control:

- ▶ Interval—Controls the interval between scroll operations. Maps to the Interval property of a constituent Timer control.
- ▶ ScrollIncrement—Controls how many pixels the text scrolls to the left after each interval elapses.

▸ XMargin—Twice the margin between the right and left borders of the control and where the text appears.

▸ YMargin—Twice the margin between the right and left borders of the control and where the text appears.

▸ ScrollEnabled—Used to start and stop the scrolling operation. Maps to the Enabled property of a constituent Timer control.

▸ ScrollText—The text to scroll. The text will scroll continuously. An extra space is automatically added to this text when the property is set to ensure spacing between one rendition of the string and the next. You can add additional strings to increase the spacing.

▸ ReplaceText—A new string that will replace the currently scrolling string. When this property is set, the current string is scrolled completely off the banner, after which the ReplaceText string is automatically assigned to the ScrollText property.

▸ AutoSizeFont—When True, the current font is automatically resized to fill the available control height (the total control height minus the YMargin value).

Listing 21.3 shows how the various control events and methods are implemented.

Listing 21.3: dwBanner Control Events and Methods

```
'WARNING! DO NOT REMOVE OR MODIFY THE FOLLOWING COMMENTED LINES!
'MappingInfo=UserControl,UserControl,-1,Refresh
Public Sub Refresh()
    UserControl.Refresh
End Sub


Private Sub Timer1_Timer()
    Call DrawTheText(UserControl.hdc)
End Sub


Private Sub UserControl_Click()
    On Error GoTo NoHyper
    UserControl.Hyperlink.NavigateTo "http://www.desaware.com"
NoHyper:
    RaiseEvent Click
End Sub


Private Sub UserControl_DblClick()
```

Listing 21.3: dwBanner Control Events and Methods (Continued)

```
      RaiseEvent DblClick
End Sub

Private Sub UserControl_MouseDown(Button As Integer, Shift As Integer, X _
As Single, Y As Single)
   RaiseEvent MouseDown(Button, Shift, X, Y)
End Sub

Private Sub UserControl_MouseMove(Button As Integer, Shift As Integer, X _
As Single, Y As Single)
   RaiseEvent MouseMove(Button, Shift, X, Y)
End Sub

Private Sub UserControl_MouseUp(Button As Integer, Shift As Integer, X _
As Single, Y As Single)
   RaiseEvent MouseUp(Button, Shift, X, Y)
End Sub

'WARNING! DO NOT REMOVE OR MODIFY THE FOLLOWING COMMENTED LINES!
'MappingInfo=UserControl,UserControl,-1,hWnd
Public Property Get hWnd() As Long
   hWnd = UserControl.hWnd
End Property

Private Sub UserControl_Resize()
   CalculateTextMetrics
End Sub

Private Sub UserControl_Paint()
   Call DrawTheText(UserControl.hdc)
End Sub

Private Sub UserControl_Show()
   CalculateTextMetrics
End Sub
```

Most of the events and methods are quite straightforward. Refresh maps directly to the UserControl object. The Paint event and Timer event call the DrawTheText function. This function takes a device context as a parameter to allow for future enhancements. The CalculateTextMetrics function is called for the first time after the control window is placed on the container during the Show event. This ensures that the window-based calculations are accurate.

The Click event will navigate the browser to Desaware's Web site if the control is contained in a browser. This line is included for demonstration purposes only. In the commercial version of this control, the Click event triggers normally. The developer can then attach whatever operation they wish to the Click event using their choice of scripting language. Listing 21.4 shows the functions that implement the scrolling.

Listing 21.4: The Control Implementation Code

```
'----------------------------------------
'
'   Private functions used internally

' Calculate the variables needed to draw text
Private Sub CalculateTextMetrics()
    Dim TxtHeight As Integer
    InitializeClippingRegion
    If m_TextClippingRegion = 0 Then
        ' Unable to draw text, just exit
        Exit Sub
    End If
    TxtHeight = UserControl.TextHeight(m_ScrollText)
    If TxtHeight > Cliprc.Bottom - Cliprc.Top Or m_AutoSizeFont Then
        ' Font size is too large at runtime, shrink it
        If Ambient.UserMode Then Call AdjustFontSize
        TxtHeight = UserControl.TextHeight(m_ScrollText)
    End If
    m_TextUpper = Cliprc.Top + (Cliprc.Bottom - Cliprc.Top - TxtHeight) \ 2

    m_TextTotalWidth = UserControl.TextWidth(m_ScrollText)
    If Ambient.UserMode Then
        m_CurrentXOffset = -(Cliprc.Right - Cliprc.Left)
        ' Start off to the right
        Timer1.Enabled = m_ScrollEnabled
    End If
    UserControl.Refresh
End Sub


' Initialize the clipping region
Private Sub InitializeClippingRegion()
    If m_TextClippingRegion <> 0 Then
        ' Delete existing region
        Call DeleteObject(m_TextClippingRegion)
    End If
```

Listing 21.4: The Control Implementation Code (Continued)

```
    Call GetClientRect(UserControl.hWnd, Cliprc)
    ' Shrink rectangle
    Cliprc.Left = Cliprc.Left + m_XMargin \ 2
    Cliprc.Right = Cliprc.Right - m_XMargin \ 2
    Cliprc.Top = Cliprc.Top + m_YMargin \ 2
    Cliprc.Bottom = Cliprc.Bottom - m_YMargin \ 2
    If Cliprc.Right > Cliprc.Left And Cliprc.Bottom > Cliprc.Top Then
        ' Drawing region is legal
        m_TextClippingRegion = CreateRectRgnIndirect(Cliprc)
    End If
End Sub


' Adjust the font size to maximum height possible
' If RetrieveOnly is True, only returns largest possible font size
Private Function AdjustFontSize(Optional ByVal RetrieveOnly As Boolean = False)
    Dim targetheight&
    Dim targetpoints&
    targetheight = (Cliprc.Bottom - Cliprc.Top - 1) * Screen.TwipsPerPixelY
    targetpoints = targetheight / 20
    UserControl.Font.Size = targetpoints
    If targetpoints < 8 Then
        ' Windows font selection trick
        UserControl.Font.Name = UserControl.Font.Name
        UserControl.Font.Size = targetpoints
    End If

End Function


' Uses the hdc because future versions will offer
' transparency
Private Function DrawTheText(ByVal hdc As Long) As Long
    Dim drawrc As RECT
    Static ReplaceMarker As Long
    Static ReplacePending As Boolean
    If m_TextClippingRegion = 0 Then Exit Function
    If m_TextTotalWidth = 0 Then
        Exit Function
    End If
    Call SelectClipRgn(hdc, m_TextClippingRegion)
    Call GetClientRect(UserControl.hWnd, drawrc)
    drawrc.Top = m_TextUpper
    drawrc.Left = Cliprc.Left - m_CurrentXOffset
    Do
        Call DrawText(hdc, m_ScrollText, -1, drawrc, DT_SINGLELINE Or DT_NOPREFIX)
```

Listing 21.4: The Control Implementation Code (Continued)

```
        If Not Ambient.UserMode Then Exit Do
        ' Exit loop if any text is on the way
        drawrc.Left = drawrc.Left + m_TextTotalWidth
        If ReplacePending And drawrc.Left > ReplaceMarker Then
            ' Follow by plenty of spaces to clear any garbage
            Call DrawText(hdc, Space$(Len(m_ScrollText)), -1, drawrc, _
                        DT_SINGLELINE Or DT_NOPREFIX)
            Exit Do  ' Replacement pending
        End If
    Loop While drawrc.Left < drawrc.Right
    If m_ReplaceText <> "" And Not ReplacePending Then
        ' Initialize replacement text
        ReplaceMarker = drawrc.Left - 1
        ReplacePending = True
    End If
    Call SelectClipRgn(hdc, 0) ' Clear clipping region
    If Ambient.UserMode Then
        ' Scrolling only happens at runtime
        m_CurrentXOffset = m_CurrentXOffset + m_ScrollIncrement
        If ReplacePending Then ReplaceMarker = ReplaceMarker - m_ScrollIncrement
        If m_CurrentXOffset > m_TextTotalWidth Then
            m_CurrentXOffset = 0
            RaiseEvent CycleComplete
            If ReplacePending And ReplaceMarker <= Cliprc.Left + _
                m_ScrollIncrement Then
                ReplaceMarker = 0
                ReplacePending = False
                m_ScrollText = m_ReplaceText
                m_ReplaceText = ""
                CalculateTextMetrics
            End If
        End If
    End If
End Function


Public Sub AboutBox()
    On Error GoTo AlreadyVisible
    frmAboutBox.Show vbModal
    Set frmAboutBox = Nothing
AlreadyVisible:
End Sub
```

The CalculateTextMetrics function begins by initializing the clipping region for the control. A clipping region masks the portion of the control that can actually be drawn. This is the mechanism used to allow the margins to work. The clipping region is set to the area in which the text should appear. The drawing function then draws text onto the entire control area, relying on Windows to clip the text that is outside of the clipping region.

The font size is then adjusted, if necessary, using the AdjustFontSize function. This function calculates the desired font size based on the current screen resolution in twips. There are 1440 twips per inch and 72 twips per point, so each point represents 20 twips. If the font size is smaller than 8 points, the size is sent and the font name is set again along with the size. This is a trick that helps Windows choose the best font at smaller sizes.

The total width of the scrolling text is calculated and the initial text position is set all the way to the right of the control.

The real work is done by the DrawTheText function. Each time it is called, it scrolls the text the number of pixels to the left specified by the ScrollIncrement property. A loop is used to draw the text repeatedly if there is room in the control for more than one copy of the text. This routine also handles text replacement if the ReplaceText property is set. At design time only a single copy of the ScrollText property is drawn, and scrolling is disabled.

As you can see, the control does not interfere with the registry, the container, the file system, or other windows in the system. I can't see any way that calling the control's methods or properties can cause any of these things to happen either during initialization or design time. Thus, this control can legitimately be marked as safe.

The control also implements a property page and an About Box. The code for those elements can be found on the CD-ROM that comes with this book. You'll find a test program that demonstrates use of the control as well.

There is room for improvement with this control, including the use of the ScrollWindow function to improve the scrolling performance. But that will have to wait for a later version of the control.

CONCLUSION

The dwBanner control is perhaps the only example in this book that can be considered a complete control. It meets all of the requirements for a commercial quality ActiveX control, except that testing of the version included here was very limited due to the tight production schedule on this book.

Here is a brief summary of the key tasks you must perform when authoring an ActiveX control. While I have made some attempt to place them in a logical order, you should not read this sequence as anything more than a suggested approach.

- ▸ Define the user interface. Unless your control is invisible at runtime, it will have a user interface. Don't forget to consider the keyboard interface as well as the mouse interface, especially for graphic intensive controls.

- ▸ Define the programmatic interface. Before you write your first line of code, you should list the properties, methods, and events of the control and how you expect them to interact.

- ▸ Implement the property procedures. Remember to change property types from variants to specific data types unless you clearly need to use a variant. Variants are slower and less efficient than other data types and require more sophisticated error checking.

- ▸ Map properties to the UserControl object and constituent controls. Some of your control's public properties and methods will simply reference properties and methods of the UserControl object or constituent controls. Remember that a single public member of your control can map to more than one constituent control.

- ▸ Add data validation to properties. Raise errors on any attempt to set a property to an illegal value. Remember that Visual Basic does not provide automatic verification for enumerated types; you must test their values yourself.

- ▸ Add runtime/design time characteristics to properties and methods. Raise errors on attempts to set a property at an invalid time. For example: try to set a property at runtime that you wish to be read-only at runtime.

- ▸ Implement property initialization and persistence. Verify the values of all default values for properties.

- ▸ Define property pages. You should implement property pages for all of your control's properties, since you can never assume that a container will provide a property browser for setting your control properties.

- ▸ Implement events. Remember that you can map UserControl events or events from constituent controls to the public events of your control.

- ▸ Assign descriptions, standard procedure IDs, and property pages for properties, methods, and events. The descriptions you set will appear in the object browser for your control. Standard procedure IDs (also known as Dispatch IDs) are used to notify the container to implement property-specific behavior. Under Visual Basic, this is especially critical for the Enabled property.

▶ Implement drawing code if necessary. Controls that are entirely made up of constituent controls may not require additional drawing operations, whereas with user-drawn controls, drawing may represent the bulk of the work.

▶ Create and set a toolbar bitmap.

▶ Create the About Box.

▶ Create a help file and assign help contexts.

▶ Test, test, test!

▶ Verify operation on target containers. This is especially critical if you make use of the Extender object, which differs from one container to the next. Visual Basic itself is one of the most sophisticated containers you will use. Most other containers will be less capable. Be sure that your control fails gracefully when container functionality is missing.

This concludes our discussion of ActiveX controls for the Internet. We'll return to the subject of Internet- and intranet-based components in Part 4, where we discuss ActiveX documents. But first, now that you know all of the fundamentals of control development, it's time to shoot for the stratosphere and cover some of the more advanced techniques that can be incorporated into your controls.

Advanced Techniques

Visual Basic versus Visual C++

Overview of Windows Messaging

Messaging Examples

A Tale of Four Listboxes

Y ou've probably noticed that I like to start each chapter with a welcoming paragraph to introduce you to what you are about to read and why it is important. I started doing so with this chapter, but 1,500 words later I realized that what I was writing was the chapter itself.

So instead of the usual introduction, I would like to offer a few words of caution. This chapter discusses some of the most advanced functionality supported by Windows. Many of the techniques I demonstrate are difficult to understand and debug, and when they fail, they are likely to cause your application or your system to hang or raise a memory exception. While I will try to briefly introduce the fundamental ideas behind the techniques shown, you probably won't really understand them without a good understanding of Windows and the Win32 API. So, if you get lost, all I can do is encourage you to read my other book, *Dan Appleman's Visual Basic 5.0 Programmer's Guide to the Win32 API*, which is referenced throughout this book. Its sole reason for existence is to give Visual Basic programmers a good understanding of Windows and the Win32 API. Since it consists of more than 1500 pages, I'm sure you can appreciate why I don't try to include the information in this chapter.

VISUAL BASIC VERSUS VISUAL C++

Now that we have discussed the creation of ActiveX controls with Visual Basic at some length, allow me to ask two simple questions. Does Visual Basic 5 make it easy to create ActiveX controls? Does Visual Basic 5 make it possible to create serious, robust, professional-quality ActiveX controls? The answer to both questions is clearly yes—and no. To explain what I mean by this, I first need to discuss a completely different language: Visual C++.

If you have used both Visual Basic and Visual C++, you know they are completely different, and not only because the underlying language is different. You see, Visual C++ is not really "Visual" in the same sense as Visual Basic.

Visual Basic is a highly interactive development environment, where you can interact easily with user interface elements and other objects and attach code directly to their events. The Visual Basic environment encapsulates the underlying Windows and OLE technology so you don't have to deal with it. This encapsulation makes Visual Basic relatively easy to learn and use but does result in some loss of functionality. You can only use those capabilities that are either exposed by Visual Basic or can be accessed by bypassing Visual Basic via API calls or third-party tools.

Visual C++ is a combination of a compiler, class library (called the Microsoft Foundation Classes, or MFC), and set of sophisticated wizards. The class library provides a framework for working with Windows and OLE that can be programmed using the wizards. The wizards know how to create code to accomplish a wide variety of tasks using this framework. The framework itself provides pretty much full access to all of the underlying capability of Windows and OLE. The catch to this approach is: As long as you are trying to implement functionality that is known by one of the wizards, Visual C++ is easy to learn and use. However, the instant you go beyond this built-in functionality, Visual C++ requires a substantial knowledge of Windows and its extension libraries in order to accomplish anything. And while the wizards and class libraries do implement most of the "grunge work" involved in common Windows tasks, they do little or nothing when it comes to implementing features unique to your applications. With Visual Basic, all you need to learn to write simple controls is Visual Basic itself. With Visual C++, you need to know C++, Windows API functions, MFC classes, and OLE. Ultimately, Visual C++ is much harder to learn and use than Visual Basic (and this is from the perspective of someone who routinely uses both).

Here is another thing to keep in mind about Visual C++: If you use the MFC classes and their associated wizards, you will need to distribute the MFC run-time libraries with your control. So despite the fact that you are using C++, you are still stuck with distributing a run-time library—exactly the same situation you face with Visual Basic. It is possible to use Visual C++ to create controls without MFC, but in doing so you lose the benefits of the wizards and the functionality provided by the classes. Learning to create these "lightweight" controls is a significant undertaking, since they require an excellent understanding of both Windows and OLE technology.

VISUAL BASIC'S "LIMITATIONS"

I've heard a number of people complain about perceived limitations in Visual Basic's ability to create ActiveX controls. These limitations derive from two distinct facts:

First, there are some definite limitations in Visual Basic's implementation of ActiveX controls. These result from the very encapsulation that makes it easy to create controls in VB in the first place. Most of these can be worked around with the aid of API and OLE techniques or third-party tools such as SpyWorks.

Second, there is the problem of expectations. When Visual Basic first appeared, some people considered it a toy language because it didn't do everything they wanted. Features were missing from the core language that could not be implemented without direct access to the Windows API or use of third-party tools. Now we understand that the very nature of the encapsulation VB provides requires that some functionality be left out of the core language. If Visual Basic did everything, it would just be another Visual C++ and be just as hard to learn and use. VB programmers became accustomed to taking advantage of those features built into the language directly, while using API calls or third-party tools to selectively extend Visual Basic where necessary for their own applications. That is perhaps Visual Basic's greatest strength, that it gives you the power to choose for yourself which tasks to perform at a high (VB) level and which to perform at a low (API) level. I believe that many of those programmers who are complaining about Visual Basic's implementation of ActiveX controls are forgetting this trade-off. They've decided that just because Visual Basic does not make it easy to do everything possible in a Visual C++ ActiveX control, it is somehow not suitable for serious control development. This is as silly now as it was then.

You should also keep in mind that Visual Basic's ActiveX control implementation has some unique advantages over the approach taken in Visual C++. It is extraordinarily difficult to build controls out of constituent controls using VC++. The vast majority of VC++ controls are either pure user-drawn controls or are subclassed from a standard control—a technique similar to one you will see shortly in this chapter.

So now let us revisit the opening questions in this chapter. Does Visual Basic 5.0 make it easy to create ActiveX controls? The key word here is *easy*. The answer is yes, so long as the controls fit closely into the functionality encapsulated by Visual Basic itself. The answer is no, as soon as you need to implement functionality that goes beyond what Visual Basic is designed to handle easily.

Does Visual Basic 5 make it possible to create serious, robust, professional-quality ActiveX controls? The key word here is *possible*. The answer again is yes, as long as you are willing to put in the effort to take full advantage of all of the resources available to you. If you know the functionality provided by Visual Basic, understand Win32 API programming techniques, understand how to take advantage of advanced API techniques such as subclassing and hooks, understand the nature of COM interfaces, and are willing to use third-party tools that can manipulate those interfaces, then almost anything you can imagine will be possible. But if you are unwilling to learn or use these additional resources, the answer will be no. You will be stuck with using Visual C++, where you may ultimately be forced to use all of those techniques anyway, whether you like it or not!

One of the consequences of this situation is that a sophisticated control can be as complex and difficult to write in Visual Basic as it is in Visual C++. I believe that even in these situations Visual Basic will often have the advantage, if only because it provides a much more interactive development environment with regard to testing and debugging.

Overview of Windows Messaging

Creating advanced controls demands a good understanding of the fundamentals of Windows messaging. If you are already acquainted with Windows messaging, you can skip this section. For everyone else, it should provide enough of a background to allow you to follow the techniques described later in this chapter.

What is a Message?

Consider what happens when you click your mouse on a window. The mouse driver for the Windows operating system detects the mouse click and notifies the operating system that a click has occurred. The operating system detects which window appears under the mouse pointer location and determines which application needs to receive the information.

The operating system maintains a queue for each application that contains a list of events, such as mouse clicks and keystrokes, that need to be sent to the application. Each of these events is called a message, and the queue is thus called the *message queue*. Each message has associated information, as shown in Table 22.1.

How does the operating system actually send a message to a window? Within each Windows application, there is a loop in which the program continuously polls the operating system to see if any messages are available. This loop, called the application *message loop*, does not exit until the application is closed. This loop is also completely hidden from Visual Basic programmers. When the loop

Table 22.1: Message Parameters

Message Parameter	Description	Mouse Click Example
hWnd	The 32-bit window handle that is the destination for the message.	The window handle of the window that was clicked.
Message	A 32-bit number assigned to a particular message.	&H201, also called WM_LBUTTONDOWN.
wParam	A 32-bit parameter whose meaning depends on the message.	Flags indicating whether the control and/or shift key is pressed and whether any of the other mouse buttons are currently pressed.
lParam	A 32-bit parameter whose meaning depends on the message.	The low 16 bits contain the horizontal location within the window of the mouse click position. The high 16 bits contain the vertical location.

sees that a message is available, it dispatches it to the window that is supposed to receive the message.

How does it do this? Every window in the system has a function defined called a *window function*. The window function for the window has four parameters. A window function written in Visual Basic would take the form:

```
Public Function MyWindowFunction(ByVal hWnd As Long, ByVal message As _
Long, ByVal wParam As Long, ByVal lParam As Long) As Long
```

In other words, the message loop for the application calls an API function that looks up the window function for a window and calls the function with the message parameters.

It is also possible to call the window function for any window directly, in effect sending a message to the window. There are two API functions you will typically use to do this, each of which takes the standard message parameters (hWnd, message, wParam, and lParam):

▶ PostMessage—This API function loads the message into the message queue for the application. The function returns immediately and the message is processed when the application's message loop reaches that message in the queue. Because the message is processed after the Post-Message call returns, it is not possible for the window to return values to functions calling PostMessage.

▶ SendMessage—This API function calls the window function for the specified window directly. The SendMessage function does not return until the window function has finished processing the message. Because the message is processed before SendMessage returns, the SendMessage function makes it possible for a window function to return a value to the calling function.

When working with Windows, the term *posting a message* always refers to the use of the PostMessage or related API functions to post a message into an application's message queue. The term *sending a message* always refers to the use of SendMessage or related API functions to call the window function for a window immediately.

WHAT HAPPENS WHEN A WINDOW IS CREATED?

When a window is created, whether it is a form, a control, or a custom window, it is always given a window function by the application that creates it. This is another one of those tasks that Visual Basic handles for you. When an application receives messages, it can handle them as it chooses or send them on to a *class window function* that is provided by Windows. For example: Windows defines a class of windows called LISTBOX. When a window belongs to this class, it can call a class window function provided by Windows which implements the default behavior of a list box. This is what makes it possible for applications to create list boxes without implementing all the complexity of a list box itself.

Figure 22.1 illustrates the control flow when a message is sent to a window. The application (or operating system) calls the window function. The window function can either call the class window function to implement a standard behavior provided by the class or handle the message itself. The arrows with broken lines indicate an optional path for the program's flow.

WHAT IS SUBCLASSING?

Visual Basic provides window functions for forms and controls it creates. Not only does this window function implement the behavior of forms and controls, it also raises Visual Basic events for selected incoming messages.

But it does not raise events for every incoming message. And there are cases where you may wish to override the standard behavior of the form or control provided by the window function that VB furnishes. In cases like this, it is possible to subclass the window. The SetWindowLong API function can be used to set the window function for a window to a function that you specify. Then you have the option of calling the previous window function if you wish. This situation is illustrated in Figure 22.2.

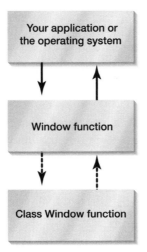

Figure 22.1: Execution flow for a window

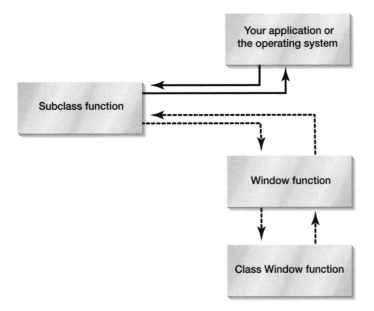

Figure 22.2: Execution flow for a subclassed window

WHAT IS A WINDOWS HOOK?

A Windows hook is a technique for intercepting messages at various points along the normal message processing sequence. Hooks are installed by providing an address of a hook function to the SetWindowsHookEx function call. Some of the more common hook types are as follows:

- ▸ WH_GETMESSAGE hook: Windows calls your hook function each time your application requests a message from the application's message queue. The hook function can change or remove the message before the application processes it.

- ▸ WH_CALLWNDPROC hook: Windows calls your hook function immediately before the window function is called for every window in your application thread. The hook function can change or remove the message. However, this type of hook is extremely inefficient, because the hook function is called for every message.

- ▸ WH_KEYBOARD hook: Windows calls your hook function for each keystroke message (key up and key down) before the message is placed in the application's message queue. The hook function can change or discard keystrokes.

- ▸ WH_MOUSE hook: Windows calls your hook function for each mouse message before the message is placed in the application's message queue. The hook function can change or discard mouse messages.

Hooks must be handled very carefully, since it is possible to confuse Windows as to what is happening in the system.

It is also possible to establish hooks that work on a system-wide basis or that hook processes other than your own. However, I have serious doubts as to whether this can be done safely (if at all) with Visual Basic. The cross-process hook controls provided with SpyWorks are all written in C++.

CUSTOM WINDOWS, SUBCLASSING, AND VISUAL BASIC

One of the intriguing new features of Visual Basic 5.0 is the fact that it is possible to obtain the address of a function using the AddressOf operator. You can pass this address to the CreateWindow API function and create and manage your own private windows. Or, you can pass this address to the SetWindowLong API function to subclass an existing window. This approach is illustrated in the Visual Basic documentation. This means that Visual Basic is now able to create private windows and subclass existing windows, a task that previously required third-party tools.

There are, however, a number of crucial issues relating to these techniques that the Visual Basic documentation does not address:

▶ Functions using the AddressOf operator must be in standard modules. Yet, in most cases, when you subclass a form or control, you need an object reference in order to do anything useful with the incoming message. This means you need to implement an efficient way to obtain an object reference for a window—and let me stress the word *efficient*. This function will be called for all incoming messages; the last thing you want to do is add significant overhead at this point in your code. Use of the VB collection object and late bound references can be deadly.

▶ It is not uncommon for Visual Basic controls to subclass each other or their containers. If any one of them behaves incorrectly, it can sabotage the operation of other controls that are subclassing the same window— even to the point of causing a memory exception. Problems are especially likely during window destruction or application termination. Your own cleanup operation must be well behaved as well.

▶ Use of subclassing is inherently dangerous. It bypasses all of the safety mechanisms built into Visual Basic. Failure to handle a message properly may not just lead to a Visual Basic run-time error. It is very likely to cause a memory exception and can even interfere with the normal functioning of your operating system (especially under Windows 95, which is significantly less robust than Windows NT in this regard).

▶ Reliable use of these techniques demands that every message be processed. But when you stop your program or enter break mode, your Visual Basic code—including the code for your windows function—stops executing immediately. For this reason, I strongly recommend that, regardless of whether you use a third-party product or your own code, you implement your window functions in a separate ActiveX control or DLL.

These issues posed a significant dilemma for me in terms of how I would demonstrate these techniques in this book. You see, my staff just invested a significant effort in adding a Visual Basic-authored component that handles subclassing, private windows, hooks, and more to version 5 of our SpyWorks product. This product is intended to provide VB programmers with the safest and most efficient possible solution to handle this type of low-level windows functionality. It also includes some high-level solutions that are based on this technology and designed specifically to help with ActiveX control development. It is also intended to be educational, in that it includes complete source code. As such, a number of possibilities faced me.

I could have included a subset of the component with some source code. But the schedule for this book did not permit an adequate explanation of the code. I could have included the whole component, but frankly, I couldn't afford to. Our customers understand that what they pay for our software goes directly towards providing them with support and with new features and new products as time goes on. I could have avoided using the component and instead used the techniques shown in the VB documentation. But then I would have been guilty of misleading you by demonstrating code that I would never consider using in my own projects. I could have included a demo version of the component that is fully functional, as long as the component is being run from within Visual Basic itself.

I finally decided on the latter approach. The first customer that every SpyWorks component is designed for is our own technical staff. I personally implemented most of the features in this particular component during the course of my own ActiveX control development (and the writing of this book). I believe that no programmer should ever ship software they are not willing to use in their own applications. These are the components I personally use. So, I do hope you will find this component (and the others in SpyWorks) useful and cost effective. Along the way here I'll try to explain what each call to the component does so you can reproduce the component's functionality yourself if you choose. For those who are interested, SpyWorks includes the full source code for the components used in this chapter.

MESSAGING EXAMPLES

It is simply not possible to discuss the enormous array of advanced techniques that are made possible through the use of API and messaging techniques. All I can hope to do is offer a few representative examples. In this section you will see two of the most common examples for use with ActiveX controls. In the next section you will see how a number of these techniques can be combined to create advanced controls.

ADVANCED KEYSTROKE HANDLING

The dwCounter control illustrates a common problem relating to user-drawn controls. You have already seen that the ability to tab between constituent controls within a control is provided by Visual Basic. And you know that you can tab to a user-drawn control. But what if you want to be able to tab between elements in a user-drawn control?

This is the case with the dwCounter control shown in Figure 22.3. This control can be thought of as a digit counter, where each digit can be clicked or changed individually. The version of this control shown here is a simplified version of the dwCounter control from Desaware's ActiveX Gallimaufry.

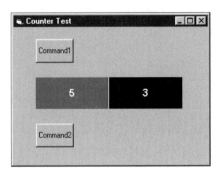

Figure 22.3: Counter control

The control treats each digit individually, meaning that it must be possible not only to set the focus to the control, but also to switch easily between the digits. This is representative of a more complex type of problem, where you have a control that contains a complex form and you want to be able to switch between the elements on the form and edit them individually, without using multiple constituent text boxes.

Listing 22.1 begins our exploration of how this control is implemented by showing the code that implements the control's properties. The listing also includes event and API declarations that will be described later.

Listing 22.1: Counter Control Code Relating to Properties

```
' dwCounter control
' Part of Desaware's ActiveX Gallimaufry
' Copyright Ö 1997 by Desaware Inc.  All Rights Reserved.

Option Explicit
'Default Property Values:
Const m_def_Digits = 2
Const m_def_Value = Ø
Const m_def_FocusColor = &HFF&    ' Red
'Property Variables:
Dim m_Digits As Integer
Dim m_Value As Long
Dim m_FocusColor As OLE_COLOR
```

Listing 22.1: Counter Control Code Relating to Properties (Continued)

```
'Event Declarations:
Event Click() 'MappingInfo=UserControl,UserControl,-1,Click
Event KeyDown(KeyCode As Integer, Shift As Integer) 'MappingInfo=UserControl, _
UserControl,-1,KeyDown
Event KeyPress(KeyAscii As Integer) 'MappingInfo=UserControl,UserControl _
,-1,KeyPress
Event KeyUp(KeyCode As Integer, Shift As Integer)
'MappingInfo=UserControl,UserControl,-1,KeyUp


' API stuff
Private Const WM_KEYDOWN = &H100
Private Const WM_KEYUP = &H101
' Not redeclaration of InvalidateRect from standard
Private Declare Function InvalidateRect Lib "user32" (ByVal hwnd As Long, _
ByVal lpRect As Long, ByVal bErase As Long) As Long


' Other values
Dim m_DigitWidth As Long
Dim m_FocusIsAt As Integer
Dim WithEvents PretranslateHook As dwPretranslate
Dim m_ClickedDigit As Integer


Private Sub UserControl_Initialize()
    m_ClickedDigit = 1
End Sub


'WARNING! DO NOT REMOVE OR MODIFY THE FOLLOWING COMMENTED LINES!
'MappingInfo=UserControl,UserControl,-1,BackColor
Public Property Get BackColor() As OLE_COLOR
    BackColor = UserControl.BackColor
End Property


Public Property Let BackColor(ByVal New_BackColor As OLE_COLOR)
    UserControl.BackColor() = New_BackColor
    PropertyChanged "BackColor"
End Property


'WARNING! DO NOT REMOVE OR MODIFY THE FOLLOWING COMMENTED LINES!
'MappingInfo=UserControl,UserControl,-1,BorderStyle
Public Property Get BorderStyle() As Integer
    BorderStyle = UserControl.BorderStyle
End Property


Public Property Let BorderStyle(ByVal New_BorderStyle As Integer)
```

Listing 22.1: Counter Control Code Relating to Properties (Continued)

```
    UserControl.BorderStyle() = New_BorderStyle
    PropertyChanged "BorderStyle"
End Property

'WARNING! DO NOT REMOVE OR MODIFY THE FOLLOWING COMMENTED LINES!
'MappingInfo=UserControl,UserControl,-1,Enabled
Public Property Get Enabled() As Boolean
    Enabled = UserControl.Enabled
End Property

Public Property Let Enabled(ByVal New_Enabled As Boolean)
    UserControl.Enabled() = New_Enabled
    PropertyChanged "Enabled"
End Property

'WARNING! DO NOT REMOVE OR MODIFY THE FOLLOWING COMMENTED LINES!
'MappingInfo=UserControl,UserControl,-1,Font
Public Property Get Font() As Font
    Set Font = UserControl.Font
End Property

Public Property Set Font(ByVal New_Font As Font)
    Set UserControl.Font = New_Font
    PropertyChanged "Font"
    UserControl.Refresh
End Property

'WARNING! DO NOT REMOVE OR MODIFY THE FOLLOWING COMMENTED LINES!
'MappingInfo=UserControl,UserControl,-1,ForeColor
Public Property Get ForeColor() As OLE_COLOR
    ForeColor = UserControl.ForeColor
End Property

Public Property Let ForeColor(ByVal New_ForeColor As OLE_COLOR)
    UserControl.ForeColor() = New_ForeColor
    PropertyChanged "ForeColor"
End Property

Public Property Get FocusColor() As OLE_COLOR
    FocusColor = m_FocusColor
End Property

Public Property Let FocusColor(ByVal New_FocusColor As OLE_COLOR)
    m_FocusColor = New_FocusColor
    PropertyChanged "FocusColor"
```

Listing 22.1: Counter Control Code Relating to Properties (Continued)

```
End Property


'WARNING! DO NOT REMOVE OR MODIFY THE FOLLOWING COMMENTED LINES!
'MappingInfo=UserControl,UserControl,-1,hWnd
Public Property Get hwnd() As Long
    hwnd = UserControl.hwnd
End Property


Public Property Get Digits() As Integer
    Digits = m_Digits
End Property


Public Property Let Digits(ByVal New_Digits As Integer)
    If New_Digits < 0 Or New_Digits > 10 Then
        Err.Raise 380
    End If
    If Ambient.UserMode Then
        ' In this preliminary edition, digits is design time only
        Err.Raise 382
    End If
    m_Digits = New_Digits
    PropertyChanged "Digits"
    SetSize
    UserControl.Refresh
End Property


Public Property Get Value() As Long
    Value = m_Value
End Property


Public Property Let Value(ByVal New_Value As Long)
    Dim MaxValue&
    ' Trick to get maximum value -
    ' example: 4 digits is 999
    MaxValue = Val(String$(m_Digits, "9"))
    If New_Value > MaxValue Then
        ' In this preliminary version, no auto digit setting
        Err.Raise 380
    End If
    m_Value = New_Value
    PropertyChanged "Value"
    UserControl.Refresh
End Property


'Initialize Properties for User Control
```

Listing 22.1: Counter Control Code Relating to Properties (Continued)

```
Private Sub UserControl_InitProperties()
   Set Font = Ambient.Font
   m_Digits = m_def_Digits
   m_Value = m_def_Value
   m_FocusColor = m_def_FocusColor
End Sub


'Load property values from storage
Private Sub UserControl_ReadProperties(PropBag As PropertyBag)
   UserControl.BackColor = PropBag.ReadProperty("BackColor", &H8000000F)
   UserControl.BorderStyle = PropBag.ReadProperty("BorderStyle", 0)
   UserControl.Enabled = PropBag.ReadProperty("Enabled", True)
   Set Font = PropBag.ReadProperty("Font", Ambient.Font)
   UserControl.ForeColor = PropBag.ReadProperty("ForeColor", &H80000012)
   m_FocusColor = PropBag.ReadProperty("FocusColor", m_def_FocusColor)
   m_Digits = PropBag.ReadProperty("Digits", m_def_Digits)
   m_Value = PropBag.ReadProperty("Value", m_def_Value)
End Sub


'Write property values to storage
Private Sub UserControl_WriteProperties(PropBag As PropertyBag)
   Call PropBag.WriteProperty("BackColor", UserControl.BackColor, &H8000000F)
   Call PropBag.WriteProperty("BorderStyle", UserControl.BorderStyle, 0)
   Call PropBag.WriteProperty("Enabled", UserControl.Enabled, True)
   Call PropBag.WriteProperty("Font", Font, Ambient.Font)
   Call PropBag.WriteProperty("ForeColor", UserControl.ForeColor, &H80000012)
   Call PropBag.WriteProperty("FocusColor", m_FocusColor, m_def_FocusColor)
   Call PropBag.WriteProperty("Digits", m_Digits, m_def_Digits)
   Call PropBag.WriteProperty("Value", m_Value, m_def_Value)
End Sub
```

Most of the properties are implemented using standard techniques and were, in fact, generated using the ActiveX Interface Wizard. There are three custom properties in this version of the control:

▶ FocusColor—the background color for a digit that has the focus. You can switch focus among the digits using the keypad or the tab key.

▶ Digits—the number of digits to display.

▶ Value—the current numeric value to display.

Both the Digits and Value property have simple range checking to make sure that the properties are valid. They raise error 380 (Invalid Property Value)

if they are not. The Digits property procedure and the control's Resize event
also call the Following function to make sure the control is large enough to display the digits for the currently selected font:

```
' Sets the minimum control size
Private Sub SetSize()
    Dim minwidth&
    Dim useheight&
    ' Calculate the width of each digit
    m_DigitWidth = ScaleWidth / Digits
    minwidth = Digits * TextWidth("W")
    useheight = TextHeight("1")
    If ScaleWidth < minwidth Or ScaleHeight < useheight Then
        ' Control is too small
        If ScaleHeight > useheight Then useheight = ScaleHeight
        UserControl.Size ScaleWidth, useheight
        Exit Sub
    End If
End Sub


Private Sub UserControl_Resize()
    SetSize
End Sub
```

The control has an internal variable named m_FocusIsAt that indicates the
focus status of the control. If the control does not have the focus, the variable
is set to 0. If the control does have the focus, the variable is set to the digit in
the control (starting from 1) that has the focus. The control's EnterFocus and
ExitFocus events control the initial setting of the variable when the control receives the focus. They set it to 0 when the control loses the focus as follows:

```
Private Sub UserControl_EnterFocus()
    m_FocusIsAt = m_ClickedDigit
    UserControl.Refresh
End Sub

Private Sub UserControl_ExitFocus()
    m_FocusIsAt = 0
    m_ClickedDigit = 1    ' Reset to first digit
    UserControl.Refresh
End Sub

Private Sub UserControl_MouseDown(Button As Integer, Shift As Integer, X As
Single, Y As Single)
    m_ClickedDigit = Int(X / m_DigitWidth) + 1
    If m_FocusIsAt > 0 Then ' Change now if already have focus
```

```
      m_FocusIsAt = m_ClickedDigit
      UserControl.Refresh
   End If
End Sub
```

The m_ClickedDigit variable is used to keep track of which digit was clicked in cases where the focus is set to the control due to a mouse click. This digit is given the focus immediately if the control already has the focus, or during the EnterFocus event if the control is about to gain the focus due to the click.

The control's appearance is defined by the Paint event, which is shown here:

```
' This preliminary version has no sophisticated
' border setting
Private Sub UserControl_Paint()
    Dim ypos&
    Dim txt$, fmt$
    Dim charpos%
    Dim thischar$
    If Not Ambient.UserMode Then
        ' Design time shows control name
        txt$ = Ambient.DisplayName
        CurrentY = (ScaleHeight - TextHeight(txt)) / 2
        CurrentX = (ScaleWidth - TextWidth(txt)) / 2
        If CurrentX < 0 Then CurrentX = 0
        Print txt
        Exit Sub
    End If
    ypos = (ScaleHeight - TextHeight("1")) / 2
    fmt$ = String$(m_Digits, "0")
    txt$ = Format$(m_Value, fmt$)
    For charpos = 1 To m_Digits
        If charpos = m_FocusIsAt Then
            UserControl.Line ((charpos - 1) * m_DigitWidth, 0)-(charpos _
                * m_DigitWidth, ScaleHeight), m_FocusColor, BF
        End If
        thischar$ = Mid$(txt$, charpos, 1)
        CurrentX = m_DigitWidth * (charpos - 1) + (m_DigitWidth _
        - TextWidth(thischar)) / 2
        CurrentY = ypos
        UserControl.Print thischar
    Next charpos
    For charpos = 1 To m_Digits - 1
        UserControl.Line (m_DigitWidth * charpos, 0)-(m_DigitWidth * _
        charpos, ScaleHeight)
    Next charpos
End Sub
```

The appearance of the control at design time differs radically from that at runtime. At design time, the control simply displays the Ambient DisplayName property in the center of the control using the currently selected font. The DisplayName is the name the developer assigned to the control.

At runtime, the routine first obtains a string where each character represents a digit in the control. A format string is defined with the correct length. This string is used with the VB Format function to load a string with the correct number of leading zeros.

The position of each digit is calculated separately so it will appear in the center of the area allocated for that digit. If the digit currently has the focus, the background color for that digit is first filled with the color defined by the FocusColor property. Finally, a line is drawn between the digits. A later version of this control will have a more sophisticated look but, for now, this approach is adequate.

The last problem we face with this control is to provide a way for the user to switch focus between the digits within the control. A first cut at this is to use the arrow keys for this purpose. The right and down arrow keys are defined as switching to the next digit. The left and up keys switch to the previous digit. This is accomplished using the following code:

```
Private Sub UserControl_KeyDown(KeyCode As Integer, Shift As Integer)
    RaiseEvent KeyDown(KeyCode, Shift)
    If KeyCode = vbKeyRight Or KeyCode = vbKeyDown Then
        If m_FocusIsAt < m_Digits Then
            m_FocusIsAt = m_FocusIsAt + 1
            UserControl.Refresh
            Exit Sub
        End If
    End If
    If KeyCode = vbKeyLeft Or KeyCode = vbKeyUp Then
        If m_FocusIsAt > 1 Then
            m_FocusIsAt = m_FocusIsAt - 1
            UserControl.Refresh
            Exit Sub
        End If
    End If
End Sub
Private Sub UserControl_KeyUp(KeyCode As Integer, Shift As Integer)
    RaiseEvent KeyUp(KeyCode, Shift)
End Sub
```

The first thing the UserControl_KeyDown event does is raise the control's KeyDown event. This allows the developer to override the keystroke. Next, the routine looks for the arrow keys. If it finds one, it changes the m_FocusIsAt variable and redraws the control. The control currently does not allow you to use the arrow keys to change the focus to another control.

The KeyPress event shown below demonstrates how typing a number when a digit has the focus can change the value of that digit. A developer could easily disable this behavior by setting the KeyAscii parameter to 0 during the control's KeyPress event. This is possible because the control's KeyPress event is raised before the KeyAscii value is processed by this routine.

```
Private Sub UserControl_KeyPress(KeyAscii As Integer)
    Dim fmt$, txt$
    RaiseEvent KeyPress(KeyAscii)
    If KeyAscii >= vbKey0 And KeyAscii <= vbKey9 Then
        fmt$ = String$(m_Digits, "0")
        txt$ = Format$(m_Value, fmt$)
        Mid$(txt$, m_FocusIsAt, 1) = Chr$(KeyAscii)
        Value = txt$
    End If

End Sub
```

The one problem with the implementation so far is that you cannot use the tab key to switch focus between the digits of the control. This is because the tab key is intercepted by the container so it can tab between controls. Your control's KeyDown and KeyUp events never see it (even if the KeyPreview property for the control is set to True).

The solution for this problem is to intercept the tab key before it gets to the container. This is accomplished using a WH_GETMESSAGE hook. The dwspyvb.dll component contains an object called dwPretranslate, which uses this hook internally to implement a function similar to the PreTranslateMessage method of the Visual C++ MFC control class. This allows you to see every message before the application processes it. The dwPretranslate object uses internal filtering to retrieve messages destined only for the window that you specify, in this case, the control's window. This reduces the control's overhead considerably. Since Pre-translate functionality is typically used for keyboard messages, an additional filter in this control lets you restrict it to intercepting the WM_KEYDOWN and WM_KEYUP messages.

The PretranslateHook variable is initialized in the following code:

```
Private Sub UserControl_Show()
    If Ambient.UserMode And PretranslateHook Is Nothing Then
        ' Not yet initialized
        Set PretranslateHook = New dwPretranslate
```

```
            PretranslateHook.KeyMessagesOnly = True
            PretranslateHook.hwnd = UserControl.hwnd
        End If
    End Sub
```

Since there is no need for pre-translation at design time, the PretranslateHook object is only set at runtime. The object raises a single event called PreTranslate-Message which is shown below:

```
Private Sub PretranslateHook_PreTranslateMessage(ByVal hwnd As Long, _
Msg As Long, wParam As Long, lParam As Long, nodef As Boolean)
    Static UpPending As Boolean
    Dim IsShiftPressed As Boolean

    IsShiftPressed = GetKeyState(vbKeyShift) < 0
    ' Watch for tab key
    If Msg = WM_KEYDOWN And wParam = vbKeyTab Then
        If m_FocusIsAt < m_Digits And Not IsShiftPressed Then
            m_FocusIsAt = m_FocusIsAt + 1
            Call InvalidateRect(UserControl.hwnd, 0, True)
            UpPending = True
            Msg = 0
            nodef = True
        End If
        If m_FocusIsAt > 1 And IsShiftPressed Then
            m_FocusIsAt = m_FocusIsAt - 1
            Call InvalidateRect(UserControl.hwnd, 0, True)
            UpPending = True
            Msg = 0
            nodef = True
        End If
        Exit Sub
    End If
    If Msg = WM_KEYUP And wParam = vbKeyTab And UpPending Then
        ' Kill the pending keyup tab
        Msg = 0
        nodef = True
        UpPending = False
    End If
End Sub
```

This event includes the standard message parameters. The Msg, wParam, lParam, and nodef parameters are passed by reference, meaning that the functions can change their values before they are processed by the application. If you set the nodef parameter to True, you prevent subsequent controls that have placed windows hooks from intercepting the message.

The routine first checks the current state of the shift key, which allows it to determine in which direction the focus is changing. The current implementation always sets the focus to the first digit when the control receives the focus, so performing a shift tab into the control will go to the first digit instead of the last. It is possible to change this behavior, but it is a great deal of trouble since you must figure out which control previously had the focus. However, this is a minor limitation, since few people use the shift-tab combination to tab backward.

When a tab key arrives, the control determines whether a focus change is necessary. If so, it changes the value of the m_FocusIsAt variable.

It then sets the UpPending static variable to True. This is a static variable that belongs to the event procedure. It is used when the WM_KEYUP message arrives indicating that the tab key has been released. You see, the event procedure throws away the WM_KEYDOWN message, and Windows might become confused if it sees the tab key being released without its first being pressed. So this variable is set to True before the tab key press message is discarded as a signal to throw away the release message as well.

The message is thrown away by setting the Msg value to 0. The null message is ignored by all windows. The nodef parameter is also set to True to prevent other hooks from seeing the message as well.

The InvalidateRect API function is used to update the control display. Why not use the UserControl Refresh method? Because this event is occurring during a Windows message hook, which is a dangerous time for many operations. It is always a good idea to keep hook functions as simple as possible and avoid performing complex operations that might confuse the system if they occur in the middle of a message dispatch operation. A refresh operation, with all of the code associated in the Paint event, is a vast unknown. It may work safely, but it's a risk. The InvalidateRect API is a fast call that simply notifies Windows that the entire area of the control window is now invalid and needs to be redrawn. Windows will itself post a WM_PAINT message for the window into the application's message queue, which in turn will trigger the control's Paint event.

One thing this control does not do is properly set the focus for a digit when you click on the control. This is left as an exercise for the reader. (Hint: use the UserControl's MouseDown event.)

MANAGING UPDATE AREAS

One of the limitations of the Visual Basic model of ActiveX control development with regard to user-drawn controls relates to the Paint event. The problem is that when this event occurs, you must redraw the entire control. This can be a very time-consuming operation for a complex control, and much of that time may be wasted in cases where the Paint event is triggered and only a small portion of the control needs to be redrawn. This often happens when dragging windows over each other or when a dialog box or message box is hidden.

If your control's drawing routine can be designed to only update those parts of the window that have changed, you might be able to gain a substantial performance benefit. You can determine the update area of a window using subclassing by calling the GetUpdateRect API function during the WM_PAINT message for the window. Listing 22.2 shows a control that does not use this technique to update itself. Instead, it subclasses its container so the container can determine its update area.

Listing 22.2: The PaintUpdate Control Code

```
' Guide to the Perplexed
' Paint update example
' Copyright Ö 1997 by Desaware Inc. All Rights Reserved

Option Explicit

Private Type RECT
        Left As Long
        Top As Long
        Right As Long
        Bottom As Long
End Type

Private Declare Function GetUpdateRect Lib "user32" (ByVal hwnd As Long, _
lpRect As RECT, ByVal bErase As Long) As Long

Private Const WM_PAINT = &HF

Dim m_UpdateRect As RECT

Dim WithEvents UpdateHook As dwSubClass

Private Sub UpdateHook_WndMessage(ByVal hwnd As Long, Msg As Long, wp As _
Long, lp As Long, retval As Long, nodef As Boolean)
    Call GetUpdateRect(Extender.Parent.hwnd, m_UpdateRect, False)
End Sub

Private Sub UserControl_ReadProperties(PropBag As PropertyBag)
    If Ambient.UserMode Then
        Set UpdateHook = New dwSubClass
        UpdateHook.AddMessage WM_PAINT
```

Listing 22.2: The PaintUpdate Control Code (Continued)

```
        UpdateHook.HwndParam = Extender.Parent.hwnd
    End If
End Sub

Private Sub UserControl_Resize()
    UserControl.Size UserControl.Picture.Width, UserControl.Picture.Height
End Sub

Private Sub UserControl_Terminate()
    Set UpdateHook = Nothing
End Sub

Public Property Get UpdateLeft() As Long
    UpdateLeft = m_UpdateRect.Left * Screen.TwipsPerPixelX
End Property

Public Property Get UpdateTop() As Long
    UpdateTop = m_UpdateRect.Top * Screen.TwipsPerPixelY
End Property

Public Property Get UpdateRight() As Long
    UpdateRight = m_UpdateRect.Right * Screen.TwipsPerPixelX
End Property

Public Property Get UpdateBottom() As Long
    UpdateBottom = m_UpdateRect.Bottom * Screen.TwipsPerPixelY
End Property
```

The dwSubClass object is part of the dwspyvb.dll component. The UpdateHook variable is initialized during the ReadProperties event, by which time the Extender property is valid. The HwndParam property of the UpdateHook object sets the window to be subclassed, in this case using the window handle of the container. The control could detect its own update area by using the hWnd property of the UserControl object instead.

The AddMessage method sets the WM_PAINT message as the only message to be detected. The object performs message filtering at a low level to provide the best possible performance. This also eliminates the need to check for messages during the object's WndMessage event. The WM_PAINT message is the only one that will arrive.

During the WndMessage event, the update rectangle is retrieved using the GetUpdateRect function and stored in the m_UpdateRect variable. The fields of this variable can be read using the UpdateLeft, UpdateTop, UpdateRight, and UpdateBottom properties.

The UpdateTest program demonstrates this by displaying the update coordinates in a Label control on the frmUpdate form. Try dragging a window over part of the form to see how this works.

A TALE OF FOUR LISTBOXES

We will conclude both our discussion of advanced controls, and our discussion of controls in general, with a look at four different approaches towards implementing a custom Listbox control. These will include:

- ▶ A constituent-based control

- ▶ A user-drawn control

- ▶ A better user-drawn control

- ▶ A custom window-based control

Before beginning, I should stress that none of these controls are intended as examples of complete or robust controls. In most cases only a few properties and events are implemented—just enough to illustrate the techniques associated with the particular approach. They have undergone minimal testing and have little or no error checking.

The ListCtls.vbg project group contains two projects. ListCtls.vbp contains the four controls that demonstrate the approaches listed above. ListTest.vbp contains four forms that demonstrate some of the characteristics of the four controls.

A CONSTITUENT-BASED CONTROL

Listing 22.3 contains the code for the constituent control-based example. This control illustrates the main limitation of this approach—that it is impossible for a developer using your control to set the design-time properties of a constituent control. This is because your control is in run mode even during the container's design time. The MultiSelect property is an example of a property that cannot be changed at runtime. The ListCtlA supports the MultiSelect property by including two separate list controls, one that is set to multi-select mode, the other to single-select.

Listing 22.3: Listing for Control ListCtlA.ctl

```
' Constituent control based list example
' Copyright (c) 1997, by Desaware Inc. All Rights Reserved

Option Explicit
'Event Declarations:
Event Click()
Event DblClick()
Event KEYDOWN(KeyCode As Integer, Shift As Integer)
Event KeyPress(KeyAscii As Integer)
Event KEYUP(KeyCode As Integer, Shift As Integer)
Event MouseDown(Button As Integer, Shift As Integer, x As Single, Y As Single)
Event MouseMove(Button As Integer, Shift As Integer, x As Single, Y As Single)
Event MouseUp(Button As Integer, Shift As Integer, x As Single, Y As Single)

Dim CurrentListBox As ListBox
Dim m_MultiSelect As Boolean

Public Property Get MultiSelect() As Boolean
    MultiSelect = m_MultiSelect
End Property


Public Property Get BackColor() As OLE_COLOR
    BackColor = CurrentListBox.BackColor
End Property

Public Property Let BackColor(ByVal New_BackColor As OLE_COLOR)
    List1.BackColor = New_BackColor
    List2.BackColor = New_BackColor
    PropertyChanged "BackColor"
End Property

Public Property Get ForeColor() As OLE_COLOR
    ForeColor = CurrentListBox.ForeColor
End Property

Public Property Let ForeColor(ByVal New_ForeColor As OLE_COLOR)
    List1.ForeColor = New_ForeColor
    List2.ForeColor = New_ForeColor
    PropertyChanged "ForeColor"
End Property

Public Property Get Enabled() As Boolean
    Enabled = CurrentListBox.Enabled
```

Listing 22.3: Listing for Control ListCtlA.ctl (Continued)

```
End Property

Public Property Let Enabled(ByVal New_Enabled As Boolean)
    List1.Enabled = New_Enabled
    List2.Enabled = New_Enabled
    PropertyChanged "Enabled"
End Property

Public Property Get Font() As Font
    Set Font = CurrentListBox.Font
End Property

Public Property Set Font(ByVal New_Font As Font)
    Set List1.Font = New_Font
    Set List2.Font = New_Font
    PropertyChanged "Font"
End Property

Public Sub Refresh()
    CurrentListBox.Refresh
End Sub

Private Sub List1_Click()
    RaiseEvent Click
End Sub

Private Sub List2_Click()
    RaiseEvent Click
End Sub


Private Sub List1_DblClick()
    RaiseEvent DblClick
End Sub

Private Sub List2_DblClick()
    RaiseEvent DblClick
End Sub

Private Sub List1_KeyDown(KeyCode As Integer, Shift As Integer)
    RaiseEvent KEYDOWN(KeyCode, Shift)
End Sub

Private Sub List2_KeyDown(KeyCode As Integer, Shift As Integer)
    RaiseEvent KEYDOWN(KeyCode, Shift)
```

Listing 22.3: Listing for Control ListCtlA.ctl (Continued)

```
End Sub

Private Sub List1_KeyPress(KeyAscii As Integer)
   RaiseEvent KeyPress(KeyAscii)
End Sub

Private Sub List2_KeyPress(KeyAscii As Integer)
   RaiseEvent KeyPress(KeyAscii)
End Sub

Private Sub List1_KeyUp(KeyCode As Integer, Shift As Integer)
   RaiseEvent KEYUP(KeyCode, Shift)
End Sub

Private Sub List2_KeyUp(KeyCode As Integer, Shift As Integer)
   RaiseEvent KEYUP(KeyCode, Shift)
End Sub

Private Sub List1_MouseDown(Button As Integer, Shift As Integer, x As Single, _
                        Y As Single)
   RaiseEvent MouseDown(Button, Shift, x, Y)
End Sub

Private Sub List2_MouseDown(Button As Integer, Shift As Integer, x As Single, _
                        Y As Single)
   RaiseEvent MouseDown(Button, Shift, x, Y)
End Sub

Private Sub List1_MouseMove(Button As Integer, Shift As Integer, x As Single, _
                        Y As Single)
   RaiseEvent MouseMove(Button, Shift, x, Y)
End Sub

Private Sub List2_MouseMove(Button As Integer, Shift As Integer, x As Single, _
                        Y As Single)
   RaiseEvent MouseMove(Button, Shift, x, Y)
End Sub

Private Sub List1_MouseUp(Button As Integer, Shift As Integer, x As Single, _
                        Y As Single)
   RaiseEvent MouseUp(Button, Shift, x, Y)
End Sub

Private Sub List2_MouseUp(Button As Integer, Shift As Integer, x As Single, _
                        Y As Single)
```

Listing 22.3: Listing for Control ListCtlA.ctl (Continued)

```
      RaiseEvent MouseUp(Button, Shift, x, Y)
End Sub

Public Sub AddItem(item As String, Optional Index As Variant)
   CurrentListBox.AddItem item, Index
End Sub

Public Sub Clear()
   CurrentListBox.Clear
End Sub


Public Property Get hwnd() As Long
   hwnd = CurrentListBox.hwnd
End Property

Public Property Get ItemData(ByVal ItemIndex As Long) As Long
   ItemData = CurrentListBox.ItemData(ItemIndex)
End Property

Public Property Let ItemData(ByVal ItemIndex As Long, ByVal New_ItemData _
                     As Long)
   CurrentListBox.ItemData(ItemIndex) = New_ItemData
   PropertyChanged "ItemData"
End Property

Public Property Get List(ByVal ItemIndex As Long) As String
   List = CurrentListBox.List(ItemIndex)
End Property

Public Property Let List(ByVal ItemIndex As Long, ByVal New_List As String)
   CurrentListBox.List(ItemIndex) = New_List
   PropertyChanged "List"
End Property

Public Property Get ListCount() As Integer
   ListCount = CurrentListBox.ListCount
End Property

Public Property Get ListIndex() As Integer
   ListIndex = CurrentListBox.ListIndex
End Property

Public Property Let ListIndex(ByVal New_ListIndex As Integer)
   CurrentListBox.ListIndex = New_ListIndex
```

Listing 22.3: Listing for Control ListCtlA.ctl (Continued)

```
    PropertyChanged "ListIndex"
End Property


Public Property Get MouseIcon() As Picture
    Set MouseIcon = CurrentListBox.MouseIcon
End Property


Public Property Set MouseIcon(ByVal New_MouseIcon As Picture)
    Set List1.MouseIcon = New_MouseIcon
    Set List2.MouseIcon = New_MouseIcon
    PropertyChanged "MouseIcon"
End Property


Public Property Get NewIndex() As Integer
    NewIndex = CurrentListBox.NewIndex
End Property


Public Sub RemoveItem(Index As Integer)
    CurrentListBox.RemoveItem Index
End Sub


Public Property Get Selected(ByVal ItemIndex As Long) As Boolean
    If CurrentListBox Is List2 Then
        Selected = CurrentListBox.Selected(ItemIndex)
    Else
        ListError 1000
    End If
End Property


Public Property Let Selected(ByVal ItemIndex As Long, ByVal New_Selected _
As Boolean)
    If CurrentListBox Is List2 Then
        CurrentListBox.Selected(ItemIndex) = New_Selected
        PropertyChanged "Selected"
    Else
        ListError 1000
    End If
End Property



Private Sub UserControl_InitProperties()
    Set CurrentListBox = List1
End Sub

'Load property values from storage
```

Listing 22.3: Listing for Control ListCtlA.ctl (Continued)

```
Private Sub UserControl_ReadProperties(PropBag As PropertyBag)
   m_MultiSelect = PropBag.ReadProperty("MultiSelect", False)
   If m_MultiSelect Then
      Set CurrentListBox = List2
      List1.Visible = False
      List2.Visible = True
   Else
      Set CurrentListBox = List1
      List2.Visible = False
      List1.Visible = True
   End If
   BackColor = PropBag.ReadProperty("BackColor", &H80000005)
   ForeColor = PropBag.ReadProperty("ForeColor", &H80000008)
   Enabled = PropBag.ReadProperty("Enabled", True)
   Set CurrentListBox.Font = PropBag.ReadProperty("Font")
   Set CurrentListBox.MouseIcon = PropBag.ReadProperty("MouseIcon", Nothing)
End Sub


'Write property values to storage
Private Sub UserControl_WriteProperties(PropBag As PropertyBag)
   Call PropBag.WriteProperty("MultiSelect", m_MultiSelect, False)
   Call PropBag.WriteProperty("BackColor", CurrentListBox.BackColor, &H80000005)
   Call PropBag.WriteProperty("ForeColor", CurrentListBox.ForeColor, &H80000008)
   Call PropBag.WriteProperty("Enabled", CurrentListBox.Enabled, True)
   Call PropBag.WriteProperty("Font", CurrentListBox.Font)
   Call PropBag.WriteProperty("MouseIcon", CurrentListBox.MouseIcon, Nothing)
End Sub
```

As you can see, most of the standard properties and events are implemented in the same manner that we have seen throughout this book.

In this implementation, the properties are mapped to both controls. It might be more efficient to use variables to hold the property values and only set the constituent properties for the control that is currently visible. However, this would also require additional code to load all of the constituent control's properties when you switch from one control to the other.

A variable called CurrentListBox serves as a handy reference to the constituent control that is in use. It is set during both the ReadProperties event and the Property Let procedure for the MultiSelect property as shown below.

```
Public Property Let MultiSelect(ByVal vNewValue As Boolean)
   If UserControl.Ambient.UserMode Then
      ' Can't change list type at runtime
```

```
        SetNotSupportedAtRuntime
    End If
    m_MultiSelect = vNewValue
    If m_MultiSelect Then
        Set CurrentListBox = List2
        List1.Visible = False
        List2.Visible = True
    Else
        Set CurrentListBox = List1
        List1.Visible = True
        List2.Visible = False
    End If


    PropertyChanged "MultiSelect"
End Property
```

Note that it is possible using this approach to allow the user to switch between multiple-select and single-select mode at the container's runtime as well, though that functionality is not implemented here. If you decide to allow that feature, you would also have to decide whether the current contents of the listbox should be copied from one constituent control to the other during the switch. This example raises an error in this case to remain compatible with the standard listbox.

The Resize event positions both listboxes so they fill the client area of your control as shown here in the UserControl_Resize event:

```
Private Sub UserControl_Resize()
    List1.Move 0, 0, ScaleWidth - Screen.TwipsPerPixelX, _
    ScaleHeight - Screen.TwipsPerPixelY
    List2.Move 0, 0, ScaleWidth - Screen.TwipsPerPixelX, _
    ScaleHeight - Screen.TwipsPerPixelY
End Sub
```

What if you wanted to handle the constituent control's Appearance property as well? This is another design-time-only property, so you would need four separate constituent list controls in order to support it. The Integral property would bring you to eight controls. Add the Sorted property, and you would be up to 16 constituent controls...

As you see, this approach can verge on the ridiculous very quickly. The overhead of supporting 17 windows for each control (the 16 listboxes plus the UserControl object) is horrendous. Any programmer who chooses this approach should (hopefully) quit the profession in embarrassment.

This is not to say that you should never use the constituent approach. Just that it is impractical if you require that your developer be able to change more than one design-time property (two at the most).

A USER-DRAWN CONTROL

Consider, for a moment, the standard listbox window class implemented by Windows. This is the class used by Visual Basic to implement its standard listbox control. How is the class itself implemented?

When a listbox window is created, the system first creates a window (which is just like any other window in the system). It assigns the class window function for the listbox class to the window. This window function receives incoming messages sent or posted to the window. When a paint message arrives, the code draws the listbox using API functions. Mouse or keyboard messages perform various selection and scrolling operations. Control messages can be sent to the window in order to perform tasks such as adding and deleting strings. The listbox is able to send messages to its parent window to notify it when certain events occur, such as a selection change. The characteristics of the listbox, such as whether it is sorted, or if it is a single- or multiple-selection listbox, are determined by the style characteristics of the window. Every window has two 32-bit style variables. Some of the bits in these variables are standardized, such as whether the window has a border. Others depend on the type of window.

We'll revisit this subject in slightly more detail later. For now, consider this: A Visual Basic-authored ActiveX control receives events. It can define internal variables. It can expose methods and properties to the outside world. It can paint whatever it chooses into its control window. The mechanism might not be the same as a window class defined by the system, but the effect is the same.

A listbox window is a window with code that processes incoming messages. An ActiveX control is a window with code that processes incoming messages. Obviously, you could implement your own list control from scratch, duplicating all or part of the functionality of a standard listbox window. If the thought of doing this seems a bit intimidating, it's probably because the task is quite intimidating. But it can be done, and with Visual Basic's new support for native code compilation, you can obtain excellent performance from this approach.

And keep in mind one important fact: If you do choose this approach, you are not limited to the features or characteristics of either the standard Visual Basic Listbox control or the Listbox window class. Your List control could include bitmaps, or even audio or video clips.

The ListCtlB example demonstrates this approach. In this case the control is designed to mimic the appearance and much of the behavior of the standard listbox, just to show it can be done. Once again, let me stress that what you see here is an experimental control designed purely for educational purposes. It is based on code I have been using in conference and training sessions over the past few years to demonstrate some of the possibilities that Visual Basic offers. It has gradually evolved over that time, and this is its first incarnation as an ActiveX control. Note that the multiple-selection capability, as it is implemented here, is a hack that was added to demonstrate the possibility of supporting both single and multiple selection in such a control. The multiple-selection behavior does not duplicate that of a standard listbox, nor is it a demonstration of good design. A proper redesign and implementation is a task for some future version.

The declarations and variables for the ListCtlB control are shown below. As you can see, this control takes advantages of a number of Win32 API functions.

```
' User drawn list example
' Copyright (c) 1997, by Desaware Inc. All Rights Reserved
Option Explicit

Private Type RECT    '16 Bytes
    left As Long
    top As Long
    right As Long
    bottom As Long
End Type

Private Type POINTAPI  '8 Bytes - Synonymous with LONG
    x As Long
    Y As Long
End Type

Private Declare Function DrawFocusRect& Lib "user32" (ByVal hdc As Long, _
lpRect As RECT)
Private Declare Function DrawText& Lib "user32" Alias "DrawTextA" (ByVal hdc _
As Long, ByVal lpStr As String, ByVal nCount As Long, lpRect As RECT, ByVal _
wFormat As Long)
Private Declare Function GetSysColor& Lib "user32" (ByVal nIndex As Long)
Private Declare Function InflateRect& Lib "user32" (lpRect As RECT, ByVal x _
As Long, ByVal Y As Long)
Private Declare Function ScrollWindowByNum& Lib "user32" Alias "ScrollWindow" _
(ByVal hwnd As Long, ByVal XAmount As Long, ByVal YAmount As Long, lpRect As _
RECT, ByVal lpClipRect As Long)
Private Declare Function GetCursorPos& Lib "user32" (lpPoint As POINTAPI)
Private Declare Function SetCursorPos& Lib "user32" (ByVal x As Long, ByVal Y _
As Long)
```

```
Private Declare Function SetCapture& Lib "user32" (ByVal hwnd As Long)
Private Declare Function ReleaseCapture& Lib "user32" ()
Private Declare Function GetFocus Lib "user32" () As Long
Private Declare Function SetTextColor& Lib "gdi32" (ByVal hdc As Long, _
ByVal crColor As Long)
Private Declare Function SelectObject Lib "gdi32" (ByVal hdc As Long, ByVal _
hObject As Long) As Long


Private CurrentTop As Long
Private TotalLines As Long
Private PixelsPerLine As Integer
Private Selected() As Long        ' The number of the selected line
Private HasFocus As Long
Private highlight As Long
Private HighlightText As Long
' Note, -1,-1 on these means to draw it all
Private LowDrawRange As Long      ' Lowest that needs drawing
Private HighDrawRange As Long     ' Highest that needs drawing
Private ClickLine As Long         ' Line on which click is detected
Private InContext As Integer      ' Prevent reentrant mousemove events
Private Light3D As Long           ' 3D highlight
Private Dark3D As Long            ' 3D shadow
Private DarkShadow As Long        ' 3D dark shadow
Private FixNextScroll As Long


Private Const KEYDOWN = 40
Private Const KEYUP = 38
Private Const COLOR_HIGHLIGHT = 13
Private Const COLOR_HIGHLIGHTTEXT = 14
Private Const COLOR_BTNSHADOW = 16
Private Const COLOR_BTNHIGHLIGHT = 20
Private Const COLOR_3DDKSHADOW = 21
Private m_BorderStyle As Integer  ' 1 = Single, 2 = 3D, 0 = None
Private m_MultiSelect As Boolean  ' Multiple selection dialog


Private Const DT_LEFT = &H0
Private Const DT_SINGLELINE = &H20
Private Const DT_NOPREFIX = &H800
```

The control has a number of internal variables that hold precalculated values such as the number of pixels per line. The control has a single constituent scroll bar to allow the listbox to scroll.

This List control does not actually hold string data. Instead, it requests the string data for each item from the container using the GetText event. This approach does require additional work from the container, but it can be extremely efficient in that it does not require that you preload the listbox with data ahead of time. This can be ideal for database applications, where you would only need to retrieve those few items visible when the control is first displayed. It also makes it easy to handle very large numbers of entries efficiently.

The code for the properties and methods for the control is shown below. As you can see, it is possible to set both the BorderStyle and MultiSelect properties at the container's design time and runtime. This is because these characteristics impact the control's behavior and appearance, and these are implemented entirely in the control's code.

```
'--------------------------------------------------------
'
'  Control Public Methods and Events
'
Event GetText(ByVal location As Long, ListBoxString As String)
Event Click()
Event DblClick()

Public Property Get BorderStyle() As dwBorderStyle
   BorderStyle = m_BorderStyle
End Property

Public Property Let BorderStyle(vNewBorder As dwBorderStyle)
   If vNewBorder < 0 Or vNewBorder > 2 Then
      ListError 380
   End If
   m_BorderStyle = vNewBorder
   PropertyChanged "BorderStyle"
   CalculateValues
   PositionScrollBar
   lbInvalidateRange
   Refresh
End Property

Public Property Get MultiSelect() As Boolean
   MultiSelect = m_MultiSelect
End Property

Public Property Let MultiSelect(ByVal vNewValue As Boolean)
   m_MultiSelect = vNewValue
   ReDim Preserve Selected(0)
   lbInvalidateRange
   Refresh
   PropertyChanged "MultiSelect"
End Property
```

```
Public Property Get BackColor() As OLE_COLOR
    BackColor = UserControl.BackColor
End Property

Public Property Let BackColor(vNewColor As OLE_COLOR)
    UserControl.BackColor = vNewColor
    PropertyChanged "BackColor"
End Property

Public Property Get Font() As Font
    Set Font = UserControl.Font
End Property

Public Property Set Font(ByVal vNewValue As Font)
    Set UserControl.Font = vNewValue
    PropertyChanged "Font"
    CalculateValues
    lbInvalidateRange
    Refresh
End Property
```

The UserControl_Initialize event initializes the internal listbox variables to their default values. The listbox colors are retrieved at this time based on the standard system colors. You can add new properties to override their values if you wish.

Those user events that control the operation of the listbox call a set of private functions with the LB prefix. This arrangement is intended to improve the readability and modularity of the code. Some events, such as the Resize event, require that some of the listbox variables be recalculated. One of the important tasks you must perform with any user-drawn control is to check the impact each variable has on the appearance of the control and handle it correctly. This control does demonstrate a good approach for handling this, where the calculations are isolated into a few routines that can be called as necessary.

```
'---------------------------------------------------------
'
'  UserControl Methods and Events
'


Private Sub UserControl_Initialize()
    CurrentTop = 0
    LowDrawRange = -1
    HighDrawRange = -1
```

```
    m_BorderStyle = dw3d
    UserControl.BackColor = &HFFFFFF
    ReDim Selected(0)
    Selected(0) = -1
    FixNextScroll = -1
    PixelsPerLine = TextHeight("W") + 1
    highlight = GetSysColor(COLOR_HIGHLIGHT)
    HighlightText = GetSysColor(COLOR_HIGHLIGHTTEXT)
    Light3D = GetSysColor(COLOR_BTNHIGHLIGHT)
    Dark3D = GetSysColor(COLOR_BTNSHADOW)
    DarkShadow = GetSysColor(COLOR_3DDKSHADOW)
End Sub


Private Sub UserControl_Click()
    RaiseEvent Click
End Sub


Private Sub UserControl_DblClick()
    RaiseEvent DblClick
End Sub


Private Sub UserControl_MouseDown(Button As Integer, Shift As Integer, x _
As Single, Y As Single)
    LBMouseDown x, Y
End Sub


Private Sub UserControl_MouseMove(Button As Integer, Shift As Integer, x _
As Single, Y As Single)
    LBMouseMove Button, x, Y
End Sub


Private Sub UserControl_MouseUp(Button As Integer, Shift As Integer, x _
As Single, Y As Single)
    LBMouseUp
End Sub


Private Sub UserControl_Paint()
    LBDraw
End Sub


Private Sub UserControl_Resize()
    CalculateValues
    PositionScrollBar
    lbInvalidateRange
End Sub


Private Sub UserControl_EnterFocus()
```

```
        LBGotFocus
    End Sub

    Private Sub UserControl_ExitFocus()
        LBLostFocus
    End Sub

    Private Sub UserControl_ReadProperties(PropBag As PropertyBag)
        m_BorderStyle = PropBag.ReadProperty("BorderStyle", dw3d)
        m_MultiSelect = PropBag.ReadProperty("MultiSelect", False)
        UserControl.BackColor = PropBag.ReadProperty("BackColor", &HFFFFFF)
        Set UserControl.Font = PropBag.ReadProperty("Font", Ambient.Font)
        CalculateValues
    End Sub

    Private Sub UserControl_WriteProperties(PropBag As PropertyBag)
        Call PropBag.WriteProperty("BorderStyle", m_BorderStyle, dw3d)
        Call PropBag.WriteProperty("MultiSelect", m_MultiSelect, 0)
        Call PropBag.WriteProperty("BackColor", UserControl.BackColor, &HFFFFFF)
        Call PropBag.WriteProperty("Font", UserControl.Font, Ambient.Font)
    End Sub

    Private Sub UserControl_InitProperties()
        m_BorderStyle = dw3d
    End Sub
```

The ListCtlB control uses a constituent scrollbar to provide scrolling capability for the listbox. The prospect of creating an owner-drawn scrollbar on the control window was too depressing to contemplate. This approach does have one major disadvantage. As you may recall, when you use a visible constituent control in a Visual Basic-authored control, the control itself cannot receive the focus. Focus will always go to the constituent control. This means all keystroke events will come in by way of the scrollbar control instead of the UserControl object. It also means that the scrollbar will appear to have the focus when your control has the focus, which will not produce the appearance of a standard list control. This is unavoidable using this particular implementation, but you'll see an easy solution in the next example.

```
'----------------------------------------------------------
'
'   VScroll1 Methods and Events
'

Private Sub VScroll1_Change()
    If FixNextScroll >= 0 Then
        If VScroll1.Value <> FixNextScroll Then
```

```
            VScroll1.Value = FixNextScroll
            Exit Sub
        End If
        FixNextScroll = -1
        Exit Sub
    End If
    Debug.Print "Change"
    LBScrollChange
End Sub

Private Sub VScroll1_KeyDown(KeyCode As Integer, Shift As Integer)
    FixNextScroll = VScroll1.Value
    LBArrow KeyCode
End Sub

Private Sub VScroll1_Scroll()
    Debug.Print "Scroll"
    LBScroll
End Sub

Private Sub VScroll1_KeyPress(KeyAscii As Integer)
    If KeyAscii = vbKeySpace And m_MultiSelect Then
        LBSelect ClickLine
        lbInvalidateRange ClickLine, ClickLine
        Refresh
    End If
End Sub
```

The user-drawn List control is actually implemented using the functions that follow. Now, I'll admit that this code looks somewhat complex. The truth is, I could probably spend the better part of an entire chapter describing it, but time and space do not permit that. My best suggestion is that you tackle it the way you would any other complex piece of code. Try to follow the logic, and trace through the code at runtime.

```
'-------------------------------------------------------
'
'   Functions that implement the user drawn list control
'
'
' Call this from the keydown event in the control
'
Private Sub LBArrow(keyid%)
    Dim newClickLine&
    Dim NewScrollValue&
    Select Case keyid%
```

```
        Case KEYDOWN
            newClickLine = ClickLine + 1
        Case KEYUP
            newClickLine = ClickLine - 1
        Case Else
            Exit Sub
    End Select
    If newClickLine < 0 Or newClickLine > VScroll1.Max Then
        ' No change, so block the redraw caused by the container
        Exit Sub
    End If
    ClickLine = newClickLine
    HasFocus = ClickLine
    If Not m_MultiSelect Then LBSelect ClickLine

    If ClickLine < CurrentTop Then
        FixNextScroll = -1
        NewScrollValue = VScroll1.Value - 1
        VScroll1.Value = NewScrollValue
        FixNextScroll = NewScrollValue
        Exit Sub
    End If

    If ClickLine > CurrentTop + TotalLines - 1 Then
        FixNextScroll = -1
        NewScrollValue = VScroll1.Value + 1
        VScroll1.Value = NewScrollValue
        FixNextScroll = NewScrollValue
        Exit Sub
    End If
    LBDraw
End Sub
```

Each line obtains the text to draw using the GetText event. It calculates the exact area in the window that will be covered by the line, taking the current border and scrollbar position into account. If the line is not visible, it doesn't bother drawing the line at all.

```
' Draw the specified line number in the list box
'
Private Sub LBDrawLine(tloc&)
    Dim rc As RECT
    Dim rc2 As RECT
    Dim di&
    Dim oldcolor&
    Dim txt$
    Dim usefont As IFont
```

```
Dim oldfont As Long
If tloc < CurrentTop Or tloc > CurrentTop + TotalLines Then
    ' It's not visible
    Exit Sub
End If
If Ambient.UserMode Then
    RaiseEvent GetText(tloc, txt$)
Else
    If tloc = 0 Then txt = Extender.Name
End If

rc.left = m_BorderStyle + 1
rc.right = ScaleWidth - VScroll1.Width - m_BorderStyle * 2
rc.top = (tloc - CurrentTop) * PixelsPerLine + m_BorderStyle
rc.bottom = rc.top + PixelsPerLine - 1
Line (m_BorderStyle, rc.top + m_BorderStyle)-(ScaleWidth - _
VScroll1.Width, rc.bottom + m_BorderStyle), BackColor, BF
If IsSelected(tloc) Then
    If VScroll1.hwnd = GetFocus() And HasFocus = tloc Then      _
    ' This line has the focus
        LSet rc2 = rc
        rc2.left = m_BorderStyle
        rc2.right = ScaleWidth - VScroll1.Width - m_BorderStyle
        di = DrawFocusRect(hdc, rc2)
        di = InflateRect(rc2, -1, -1)
        Line (rc2.left, rc2.top)-(rc2.right - 1, rc2.bottom - 1), highlight, BF
    Else
        Line (m_BorderStyle, rc.top)-(ScaleWidth - VScroll1.Width - _
        m_BorderStyle, rc.bottom), highlight, BF
    End If
    oldcolor = SetTextColor(hdc, HighlightText)

Else
    If VScroll1.hwnd = GetFocus() And HasFocus = tloc Then
        ' This line has the focus
        LSet rc2 = rc
        rc2.left = m_BorderStyle
        rc2.right = ScaleWidth - m_BorderStyle
        di = DrawFocusRect(hdc, rc2)
        di = InflateRect(rc2, -1, -1)
        Line (rc2.left, rc2.top)-(rc2.right - 1, rc2.bottom - 1), BackColor, BF
    Else
        Line (m_BorderStyle, rc.top)-(ScaleWidth - m_BorderStyle, rc.bottom), _
            BackColor, BF
    End If
End If
```

```
'Set usefont = UserControl.Font
'oldfont = SelectObject(hdc, usefont.hFont)
di = DrawText(hdc, txt, Len(txt), rc, DT_LEFT Or DT_SINGLELINE Or _
              DT_NOPREFIX)
'Call SelectObject(hdc, oldfont)
If IsSelected(tloc) Then
   oldcolor = SetTextColor(hdc, oldcolor)
End If

End Sub
```

It would be very inefficient for the control to display every entry in the list-box any time a change occurs. For example: when the list is scrolled one item up or down, it should be possible to just scroll the window contents and draw the one line that has just appeared. This feature is supported by this implementation. The lbInvalidateRange function is used to mark which entries in the listbox actually need to be drawn.

```
'
' Invalidate a range of entries
'
Private Sub lbInvalidateRange(Optional ByVal lowval& = 0, Optional _
ByVal highval& = &H7FFFFFFF)
    Dim tval&
    Dim highest&
    If LowDrawRange = -1 And HighDrawRange = -1 Then
       LowDrawRange = &H7FFFFFFF
    End If
    If highval < lowval Then
       ' Swap if necessary to keep range in order
       tval = lowval
       lowval = highval
       highval = tval
    End If
    If lowval < LowDrawRange Then LowDrawRange = lowval
    If highval > HighDrawRange Then HighDrawRange = highval
    If LowDrawRange < CurrentTop Then LowDrawRange = CurrentTop
    highest = CurrentTop + TotalLines
    If HighDrawRange > highest Then HighDrawRange = highest

End Sub
```

When an entry is clicked, it may need to be redrawn if the selection state changed. This is handled by the LBMouseDown function as shown here. Note how it shifts the entry that has the focus as well. The function also captures mouse input. This will be described further in the LBMouseMove function.

```
'
' Called this by the mouse down event for the control
'
Private Sub LBMouseDown(ByVal x&, ByVal Y&)
    Dim newClickLine&
    Dim li&
    li = SetCapture(hwnd)
    newClickLine = (Y - m_BorderStyle) \ PixelsPerLine + CurrentTop
    ' Listbox line did not change
    If HasFocus <> newClickLine Then
        HasFocus = newClickLine
        lbInvalidateRange HasFocus, HasFocus
    End If
    If IsSelected(newClickLine) And Not m_MultiSelect Then
        Exit Sub
    End If
    ClickLine = newClickLine
    LBSelect ClickLine
    LBDraw
End Sub
```

The LBScroll function handles the scrolling operation that was described earlier. It calculates how far the list needs to scroll and calls the ScrollWindow API function to scroll the contents of the window the correct amount. It then uses the lbInvalidateRange function to mark the lines that need to be drawn from scratch. This approach provides for very fast and smooth scrolling.

```
'
' Call from the scroll event of the vertical scroll bar
'
Private Sub LBScroll()
    Dim howmuch&
    Dim newtop&
    Dim dl&
    Dim rc As RECT
    rc.left = m_BorderStyle
    rc.right = ScaleWidth - VScroll1.Width - m_BorderStyle
    rc.top = m_BorderStyle
    rc.bottom = ScaleHeight - m_BorderStyle
    newtop& = VScroll1.Value
    howmuch& = CurrentTop - newtop&
    If howmuch& = 0 Then
        Exit Sub
    End If
```

```
            If Abs(howmuch) >= TotalLines Then
                ' Set to redraw it all
                LowDrawRange = -1
                HighDrawRange = -1
                CurrentTop = newtop
                LBDraw
                Exit Sub
            End If
            CurrentTop = newtop
            dl& = ScrollWindowByNum(hwnd, 0, howmuch& * PixelsPerLine, rc, 0)
            ' Now invalidate
            If howmuch < 0 Then ' We scrolled up
                lbInvalidateRange newtop + TotalLines + howmuch, newtop + TotalLines
            Else
                lbInvalidateRange newtop, newtop + howmuch
            End If
            LBDraw

End Sub
```

The selection operation is quite straightforward. In single-selection mode, the first entry in the selected array specifies the entry currently selected. In multiple-selection mode, the Selected array is dynamically sized using the Set-Selection function to contain a list of lines that are currently selected.

```
'
' Select the specified entry
'
Private Sub LBSelect(ByVal tloc&)
    If m_MultiSelect Then
        SetSelection tloc, Not IsSelected(tloc)
        lbInvalidateRange
    Else
        lbInvalidateRange Selected(0), tloc
        Selected(0) = tloc
    End If
End Sub
```

The LBDraw function draws those lines that are currently marked as invalid. Its most interesting characteristic, however, is the border implementation. As you can see, it is quite easy to implement 3D effects using simple VB code. Remember this the next time you consider using an ActiveX control solely to provide a 3D appearance. The code approach is much more efficient in terms of memory and resources, and its performance is excellent.

```
Private Sub LBDraw()
    Dim startline&, lastline&
```

```
Dim x&
Dim sw As Long
Dim sh As Long
sw = ScaleWidth
sh = ScaleHeight

If LowDrawRange = -1 And HighDrawRange = -1 Then
    startline& = CurrentTop
    lastline& = TotalLines + CurrentTop
Else
    startline& = LowDrawRange
    lastline& = HighDrawRange
End If
For x& = startline& - 1 To lastline& + 1
   LBDrawLine x
Next x&
LowDrawRange = -1
HighDrawRange = -1

Select Case m_BorderStyle
    Case dw3d
        UserControl.Line (0, 0)-(sw, 0), Dark3D
        UserControl.Line (1, 1)-(sw, 1), DarkShadow
        UserControl.Line (0, 0)-(0, sh), Dark3D
        UserControl.Line (1, 1)-(1, sh), DarkShadow
        UserControl.Line (sw - 1, 0)-(sw - 1, sh), Light3D
        UserControl.Line (sw - 1, sh - 1)-(1, sh - 1), Light3D
        UserControl.Line (sw - 2, sh - 2)-(2, sh - 2), Dark3D
    Case dwSingle
        UserControl.Line (0, 0)-(sw, 0), 0
        UserControl.Line (0, 0)-(0, sh), 0
        UserControl.Line (sw - 1, 0)-(sw - 1, sh), 0
        UserControl.Line (sw - 1, sh - 1)-(1, sh - 1), 0
    End Select
End Sub
```

What happens when you click on an entry in a listbox and drag the mouse outside of the top or bottom border of the listbox. The listbox continues to scroll. The LBMouseMove uses an API trick to accomplish this. If a MouseMove event appears from a coordinate outside of the listbox, it checks to see if the location is above or below the control. If it is, the code first scrolls the listbox. Then it performs a DoEvents operation to allow the update to occur. A module level context variable named incontext is used to prevent reentrancy at this time. Thus, any other MouseMove events are ignored at this time. Next, the function uses the GetCursorPos and SetCursorPos to set the mouse pointer position to its

current location. This does not move the mouse, but it does generate another
MouseMove event, causing the scroll operation to repeat.

How can a MouseMove event appear for a point outside of the control? During the LBMouseDown function, the SetCapture API function was called to
capture the mouse input. Under Win32, mouse capture is only guaranteed to
remain in effect while the mouse button is held down, which is perfect for this
application. The LBMouseUp function releases the capture using the Release-
Capture API function.

```
'
' Call this from the MouseMove event of the control
'
Private Sub LBMouseMove(ByVal Button%, ByVal x&, ByVal Y&)
    Dim pt As POINTAPI
    Dim dl&
    If InContext% Then Exit Sub
    If (Button And 1) = 0 Then Exit Sub
    If Y < 0 Or Y > ScaleHeight Then ' We be scrolling
        InContext% = True
        If Y < 0 Then
            If VScroll1.Value > 0 Then VScroll1.Value = VScroll1.Value - 1
        Else
            If VScroll1.Value < VScroll1.Max Then VScroll1.Value = _
            VScroll1.Value + 1
        End If
        DoEvents
        ' Force another mouse event so it will scroll again
        InContext% = False
        dl& = GetCursorPos(pt)
        dl& = SetCursorPos(pt.x, pt.Y)
        Exit Sub
    End If
    If Not m_MultiSelect Then LBMouseDown x, Y
End Sub

Private Sub LBMouseUp()
    Dim dl&
    dl& = ReleaseCapture()
End Sub

Private Property Get LBClickLine()
    LBClickLine = ClickLine
End Property
```

```
' Call this from the GotFocus event
'
Private Sub LBGotFocus()
   If m_MultiSelect Then
      lbInvalidateRange
   Else
      lbInvalidateRange Selected(0), Selected(0)
   End If
   LBDraw
End Sub


'
' Call this from the Change event of the scrollbar
'
Private Sub LBScrollChange()
    LBScroll
End Sub


'
' Call this from the control LostFocus event
'
Private Sub LBLostFocus()
   If m_MultiSelect Then
      lbInvalidateRange
   Else
      lbInvalidateRange Selected(0), Selected(0)
   End If
   LBDraw
End Sub



Private Sub PositionScrollBar()
   Dim slidescroll%
   If m_BorderStyle = dw3d Then slidescroll = 1
   VScroll1.Move ScaleWidth - (VScroll1.Width + slidescroll), _
   slidescroll, VScroll1.Width, ScaleHeight - m_BorderStyle
End Sub

Private Function IsSelected(ByVal location&) As Boolean
   Dim x&
   For x = 0 To UBound(Selected)
      If Selected(x) = location Then
         IsSelected = True
         Exit Function
      End If
   Next x
End Function
```

The SetSelection subroutine manages the selection array. This is one of the hacks that were described earlier and does not represent the most efficient way of handling this task. But it does the trick.

```
Private Sub SetSelection(ByVal location&, ByVal newstate As Boolean)
    Dim x&
    Dim firstfree&
    firstfree = -1
    For x = 0 To UBound(Selected)
        If Selected(x) = location Then
            If Not newstate Then Selected(x) = -1
            Exit Sub
        End If
        If firstfree < 0 And Selected(x) = -1 Then firstfree = x
    Next x
    If newstate Then
        If firstfree >= 0 Then
            Selected(firstfree) = location
            Exit Sub
        End If
        ReDim Preserve Selected(UBound(Selected) + 1)
        Selected(UBound(Selected)) = location
    End If

End Sub


Private Sub CalculateValues()
    PixelsPerLine = UserControl.TextHeight("W") + 1
    TotalLines = (ScaleHeight - m_BorderStyle * 2) \ PixelsPerLine
End Sub
```

As you can see, the user-drawn approach does require substantially more work, but you gain a great deal of flexibility in the process. Before leaving this approach behind, there is one more example to look at that fixes the focus problem that exists with this implementation.

A BETTER USER-DRAWN CONTROL

The ListCtlC.ctl example eliminates the problems relating to focus that result from having a visible constituent control. It turns out that Windows has built-in scrollbar support that is available to virtually every type of window. This scrollbar support can be turned on using API functions but requires subclassing to obtain the necessary messages. You can turn on these built-in scrollbars for the UserControl window as well. Doing so does not count as a visible constituent control. Thus the control itself will receive the focus.

Turning on scrollbars and managing the incoming messages turns out to be quite a bit of work, but the dwspyvb.dll component includes an object that does the work for you: the dwScrollBars object. It works with many types of windows including ActiveX control windows, forms, and picture controls. The object is declared and initialized as follows:

```
Private WithEvents VScroll As dwScrollBars
```

The object is initialized in the UserControl_Initialize event as follows:

```
Set VScroll = New dwScrollBars
```

The vertical scrollbar is turned on during the UserControl_Show event as follows:

```
Private Sub UserControl_Show()
    If Ambient.UserMode Then
        VScroll.hwnd = UserControl.hwnd
        VScroll.ScrollBars = sbeVerticalScrollbar
    End If
End Sub
```

There is no need to display the scrollbar at design time.

The control itself now receives keyboard input, which is handled as follows:

```
Private Sub UserControl_KeyDown(KeyCode As Integer, Shift As Integer)
    FixNextScroll = VScroll.VValue
    LBArrow KeyCode
End Sub

Private Sub UserControl_KeyPress(KeyAscii As Integer)
    If KeyAscii = vbKeySpace And m_MultiSelect Then
        LBSelect ClickLine
        lbInvalidateRange ClickLine, ClickLine
        Refresh
    End If
End Sub
```

The VScroll object properties and events are similar to those of the standard scrollbar control. The only difference is that each event or property name is prefixed with an H or V character indicating whether it belongs to the vertical or horizontal scrollbar. This control only uses the vertical scrollbar, but the object supports both, either individually or simultaneously.

```
'- - - - - - - - - - - - - - - - - - - - - - - - - - - - - - - - - -
'
' VScroll Methods and Events
'
Private Sub VScroll_VChange()
```

```
    If FixNextScroll >= 0 Then
        If VScroll.VValue <> FixNextScroll Then
            VScroll.VValue = FixNextScroll
            Exit Sub
        End If
        FixNextScroll = -1
        Exit Sub
    End If
    Debug.Print "Change"
    LBScrollChange
End Sub

Private Sub VScroll_VScroll()
    LBScroll
End Sub
```

The remaining control functions are virtually identical except for the change from the VScroll1 control to VScroll object and the change in name to the scrolling property and event names.

This concludes our discussion of user-drawn controls and leaves us with one more approach to discuss: the fourth model of control creation, which is the window-based control.

A CUSTOM WINDOW-BASED CONTROL

The major limitation of constituent-based controls is that you cannot change the design properties of the constituent controls. This is because those properties are based on window styles that must be defined when the window is created. Visual Basic 5.0 does not provide a mechanism to destroy and recreate a control. But if you were to create your own window from scratch, you could destroy and re-create the window any time you wanted, including the container's design time and runtime. Of course, in doing so your control would take on a number of responsibilities:

▶ You would have to handle incoming messages to the window.

▶ You would need to intercept messages sent by the window to its parent (your UserControl object).

▶ All communication with the window would be through messages.

But that really isn't as bad as it might sound, as you will soon see.

The ListCtlD sample control creates a standard listbox window and places it over the UserControl window for your control. The sample begins with a number of standard API declarations.

The WS and LBS prefixed constants describe the styles of the window. You can guess the meanings of most of them by their names. Detailed explanations can be found in any good API reference. Only a few of the styles shown here are actually used in this control.

```
' CreateWindow list example
' Copyright (c) 1997, by Desaware Inc. All Rights Reserved

Option Explicit

Private Const WS_CHILD = &H40000000
Private Const WS_VISIBLE = &H10000000
Private Const WS_CLIPSIBLINGS = &H4000000
Private Const WS_BORDER = &H800000
Private Const WS_GROUP = &H20000
Private Const WS_TABSTOP = &H10000
Private Const WS_VSCROLL = &H200000
Private Const WS_EX_APPWINDOW = &H40000
Private Const WS_EX_CLIENTEDGE = &H200&
Private Const WS_EX_CONTEXTHELP = &H400&
Private Const WS_EX_CONTROLPARENT = &H10000
Private Const WS_EX_LEFT = &H0&
Private Const WS_EX_LEFTSCROLLBAR = &H4000&
Private Const WS_EX_LTRREADING = &H0&
Private Const WS_EX_MDICHILD = &H40&
Private Const WS_EX_RIGHT = &H1000&
Private Const WS_EX_RIGHTSCROLLBAR = &H0&
Private Const WS_EX_RTLREADING = &H2000&
Private Const WS_EX_STATICEDGE = &H20000
Private Const WS_EX_TOOLWINDOW = &H80&
Private Const WS_EX_WINDOWEDGE = &H100&


' Listbox Styles
Private Const LBS_NOTIFY = &H1&
Private Const LBS_SORT = &H2&
Private Const LBS_NOREDRAW = &H4&
Private Const LBS_MULTIPLESEL = &H8&
Private Const LBS_OWNERDRAWFIXED = &H10&
Private Const LBS_OWNERDRAWVARIABLE = &H20&
Private Const LBS_HASSTRINGS = &H40&
Private Const LBS_USETABSTOPS = &H80&
Private Const LBS_NOINTEGRALHEIGHT = &H100&
Private Const LBS_MULTICOLUMN = &H200&
Private Const LBS_WANTKEYBOARDINPUT = &H400&
Private Const LBS_EXTENDEDSEL = &H800&
Private Const LBS_DISABLENOSCROLL = &H1000&
```

```
Private Const LBS_NODATA = &H2000&
Private Const LBS_NOSEL = &H4000&
Private Const LBS_STANDARD = (LBS_NOTIFY Or LBS_SORT Or WS_VSCROLL Or WS_BORDER)
```

Notification codes are types of WM_COMMAND messages that are sent from the window to the parent, in this case, the UserControl window.

```
' Listbox Notification Codes
Private Const LBN_ERRSPACE = (-2)
Private Const LBN_SELCHANGE = 1
Private Const LBN_DBLCLK = 2
Private Const LBN_SELCANCEL = 3
Private Const LBN_SETFOCUS = 4
Private Const LBN_KILLFOCUS = 5
```

The LB_ prefixed messages are used to control the operation of the listbox window. Only a few of the commands shown here are actually implemented in this example.

```
' Listbox messages
Private Const LB_ADDSTRING = &H180
Private Const LB_INSERTSTRING = &H181
Private Const LB_DELETESTRING = &H182
Private Const LB_SELITEMRANGEEX = &H183
Private Const LB_RESETCONTENT = &H184
Private Const LB_SETSEL = &H185
Private Const LB_SETCURSEL = &H186
Private Const LB_GETSEL = &H187
Private Const LB_GETCURSEL = &H188
Private Const LB_GETTEXT = &H189
Private Const LB_GETTEXTLEN = &H18A
Private Const LB_GETCOUNT = &H18B
Private Const LB_SELECTSTRING = &H18C
Private Const LB_DIR = &H18D
Private Const LB_GETTOPINDEX = &H18E
Private Const LB_FINDSTRING = &H18F
Private Const LB_GETSELCOUNT = &H190
Private Const LB_GETSELITEMS = &H191
Private Const LB_SETTABSTOPS = &H192
Private Const LB_GETHORIZONTALEXTENT = &H193
Private Const LB_SETHORIZONTALEXTENT = &H194
Private Const LB_SETCOLUMNWIDTH = &H195
Private Const LB_ADDFILE = &H196
Private Const LB_SETTOPINDEX = &H197
Private Const LB_GETITEMRECT = &H198
Private Const LB_GETITEMDATA = &H199
Private Const LB_SETITEMDATA = &H19A
Private Const LB_SELITEMRANGE = &H19B
```

```
Private Const LB_SETANCHORINDEX = &H19C
Private Const LB_GETANCHORINDEX = &H19D
Private Const LB_SETCARETINDEX = &H19E
Private Const LB_GETCARETINDEX = &H19F
Private Const LB_SETITEMHEIGHT = &H1A0
Private Const LB_GETITEMHEIGHT = &H1A1
Private Const LB_FINDSTRINGEXACT = &H1A2
Private Const LB_SETLOCALE = &H1A5
Private Const LB_GETLOCALE = &H1A6
Private Const LB_SETCOUNT = &H1A7
Private Const LB_MSGMAX = &H1A8
Private Const WM_CTLCOLORLISTBOX = &H134


Private Const WM_LBUTTONDOWN = &H201
Private Const WM_LBUTTONUP = &H202
Private Const WM_SETFONT = &H30

Private Const WHITE_BRUSH = 0
Private Declare Function GetStockObject Lib "gdi32" (ByVal nIndex As Long) As Long

Event Click()
Event DblClick()
```

This sample uses two objects from the dwSpyvb.dll component. The dwPrivateWindow class is used to manage the creation and use of private windows. The dwSubClass object you saw earlier is used to intercept the listbox window notifications.

```
Dim WithEvents listwnd As dwPrivateWindow
Dim WithEvents cmdhook As dwSubClass


Private Const defClassName = "LISTBOX"


Private m_MultiSelect As Boolean
Private m_BorderStyle As Integer
```

Changing the MultiSelect and BorderStyle properties both require that the listbox window be destroyed and re-created, as you can see in their property procedures.

```
Public Property Get MultiSelect() As Boolean
    MultiSelect = m_MultiSelect
End Property

Public Property Let MultiSelect(ByVal vNewValue As Boolean)
    m_MultiSelect = vNewValue
    PropertyChanged "MultiSelect"
```

```
        InitTheWindow   ' Change the appearance now!
End Property

Public Property Get BorderStyle() As dwBorderStyle
    BorderStyle = m_BorderStyle
End Property

Public Property Let BorderStyle(ByVal vNewValue As dwBorderStyle)
    If vNewValue > 2 or vNewValue < 0 Then
        Err.Raise 380
    End If
    m_BorderStyle = vNewValue
    PropertyChanged "BorderStyle"
    InitTheWindow
End Property


Public Property Get Font() As Font
    Set Font = UserControl.Font
End Property

Public Property Set Font(ByVal vNewValue As Font)
    Set UserControl.Font = vNewValue
    PropertyChanged "Font"
    UpdateTheFont
End Property
```

When your control receives the focus, you must set the focus to the contained listbox window. This is necessary because a private window is not really a constituent control, so Visual Basic doesn't know that it should receive the focus when the control does. The SetFocus method you see here is a method of the dwPrivateWindow object that calls the API SetFocus command.

```
'---------------------------------------------
'
'     UserControl events and properties
'
Private Sub UserControl_EnterFocus()
    listwnd.SetFocus
End Sub


Private Sub UserControl_Initialize()
    Set listwnd = New dwPrivateWindow
    Set cmdhook = New dwSubClass
End Sub
```

The InitWindow function is called when the control is initialized or loaded.

```
Private Sub UserControl_InitProperties()
   ' Create the child window after properties are read
   InitTheWindow
End Sub

Private Sub UserControl_ReadProperties(PropBag As PropertyBag)
   ' Create the child window after properties are read
   m_MultiSelect = PropBag.ReadProperty("MultiSelect", False)
   m_BorderStyle = PropBag.ReadProperty("BorderStyle", False)
   Set UserControl.Font = PropBag.ReadProperty("Font", Ambient.Font)
   InitTheWindow
End Sub

Private Sub UserControl_WriteProperties(PropBag As PropertyBag)
   Call PropBag.WriteProperty("MultiSelect", m_MultiSelect, False)
   Call PropBag.WriteProperty("BorderStyle", m_BorderStyle, False)
   Call PropBag.WriteProperty("Font", UserControl.Font, Ambient.Font)
End Sub
```

The following cleanup on termination is mostly a matter of good style. Both the dwPrivateWindow and dwSubClass objects know how to clean up after themselves when they are destroyed.

```
Private Sub UserControl_Terminate()
   listwnd.DestroyWindow
   cmdhook.HwndParam = 0
   Set listwnd = Nothing
   Set cmdhook = Nothing
End Sub
```

You cannot obtain a font handle from the Font object directly, but the Font object implements an interface called IFont that allows you to retrieve the handle to the font. This can be sent to the listbox window using the WM_SETFONT message.

```
'-------------------------------------
'
'      Functions used internally
'

Private Sub UpdateTheFont()
   Dim usefont As IFont
   Set usefont = UserControl.Font
   Call listwnd.SendMessageNumber(WM_SETFONT, usefont.hFont, 1)
End Sub
```

The GetListboxStyle function is a utility function that retrieves the correct window style to use for the given multiple-select and border settings.

```
Private Function GetListboxStyle() As Long
    Dim LS As Long
    LS = WS_CHILD Or WS_TABSTOP Or WS_CLIPSIBLINGS Or WS_VISIBLE Or WS_VSCROLL
    LS = LS Or LBS_NOTIFY Or LBS_HASSTRINGS
    If m_MultiSelect Then LS = LS Or LBS_MULTIPLESEL Or LBS_EXTENDEDSEL
    If m_BorderStyle Then LS = LS Or WS_BORDER
    GetListboxStyle = LS
End Function
```

The InitTheWindow function creates the contained listbox window. The cmdhook object is set to subclass the user control window. It is set to detect command messages using the CommandMessage event, which breaks the WM_COMMAND message parameters into their individual components. It is also set to detect the WM_CTLCOLORLISTBOX message, which allows you to set the background color of the listbox. The listwnd CreateWindowEx method creates the new window. There is no need to destroy the previous window—that operation is handled automatically when you create the new one.

```
Private Sub InitTheWindow()
    cmdhook.EnableCommandEvent = True
    cmdhook.HwndParam = UserControl.hwnd
    cmdhook.AddMessage WM_CTLCOLORLISTBOX
    Call listwnd.CreateWindowEx(0, defClassName, "", GetListboxStyle, _
        0, 0, ScaleWidth, ScaleHeight, hwnd, 0)
    If Not Ambient.UserMode Then AddItem Ambient.DisplayName
    UpdateTheFont
End Sub
```

WM_COMMAND messages from the listbox window are intercepted on their way to the UserControl window. The UserControl window receives WM_COMMAND messages from many sources, including other controls and menus. In this example, no other window exists, so the only source of WM_COMMAND messages is the listbox window. However, it is still good practice to double check. The messages are mapped directly into Control events.

```
' Here is where command notifications come in
Private Sub cmdhook_CommandMessage(ByVal hwnd As Long, ByVal wID As Long, _
ByVal wNotifyCode As Long, ByVal hwndCtl As Long, retval As Long, nodef _
As Boolean)
    If hwndCtl <> listwnd.hwnd Then Exit Sub  ' It's not for the list box
    Select Case wNotifyCode
        Case LBN_SELCHANGE
```

```
      RaiseEvent Click
    Case LBN_DBLCLK
        RaiseEvent DblClick
  End Select
  ' Default result for notification messages
  nodef = True
  retval = 0
End Sub

Private Sub cmdhook_WndMessage(ByVal hwnd As Long, Msg As Long, wp As Long, lp As_
Long, retval As Long, nodef As Boolean)
  If lp <> listwnd.hwnd Then Exit Sub  ' It's not for the list box
  Select Case Msg
    Case WM_CTLCOLORLISTBOX
        retval = GetStockObject(WHITE_BRUSH)   ' Return white brush
        nodef = True   ' Block default processing
  End Select
End Sub
```

The cmdhook_WndMessage function intercepts the WM_CTLCOLORLIST-
BOX message and returns a handle to a white brush to force the background
color of the list box to white. You could, of course, set this value based on a
BackColor property should you choose to implement one. The nodef event parameter must be set to True to prevent default processing for the message,
which would set the color to the default background color for listboxes.

Adding and removing a string is a simple matter of sending the appropriate
message.

```
' Add a string to the list box
Public Sub AddItem(item As String, Optional Index As Long = -1)
  Dim res&
  If Index = -1 Then
    res = listwnd.SendMessageString(LB_ADDSTRING, 0, item)
    ' TODO - on fail raise error
  Else
    res = listwnd.SendMessageString(LB_INSERTSTRING, Index, item)
    ' TODO - on fail raise error
  End If
End Sub


' Remove a string from the list box
Public Sub RemoveItem(ByVal Index As Long)
  If Index < 0 Or Index > ListCount Then
    Err.Raise 380
  Else
    Call listwnd.SendMessageNumber(LB_DELETESTRING, Index, 0)
```

```
      End If
End Sub

Public Property Get ListCount() As Long
   ListCount = listwnd.SendMessageNumber(LB_GETCOUNT, 0, 0)
End Property
```

What about the messages that are being sent to the private listbox window? Unless you specify otherwise, they are automatically sent by the listwnd object to the default window function—the class window function that implements the listbox functionality. You can override the handling of these messages if you wish, but in this case there is no need to do so. The nice thing about this approach is that if you break or pause your application, window messages will continue to receive their default processing, thus allowing Windows message processing to continue in a normal manner. This is because default message processing is built into the dwPrivateWindow object. You can override it if you choose, but if your code is stopped, the default message processing will always take place.

```
Private Sub listwnd_WndMessage(ByVal hwnd As Long, ByVal Msg As Long, _
ByVal wParam As Long, ByVal lParam As Long, retval As Long, nodef As Boolean)
   Select Case Msg
      ' We can handle window messages here
   End Select
End Sub
```

The approach shown here can become much more useful when using a technique called *owner drawn listboxes*. In this case the standard listbox window does not actually draw the list box. Instead, it sends a message to the parent window telling it which line to draw and whether it is selected or has the focus. It also provides a device context that is ready for drawing.

You may feel you need to be a bit of a Windows expert to take full advantage of the private window approach. There is some truth to this. But it just serves to stress the point I made at the beginning of this chapter: that you can take advantage of virtually all of the control development techniques that are possible using other languages when writing controls using Visual Basic. However, to do so you must learn those techniques and handle them at the same level—the API and windows messaging level. Visual Basic may be the easiest way to create advanced controls, but this is empathetically not the same as saying that it is easy.

This concludes our coverage of developing ActiveX controls using Visual Basic. We'll return to the subject again in Part 4, where we cover the related topics of versioning and licensing. Meanwhile, let's turn our attention to a closely related component type: the ActiveX document.

Part 4

ActiveX Documents

ACTIVEX DOCUMENT FUNDAMENTALS

ACTIVEX DOCUMENTS AND
THE INTERNET

This part of the book posed a truly unique challenge for me. You see, any book, by definition, is influenced by the opinions of the author as to what is important. Since this book is designed to supplement rather than replace the Visual Basic documentation, this perspective becomes significant. Everything I have written so far is something I believe you either must know or will find extremely useful in creating ActiveX components. And creating ActiveX components is, in and of itself, extremely important for every Visual Basic programmer to know how to do.

So now we come to ActiveX documents. What are they good for? They can be used with the Microsoft Office Binder. Cool. But does anyone actually use the Microsoft Office Binder? They can be used to help create new tool windows for the Visual Basic design environment. But this is mostly of interest to add-on vendors. How many typical VB programmers create their own VB add-ins? They can run within Web browsers. But if ActiveX controls run on Web pages, where do ActiveX documents fit in? And is anyone actually using ActiveX documents in this manner?

The importance of ActiveX code components (DLL and EXE servers) is self-evident: every major Windows application from most vendors, including Visual Basic itself, is now based on this technology. The importance of ActiveX controls is also clear: all Visual Basic programmers use controls in their applications. Even if ActiveX controls do not catch on for the Internet or intranets, their importance for application development under Windows will continue to grow.

But at this time it is not completely clear to me that ActiveX documents are actually going to become widely accepted. I'm not even convinced that this technology is truly important in the long run.

Given this book's philosophy, I could not even begin to write the next two chapters without first establishing a reasonable scenario of how and why most Visual Basic programmers might use ActiveX documents. To help me accomplish this, I turned to a friend of mine, Carl Franklin, who is a well-known author and speaker on Visual Basic-related subjects and co-founder of "Carl and Gary's Home Page" (http://www.apexsc.com/vb). Their page is an excellent resource site for Visual Basic programmers.

I've had several discussions with Carl, during which he waxed eloquent about the wonders of this technology. So I asked him to write a few paragraphs about ActiveX documents. My hope was that this would not only provide me with a framework for this part of the book but also provide a good balance for the skepticism I have expressed here. This was his response.

"I always go by the rule 'Use the right tool for the job.' There are four main types of Web pages. Static HTML, Dynamic, Forms, and Applications. Granted, the world hasn't seen many applications on the Web, but I believe this is only because when we think of the Internet we think of words like *download* and *Web site*. If there are applications on the Net, we think of first downloading them and then running them.

"This is a natural way to think when you are limited to the speed that modems deliver. In fact, historically you can see a reoccurring trend where people fail to think in the future because our knowledge has been shaped by the past. We bring forward all the bad habits we've learned when our hands were tied. Now that we have a wide open frontier, it is difficult to change the way we think about what is and is not feasible.

"Getting back to my point, Mr. Gates in Redmond is betting the bank that Web sites and applications are on a collision course. So much so that the next version of Windows 95 will (for better or for worse) blur the lines between applications and Web sites so much. The two ideas will become one.

"Think back to the late '80s, when everyone wanted a VB front end to their particular database, DOS app, or what have you. As features became more in demand, it became harder to do things using the same old tools, and the third-party VB tools had begun. Well, HTML forms are the starting point for doing the same thing on the Internet.

"An ActiveX Document is a program. (Think of it as a VB Form, in which the menus and toolbars merge with its host viewer, Internet Explorer.) To me, ActiveX Documents represent an opportunity for application developers to reach the widest audience possible: The world. By now we should have figured out that in the software business, perception is everything. Without good packaging, software does not sell. There is nothing new about downloading and running a program. *But,* people are more willing to check it out if it's on the Net. Even though an ActiveX Document downloads, registers, and runs locally, it runs *in the browser,* giving the user the perception that it's on the Internet. And in fact, it is. Where else can you give someone a URL that installs your software and runs it, all without user intervention? That's a distribution dream come true! And updates? Hit refresh. How totally cool!

"There are countless possibilities for ActiveX Documents: games, training, truly interactive Web pages, as well as complete applications. Almost any Windows application can run as an ActiveX Document. They load fast too. Now how much would you pay? If I seem excited it's because I can see the potential here. Write any kind of application for the Net. Cool."

That was what Carl said. So for the next two chapters, I will mostly set my skepticism aside and try to look at ActiveX documents from Carl's point of view.

My first step was to imagine how a business, say, for example, a realtor's office, might deploy this technology. I think you'll find the results intriguing. But first, we have to cover the fundamentals, so come along with me and take the next leg of our journey.

ActiveX Document Fundamentals

WHAT IS AN ACTIVEX DOCUMENT?

ACTIVEX DOCUMENT PROGRAMMING

THE USERDOCUMENT OBJECT

Chapter 23

F rom a programming perspective, ActiveX documents are almost
identical to ActiveX controls. In fact, the greatest challenge you are
likely to face is understanding exactly what ActiveX documents are
and how they differ from controls.

So we'll begin this chapter with a discussion of the philosophy of ActiveX
documents, focusing on the assumption that the most likely use for this type
of component is on Internet and intranet Web sites. We'll conclude with a surprisingly short section discussing ActiveX document programming. Short,
because you already know almost everything you need to know from our discussions relating to other types of components.

And what if you have skipped directly to this chapter because all you want to
do is write ActiveX documents and you don't want to waste your time learning
how to write ActiveX code components and controls first? Sorry, but you are
about to become extremely confused, because I am definitely assuming that
you have read the entire book before reaching this point.

WHAT IS AN ACTIVEX DOCUMENT?

In order to really understand ActiveX documents, you need to go back to
Chapter 2 and recall our discussion on the idea of docu-centric programming.
In this approach we distinguish between a document, such as a word document or video clip, and the application that can service (open, edit, display,
save) the document. So when you talk about ActiveX documents, you are really talking about two different things: the document itself and the ActiveX
DLL or EXE server that supports it.

When you create a new ActiveX document project, you are actually creating both of these elements: the server, and an empty document. A single server can support an unlimited number of documents, just as Microsoft Word can support any number of document files. The server for an ActiveX document can be an EXE or a DLL server. The document generally has the extension .VBD, though ActiveX documents can be stored within other files as well, using a mechanism called OLE structured storage.

This division between server and document may seem obvious, but I found that it is very easy to lose sight of when reading the Visual Basic documentation for ActiveX documents. Table 23.1 illustrates the similarities between Word documents and ActiveX documents.

When you compile or run a new ActiveX document server, Visual Basic creates an empty .VBD file that has no properties set. When you load an empty .VBD file, the UserDocument's InitProperties event will trigger. If you save the object, the object will write out its properties into the .VBD file during the UserDocument's WriteProperties event. From then on, when you open the .VBD file, a ReadProperties event will trigger to prompt the server to read the properties from the .VBD file. Sounds just like an ActiveX control, doesn't it?

ACTIVEX DOCUMENTS AND ACTIVEX CONTROLS

Even though ActiveX documents and ActiveX controls are extremely similar when it comes to programming, there are substantial differences in how they work and how they are deployed.

Table 23.2 compares ActiveX controls and ActiveX documents. The table limits itself to a comparison of deploying these two technologies on Web pages, since we resolved earlier that from our perspective in this chapter, the Internet and intranets are the most likely uses for ActiveX documents.

This suggests another way of looking at ActiveX documents.

Think of your Internet browser as a window onto the Internet or an intranet. When it is displaying a Web page, what it is really doing is interpreting a simple text markup language called HTML. An advanced browser such as Microsoft's Internet Explorer or Netscape's Navigator can execute scripts that are included on the HTML page. These scripts can be in Javascript or in VBScript, but there is nothing to prevent other scripting languages from being defined.

But an Internet browser window can display other things as well. It might be able to display a directory when you are looking at an FTP site. Or perhaps an image when you ask it to display a bitmap file.

Table 23.1: Comparison of Microsoft Word with an ActiveX Document

Operation	Microsoft Word	ActiveX Document
Open a document file	Double-click on a .DOC file.	Double-click on an HTML page that references a .VBD file, or open the .VBD file using MS Explorer.
The server is found.	Windows checks the registry and finds that files with the extension .DOC should be opened by Word.	OLE looks inside the .VBD file to find the CLSID of the server.
The document is opened.	Word is loaded and opens the .DOC file. The contents of the document are loaded.	The ActiveX document server is loaded and opens the .VBD document file. An ActiveX document object is created that loads the document by reading properties from the file.
The document is displayed.	Word displays the .DOC file.	The browser allocates a window in which the ActiveX document object is sited. The server then displays this object.
The document is edited.	You can use all of the functionality of Word to manipulate the data for the document.	You can use all of the functionality that has been programmed into the server to manipulate the data for the object.
The server is closed.	Word prompts you to save the changed document data into the .DOC file if you wish.	Explorer prompts you to save the changed document data if you wish. If you say yes, the object saves the document data by writing properties into the .VBD file (or a separate file if it can't write into the current document file).

Table 23.2: Comparison of ActiveX Controls and ActiveX Documents on a Web Page

Operation	ActiveX Control	ActiveX Document
Finding the component	The control is defined by an Object tag in an HTML file.	The document server DLL or EXE is defined by an Object tag in an HTML file.
Downloading the server	The browser downloads the control or .CAB file. Code signing can be used to identify the file.	The browser downloads the document server DLL or EXE, or the .CAB file. Code signing can be used to identify the file.
Initializing the Server object	Properties are defined by PARAM commands in the HTML file. The control is in run mode on the container and thus will never need to write properties. Each object reference creates an instance of the control on the container.	The required server and current property settings are loaded from a .VBD document file. The object reference loads the server DLL or EXE, but does not create an instance of the Document object. Document objects are only created when .VBD document files are referenced.
Siting the Server object	The Object reference defines a location for the control on the current Web page.	The ActiveX document is best thought of as its own Web page. You can link to it as you would link to any page. You can't mix HTML and an ActiveX document on a page. However, an ActiveX document can be loaded into a browser frame. Each frame contains an independent Web page.
Changing Object properties	You can change control properties through user interaction or HTML scripting. Changes will not be saved unless you provide a mechanism to do so yourself—and never through the WriteProperties event. The control can't rewrite the HTML page that loaded it.	You can change ActiveX document properties through user interaction and, depending on the container, through scripting. The browser will give you the opportunity to save changes before you leave the page. If you do so, a .VBD file will be written with the new properties.

Microsoft's Internet Explorer can display ActiveX documents. Unlike an ActiveX control, which is designed to appear as an object on an HTML page, an ActiveX document is a completely independent type of object the browser can display instead of a Web page. This leads us to a staggering possibility: Because ActiveX documents support the Hyperlink object, which allows navigation among pages, it is theoretically possible to create a Web site that contains only ActiveX documents, with no HTML code whatsoever (other than perhaps a single initial page to download the server components).

Now add to this the fact that an ActiveX document has virtually all of the same capabilities as Visual Basic, including the ability to bring up additional forms, and that both the UserDocument object and the document's forms can contain additional controls. In other words: An ActiveX document is a Visual Basic application. The logical conclusion is inescapable: ActiveX documents allow you to create a site that is actually an application that runs on the client system.

Hmmm. Perhaps Carl was right about the importance of ActiveX documents after all.

On the other hand, a site created in this fashion could, at the time of this writing, only support people using Microsoft's Internet Explorer 3.01 or later on Windows 95 or Windows NT 4.0. This leaves a number of possible strategies for deploying this technology:

▸ You could create a site only for these people. This approach works best for Microsoft-specific sites where you don't care about people using other tools, or corporate intranets where you can dictate the client's environment.

▸ You could create a site in the hope that ActiveX documents will ultimately be supported by more operating systems and more browsers, and the expectation that your target audience will upgrade to the necessary tools as soon as possible.

▸ You could create a site in the expectation that it won't be long before everyone is running Microsoft Internet Explorer on Windows 95 or NT 4.0. (I think this is the one Microsoft would like you to choose.)

▸ You could create a hybrid site in which some scripting code in the HTML page detects the browser in use and sends the user to the ActiveX document pages if they have the right tools to support it. This is a good solution but does require that you effectively support two sites—one based on ActiveX documents and the other based on other technologies.

▸ You can stay away from ActiveX documents and go for technologies that may be less powerful but are designed to run on any possible system. (I think this is the one Netscape would like you to choose.)

▸ And, of course, you can choose any combination of the above.

Hmmm. Perhaps my skepticism about the importance of ActiveX documents is justified after all?

You can probably see why this chapter is short on good advice. I can see the advantages of ActiveX documents. I can see their potential. I can see they comprise a very cool technology that has the potential to bring about as great a revolution on the Internet as the invention of HTML. But I can't predict how ActiveX technology will spread to other platforms, or how important those platforms will be, or whether competing technologies might provide viable alternatives. It's just too soon to tell.

So I will leave the decision on whether or not to deploy this technology up to you, as we look into how these creatures are built.

ActiveX Document Programming

You already know 99 percent of everything you need to know in order to create ActiveX documents. So here, without further ado, is most of the other 1 percent.

SHOULD YOU USE A DLL OR AN EXE SERVER?

You are already well versed in the differences between the two approaches. All of the issues that have been discussed throughout this book regarding these apply to ActiveX documents as well.

DLL servers tend to be more efficient because they run in the process space of the browser. EXE servers run in their own thread, making some background operations easier to implement. An EXE server can be configured to run as a stand-alone executable as well. (Though you will not be able to use the User-Document, you can load and display forms during the Sub Main procedure.) A single EXE server will support all of the user documents of a given type that are loaded.

Personally, I have yet to run into a case where I wanted to use an EXE server for an ActiveX document. The most likely case where you would do so is if you wanted to control access to a shared resource, as was the case with the Stock-Quote server in Chapter 15.

ACTIVEX DOCUMENT DISPLAY

ActiveX documents differ from both forms and controls in the way they are displayed.

As a programmer, you define the size of your document. You have no control over the amount of screen space that is actually allocated to your document display, but you do have complete information about the available space. If the space is smaller than the document size, the container will make it possible to view a portion of the document in a viewport. This is shown in Figure 23.1.

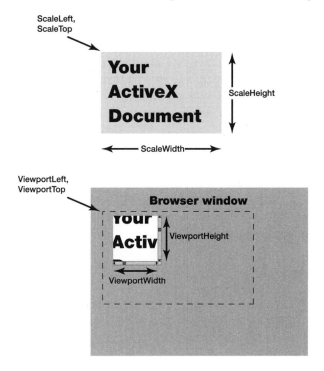

Figure 23.1: ActiveX Document Viewports

The ScaleLeft, ScaleTop, ScaleWidth, and ScaleHeight properties work as they do with forms and ActiveX controls. They reflect the coordinates of the control from the programmer's perspective. The viewport defines the area that is actually displayed. The ViewportLeft and ViewportTop properties define the location within the document area that appears in the upper left corner of the viewport area. The ViewportWidth and ViewportHeight properties define the width and height of the viewport.

The UserDocument's SetViewport method can be used to set the apparent position of the document within the viewport. It, in turn, sets the ViewportLeft and ViewportTop properties.

The UserDocument's Resize event is triggered any time the size of the document's container is changed. It occurs even if the container is larger than the current ScaleWidth and ScaleHeight settings.

If the container width is smaller than the UserDocument's MinWidth property, and the UserDocument's ScrollBars is set to display horizontal scrollbars, scrollbars will appear around the container window. This allows you to scroll the horizontal position of the document in the viewport. If the container height is smaller than the UserDocument's MinHeight property and the UserDocument's ScrollBars is set to display vertical scrollbars, scrollbars will appear around the container window. They allow you to scroll the vertical position of the document in the viewport. The HScrollSmallChange and VScrollSmallChange indicate the distance the document window scrolls when the user clicks on one of the scrollbars.

The Scroll event is triggered when the user scrolls the document within the container. If the ContinuousScroll property is True, Scroll events will be triggered as the user drags the scrollbar thumb.

The scroll.vbp project demonstrates a simple ActiveX document that displays the viewport property values and allows you to experiment with scrolling as the size of the container changes.

```
' Guide to the Perplexed
' Simple scrolling example
Option Explicit

Private m_ScrollCount&

Private Sub UpdateLabels()
    lblViewportLeft.Caption = ViewportLeft
    lblViewportTop.Caption = ViewportTop
    lblViewportWidth.Caption = ViewportWidth
    lblViewportHeight.Caption = ViewportHeight
    lblScrollCount.Caption = m_ScrollCount
End Sub

Private Sub UserDocument_Resize()
    Debug.Print "Resize"
End Sub

Private Sub UserDocument_Scroll()
    m_ScrollCount = m_ScrollCount + 1
```

```
    UpdateLabels
End Sub

Private Sub UserDocument_Show()
    UpdateLabels
End Sub
```

THE LIFE AND TIMES OF AN ACTIVEX DOCUMENT

The Visual Basic documentation goes into quite a bit of depth regarding the life cycle of an ActiveX document. In a sense this is odd, because the key events (Initialize, InitProperties, Show, ReadProperties, WriteProperties, Hide, and Terminate) work the same way as they do with ActiveX controls. The biggest difference is that the container no longer has separate design-time and run-time modes.

While the behavior of the Microsoft Internet Explorer is very interesting as described in the VB documentation, it is also largely irrelevant. This is because you cannot assume that future versions of the browser will have the same cache size and behavior. Nor can you assume that other containers will behave similarly. So design your controls under the following assumptions:

▸ The container can ask your document to save itself using the WriteProperties event any time it feels like it. Generally speaking this will occur whenever you navigate away from a page containing the document and the UserDocument's PropertyChanged method has been called.

▸ The container can navigate to and from your document whenever it wishes. The document is reloaded from the .VBD file any time you navigate to the document.

▸ The container can hide and redisplay your document at any time.

VERSIONING

Chapter 25 will discuss the issues of versioning and preserving backward compatibility when you upgrade your control. This issue is absolutely critical with regard to ActiveX documents, because if you break backward compatibility, all of your existing .VBD files supported by that server will fail to work.

CONTAINERS

You cannot test ActiveX documents using Visual Basic. You can use the Microsoft Office Binder, but I would recommend that you use the Microsoft Internet Explorer (version 3.01 or greater). This is in following our scenario that the most likely use for ActiveX documents is on Web sites. To load an ActiveX document, simply open the .VBD file using the browser's File, Open command.

The Microsoft Office Binder has its own metaphor for dealing with ActiveX documents, calling them Sections and saving properties into .OBD (Office BinDer) files instead of the .VBD files. You should refer to your Office Binder documentation for specifics on using ActiveX documents with this container.

MENUS

ActiveX documents can have a menu. However, the menu will not appear on the document page. Instead, it is merged into the container application's menu bar. In order for this to occur, you must set the NegotiatePosition option to a value other than 0.

If the top-level menu name is &Help, the menu will appear as a submenu under the container's Help menu, at least under Internet Explorer.

ERROR CHECKING

It is imperative that you trap run-time errors in your project. When a run-time error occurs, your server will stop executing. The browser will indicate that it cannot display documents that are handled by that server, typically by displaying a cross-hatched pattern over the page or an error message. The browser will not reload the server until it exits or unloads all of the cached page information, making it difficult for clients to figure out what is wrong.

THE USERDOCUMENT OBJECT

The UserDocument object is to ActiveX document servers what the UserControl object is to ActiveX controls. It is the heart of the server.

More importantly, the UserDocument works almost identically to the UserControl object. So much so, in fact, that this short section will only focus on those areas in which the two differ.

AMBIENT AND EXTENDER PROPERTIES

An ActiveX control is sited on a container that also contains other controls and objects. Thus the control has the need and ability to access ambient properties of the container.

An ActiveX document takes over the entire page or frame in which it is loaded. Whether this is enough of a reason to abandon the idea of ambient properties is not for me to say. But for good or for ill, the UserDocument object does not have an AmbientProperties property or Ambient object to access. Nor does an ActiveX document support an Extender object. It does, however, support a Parent property.

PARENT AND OTHER CLIENT PROPERTIES

The UserDocument object in an ActiveX document server has a Parent property, which allows you to access properties or methods the container chooses to provide. For example, the property UserDocument.Parent.Name returns the name of the container, such as Microsoft Internet Explorer.

The Parent object and other properties that relate to the container are not accessible until the document is sited. The property will be valid after the Show event occurs (assuming it is supported under the container) but may be valid during the InitProperties and ReadProperties events, depending on the container. It will not be valid during the Initialize event.

The Parent property provides access to the object model of the container. This can provide your server with a great deal of functionality, depending on the container. Specifics of individual containers are beyond the scope of this book. The object model for the Microsoft Internet Explorer can be found in the ActiveX SDK, which is available from Microsoft.

Naturally, any code you write that uses the container's object model will be highly container-dependent.

PROPERTY PERSISTENCE

The initial .VBD document file that is created with your ActiveX document server is empty. It essentially contains nothing more than the information needed to create a default document. Every time this document is loaded, the UserDocument's InitProperties event is triggered. It is only after information has been written into the document that the ReadProperties event will be triggered. Once that happens, the InitProperties event will not be triggered again for that particular .VBD document file.

The container will only try to write out properties using the WriteProperties event if the UserDocument object's PropertyChanged method has been called for the document. This differs from ActiveX controls where the InitProperties event occurs only once, and that in the development environment.

Documents downloaded from a Web site using a browser cannot be saved directly back to the site, and it is not clear what kind of applications can benefit from having a user modify a downloaded ActiveX document and save it locally. This suggests two likely scenarios with regard to your deployment of ActiveX documents on a Web site:

▶ The blank document approach—There is no requirement that an ActiveX document save persisted information at all. This is especially true on documents downloaded through the Internet. The document server is, after all, a fully functional program, and there are any number of possible applications that do not require the use of properties at all. With this approach, the InitProperties event will occur every time the document is loaded.

▶ The predefined document approach—With this approach you provide your server with two different operating modes. One is an edit mode, which is triggered when the empty document is loaded as indicated by the InitProperties event. The other is a standard mode, which is indicated by the ReadProperties event. In edit mode, you would open the file locally on your system, edit the properties, and save the changes when you are done. In standard mode, the document might be downloaded through a Web server. The ActiveX server loads properties during the ReadProperties event and disables any options that could change the property values. This approach is demonstrated in the realty example in Chapter 24.

Naturally, you can use any combination of the two approaches. The most important thing is that you consider how you wish your ActiveX document to be used and support it by handling the InitProperties and ReadProperties events accordingly.

TIPS AND TRICKS

Here are some additional techniques you can use with ActiveX Documents.

You can set the MinHeight and MinWidth properties to a very large value to force scrollbars to always be displayed.

Remember that you control the appearance of the document. Let's say you need a document with 100 text boxes in a vertical column (not that you would ever really want to do this). You could try to create one enormous document. A better approach would be to use a control array to create only enough text boxes to fill the available viewport, then turn on the scrollbars. When the user scrolls, you can programmatically redefine the meaning of the text boxes that are visible to make them appear as if they had scrolled, then use the SetViewport property to force the document to appear correctly in the window.

An ActiveX document can appear in a browser frame as well as in an independent window. This allows you to use any Web designer to create the navigation portion of your site (the links between the various pages), instead of coding navigation links into the document server. You'll see how this works in Chapter 24.

The Show event occurs after the document is fully sited on the container. It also occurs any time you return to the page after moving to another page. You can improve your document's performance by performing any initialization necessary the first time the Show event is called, then setting a module or static variable to indicate that the initialization is complete so you need not repeat it on subsequent Show events.

Visual Basic includes a wizard that does much of the work of converting a stand-alone application into an ActiveX document.

Given our scenario that ActiveX documents will be used primarily on Web sites, it seems clear that our next step must be to take a closer look at how ActiveX documents can be deployed on an Internet or intranet site. This is the step that forms the basis for Chapter 24.

ActiveX Documents and the Internet

THE REALTY ACTIVEX DOCUMENT

ACTIVEX DOCUMENTS AND HTML

I read through the documentation on ActiveX documents several times trying to understand the implications of this technology. But it wasn't until I actually used these documents that I began to realize the possibilities. In this chapter, my intent is not so much to tell you about ActiveX documents, as it is to show you. To do this, I had the pleasure of inventing a fictitious real estate company. I hope you enjoy its site, which makes extensive use of ActiveX documents. However, I encourage you to use extreme caution before sending a check or your credit card number there!

THE REALTY ACTIVEX DOCUMENT

Really Realty Services Inc. is a small fictitious outfit with big goals. They don't want to just display properties on the Web. They want to display the current information about a property along with an interactive program that allows potential customers to calculate their mortgage payments and even submit on-line bids. They could come up with some sophisticated form-based Web pages to do this, but they've figured out that there is no reason to tie up their server with tasks such as calculating loans. It's much better to have those types of programs just run on the client machine.

Besides, they are Visual Basic programming wizards and don't know much about complex form-based HTML code and server-side programming. By using an ActiveX document, they are able to use the full resources of the local system. They're not quite sure what to do with that capability yet, but they know it will come in handy in the future.

Figure 24.1 shows the page they've created to display information about a property. There is a Picture Box that will contain a picture of the property, a Label to show the current asking price, and a Text Box that will display the current property description.

Figure 24.1: Design-time view of the realty.dob ActiveX document

The ActiveX document has three properties: Price, Picture, and Description. The property procedures for these properties and persistence functions are shown below:

```
' Guide to the Perplexed
' Realty Example
' Copyright Ö 1997 by Desaware Inc. All Rights Reserved.
' Really Realty Services Inc. is a fictional company, and
' any resemblance to a real company is entirely unintentional
Option Explicit

Dim m_Price As Currency


Public Property Get Picture() As Picture
    Set Picture = Picture1.Picture
End Property

Public Property Set Picture(ByVal vNewValue As Picture)
    Set Picture1.Picture = vNewValue
    PropertyChanged "Picture"
End Property
```

```
Public Property Get Price() As Currency
   Price = m_Price
End Property

Public Property Let Price(ByVal new_Price As Currency)
   If new_Price < 0 Then Exit Property
   m_Price = new_Price
   lblPrice.Caption = Format$(m_Price, "Currency")
   PropertyChanged "Price"
End Property

Public Property Get Description() As String
   Description = txtDescription.Text
End Property

Public Property Let Description(new_Description As String)
   txtDescription.Text = new_Description
   PropertyChanged "Description"
End Property

Private Sub UserDocument_InitProperties()
   cmdEdit.Visible = True
   cmdNew.Visible = True
End Sub

Private Sub UserDocument_ReadProperties(PropBag As PropertyBag)
   txtDescription.Text = PropBag.ReadProperty("Description")
   m_Price = PropBag.ReadProperty("Price")
   lblPrice.Caption = Format$(m_Price, "Currency")
   Set Picture1.Picture = PropBag.ReadProperty("Picture")
End Sub

Private Sub UserDocument_WriteProperties(PropBag As PropertyBag)
   Call PropBag.WriteProperty("Description", txtDescription.Text)
   Call PropBag.WriteProperty("Price", m_Price)
   Call PropBag.WriteProperty("Picture", Picture1.Picture)
   ' Once data is written, this page is not editable
   cmdEdit.Visible = False
   cmdNew.Visible = False
End Sub
```

There are also four buttons. The Bid button is used to bring up a bid submission form, which is a separate Visual Basic modal form that not only allows the client to submit bids on the property, but to perform any other tasks they decide will be related to submitting a bid. The Back button is just a navigation aid to allow the client to return to the previous browser page without having to use the browser toolbar or menu.

This ActiveX document is designed to work in two modes. When the browser opens an empty .VBD file, the InitProperties event is triggered and the Edit and New buttons are made visible (they are invisible by default). This is done in the following code:

```
Private Sub UserDocument_InitProperties()
    cmdEdit.Visible = True
    cmdNew.Visible = True
End Sub
```

This mode is intended for their own use when developing the site. They use Microsoft's Internet browser to open the empty RealtyDoc.vbd file, then use the Edit and New buttons to create new VBD documents that have the picture, price, and description properties set. When those documents are loaded, the ReadProperties event will be triggered, which does not make the Edit and New buttons visible. These two buttons are also hidden after the WriteProperties event occurs, to prevent the pages from being edited again. (Note that the RealtyDoc.vbd file has been renamed ReltyDoc.vbd in the CH24 sample directory in order to fit within the 8.3 filename format required by the CD-ROM.)

Editing the current page is a simple task. A separate form named frmEdit is used to edit the document's properties. It is brought up using the following code when the Edit button is clicked. The Edit form is shown in Figure 24.2.

```
Private Sub cmdEdit_Click()
    Set frmEdit.OwnerDoc = Me
    frmEdit.Show vbModal
    Set frmEdit = Nothing
End Sub
```

This form has a preview window to display a picture of the property. It has two text boxes for editing the price and the description, and it uses a common dialog control to load the picture file. The code for this form is shown below:

```
Option Explicit

Public OwnerDoc As RealtyDoc

Private Sub cmdCancel_Click()
    Unload Me
End Sub

Private Sub cmdLoadImage_Click()
    Dim newfile$
```

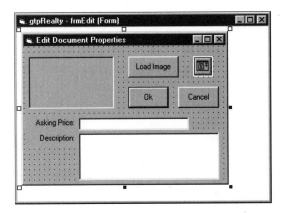

Figure 24.2: The document editing form

```
    CmnDialog1.ShowOpen
    If CmnDialog1.FileTitle = "" Then Exit Sub
    newfile = CmnDialog1.filename
    On Error GoTo badimage
    Set Picture1.Picture = LoadPicture(newfile)
    Exit Sub
badimage:
End Sub

Private Sub cmdOk_Click()
    OwnerDoc.Price = txtPrice.Text
    OwnerDoc.Description = txtDescription.Text
    Set OwnerDoc.Picture = Picture1.Picture
    Unload Me
End Sub

Private Sub Form_Load()
    txtPrice.Text = OwnerDoc.Price
    txtDescription.Text = OwnerDoc.Description
    Set Picture1.Picture = OwnerDoc.Picture
End Sub
```

The OwnerDoc variable is a public property of the form that is set by the realty Document object before the form is shown. This allows the form to access the public properties of the document. You can also access Friend properties and methods of the Document object, though this is not shown in this particular example.

If you look at the settings for the common dialog control, you'll find that its filter property is set to Pictures (*.bmp;*.ico;*.wmf;*.gif). WMF? That's a Windows metafile. Since when can a Web browser download and display a Windows metafile? Well, most of them can't. But it doesn't matter. You see, the Web browser does not download and display the metafile. It downloads the VBD ActiveX document file. That document file contains the metafile, and Visual Basic knows how to read and display metafiles in picture boxes.

Does this mean that ActiveX documents can allow you to potentially handle any file format or even create custom file formats of your own that you can edit and display, regardless of the capabilities of the browser? Yes. In fact, this example uses metafile pictures for all of its graphics. A complete discussion of metafiles is beyond the scope of this book but, in short, they differ from bitmaps in two major characteristics:

▸ They contain graphic drawing commands instead of bitmap information. This means they may be smaller than a bitmap.

▸ They are fully scaleable and do not lose image quality as they are resized.

The Edit button edits the current document. But you don't want to edit the empty RealtyDoc document. You need to keep it around as a blank template for other documents. For this reason, it should be set to read-only. Instead, there needs to be a way to create new documents.

One method to do so is shown below in the cmdNew_Click command code:

```
Private Sub cmdNew_Click()
    Dim newname$
    Dim newpath$, oldpath$
    Dim searchloc&, curloc&, curchar$
    newname$ = InputBox("Enter new document name", "New")
    If newname$ = "" Then Exit Sub
    oldpath = Parent.locationname
    newpath = oldpath
    curloc = Len(newpath)
    Do While curloc > 0
        curchar$ = Mid$(newpath, curloc, 1)
        If curchar = "/" Or curchar = "\" Then
            newpath = Left$(newpath, curloc)
            Exit Do
        End If
        curloc = curloc - 1
    Loop
    newpath = newpath & newname$ & ".vbd"
    ' Add test for existing file here
    FileCopy oldpath, newpath
    m_HyperLinked = True
```

```
   Hyperlink.NavigateTo "file://" & newpath
End Sub
```

The Parent object's Locationname property provides the document name. You can't use the App.Path property in Visual Basic because it gives you the location of the server, not the current document.

The document name is assumed to be on the local system. If you loaded it through a Web site, this code will fail with an error. But in this particular application, it is assumed that new properties will only be defined on the local system. The routine strips the final document name from the path and appends in a new document name that is entered using an input box. The name should be added without an extension; a more robust example would verify this. The FileCopy command is used to create the new document file. Note that this will be a blank document.

The next step is to navigate to the new document. This is done by setting a global variable called m_HyperLinked to True. This variable is used to indicate to a newly loaded document that it has been loaded as a result of a New operation and to tell it to bring up its edit form during the Show event. The Hyperlink object is then used to navigate to the new page.

The m_HyperLinked variable is defined in a standard form so it will be global to all document objects. If it is True, the edit form is shown, as you can see below:

```
Private Sub UserDocument_Show()
   If m_HyperLinked Then
      m_HyperLinked = False
      Set frmEdit.OwnerDoc = Me
      frmEdit.Show vbModal
      Set frmEdit = Nothing
   End If
End Sub
```

The ActiveX document includes an About Box implemented in the usual way as shown below: The document has a menu that includes both a Help and an About command. The Negotiate attribute for the menu is set so it will be merged with the container's menu.

```
Private Sub mnuAbout_Click()
   frmAbout.Show vbModal
End Sub
```

A text box is used for the description because it supports scrolling. However, the document does not allow editing of the description on the document page itself. In order to prevent editing, keypresses are intercepted to block editing and deleting in the text box, as shown below:

```
Private Sub txtDescription_KeyDown(KeyCode As Integer, Shift As Integer)
    If KeyCode = vbKeyDelete Then
        KeyCode = 0
    End If
End Sub
```

```
Private Sub txtDescription_KeyPress(KeyAscii As Integer)
    KeyAscii = 0
End Sub
```

Implementing the Back browser command is trivial:

```
Private Sub cmdBack_Click()
    Hyperlink.GoBack
End Sub
```

The Bid form is brought up using the following code:

```
Private Sub cmdBid_Click()
    Set frmBid.OwnerDoc = Me
    frmBid.Show vbModal
    Set frmBid = Nothing
End Sub
```

The form is shown in Figure 24.3.

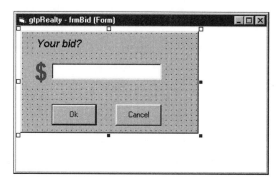

Figure 24.3: The Bid form at design time

Right now the form does nothing with the information that is entered. But this is a standard Visual Basic form, so you can do anything you want at this point. You could generate an e-mail message with the bid. You could calculate a loan payment and send information based on the results. You could allow the user to record an audio message and upload it to an FTP site somewhere.

This brings up an important point. Standard Web sites are designed to accept small amounts of data from the client while sending large amounts of data back to the client. Relatively short text command lines are used in HTML to request information from a server. Once in Visual Basic, you have a great deal more flexibility for sending information to the server. You could, for example, upload data to an FTP site, then send a command with the name of the file. Or use a separate direct Internet connection using a Winsock control. ActiveX documents may prove to be an excellent solution for this type of situation. For example: If the fictitious folks that run Really Realty Services, Inc. ever go out of business, they could set up an ActiveX document-based dating service, where you can use a VB form to submit your picture and perhaps a short video clip directly to the services computer systems via the Internet.

Now let's take a look at what it takes to make this document work on a Web site.

ACTIVEX DOCUMENTS AND HTML

The process of setting up an ActiveX document for Internet distribution is identical to that of ActiveX controls and will not be repeated here. The only difference is that what you are distributing is the document server, not the document itself.

If you look at the Setup subdirectory under the Chapter 24 sample directory on the CD-ROM that comes with this book, you will find the file Realty.htm HTML page that is created by the Visual Basic setup wizard.

```
<HTML>
<OBJECT ID="RealtyDoc"
CLASSID="CLSID:18C62902-7B03-11D0-91BB-00AA0036005A"
CODEBASE="realty.CAB#version=1,0,0,1">
</OBJECT>

<SCRIPT LANGUAGE="VBScript">
Sub Window_OnLoad
     Document.Open
     Document.Write "<FRAMESET>"
     Document.Write "<FRAME SRC=""RealtyDoc.VBD"">"
     Document.Write "</FRAMESET>"
     Document.Close
End Sub
</SCRIPT>
</HTML>
```

The Object tag should be familiar to you from the ActiveX control example. The .CAB file can be signed just as it was in the ActiveX control example. The servers within the file can be marked as safe for initialization and safe for scripting using either the registry technique or the IObjectSafety technique described in Chapter 21. Note that this sample code does use scripting and thus will generate a warning message if the component is not marked as safe for scripting.

Speaking of scripting, what is the script that appears below the Object tag? When this HTML page is loaded by the browser, it will first verify that the object is present on the system, downloading it if necessary. It will then run the VB Script code shown. This code opens the current page and starts writing new HTML code into the page. It first writes a <FRAMESET> tag, which defines what follows as being a frame that takes over the entire browser window. It then specifies that the frame should be loaded with the ActiveX document, in this case, the default RealtyDoc.VBD file. Finally it closes the frameset and the document. In effect, it tells the browser to load the .VBD file and display it.

The page shown here will, in fact, download a document server if necessary and then display a document. However, it is somewhat misleading. I'm afraid that many ActiveX document developers will get the idea that this is the only way to display an ActiveX document and that each ActiveX document requires its own HTML page to load and display. That may be true if you are using a single ActiveX document, but if your site uses many documents, it is terribly inefficient.

The programmers at the Really Realty Services company knew better. You can see their handiwork by opening the default.htm file in Chapter 24 on the CD-ROM with Microsoft Internet Explorer. This page is shown below:

```
<!DOCTYPE HTML PUBLIC "-//W30/DTD HTML//EN">

<html>
<OBJECT ID="RealtyDoc"
CLASSID="CLSID:18C62902-7B03-11D0-91BB-00AA0036005A"
CODEBASE="realty.CAB#version=1,0,0,1">
</OBJECT>
<head>
<title>mainpage</title>
<meta name="FORMATTER" content="Microsoft FrontPage 1.1">
</head>
<frameset rows="23%,77%">
    <frame src="frbanner.htm" name="banner" marginwidth="1"
    marginheight="1">
    <frameset cols="30%,70%">
        <frame src="frconten.htm" name="contents" marginwidth="1"
```

```
        marginheight="1">
        <frame src="frmain.htm" name="main" marginwidth="1"
        marginheight="1">
    </frameset>
    <noframes>
    <body>
    <p> </p>
    <p>This web page uses frames, but your browser doesn't
    support them.</p>
    </body>
    </noframes>
</frameset>
</html>
```

This is the root page for the site. The company expects everyone viewing the site to go through this page at least the first time they access the site. Thus, the document server download takes place at this time. The page has a banner frame with the company name at the top and a list of properties on the left. The main portion of the page, on the right, contains an introductory text at first. The contents page, frconten.htm, contains jumps that go directly to the ActiveX documents. For example, the line:

```
<h3><a href="bigben.vbd">Big Ben</a></h3>
```

will appear as <u>Big Ben</u> on the Web page in blue text (or whichever color your browser is using to indicate a jump). When you click on the link, the browser will download file bigben.vbd from the site. It examines the file and sees that it is a structured storage file that meets the standard of ActiveX documents. It extracts the CLSID identifier of the server and checks the server, to find that it is registered to realty.dll, which was downloaded earlier. The browser then asks the server to create a RealtyDoc object. The object's ReadProperties event is then triggered, allowing it to read the property information from file bigben.vbd, which had just been downloaded. The browser then displays the ActiveX document in the main frame, which is the default target for all links on the current page.

It is conceivable that a client will run into trouble if they set bookmarks directly to one of these documents and lose access to their server, but if this occurs they will be notified by the browser. All they need to do is go back to the home page to reload the document server. The contents page code is shown below.

```
<!DOCTYPE HTML PUBLIC "-//IETF//DTD HTML//EN">

<html>

<head>
<title>Table of Contents Frame in mainpage</title>
```

```
<meta name="GENERATOR" content="Microsoft FrontPage 1.1">
<base target="main">
</head>

<body>
<h3>Choose from among <br>
these fine properties:</h3>
<h3><a href="bigben.vbd">Big Ben</a></h3>
<h3><a href="capitol.vbd">U.S. Capitol</a></h3>
<h3><a href="eiffel.vbd">Eiffel Tower</a></h3>
<h3><a href="empire.vbd">Empire State</a></h3>
<h3><a href="sydney.vbd">Opera House</a></h3>
<h3><a href="tajmahal.vbd">Taj Mahal</a></h3>
</body>

</html>
```

It is up to you whether you want to have a separate HTML page for each ActiveX document or implement direct links as shown here. The end result can be seen in Figure 24.4.

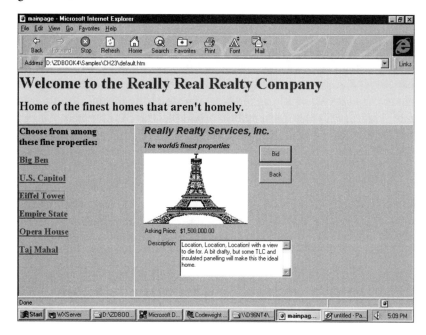

Figure 24.4: Sample page from the Realty site

I encourage you to explore this small site and to create some documents of your own. This concludes our coverage of ActiveX documents. Are they the future of Internet and intranet Web sites? Or are they a solution to a problem that doesn't really exist? Or perhaps a good idea that just won't catch on. Time will tell.

Part 5

Selected Topics

VERSIONING

LICENSING AND DISTRIBUTION

There is a saying that in order to ask a question, you must already know 80 percent of the answer.

I don't know if this is true, but I do know that knowledge is a pyramid, that newly learned knowledge must be based on what you already know. This is one of the reasons I prefer to avoid writing "tips and techniques" books. They do have value, but they are no substitute for learning from the fundamentals up. If you learn an advanced technique, you know that technique. If you make the extra effort to learn the technology on which that technique is based, including how and why it works, you will know more than the technique. You will be able to build on it to develop your own solutions. When trouble occurs, you'll be able to figure out why the technique doesn't work and fix the problem. You'll be able to develop and discover new approaches to solving problems on your own. You will be able to derive variations on the technique and take full advantage of them from the earliest design stages of your project.

This book was written with this philosophy in mind. Every chapter was designed as much as possible to build on the knowledge gained in earlier chapters. The entire book was intended from the start to build on the knowledge you already have, both from programming Visual Basic and from reading the Microsoft Visual Basic documentation. Much of the general information presented at the beginning of the book applied to all of the component types discussed in later chapters. This information formed the foundation on which the component-specific chapters were built.

But there is another type of general information. This is information that also applies to every type of component but that requires a good understanding of all of the component types to use effectively. Which brings us to this final part of the book. In the following brief, but important chapters, you'll find selected topics that apply to all of the component types.

Enjoy…

Versioning

VERSION RESOURCES

VERSION COMPATIBILITY

Chapter 25

Windows 3.0. Windows 3.1. Windows 95. Windows NT 3.51. Windows NT 4.0. Visual Basic 1.0. Visual Basic 2.0. Visual Basic 3.0. Visual Basic 4.0. Visual Basic 5.0.

We are well accustomed to dealing with different versions of software packages. As consumers we look at each version number as a package with a new set of features. This used to be the way developers would look at software packages, but that is no longer the case.

A typical Windows application depends on many different components. It uses functions provided by dynamic link libraries that are part of the operating system. It uses functions provided by dynamic link libraries that are part of the operating system's implementation of OLE. It uses standard window classes that are provided by additional dynamic link libraries, such as the common control library and the common dialog library. It uses system services, such as Mail and Winsock, that are implemented by other dynamic link libraries. It may use ActiveX controls, each of which is implemented by a dynamic link library (typically with the .OCX extension). A Visual Basic application always requires the Visual Basic run-time DLL and may also depend upon additional run-time DLLs used by the various ActiveX controls. And now, your program will also be dependent on any new ActiveX components or controls that you create for use in the application.

That is a lot of dependencies. And each and every one of those components has its own version, which is completely independent of the version number of the application. When you create your application, you build and test it based on a particular set of components. If you try to run your application on a system where any single one of those components is obsolete, your program may not run correctly. This is a fundamental problem with component-based software, and it is a very serious problem indeed.

In this chapter you'll find out how to deal with it, both with regard to developing components and with regard to distributing them.

Version Resources

An obvious necessity for dealing with the problem of component versions is the ability to mark each component with a version number. Windows allows each executable or dynamic link library to be embedded with a version resource. This resource contains both the version number and descriptive string information.

Figure 25.1 shows the Project Make dialog box for the project properties settings. You can set descriptive strings including the company name, file description, product name, and copyright and trademark information. But you should always set the version number.

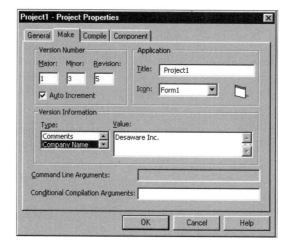

Figure 25.1: The Project Make dialog box

In fact, the very first thing you should do is to select the Auto Increment checkbox. This insures that every time you build your component, it will have an updated version number.

Why is this important? Because the version resource is almost universally used by installation programs to prevent newer components from being overwritten by older components. You see, version resources mark a component or executable, but there is nothing in the system or in Visual Basic that automatically verifies that dependent components are present and correct when an application is run. Worse yet, it is often impossible to detect that a problem was caused by a component-related issue. For example: a component error that prevents a control or ActiveX document from loading might simply cause a trapped run-time error, which is then reported by the container as an HTML or scripting error.

It is possible for a component to be overwritten by an older component in several ways. Some installation programs signal when they are about to overwrite a newer component and allow the user to do so if they wish. Some installation programs do not check version numbers correctly. Sometimes individuals simply copy files from one system to another.

Keep in mind that with OLE technology, the component used depends on the contents of the system registry. Any application can register an older version of a component and thus effectively replace a newer version without overwriting it. The old solution of keeping components in a private directory no longer works.

All of these scenarios illustrate that it is possible for obsolete components to appear on a system at any time. Then, they can interfere with the correct operation of your application, even if your application was installed correctly. There are several approaches you can take to deal with this situation:

▶ Reinstall your application any time it starts exhibiting unusual behavior or fails to run correctly.

▶ Have your component or application perform its own dependency verification. The Win32 API has a number of functions that allow you to read version information from any executable or component that has a version resource.

▶ Use a component verification toolkit such as Desaware's VersionStamper. It can be used to add dependency verification to your component or application, including the ability to update components via the Internet or corporate intranet.

▶ Ignore the problem and expect to spend quite a bit of time dealing with support calls when problems occur.

You should decide which of these strategies you wish to use in distributing your own component-based applications. The problem is not as serious for controls and components that are downloaded by Web pages. This is because the browser is essentially filling the role of an installation program, downloading the latest components each time they are needed. But regardless of the approach you take for distributing your components, it is clear that as a component developer you have a responsibility to your users to make sure that your components are marked correctly.

Version Compatibility

Consider the following scenario. You have created an application that uses version 1.0 of control xyz.ocx. The vendor who developed the xyz.ocx control releases a new version numbered 2.0. However, the developer removed one of the control's properties, figuring that it was not particularly useful.

Your application continues to run correctly, because you are still shipping version 1.0 of the control. However, one day you install a different application that uses version 2.0 of the control. The installation program for that application detected version 1.0 on your system and replaced it with the upgraded version. Next time you run your application, it uses version 2.0 of the control. However, as soon as it tries to access the missing property, the control will fail, probably with a memory exception.

The version number in the version resource is just an identifier. It has no functionality. There is nothing to guarantee that version 2.0 of a component will successfully run with an application that was compiled using version 1.0 of a component. Yet the entire system of component upgrades assumes that a later version of a component will support all of the features of the earlier version.

It is absolutely critical that you, as a component developer, make certain that your upgraded components are backward compatible with previous versions. This means that an upgraded component must do the following:

▶ Have the same CLSID component identifiers and type library identifiers as the earlier version.

▶ Support all previous properties, methods, and events.

▶ All properties, methods, and events must have the same Dispatch ID number (procedure ID).

▶ All properties, methods, and events must have the same parameters and parameter types.

▶ All properties, methods, and events must exhibit the same functionality as the earlier version.

Now we'll return to a discussion of how to accomplish this in a moment.

If you decide to abandon backward compatibility, you should do the following:

▶ Change the project name using the General tab of the Project Properties dialog box.

▶ Turn off compatibility by setting the No Compatibility option in the Components tab of the Project Properties dialog box.

▶ Rebuild the project, changing the name of the executable file or DLL.

You have seen how Microsoft handled this situation in the history of Visual Basic. When switching from version 3 to version 4, the run-time file used by Visual Basic was changed from VBRUN300.DLL to VB40032.DLL. But when they did a minor upgrade to Visual Basic 4.0 called version 4.0A, they kept backward compatibility with the previous VB40032.DLL and just changed the version number in the resource file.

How do you maintain backward compatibility? Keeping the same properties, members, and events and their parameters is easy. But Visual Basic hides the assignment of CLSID values and procedure identifiers. This means there must be a way to tell Visual Basic you want to keep the previous values. This is accomplished using the Components tab of the Property Procedures dialog box. It provides three possible types of compatibility:

▶ No compatibility

▶ Project compatibility

▶ Binary compatibility

No compatibility is obvious. Visual Basic redefines the type library identifier and all interface and procedure identifiers every time the project is built. Project compatibility is not really compatible at all. The only thing it does is reuse the current type library identifier. It's convenient because you don't have to keep reestablishing references to the component, but Visual Basic does nothing to check that the project is, in fact, backward compatible.

Selecting binary compatibility is a way to tell Visual Basic that you want to make sure the newly compiled component will be backward compatible with a previous version of the component. Visual Basic will continue to use the same type library identifier and will continue to support existing interface and procedure identifiers. If you make a change that might break backward compatibility, Visual Basic will warn you. Take those warnings seriously! Accepting changes in this case is effectively the same as choosing the no-compatibility option. Visual

Basic can preserve compatibility of the interface and procedure definitions, but it is still your job to ensure functional compatibility.

Here's a true story from about five years ago that illustrates what I mean. Desaware's first product was the Custom Control Factory, a flexible button control that supports multiple states and animation. We licensed a subset of the control called the *animated button* to Microsoft for inclusion with Visual Basic. This control had a property called Frame, which could be set to the current animation frame to display. If you tried to set the property to a negative number, it would simply ignore the setting and would not raise an error. In hindsight, we should have raised an error in that case. Keep in mind, though, that the control was written in the early days of VBX technology. We were still getting accustomed to the whole idea of custom controls and Visual Basic, so the conventions we observe today were not yet clearly defined.

During one of the upgrades—I think it was from version 1 to version 2—Microsoft asked us to add an error test to the property and raise an error if it was set to a negative number. I protested this, saying that in the unlikely event some program actually did set a negative number, the change could break backward compatibility. But they insisted I make the change. By this time it was well established that errors should be raised in cases such as this. Besides, any program that did set the Frame property to a negative number had a bug in it anyway, so it would really be their fault if a problem occurred.

Under the terms of the license, they were paying for the work and had the right to dictate things like that, so I did make the change to their version of the control. However, I kept the existing behavior in the full Custom Control Factory product, just in case. Well, wouldn't you know it. Turns out that a program out there had a bug in it that sometimes set the property to a negative number. It was one of the early versions of Microsoft Encarta. Go figure!

The moral of this story is clear: Visual Basic's binary compatibility mode will do its best to make sure that your interfaces and registry information support backward compatibility. But maintaining functional compatibility is equally important, and that is entirely up to you.

INSIDE BINARY COMPATIBILITY

Let's take a closer look at what happens when you specify Binary Compatibility.

The gtpComp.vbp project in the Chapter 25 sample directory on your CD-ROM was used to generate the examples that follow. It contains the final version of the project. You can follow its creation step by step. However the explanation that follows should prove sufficiently clear without your having to go through the process of verifying it for yourself.

The gtpComp.vbp is an ActiveX DLL project that contains a single class called gtpComp. The class module is initially defined as follows:

```
Public Sub A()
    Debug.Print "A called"
End Sub
```

When compiled, the following type library is produced:

```
'===================================================================
' Type Library: gtpCompatibility, Library Version 1.000
' GUID: {3A33201F-7F29-11D0-93A2-00AA0036005A}
' LCID: 0X00000000
' Documentation: (o vial)Tx ie *tt' Help: (o vial)Tx ie
*tt'=============================================================


'===================================================================
' Type Info: _gtpComp, TypeInfo Version 1.000
' GUID: {3A33201D-7F29-11D0-93A2-00AA0036005A}
' LCID: 0X00000000
' TypeKind: dispinterface
'-------------------------------------------------------------


' Function: QueryInterface
'
Declare Sub QueryInterface (ByRef riid As Variant, ByRef ppvObj As Variant)

' Function: AddRef
'
Declare Function AddRef () As ULONG

' Function: Release
'
Declare Function Release () As ULONG

' Function: GetTypeInfoCount
'
Declare Sub GetTypeInfoCount (ByRef pctinfo As Variant)

' Function: GetTypeInfo
'
Declare Sub GetTypeInfo (ByVal itinfo As UINT, ByVal lcid As ULONG, ByRef pptinfo_
As Variant)

' Function: GetIDsOfNames
'
Declare Sub GetIDsOfNames (ByRef riid As Variant, ByRef rgszNames As Variant,_
ByVal cNames As UINT, ByVal lcid As ULONG, ByRef rgdispid As Variant)
```

```
' Function: Invoke
'
Declare Sub Invoke (ByVal dispidMember As Long, ByRef riid As Variant, ByVal lcid
As ULONG, ByVal wFlags As USHORT, ByRef pdispparams As Variant, ByRef pvarResult
As Variant, ByRef pexcepinfo As Variant, ByRef puArgErr As Variant)

' Function: A
'
Declare Sub A ()

'================================================================
' Type Info: gtpComp, TypeInfo Version 1.000
' GUID: {3A33201E-7F29-11D0-93A2-00AA0036005A}
' LCID: 0X00000000
' TypeKind: coclass
'----------------------------------------------------------------
```

Note that the actual GUID values that appear in this listing may not match those for the components on the CD-ROM.

I encourage you to turn your attention to several parts of the type library. The GUID specifies the type library identifier. _gtpComp is the name of the main interface for the class. The class is an automation-compatible interface, as you can tell by the fact that it has the standard IDispatch members, including GetTypeInfoCount, GetTypeInfo, GetIDsOfNames, and Invoke. It also includes subroutine A.

Next, make a reference copy of the compiled DLL. This will be version 1. Bring up the Components tab of the Project Properties dialog box and set binary compatibility to the version 1 reference.

Go ahead and recompile the project as many times as you wish. The type library will remain the same. This means you can safely change the code without impacting the type library information. You should, of course, make sure that the code changes remain compatible with earlier versions. You should increment the version number in the resource so installation programs will know to replace earlier versions of your component with the improved versions.

Now, change the class code by adding a new procedure B. Unregister the current DLL using the regsvr32 command with the /u option. This cleans up the registry so we know we are starting with a clean slate with this application. Now recompile and look at the type library.

```
'================================================================
' Type Library: gtpCompatibility, Library Version 1.001
' GUID: {3A33201F-7F29-11D0-93A2-00AA0036005A}
' LCID: 0X00000000
```

```
' Documentation: (o vial)Tx ie *tt' Help: (o vial)Tx ie
*tt'=========================================================
'=========================================================
' Type Info: _gtpComp, TypeInfo Version 1.001
' GUID: {3A332029-7F29-11D0-93A2-00AA0036005A}
' LCID: 0X00000000
' TypeKind: dispinterface
'----------------------------------------------------------

' Function: QueryInterface
'
Declare Sub QueryInterface (ByRef riid As Variant, ByRef ppvObj As Variant)

' Function: AddRef
'
Declare Function AddRef () As ULONG

' Function: Release
'
Declare Function Release () As ULONG

' Function: GetTypeInfoCount
'
Declare Sub GetTypeInfoCount (ByRef pctinfo As Variant)

' Function: GetTypeInfo
'
Declare Sub GetTypeInfo (ByVal itinfo As UINT, ByVal lcid As ULONG, ByRef pptinfo_
As Variant)

' Function: GetIDsOfNames
'
Declare Sub GetIDsOfNames (ByRef riid As Variant, ByRef rgszNames As Variant,_
ByVal cNames As UINT, ByVal lcid As ULONG, ByRef rgdispid As Variant)

' Function: Invoke
'
Declare Sub Invoke (ByVal dispidMember As Long, ByRef riid As Variant, ByVal lcid_
As ULONG, ByVal wFlags As USHORT, ByRef pdispparams As Variant, ByRef pvarResult_
As Variant, ByRef pexcepinfo As Variant, ByRef puArgErr As Variant)

' Function: A
'
Declare Sub A ()

' Function: B
```

```
'
Declare Sub B ()

'===========================================================
' Type Info: gtpComp, TypeInfo Version 1.001
' GUID: {3A33201E-7F29-11D0-93A2-00AA0036005A}
' LCID: 0X00000000
' TypeKind: coclass
'-----------------------------------------------------------
```

The type library version has been increased to version 1.001. Let me stress an important point at this time: The type library version number bears absolutely no relationship to the version number specified in the version resource. None whatsoever. Despite the change in type library version number, the type library GUID remains the same. However, the _gtpComp interface has a new interface identifier. How then, can existing versions of the program use the interface?

The answer is that both interfaces are preserved. If you look in the registry for the interfaces, you will find an entry for both interfaces in the HKEY_CLASSES_ROOT/Interfaces key. First, the original version 1.0 interface is defined as follows:

```
Key Name:         Interface\{3A33201D-7F29-11D0-93A2-00AA0036005A}
Class Name:       <NO CLASS>
Last Write Time:  2/4/97 - 11:55 PM
Value 0
  Name:           <NO NAME>
  Type:           REG_SZ
  Data:           gtpComp


Key Name:         Interface\{3A33201D-7F29-11D0-93A2-00AA0036005A}\Forward
Class Name:       <NO CLASS>
Last Write Time:  2/4/97 - 11:55 PM
Value 0
  Name:           <NO NAME>
  Type:           REG_SZ
  Data:           {3A332029-7F29-11D0-93A2-00AA0036005A}
```

This interface has an entry marked Forward, which indicates that an updated version of the interface is available. This interface is shown here:

```
Key Name:         Interface\{3A332029-7F29-11D0-93A2-00AA0036005A}
Class Name:       <NO CLASS>
Last Write Time:  2/4/97 - 11:55 PM
Value 0
  Name:           <NO NAME>
```

```
        Type:              REG_SZ
        Data:              gtpComp


Key Name:                  Interface\{3A332029-7F29-11D0-93A2-00AA0036005A}\TypeLib
Class Name:                <NO CLASS>
Last Write Time:           2/4/97 - 11:55 PM
Value 0
    Name:                  <NO NAME>
    Type:                  REG_SZ
    Data:                  {3A33201F-7F29-11D0-93A2-00AA0036005A}

Value 1
    Name:                  Version
    Type:                  REG_SZ
    Data:                  1.1
```

Applications that were compiled to use the earlier component can request the original _gtpComp interface and still work correctly. Newer applications will always get the later interface.

If you refer back to the type library listing, you'll see that the new subroutine has been added to the end of the list of procedures for the interface. This means that from a coding point of view, an application using the interface is fully compatible with the new one, even if it used early binding to call those functions directly. Older applications simply will not see the new B function.

There are two additional points to learn from this example:

▶ Every time you create a new release that redefines an interface, you increase the overhead of your application because Visual Basic must store the additional type library information and register both versions of the interface.

▶ If you try to run a new application with an old component, any number of problems can occur. The most likely one is that Visual Basic will report a run-time error when it finds that the desired interface is missing. Other run-time errors will occur if you are using late binding. This is the type of problem that was discussed in the Version Resource section at the start of this chapter.

The sequence for creating upgraded components that was described here is exactly what you should do in your own applications. A newly created project will have No Compatibility specified. The first time that you compile the application, you should select Project compatibility and set the project to be compatible with the newly compiled file. This allows you to reuse the type library identifiers. When you first release the component for use by other applications, you should compile the component and make a reference copy somewhere. You should then choose Binary Compatibility and set it to the reference copy, not the original.

You can now rebuild the component as many times as you wish with confidence that the type library and interface information will remain compatible with the reference copy. You will not accumulate multiple interface versions in your component, because you are basing compatibility on the reference. Let's say that the reference version is type library version 1.0. You then build version 1.1. If you were to base binary compatibility on the newly built component, the next build would be version 1.2. However, by basing it on the reference copy, your next build will again be 1.1.

Now try changing the declaration of the procedure A in the gtpComp class to include a parameter, for example:

```
Public Sub A(param As Integer)
    MsgBox "A Called"
End Sub
```

When you try to compile the project, Visual Basic will warn you that you are breaking backward compatibility of your component. Don't do it.

CREATING NEW INTERFACES

Why does Visual Basic go to the trouble of defining a new interface identifier for the updated interface, even though they are functionally compatible? To see the answer, you can go back to the original discussions of the Component Object Model in Chapters 3 and 4. An interface was defined as a contract. Once you define an interface to contain a certain set of properties, methods, and their parameters, you are not allowed to change it.

When you add properties or methods to an interface, you are in effect creating a new interface. It may be compatible in that the newer interface can fully support the older one. It may also have the same name, but it is nonetheless a different interface and thus has a unique interface identifier.

This serves to emphasize the importance of preserving backward compatibility. If you allow a member of an interface or its parameters to change, not only are you breaking backward compatibility in your component, you are violating one of the cardinal principles on which COM is based.

But this also brings up another approach to preserving backward compatibility. Instead of letting Visual Basic add new interface identifiers using binary compatibility, you can create your own alternate interfaces using the Implements statement. This situation was discussed in Chapter 4, which described the example of the IViewObject interface, which is used by containers to display ActiveX objects. When Microsoft needed to add functionality to the interface, they defined a new interface called IViewObject2. You can take this approach as well.

If you do take this approach, be careful not to change any of the interfaces you are using with the Implements statement in other classes. Even with binary compatibility, changing the base class members will change the interface identifier and cause compatibility problems with any object that uses the Implement statement to aggregate that interface. Binary compatibility only works with the default interface of a class. It won't detect if an interface being implemented has changed.

CONCLUSION

The Visual Basic documentation relating to version compatibility is quite thorough, and I encourage you to review it. Among other things, it goes into some grizzly discussions of what can happen if you allow version trees by basing versions of your component on more than one reference point.

In this chapter you've learned how version compatibility works internally and what happens in both the type library and registry as you upgrade components. Most of all, I would like to stress two issues: Interface compatibility is indeed important, but do not neglect functional compatibility. In some ways it is deserving of even more attention than interface compatibility because Visual Basic provides no help or tools to help insure that your components are functionally backward compatible with previous versions. This is not a fault in Visual Basic; it's your code, and no other language does better in this area.

Second, don't neglect distribution issues. Making sure that your component-based application runs reliably goes beyond making sure that it is installed correctly. You also need a mechanism to detect when component problems and conflicts occur on the target system even after installation. And you need a strategy for dealing with those situations.

Licensing and Distribution

ACTIVEX CONTROL LICENSING

ALTERNATIVE LICENSING APPROACHES

CLOSING NOTE

Chapter

26

The computer business must be one of the oddest industries that has ever existed. There's the incredible and overwhelming rate of change we are all experiencing. And there is the enormous impact that computers are having on society, which I think we have only begun to experience. Those are perhaps subjects for another book. Right now I want to talk about money.

Sometimes I think we programmers have a love/hate relationship with money. On one hand there is an ongoing theme that information and software should be free. There are thousands of freeware and public domain applications out there, many of which are excellent. There are uncounted programmers who write great software just for the fun of it or for the principle involved. I'm hard pressed to think of any other industry where this is the case.

On the other hand, how many programmers do you know who are doing some software development "on the side" in the hope of ultimately founding the next Netscape or Microsoft? I know quite a few myself. (And no, I neither expect, nor want, to run the next Netscape or Microsoft.)

This dichotomy also appears during a typical development cycle. We tend to be perfectionists, looking for the most creative and elegant solution to software problems, preferring sometimes to write our own code rather than purchase someone else's. Yet there is also pressure to meet tight schedules and to find the most economical solution to the task at hand. The two forces are in perpetual conflict. So part of what we do as software developers is try to find a balance between the two.

I don't know to what degree today's computer science degree programs discuss this issue. I know the economics of a software project was not a large part of my curriculum when I was in school. However, at the same time as I was studying computer science, I also picked up an engineering degree. The economic implications of a project was a very strong theme in that program, even to the point of having a class dedicated to the subject. I must confess that this economics background has influenced the way I approach software development. Which brings us to the subject of software licensing.

THE PURPOSE OF LICENSING

When I started this chapter, I tried to imagine the needs of the typical Visual Basic programmer with regard to licensing and distribution issues.

My background is that of an Independent Software Vendor (ISV) who develops and markets commercial controls. Up until Visual Basic 5.0, I had assumed that the vast majority of readers would have no intention of becoming control or component vendors. Authoring controls in Visual C++ is too difficult to attract large numbers of developers.

But Visual Basic 5.0 makes the development of ActiveX code components and controls easy. And there is a chance that large numbers of programmers will begin creating controls and ActiveX documents for the Internet. The question is simply this: If Visual Basic 5.0 makes it possible for anyone to create ActiveX components, will they? I will assume for now that the answer is yes.

This chapter is thus premised upon the idea that whether you are working for a large corporation or are an independent software developer or want to create commercial or shareware controls, you will have an interest in incorporating some licensing mechanism to protect your technology.

Degrees of Security   The first question you need to ask is how much security you require. There is a real trade-off here, since the more secure your component is, the harder it will be to use.

One could imagine a component that requires one of those hardware security devices or "dongles" that are attached to a parallel port. Imagine if every component vendor took this approach. A fairly complex program could require dozens of dongles chained to the back of each computer—a frightening thought.

Barring a hardware solution (and possibly including a hardware solution), it is probably impossible to come up with a 100 percent fail-safe licensing scheme. If there is one, I don't know about it.

The approaches you'll read about in this chapter do not claim to be perfect. In fact, they don't even claim to be secure. Instead, they follow the approach that has been adopted by both Microsoft and most component vendors, that component licensing exists to make it inconvenient to use components that are unlicensed. In other words, you distribute the control with a license agreement that threatens dire consequences if the license is violated. You include a simple licensing scheme that effectively warns users when they are about to violate the license. And then you ultimately trust them to be honest.

So each technique you will read about shortly is really more of a warning mechanism than a secure licensing mechanism. I will provide some suggestions that can help you improve the security of your licensing approach through use of hidden files or passwords, but they will not be the real focus of the chapter.

Licensing Models   The Visual Basic documentation discusses ActiveX control licensing at great length. But the approach it describes only covers one licensing model and does not cover ActiveX code components at all. What are licensing models? They represent different approaches to distributing components. Consider the following examples:

Design-Time Licensing. This is the model that is supported by Visual Basic for ActiveX controls and is frequently used by control vendors. Controls must be licensed in order to load within the container's design-time environment. Controls do not need to be licensed to work in the runtime environment. This approach is also supported by the ActiveX specification in the form of a special interface called IClassFactory2 that is built into every Visual Basic control to support licensing. The functioning of this interface is built into Visual Basic and is transparent to VB programmers.

License File/Component. This approach can be used with both controls and ActiveX DLL code components. It uses separate files or ActiveX components for licensing instead of adding license keys to the system registry.

Runtime Licensing. This approach uses a separate file or ActiveX component to provide licensing in all situations. It is used in cases where you wish to license runtime distribution of components as well as their design-time use. Runtime licensing is not common in the current market for Visual Basic add-on components. However, this approach may be useful for applications you intend to use on a corporate intranet to help prevent them from being distributed outside of your company.

Separate Demo Components. This model is especially useful for ActiveX code components. It consists of compiling separate demo components that either have limited functionality or only run when called within the context of certain development tools such as Visual Basic. This approach is designed to allow you to distribute demonstration versions of a control while controlling access to the release version.

Limited Duration Components. This approach involves enabling a control or ActiveX code component for a limited time period. After this period, it disables itself, perhaps until a unique password is provided.

Which of these approaches should you use? Other than the obvious fact that some of them can be used with code components and ActiveX documents, the decision is largely dependent on what it is that you are trying to accomplish. If you want to provide a mechanism for people to evaluate your controls, you might take the demo or limited duration approach. If you are only interested in limiting unauthorized use of your controls, you might choose one of the file or registry-based approaches. You can combine the approaches as needed.

ActiveX Control Licensing

Let us begin with a quick summary of the licensing approach supported directly by Visual Basic.

You can create a licensed control by selecting the Require License Key checkbox in the General tab of the Project Properties dialog box. When you do this, the following occurs:

- ▸ The control will always require a license key in order to load.

- ▸ Visual Basic creates a VBL license file for the control.

- ▸ When the control is compiled, Visual Basic registers the license key.

Let's take a closer look at these issues.

Every licensed control supports an interface called IClassFactory2, which is used during the control's creation. This is a standard ActiveX interface designed specifically to support this type of licensing. The container that loads the control is required to pass it a license key, a unique string defined by the control. If the key that is provided by the container matches that of the control, the control loads successfully.

Where does this license key come from? Visual Basic pulls the key from one of two sources, depending on whether the container is in design time or runtime. If the container is in design time, Visual Basic looks in the registry for a license key for the control.

When a control is compiled into an application, Visual Basic stores the license keys for each control with the application. That way, when a control is loaded into the running application, Visual Basic can use the stored key and allow the control to run.

Controls built from constituent controls are handled the same way. Each of the constituent controls must load in order for the main control to run. When the control's container is in design mode, Visual Basic attempts to find a license key for each constituent control. If any of the constituent controls are licensed and a license key cannot be found, the control will fail to load. By the same token, when a control is compiled into an application, Visual Basic stores the license key for each of the constituent controls with the application so it can create them at runtime.

This means that if you use licensed constituent controls in your controls, you must distribute license keys for each of the constituent controls for your control to be usable at design time. Naturally, you should never distribute a license key unless you have the right to do so. You'll have to contact the vendors of any components you use to obtain the right to use them.

License keys are stored in the registry under the HKEY_CLASSES_ROOT\Licenses key. Let's say that you create a control called xyz.ocx with GUID:

```
93A7C69D-7FEE-11D0-93A6-00AA0036005A.
```

When you create the project, a VBL file is created that might look something like this:

```
Key Name:         Licenses\93A7C69D-7FEE-11D0-93A6-00AA0036005A
Class Name:       <NO CLASS>
Last Write Time:  2/5/97 - 11:01 PM
Value 0
  Name:           <NO NAME>
  Type:           REG_SZ
  Data:           onmghnnglnlgpgknsmmnmnlnomrhgnigtnth
```

This VBL file contains instructions for registering the license key and the key itself—typically a random string of data. This GUID will appear as a subkey in the registry as follows:

```
HKEY_CLASSES_ROOT\Licenses\93A7C69D-7FEE-11D0-93A6-00AA0036005A =
onmghnnglnlgpgknsmmnmnlnomrhgnigtnth
```

The Visual Basic setup wizard uses the VBL file to add licensing registration instructions to the setup program. When you run the setup program, it will add the license key to the registry. If someone just copies the control onto their system, it will work fine with applications; they will have the license key compiled into the application itself. But if a user tries to place or load the control on a Visual Basic form at design time, Visual Basic will fail to find the license key and will not load the control.

This approach has one major limitation: it does not help you with environments that do not have separate design-time and stand-alone runtime modes. For example: Microsoft Office applications always check the registry for a license key. This means that if you want your control to be usable within Office applications, you must always provide the license key, which is effectively the same as providing no licensing at all. ActiveX documents are also not able to store license keys. Thus, they also check the registry for license keys any time a control is loaded. An alternative approach that allows additional control over licensed environments will be described shortly.

A slight variation of the control licensing approach described here relates to using controls on Web pages. Clearly these controls require license keys to work. It's also clear that registering license keys for each control that is downloaded would not be acceptable. It would be the equivalent of providing an unlimited license for the use of each downloaded control. Including the key on the Web page itself would make accessing the key just a little bit too easy.

Thus, browsers that support ActiveX controls provide a mechanism to download a license package file, or .LPK file. This file is created using a program called lpk_tool.exe, which can be found in the Tools directory on your Visual Basic CD-ROM. This program allows you to combine the license keys for all of the controls on a Web page into a file with the extension .LPK. You can then add a parameter to the Object tag of the Web page as follows:

```
<PARAM NAME="LPKPath" VALUE = "mylpk.lpk">
```

This adds to the object a special parameter named LPKPath, which tells the browser the name of the .LPK file to retrieve. This file name should be relative to the page and not an absolute URL, to make it more difficult to copy pages and run them on your local system.

Why do you have to use a special tool to create the license package file? Why can't Visual Basic do it for you? Because the file must contain the license keys for every control on a Web page and Visual Basic cannot possibly know which controls will be on a particular page. The license keys provided in this file are only used by the browser to load the controls. They are not added to the registry.

ALTERNATIVE LICENSING APPROACHES

You've seen that the standard control licensing approach does not work well with containers that always use the registry for license keys. It also does not help with regard to licensing ActiveX documents and ActiveX code components. I'll address both of these issues in a moment. But first, let's take a look at how to implement a demonstration component. The techniques used to do this are a good introduction to those used in other control licensing schemes.

CREATING DEMONSTRATION COMPONENTS

The gtpDT.vbg program group demonstrates an alternative approach for licensing. The gtpLicDT.vbp and gtpLicRT.vbp projects both expose a class named gtpLicensed, which contains the following code:

```
Option Explicit

Public Sub A()
    ' Prevent key functionality
    If Not VerifyLicense() Then
        MsgBox "License failure won't allow this operation"
        Exit Sub
    End If
    MsgBox "Subroutine A was invoked"
End Sub

Private Sub Class_Initialize()
    MsgBox "gtpLicensed object created"
End Sub
```

In this example, the functionality of function A is blocked if a license test fails. You could take a more extreme approach and raise an error, possibly during the class initialization, if the licensing fails. Normally, you should never raise arbitrary errors in a code component, but in this case you probably won't mind if the application fails in an unpleasant manner. Just be sure to first bring up a message box or dialog explaining the problem so the end user will not spend hours trying to figure out what is wrong.

The VerifyLicense function can be found in module Licenser.bas that contains the following code:

```
' Guide to the Perplexed
' Copyright © 1997 by Desaware Inc. All Rights Reserved

' Options supported by this module include:
' DEMOVERSION - Verifies ok in VB environment only
' DLLCHECK - Requires license file in VB environment


Option Explicit

Private Declare Function GetModuleFileName Lib "kernel32" Alias
"GetModuleFileNameA" (ByVal hModule As Long, ByVal lpFileName As String, ByVal_
```

```
nSize As Long) As Long
Private Declare Function GetModuleHandle Lib "kernel32" Alias "GetModuleHandleA"_
(ByVal lpModuleName As Long) As Long

#If DEMOVERSION Or DLLCHECK Then
' Return True if
' The demo can run on any VB platform, design
' or runtime
Public Function IsVBEnvironment() As Boolean
    Dim thismod&
    Dim thisfile$
    Dim basename$
    Dim thispos%
    Dim thischar$

    On Error GoTo nogo
    thismod = GetModuleHandle(0)
    thisfile = String$(262, Chr$(0))
    Call GetModuleFileName(thismod, thisfile, 261)
    thisfile = Left$(thisfile, InStr(thisfile, Chr$(0)) - 1)
    thispos = Len(thisfile)
    Do
        thischar = Mid$(thisfile, thispos, 1)
        If thischar = "\" Or thischar = ":" Then Exit Do
        thispos = thispos - 1
    Loop While thispos > 0
    basename = LCase$(Mid$(thisfile, thispos + 1))
    If basename = "vb.exe" Or basename = "vb32.exe" Or _
        basename = "vb5.exe" Then
            IsVBEnvironment = True
    End If
    Exit Function
nogo:
End Function
#End If

Public Function VerifyLicense() As Boolean
    Static PriorVerification As Boolean
    Static VerifiedOnce As Boolean
    ' Fast return 2nd time through
    If PriorVerification Then
        VerifyLicense = VerifiedOnce
        Exit Function
    End If
    PriorVerification = True
    #If DEMOVERSION Then
        If Not IsVBEnvironment() Then
```

```
            ' License failure screen
            frmAbout.MessageType = 1
            frmAbout.Show vbModal
            VerifiedOnce = False
        Else
            ' Optional splash screen
            frmAbout.MessageType = 0
            frmAbout.Show vbModal
            VerifiedOnce = True
        End If
        VerifyLicense = VerifiedOnce
        Exit Function
    #End If
    #If DLLCHECK Then
        If IsVBEnvironment Then
            ' Check for DLL or object here.
            ' If not found, Set VerifyLicense to False
            VerifiedOnce = False
        Else
            VerifiedOnce = True
        End If
        VerifyLicense = VerifiedOnce
        Exit Function
    #End If
    VerifiedOnce = True     ' Default ok
    VerifyLicense = True
End Function
```

The behavior of this module depends on two conditional compilation constants. For now, we'll look at the DEMOVERSION constant.

ActiveX components cannot detect the difference between design time and runtime. The DEMOVERSION conditional compilation constant is intended to allow you to compile two versions of a component easily: one that always runs, the other that only works within the Visual Basic environment.

When this constant and the DLLCHECK constant (which will be described later) is undefined or is 0, the VerifyLicense function always returns True. This provides a very fast verification for the regular component. When the constant is True, the VerifyLicense function first calls the IsVBEnvironment function to see if the current process is Visual Basic. It does this by using the GetModule-Handle function with a null parameter to retrieve the instance handle of the running application. The GetModuleFileName function can then be used to retrieve the name of the executable file for the application. If it is one of the possible Visual Basic executable names, the function returns True, indicating that the component is running under Visual Basic.

Naturally, you can extend the list to include any applications you wish. You can even use a separate file or set of registry entries to indicate which applications the demo component is allowed to run in.

The VerifyLicense function performs the verification only once. From then on, it returns the results of the initial test. This serves two purposes. First, it improves efficiency. Second, it makes it easy to support a splash screen that will appear only on first load of the DLL.

The first time VerifyLicense is called, the frmAbout form is shown. The code for this form is shown below:

```
' Guide to the Perplexed
' Licensing dialog example

Option Explicit

Public MessageType As Integer

Private Sub Command1_Click()
    Unload Me
End Sub

Private Sub Form_Load()
    Select Case MessageType
        Case 0
            lblMessage.Caption = "This is a demo version of the gtpLicensed_
            component"
        Case 1
            lblMessage.Caption = "This component is unlicensed."
    End Select
End Sub
```

The MessageType public variable allows the calling module to specify which warning message to display: the standard splash screen identifying the component or a licensing warning. There is one thing you should keep in mind if you choose to display a splash screen. If you create an object from the DLL and then release it, after a while the DLL will unload. When you reload it, the splash screen will appear again.

There are only three differences between the gtpLicDT and gtpLicRT projects:

▶ The gtpLicDT project has the DEMOVERSION conditional compilation variable set to 1.

▶ The project names are different.

▶ The gtpLicRT project does not include the frmAbout form.

Why use conditional compilation to differentiate between the components instead of just a global constant? Because:

▶ You can provide the best possible performance with the non-demo version.

▶ The two projects can share the exact same code base. The only differences are in the project file.

▶ The runtime component can safely exclude any forms that are only used by the demonstration version. In this case the frmAbout form is never referenced in the code that is compiled for the gtpLicRT project.

If you look in the frmLicTest.frm form in the LicTest project you'll see the following code:

```
' Changing reference is easy
Dim obj As New gtpLicensed

Private Sub Command1_Click()
    obj.A
End Sub
```

Let's say the project is initially created using the demo component gtpLicDT. How can you switch over to the other component? Easy. Just change the reference in the Project-References dialog box to reference the gtpLicRT project instead of the gtpLicDT project. No other code changes are necessary.

FILE-BASED CONTROL LICENSING

A slight variation on this approach can be seen in the ctlTest.vbg program group, which contains LicCtl.vbp project and a test project, ctltest.vbp. The control uses the same Licenser module that you saw in the previous example, but in this case it defines the DLLCHECK conditional compilation variable.

The VerifyLicense procedure can be called at two possible times: during the control's initialization or during the InitProperties and ReadProperties events. If you choose the latter, be sure to perform the license test during both InitProperties and ReadProperties, to cover the creation of new controls and the loading of existing projects.

```
Option Explicit

Private Sub UserControl_Initialize()
    If Not VerifyLicense Then
        MsgBox "Licensing error"
```

```
    Err.Raise vbObjectError + 1000, "Control", "Control is not licensed for
this platform"
    End If
End Sub

Private Sub UserControl_InitProperties()
    ' An alternate approach
    'If (Not Ambient.UserMode) And (Not VerifyLicense) Then
    '    MsgBox "Licensing error"
    '    Err.Raise vbObjectError + 1000, "Control", "Control is not licensed for_
    this platform"
    'End If
End Sub
```

You would perform the verification during initialization only if you do not care whether the control is in design time or runtime. For example: you might use this approach to enable or disable operation of the control for use with Office applications. If you do want to base verification on the container's User-Mode, you must wait until the InitProperties or ReadProperties event, when the Ambient object exists. With ActiveX documents you might wait until the Show event, when you can also base the operation on the container, which is accessible through the Parent property.

The verification itself can be based on any criteria you wish. One common approach is to distribute a separate DLL or ActiveX DLL that contains design-time licensing information. You can test for the existence of version information in this DLL at the times you choose.

```
#If DLLCHECK Then
    If IsVBEnvironment Then
        ' Check for DLL or object here.
        ' If not found, Set VerifyLicense to False
    Else
        VerifiedOnce = True
    End If
    VerifyLicense = VerifiedOnce
    Exit Function
#End If
```

When licensing fails, you have a number of choices. The Visual Basic documentation correctly warns you against raising errors at times when the container does not expect it, such as during InitProperties, ReadProperties, and component Initialization. Why do I break this rule here? Because I assume that an attempt to run an unlicensed component is a fatal error. I want the container to abort if possible. But raising an error does not guarantee the control will fail to load (though it does have that effect in the containers I've tested this with).

Thus, you should keep track of the fact that licensing failed in a module-level variable and use that variable to disable various parts of the control's operation if licensing fails.

As before, the control does bring up a message box to inform the end user that the problem is due to licensing. A better approach is to include a modal dialog box with information on how to obtain a license.

These two simple examples illustrate some important principles for licensing. Consider first the information that you have available:

▶ The name of the executable that is running the current process (the calling process for ActiveX DLLs, DLL-based ActiveX Documents, and ActiveX controls).

▶ Whether the container is in design mode or run mode (ActiveX controls only).

Now consider the tools you have available to indicate that a control is licensed:

▶ You can distribute a text license file.

▶ You can create hidden files for licensing purposes.

▶ You can distribute a DLL or ActiveX DLL for licensing.

▶ You can add your own entries in the registry.

Combine the two and you see there are almost unlimited variations available for controlling the licensing of any type of ActiveX component.

For example: a limited duration component could be implemented as follows:

▶ When the control loads for the first time it adds a registry entry or hidden file that indicates the date of first use.

▶ The control then tests this hidden entry every time it is loaded. If the control is running in Visual Basic and has expired, it terminates with an error.

▶ You can have a registration program that you ship out to the customer when they purchase the control. This program updates the registry entry or file to indicate that the control is now licensed.

Sure, the user could figure out which registry entry you used or find the hidden file and restart the trial period. They can also set back the clock on their system. Remember that the intent here is to warn the user, because all of these approaches are based on the assumption that most developers are honest.

CLOSING NOTE

This brings us to the end of the first edition of *Developing ActiveX Components with Visual Basic 5.0: A Guide to the Perplexed*. While I suppose we can take it for granted there will be a Visual Basic 6.0 someday, whether there will be a second edition of this book depends largely on how well I've done my job here—how much this book helps you in your work.

I leave you with this last request. Visual Basic has grown from a small and easy programming environment to a large, complex environment that, while not easy, is still easier to use than anything else out there. I am sure there are some areas that could use additional explanation or commentary beyond what I was able to include here. In order to decide which subjects should be covered in future editions, I would like your input. What subjects do you still find confusing? Which areas need additional clarification or examples? Drop me a line at dan@desaware.com. I can't promise to answer every message (I get a lot of e-mail), but I will keep your comments and consider them carefully.

Remember, too, to check www.desaware.com for corrections. No book is perfect. While I don't know of any errors as it goes to press, I'm sure a few have crept in somewhere.

Even though the main title of this book is *Developing ActiveX Components with Visual Basic 5.0*, I've tended to refer to it by its subtitle, *A Guide to the Perplexed*. This is how I've thought about it during the process of writing the book. So, if you find yourself reaching this point just a little bit less perplexed than you were when you started out, then I'll count this book a success.

Daniel Appleman
March 1997

Index

N

O

GMAT

PREMIUM PREP

2021 Edition

The Staff of The Princeton Review

PrincetonReview.com

Penguin
Random
House

The Princeton Review
110 East 42nd Street, 7th Floor
New York, NY 10017
Email: editorialsupport@review.com

Published in the United States by Penguin Random House LLC,
New York, and in Canada by Random House of Canada, a division
of Penguin Random House Ltd., Toronto.

Terms of Service: The Princeton Review Online Companion Tools
("Student Tools") for retail books are available for only the two
most recent editions of that book. Student Tools may be activated
only once per eligible book purchased for a total of 24 months
of access. Activation of Student Tools more than once per book
is in direct violation of these Terms of Service and may result in
discontinuation of access to Student Tools Services.

ISBN: 978-0-525-56936-7
eBook ISBN: 978-0-525-56975-6
ISSN: 2687-9646

GMAT is a registered trademark and owned by the Graduate
Management Admission Council (GMAC).

The material in this book is up-to-date at the time of publication.
However, changes may have been instituted by the testing body
in the test after this book was published.

If there are any important late-breaking developments, changes, or
corrections to the materials in this book, we will post that information online in the Student Tools. Register your book and check your
Student Tools to see if there are any updates posted there.

The Princeton Review is not affiliated with Princeton University.

Editor: Eleanor Green
Production Artist: Jason Ullmeyer
Production Editors: Kathy Carter and Sarah Litt

Printed in the United States of America.

10 9 8 7 6 5 4 3 2 1

2021 Edition

Editorial
Rob Franek, Editor-in-Chief
David Soto, Director of Content Development
Stephen Koch, Student Survey Manager
Deborah Weber, Director of Production
Gabriel Berlin, Production Design Manager
Selena Coppock, Managing Editor
Aaron Riccio, Senior Editor
Meave Shelton, Senior Editor
Chris Chimera, Editor
Eleanor Green, Editor
Orion McBean, Editor
Brian Saladino, Editor
Patricia Murphy, Editorial Assistant

Penguin Random House Publishing Team
Tom Russell, VP, Publisher
Alison Stoltzfus, Publishing Director
Amanda Yee, Associate Managing Editor
Ellen Reed, Production Manager
Suzanne Lee, Designer